William Grimshaw

The ladies' lexicon and parlour companion

Containing nearly every word in the English language

William Grimshaw

The ladies' lexicon and parlour companion
Containing nearly every word in the English language

ISBN/EAN: 9783337223984

Hergestellt in Europa, USA, Kanada, Australien, Japan

Cover: Foto ©Paul-Georg Meister /pixelio.de

Weitere Bücher finden Sie auf **www.hansebooks.com**

THE LADIES' LEXICON,

AND

PARLOUR COMPANION,

CONTAINING

NEARLY EVERY WORD IN THE ENGLISH LANGUAGE, AND EXHIBITING THE PLURALS OF NOUNS AND THE PARTICIPLES OF VERBS;

BEING ALSO

PARTICULARLY ADAPTED TO THE USE OF

ACADEMIES AND SCHOOLS.

BY WILLIAM GRIMSHAW,

Author of a History of the United States, England, &c. &c.

PHILADELPHIA:
J. B LIPPINCOTT & CO.
1863.

Eastern District of Pennsylvania, to wit:

[L. S.] BE IT REMEMBERED, That on the twenty-fourth day of April, in the fifty-third year of the independence of the United States of America, A. D. 1829, JOHN GRIGG, of the said district, has deposited in this office the title of a Book, the right whereof he claims as proprietor, in the words following, to wit:

"The Ladies Lexicon, and Parlour Companion, containing nearly every word in the English Language, and exhibiting the plurals of nouns and the participles of verbs; being also particularly adapted to the use of Academies and Schools. By William Grimshaw, Author of a History of the United States, England, &c. &c."

In conformity to the Act of the Congress of the United States, entitled, "An Act for the encouragement of Learning, by securing the copies of Maps, Charts, and Books, to the Authors and Proprietors of such copies, during the times therein mentioned." And also to the Act entitled, "An Act supplementary to an Act, entitled 'An Act for the Encouragement of Learning, by securing the copies of Maps, Charts, and Books, to the Authors and Proprietors of such copies, during the times therein mentioned,' and extending the benefits thereof to the arts of designing, engraving, and etching, historical and other Prints."

D. CALDWELL, *Clerk of the*
Eastern District of Pennsylvania.

PREFACE.

In offering this dictionary to the public, some explanation seems required, in relation to the plan, and the improvements which it professes to contain. It differs from every preceding work of the kind, principally in this:—that it exhibits the plurals of all nouns, which are not formed by the mere addition of the letter *s;* and also the participles of every verb that is now generally used

These additions will perhaps be pronounced, by some, to be innovations; but they are innovations of a very useful character, and such as should have been made, centuries ago, not only in a dictionary of our own tongue, but in that of every other language, ancient or modern. Fifty years from the present time, a dictionary which does not exhibit the plurals of nouns, as well as the participles of verbs, will be viewed as a curiosity; and considered as an example of that irrational pertinacity, with which men cling to ancient forms, for ages after their impropriety and insufficiency have been fully discovered and acknowledged.

A dictionary which does not contain the plurals and the participles, contains not more than half the language. Every verb, except those that are defective, has at least two participles—the present and the past—both of which have been excluded from every vocabulary that has yet been published. Thus, the verb *to advise,* has *advising* and *advised; differ* has *differing* and *differed; confer* has *conferring* and *conferred.* Whether the final *e* is to be retained or not, in the present participle, is a question involving some difficulty, even to persons who have received a good common education; and why the final *r* should remain single in the word *differing,* and be doubled in *conferring,* is a question not easily solved, by writers of considerable experience in composition. Nor is the like-lihood of error in any degree less, in forming the plurals of a numerous class of nouns. Thus, *ability* has *abilities*, in the plural; *adversary* has *adversaries*; *ally, allies*; *alley, alleys*; *potato, potatoes*; yet, why the final *y*, in one class of words, (as *ally,*) should be changed into *ies*, to form the plural, and in another class, ending also in *y*, (as *alley,*) it should be formed by adding *s*; and why the plural of *potato* should be formed by the addition of *es*; why *box* should become *boxes*, and *knife, knives*, all of which are variations from the general mode of forming the plural of English nouns by adding a single *s*—is known only to those who have had a regular grammatical education, and remembered only by persons who have frequent occasion to write for the public eye.

THIS POCKET DICTIONARY professes to supply the deficiencies of all preceding dictionaries; and therefore to contain, already formed, every word in the English language, that may be necessary in the composition of a Letter.

The rules, on which is founded the orthography of plurals and of participles, are here subjoined; taken substantially from the grammar of Lindley Murray.

It has not been judged requisite, in this dictionary, to exhibit the *definitions* of *all* the parts of speech: but in general only of the *parent word;* the meaning of the derivative formations, being, for the most part, so obviously deducible from their respective roots, as not to require any particular explanation.

RULE I.—Monosyllables, ending with *f, l,* or *s,* preceded by a single vowel, double the final consonant: as, *staff, mill, pass,* &c. The only exceptions are, *of, if, as, is, has, was, yes, his, this, us,* and *thus*.

RULE II.—Monosyllables ending with any consonant but *f, l,* or *s,* and preceded by a single vowel, never double the final consonant; excepting *add, ebb, butt, egg, odd, err, inn, bunn, purr,* and *buzz*.

RULE III.—Words ending with *y,* preceded by a consonant, form the plurals of nouns, the persons of verbs, verbal nouns, past participles, comparatives, and superlatives, by changing *y* into *i*: as,

PREFACE.

-y, spies; I carry, thou carriest; he carrieth, or *carries; carrier, carried; happy, happier, happiest.*

The present participle in *ing,* retains the *y,* that *i* may not be doubled; as, *carry, carrying; bury, burying,* &c.

But *y,* preceded by a vowel, in such instances as the above, is not changed: as, *boy, boys; I cloy, he cloys, cloyed,* &c.; except in *lay, pay,* and *say;* from which are formed, *laid, paid,* and *said;* and their compounds, *unlaid, unpaid, unsaid,* &c.

RULE IV.—Words ending with *y,* preceded by a consonant, upon assuming an additional syllable beginning with a consonant, commonly change *y* into *i:* as, *happy, happily, happiness.* But when *y* is preceded by a vowel, it is very rarely changed in the additional syllable; as, *coy, coyly; boy, boyish, boyhood; annoy, annoyer, annoyance; joy, joyless, joyful.*

RULE V.—Monosyllables, and words accented on the last syllable, ending with a single consonant preceded by a single vowel double that consonant, when they take another syllable beginning with a vowel: as, *wit, witty; thin, thinnish; to abet, an abettor; to begin, a beginner.*

But if a diphthong precedes, or the accent is on the preceding syllable, the consonant remains single; as, *to toil, toiling; to offer, an offering; maid, maiden,* &c.

But to this rule, there seem to be a few exceptions, not noticed, and perhaps not approved by Lindley Murray. The participles of verbs ending in *l,* whether the accent be on the last, or on the preceding syllable, are almost universally, though erroneously, spelled with double *l,* as *level, levelling, levelled; revel, revelling, revelled;* instead of *leveling* and *leveled; reveling* and *reveled.* The word *tranquil,* though the final consonant is preceded by a *diphthong,* generally forms its substantive with *ll,* as *tranquillity,* instead of *tranquility:* we often see *worshipping,* and *worshipped,* instead of *worshiping,* and *worshiped;* and we believe that the participles of the verb *bias,* are almost universally written *biassing* and *biassed,* instead of *biasing* and *biased.*

RULE VI.—Words ending with any double letter but *l,* and taking *ness, less, ly,* or *ful,* after them, preserve the letter double: as, *harmlessness, carelessness, carelessly, stiffly, successful, distressful,* &c But those words which end with double *l,* and take *ness, less, ly,* or *ful,* after them, generally omit one *l:* as, *fulness, skilless, fully, skilful,* &c.

RULE VII.—*Ness, less, ly,* and *ful,* added to words ending with silent *e,* do not cut it off; as, *paleness, guileless, closely, peaceful;* except in a few words; as, *duly, truly, awful.*

RULE VIII.—*Ment,* added to words ending with silent *e,* generally preserves the *e* from elision; as, *abatement, chastisement, incitement,* &c. The words *judgment, abridgment, acknowledgment,* are deviations from the rule.

Like other terminations, *ment* changes *y* into *i,* when preceded by a consonant: as, *accompany, accompaniment; merry, merriment.*

RULE IX.—*Able* and *ible,* when incorporated into words ending with silent *e,* almost always cut it off: as, *blame, blamable; cure, curable; sense, sensible,* &c.; but if *c* or *g* soft comes before *e* in the original word, the *e* is then preserved in words compounded with *able*: as, *change, changeable; peace, peaceable,* &c.

RULE X.—When *ing* or *ish* is added to words ending with silent *e,* the *e* is almost universally omitted: as, *place, placing; lodge, lodging; slave, slavish; prude, prudish.*

RULE XI.—Compounded words are generally spelled in the same manner as the simple words of which they are formed: as, *glasshouse, skylight, thereby, hereafter.* Many words ending with double *l,* are exceptions to this rule: as, *already, welfare, wilful, fulfil:* and also the words *wherever, christmas, lammas,* &c.

Some nouns, from the nature of the things which they express, are used only in the singular form: as, *wheat, pitch, gold, sloth, pride,* &c.; others, only in the plural form: as, *bellows, scissors, lungs, riches,* &c.

Some words are the same in both numbers: as, *deer, sheep, swine,* &c.

The plural number of nouns is generally formed by adding *s* to the singular: as, *dove, doves; face, faces; thought, thoughts.* But when the substantive singular ends in *x, ch,* soft, *sh, ss,* or *s,* we add *es* in the plural: as, *box, boxes; church, churches; lash, lashes; kiss, kisses; rebus, rebuses.* If the singular ends in *ch* hard, the plural is formed by adding *s*: as, *monarch, monarchs; distich, distichs.*

Nouns which end in *o,* have sometimes *es* added to the plural. as, *cargo, echo, hero, negro, manifesto, potato, volcano, vo*: and sometimes only *s*; as, *folio, nuncio, punctilio, seraglio.*

Nouns ending in *f,* or *fe,* are rendered plural by the change of those terminations into *ves*: as, *loaf, loaves; half, halves; wife, wives;* except *grief, relief, reproof,* and several others, which form the plural by the addition of *s.* Those which end in *ff,* have the regular plural: as, *ruff, ruffs;* except *staff, staves.*

Some nouns become plural by changing the *a* of the singular into *e*: as, *man, men; woman, women; alderman, aldermen.* The words, ox and *child*, form *oxen* and *children*; *brother*, makes either *brothers* or *brethren*. Sometimes the diphthong *oo* is changed into *ee* in the plural: as, *foot, feet; goose, geese; tooth, teeth. Louse* and *mouse*. make *lice* and *mice*. *Penny* makes *pence*; or *pennies*, when the coin is meant; *die, dice* (for play;) *die, dies* (for coining.)

It is agreeable to analogy, and the practice of the generality of correct writers, to construe the following words as plural nouns *pains, riches, alms*: and also, *mathematics, metaphysics politics, ethics, optics, pneumatics*, with other similar names of sciences.

As a general rule for the use of the word *means*, as either singular or plural, it would render the construction less vague, and the expression therefore less ambiguous, were we to employ it as singular, when the mediation or instrumentality of one thing is implied; and, as plural, when two or more mediating causes are referred to. " He was careful to observe what means *were* employed by his adversaries, to counteract his schemes." Here *means* is properly joined with a plural verb, several methods of counteraction being signified. " The king consented; and, by *this* means all hope of success was lost." Here but one mediating circumstance is implied; and the noun is, therefore, used as singular.

The following words, which have been adopted from the Hebrew, Greek, and Latin languages, are thus distinguished, with respect to number.

Singular.	Plural.	Singular.	Plural.
Cherub,	Cherubim.	Datum,	Data.
Seraph,	Seraphim.	Effluvium,	Effluvia.
Antithesis,	Antitheses.	Encomium,	{ Encomia *or* { Encomiums.
Automaton,	Automata.		
Basis,	Bases.	Erratum,	Errata.
Crisis,	Crises.	Genius,	Genii.*
Criterion,	Criteria.	Genus,	Genera.
Diæresis,	Diæreses.	Index,	{ Indices *or* { Indexes.†
Ellipsis,	Ellipses.		
Emphasis,	Emphases.	Lamina,	Laminæ.
Hypothesis,	Hypotheses.	Medium,	Media.
Metamorphosis,	Metamorphoses.	Magus,	Magi.
Phœnomenon,	Phœnomena.	Memorandum,	{ Memoranda *or* { Memorandums.
Appendix,	{ Appendices *or* { Appendixes.		
		Radius,	Radii.
Arcanum,	Arcana.	Stamen,	Stamina.
Axis,	Axes.	Stratum,	Strata.
Calx,	Calces.	Vortex,	Vortices.

---

* *Genii*, when denoting aerial spirits; *Geniuses*, when signifying persons of genius.

† *Indexes*, when it signifies pointers, or Tables of Contents· *Indices*, when referring to algebraic quantities.

Some words, derived from the learned languages, are confined to the plural number as, *antipodes, credenda, literati, minutiæ.*

The following nouns, being in Latin, both singular and plural are used in the same manner, when adopted into our tongue: *hiatus, apparatus, series, species.*

It is a general rule, that all names of things measured or weighed, have no plural; for in them not number, but quantity is regarded: as *wool, wine, oil.* When we speak, however, of different kinds, we use the plural: as, *the coarser wools, the richer wines, the finer oils.*

The word *news* is now almost universally considered as belonging to the singular number.

The noun *means* is used both in the singular and the plural number.

We shall conclude, with the following observation, in relation to the claim of this little volume to a preference over all other vocabularies by which it has been preceded. We allude to the selection of words. Unless accompanied by a particular caution, no word has been admitted, which is not now of polite or popular use; and no word has been excluded, which is required either in epistolary composition or in conversation.

Philadelphia, Dec. 1, 1828.

ABBREVIATIONS.

Art. article: *s.* substantive: *adj.* adjective: *pron.* pronoun: *v.* verb: *adv.* adverb: *prep.* preposition: *conj.* conjunction: *int.* interjection: pr. present· par. participle: pl. plura · fem. feminine: comp. comparative: sup. superlative.

THE LADIES' LEXICON.

A

ABAFT. *adv.* From the fore part of a ship, towards the stern.

ABAN'DON. *v.* To give up, resign, or quit; to desert, to forsake. pr. par. *abandoning;* past, *abandoned:* s. *abandonment.*

ABA'SE. *v.* To cast down; to depress; to perform an act of self-humiliation. pr. par. *abasing;* past, *abased:* s. *abasement.*

ABASH'. *v.* To make ashamed. pr. par. *abashing;* past, *abashed:* s. *abashment.*

ABA'TE. *v.* To lessen, to diminish, to quash. pr. par. *abating;* past, *abated:* s. *abatement, abater.*

ABAT'IS. *s.* A military term—Trees cut down, and laid so as to form a defence for troops.

AB'BACY. *s.* The rights or privileges of an abbot. pl. *abbacies.* adj. *abbatial.*

AB'BESS. *s.* The superior or governess of a nunnery, or convent of women. pl. *abbesses.*

AB'BEY. *s.* A monastery of religious persons, either male or female.

AB'BOT. *s.* The chief of a convent of men.

ABBRE'VIATE. *v.* To shorten; to abridge. pr. par. *abbreviating;* past, *abbreviated:* s. *abbreviation, abbreviator, abbreviature.*

AB'DICATE. *v.* To resign. pr. par. *abdicating;* past, *abdicated:* s. *abdication, abdicator:* adj. *abdicative, abdicant.*

AB'DITORY. *s.* A hiding place. pl. *abditories.*

ABDU'CE. *v* To draw away; to draw one part from another. pr. par. *abducing;* past, *abduced:* adj. *abducent.*

ABDUC'TION. *s.* Act of abducing s. *abductor.*

ABECEDA'RIAN. *s.* A teacher of the alphabet.

ABER'RANCE, ABER'RANCY. *s.* Deviation from the right way; error. pl. *aberrances, aberrancies:*—*aberration:* adj. *aberrant:* par. adj. *aberring*

ABET'. *v.* To support another in his illegal designs. pr. par. *abetting,* past, *abetted:* s. *abetter, or abettor, abetment.*

ABEY'ANCE. *s.* In law, a state of suspense.

ABHOR'. *v.* To detest, to hate with acrimony. pr. par. *abhorring;* past, *abhorred:* s. *abhorrence, or abhorrency; abhorrer:* aoj. *abhorrent:* adv. *abhorrently.*

ABI'DE. *v.* To stay in a place; to dwell; to remain. pr. par. *abiding;* past, *abode:* s. *abider, abode.*

ABIL'ITY. *s.* Power, mental efficiency. pl. *abilities.*

AB'JECT. *adj.* Worthless, mean groveling. s. *abjection, abjectness* adv. *abjectly.*

AB'JUGATE. *v.* To unyoke. pr par. *abjugating;* past, *abjugated*

ABJU'RE. *v.* To retract; to swear not to do, or not to have. pr. par. *abjuring;* past, *abjured:* s. *abjuration, abjurement, abjurer.*

AB'LATIVE. *s.* That which takes away; the sixth case of the Latin nouns.

9

A'BLE. *adj.* Having ability; adv. *ably.*
A'BLE-BOD'IED. *adj.* Strong of body.
ABLU'TION. *s.* The act of cleansing. adj. *abluent.*
ABO'ARD. *adv.* On board; in a ship; into a ship.
ABO'DE. The preterit of *abide.* s. *abode.*
ABOL'ISH. *v.* To annul; to put an end to; to destroy. pr. par. *abolishing;* past, *abolished:* s. *abolisher:* adj. *abolishable.*
ABOLI'TION. *s.* Act of abolishing.
ABOM'INABLE. *adj.* Hateful, detestable. adv. *abominably:* s. *abominableness.*
ABOM'INATE. *v.* To abhor, to detest. pr. par. *abominating;* past, *abominated:* s. *abomination.*
ABORI'GINES. *s.* The earliest inhabitants of a country. adj. *aboriginal:* adv. *aboriginally.*
ABOR'TION. *s.* Act of bringing forth prematurely; the produce of a premature birth. adj. *abortive:* adv. *abortively:* s. *abortiveness.*
ABOUND'. *v.* To have in great plenty; to be in great plenty. pr. par. *abounding;* past, *abounded.*
ABOUT'. *prep.* Around; surrounding; near to, &c. adv. *about.*
ABO'VE. *prep.* Higher in place; higher in rank; more than; too proud for. adv. *above.*
ABO'VE-BOARD. *adv.* In open sight; without disguise or concealment.
ABO'VE-MENTIONED. *adj.* Mentioned previously.
ABRA'DE. *v.* To rub off. pr. par. *abrading;* past. *abraded.*
ABRA'SION. *s.* Act of abrading. adj. *abrasive.*
ABREAST'. *adv.* Side by side.
ABRI'DGE. *v.* To contract, to diminish, to cut short. pr. par. *abridging;* past, *abridged:* s. *abridger, abridgment.*
ABROAD'. *adv.* Without confinement; from home, in another country.

AB'ROGATE. *v.* To repeal, to annul. pr. par. *abrogating;* past, *abrogated:* s. *abrogator, abrogation*
ABRUPT'. *adj.* Broken, craggy sudden, unexpected. adv. *abruptly:* s. *abruption, abruptness.*
AB'SCESS. *s.* A tumour filled with matter. pl. *abscesses.*
ABSCIND'. *v.* To cut off. pr. par. *abscinding;* past. *abscinded.*
ABSCIS'SION. *s.* Act of abscinding.
ABSCOND'. *v.* To hide; to depart secretly. pr. par. *absconding;* past, *absconded:* s. *absconder.*
AB'SENT. *adj.* Not present; inattentive. v. *absent';* pr. par. *absenting;* past, *absented:* s. *absence.*
ABSENTEE'. *s.* A word applied, by the British and the Irish, to men of large estate who reside out of their country.
AB'SOLUTE. *adj.* Unconditional; not relative; not limited; positive; certain. adv. *absolutely:* s *absoluteness.*
ABSOLU'TION. *s.* Act of absolving; acquittal; remission of sins. adj. *absolutory.*
ABSO'LVE. *v.* To free, to acquit, to discharge. pr. par. *absolving,* past, *absolved:* s. *absolver.*
ABSO'NANT. *adj.* Contrary to reason; not to the purpose; inconsistent. adv. *absonantly.*
ABSORB'. *v.* To suck in; to swallow up. pr. par. *absorbing;* past, *absorbed:* adj. *absorbent.*
ABSORP'TION. *s.* Act of absorbing. adj. *absorptive.*
ABSTAIN'. *v.* To keep from; to forbear. pr. par. *abstaining;* past, *abstained:* s. *abstainer.*
ABSTE'MIOUS. *adj.* Temperate, sober, abstinent. s. *abstemiousness* adv. *abstemiously.*
ABSTER'GENT, ABSTER'SIVE. *adj.* Of a cleansing quality. s. *abstersion.*
ABS'TINENCE. *s.* Act of abstaining. adj. *abstinent* adv. *abstinently.*

10

ABSTRACT'. *v.* To take from; to separate. pr. par. *abstracting;* past, *abstracted:* adj. *ab'stract, abstractive:* s. *ab'stract, abstraction, abstractedness:* adv. *abstractedly.*

ABSTRU'SE. adj. Hidden; difficult. s. *abstruseness:* adv. *abstrusely.*

ABSURD'. adj. Unreasonable; inconsistent; contrary to reason. s. *absurdity,* pl. *absurdities:* adv. *ubsurdly.*

ABUN'DANCE. s. Plenty; more than sufficient. adj. *abundant:* adv. *abundantly.*

ABU'SE. *v.* To make an ill use of; to treat with rudeness. pr. par. *abusing;* past, *abused:* s. *abuse, abusiveness, abuser:* adj. *abusive:* adv. *abusively.*

ABUT'MENT. s. That which abuts or borders on.

ABYSS'. s. Depth without bottom; a prodigious gulf. pl. *abysses.*

ACA'CIA. s. A species of drug.

ACAD'EMY. s. A society united for the promotion of some art or science; the place where sciences are taught. pl. *academies;* s. *academician:* adj. *academial, academic, academical:* adv. *academically.*

ACAN'THUS. s. A species of plant. pl. *acanthuses.*

ACCE'DE. *v.* To be added to; to come to; to assign over; to agree. pr. par. *acceding;* past, *acceded.*

ACCEL'ERATE. *v.* To hasten, to quicken. pr. par. *accelerating;* past, *accelerated:* s. *acceleration:* adv. *accelerative.*

AC'CENT. s. Manner of speaking, or pronouncing; sound given to a particular syllable; mark of that sound. *v. accent';* pr. par. *accenting;* past, *accented:* adj. *accentual.*

ACCEN'TUATE. *v.* To place the accents properly. pr. par. *accentuating;* past, *accentuated:* s. *accentuation.*

ACCEPT'. *v.* To receive willingly; to admit with approbation. pr. par. *accepting;* past, *accepted* adj *acceptable:* adv. *acceptably.* s. *acceptability, acceptance, acceptation, accepter.*

ACCESS'. s. Means or liberty of approaching; increase. pl. *accesses* s. *accession, accessary* —pl. *accessaries:* adj. *accessory.*

ACCES'SIBLE. adj. Possible to be approached, or reached. s. *access sibility,* pl. *accessibilities.*

AC'CIDENT. s. The property or quality of any being which may be separated from it, at least in thought; casualty; chance. adj *accidental:* adv. *accidentally.*

ACCES'SORY. adj. Joined to; additional. s. *accessory,* pl. *accessori s*

ACCIP'IENT. s. A receiver.

ACCI'TE. *v.* To call, to summon pr. par. *acciting;* past, *accited:* a. *acciter, accitor.*

ACCLAIM'. s. A shout of praise; acclamation. (little used.)

ACCLAMA'TION. s. Shouts of applause. adj. *acclamatory.*

AC'CLIMATE. *v.* To habituate to a new climate. pr. par. *acclimating;* past, *acclimated:* adj. *acclimative.*

ACCLIV'ITY. s. Steepness, reckoned upwards. pl. *acclivities:* adj *acclivous.*

ACCOM'MODATE. *v.* To render a convenience; to make suitable; to compromise. pr. par. *accommodating;* past, *accommodated:* s *accommodation, accommodator* adj. *accommodable.*

ACCOM'PANY. *v.* To go with, as a companion; to escort. pr. par. *accompanying;* past, *accompanied;* s. *accompaniment.*

ACCOM'PLICE. s. A partner in crime.

ACCOM'PLISH. *v.* To complete; to execute fully; to obtain, to adorn. pr. par. *accomplishing;* past *accomplished:* s. *accomplishment.* adj. *accomplishable.*

ACCORD'. *v.* To agree. pr. par. *according;* past, *accorded:* s. *accord,*

11

accordance: adj. *accordant:* adv. *accordantly, accordingly.*

ACCOST'. *v.* To speak to; to address; to salute. pr. par. *accosting;* past, *accosted:* adj. *accostable.*

ACCOUCHEUR'. *s.* A surgeon who attends a female during her confinement.

ACCOUNT'. *s.* A computation of debts or expenses; profit; advantage; distinction; sake; narrative. *v. account;* pr. par. *accounting;* past, *accounted:* s. *accountant, accountability* — pl. *accountabilities:* adj. *accountable:* adv. *accountably.*

ACCOU'TRE. *v.* To equip, to dress. pr. par. *accoutring;* past, *accoutred:* s. *accoutrement.*

ACCRED'IT. *v.* To procure or give honour or credit to. pr. par. *accrediting;* past, *accredited.*

ACCRES'CENT. adj. Increasing.

ACCRE'TION. *s.* Act of increasing; increase. adj. *accretive.*

ACCRUE'. *v.* To be added to; to arise from. pr. par. *accruing;* past, *accrued:* s. *accruement.*

ACCU'MULATE. *v.* To pile up; to heap together; to increase. pr. par. *accumulating;* past, *accumulated:* s. *accumulation, accumulator:* adj. *accumulative:* adv. *accumulatively.*

AC'CURATE. adj. Exact; very correct. s. *accuracy,* pl. *accuracies:* adv. *accurately.*

ACCURSE'. *v.* To doom to misery; to invoke a curse. pr. par. *accursing;* past, *accursed.*

ACCU'SE. *v.* To charge with a crime; to blame; to censure. pr. par. *accusing;* past, *accused:* s. *accusation, accuser:* adj. *accusable, accusative, accusatory.*

ACCUS'TOM. *v.* To habituate; to inure. pr. par. *accustoming;* past, *accustomed:* adj. *accustomary:* adv. *accustomarily*

ACE. *s.* One; a single point, or cards or dice.

ACER'BATE. *v.* To make sour. pr. par. *acerbating;* past, *acerbated.*

ACER'BITY. *s.* Sourness, severity pl. *acerbities.*

ASCES'CENT. adj. Growing sour

ACE'TOUS. adj. Sour.

ACHE. *s.* Continued pain. *v. ache* pr par. *aching;* past, *ached: s aching.*

ACHIE'VE. *v.* To perform, to accomplish. pr. par. *achieving;* past, *achieved:* s. *achiever, achievement.* adj. *achievable.*

A'CID. *s.* A sour substance. adj. *acid:* s. *acidity,* pl. *acidities:* adj. *acidulous.*

ACHROMAT'IC. adj. In optics, applied to telescopes,—" contrived to remedy aberrations."

ACID'ULATE. *v.* To make sour. pr. par. *acidulating;* past, *acidulated:* adj. *acidulative, acidulous.*

AC'ME. *s.* The height.

ACKNOWL'EDGE. *v.* To confess as a fault; to own as a benefit, pr. par. *acknowledging;* past, *acknowledged:* s. *acknowledgment*

A'CORN. *s.* The seed of the oak.

ACOUS'TICS. *s.* The doctrine of sounds.

ACQUAINT'. *v.* To inform; to make familiar with. pr. par. *acquainting;* past, *acquainted: s. acquaintance.*

ACQUIESCE'. *v.* To be satisfied with, either really or apparently, pr. par. *acquiescing;* past, *acquiesced:* s. *acquiescencce:* adj. *acquiescent.*

ACQUI'RE. *v.* To gain, to obtain. pr. par. *acquiring;* past, *acquired:* s. *acquirement, acquirer:* adj. *acquirable.*

ACQUISI'TION. *s.* Act of acquiring; thing acquired.

ACQUIT'. *v.* To declare innocent; to absolve. pr. par. *acquitting;* past, *acquitted:* s. *acquittance.*

A'CRE. *s.* A quantity of land, containing 160 square perches.

A'CRID. adj. Of a hot, biting taste; bitter.

A'CRIMONY. *s.* Sharpness, severity, corrosiveness. pl. *acrimonies:* adj. *acrimonious:* adv. *acrimoniously.*

ACROMATIC, ACROMATICAL. adj. Belonging to profound learning.

ACROSS'. *adv.* Athwart; laid over, so as to cross.

ACROS'TIC. *s.* A kind of verses, of which the first letter of every line being taken, a particular name is found. adj. *acrostic, acrostical:* adv. *acrostically.*

ACT. *v.* To be in action; to produce effect; to perform a borrowed character. pr. par. *acting;* past, *acted:* s. *act, action, actor.*

ACTIONABLE. *adj.* Admitting an action in law; liable to an action.

ACTIVE. *adj.* Having the power or quality of acting; busy; nimble; quick. adv. *actively:* s. *activity,* pl. *activities.*

ACTRESS. *s.* She that performs any thing. pl. *actresses.*

ACTUAL. *adj.* Real; not speculative. adv. *actually.*

ACTUARY. *s.* A clerk who compiles minutes of the proceedings of a court, or society. pl. *actuaries.*

ACTUATE. *v.* To put into action. pr. par. *actuating;* past, *actuated:* s. *actuation:* adj. *actuative.*

ACUMEN. *s.* A sharp point; acuteness.

ACUTE. *adj.* Ending in a point; sharp; of a penetrating mind. adv. *acutely:* s. *acuteness.*

AD'AGE. *s.* A maxim, a proverb.

ADAGIO. A term in music, denoting slow time.

AD'AMANT. *s.* A stone of impenetrable hardness; the diamond. adj. *adamantine.*

AD'AMITE. *s.* The name of a religious sect, who used to pray naked.

ADAPT'. *v.* To fit, to suit. pr. par. *adapting;* past, *adapted:* s. *adaptation, adaption:* adj. *adaptable:* s *adaptability,* pl. *adaptabilities*

ADD. *v.* To join; to perform addition. pr. par. *adding;* past, *added.*

AD'DER. *s.* A serpent, a viper.

ADDENDA. *s.* Things to be added.

ADDICT'. *v.* To devote, to dedicate. pr. par. *addicting;* past, *addicted.* s. *addiction.*

ADDITION. *s.* Act of adding; thing added. adj. *additional:* adv. *additionally.*

AD'DLE. *v.* To make stupid; to confuse. pr. par. *addling;* past, *addled.*

ADDRESS'. *v.* To prepare one's-self to enter upon any action; to apply to another, by words; to accost. pr. par. *addressing;* past, *addressed:* s. *address, addresser.*

ADDUCE. *v.* To bring forward; to offer in argument. pr. par. *adducing;* past, *adduced:* adj. *adducent, adducible.*

ADDUCTION. *s.* Act of adducing.

ADEMPTION. *s.* Act of taking away; privation. adj. *ademptive.*

ADEPT'. *s.* One completely skilled in any particular art. adv. *adeptly.*

AD'EQUATE. *adj.* Equal to; proportionate. adv. *adequately:* s *adequateness.*

ADHERE. *v.* To stick; to continue firmly fixed. pr. par. *adhering;* past, *adhered.* s. *adherence, adherent:* adj. *adherent:* adv. *adherently.*

ADHESION. *s.* Act of adhering. adj. *adhesive:* adv. *adhesively.* s. *adhesiveness.*

ADIEU'. *int.* Farewell. s. *adieu.*

ADJA'CENT. *adj.* Lying near; neighbouring. s. *adjacency,* pl. *adjacencies.*

AD'JECTIVE. *s.* A word added to a noun to signify some quality. adv. *adjectively.*

ADJOIN'. *v* To join to; to be contiguous to. pr. par. *adjoining,* past, *adjoined.*

ADJOURN'. *v.* To put off to another day, or to another time of the same day. pr. par. *adjourning;*

past, *adjourned:* s. *adjournment, adjourner.*

ADJUDGE'. *v.* To give a judicial sentence; to judge; to decree. pr. par. *adjudging;* past, *adjudged.*

ADJUDICA'TION. *s.* Act of adjudging.

ADJUNCT. *s.* Something adherent or united to another; a person united to another. s. *adjunction:* adj. *adjunct, adjunctive;* adv. *adjunctively.*

ADJU'RE. *v.* To impose an oath upon; to charge earnestly. pr. par. *adjuring;* past, *adjured:* s. *adjuration, adjurer.*

ADJUST'. *v.* To regulate, to render conformable. pr. par. *adjusting;* past, *adjusted:* s. *adjuster, adjustment.*

AD'JUTANT. *s.* An assistant regimental officer. s. *adjutancy,* pl. *adjutancies.*

ADMEA'SUREMENT. *s.* Adjustment of proportions; act of measurement.

ADMIN'ISTER. *v.* To give, to afford, to perform; to act as minister or agent. pr. par. *administering;* past, *administered:* adj. *administrable.*

ADMIN'ISTRATE. *v.* To act as a minister or agent. pr. par. *administrating;* past, *administrated:* s. *administration, administrator, administratrix,*(pl.*administratrixes*): adj. *administrative.*

AD'MIRAL. *s.* The chief commander of a large fleet. s. *admiralty,* pl. *admiralties.*

ADMI'RE. *v.* To regard with wonder or pleasure. pr. par. *admiring;* past, *admired:* s. *admiration, admirer:* adj. *admirable:* adv. *admirably, admiringly.*

ADMIS'SION. *s.* The act or practice of admitting. s. *admissibility:* adj. *admissible* · adv. *admissively.*

ADMIT'. *v.* To let in; to grant. pr. par. *admitting;* past, *admitted:* s. *admittance, admitter.*

ADMIX'. *v.* To mingle with. pr par. *admixing;* past, *admixed:* s *admixtion, admixture.*

ADMON'ISH. *v.* To warn of a fault; to reprove gently; to inform. pr. par. *admonishing;* past, *admonished:* s. *admonisher.*

ADMONI'TION. *s.* Act of admonishing; advice or information given. s. *admonitor:* adj. *admonitive, admonitory:* adv. *admonitorily.*

ADOLES'CENCE, ADOLES'CENCY. *s.* The age succeeding childhood. pl. of *adolescency, adolescencies.*

ADOPT'. *v.* To receive as our own, to receive for use. pr. par. *adopting;* past, *adopted.* s. *adopter, adoption:* adj. *adoptive:* adv. *adoptively.*

ADO'RE. *v.* To worship with ext ir nal homage. pr. par. *adoring;* past, *adored:* s. *adoration, adorer:* adj *adorable.*

ADROIT'. *adj.* Dexterous, skilful, active. s. *adroitness:* adv. *adroitly.*

ADORN'. *v.* To dress; to deck with ornaments. pr. par. *adorning;* past, *adorned:* s. *adorner, adornment.*

ADRIFT'. *adv.* Floating withou' a guide.

ADSTRIC'TION. *s.* Act of binding together. adj. *adstrictive.*

ADULA'TION. *s.* Extreme flattery s. *adulator:* adj. *adulatory, adulative.*

ADULT' *s.* A person full grown.

ADUL'TERATE. *v.* To corrupt by some admixture. p. par. *adulterating;* past, *adulterated* · adj. *adulterate:* s. *adulteration.*

ADUL'TERY. *s.* Violation of the marriage bed. pl. *adulteries:* s. *adulterer,* fem. *adultress,* pl. *adultresses.*

ADUST'. *adj.* Burned up; scorched. s. *adustion.*

ADVANCE'. *v.* To move forward; to promote; to accelerate; to propose. pr. par. *advancing;* past, *advanced:* s. *advance, advancer, advancement.*

ADVAN'TAGE. *s.* Superiority, op-

14

portunity. v. *advantage;* pr. par. *advantaging;* past, *advantaged:* adj. *advantageous:* adv. *advantageously:* s. *advantageousness.*

AD'VENT. *s.* The name of one of the holy seasons, signifying "the coming",—that is, the coming of Jesus Christ, which is made the subject of Christian devotion during the four weeks immediately before Christmas.

ADVENTI'TIOUS. *adj.* Accidental, extrinsic. adv. *adventitiously.*

ADVEN'TURE. *s.* Accident; a chance; an enterprize. v. *adventure;* pr. par. *adventuring;* past, *adventured:* s. *adventurer:* adj. *adventurous:* adv. *adventurously.*

AD'VERB. *s.* A word joined to another word, to signify some quality or circumstance respecting it. adv. *adverbially.*

AD'VERSARY. *s.* An opponent; an enemy. pl. *adversaries.*

AD'VERSE. *adj.* Opposing, hostile, calamitous. adv. *adversely:* s. *adverseness, adversity,* pl. *adversities.*

ADVERT'. *v.* To attend to; to speak of. pr. par. *adverting;* past, *adverted:* s. *advertence:* adj. *advertent.*

ADVERTI'SE. *v.* To inform; to make public. pr. par. *advertising;* past, *advertised:* s. *advertisement, advertiser.*

ADVI'CE. *s.* Counsel, instruction, notice.

ADVI'SE. *v.* To counsel, to inform, to make acquainted. pr. par. *advising;* past, *advised:* adj. *advisable:* adv. *advisably:* s. *adviser.*

AD'VOCATE. *v.* To plead or espouse the cause of another. pr. par. *advocating;* past, *advocated:* s. *advocate, advocation, advocacy,* pl. *advocacies:* adj. *advocative.*

ADVOLU'TION. *s.* Act of rolling towards. adj. *advolutory.*

ADVOU'SON. *s.* The right of presentation to a church, or ecclesiastical benefice.

AE'RIAL. *adj.* Belonging to, or inhabiting the air; placed in the air.

Æ'RIE. *s.* A young brood or nest of hawks.

Æ'REFORM. *adj.* Gaseous; having the form of air.

Æ'ROLITE. *s.* A solid substance which has fallen out of the air, as a meteoric stone.

ÆROL'OGY. *s.* The doctrine of the air. pl. *ærologies:* adj. *ærological.*

ÆROM'ETER. *s.* An instrument for weighing the air.

ÆROSTA'TION. *s.* The science of weighing air.

Æ'RONAUT. *s.* One who ascends in a balloon. adj. *æronautical.*

AF'FABLE. *adj.* Of easy manners; courteous; complaisant. adv. *affably:* s. *affability,* pl. *affabilities.*

AFFAI'R. *s.* Business; something to be managed or transacted; in military language, a skirmish.

AFFECT'. *v.* To act upon; to influence; to pretend. pr. par. *affecting;* past, *affected:* s. *affectation:* adv. *affectedly, affectingly.*

AFFEC'TION. *s.* State of being affected; love; personal attachment. adj. *affectionate:* adv. *affectionately.*

AFFETUO'SO. A term of music, signifying to be sung or played tenderly.

AFFI'ANCE. *v.* To betroth; to bind, by promise, to marriage. pr. par. *affiancing;* past, *affianced.*

AFFIDA'VIT. *s.* A declaration upon oath.

AFFIL'IATE. *v.* To associate, ally, or unite with. pr. par. *affiliating,* past, *affiliated.*

AFFILIA'TION. *s.* Adoption; act of taking a son or a daughter.

AFFIN'ITY. *s.* Connexion with; relation to; relation by marriage, opposed to consanguinity. pl. *affinities.*

AFFIRM'. *v.* To ratify; to declare. pr. par. *affirming;* past, *affirmed:* s. *affirmance, affirmant, affirmation, affirmer:* adj. *affirmative, affirmable:* adv. *affirmatively.*

AFFIX. *v.* To unite to the end; to subjoin; to connect with. pr. par. *affixing;* past, *affixed:* s. *affix, affixion.*

AFFLA'TION. *s.* Act of breathing upon. adj. *afflative.*

AFFLICT'. *v.* To cause pain; to grieve. pr. par. *afflicting;* past, *afflicted:* s. *afflicter, affliction:* adj. *afflictive:* adv. *afflictively.*

AFFLUENCE. *s.* Act of flowing; exuberance of riches: plenty. adj. *affluent:* adv. *affluently.*

AFFLUX. *s.* Act of flowing to; the thing which flows. pl. *affluxes:* s. *affluxion.*

AFFORD'. *v.* To yield or produce; to grant or confer any thing. pr. par. *affording;* past, *afforded.*

AFFRAN'CHISE. *v.* To make free. pr. par. *affranchising;* past, *affranchised.*

AFFRAY'. *s.* The fighting of two or more persons, in some public place, and causing terror to others.

AFFRIC'TION. *s.* Act of rubbing one thing upon another.

AFFRIGHT'. *v.* To affect with fear; to terrify. pr. par. *affrighting;* past, *affrighted:* s. *affright, affrighter.*

AFFRONT'. *v.* To insult, to offend. pr. par. *affronting;* past, *affronted:* s. *affront, affronter.*

AFFU'SE. *v.* To pour one thing upon another. pr. par. *affusing;* past, *affused:* s. *affusion.*

AFLOAT'. adv. and adj. Floating.

AFORE'SAID. adj. Mentioned before.

AFRAID'. adj. Struck with fear; terrified; fearful.

AFRESH'. adv. Anew; over again.

AFRICAN. adj. Belonging or relating to Africa.

AFT. adv. Abaft; at the stern; to the stern.

AF'TER. prep. Following in place: in pursuit of; behind; in imitation of adv. *after.*

AF'TERCLAP. s. An event happening after an affair is supposed to be at an end.

AF'TERMOST. adj. Hindmost.

AF'TERPART. s. The latter part.

AF'TERPIECE. s. A farce, or any smaller entertainment, after the play.

AF'TERWARDS. adv. In succeeding time.

AF'TERNOON. s. The time from the meridian to the evening.

AGAIN'. adv. A second time; once more; on the other hand; besides.

AGAINST'. prep. In opposition to; contrary; in provision for.

A'GATE. s. A precious stone, of the lowest class.

AGE. s. A period of time; a hundred years; the latter part of life; old age; number of years. adj. *aged.*

A'GENT. s. That which acts; a substitute; a deputy; a factor.

A'GENCY. s. The quality of acting: state of being in action; the office of an agent. pl. *agencies.*

AG'GERATE. v. To heap up. pr. part. *aggerating;* past, *aggerated.*

AGGLOM'ERATE. v. To come together, in a ball, as thread. pr. par. *agglomerating;* past, *agglomerated:* s. *agglomeration:* adj. *agglomerative.*

AGGLU'TINATE. v. To join, as it by glue or some other mucilage pr. par. *agglutinating;* past, *agglutinated:* s. *agglutination:* adj. *agglutinative.*

AG'GRANDIZE. v. To make great: to enlarge; to increase in power. pr. par. *aggrandizing;* past, *aggrandized:* s. *aggrandizement, aggrandizer.*

AG'GRAVATE. v. To make heavier; to make worse. pr. par. *aggravating;* past, *aggravated:* s. *aggravation.*

AG'GREGATE. s. The entire; collective result. pr. par. *aggregating;* past, *aggregated:* s. *aggregation.*

AGGRESS'. v. To commit the first act of violence. pr. par. *aggress-*

ing; past, *aggressed:* s. *aggression, aggressor:* adj. *aggressive:* adv. *aggressively.*

AGGRIE'VE. *v.* To give sorrow; to vex. pr. par. *aggrieving;* past, *aggrieved:* s. *aggrievance, aggriever.*

AGHAST'. *adv.* Struck with terror; amazed.

A'GILE. *adj.* Nimble, ready, active. s. *agility,* pl. *agilities.*

A'GITATE. *v.* To affect with perturbation. pr. par. *agitating;* past, *agitated;* s. *agitation, agitator.*

AGO'. *adv.* Past; as, *long ago,* a *year ago.*

AGOG'. *adv.* In a state of warm imagination, or mental intoxication.

AGONIS'TIC, AGONIS'TICAL. *adj.* Relating to prize-fighting.

AG'ONY. *s.* The pangs of death; violent pain. pl. *agonies:* v. *agonize;* pr. par. *agonizing;* past, *agonized:* s. *agonizer.*

AGRA'RIAN. *adj.* Relating to land.

AGREE'. *v.* To be in concord; to be of the same opinion; to suit with. pr. par. *agreeing;* past, *agreed:* adj. *agreeable:* adv. *agreeably:* s. *agreeableness, agreement.*

AGRICUL'TURE. *s.* The art of cultivating land. adj. *agricultural:* s. *agriculturist.*

AGROUND'. *adv.* Touching the bottom.

A'GUE. *s.* An intermitting fever, with cold fits, succeeded by hot. adj. *aguish.*

AHA! *int.* A word intimating triumph and contempt.

AHEAD'. *adv.* Further onward than another; forward.

AID. *v.* To help, to support, to succour. pr. par. *aiding;* past, *aided:* s. *aid, aidance, aider:* adj. *aidless.*

AID'-DE-CAMP. *s.* An officer who conveys the orders of a military commander.

AIL. *v.* To pain, to trouble. pr. par. *ailing;* past, *ailed:* s. *ailment.*

AIM. *v.* To point the view; to direct the steps towards. pr. par *aiming;* past, *aimed:* s. *aim, aimer.*

AIR. *s.* The element encompassing the earth; a gentle gale; a species of music; the mien or manner of the person. adj. *airy:* v. *air:* pr. par. *airing;* past, *aired.*

AIR'DRAWN. *adj.* Drawn or painted in the air; imaginary.

AIR'ING. *s.* Salutary exposure to the air; a short journey, to enjoy the free air.

AIR'-GUN. *s.* A species of gun charged with condensed air.

AIR'-PUMP. *s.* A machine for exhausting air out of proper vessels.

AISLE. *s.* The walk in a church, or wing in a choir.

AJAR'. *adv.* Partly open, in relation to a door.

AKIN'. *adj.* Related to; allied to by nature.

ALABAS'TER. *s.* A kind of soft marble.

ALAC'RITY. *s.* Nimbleness, cheerfulness. pl. *alacrities.*

ALAMO'DE. *adv.* According to the fashion.

ALARM'. *v.* To call to arms; to surprise with the apprehension of danger; to disturb. pr. par. *alarming;* past, *alarmed.* s. *alarm, alarmist.*

ALA'RUM. *s.* See ALARM.

ALAS'! *int.* A word expressing lamentation, pity, or concern.

AL'BUM. *s.* A book with unwritten leaves.

AL'BUMEN. *s.* That which forms the serum of the blood; the white of an egg. adj. *albuminous.*

AL'CHYMY. *s.* Anciently, signified the most abstruse part of chymistry, as the attempt to transmute common metals into gold; but it is no longer ranked amongst the sciences. s. *alchymist.*

AL'COHOL. *s.* A highly rectified spirit of wine. v *alcoholize:* pr par. *alcoholizing*, past, *alcoholized.*

AL'CORAN. s. The Koran, the book of the Mahometan precepts.

AL'COVE. s. A recess.

AL'DER. s. A species of tree.

AL'DERMAN. s. An elder-man; a magistrate of an incorporated town. adj. *aldermanic*.

ALE. s. Strong beer.

ALEM'BIC. s. A vessel used in distilling.

ALERT. adj. Brisk, watchful. s. *alertness*. adv. *alertly*.

ALEXAN'DRINE. s. A line of verse, containing in English poetry 12 syllables.

ALGE'BRA. s. A kind of arithmetic. adj. *algebraic*: adv. *algebraically*: s. *algebraist*.

AL'IBI. Elsewhere; in law, a plea which alleges the defendant to have been distant from any certain place, when the crime was committed.

A'LIEN. s. A foreigner; a person not naturalized in the country into which he has emigrated.

A'LIENATE. v. To transfer to another; to withdraw the affections. pr. par. *alienating*; past, *alienated*: adj. *alienable*: s. *alienation*, *alienator*.

ALIF'EROUS, ALIG'EROUS. adj. Having wings.

AL'IMENT. s. Food, nourishment. adj. *alimental*, *alimentary*.

AL'IMONY. s. Legal allowance, by the husband to his wife, after separation. pl. *alimonies*.

AL'IQUOT. adj. Even; without a remainder, as 2 is an aliquot part of 6.

ALI'VE. adj. In the state of life; sprightly.

AL'KALI. s. A species of vegetable; a kind of chymical salt. adj. *alkaline*.

ALL. adj. The whole number; every one; every part. adv. *all*: s. *all*.

ALLAY'. v. To quiet, to pacify. pr par. *allaying*; past, *allayed*.

ALL-FOURS. s. A kind of game at cards; on both hands and feet, at the same time.

ALLEGA'TION. s. Act of alleging declaration; plea.

ALLE'GE. v. To affirm, to maintain, to declare. pr. par. *alleging*, past, *alleged*: s. *allegation*, *alleger*: adj. *allegable*.

ALLE'GIANCE. s. The duty of a subject to his superior: adj. *allegiant*.

AL'LEGORY. s. A figurative relation. pl. *allegories*: adj. *allegoric*, *allegorical*: adv. *allegorically*: v *allegorize*; pr. par. *allegorizing* past, *allegorized*: s. *allegorist*.

ALLE'GRO. A term in music, denoting a sprightly motion.

ALLELU'JAH. s. A word of spiritual exultation, signifying "give praise to God."

AL'LEMAND. A term in dancing.

ALLE'VIATE. v. To lighten, to ease. pr. par. *alleviating*; past, *alleviated*: s. *alleviation*, *alleviator*; adj. *alleviative*.

AL'LEY. s. A narrow walk or street.

ALLI'ANCE. s. State of being allied.

ALLIGA'TION. s. Act of binding together; the arithmetical rule which teaches to adjust the price of compounds formed of several ingredients of different value.

AL'LIGATOR. s. The crocodile; used chiefly for the crocodile of America.

ALLITERA'TION. s. Beginning several successive words with the same letter.

ALLOCA'TION. s. Act of putting one thing to another.

ALLO'DIAL. adj. Not feudal; independent.

ALLOT'. v. To distribute by lot; to grant; to distribute. pr. par. *allotting*; past, *allotted*: s. *allotment*.

ALLOW. v. To admit, to grant, to yield. pr. par. *allowing*: past, *allowed*: s. *allowance*: adj. *allowable*.

18

ALLOY. *s.* Baser metal mixed with that which is of greater value; abatement. *v. alloy;* pr. par. *alloying;* past, *alloyed.*

ALL-SAINTS-DAY. *s.* The day on which there is a general celebration of the saints; the first of November.

ALL'SPICE. *s.* A kind of spice.

ALL'SUFFICIENT. *adj.* Sufficient for every thing.

ALLU'DE. *v.* To speak of indirectly; to hint at. pr. par. *alluding;* past, *alluded.*

ALLU'RE. *v.* To entice. pr. par. *alluring;* past, *allured:* s. *allurer, allurement:* adj. *alluring:* adv. *alluringly.*

ALLU'SION. *s.* Act of alluding; indirect reference. adj. *allusive:* adv. *allusively.*

ALLU'VIAL. *adj.* Relating to alluvion; consisting of alluvion.

ALLU'VION. *s.* That which is carried by a flood, as land formed near a river.

ALLWI'SE. *adj.* Having infinite wisdom.

ALLY'. *v.* To unite by kindred, friendship, or confederacy; to confederate. pr. par. *allying,* past, *allied:* s. *ally,* pl. *allies.*

AL'MANAC. *s.* A calendar of the year.

ALMIGH'TY. *adj.* Omnipotent, all-powerful. s. *Almighty.*

ALM'OND. *s.* The nut of the almond-tree.

AL'MONER. *s.* One employed, by another, in the distribution of alms.

ALMOST'. *adv.* Nearly.

ALMS. *s.* Something given gratuitously, in relief of the poor.

ALMS'HOUSE. *s.* A house appropriated to the use of the poor.

ALOE. *s.* A kind of plant.

ALOFT'. *adv.* On high, above.

ALO'NE. *adj.* Without another; solitary.

ALONG'. *adv.* At length; lengthwise, throughout; onward.

ALOOF'. *adv.* At a distance.

ALOUD'. *adv.* Loudly.

AL'PHABET. *s.* The letters of a language. adj. *alphabetical*· adv. *alphabetically.*

AL'PINE. *adj.* Relating or belonging to the Alps.

ALREA'DY. *adv.* At the present time; before the present.

AL'SO. *adv.* In the same manner; likewise.

AL'TAR. *s.* A place raised for worship.

AL'TER. *v.* To change; to make otherwise than it is. pr. par. *altering;* past, *altered:* s. *alteration*· adj. *alterative, alterable.*

ALTERCA'TION. *s.* Dispute, debate, controversy. v. *altercate;* pr par. *altercating;* past, *altercated.*

ALTER'NATIVE. *s.* Choice of two things. s. *alternatively.*

ALTER'NATE. *v.* To perform alternately; to change one thing for another, reciprocally. pr. par. *alternating;* past, *alternated:* s. *alternation, alternative:* adj. *alternate:* adv. *alternately.*

ALTHE'A. *s.* A kind of shrub.

ALTHO'UGH. *conj.* Notwithstanding; however.

AL'TITUDE. *s.* Height.

ALTOGETHER. *adj.* Conjunctly, completely.

AL'UM. *s.* A kind of mineral salt. adj. *aluminous.*

ALUM'NI. *s.* Pupils; youths who have been educated at any particular college.

AL'WAYS. *adv.* Perpetually.

AM. *v.* The indicative mood, first person singular, of the verb *to be.*

AMAIN'. *adv.* With vehemence; with vigour.

AMAL'GAM. *s.* A composition of metals.

AMAL'GAMATE. *v.* To form into amalgam; to unite intimately. pr. par. *amalgamating;* past, *amalgamated:* s. *amalgamation:* adj. *amalgamative.*

AMANUEN'SIS. *s.* A person who

writes what another dictates, or copies what another has written. pl. *amanuenses*.

AM'ARANTH. *s.* A kind of plant.

AMASS'. *v.* To accumulate. pr. par. *amassing*; past, *amassed*: *s. amassment*.

AMATEU'R. *s.* A lover of any particular pursuit, or system.

AM'ATORY. *adj.* Relating to love; containing sentiments of love.

AMA'ZE. *v.* To confuse with terror; to put into confusion, with wonder. pr. par. *amazing*; past, *amazed*: *s. amazement*: adj. *amazing*: adv. *amazingly*.

AM'AZON. *s.* One of an ancient race of women, famous for valour; a virago. adj. *amazonian*.

AMBAS'SADOR. *s.* A person sent, in a public manner, from one government to another. fem. *ambassadress*: adj. *ambassadorial*.

AM'BER. *s.* A species of resinous gum.

AMBIDEX'TROUS. *adj.* Expert with both hands.

AMB'IENT. *adj.* Surrounding, encompassing.

AMBIG'UOUS. *adj.* Having a double meaning. *s. ambiguity*, pl. *ambiguities*: adv. *ambiguously*.

AMBI'TION. *s.* Desire of eminence. adj. *ambitious*: adv. *ambitiously*.

AM'BLE. *v.* To move easily; to walk affectedly. pr. par. *ambling*; past, *ambled*: *s. amble, ambler*: adv. *amblingly*.

AMBRO'SIA. *s.* The imaginary food of the gods. adj. *ambrosial*.

AM'BULATE. *v.* To walk about. pr. par. *ambulating*; past, *ambulated*: *s. ambulation, ambulator*: adj. *ambulatory, ambulative*.

AMBUSCA'DE. *s.* A hostile concealment; ambush. v. *ambuscade*; pr. par. *ambuscading*; past, *ambuscaded*.

AM'BUSH. *s.* The post where soldiers are placed, in order to fall unexpectedly upon an enemy.

AME'LIORATE. *v.* To make better; to improve. pr. par. *ameliorating*; past, *ameliorated*: *s. amelioration*: adj. *ameliorative*.

AMEN'. A Hebrew word, used in devotions, meaning, at the end of a prayer, *so be it*—at the end of a creed, *so it is*.

AME'NABLE. *adj.* Responsible, tractable. adj. *amenably*.

AMEND'. *v.* To reform, to correct. pr. par. *amending*; past, *amended*: *s. amendment, amender*.

AMENDS'. *s.* Recompense, compensation.

AMEN'ITY. *s.* Pleasantness, agreeableness of situation or of manners. pl. *amenities*.

AMERCE'. *v.* To punish with a pecuniary fine. pr. par. *amercing*; past, *amerced*: *s. amercement, amercer*.

AMER'ICAN. *adj.* Relating or belonging to America. *s. American*.

AMER'ICANISM. *s.* A word or phrase peculiar to the people of America.

AM'ETHYST. *s.* A precious stone, of a violet colour bordering on purple.

A'MIABLE. *adj.* Lovely, virtuous, pleasing. *s. amiability*, pl. *amiabilities*: adv. *amiably*.

AM'ICABLE. *adj.* Friendly, kind. adv. *amicably*: *s. amicability*, pl. *amicabilities, amicableness*.

AMID', AMIDST'. *prep.* In the midst; mingled with.

AMISS'. *adv.* Faulty, criminal.

AM'ITY. *s.* Friendship, peace. pl. *amities*.

AMMO'NIA. *s.* Volatile alkali. adj *ammoniac, ammoniacal*.

AMMUNI'TION. *s.* Military stores

AM'NESTY. *s.* Act of oblivion, pl *amnesties*.

AMONG', AMONGST'. *prep.* Mingled with.

AMORO'SO. A term in music, signifying in a soft or loving manner

AM'OROUS. *adj.* Loving; naturally inclined to love. adv. *omorously* *s. amorousness, amorist, amour*.

20

AMOTION. *s.* Act of removing.

AMPHIB'IOUS. *adj.* Capable of living on land or in water. *adv. amphibiously:* *s. amphibiousness.*

AMPHITHE'ATRE. *s.* A circular or oval building, of which the area or pit is reserved for exhibitions, and surrounded by seats, one above another. *adj. amphitheatric, amphitheatrical:* *adv. amphitheatrically.*

AM'PLE. *adj.* Large, wide, sufficient. *s. amplitude:* *adv. amply.*

AM'PLIFY. *v.* To enlarge, to exaggerate, to improve by new additions. *pr. par. amplifying;* past, *amplified:* *s. amplification, amplifier.*

AM'PUTATE. *v.* To cut off; a term applied peculiarly to limbs. *pr. par. amputating;* past, *amputated:* *s. amputation.*

AM'ULET. *s.* A sort of charm, worn about the person.

AMU'SE. *v.* To entertain; to gain the attention; to deceive, by artful management. *pr. par. amusing;* past, *amused:* *s. amusement, amuser:* *adj. amusive:* *adv. amusingly.*

AN. One of the indefinite articles.

ANABAP'TIST. *s.* One who opposes the baptism of infants. *s. anabaptism:* *adj. anabaptistic, anabaptistical.*

ANA'CHRONISM. *s.* Error in computing time; application of a wrong date to any event.

ANACREON'TIQUE. *s.* A poem in the manner of Anacreon.

AN'AGRAM. *s.* A conceit, arising from the transposition of letters. *adj. anagrammatical:* *adv. anagrammatically:* *s. anagrammatism, anagrammatist.*

ANALEC'TIC, ANALEC'TICAL. *adj.* Selecting.

ANAL'OGY. *s.* Resemblance, with regard to some circumstance or effect. *pl. analogies:* *adj. analogical:* *adv. analogically:* *v. analogize;* *pr. par. analogizing;* past, *analogized:* *s. analogism.*

ANAL'YSIS. *s.* Separation of elementary parts. *pl. analyses.*

ANALYT'IC, ANALYT'ICAL. *adj.* By analysis; by minute separation and examination of parts. *adv. analytically.*

AN'ALYZE. *v.* To resolve a compound into its first elements. *pr. par. analyzing;* past, *analyzed.* *s. analyzer, analyzation.*

AN'ARCHY. *s.* Want of government; national confusion. *pl. anarchies:* *s. anarchist:* *adj. anarchal.*

ANA'THEMA. *s.* A curse pronounced by ecclesiastical authority. *v. anathematize;* *pr. par. anathematizing;* past, *anathematized:* *s. anathematizer:* *adj. anathematical* *adv. anathematically.*

ANAT'OMY. *s.* The art of dissection. *pl. anatomies:* *s. anatomist* *v. anatomize;* *pr. par. anatomizing;* past, *anatomized:* *adj. anatomical:* *adv. anatomically.*

AN'CESTOR. *s.* One from whom a person is remotely descended. *s. ancestry,* *pl. ancestries:* *adj. ancestral.*

ANC'HOR. *s.* An instrument for holding a ship in a certain place. *v. anchor;* *pr. par. anchoring,* past, *anchored:* *s. anchorage.*

ANCH'ORET, ANCH'ORITE. *s.* A religious recluse; a hermit.

ANCHO'VY. *s.* A little sea-fish, used for sauce. *pl. anchovies.*

AN'CIENT. *adj.* Past, former, of great age. *adv. anciently.*

ANCIL'LARY. *adj.* Subservient.

AND. A copulative conjunction.

ANDAN'TE. In music;—expressive, distinct, exact.

AN'ECDOTE. *s.* Secret history; biographical incident; a minute passage of private life. *adj. anecdotal.*

ANEMOG'RAPHY. *s.* Description of the cause of the winds.

ANEMOM'ETER. *s.* An instrument

21

for measuring the power or velocity of the wind.

ANEM'ONE. *s.* A species of garden plant.

ANEM'OSCOPE. *s.* An instrument to show the direction of the wind.

AN'EURISM. *s.* An irregular dilation of an artery.

ANEW'. *adv.* Over again.

AN'GEL. *s.* A messenger; a celestial inhabitant or messenger. adj. *angelic, angelical:* adv. *angelically.*

ANG'ER. *s.* Severe displeasure; wrath. v. *anger;* pr. par. *angering;* past, *angered:* adj. *angry:* adv. *angrily.*

ANG'LE. *s.* A term in geometry. adj. *angular:* adv. *angularly:* s. *angularity,* pl. *angularities.*

ANG'LE. *v.* To fish with a rod and hook. pr. par. *angling;* past, *angled:* s. *angle, angler.*

ANG'LICISM. *s.* An English idiom. v. *anglicise;* pr. par. *anglicising;* past, *anglicised.*

ANG'UISH. *s.* Excessive pain, either of mind or body. adj. *anguished.*

ANHELA'TION. *s.* Act of panting; being out of breath.

ANIMADVER'T. *v.* To consider, to observe, to censure. pr. par. *animadverting;* past, *animadverted:* s. *animadverter.*

ANIMADVER'SION. *s.* Act of animadverting; reproof. adj. *animadversive.*

AN'IMAL. *s.* A living creature. adj. *animal.*

ANIMAL'CULE. *s.* A small animal.

AN'IMATE. *v.* To give life, to enliven, to encourage, to incite. pr. par. *animating;* past, *animated:* s. *animation, animator;* adj. *animative:* adv. *animatedly.*

ANIMOS'ITY. *s.* Vehement hatred; passionate malignity. pl. *animosities.*

AN'ISE. *s.* A species of aromatic plant.

ANK'LE. *s.* The joint which connects the foot with the leg.

AN'NALIST. *s.* A writer of annals. adj. *annalistic, annalistical:* adv *annalistically.*

AN'NALS. *s.* History, in which the events are recorded in yearly succession.

ANNEAL'. *v.* To heat glass, so that the colours laid on may pass through; to heat any thing in such a manner as to give it the proper temper. pr. par. *annealing,* past, *annealed.*

ANNEX'. *v.* To join to, at the end; to unite. pr. par. *annexing;* past, *annexed:* s. *annexation.*

ANNI'HILATE. *v.* To destroy, to annul. pr. par. *annihilating;* past, *annihilated:* s. *annihilation:* adj *annihilable.*

ANNIVER'SARY. *s.* A day celebrated as it annually returns. pl. *anniversaries:* adj. *anniversary*

ANNO DOM'INI. In the year of our Lord. A. D.

ANNO MUN'DI. In the year of the world. A. M.

AN'NOTATE. *v.* To add notes. pr par. *annotating;* past, *annotated.* s. *annotation, annotator:* adj. *annotative, annotatorial.*

ANNOUNCE'. *v.* To proclaim, to publish. pr. par. *announcing,* past, *announced:* s. *announcer.*

ANNOY'. *v.* To molest, to tease. pr. par. *annoying:* past, *annoyed.* s. *annoyance, annoyer.*

AN'NUAL. adj. Yearly, lasting only a year. adv. *annually.*

ANNU'ITY. *s.* Yearly rent; yearly income or allowance. pl. *annuities:* s. *annuitant.*

ANNUL'. *v.* To make void. pr. par. *annulling;* past, *annulled:* s. *annulment.*

AN'NULAR. adj. In the form of a ring. adj. *annularly.*

ANNUNCIA'TION. *s.* Act of announcing.

AN'ODYNE. *s.* A mitigator of pain.

ANOINT'. *v.* To rub with ointment; to consecrate by unction pr. par. *anointing;* past, *anointed:* s. *anointer.*

ANOM'ALY. s. Irregularity; deviation from the common rule. pl. *anomalies:* adj. *anomalous.*

ANON'. adv. Quickly, soon, sometimes.

ANON'YMOUS. adj. Without a name. adv. *anonymously.*

ANOTH'ER. adj. Not the same; one more; widely different.

AN'SWER. v. To speak in return to a question; to speak in opposition; to be accountable for; to correspond with. pr. par. *answering;* past, *answered:* s. *answer:* adj. *answerable:* adv. *answerably.*

ANT. s. An emmet.

ANTAG'ONIST. s. One who contends; an opponent. s. *antagonism.*

ANTARC'TIC. adj. A term in astronomy, relating to the southern pole.

ANTECE'DE. v. To precede; to go before. pr. par. *anteceding;* past, *anteceded:* s. *antecedence:* adj. *antecedent:* adv. *antecedently.*

ANTECES'SOR. s. One that goes before.

ANTECHAM'BER. s. A chamber that leads to the chief apartment.

ANTEDA'TE. v. To date earlier than the true time. pr. par. *antedating;* past, *antedated.*

ANTEDILU'VIAN. adj. Existing before the flood.

AN'TELOPE. s. A species of quadruped.

ANTEMERID'IAN. adj. Before noon. A. M.

ANTEMUN'DANE. adj. Before the creation of the world.

ANTEPE'NULT, ANTEPENUL'TIMATE. s. The last syllable in a word, or line of verse, except two.

ANTE'RIOR. adj. Going before; previous. s. *anteriority,* pl. *anteriorities:* adv. *anteriorly.*

AN'THEM. s. A hymn, sung in alternate parts.

AN'THRACITE. adj. Composed chiefly of carbon; not bituminous.

ANTHROPOPH'AGI. s. Eaters of human flesh; cannibals.

ANTICHRIS'TIAN. adj. Opposed to christianity. s. *antichristianity.*

ANTI'CIPATE. v. To act or think before an event. pr. par. *anticipating;* past, *anticipated:* s. *anticipation, anticipator:* adj. *anticipatory.*

AN'TIC. adj. Strange, ridiculous. s. *antic:* adv. *anticly.*

ANTICLI'MAX. s. A sentence, o. which the last part expresses something lower than the first. pl. *anticlimaxes.*

ANTICOSMET'IC. adj. Destructive of beauty.

AN'TIDOTE. s. A remedy for poison. adj. *antidotal.*

AN'TIENT. adj. See ANCIENT.

ANTIFE'BRILE. adj. Efficacious against fever.

ANTIMONARCH'AL. adj. Against government by a single person s. *antimonarchist.*

AN'TIMONY. s. A mineral substance, of a metalline nature. pl. *antimonies:* adj. *antimonial.*

ANTIFED'ERALIST. s. A person who was opposed to the establishment of the Federal Constitution of the United States.

ANTIPA'PAL. adj. Opposing popery.

ANTIP'ATHY. s. Natural dislike, aversion. pl. *antipathies.*

ANTIPH'ONY. s. An echo, or response. pl. *antiphonies.*

ANTIPESTILEN'TIAL. adj. Efficacious against the plague.

ANTIPH'RASIS. s. An expression in which the words are used in a sense opposite to their just meaning. pl. *antiphrases:* adj. *antiphrastic:* adv. *antiphrastically.*

ANTIP'ODES. s. People who live on opposite meridians, and in opposite latitudes. adj. *antipodal.*

ANTIPOL'OMIST. s. One opposed to war. adj. *antipolomistic.*

ANTIQUA'RIAN. adj. Relating to antiquity. s. *antiquarian, antiquary,* pl. *antiquaries.*

AN'TIQUATE. v. To make obsolete. pr. par. *antiquating;* past, *antiquated.*

ANTIQUE'. adj. Ancient, old. adv. *antiquely:* s. *antiquity,* pl. *antiquities.*

ANTISCORBU'TIC. adj. Efficacious against scurvy.

ANTISEP'TIC. adj. Preventive of putrefaction.

ANTISPASMOD'IC. adj. Efficacious against cramp.

ANTITH'ESIS. s. Contrast in words. pl. *antitheses.*

ANTITHET'IC, ANTITHETI-CAL. adj. Placed in contrast. adv. *antithetically.*

ANT'LER. s. Branch of a stag's horn. adj. *antlered.*

ANTŒ'CI. s. People who live in opposite latitudes, on the same meridian.

AN'VIL. s. The iron block on which a smith lays his metal, to be forged.

ANXI'ETY. s. Trouble of mind, about a future event. pl. *anxieties:* adj. *anxious:* adv. *anxiously.*

AN'Y. adj. Whoever, whatever; one of many.

APA'CE. adv. Quickly, speedily.

APART'. adv. Separately; at a distance.

APART'MENT. s. A separate room; a chamber.

AP'ATHY. s. Want of feeling, or of passion. pl. *apathies.*

APE. s. A kind of monkey. v. *ape;* pr. par. *aping;* past, *aped:* s. *aper:* adj. *apish:* adv. *apishly:* s. *apishness.*

APEP'SIA, APEP'SY. s. Want of natural concoction.

APE'RIENT. adj. Gently purgative. adv. *aperiently.*

AP'ERTURE. s. An open place.

AP'EX. s. The tip or point. Lat. pl. *apices;* English, *apexes.*

APHÆ'RISIS. s. A figure in grammar, by which a letter or syllable is taken from the beginning of a word. pl. *aphærises.*

APHE'LION. s. That part in the orbit of a planet, which is the most remote from the sun.

APH'ORISM. s. A maxim; a precept contracted into a short sentence. adj. *aphoristical:* adv. *aphoristically.*

AP'IARY. s. A place for bees. pl. *apiaries.*

APIECE'. adv. To the part or share of each.

APOC'ALYPSE. s. Revelation; the last book of the new testament. adj. *apocalyptical.*

APOC'RYPHA. s. Books added to the sacred writings, of doubtful authority. adj. *apocryphal:* adv. *apocryphally.*

APOGEE. s. A point in the heavens, in which the sun, or a planet, is at the greatest distance from the earth.

AP'OLOGUE. s. A kind of fable.

APOL'OGY. s. Excuse, defence. pl. *apologies;* v. *apologize,* pr. par. *apologizing;* past, *apologized:* adj. *apologetic, apologetical:* adv. *apologetically.*

AP'OPHTHEGM, AP'OTHEGM. s. A remarkable saying; a valuable maxim.

AP'OPLEXY. s. A general deprivation of animal sensation. pl. *apoplexies:* adj. *apoplectic, apoplectical:* adv. *apoplectically.*

APOS'TATE. s. One who has deserted his former profession, either in politics or religion. v. *apostatize;* pr. par. *apostatizing,* past, *apostatized:* adj. *apostatical:* s. *apostacy,* pl. *apostacies.*

APOS'TLE. s. A person sent with mandates; a title particularly applied to those whom Christ deputed to preach the gospel. adj. *apostolic, apostolical:* adv. *apostolically.*

APOS'TROPHE. s. A diversion of

24

speech, to another person or thing; in grammar, the contraction of a word, by the use of a comma. v. *apostrophize;* pr. par. *apostrophizing;* past, *apostrophized:* adj. *apostrophic.*
APOS'TUME. *s.* An abscess.
APOTH'ECARY. *s.* A compounder and vender of medicines. pl. *apothecaries.*
APO'THEGM, AP'OPHTHEGM. *s.* A remarkable saying; a valuable maxim.
APOTHE'OSIS. *s.* Heathenish deification. pl. *apotheoses.*
APPAL'. *v.* To affright, to dismay. pr. par. *appalling;* past, *appalled.*
AP'PANAGE. *s.* An appurtenance of land.
APPARA'TUS. *s.* Utensils; philosophical instruments. Latin, pl. *apparatus.*
APPAR'EL. *s.* Dress, habiliments. v. *apparel;* pr. par. *appareling;* past, *appareled.*
APPA'RENT. *adj.* Easily seen; certain; different from what a thing appears to be; seeming; not real. adv. *apparently.*
APPARI'TION. *s.* Appearance; a spectre.
APPEAL'. *v.* To remove a cause from a lower to a higher tribunal; to refer. pr. par. *appealing;* past, *appealed:* s. *appeal.*
APPE'AR. *v.* To come in view; to be apparent. pr. par. *appearing;* past, *appeared:* s. *appearance.*
APPE'ASE. *v.* To quiet, to pacify, to reconcile. pr. par. *appeasing;* past, *appeased:* adj. *appeasable:* s. *appeasement, appeaser.*
APPEL'LANT. *s.* One who appeals.
APPEL'LATE. *adj.* Created on appeal; having the power to hear and determine an appeal.
APPELLA'TION. *s.* A name.
APPEL'LATIVE. *adj.* Common, usual. adv. *appellatively.*
APPEND'. *v.* To hang, or attach. pr. par. *appending;* past, *appended:* s. *appendage:* adj. *appendant.*

APPEN'DIX. *s.* Something appended; a supplement, pl. *appendixes.*
APPERTAIN'. *v.* To belong to. pr. par. *appertaining;* past, *appertained:* s. *appertainment:* adj. *appertinent.*
AP'PETENCE, AP'PETENCY. *s.* Strong desire. pl. *appetences, appetencies.*
AP'PETITE. *s.* Desire; keenness of stomach.
APPLAUD'. *v.* To praise, by clapping the hands; to praise aloud. pr. par. *applauding;* past, *applauded:* s. *applauder, applause:* adj. *applausive.*
AP'PLE. *s.* A species of fruit.
AP'PLICABLE. *adj.* Suitable; attributable. s. *applicability,* pl. *applicabilities:* adv. *applicably.*
APPLICA'TION. *s.* Act of applying; attention to some particular affair; thing applied. adj *applicative, applicatory.*
APPLY'. *v.* To join; to lay upon; to use as means; to fix the mind upon; to have recourse. pr. par *applying;* past, *applied:* s. *applied appliance, applicant.*
APPOINT'. *v.* To fix; to mark out; to elect. pr. par. *appointing,* past, *appointed:* s. *appointer, appointment.*
APPOR'TION. *v.* To assign in just proportion. pr. par. *apportioning* past, *apportioned:* s. *apportioner apportionment.*
AP'POSITE. *adj.* Proper, appropriate. adv. *appositely:* s. *appositeness.*
APPOSI'TION. *s.* Addition of new matter; agreement of nouns with each other.
APPRA'ISE. *v.* To fix a price on pr. par. *appraising;* past, *appraised:* s. *appraiser, appraisement.*
APPRE'CIATE. *v.* To value at a just rate or price. pr. par. *appreciating;* past, *appreciated:* s. *appreciation:* adj. *appreciable.*
APPREHEND'. *v.* To seize, to understand; to think on with fear.

pr. par. *apprehending*; past, *apprehended*: s. *apprehender, apprehension*: adj. *apprehensive*: adv. *apprehensively*.

APPREN'TICE. *s.* One who is bound, by covenant, to remain with another, for a certain period, in order that he may acquire a knowledge of an art or a trade. v. *apprentice*; pr. par. *apprenticing*; past, *apprenticed*: s. *apprenticeship*.

APPRI'ZE. *v.* To inform. pr. par. *apprizing*; past, *apprized*.

APPROACH'. *v.* To come towards; to come near. pr. par. *approaching*; past, *approached*: s. *approach, approacher*: adj. *approachable*.

APPROBA'TION. *s.* Act of approving; approval. adj. *approbatory*.

APPRO'PRIATE. *v.* To assign to some particular use. pr. par. *appropriating*; past, *appropriated*: adj. *appropriate, appropriative*: s. *appropriateness, appropriation, appropriator*.

APPRO'VE. *v.* To like; to be pleased with; to prove. pr. par. *approving*; past, *approved*: adj. *approvable*: s. *approval, approver*.

APPROX'IMATE. *v.* To bring near; to approach. pr. par. *approximating*; past, *approximated*: s. *approximation*.

APRICOT. *s.* A kind of fruit.

A'PRIL. *s.* The fourth month.

A'PRON. *s.* A cloth hung before, to keep the other dress clean. adj. *aproned*.

APROPO'S. To the purpose; well-timed (pronounced *apropo'*.)

APT. adj. Fit, inclined, ready. adv. *aptly*: s. *aptness, aptitude*.

AP'TOTE. *s.* An indeclinable noun.

A'QUA. *s.* In Latin, signifies water.

AQUA-FOR'TIS. *s.* Nitric acid.

AQUA-RE'GIA. *s.* Nitro-muriatic acid.

AQUA'RIUS. *s.* A sign of the zodiac; the waterman.

AQUAT'IC. *adj.* Relating to any thing that inhabits water.

AQUA-TIN'TA. *s.* A species of engraving, imitating drawings made with Indian ink, or bistre.

AQUA-VI'TÆ. *s.* Brandy, or spirit of wine.

A'QUEOUS. *adj.* Watery.

A'QUEDUCT. *s.* An artificial conveyance for water.

A'QUILINE. *adj.* Resembling an eagle; (when applied to the nose) hooked, or Roman.

ARA'BIAN. *adj.* Relating or belonging to Arabia.

A'RABLE. *adj.* Fit for cultivation. s. *arability*, pl. *arabilities*.

AR'BITER. *s.* A judge; one who has the power of decision. fem *arbitress*, pl. *arbitresses*.

AR'BITRARY. *adj.* Despotic; independent of rules. adv. *arbitrarily*.

AR'BITRATE. *v.* To decide, to determine; to submit to arbitrators pr. par. *arbitrating*; past, *arbitrated*: s. *arbitration, arbitrator*

ARBORES'CENT. *adj.* Growing in the form of a tree.

AR'BORIST. *s.* One who makes trees his study.

AR'BOUR. *s.* A bower.

ARC. *s.* A segment of a circle; an arch.

ARCA'DE. *s.* A continued arch; a walk covered with an arched roof.

ARCA'NUM. *s.* A secret. pl. *arcana*.

ARCH. *s.* Part of a circle, not more than a half. v. *arch*; pr. par *arching*; past, *arched*.

ARCH. adj. Pronounced *ark*; when prefixed to a word beginning with a vowel, Chief.

ARCH. *adj.* Waggish, mirthful adv. *archly*: s. *archness*.

ARCHAN'GEL. *s.* One of the highest order of angels. (pronounced *ark-angel*.) adj. *archangelic*.

26

ARCHBISB'OP. *s.* A chief bishop. s. *archbishopric.*

ARCHDEA'CON. *s.* One who supplies the bishop's place and office. s. *archdeaconry,* pl. *archdeaconries.*

ARCHDUCH'ESS. *s.* A title given to certain princesses. pl. *archduchesses.*

ARCH'DUKE. *s.* A title given to certain princes.

ARCH'ER. *s.* One who uses a bow. s. *archery.*

ARCH'ETYPE. *s.* The original. pronounced *ark'-e-type:* adj. *archetypal.*

ARCHEOL'OGY. *s.* A discourse on antiquity. pronounced *ark-e-ol'ogy.* pl. *archiologies.*

ARCHIEPIS'COPAL, ARCHEPIS'COPAL. *adj.* Belonging to an archbishop. pronounced *ark-i-epis'copal,* or *ark-epis'copal.*

ARCH'ITECT. *s.* A professor of the art of building. pronounced *ark'-e-tect.* s. *architecture:* adj. *architectural, architective.*

ARCH'ITRAVE. *s.* The moulding next above the capital of a column. pronounced *ark'-e-trave.*

ARCH'IVES. *s.* A place for public records; or, the records themselves. pronounced *ark'-eeves.*

ARCH'ON. *s.* One of the nine chief magistrates of Athens. pronounced *ark'-on.*

ARC'TIC. *adj.* Relating to the arctic circle, or to the north. pronounced *ark'-tic.*

ARCUA'TION. *s.* Act of bending; curvity.

AR'DENT. *adj.* Hot, eager. s. *ardency,* pl. *ardencies:* adv. *ardently.*

AR'DOUR. *s.* Heat; heat of affection; desire; courage.

AR'DUOUS. *adj.* Hard to climb; difficult. adv. *arduously:* s. *arduousness.*

ARE. *v.* An inflexion of the verb *to be.*

A'REA. *s.* The surface contained between any lines.

ARE'NA. *s.* That part of a theatre which is left vacant for the contests or sports.

AR'GENT. *s.* The white colour. used in coats of arms, bright, like silver.

ARGILLA'CEOUS. *adj.* Partaking of clay.

AR'GUE. *v.* To reason, to dispute. pr. par. *arguing;* past, *argued:* s. *arguer, argument, argumentation:* adj. *argumentative:* adv *argumentatively:* adj. *argumentable.*

A'RID. *adj.* Dry, parched. s. *aridity,* pl. *aridities.*

A'RIES. *s.* A sign of the zodiac; the ram.

ARIET'TA. *s.* A short air, song, or tune.

ARIGHT'. *adv.* Rightly.

ARIO'SO. The movement of a common air.

ARI'SE. *v.* To mount upwards; to get up; to proceed from. pr. par. *arising;* past, *arisen.*

ARISTOC'RACY. *s.* A government by nobles; the highest class in society. pl. *aristocracies.*

ARIS'TOCRAT. *s.* One who favours aristocracy. adj. *aristocratic, aristocratical:* adv. *aristocratically.*

ARITH'METIC. *s.* The science of numbers; the art of computation. s. *arithmetician:* adj. *arithmetical:* adv. *arithmetically.*

ARITHMOM'ETER. *s.* An instrument for solving questions in arithmetic.

ARK. *s.* A large chest; a vessel to swim on the water, as the ark of Noah.

ARM. *s.* The limb which reaches from the hand to the shoulder; a branch.

ARM. *v.* To take arms; to furnish with arms. pr. par. *arming:* past, *armed.*

ARMA'DA *s.* A fleet of war

ARM'AMENT. *s.* A force equipped for war; implements of war.

ARM'FUL. *s.* As much as the arms can hold.

ARMIL'LARY. *adj.* Resembling a bracelet. *adj. armillated.*

ARM'ISTICE. *s.* A suspension of arms; a short truce.

ARM'LET. *s.* A little arm, as an *armlet* of the sea; a bracelet for the arm.

ARMO'RIAL. *adj.* Belonging to the arms of a family; belonging to armour.

ARM'OUR. *s.* Defensive arms. *s. armoury,* pl. *armouries; armourer.*

ARM'PIT. *s.* The hollow place under the shoulder.

ARMS. *s.* Weapons of offence

ARM'Y. *s.* A numerous body of soldiers. pl. *armies.*

AROMAT'IC. *adj.* Spicy, fragrant.

ARO'SE. *v.* Did arise.

AROUND'. *adv.* In a circle; on every side. *prep. around.*

AROU'SE. *v.* To wake from sleep; to excite. pr. par. *arousing;* past, *aroused.*

AR'QUEBUSS. *s.* A hand-gun. pl. *arquebusses.*

AR'RACK. *s.* Commonly called *rack.* A species of distilled liquor.

ARRAIGN'. *v.* A prisoner is said to be arraigned, when he is brought forth, and put upon his trial. pr. par. *arraigning;* past, *arraigned:* s. *arraignment.*

ARRANGE'. *v.* To place in order: to settle. pr. par. *arranging;* past, *arranged:* s. *arrangement, arranger.*

AR'RANT. *adj.* Bad in a high degree. adv. *arrantly.*

AR'RAS. *s* Tapestry.

ARRAY'. *v.* To put in order; to deck; to dress. pr. par. *arraying;* past, *arrayed.*

ARRE'AR. *s.* That which is left unpaid, or not done. *s. arrearage:* adv. *arrear,* behind.

ARREST'. *v.* To seize; to stop. pr. par *arresting* · past, *arrested.*

ARRE'T. *s.* A decree. pronounced *ar-ray.*

ARRI'VE. *v.* To come to; to reach pr. par. *arriving;* past, *arrived* s. *arrival.*

AR'ROGANCE. *s.* Undue assumption; haughtiness. adj. *arrogant* adv. *arrogantly.*

AR'ROGATE. *v.* To claim unjustly pr. par. *arrogating;* past, *arrogated:* s. *arrogation.*

AR'ROW. *s.* A dart; the pointed weapon which is shot from a bow.

AR'SENAL. *s.* A depositary for things requisite to war.

AR'SENIC. *s.* A mineral substance, which is a violent corrosive poison.

AR'SON. *s.* The crime of feloniously burning houses, and other things defined by law.

ART. *s.* The power of doing something not taught by nature; skill; dexterity. s. *artist.*

AR'TERY. *s.* A conical canal, which conveys the blood from the heart to all parts of the body. pl. *arteries:* adj. *arterial.*

ART'FUL. *adj.* Performed with art, cunning. adv. *artfully:* s. *artfulness.*

AR'TICHOKE. *s.* A species of esculent plant.

AR'TICLE. *s.* A part of speech; a particular part; terms; stipulation. *v. article;* pr. par. *articling,* past, *articled.*

ARTIC'ULATE. *v.* To pronounce distinctly. pr. par. *articulating,* past, *articulated:* s. *articulation:* adj. *articulate:* adv. *articulately.*

ART'IFICE. *s.* Trick, stratagem, fraud, art.

ARTIFI'CIAL. *adj.* Made by art fictitious. adv. *artificially.*

ART'IFICER. *s.* An artist. a manufacturer, a contriver.

ARTIL'LERY. *s.* Missive weapons; cannon. pl. *artilleries.*

ARTISAN'. *s.* A practiser of an art.

ART'LESS. *adj.* Unskilful, without fraud. adv. *artlessly:* s. *artlessness*

ASBES'TOS. *s.* A kind of stone.
ASCEND'. *v.* To go upwards. pr. par. *ascending;* past, *ascended;* adj. *ascendant:* s. *ascendency,* pl. *ascendencies.*
ASCEN'SION. *s.* Act of ascending. adj. *ascensive.*
ASCENT. *s.* Rise; an eminence or high place.
ASCERTAIN'. *v.* To know surely; to make certain; to fix; to establish pr. par. *ascertaining;* past, *ascertained:* adj. *ascertainable.*
ASCET'IC. *s.* A disagreeable professor of religion.
ASCRI'BE. *v.* To attribute. pr. par. *ascribing;* past, *ascribed:* adj. *ascribable.*
ASCRIP'TION. *s.* Act of ascribing.
ASHAM'ED. *adj.* Touched with shame.
ASH'ES. *s.* Remains of any thing burned.
ASHO'RE. *adv.* On shore; to the shore.
ASIAT'IC. *adj.* Relating or belonging to Asia.
ASI DE. *adv.* To one side; to another part; from the company.
ASK. *v.* To petition, to beg, to demand, to enquire, to question; to require. pr. par. *asking;* past, *asked.*
ASKANSE', ASKAUNSE'. *adv.* Sideways, obliquely.
ASKEW'. *adv.* Aside; with contempt or envy; obliquely.
ASLANT'. *adv.* Obliquely.
ASLEEP. *adv.* Sleeping; at rest.
ASP. *s.* A kind of poisonous serpent.
ASPAR'AGUS. *s* A kind of esculent plant
AS PECT. *s.* Appearance; direction towards.
ASP'EN. *adj.* Belonging to the asp-tree.
ASPER'ITY. *s.* Roughness, severity. pl. *asperities.*
ASPERSE'. *v.* To calumniate. pr. par. *aspersing;* past, *aspersed:* s. *asperser,* *aspersion:* adj. *aspersive.*
AS'PIRATE. *v.* To pronounce with full breath. pr. par. *aspirating;* past, *aspirated:* s. *aspirate, aspiration.*
ASPI'RE. *v.* To pant after; to desire eagerly. pr. par. *aspiring;* past, *aspired:* s. *aspirant.*
ASSAFŒT'IDA. *s.* A kind of ill smelling drug.
ASSAIL'. *v.* To assault, to attack pr. par. *assailing;* past, *assailed* s. *assailant:* adj. *assailable.*
ASSAS'SIN. *s.* A murderer; one who kills by secret violence. v *assassinate;* pr. par. *assassinating;* past, *assassinated:* s. *assassination.*
ASSAULT'. *v.* To attack, to assail pr. par. *assaulting;* past, *assaulted:* s. *assault.*
ASSAY'. *v.* To make trial; to try; to endeavour. pr. par. *assaying,* past, *assayed:* s. *assay.*
ASSEM'BLE. *v.* To bring together; to meet together. pr. par. *assembling;* past, *assembled:* s. *assembly,* pl. *assemblies* s. *assemblage.*
ASSENT'. *v.* To agree to. pr par. *assenting;* past, *assented:* s. *assent.*
ASSERT'. *v.* To maintain, to defend. pr. par. *asserting;* past, *asserted:* s. *assertion, assertor.*
ASSESS'. *v.* To apportion, or tax pr. par. *assessing;* past, *assessed* adj. *assessable:* s. *assessment, assessor.*
AS'SETS. *s.* Funds or property for distribution.
ASSEV'ERATE. *v.* To declare earnestly. pr. par. *asseverating;* past, *asseverated:* s. *asseveration.*
ASSIDU'ITY. *s.* Diligence. pl. *assiduities:* adj. *assiduous:* adv. *assiduously.*
ASSIGN'. *v.* To mark out; to convey a right; to appoint or depute. pr. par. *assigning;* past, *assigned* adj. *assignable:* s. *assignation.*
ASSIGNEE'. *s.* One to whom any thing is assigned.

ASSIM'ILATE. *v.* To convert to the same nature; to cause resemblance. pr. par. *assimilating;* past, *assimilated:* s. *assimilation.*

ASSIST'. *v.* To help. pr. par. *assisting;* past, *assisted:* s. *assistance:* adj. *assistant:* s. *assistant.*

ASSI'ZE. *s.* Regulation. (*assizes,* meeting of provincial law-courts.)

ASSO'CIATE. *v.* To join as a companion; to unite. pr. par. *associating;* past, *associated:* s. *associate, association.*

ASSORT'. *v.* To place in classes. pr. par. *assorting;* past, *assorted:* s. *assortment.*

ASSUAGE'. *v.* To mitigate, to ease, pr. par. *assuaging;* past, *assuaged:* s. *assuager.*

ASSUA'SIVE. *adj.* Softening, mitigating.

ASSU'ME. *v.* To take, to usurp. pr. par. *assuming;* past, *assumed.*

ASSUMP'TION. *s.* Act of assuming. adj. *assumptive:* adv. *assumptively.*

ASSU'RE. *v.* To give confidence; to insure. pr. par. *assuring;* past, *assured:* s. *assurance:* adj. *assuredly.*

AS'TERISK. *s.* A mark (*) used in printing.

ASTERN'. *adv.* In the hinder part of a ship; behind another ship.

AS'TEROIDE. *s.* Something partaking of the form of a star. adj. *asteroidal.*

AST'HMA. *s.* A difficult, short respiration. adj. *asthmatic, asthmatical.*

ASTON'ISH. *v.* To confound, to amaze. pr. par. *astonishing;* past, *astonished:* s. *astonishment:* adv. *astonishingly.*

ASTOUND'. *v.* To astonish, to stun. pr. par. *astounding;* past, *astounded.*

AS'TRAL. adj. Relating to the stars.

ASTRAY'. *adv.* Out of the right way, or place.

ASTRIC'TION. *s.* Act of contracting by medical applications; adj *astrictive.*

ASTRI'DE. *adv.* With the legs open; with a leg on each side.

ASTRIN'GENT. *adj.* Binding, contracting. s. *astringency,* pl. *astringencies.*

AS'TROLABE. *s.* An instrument formerly used for ascertaining latitudes.

ASTROL'OGY. *s.* The pretended science of foretelling by the stars. s. *astrologer:* adj. *astrological.*

ASTRON'OMY. *s.* The science of the heavenly bodies. s. *astronomer:* adj. *astronomical:* adv. *astronomically.*

ASTU'TE. *adj.* Subtle, cunning. adv. *astutely.*

ASUN'DER. *adv.* Apart, separately.

ASY'LUM. *s.* Place of safety.

AT. One of the prepositions.

ATE. *v.* Did eat. Little used.

A'THEIST. *s.* One who denies the existence of God. adj. *atheistical:* adv. *atheistically:* s. *atheism.*

ATHLET'IC. *adj.* Of a strong and vigorous body.

ATHWART'. *prep.* Across, through. adv. *athwart.*

AT'MOSPHERE. *s.* The air which surrounds the earth. adj. *atmospheric, atmospherical.*

AT'OM. *s.* A very small particle. adj. *atomic, atomical.*

ATO'NE. *v.* To expiate. pr. par. *atoning;* past, *atoned:* s. *atonement.*

ATRO'CITY. *s.* Horrible wickedness. pl. *atrocities:* adj. *atrocious,* adv. *atrociously.*

AT'ROPHY. *s.* Debility, for want of nourishment. pl. *atrophies.*

ATTACH'. *v.* To join, to arrest, to seize. pr. par. *attaching;* past, *attached:* s. *attachment.*

ATTACK'. *v.* To assault; to begin a contest. pr. par. *attacking;* past, *attacked:* s. *attack.*

ATTAIN'. *v.* To procure, to reach. pr. par. *attaining;* past, *attained.* s. *attainment.*

ATTAIN'DER. *s.* The act of attainting: state of being attainted.

ATTAINT'. *v.* To disgrace; to corrupt the blood, by a judgment after conviction of felony or treason. pr. par. *attainting*; past, *attainted*: *s. attaint.*

ATTEM'PER. *v.* To mingle, to soften, to fit to. pr. par. *attempering*; past, *attempered*: *s. attemperment.*

ATTEMPT'. *v.* To endeavour, to try. pr. par. *attempting*; past, *attempted*: *s. attempt.*

ATTEND'. *v.* To give attention, or aid; to be present at. pr. par. *attending*; past, *attended*: *s. attendance, attendant.*

ATTEN'TION. *s.* The act of attending: particular respect. adj. *attentive*: adv. *attentively*: *s. attentiveness.*

ATTEN'UATE. *v.* To make thin, or slender. pr. par. *attenuating*; past, *attenuated*: *s. attenuation.*

ATTEST'. *v.* To sign as a witness; to bear witness. pr. par. *attesting*; past, *attested*: *s. attestation, attester, attestor.*

AT'TIC. *adj.* Belonging or relating to Attica, or to Athens; pure; classical; elegant. *s. atticism.*

AT'TIC. *s.* The garret or uppermost room in a house.

ATTI'RE. *v.* To dress, to habit, to array. pr. par. *attiring*; past, *attired*: *s. attire.*

AT'TITUDE. *s.* A posture.

ATTOR'NEY. *s.* One appointed to transact business for another; a species of officer, in courts of law, proper. pl. *attorneys*; but often erroneously spelled *attornies.*

ATTRACT'. *v.* To draw towards. pr. par. *attracting*; past, *attracted*: *s. attraction*: adj. *attractive*: adv. *attractively.*

ATTRIB'UTE. *v.* To ascribe. pr. par. *attributing*; past, *attributed*: *s. attribute*: adj. *attributable.*

ATTRI'TION. *s.* Act of wearing any thing, by rubbing.

ATTU'NE. *v.* To make musical to tune. pr. par. *attuning*, past, *attuned.*

AU'BURN. *adj.* Brown; of a dark, reddish brown.

AUC'TION. *s.* A mode of public sale. v. *auction*; pr. par. *auctioning*; past, *auctioned*: *s. auctioneer.*

AUDA'CIOUS. *adj.* Impudently daring. adv. *audaciously*: *s. audacity*, pl. *audacities.*

AU'DIBLE. *adj.* Loud enough to be heard. adv. *audibly.*

AU'DIENCE. *s.* The act of hearing; a hearing; hearers.

AU'DIT. *v.* To examine the accounts of another. pr. par. *auditing*; past, *audited.*

AU'DITOR. *s.* A hearer; an examiner of public accounts. adj. *auditory*, pl. *auditories.*

AU'GER. *s.* A tool for boring holes.

AUGHT. *s.* Any thing.

AUGMENT'. *v.* To increase, to become larger, or more. pr. par. *augmenting*; past, *augmented*: *s. augmentation*: adj. *augmentative*: *s. augmenter.*

AU'GUR. *v.* To conjecture by signs; to portend. pr. par. *auguring*; past, *augured*: *s. augur, augury*, pl. *auguries.*

AUGUST'. *adj.* Great, magnificent. adv. *augustly*: *s. augustness.*

AU'GUST. *s.* The eighth month.

AUNT. *s.* A father's or mother's sister.

AURE'LIA. *s.* The first apparent change of the maggot of insects.

AURIC'ULAR. *adj.* Within the sense or reach of hearing; secret. adv. *auricularly.*

AU'RIST. *s.* An ear-surgeon.

AURO'RA-BOREA'LIS. *s.* A luminous meteor, peculiar to northern latitudes.

AUS'PICE. *s.* An omen, protection. adj. *auspicious*: adv. *auspiciously*: *s. auspiciousness.*

AUSTE'RE. *adj.* Harsh; of a distant manner. adv. *austerely*: *s. austerity*, pl. *austerities.*

AUS'TRAL. *adj.* Southern.

AUTHEN'TIC. *adj.* Proceeding from sufficient authority. *v. authenticate;* pr. par. *authenticating;* past, *authenticated:* adv *authentically:* s. *authenticity,* pl. *authenticities.*

AU'THOR. *s.* One who first effects or produces any thing. s. *authorship.*

AUTHOR'ITY. *s.* Testimony, influence, power. pl. *authorities:* adj. *authoritative:* adv. *authoritatively.*

AUTOBIOG'RAPHY. *s* Memoirs of any person, written by himself. pl. *autobiographies.*

AU'THORIZE. *v.* To make legal; to justify. pr. par. *authorizing;* past, *authorized:* s. *authorization.*

AU'TOCRAT. *s.* An absolute prince. adj. *autocratic:* adv. *autocratically:* s. *autocracy,* pl. *autocracies.*

AU'TOGRAPHY. *s.* A particular person's own hand-writing; or the original manuscript, distinguished from a copy. pl. *autographies:* adj. *autographical.*

AUTOM'ATON. *s.* A machine which has a power of motion within itself. adj. *automatical.*

AU'TUMN. *s.* The season of the year between summer and winter. adj. *autumnal.*

AUXIL'IARY. *s.* An assistant. pl. *auxiliaries:* adj. *auxiliary.*

AVAIL'. *v.* To aid in promoting; to profit. pr. par. *availing;* past, *availed:* s. *avail:* adj. *available:* adv. *availably.*

AV'ALANCHES. *s.* Prodigious snow-balls, that frequently roll down the mountains, in Savoy.

AVANT-COU'RIER. *s.* One who is despatched before the rest, to notify their approach.

A'VARICE. *s.* Insatiable desire of wealth. adj. *avaricious:* adv. *avariciously:* s. *avariciousness.*

AVAST'. *int.* Enough, stop.

AVAUNT'. *int.* A word of abhorrence, used to drive a person away.

AVENGE'. *v.* To punish in behalf of another; to revenge. pr. par *avenging;* past, *avenged:* s *avenger.*

A'VENUE. *s.* A way of approach.

AVER'. *v.* To declare solemnly. pr. par. *averring;* past, *averred:* s. *averment.*

A'VERAGE. *v.* To fix one degree of value upon things of different qualities. pr. par. *averaging,* past, *averaged:* s. *average.*

AVERSE'. *adj.* Not favourable opposed to. s. *aversion:* adv *aversely.*

AVERT'. *v.* To turn aside; to keep off. pr. par. *averting;* past, *averted:* s. *averter.*

A'VIARY. *s.* A place inclosed for birds. pl. *aviaries.*

AVID'ITY. *s.* Greediness, eagerness. pl. *avidities.*

AVOCA'TION. *s.* Business which calls a person away from his usual employment; opposed to vocation. adj. *avocative.*

AVOID'. *v.* To make void; to shun; to decline; to escape. pr. par. *avoiding;* past, *avoided:* s. *avoidance.*

AVOIRDUPOIS'. *adj.* A kind of weight, having 16 ounces in the pound.

AVOUCH'. *v.* To affirm, to maintain, to vindicate, to justify. pr. par. *avouching;* past, *avouched.*

AVOW'. *v.* To declare with confidence: to own or confess. pr. par. *avowing;* past, *avowed:* s. *avowal:* adj. *avowable:* adv. *avowedly.*

AVUL'SION. *s.* Act of pulling one thing from another. adj. *avulsive.*

AWAIT'. *v.* To expect, to attend. pr. par. *awaiting;* past, *awaited* s *awaiter.*

AWAKE'. *v.* To rouse out of sleep to put into new action pr. par *awaking;* past, *awoke.*

AWARD'. *v.* To adjudge, to deter

mine. pr. par. *awarding;* past, *awarded:* s. *award.*
AWE. s. Reverential fear; reverence; dread. adj. *awful:* adv. *awfully.*
AWK'WARD. adj. Inelegant, unpolite, clumsy. s. *awkwardness:* adv. *awkwardly.*
AWL. s. A pointed instrument, for boring holes in leather.
AWN'ING. s. A covering spread over a boat or ship, to keep off the sun and rain.
AXE. s. A kind of hatchet.
AX'IOM. s. A proposition, evident at the first view, and which cannot be made plainer by demonstration.

AX'IS. s. The line, real or imaginary, that passes through any thing, and on which it may revolve. pl. *axes.*
AX'LE, AX'LETREE. s. The pin which passes through the midst of a wheel.
AYE. adv. Yes.
AY'RY. s. The nest of a bird of prey. pl. *ayries.*
A'ZOTE. s. Nitrogen; that part of the atmospheric air, which will not support life.
AZ'IMUTH. s. A term in astronomy.
A'ZURE. s. Light blue.

B

BAB'BLE. v. To prate like a child; to talk idly. pr. par. *babbling;* past, *babbled:* s. *babble, babbler.*
BABE, BA'BY. s. An infant. pl. *babes, babies:* adj. *babyish:* adv. *babyishly.*
BABOON'. s. A kind of monkey.
BAC'CHANAL, BACCHANA'LIAN. s. A devotee to Bacchus, the god of wine. adj. *bacchanalian.*
BACH'ELOR. s. An unmarried man; one who has taken his first degree, at a college.
BACK. s. The hinder part of the body; the rear; the place behind; a large vat. adj. *back.*
BACK. v. To mount on the back of a horse; to maintain, as a second. pr. par. *backing;* past, *backed.*
BACK'BITE. v. To censure the absent. v. *backbite;* pr. par. *backbiting;* past, *backbitten:* s. *backbiter.*
BACKGAM'MON. s. A kind of game.
BACK'SLIDE. v. To fall off; to apostatize. pr. par. *backsliding;* past, *backslided:* s. *backslider.*
BACK'WARD. adj. Unwilling, hes-

itating, sluggish, dull. adv. *backwardly:* s. *backwardness.*
BACK'WARDS. adv. With the back forwards; towards the back; regressively.
BA'CON. s. The dried flesh of a hog.
BAD. adj. Ill, not good, vicious, unfortunate. adv. *badly:* s. *badness.*
BADE. The preterit of *bid.*
BADGE. s. A token by which a person is known; a mark.
BAD'GER. s. A kind of quadruped.
BAD'INAGE. s. Light or playful discourse.
BAF'FLE. v. To elude, to confound, to defeat. pr. par. *baffling;* past, *baffled:* s. *baffler.*
BAG. s. A sack or pouch. v. *bag;* pr. par. *bagging;* past, *bagged.*
BAGATELL'E. s. A trifle.
BAG'GAGE. s. The furniture of an army; luggage.
BA'GNIO. s. A house for bathing.
BAG'PIPE. s. A kind of musical instrument.
BAIL. s. Surety given for a person's appearance at court: he who bails

another. v. *bail;* pr par. *bailing* past, *bailed:* adj *bailable.*

BAI'LIFF. *s.* The chief magistrate of a certain class of corporate towns; a sheriff's officer who executes arrests; an under-steward of a manor.

BAIL'IWICK. *s.* The jurisdiction of a bailiff, or of a sheriff.

BAIT. *v.* To put meat upon a fishhook; to feed on a journey. pr. par. *baiting;* past, *baited:* s. *bait.*

BAIT. *v.* To attack with violence; to harass by the help of others. pr. par. *baiting;* past, *baited.*

BAIZE. *s.* A kind of coarse cloth.

BAKE. *v.* To harden in the fire; to harden with heat. pr. par. *baking;* past, *baked:* s. *baker.*

BAL'ANCE. *s.* An instrument for weighing; difference of weight or amount; equipoise. v. *balance;* pr. par. *balancing;* past, *balanced:* s. *balancer.*

BAL'CONY. *s.* A frame before the window of a room. pl. *balconies.*

BALD. *adj.* Wanting hair; naked; inelegant; mean. s. *baldness.*

BAL'DERDASH. *s.* Words jumbled together, without judgment.

BALE. *s.* A large bundle; a package. v. *bale;* pr. par. *baling;* past, *baled.*

BALE'FUL. *adj.* Full of misery; full of mischief. adv. *balefully.*

BALIS'TA. *s.* A warlike instrument, anciently used to throw stones and darts.

BALK. *s.* A great beam, used in building; a disappointment. v. *balk;* pr. par. *balking;* past, *balked.*

BALL. *s.* Any thing made in a round form; an entertainment of dancing.

BAL'LAD. *s.* A species of song.

BAL'LAST. *s.* Something put at the bottom of a ship, to keep it steady. v. *ballast;* pr. par. *ballasting;* past, *ballasted.*

BAL'LET. *s.* A kind of dance. (pronounced *hal-lay.*)

BALLOON'. *s.* A spheroid, formed of silk; which, when inflated with hydrogen gas, or rarefied air, ascends.

BAL'LOT. *s.* A mode of giving votes, originally by means of little balls. v. *ballot;* pr. par. *balloting;* past, *balloted.*

BALM. *s.* A species of aromatic herb; any thing that soothes or mitigates pain. adj. *balmy.*

BAL'SAM. *s.* Ointment; unguent; a kind of plant. adj. *balsamic.*

BALUSTRA'DE. *s.* An assemblage of balusters, fixed on a terrace, or on the top of a building.

BAMBOO'. *s.* An Indian plant, of the reed kind.

BAN. *s.* A curse, excommunication, interdiction.

BANA'NA. *s.* A species of plantain

BAND. *s.* Means of union or connexion; any thing bound round another; a company of soldiers, or of other persons. v. *band;* pr. par. *banding;* past, *banded.*

BAND'AGE. *s.* Something bound over another. v. *bandage;* pr. par. *bandaging;* past, *bandaged.*

BAND'BOX. *s.* A slight box, used for things of small weight. pl *bandboxes.*

BAN'DIT. *s.* An outlawed robber. pl. *banditti.*

BAN'DY. *adj.* Crooked.

BAN'DY. *v.* To beat to and fro; to exchange; to agitate. pr. par. *bandying;* past, *bandied.*

BANE. *s.* Poison; that which destroys. adj. *baneful;* s. *banefulness.*

BANG. *v.* To beat, to thump, to handle roughly. pr. par. *banging,* past, *banged:* s. *bang.*

BAN'ISH. *v.* To condemn to leave the country; to drive away. pr. par. *banishing;* past, *banished* s. *banishment.*

BAN'ISTRE. *s.* A kind of railing.

BANK. *s.* The earth which confines a river or lake; any heap piled up; a place where money is de-

34

posited. v. b*nk*; pr. par. *banking:* past, *banked:* s. *banker.*

BAN'KRUPT. *adj.* In debt, beyond the power of paying. s. *bankrupt, bankruptcy,* pl. *bankruptcies.*

BAN'NER. *s.* A flag, a standard.

BAN'NERET. *s.* A little banner.

BAN'QUET. *s.* A feast. v. *banquet;* pr. par. *banqueting;* past, *banqueted.*

BAN'TER. *v.* To challenge idly, to tease. pr. par. *bantering;* past, *bantered:* s. *banter, banterer.*

BANT'LING. *s.* A little child.

BAPTI'ZE. *v.* To administer baptism; to christen. pr. par. *baptizing;* past, *baptized.* s. *baptism:* adj. *baptismal.*

BAP'TIST. *s.* One who practises adult baptism, by immersion.

BAR. *s.* That which is laid across a passage, to hinder entrance; a bolt; obstruction; the place where causes of law are tried, or where criminals stand; members of the profession of law, &c.

BAR. *v.* To fasten or shut with a bolt; to prevent. pr. par. *barring;* past, *barred.*

BARB. *s.* The points that stand backwards, in an arrow. v. *barb;* pr. par. *barbing;* past, *barbed.*

BARBA'RIAN. *s.* A man uncivilized; a brutal monster. adj. *barbarian.*

BAR'BAROUS. *adj.* Uncivilized, cruel. s. *barbarism, barbarity,* pl. *barbarities:* adv. *barbarously.*

BARBECUE, BAR'BACUE. *s.* A large animal roasted whole. v. *barbecue;* pr. par. *barbecuing;* past, *barbecued.*

BAR'BER. *s.* A man who shaves beards for hire.

BARD. *s.* A poet. adj. *bardic.*

BARE. *adj.* Naked, unadorned, indigent, threadbare. v. *bare;* pr. par. *baring;* past, *bared:* adv. *barely:* s. *bareness.*

BARE'FACED. *adj.* With the face naked; impudent. adv. *barefacedly* s. *barefacedness.*

BARE'FOOTED. *adj.* Without shoes or stockings.

BARE'HEADED. *adj.* With the head uncovered.

BARE'LEGGED. *adj.* Having the legs bare.

BARE'NECKED. *adj.* Having the neck bare.

BAR'GAIN. *s.* A contract; a stipulation; the thing bought or sold v. *bargain;* pr. par. *bargaining* past, *bargained:* s. *bargainer.*

BARGE. *s.* A pleasure-boat; a sea-commander's boat.

BARK. *s.* The rind or covering of a tree; a small ship. v. *bark;* pr. par. *barking;* past, *barked.*

BARK. *v.* To make the loud noise uttered by a dog. v. *bark;* pr par. *barking;* past, *barked:* s. *bark, barker.*

BAR'LEY. *s.* A species of grain.

BARM. *s.* Yeast; the matter put into a liquid, to cause it to ferment. adj. *barmy.*

BARN. *s.* A house in which is preserved any sort of grain, hay, or straw.

BAR'NACLE. *s.* A kind of shell fish; a species of sea-fowl.

BAROM'ETER. *s.* An instrumen for ascertaining the pressure o the atmosphere. adj. *barometrical* adv. *barometrically.*

BAR'ON. *s.* A degree of nobility next to a viscount. fem. *baroness* pl. *baronesses:* s. *barony,* pl. *baronies:* adj. *baronial.*

BAR'ONET. *s.* The lowest degree of honour in Great Britain and Ireland, that is hereditary. s. *baronetcy,* pl. *baronetcies.*

BAR'RACK. *s.* A building to lodge soldiers; a temporary barn.

BAR'REL. *s.* A round, wooden vessel; a cylinder. v. *barrel;* pr par. *barreling;* past, *barreled.*

BAR'REN. *adj.* Unfruitful, not fertile. s. *barrenness.*

BARRICA'DE. *v.* To stop up a passage. pr. par. *barricading;* past, *barricaded:* s. *barricade.*

35

BAR—BAS

BAR'RIER. *s.* A barricade, a fortification.
BAR'RISTER. *s.* A person qualified to plead the cause of clients, in a court of justice.
BAR'ROW. *s.* A kind of carriage, moved or supported by the hand.
BAR'ROW. *s.* A hillock over a grave.
BAR'TER. *v.* To exchange one thing for another. pr. par. *bartering;* past, *bartered:* s. *barter, barterer.*
BASAL'TES. *s.* A kind of stone, found in perpendicular blocks. adj. *basaltic.*
BASE. *s.* The bottom of any thing; the string which produces a base sound. v. *base;* pr. par. *basing;* past, *based.*
BASE. *adj.* Mean, dishonest. adv. *basely:* s. *baseness.*
BASE'MENT. *s.* A continued base, extending a considerable length.
BASHAW'. *s.* A pacha, or viceroy of a Turkish province.
BASH'FUL. *adj.* Modest, shy, sheepish. s. *bashfulness:* adv. *bashfully.*
BASIL'IKON. *s.* An ointment.
BAS'ILISK. *s.* A kind of serpent.
BA'SIN. *s.* A small vessel to hold water, for washing; a pond.
BA'SIS. *s.* The foundation, first principle. pl. *bases.*
BASK. *v.* To lie in a place, in order to receive heat. pr. par. *basking;* past, *basked.*
BAS'KET. *s.* A vessel made of twigs, rushes, or splinters.
BASS. *adj.* In music—grave, deep.
BASS-RELIE'F. *s.* Sculpture, the figures of which do not stand out from the ground, in their full proportion.
BASSOON'. *s.* A species of musical instrument.
BAS'TARD. *s.* An illegitimate child; any thing spurious. adj. *bastard;* s. *bastardy,* pl. *bastardies:* v. *bastardize;* pr. par. *bastardizing;* past, *bastardized.*

BAS—BAY

BASTE. *v.* To beat with a stick; to soften with butter, when roasting; to sew slightly. pr. par. *basting;* past, *basted.*
BASTINA'DE, BASTINA'DO. *s.* A Turkish punishment. v. *bastinade,* pr. par. *bastinading;* past, *bastinadoed.*
BAS'TION. *s.* A huge mass of earth, standing out from a rampart; a bulwark.
BAT. *s.* A kind of animal.
BATCH. *s.* A quantity of bread baked at one time.
BATCH'ELOR. See BACHELOR.
BATE. *v.* To lessen; to lower the price. pr. par. *bating;* past, *bated.*
BATH. *s.* A vessel for bathing in.
BATHE. *v.* To wash; to go into a bath. pr. par. *bathing;* past, *bathed.*
BATH'OS. *s.* The art of sinking, in poetry, or other literary composition.
BA'TON. *s.* A marshal's staff.
BATTAL'ION. *s.* A certain division of an army.
BAT'TER. *v.* To beat against, with violence. pr. par. *battering;* past, *battered:* s. *batter, battery,* pl. *batteries.*
BAT'TLE. *s.* A fight; an encounter between opposite armies. pr. par *battling;* past, *battled:* s. *battler.*
BAT'TLEDORE. *s.* An instrument used for striking a shuttlecock.
BAT'TLEMENT. *s.* A wall with open places, to look through, or annoy an enemy.
BAULK. See BALK.
BAW'BLE. *s.* A gewgaw; a trifling piece of finery.
BAWD. *s.* A procurer, or procuress. s. *bawdry,* pl. *bawdries:* adj. *bawdy:* adv. *bawdily.*
BAWL. *v.* To cry out with great vehemence. pr. par. *bawling,* past, *bawled:* s. *bawl, bawler.*
BAY. *adj.* Inclining to a chesnut colour.
BAY. *s.* An opening into the land; a harbour; the state of any ani-

mal being on the defensive, and surrounded by enemies; as, "a stag at bay."

BAY. *s.* A kind of laurel.

BAY'ONET. *s.* A kind of short sword, fixed at the end of a musket. v. *bayonet;* pr. par. *bayoneting;* past, *bayoneted.*

BAZAR'. *s.* A constant market; a covered market-place.

BE. *v.* To have some certain state; to exist. pr. par. *being;* past, *been:* s. *being.*

BEACH. *s.* The shore, or strand.

BEA'CON. *s.* A mark erected, to direct navigators. s. *beaconage.*

BEAD. *s.* A very small globe. pl. *beads,* small globes strung on a thread, and used by the Romanists, to count their prayers.

BEA'DLE. *s.* A petty officer in parishes.

BEAD'ROLL. *s.* A catalogue of those who are to be mentioned in prayers.

BEADS'MAN. *s.* A man employed in praying, generally for another.

BEA'GLE. *s.* A small hound.

BEAK. *s.* The bill or horny mouth of a bird; the head of a ship. adj. *beaked.*

BEAM. *s.* The main piece of timber which supports the lofts of a house; any long piece of timber; that part of a balance at the end of which the scales are suspended; the pole of a chariot; a ray of light. adj. *beamy.*

BEAM. *v.* To shoot forth; to emit; to emit rays or beams. pr. par. *beaming;* past, *beamed.*

BEAN. *s.* A species of leguminous fruit, for food.

BEAR. *v.* To convey or carry; to suffer pain; to endure. pr. par. *bearing;* past, *borne:* s. *bearer.*

BEAR. *s.* A species of quadruped. adj. *bearish.*

BEAR'ING. *s.* The site of any thing, with regard to something else; gesture; mien.

BEARD. *s.* The hair that grows on the lips and chin. v. *beard;* pr. par. *bearding;* past, *bearded.* adj. *beardless, beardy.*

BEAST. *s.* An animal distinguished from birds, insects, fishes, and man. adj. *beastlike, beastly:* s. *beastliness.*

BEAT. *v.* To strike, to conquer, to throb. pr. par. *beating;* past, *beaten:* s. *beat.*

BEAT'IFY. *v.* To make happy; to bless. pr. par. *beatifying;* past, *beatified:* adj. *beatific, beatifical:* adv. *beatifically:* s. *beatification, beatitude.*

BEAU. *s.* A fop. French plural *beaux.*

BEAU-MOND'E. *s.* The gay or fashionable world.

BEAU'TY. *s.* That assemblage o graces which pleases the eye. v *beautify;* pr. par. *beautifying* past, *beautified:* adj. *beautiful, beauteous:* adv. *beautifully, beauteously.*

BEA'VER. *s.* A species of amphibious animal, covered with a fine fur; a hat, made of the fine fur o. the beaver.

BEA'VER. *s.* That part of a helmet which can be raised whe drinking.

BECALM'. *v.* To still the elements to deprive of wind. pr. par. *becalming;* past, *becalmed.*

BECA'ME. *v.* The preterit of *become.*

BECAU'SE. *conj.* For this reason; for; on this account.

BECK. *s.* A sign with the hand; nod of command.

BECK'ON. *v.* To make a sign. pr. par. *beckoning;* past, *beckoned*

BECO'ME. *v.* To enter into some state or condition; to appear in a manner suitable and pleasing. pr. par. *becoming;* past, *become* adv. *becomingly.*

BED. *s.* That on which any thing lies; a bank of earth raised in a garden. v. bed; pr. par. bedding; past, bedded.

BEDAUB'. v. To daub over. pr. par. bedaubing; past, bedaubed.

BED'DING. s. The furniture of a bed.

BEDEW'. v. To moisten with dew; to moisten gently. pr. par. bedewing; past, bedewed.

BED'FELLOW. s. One that lies in the same bed.

BEDIM'. v. To make dim. pr. par. bedimming; past, bedimmed.

BEDIZ'EN. v. To dress out. pr. par. bedizening; past, bedizened.

BED'LAM. s. Corrupted from Bethlehem; the name of a religious house in London, converted into an hospital for the insane. s. bedlamite.

BED'RIDDEN. adj. Confined to bed, by age or sickness.

BED'ROOM. s. A bed-chamber.

BED'STEAD. s. The frame on which a bed is placed.

BEE. s. The insect that makes honey.

BEE'HIVE. s. The case in which bees are kept.

BEACH. s. A kind of deciduous tree. adj. beachen.

BEEF. s. The flesh of an ox, bull, or cow. pl. beeves, fat oxen for killing.

BEEN. v. The past par. of the v. to be.

BEER. s. A beverage made of malt and hops.

BEET. s. The name of an esculent plant.

BEET'LE. s. A species of insect; a heavy mallet.

BEET'LE. v. To jut out; to beat with a beetle. pr. par. beetling; past, beetled: s. beetler.

BEFAL'. v. To happen to. pr. par. befalling; past, befallen; pret. befel.

BEFIT'. v. To suit, to become. pr. par. befitting; past, befitted.

BEFORE. prep. Farther onward, in the front of; in the presence of. adv. before.

BEFO'REHAND. adv. In a state of anticipation; previously.

BEFRIEND'. v. To favour, to be kind to. pr. par. befriending; past, befriended.

BEG. v. To ask, to seek by petition. pr. par. begging; past, begged.

BEGAN'. v. Did begin; pr. of begin.

BEGET'. v. To generate, to produce. pr. par. begetting; past, begot, begotten: s. begetter.

BEG'GAR. v. To reduce to beggary. pr. par. beggaring; past, beggared: s. beggar, beggary adj. beggarly.

BEGIN'. v. To enter upon something new. pr. par. beginning, past, begun: pret. began: s. beginner, beginning.

BEGIRD'. v. To bind with a girdle; to surround. pr. par. begirding: past. begirt.

BEGO'NE. int. Go away; hence, haste away.

BEGOT'. v. The preterit of beget past par. begotten.

BEGRI'ME. v. To soil with dirt deeply impressed. pr. par. begriming; past, begrimed.

BEGRUDG'E. v. To envy. pr. par begrudging; past, begrudged.

BEGUI'LE. v. To delude, to deceive. pr. par. beguiling; past beguiled: s. beguiler.

BEHA'VE. v. To conduct. pr. par behaving; past, behaved: s. behaviour.

BEHEAD'. v. To kill, by cutting off the head. pr. par. beheading; past beheaded: s. beheader.

BEHELD'. v. Did behold.

BEHEST'. s. Command, precept.

BEHIND'. prep. On the back of, in the rear of. adv. behind.

BEHIND'HAND. adv. In a state in which rent or profit, or any advantage, is anticipated; backward, tardy.

BEHOLD'. *v.* To view, to see. pr. par. *beholding;* past, *beheld:* s. *beholder.*

BEHOOVE. *v.* To be fit; to be meet. pr. par. *behooving;* past, *behooved.*

BE'ING. *s.* Existence, opposed to nonentity; an individual in existence.

BELA'BOUR. *v.* To beat, to thump. pr. par. *belabouring;* past, *belaboured.*

BELAY'. *v.* To splice; to mend a rope, by laying one end over another. pr. par. *belaying;* past, *belayed.*

BELCH. *v.* To eject wind from the stomach; to throw out. pr. par. *belching;* past, *belched:* s. *belcher.*

BEL'DAME. *s.* A hag.

BEL'FRY. *s.* The place where bells are suspended and rung. pl. *belfries.*

BELI'E. *v.* To give the lie to; to calumniate; to give a false representation of. pr. par. *belying;* past, *belied:* s. *belier.*

BELIE'VE. *v.* To credit upon the authority of another. pr. par. *believing;* past, *believed:* s. *believer,* *belief.*

BELL. *s.* A hollow body, of cast metal, formed to sound by something striking it.

BELLE. *s.* A young lady.

BELLE-LET'TRES. *s.* Polite literature.

BELLIG'ERENT, BELLIG'ERANT. *adj.* Waging war. s. *belligerant.*

BEL'LOW. *v.* To make a noise as a bull; to vociferate. pr. par. *bellowing;* past, *bellowed:* s. *bellow, bellower.*

BEL'LOWS. *s.* An instrument used to blow a fire.

BELONG'. *v.* To be the property of. pr. par. *belonging;* past, *belonged.*

BELOW'. *prep.* Under in place, rank, or dignity; unworthy of. adv. *below.*

BEL'LY. *s.* That part of the body which contains the bowels. pl. *bellies.*

BELT. *s.* A girdle. v. *belt;* pr. par. *belting;* past, *belted.*

BEMOAN'. *v.* To lament. pr. par. *bemoaning;* past, *bemoaned.*

BENCH. *s.* A kind of seat. pl. *benches.*

BEN'CHER. *s.* A judge.

BEND. *v.* To incline, to curve, to subdue. pr. par. *bending;* past, *bent:* s. *bend:* adj. *bendable.*

BENEATH'. *prep.* Under, lower in rank.

BENEDIC'TION. *s.* A blessing.

BENEFAC'TOR. *s.* One who confers a benefit. fem. *benefactress,* pl. *benefactresses;* s. *benefaction.*

BEN'EFICE. *s.* An ecclesiastical living. adj. *beneficed.*

BENEF'ICENCE. *s.* Active goodness. adj. *beneficent:* adv. *beneficently.*

BENEFI'CIAL. *adj.* Advantageous, helpful. adv. *beneficially.*

BEN'EFIT. *s.* Favour conferred; advantage; profit. adj. *beneficial:* adv. *beneficially:* v. *benefit;* pr. par. *benefiting;* past, *benefited.*

BENEV'OLENCE. *s.* Disposition to do good; kindness. adj. *benevolent:* adv. *benevolently.*

BENIGN'. *adj.* Kind, liberal, generous. adv. *benignly.*

BENIG'NITY. *s.* Graciousness, actual kindness. pl. *benignities* adj. *benignant:* adv. *benignantly.*

BEN'ISON. *s.* Blessing, benediction.

BENT. *v.* The pret. and past par. of *bend:* s. *bent,* inclination, determination.

BENUMB'. *v.* To make torpid; to stupify. pr. par. *benumbing;* past, *benumbed.*

BEQUEATH'. *v.* To leave by will to another. pr. par. *bequeathing,* past, *bequeathed:* s. *bequeather.*

BEQUEST'. *s.* Something left by will.

BEREAVE'. *v.* To strip of; to deprive of. pr. par. *bereaving;* past, *bereft:* s. *bereavement.*

BERGAMOT'. *s.* A kind of perfume.

BER'RY. *s.* A small fruit. pl. *berries.*

BER'YL. *s.* A kind of precious stone.

BESEECH'. *v.* To intreat, to supplicate. pr. par. *beseeching;* past, *besought.*

BESET'. *v.* To besiege, to hem in, to embarrass. pr. par. *besetting;* past, *beset.*

BESHREW'. *v.* To wish a curse to; to wish ill to. pr. par. *beshrewing;* past, *beshrewed.*

BESI'DE. *prep.* At the side of another.

BESI'DES. *prep.* Over and above. *adv. besides.*

BESIE'GE. *v.* To lay siege to. pr. par. *besieging;* past, *besieged:* s. *besieger.*

BESME'AR. *v.* To daub, to soil. pr. par. *besmearing;* past, *besmeared.*

BESOU'GHT'. *v.* The pret. and past par. of the v. *beseech.*

BESPANG'LE. *v.* To adorn with spangles. pr. par. *bespangling;* past, *bespangled.*

BESPAT'TER. *v.* To soil, by throwing filth. pr. par. *bespattering;* past, *bespattered.*

BESPEAK'. *v.* To order any thing, prospectively. pr. par. *bespeaking;* past, *bespoke, bespoken.*

BESPRINK'LE. *v.* To sprinkle over. pr. par. *besprinkling;* past, *besprinkled.*

BEST. *adj.* Superlative of good. *adv. best.*

BES'TIAL. *adj.* Belonging to a beast; brutal. s. *bestiality,* pl. *bestialities:* adv. *bestially.*

BESTIR'. *v.* To put into vigorous action. pr. par. *bestirring;* past, *bestirred.*

BESTOW'. *v.* To give, to confer upon. pr. par. *bestowing;* past, *bestowed:* s. *bestower.*

BESTRI'DE. *v.* To stride over; to ride on. pr. par. *bestriding,* past, *bestrode.*

BET. *s.* A wager. *v. bet;* pr. par. *betting;* past, *bet, betted:* s. *better*

BETI'DE. *v.* To come to pass; to happen.

BETI'MES. *adv.* Seasonably; early in the day.

BETO'KEN. *v.* To signify, to foreshow. pr. par. *betokening;* past, *betokened:* s. *betokener.*

BETRAY'. *v.* To give into the hands of an enemy; to disclose that which has been intrusted to secresy. pr. par. *betraying;* past, *betrayed:* s. *betrayer.*

BETROTH'. *v.* To contract in marriage. pr. par. *betrothing;* past, *betrothed:* s. *betrothment.*

BET'TER. *adj.* Comparative of good. v. *better;* pr. par. *bettering,* past, *bettered:* adv. *better.*

BETWEEN', BETWIXT. *prep.* In the intermediate space; from one to another, in partnership.

BEV'ERAGE. *s.* Drink.

BEV'Y. *s.* A flock of birds; a company. pl. *bevies.*

BEWAI'L. *v.* To bemoan, to lament. pr. par. *bewailing;* past, *bewailed.* s. *bewailer.*

BEWA'RE. *v.* To regard with caution.

BEWIL'DER. *v.* To lose in pathless places; to puzzle. pr. par. *bewildering;* past, *bewildered.*

BEWITCH'. *v.* To injure by witchcraft; to charm; to enrapture. pr par. *bewitching;* past, *bewitched.* s. *bewitcher, bewitchery,* pl. *bewitcheries.*

BEYOND'. *prep.* On the farther side of; farther onward than; past adv. *beyond.*

BI'AS. *s.* Inclination, either of matter or mind. v. *bias,* pr. par. *biasing;* past, *biased.*

BIB. *s.* A child's apron.

BIB'BER. *s.* A tippler.

BI'BLE. *s.* The sacred volume. adj *biblical.*

40

BIBLIOG'RAPHY. *s.* History of books. pl. *bibliographies:* s. *bibliographer.*

BIB'ULOUS. *adj.* Absorbing moisture.

BICK'ERING. *s.* A slight quarrel.

BICOR'NOUS. *adj.* Having two horns.

BID. *v.* To desire, to command, to offer a price. pr. par. *bidding;* past, *bidden:* s. *bidder.*

BIDE. *v.* To endure, to suffer, to dwell. pr. par. *biding;* past, *bode.*

BIDEN'TAL. *adj.* Having two teeth.

BIEN'NIAL. *adj.* Continuing two years; happening every two years. adv. *biennially.*

BIER. *s.* A carriage on which the dead are carried.

BIF'EROUS. *adj.* Bearing twice a year.

BIG. *adj.* Large. s. *bigness.*

BIG'AMY. *s.* The crime of having two wives, or two husbands, at once. pl. *bigamies.*

BIG'OT. *s.* A person blindly devoted to a certain party. adj. *bigoted:* s. *bigotry*, pl. *bigotries.*

BILE. *s.* A thick yellow secretion; a sore swelling. adj. *bilious.*

BILGE. *v.* To spring a leak. pr. par. *bilging;* past, *bilged:* s. *bilge.*

BILL. *s.* The beak of a fowl; a hatchet with a hooked point; a written paper of a certain kind.

BIL'LET. *s.* A small paper; a note; a ticket directing soldiers at what house to lodge. v. *billet;* pr. par. *billeting:* past, *billeted.*

BIL'LIARDS. *s.* A kind of play.

BIL'LINGSGATE. *s.* Ribaldry, foul language: A cant word, borrowed from Billingsgate, in London.

BIL'LION. *s.* A million of millions.

BIL'LOW. *s.* A wave. adj. *billowy.*

BIN. *s.* A place where corn or wine is deposited.

BIN'ACLE. *s.* A sea term, denoting the compass-box.

BI'NARY. *adj.* In couples.

BIND. *v.* To confine with bonds, to contract; to fasten together pr. par. *binding:* past, *bound:* s. *binder.*

BIOG'RAPHY. *s.* Personal history. pl. *biographies:* s. *biographer:* adj. *biographical:* adv. *biographically.*

BI'PAROUS. *adj.* Having two at birth.

BIPAR'TITE. *adj.* Having tw parts.

BI'PED. *s.* An animal having two feet. adj. *bipedal.*

BIPET'ALOUS. *adj.* Consisting of two flower leaves.

BIRCH. *s.* A kind of deciduous tree. adj. *birchen.*

BIRD. *s.* A feathered animal.

BIRD'LIME. *s.* A glutinous substance, for catching birds.

BIRTH. *s.* The act of coming into life; rank by descent; thing born; a place on board a vessel, for holding a bed.

BIRTH'DAY. *s.* The day on which any one is born; the anniversary of one's birth.

BIRTH'RIGHT. *s.* The rights to which a person is born.

BIS'CUIT. *s.* Hard bread.

BISECT'. *v.* To divide into two parts. pr. par. *bisecting;* past, *bisected:* s. *bisection, bisector.*

BISH'OP. *s.* One who is placed over several churches. s. *bishopric,* the diocese of a bishop.

BI'SON. *s.* A kind of wild ox.

BISSEX'TILE. *adj.* Relating to eve ry fourth or leap year. s. *bissextile.*

BIS'TRE. *s.* A kind of paint.

BIT. *s.* That part of a bridle which is in the mouth; a small piece; a morsel.

BIT. *v.* Did bite.

BITE. *v.* To crush or pierce with the teeth. pr par. *biting;* past, *bit, bitten:* s. *bite.*

BIT'TER. *adj.* Having a hot, acrid, biting taste. s. *bitterness:* adv *bitterly.*

BIT'TERN. *s.* A kind of bird.

BITU'MEN, BITUMEN. s. A fat, unctuous matter, dug out of the earth, or skimmed off lakes. adj. *bituminous:* adv. *bituminously.*

BIVOUAC'. s. The place where an army lies under arms. v. *bivouac;* pr. par. *bivouacking;* past, *bivouacked.*

BLAB. v. To tell what ought to be kept secret. pr. par. *blabbing;* past, *blabbed:* s. *blabber.*

BLACK. adj. Of the colour of night: dark; horrible. v. *black;* pr. par. *blacking;* past, *blacked:* adj. *blackish:* s. *blackness.*

BLACK'EN. v. To darken, to defame. pr. par. *blackening;* past, *blackened.*

BLACK'GUARD. s. A dirty fellow; a rascal.

BLACK'GUARD. v. To apply abusive and scurrilous epithets. pr. par. *blackguarding;* past, *blackguarded.*

BLACK'LEG. s. A professed gambler.

BLACK'SMITH. s. A smith who forges iron.

BLAD'DER. s. The vessel which contains the urine.

BLADE. s. A spire of grass; the leaf of an esculent plant; the sharp part of a weapon.

BLAME. v. To censure, to charge with a fault. pr. par. *blaming;* past, *blamed:* adj. *blameable, blameless:* s. *blamelessness.*

BLAME'WORTHY. adj. Deserving blame. s. *blameworthiness.*

BLANCH. v. To whiten. pr. par. *blanching;* past, *blanched.*

BLAND. adj. Mild, gentle. adv. *blandly:* s. *blandness.*

BLAND'ISHMENT. s. Act of fondness; caresses.

BLANK. s. A space not written upon; unprofitable result of a lottery chance.

BLANK'ET. s. A woolen cover for a bed. s. *blanketing.*

BLASPHE'ME. v. To speak irreverently of God. pr. par. *blasphem-ing;* past, *blasphemed:* adj. *blasphemous:* adv. *blasphemously:* s. *blasphemer, blasphemy,* pl. *blasphemies.*

BLAST. v. To wither, to injure, to invalidate. pr. par. *blasting;* past, *blasted:* s. *blast.*

BLAZE. s. A flame; a mark made in a tree with a hatchet. v. *blaze;* pr. par. *blazing;* past, *blazed:* s. *blazer.*

BLA'ZON. v. To deck, to embellish, to make public. pr. par. *blazoning;* past, *blazoned:* s. *blazonry.*

BLEACH. v. To whiten. pr. par. *bleaching;* past, *bleached:* s. *bleacher.*

BLEAK. adj. Cold, chill. adv. *bleakly:* s. *bleakness.*

BLEAR. adj. Dim with rheum or water.

BLEAT. v. To cry as a sheep. pr. par. *bleating;* past, *bleated;* s. *bleat, bleater.*

BLEED. v. To lose blood; to drop as blood: to draw blood from. pr. par. *bleeding;* past, *bled:* s. *bleeder.*

BLEM'ISH. s. A mark of deformity; a scar, a reproach; disgrace. pr. par. *blemishing;* past, *blemished.*

BLEND. v. To mingle together; to confound. pr. par. *blending,* past, *blended.*

BLESS. v. To make happy; to prosper. pr. par. *blessing;* past, *blessed:* s. *blessing:* adv. *blessedly.*

BLEW. Preterit of the v. *blow.*

BLIGHT. v. To blast. pr. par. *blighting;* past, *blighted:* s. *blight, blighter.*

BLIND. adj. Deprived of sight. v. *blind;* pr. par. *blinding:* past, *blinded:* adv. *blindly:* s. *blindness.*

BLIND'FOLD. v. To cover the eyes. pr. par. *blindfolding;* past, *blindfolded:* adj. *blindfold.*

BLINK. v. To wink: to see obscurely. pr par. *blinking;* past, *blinked.*

BLISS. *s.* The highest degree of happiness. *adj. blissful:* adv. *blissfully:* s. *blissfulness.*

BLIS'TER *s.* A pustule formed by raising the cuticle. *v. blister;* pr. par. *blistering;* past, *blistered.*

BLITHE. *adj.* Gay, airy. *adv. blithely:* s. *blitheness.*

BLOAT. *v.* To swell; to make turgid. pr. par. *bloating;* past, *bloated:* s. *bloatedness.*

BLOCK. *s.* A heavy piece of timber; a mass of matter; a sea term for a pulley; sometimes used in the United States, for a row of houses, or pile of buildings.

BLOCK. *v.* To shut up. pr. par. *blocking;* past, *blocked.*

BLOCKA'DE. *s.* A siege carried on by shutting up the place. *v. blockade;* pr. par. *blockading;* past, *blockaded.*

BLOCK'HEAD. *s.* A stupid fellow. *adj. blockheaded.*

BLOOD. *s.* The red fluid which circulates in the bodies of animals. *adj. bloody, bloodless:* adv. *bloodily.*

BLOOD'HOUND. *s.* A hound used for hunting men.

BLOOD'THIRSTY. *adj.* Desirous of shedding blood.

BLOOM. *v.* To yield blossoms. pr. par. *blooming;* past, *bloomed:* s. *bloom:* adv. *bloomingly.*

BLOS'SOM. *s.* The flower produced before the seed. *v. blossom;* pr. par. *blossoming;* past, *blossomed.*

BLOT. *v.* To obliterate, to erase, to disfigure. pr. par. *blotting;* past, *blotted:* s. *blot.*

BLOTCH. *s.* A spot on the skin. *adj blotched.*

BLOW. *s.* Bloom, blossom. *v. blow;* pr. par. *blowing:* past, *blowed.*

BLOW. *s.* A stroke.

BLOW. *v.* To make a current of air; to pant. pr. par. *blowing;* past, *blown:* s. *blow, blower.*

BLOW'PIPE. *s.* A tube used by various artificers.

BLUB'BER. *s.* The fat of a large fish.

BLUB'BER. *v.* To swell the cheeks with weeping. pr. par. *blubbering;* past, *blubbered.*

BLUD'GEON. *s.* A short, heavy stick, used as an offensive weapon.

BLUE. *s.* One of the seven original colours. *adj. bluish:* adv. *bluely* · s. *blueness.*

BLUFF. *s.* A steep bank, or high bold shore.

BLUN'DER. *v.* To err, to mistake pr. par. *blundering;* past, *blundered:* s. *blunder, blunderer.*

BLUN'DERBUSS. *s.* A kind of short gun, with a wide mouth. pl. *blunderbusses.*

BLUNT. *v.* To dull the edge or point. pr. par. *blunting;* past, *blunted:* adj. *blunt:* adv. *bluntly:* s. *bluntness.*

BLUSH. *v.* To become red. pr. par. *blushing;* past, *blushed:* s. *blush.*

BLUS'TER. *v.* To roar as a storm. pr. par. *blustering;* past, *blustered:* s. *bluster, blusterer.*

BOAR. *s.* The male swine.

BOARD. *s.* A flat piece of wood, entertainment; an assembly seated at a table. *s. boarder:* v. *board;* pr. par. *boarding;* past, *boarded.*

BOAST. *v.* To brag, to magnify, to exalt. pr. par. *boasting;* past, *boasted:* s. *boast, boaster:* adj *boastful:* adv. *boastfully.*

BOAT. *s.* A small vessel, in which persons pass over water. *v. boat,* pr. par. *boating;* past, *boated.* adj. *boatable.*

BOAT'MAN. *s.* He that manages a boat.

BOATS'WAIN. *s.* A petty officer on board a ship. pronounced *bo'-sn.*

BOB'BIN. *s.* A small roller of wood, on which thread is wound.

BODE. *v.* To portend. pr. par. *boding;* past, *boded.*

43

BOD'ICE. s. Stays.
BOD'KIN. s. An instrument used to bore holes, &c.
BODY. s. The material substance of an animal; matter, opposed to spirit; a collective mass. pl. *bodies*: adj. *bodied*: adj. and adv. *bodily*.
BOG. s. A marsh; a morass. v. *bog*; pr. par. *bogging*; past, *bogged*: adj. *boggy*.
BOHE'A. s. A species of tea.
BO'GLE. s. A bugbear; a spectre.
BOG'GLE. v. To start; to hesitate. pr. par. *boggling*; past, *boggled*: s. *boggler*.
BOIL. v. To be agitated by heat; to heat to a certain degree. pr. par. *boiling*; past, *boiled*: s. *boil*, *boiler*.
BOIS'TEROUS. adj. Violent, loud, roaring, stormy. adv. *boisterously*: s. *boisterousness*.
BOLD. adj. Daring, brave, rude. adv. *boldly*: s. *boldness*: adj. *boldfaced*.
BOLE. s. A measure containing six bushels.
BOL'STER. s. Something laid under the head; a pad. v. *bolster*; pr. par. *bolstering*; past, *bolstered*.
BOLT. s. An arrow; the bar of a door; a sieve. v. *bolt*; pr. par. *bolting*; past, *bolted*.
BO'LUS. s. A kind of large pill. pl. *boluses*.
BOMB. s. A hollow cannon-ball.
BOMBARD'. v. To attack with bombs. pr. par. *bombarding*; past, *bombarded*: s. *bombard*, *bombardier*.
BOM'BAST. s. Inflated language. adj. *bombastic*, *bombastical*: adv. *bombastically*.
BOND. s. Cords or a chain; union; imprisonment; written obligation. s. *bondage*: v. *bond*; pr. par. *bonding*; past, *bonded*.
BONDS'MAN. s. A male slave.
BONE. s. The solid parts of the body of an animal. v. *bone*; pr. par. *boning*, past, *boned*: adj. *bony*.

BONET'TA. s. A kind of sea-fish.
BON'FIRE. s. A fire made for some public cause of triumph.
BON-MOT". s. a jest, a witty reply. Fr.
BON'NET. s. A species of hat.
BON'NY. adj. Handsome, pretty. adv. *bonnily*.
BOO'BY. s. A dull, stupid fellow. pl. *boobies*.
BOOK. s. A volume in which we read or write. v. *book*; pr. par. *booking*; past, *booked*.
BOOK'BINDER. s. One who binds books.
BOOK'CASE. s. A case for holding books.
BOOK'SELLER. s. A man who sells books.
BOOK'WORM. s. A worm that eats holes in books; a student too closely devoted to books.
BOOM. s. A large spar, on which a sail is spread. v. *boom*; pr. par. *booming*; past, *boomed*.
BOON. s. A gift, a grant. adj. *boon*, gay, merry.
BOOR. s. A rustic clown. adj. *boorish*; adv. *boorishly*: s. *boorishness*.
BOOT. s. Profit, gain; over and above; a cover for the leg. adj. *booted*, *bootless*.
BOOTH. s. A temporary house, made of boards.
BOO'TY. s. Plunder. pl. *booties*.
BO'RAX. s. A kind of artificial salt.
BOR'DER. s. The outer part or edge. s. *borderer*: v. *border*, pr. par. *bordering*; past, *bordered*.
BORE. v. To pierce; to make hollow. pr. par. *boring*; past, *bored*: s. *bore*, *borer*.
BORE. v. Did bear.
BORNE. Part. passive of the verb *bear*.
BOR'OUGH. s. An incorporated town.
BOR'ROW. v. To take from another, upon credit; to use as one's own. pr. par. *borrowing* past, *borrowed*: s. *borrower*.

44

BO'SOM. *s.* The breast. *v. bosom;* pr. par *bosoming;* past, *bosomed.*
BOSS. *s.* A stud; the part rising in the midst of any thing. pl. *bosses.*
BOT'ANY. *s.* The science of plants. adj. *botanic, botanical;* adv. *botanically;* v. *botanize;* pr. par. *botanizing;* past, *botanized:* s. *botanist.*
BOTCH. *s.* A part of any thing ill finished; a bad workman. pl. *botches:* pr. par. *botching;* past, *botched:* s. *botcher.*
BOTH. *adj.* The two. conj. *both.*
BOTH'ER. *v.* To perplex and confound. pr. par. *bothering;* past, *bothered:* s. *botherer.*
BOT'TLE. *s.* A vessel with a narrow mouth, to put liquors in; a bundle of hay or grass. v. *bottle;* pr: par. *bottling;* past, *bottled:* s. *bottler.*
BOT'TOM. *s.* The lowest part; the ground under the water. v. *bottom;* pr. par. *bottoming;* past, *bottomed:* adj. *bottomless.*
BOUGH. *s.* An arm or large shoot of a tree.
BOUGHT. Preterit and past part. of *buy.*
BOUNCE. *v.* To fall or fly against any thing with great force, so as to rebound; to spring. pr. par. *bouncing;* past, *bounced:* s. *bounce, bouncer.*
BOUND. *v.* To limit; to terminate. pr. par. *bounding;* past, *bounded:* s. *bound:* adj. *boundless:* adv. *boundlessly.*
BOUND. *v.* To jump, to spring. pr. par. *bounding;* past, *bounded.*
BOUND'ARY. *s.* Limit. pl. *boundaries.*
BOUND'EN. *adj.* Required by contract.
BOUN'TY *s.* Generosity, pecuniary encouragement. pl. *bounties:* adj. *bounteous, bountiful:* adv. *bounteously, bountifully.*
BOUQUET. *s.* A nosegay. *Fr.* pronounced *boo-kay.*
BOURN. *s.* A bound, a limit.

BOW. *v.* To bend, to incline. pr par. *bowing;* past, *bowed:* s. *bow.*
BOW'ELS. *s.* The inner part; intestines.
BOW'ER. *s.* An arbour.
BOWL. *s.* A vessel to hold liquids, a basin; a round mass, which may be rolled along the ground. v. *bowl;* pr. par. *bowling;* past, *bowled:* s. *bowler.*
BOW'SPRIT. *s.* A spar running out at the head of a ship.
BOX. *s.* A case made of wood or other substance; a fight. pl. *boxes:* v. *box;* pr. par. *boxing;* past, *boxed:* s. *boxer.*
BOY. *s.* A male child. adj. *boyish:* adv. *boyishly:* s. *boyishness, boyhood.*
BRACE. *v.* To make firm; to bind. pr. par. *bracing;* past, *braced:* s. *brace, bracer.*
BRACE'LET. *s.* An ornament fo. the arm.
BRA'CHMAN. *s.* A priest of India, of the first cast of Gentoos.
BRACK'ET. *s.* A piece of wood, nailed against a wall, to support something.
BRACK'ISH. *adj.* Having a slight flavour of salt. s. *brackishness.*
BRAD. *s.* A sort of nail, with an oblong head.
BRAG. *v.* To boast; to display ostentatiously. pr. par. *bragging* past, *bragged:* s. *braggart, bragger.*
BRAID. *v.* To weave together. pr par. *braiding;* past, *braided:* s *braid.*
BRAIN. *s.* That collection of vessels and organs in the head, from which sense and motion arise. adj. *brainless:* v. *brain;* pr. par. *braining.* past, *brained:* s. *brainless.*
BRAKE. *s.* A thicket of brambles.
BRAM'BLE. *s.* Any rough, prickly shrub.
BRA'MIN. See BRACHMAN.
BRAN. *s.* The husks of corn, ground

BRANCH. *s.* The shoot of a tree, from one of the main boughs; a smaller river running into a larger; any distinct article. pl. *branches:* v. *branch;* pr. par. *branching;* past, *branched:* adj. *branchless.*

BRAND. *s.* A lighted stick; a mark made on a criminal, with a hot iron; a stigma; a sword. v. *brand;* pr. par. *branding;* past, *branded.*

BRAND'ISH. *v.* To wave or shake; to flourish. pr. par. *brandishing;* past, *brandished.*

BRAN'DY. *s.* A strong liquor, distilled from wine. pl. *brandies.*

BRA'SIER. *s.* A manufacturer that works in brass.

BRASS. *s.* A yellow metal, made by mixing copper with lapis calaminaris. pl. *brasses:* adj. *brassy.*

BRAT. *s.* A child, so called in contempt.

BRAVA'DO. *s.* A boast, a brag. pl. *bravadoes.*

BRAVE. *adj.* Courageous. adv. *bravely:* v. *brave;* pr. par. *braving;* past, *braved:* s. *bravery,* pl. *braveries.*

BRA'VO. *s.* A man who murders for hire.

BRAVU'RA. *s.* A kind of song, requiring great vocal power.

BRAWL. *v.* To quarrel noisily. pr. par. *brawling;* past, *brawled:* s. *brawl, brawler.*

BRAWN. *s.* The fleshy part of the body; the flesh of a boar, prepared in a particular manner. adj. *brawny.*

BRAY. *v.* To make a noise as an ass. pr. par. *braying;* past, *brayed:* s. *bray, brayer.*

BRAZE. *v.* To solder with brass. pr. par. *brazing;* past, *brazed:* s. *brazier.*

BRAZ'EN. *adj.* Made of brass.

BREACH. *s.* A gap: infraction; quarrel. pr. par. *breaching;* past, *breached.*

BREAD. *s.* Food made of ground corn.

BREADTH. *s.* The measure of any plain superficies, from side to side.

BREAK. *v.* To burst open by force, to divide; to overcome. pr. par. *breaking;* past, *broken:* s. *break, breaker.*

BREAK'FAST. *v.* To eat the first meal in the day. pr. par. *breakfasting;* past, *breakfasted.* s. *breakfast.*

BREAST. *s.* The middle part of the human body, between the neck and the belly. v. *breast;* pr. par. *breasting;* past, *breasted.*

BREAST'WORK. *s.* In fortification;—works thrown up as high as the breasts of the defenders.

BREATHE. *v.* To draw in air by the lungs. pr. par. *breathing;* past, *breathed:* s. *breath:* adj. *breathless.*

BRED. Preterit and past part. of the v. *breed.*

BREECH'ES. *s.* The garment worn by men, over the lower part of the body and thighs.

BREED. *v.* To procreate; to educate. pr. par. *breeding,* past, *bred* s. *breed, breeding.*

BREEZE. *s.* A gentle gale. adj *breezy.*

BRET. *s.* A kind of turbot.

BRE'THREN. *s.* The ancient plural of *brother.*

BREVE. *s.* A term in music.

BREVET'. *s.* A rank by *brevet,* signifies a title a degree higher than is denoted in the officer's commission.

BREV'IARY. *s.* An abridgment; a book containing the daily service of the church of Rome. pl. *breviaries.*

BREV'ITY. *s.* Shortness; conciseness. pl. *brevities.*

BREW. *v.* To make liquors by mixing several ingredients. pr. par. *brewing;* past, *brewed:* s. *brewer, brewery,* pl *breweries.*

BRI'AR, BRI'ER. *s.* A species of thorny plant. adj. *briary, briery*

BRIBE. *s.* A reward given corruptly. *s. briber, bribery,* pl. *briberies:* v. *bribe;* pr. par. *bribing;* past, *bribed.*

BRICK. *s.* A piece of burned clay, used in building; a loaf of bread, shaped like a brick. v. *brick;* pr. par. *bricking;* past, *bricked.*

BRICK'-KILN. *s.* A place to burn bricks.

BRICK'LAYER. *s.* A brick-mason.

BRIDE. *s.* A woman recently married. adj. *bridal.*

BRIDE'GROOM. *s.* A man recently married.

BRIDES'MAID. *s.* She who attends upon a bride.

BRIDGE. *s.* A building raised over water, for the convenience of passage; the prominent part of the nose; the supporter of the strings in a lute, fiddle, &c. v. *bridge;* pr. par. *bridging;* past, *bridged.*

BRI'DLE. *v.* To restrain, to govern. pr. par. *bridling;* past, *bridled:* s. *bridle, bridler.*

BRIEF. *adj.* Short, concise. adv. *briefly:* s. *briefness.*

BRI'ER, BRI'AR. *s.* A species of thorny plant. adj. *briery, briary.*

BRIG. *s.* A vessel with two masts, and square rigging.

BRIGA'DE. *s.* A division of forces; a body of men. v. *brigade;* pr. par. *brigading;* past, *brigaded:* adj. *brigadier.*

BRIGAND'. *s.* A robber.

BRIGHT. *adj.* Shining; full of light. s. *brightness:* adv. *brightly:* v. *brighten;* pr. par. *brightening;* past, *brightened.*

BRIL'LIANCY. *s.* Lustre, splendour. pl. *brilliancies:* adj. *brilliant:* adv. *brilliantly.*

BRIM. *s.* The edge of a small vessel.

BRIMFUL'. *adj.* Full to the top.

BRIM'STONE. *s.* Sulphur in lumps or rolls.

BRIND'LED. *adj.* Streaked.

BRINE. *s.* Water impregnated with salt. adj. *briny.*

BRING. *v.* To fetch from; to convey; to attract; to draw along pr. par. *bringing;* past, *brought.*

BRINK. *s.* The edge of any place, as of a precipice or river.

BRISK. *adj.* Lively, gay, vivid, bright. adv. *briskly:* s. *briskness*

BRISK'EN. *v.* To make brisk. pr par. *briskening;* past, *briskened.*

BRISK'ET. *s.* The breast of an animal.

BRIS'TLE. *s.* The stiff hair of swine. v. *bristle;* pr. par. *bristling;* past, *bristled:* adv. *bristly.*

BRIT'ISH. *adj.* Relating to Britain.

BRIT'TLE. *adj.* Fragile; apt to break. s. *brittleness.*

BROACH. *v.* To pierce a vessel to tap; to suggest; to utter. pr par. *broaching;* past, *broached* s. *broacher.*

BROAD. *adj.* Wide, large, open gross. adv. *broadly:* v. *broaden* pr. par. *broadening;* past, *broadened.*

BROAD'SIDE. *s.* The side of a ship; a volley of shot, fired at once, from all the guns in the side of a ship.

BROCA'DE. *s.* A species of silken stuff. adj. *brocaded.*

BROC'COLI. *s.* A species of cabbage.

BROGUE. *s.* A kind of shoe; a cant word for a provincial accent.

BROIL. *v.* To cook, by laying on the coals. pr. par. *broiling,* past *broiled:* s. *broil, broiler.*

BRO'KEN. Past part. of *break.* s *brokenness.*

BROKEN-HEART'ED. *adj.* Much depressed in spirit; grief-worn.

BROKEN-WIND'ED. *adj.* Having short breath.

BRO'KER. *s.* A factor; one that does business for another.

BRO'KERAGE. *s.* The pay or reward of a broker.

BRONZE. *s.* Brass; a metal compounded of copper and tin. v *bronze;* pr. par. *bronzing;* past, *bronzed.*

BROOD. s. Offspring; the number hatched at once.
BROOD. v. To sit as on eggs; to remain long in anxiety; to mature by care. pr. par. *brooding*; past, *brooded.*
BROOK. s. A running water, less than a river.
BROOK. v. To bear, to endure. pr. par. *brooking*; past, *brooked.*
BROOM. s. A small tree; a besom.
BROTH. s. Liquor in which flesh is boiled.
BROTH'EL. s. A house of ill fame.
BRO'THER. s. One born of the same father or mother. adj. *brotherly.*
BRO'THERHOOD. s. The state or quality of being a brother.
BROUGHT. Preterit and past part. of the v. *bring.*
BROW. s. The arch over the eye; the forehead; the edge or brink of any high place.
BROW'BEAT. v. To bully. pr. par. *browbeating*; past, *browbeaten.*
BROWN. adj. The name of a colour. adj. *brownish.*
BROWSE. v. To eat branches or shrubs. pr. par. *browsing*; past, *browsed.* s. *browser.*
BRUISE. v. To crush or mangle with a heavy blow. pr. par. *bruising*; past, *bruised*: s. *bruise, bruiser.*
BRUIT. s. Rumour, report. v. *bruit*; pr. par. *bruiting*; past, *bruited.*
BRU'MAL. adj. Belonging to winter.
BRUNETTE'. s. A woman with a brown complexion.
BRUNT. s. Shock; violence.
BRUSH. s. An instrument used for sweeping; a rude assault; a thicket. v. *brush*: pr. par. *brushing*; past, *brushed*: s. *brusher*: adj. *brushy.*
BRUSH'WOOD. s. Rough, low, close thickets.
BRUTE. s. A creature without reason. adj. *brutal*: adv. *brutally*: v. *brutalize*; pr. par. *brutalizing* past, *brutalized.*
BUB'BLE. s. A small bladder of water. v. *bubble*; pr. par. *bubbling*; past, *bubbled.*
BUC'ANIER. s. A pirate.
BUCK. s. The male of the fallow deer, and of some other quadrupeds.
BUCK'ET. s. A sort of small tub.
BUC'KLE. s. A link of metal, with a tongue or catch, made to fasten one thing to another. v. *buckle*, pr. par. *buckling*; past, *buckled.*
BUCK'LER. s. A shield.
BUCK'RAM. s. A sort of stiffened linen.
BUCK'SKIN. s. The skin of a buck.
BUCK'WHEAT. s. A species of grain.
BUCOL'IC. adj. Pastoral.
BUD. s. The first shoot of a plant. v. *bud*; pr. par. *budding*; past, *budded.*
BUDGE. v. To stir. pr. par. *budging*; past, *budged.*
BUDG'ET. s. A bag; a store of stock.
BUFF. s. A sort of leather, prepared from the skin of the buffalo; the colour of the leather, which is a very light yellow.
BUFF. v. To strike. pr. par. *buffing*; past, *buffed*: s. *buffer.*
BUF'FALO. s. A kind of wild cow. pl. *buffaloes.*
BUF'FET. s. A blow with the fist. v. *buffet*; pr. par. *buffeting*, past, *buffeted.*
BUF'FET. s. A cup-board.
BUFFOON'. s. A man whose profession is to make sport. s *buffoonery*, pl. *buffooneries.*
BUG. s. A species of insect.
BUG'BEAR. s. A frightful object.
BU'GLE, BU'GLE-HORN. s. A hunting horn.
BU'GLE. s. A kind of glass ornament, of a cylindrical form.
BUILD. v. To erect, to rest upon. pr. par. *building*; past, *built*: s *builder.*

48

BULB. *s.* A round body, or root. adj. *bulbous.*
BUL'FINCH. *s.* A species of singing bird. pl. *bulfinches.*
BULK. *s.* Magnitude, size. adj. *bulky:* s. *bulkiness.*
BULL. *s.* The male of black cattle; a papal mandate.
BUL'LET. *s.* A small metal ball.
BUL'LETIN. *s.* A military or other public document.
BUL'LION. *s.* Gold or silver in the lump.
BUL'LOCK. *s.* An ox.
BUL'LY. *s.* A noisy, blustering, quarrelsome fellow. pl. *bullies:* v. *bully;* pr. par. *bullying;* past, *bullied.*
BUL'RUSH. *s.* A species of large rush. pl. *bulrushes.*
BUL'WARK *s.* A bastion; a fortification.
BUM'BLEBEE. *s.* The wild bee.
BUMP. *s.* A swelling, a protuberance.
BUMP. *v.* To make a loud noise; to strike against. pr. par. *bumping;* past, *bumped.*
BUMP'ER. *s.* A cup filled to the brim.
BUMP'KIN. *s.* An awkward, heavy rustic.
BUNCH. *s.* A cluster; a number of things tied together. pl. *bunches:* adj. *bunchy:* s. *bunchiness.*
BUN'DLE. *s.* A number of things bound together; a roll. v. *bundle;* pr. par. *bundling;* past, *bundled.*
BUNG. *s.* A stopper for a barrel. v. *bung;* pr. par. *bunging;* past, *bunged.*
BUN'GLE. *v.* To perform clumsily; to botch. pr. par. *bungling;* past, *bungled:* s. *bungler:* adv. *bunglingly.*
BUNN. *s.* A kind of light bread.
BUNT'ING. *s.* The stuff of which a ship's colours are made.
BUOY. *s.* A light substance, floating on the water, and tied to something at the bottom. v. *buoy;* pr. par. *buoying;* past, *buoyed.*

BUOY'ANCY. *s.* The quality o floating. pl. *buoyancies:* adj. *buoyant:* adv. *buoyantly.*
BUR'DEN, BUR'THEN. *s.* A load, something grievous; the verse repeated in a song. v *burden;* pr. par. *burdening;* past, *burdened.* v. *burthen;* pr. par. *burthening;* past, *burthened:* adj. *burdensome, burthensome.*
BU'REAU. *s.* A chest of drawers.
BUR'GESS. *s.* An officer of a certain rank in a corporate town; a representative of a borough-town. pl. *burgesses.*
BURG'LARY. *s.* Act of feloniously entering a house by night. pl. *burglaries.* s. *burglar:* adj. *burglarious;* adv. *burglariously:* s. *burgler.*
BURG'OMASTER. *s.* One employed in the government of a city.
BURLES'QUE. *adj.* Ludicrous. s. *burlesque:* v. *burlesque;* pr. par. *burlesquing;* past, *burlesqued:* s. *burlesquer.*
BURLET'TA. *s.* A musical farce.
BURN. *v.* To consume or wound with fire; to be on fire. pr. par. *burning;* past, *burned, burnt:* s. *burn, burner.*
BUR'NISH. *v.* To polish. pr. par. *burnishing;* past, *burnished.* s. *burnish, burnisher.*
BURR. *s.* The rough head of a cer tain plant.
BUR'ROW. *v.* To mine as rabbits. pr. par. *burrowing;* past, *burrowed:* s. *burrow.*
BURST. *v.* To break suddenly. pr. par. *bursting;* past, *burst.*
BUR'THEN. *s.* See BURDEN.
BUR'Y. *v.* To inter; to put into a grave. pr. par. *burying;* past, *buried:* s. *burial.*
BUSH. *s.* A thick shrub. pl. *bushes* adj. *bushy:* s. *bushiness.*
BUSH'EL. *s.* A measure containing eight gallons.
BUS'KIN. *s.* A kind of half-boot, a shoe, worn by the ancient actors of tragedy. adj. *buskined.*

E 49

BUST. *s.* A statue, representing a person as far as the breast.
BUS'TARD. *s.* A wild turkey.
BUS'TLE. *v.* To be busy; to stir. pr. par. *bustling* past, *bustled:* s. *bustle, bustler.*
BUS'Y. *adj.* Fully employed; bustling; meddling. *v. busy;* pr. par. *busying;* past, *busied:* adv. *busily:* s. *business.*
BUT. A conjunction; a preposition.
BUTCH'ER. *s.* One who kills domestic animals for the purpose of food. v. *butcher;* pr. par. *butchering;* past, *butchered:* adj. *butcherly:* s. *butchery,* pl. *butcheries.*
BUT'LER. *s.* A servant who takes care of the wines, and superintends the table.
BUT'-END. *s.* The blunt end.
BUT'MENT. *s.* That part of an arch which joins it to the upright pier.
BUTT. *s.* A mark to shoot at; a blow given by a horned animal; a large barrel.
BUTT. *v.* To strike with the head. pr. par. *butting;* past, *butted.*
BUT'TER. *s.* An unctuous substance, made from milk. s. *buttery,* pl. *butteries:* v. *butter;* pr. par. *buttering;* past, *buttered.*

BUT'TERFLY. *s.* A kind of beautiful insect. pl. *butterflies.*
BUT'TON. *s.* A kind of knob or ball. v. *button;* pr. par. *buttoning;* past, *buttoned:* s. *buttoner.*
BUT'TON-HOLE. *s.* A hole to catch the button.
BUT'TRESS. *s.* A wall built to support another wall. pl. *buttresses.*
BUX'OM. *adj.* Gay, lively.
BUY. *v.* To purchase, to acquire by paying for. pr. par. *buying;* past, *bought:* s. *buyer.*
BUZZ. *v.* To hum, to whisper. pr pur. *buzzing;* past, *buzzed:* s. *buzz.*
BUZ'ZARD. *s.* A species of hawk.
BY. A preposition.
BY'-CORNER. *s.* A private corner
BY'-LANE. *s.* A lane out of the usual road.
BY'-LAW. *s.* A law made to regulate the business of a corporation
BY'-PATH. *s.* A private or obscure path.
BY'-ROAD. *s.* An obscure road.
BY'STANDER. *s.* A looker-on; one unconcerned.
BY'-WORD. *s.* A saying, a proverb
BYRE. *s.* A cow-house.

C

CABAL'. *s.* The secret science of the Hebrew rabbins; a body of men united in some close design; intrigue. s. *cavaller;* adj. *cabalistic, cabalistical:* v. *cabal;* pr. par. *caballing;* past, *caballed.*
CAB'BAGE. *s.* A species of culinary vegetable.
CAB'BAGE. *v.* To steal in cutting clothes. pr. par. *cabbaging;* past, *cabbaged:* s. *cabbage, cabbager.*
CAB'IN. *s.* A small chamber in a ship; a cottage.
CAB'INET. *s.* A set of boxes or drawers for curiosities; a private

room in which consultations are held; ministers of state, assembled in council.
CA'BLE. *s.* The great rope of a ship, to which the anchor is fastened.
CABRIOLET'. *s.* An open carriage
CACK'LE. *v.* To make a noise like a hen. pr. par. *cackling;* past, *cackled:* s. *cackle, cackler.*
CACO'PHONY. *s.* A bad sound o. words. pl. *cacophonies.*
CADA'VEROUS. *adj.* Looking like a corpse.

CA'DENCE. *s.* Fall; state of sinking; decline.

CADET'. *s.* A person who serves in expectation of an office.

CA'DI. *s.* A magistrate amongst the Turks.

CADU'CEUS. *s.* The rod or wand with which Mercury is depicted.

CÆSU'RA. *s.* A figure in poetry, by which a short syllable after a complete foot, is made long; a pause. *adj. cæsural.*

CAGE. *s.* An inclosure of twigs, wires, or bars, in which animals are confined. *v. cage;* pr. par. *caging;* past, *caged.*

CAIRN. *s.* A heap of stones.

CAJOLE'. *v.* To flatter; to cheat. pr. par. *cajoling,* past, *cajoled: s. cajoler, cajolery,* pl. *cajoleries.*

CAI'TIFF. *s.* A mean villain.

CAKE. *s.* Something of a form rather flat than high; a kind of delicate bread. *v. cake;* pr. par. *caking;* past, *caked.*

CALABASH'. *s.* A species of large gourd. pl. *calabashes.*

CALAMANC'O. *s.* A kind of woollen stuff. pl. *calamancoes.*

CALAM'ITY. *s.* Sudden misfortune. pl. *calamities:* adj. *calamitous:* adv. *calamitously.*

CALASH'. *s.* A small carriage of pleasure. pl. *calashes.*

CALCA'REOUS. *adj.* Of the nature of lime.

CALCI'NE. *v.* To reduce to a calx. pr. par. *calcining;* past, *calcined:* adj. *calcinable: s. calcination.*

CAL'CULATE. *v.* To enumerate, to conjecture. pr. par. *calculating;* past, *calculated:* adj. *calculable: s. calculation, calculator.*

CAL'DRON. *s.* A pot, a boiler.

CALEDO'NIAN. *adj.* Relating to Scotland.

CAL'ENDAR. *s.* A register of the year.

CAL'ENDER. *s.* A machine formed of rollers, in which cloth is pressed. *v. calender;* pr. par. *calendering;* past, *calendered.*

CAL'ENTURE. *s.* A distemper peculiar to sailors in hot climates.

CALF. *s.* The young of a cow; the thick part of the leg. pl. *calves.*

CAL'IBER. *s.* The bore of a gun.

CAL'ICO. *s.* A kind of cloth, made of cotton. pl. *calicoes.*

CA'LIPH. *s.* A title assumed oy the successors of Mahomet, amongst the Saracens.

CALID'ITY. *s.* Heat. pl. *calidities.*

CALIPASH', CALIPEE'. *s.* Certain parts of a turtle.

CALL. *v.* To summon, to name. pr. par. *calling;* past, *called: s. call, calling.*

CAL'LIPERS. *s.* An instrument for measuring the diameter of a cylinder.

CAL'LOUS. *adj.* Indurated, hardened, insensible. *s. callosity,* pl. *callosities:* adv. *callously: s. callousness.*

CAL'LOW. *adj.* Without feathers, unfledged.

CALM. *v.* To allay, to quiet, to pacify. pr. par. *calming;* past, *calmed: s. calm, calmer:* adj. *calm:* adv. *calmly.*

CAL'OMEL. *s.* Mercury sublimed.

CALOR'IC. *s.* The modern chymical name of heat. adj. *calorific.*

CALORIM'ETER. *s.* An instrument for ascertaining the quantity of disengaged heat.

CAL'UMNY. *s.* Slander, false charge. pl. *calumnies: s. calumniation, calumniator:* adj. *calumnious:* adv. *calumniously.*

CALVE. *v.* To produce a calf. pr. par. *calving;* past, *calved.*

CAL'VINISM. *s.* The doctrine of Calvin. *s. calvinist;* adj. *calvinistic.*

CALX. *s.* Any thing rendered reducible to powder, by burning. pl. *calxes.*

CA'LYX. *s.* The cup of a plant. pl. *calyxes.*

CAMB'LET. *s.* A kind of cloth.

CAM'BRIC. *s.* A kind of fine linen.

51

CAME. Preterit of the v. *come*.

CAM'EL. *s.* A species of beast of burthen.

CAMEL'OPARD. *s.* A species of quadruped, sometimes called a giraff.

CAM'EO. *s.* A stone, with various figures and representations of landscapes, formed by nature.

CAM'ERA-OBSCU'RA. *s.* A species of optical machine.

CAMP. *s.* A number of military tents. v. *encamp*.

CAMPAIGN'. *s.* The period of an army's operations in the field, during one season. v. *campaign:* pr. par. *campaigning;* past, *campaigned:* s. *campaigner*.

CAMPES'TRAL. *adj.* Growing in fields; relating or belonging to a field.

CAM'PHIRE. *s.* A kind of resin. adj. *camphirated*.

CAN. *s.* A cup; a vessel for carrying liquids.

CAN. *v.* To be able.

CANAIL'LE. *s.* The very lowest of the people; the rabble.

CANAL'. *s.* An artificial watercourse; a conduit, through which any of the juices of the body flow.

CAN'CEL. *v.* To cross a piece of writing; to obliterate. pr. par. *canceling;* past, *canceled*. s. *canceler*.

CAN'CER. *s.* A corroding, incurable sore. adj. *cancerous*.

CAN'DID. *adj.* Sincere, fair, open, ingenuous. adv. *candidly:* s. *candour*.

CAN DIDATE. *s.* A suitor for any place of honour or profit.

CAN'DLE. *s.* A light made of wax or tallow.

CAN'DLESTICK. *s.* The instrument which holds a candle.

CAN'DLEMAS. *s.* The feast of the purification of the Virgin Mary, which was celebrated with many lights in the churches. pl. *candlemasses*.

CAN'DOUR. *s.* Ingenuousness; openness.

CAN'DY. *v.* To become congealed pr. par. *candying;* past, *candied:* s. *candy*, pl. *candies*.

CANE. *s.* A kind of strong reed. v. *cane;* pr. par. *caning;* past, *caned*.

CANI'NE *adj.* Relating or belonging to a dog.

CAN'ISTER. *s.* A case, now generally made of tin; but formerly of canes.

CANK'ER. *s.* A worm that destroys fruit; something corrosive. v. *canker;* pr. par. *cankering;* past, *cankered:* adj. *cankerous*.

CAN'NIBAL. *s.* A person who eats human flesh. s. *cannibalism*.

CAN'NON. *s.* A great gun.

CANNONA'DE. *v.* To attack or batter with cannon. pr. par. *cannonading;* past, *cannonaded:* s. *cannonade, cannonading*.

CANO'E. *s.* A small boat, made of the trunk of a tree.

CAN'ON. *s.* A rule; a church law; a dignitary in cathedral churches. adj. *canonical:* adv. *canonically:* s. *canonicals*.

CAN'ONESS. *s.* In popish countries, women living after the example of secular canons. pl. *canonesses*.

CAN'ONIZE. *v.* To declare any person a saint. pr. par. *canonizing,* past, *canonized:* s. *canonization*.

CAN'OPY. *s.* A covering spread over the head. pl. *canopies:* adj. *canopied*.

CANT. *s.* A peculiar form of speaking; a whining pretension to goodness; barbarous jargon; auction. s. *canter:* v. *cant;* pr. par. *canting;* past, *canted*.

CANTEE'N. *s.* A small vessel, in which a soldier carries something for drinking.

CAN'TER. *v.* To gallop gently. pr. par. *cantering;* past, *cantered:* s. *canter, canterer*.

CANTHAR'IDES. *s.* Spanish flies, used to raise blisters.

CAN'TICLE. *s.* A song; the song of Solomon.

CAN'TO. *s.* A certain division of a poem. pl. *cantoes.*

CAN'TON, CANTON'. *v.* To distribute an army over a district. pr. par. *cantoning;* past, *cantoned:* s. *canton, cantonment.*

CAN'VASS. *v.* To solicit, to examine. pr. par. *canvassing;* past, *canvassed:* s. *canvass, canvasser.*

CANZONET'. *s.* A little song.

CAP. *s.* A cover for the head; the topmost; the highest. v. *cap;* pr. par. *capping;* past, *capped.*

CA'PABLE. *adj.* Endued with sufficient power; able; capacious. s. *capability,* pl. *capabilities.*

CAPA'CIOUS. *adj.* Capable of containing much; internally large. adv. *capaciously:* s. *capacity,* pl. *capacities.*

CAP à pè, CAP à piè. From head to foot.

CAPAR'ISON. *s.* A sort of cover for a horse; a pompous dress. v. *caparison;* pr. par. *caparisoning;* past, *caparisoned.*

CAPE. *s.* Headland; promontory; the neck-piece of a cloak or coat.

CA'PER. *s.* A leap, a jump; an acid pickle. v. *caper;* pr. par. *capering;* past, *capered:* s. *caperer.*

CAPILLA'IRE. *s.* A kind of syrup.

CAPIL'LARY. *adj.* Resembling hairs; relating to very small tubes.

CAPITAL. *s.* Head of a pillar; chief town; stock of a trader or company. s. *capitalist.*

CAPITAL. *adj.* Relating to the head; affecting the life; chief, principal. adv. *capitally.*

CAPITA'TION. *s.* Numeration by heads.

CAPITOL. *s.* The temple of Jupiter, at Rome; a building in which the legislature holds its sessions.

CAPIT'ULATE. *v.* To surrender by agreement. pr. par. *capitulat-*ing; past, *capitulated:* s. *capitulation.*

CA'PON. *s.* A castrated domestic fowl.

CAPOU'CH. *s.* A monk's hood.

CAPRI'CE. *s.* Freak, fancy, whim. adj. *capricious:* adv. *capriciously:* s. *capriciousness.*

CA'PRICORN. *s.* A sign of the zodiac.

CAP'STAN. *s.* In sea language, the cylinder or windlass used for winding up a great weight.

CAP'TAIN. *s.* A commander: the commander of a ship, or of a company of soldiers. s. *captaincy,* pl. *captaincies.*

CAP'TIOUS. *adj.* Eager to object; ensnaring; caviling. adv. *captiously:* s. *captiousness.*

CAP'TIVATE. *v.* To delight highly; (figuratively) to enslave. pr. par. *captivating;* past, *captivated:* s. *captivater, captivation.*

CAP'TIVE. *s.* One taken in war; a prisoner. s. *captivity,* pl. *captivities.*

CAP'TOR. *s.* He that takes a prisoner, or prize. s. *capture.*

CAP'TURE. *v.* To seize in war. pr. par. *capturing;* past, *captured:* s. *captor.*

CAPUCHIN'. *s.* A monk of the reformed order of Franciscans.

CAR. *s.* A sort of carriage.

CAR'ABINE, CAR'BINE. *s.* A small kind of fire-arms.

CAR'AVAN. *s.* A body of merchants or pilgrims.

CARAVAN'SARY. *s.* A house built for the reception of travellers, in the east. pl. *caravansaries.*

CARAVEL'. *s.* A kind of ship, formerly used by the Spanish.

CAR'AWAY. *s.* A kind of aromatic plant.

CAR'BON. *s.* Charcoal, pure coal. adj. *carbonaceous, carbonic.*

CAR'BUNCLE. *s.* A jewel which shines in the dark; a red spot or pimple, on the body. adj. *carbuncular.*

CAR'CASS. *s.* The dead body of an animal; (in gunnery) a kind of bomb. pl. *carcasses.*

CARD. *s.* A piece of very thick paper; a paper printed with figures, used in games; an instrument with which wool and flax are combed. *s. carder:* v. *card;* pr. par. *carding;* past, *carded.*

CAR'DINAL. *adj.* Principal, chief.

CAR'DINAL. *s.* One of the chief governors of the Roman church.

CARDIN'ALATE. *s.* The office of cardinal.

CARE. *s.* Solicitude, anxiety, concern, regard, heed. v. *care;* pr. par. *caring;* past, *cared:* adj. *careful, careless: s. carefulness:* adv. *carefully, carelessly.*

CAREEN'. *v.* To lay a vessel on one side, in order to repair the other. pr. par. *careening;* past, *careened.*

CAREER'. *s.* A race; course of rapid action. v. *career;* pr. par. *careering;* past, *careered.*

CARESS'. *v.* To treat in a kind, or loving manner. pr. par. *caressing;* past, *caressed: s. caress,* pl. *caresses.*

CAR'ET. *s.* A grammatical point (‸), denoting that something is omitted in its right place.

CAR'GO. *s.* The lading of a ship. pl. *cargoes.*

CARICATURE'. *s.* A ridiculous representation of a person, or a circumstance. v. *caricature;* pr. par. *caricaturing;* past, *caricatured: s. caricaturist.*

CAR'IOUS. *adj.* Decayed; rotten.

CAR'MELITE. *s.* A white friar.

CARMIN'ATIVE. *s.* A medicine for expelling wind.

CARMI'NE. *s.* A powder of bright red, or crimson colour.

CAR'NAGE. *s.* Heaps of flesh; immense slaughter.

CAR'NAL. *adj.* Fleshly, not spiritual. adv. *carnally.*

CARNA'TION. *s.* The name of the natural flesh colour; the name of a pink flower.

CAR'NIVAL. *s.* A feast before lent.

CARNIV'OROUS. *adj.* Having a natural inclination to eat flesh. adv. *carnivorously.*

CAR'OL. *v.* To sing, to warble. pr. par. *caroling;* past, *caroled. s. carol.*

CAROU'SE. *v.* To drink; to keep a festival. pr. par. *carousing,* past, *caroused: s. carousal, carouser.*

CARP. *s.* A kind of fish.

CARP. *v.* To cavil, to censure. pr. par. *carping;* past, *carped: s. carp, carper.*

CAR'PENTER. *s.* An artificer in wood.

CAR'PET. *s.* A cover for a floor. v. *carpet;* pr. par. *carpeting;* past, *carpeted.*

CAR'RIAGE. *s.* A vehicle, behaviour, conduct; act of carrying.

CAR'RION. *s.* Flesh unfit for the food of man.

CARRONA'DE. *s.* A very short cannon, used for discharging grapeshot.

CAR'ROT. *s.* A garden root.

CAR'RY. *v.* To convey from a place; to bear. pr. par. *carrying;* past, *carried: s. carrier.*

CART. *s.* A kind of carriage with two wheels. *s. carter, cartage* v. *cart,* pr. par. *carting;* past, *carted.*

CARTE-BLANCHE'. *s.* An unlimited commission.

CARTEL'. *s.* A writing containing stipulations between enemies, generally relating to an exchange of prisoners; a vessel sailing under those stipulations. v. *cartel;* pr. par. *cartelling;* past, *cartelled.*

CARTE'SIAN. *adj.* Relating to the philosophy of Des Cartes.

CARTHU'SIAN. *s.* A monk of the Chartreaux.

CAR'TILAGE. *s.* A smooth and solid body, softer than a bone, but harder than a ligament. adj. *cartilaginous.*

CAR—CAS

CARTOON'. s. A painting or drawing on large paper.
CARTOUCH'. s. A box to hold cartridges.
CARTRIDGE. s. A gun-charge, generally in paper.
CARTWRIGHT. s. A maker of carts.
CARVE. v. To cut wood, stone, or meat; to engrave. pr. par. *carving*; past, *carved*: s. *carver*.
CASCA'DE. s. A waterfall.
CASE. s. Condition, with regard to outward circumstances, state, contingence; question; variation of nouns; a sort of cover.
CASE. v. To inclose in a case. pr. par. *casing*; past, *cased*.
CASE'MATE. s. In fortification, a subterraneous or covered archwork. adj. *casemated*.
CASE'MENT. s. A window opening upon hinges.
CASH. s. Money. s. *cashier*: v. *cash*; pr. par. *cashing*; past, *cashed*.
CASHIE'R. v. To discard; to dismiss from a military office. pr. par. *cashiering*; past, *cashiered*.
CASK. s. A barrel. v. *cask*; pr. par. *casking*; past, *casked*.
CASK'ET. s. A small box or chest, for jewels.
CAS'SIA. s. A sweet spice.
CASSI'NO. s. A game at cards.
CASSIOWARY. s. A large bird of prey. pl. *cassiowaries*.
CAS'SOCK. s. A close garment.
CAST. v. To throw away, to shed, to compute, to contrive. pr. par. *casting*; past, *cast*: s. *cast, caster*.
CASTANET'. s. Small shells of ivory, or hard wood, which dancers rattle in their hands.
CASTE. s. In India, a term denoting a certain rank in life.
CAS'TELLATED. adj. Having turrets and battlements like a castle.
CAS'TIGATE. v. To chastise, to punish pr. par. *castigating*; past, *castigated*: s. *castigation*: adj. *castigatory*.

CAS—CAT

CAS'TLE. s. A fortified house. adj. *castled*.
CAS'TOR OIL. s. An oil extracted from the palma-christi.
CASTRAMETA'TION. s. Science of measuring and laying out the ground for an encampment.
CA'SUAL. adj. Accidental; arising from chance. adv. *casually*: s. *casualty*, pl. *casualties*.
CA'SUIST. s. One who justifies evil actions by argument. adj. *casuistical*: adv. *casuistically*: s. *casuistry, casuistries*.
CAT. s. An animal of the feline species.
CATACHRE'SIS. s. Abuse of words. pl. *catachreses*: adj. *catachrestical*; adv. *catachrestically*.
CA'TACOMBS. s. Subterraneou cavities for the burial of the dead.
CA'TALOGUE. s. An enumeration of particulars; a list.
CA'TAPLASM. s. A poultice.
CATAPUL'TA. s. An engine used anciently to throw stones.
CA'TARACT. s. A waterfall.
CATARRH'. s. An issue of humour from the glands. adj. *catarrhal*.
CATAS'TROPHE. s. Terminating event; unhappy conclusion.
CAT'CALL. s. A squeaking instrument, sometimes used in theatres to condemn a play. s. *catcalling*
CATCH. v. To lay hold of, to seize, to ensnare. pr. par. *catching*; past, *caught*.
CATCH. s. Seizure; advantage taken; thing caught: a sort of hook; a kind of song. pl. *catches*.
CATCH PENNY. s. A worthless pamphlet, calculated to gain money. pl. *catchpennies*.
CATCH'POLL. s. A common bailiff.
CA'TECHISE. v. To question minutely. pr. par. *catechising*; past, *catechised*: s. *catechiser, catechism, catechist*: adj. *catechistical*: adv *catechistically*.
CATEGOR'ICAL. adj. Absolute, direct. adv. *categorically*.

CA'TEGORY. *s.* A class, an order of ideas. pl. *categories.*
CATENA'RIAN. *adj.* Resembling a chain.
CA'TER. *v.* To provide food. pr. par. *catering;* past, *catered:* s. *caterer, cateress.*
CAT'ERPILLAR. *s.* A worm sustained by leaves and fruits.
CATES. *s.* Viands; food.
CAT'GUT. *s.* A string for musical instruments, made from the intestine of an animal; a species of linen or canvas, with wide interstices.
CATHAR'TIC. *adj.* Purgative.
CATHE'DRAL. *s.* The head church of a diocese.
CATH'OLIC. *adj.* Universal, general. s. *catholic, catholicism.*
CATHOL'ICON. *s.* Something of universal application or use.
CATOP'TRICS. *s.* That part of optics which relates to vision by reflection.
CAT'TLE. *s.* Domesticated beasts of pasture.
CAT'SUP. *s.* A poignant liquor, made from mushrooms, and some other vegetables.
CAU'DLE. *s.* A mixture of wine and other materials.
CAUL. *s.* The net in which women enclose their hair; a small cap.
CAUGHT. Preterit and past part. of the v. *to catch.*
CAUL'IFLOWER. *s.* A species of cabbage.
CAUSE. *s.* That which effects; subject of litigation; party. v. *cause;* pr. par. *causing;* past, *caused:* adj. *causal, causeless:* adv. *causelessly.*
CAULK. *v.* To stop the seams of a ship. pr. par. *caulking;* past, *caulked* s. *caulker.*
CAU'SEWAY. *s.* A way raised and paved above the rest of the ground.
CAUS'TIC. *adj.* Destroying the texture of any thing, by its hot, corrosive nature. s. *caustic.*

CAU'TERY. *s.* An instrument used by surgeons, for burning the flesh; a caustic substance. pl. *cauteries* v. *cauterize;* pr. par. *cauterizing* past, *cauterized.*
CAU'TION. *v.* Prudence, foresight, circumspection; warning. v. *caution;* pr. par. *cautioning;* past, *cautioned:* adj. *cautionary, cautious:* adv. *cautiously.*
CAVALCA'DE. *s.* A procession on horseback.
CAVALI'ER. *s.* A horseman or knight.
CAVALI'ER. *adj.* Warlike, haughty. adv. *cavalierly.*
CAV'ALRY. *s.* Men mounted on horses, and armed for war. pl. *cavalries.*
CAVE. *s.* A cavern; a hollow place. v. *cave;* pr. par. *caving;* past, *caved.*
CAV'ERN. *s.* A cave.
CAV'IL. *v.* To raise frivolous objections. pr. par. *caviling;* past, *caviled:* s. *cavil, caviler.*
CAV'ITY. *s.* Hollowness; a hollow place. pl. *cavities.*
CAW. *v.* To cry as a crow; pr. par. *cawing;* past, *cawed.*
CAZI'QUE. *s.* A chief of the South American Indians.
CEASE. *v.* To stop, to fail. pr. par. *ceasing;* past, *ceased:* adj. *ceaseless:* adv. *ceaselessly.*
CE'DAR. *s.* A species of tree.
CEDE. *v.* To yield, to assign by virtue of treaty. pr. par. *ceding;* past, *ceded:* s. *ceder.*
CEIL. *v.* To cover the inner roof of a building. pr. par. *ceiling;* past, *ceiled:* s. *ceiling.*
CEL'EBRATE. *v.* To solemnize, to make famous. pr. par. *celebrating,* past, *celebrated:* s. *celebration, celebrator, celebrity,* pl. *celebrities.*
CELER'ITY. *s.* Swiftness, speed, velocity, despatch. pl. *celerities.*
CEL'ERY. *s.* A species of culinary vegetable. pl. *celeries.*

CELESTIAL. *adj.* Heavenly, relating to the upper regions *adv. celestially.*

CELIBACY. *s.* Unmarried state. pl. *celibacies.*

CELL. *s.* A small cavity or hollow place; the cave or little habitation of a religious person. *adj. cellular.*

CELLAR. *s.* A subterraneous apartment. *s. cellerage.*

CELLULAR. *adj.* Consisting of little cells or cavities.

CELTIC. *adj.* Relating to the Celts.

CEMENT. *s.* Cohesive matter; bond of union. *v. cement'; pr. par. cementing;* past, *cemented: s. cementation, cementer.*

CEMETERY. *s.* A place for the dead. pl. *cemeteries.*

CENOBITE, CŒNOBITE. *s.* One of a religious order, who lives in a convent, or in a community, under a certain rule; in opposition to a hermit, who lives in solitude. *adj. cenobitical: adv. cenobitically.*

CENOTAPH. *s.* An empty tomb, erected in honour of a person buried at another place.

CENSER. *s.* A vessel in which incense is burned.

CENSOR. *s.* One empowered to correct manners. *adj. censorial, censorian: adv. censorially: s. censorship.*

CENSORIOUS. *adj.* Addicted to censure; severe. *adv. censoriously; s. censoriousness.*

CENSURE. *s.* Blame, reprimand, reproach. *v. censure; pr. par. censuring;* past, *censured:* adj. *censurable: s. censurer.*

CENSUS. *s.* An account of the inhabitants, made by public authority. Latin pl. *census.*

CENT. *s.* A hundred, a coin equal to the hundredth part of a dollar.

CENTAUR. *s.* An imaginary being, supposed to be compounded of a man and a horse; the archer in the zodiac.

CENTENARY. *adj.* The number of a hundred. *s. centenarian: adj. centennial.*

CENTIPEDE. *s.* An insect with many feet.

CENTRE. *s.* The middle; that which is equally distant from all extremities. *adj. central: s. centrality: adv. centrally: v. centre; pr. par. centring;* past, *centred.*

CENTRIFUGAL. *adj.* Receding from the centre. *adv. centrifugally.*

CENTRIPETAL. *adj.* Approaching the centre. *adv. centripetally.*

CENTRIPLE. *adj.* A hundred-fold.

CENTURION. *s.* A Roman officer who commanded a hundred men.

CENTURY. *s.* A hundred; a hundred years. pl. *centuries.*

CEPHALIC. *adj.* Medicinal to the head.

CERATE. *s.* An ointment made of wax. *adj. cerated.*

CERECLOTH. *s.* Cloth dipped in wax or gum.

CEREMONY. *s.* Outward rite; external form in religion, or state. pl. *ceremonies:* adj. *ceremonial, ceremonious: adv. ceremoniously: s. ceremoniousness.*

CERTAIN. *adj.* Sure, indubitable, determined. *adv. certainly: s. certainty,* pl. *certainties.*

CERTIFICATE. *s.* Written testimony. *adj. certificated.*

CERTIFY. *v.* To make a formal attestation. *pr. par. certifying,* past, *certified: s. certification, certifier.*

CERULEAN. *adj.* Sky-coloured; light blue.

CERUMEN. *s.* The wax formed in the ear.

CESS. *s.* A levy upon the inhabitants of a place, according to their property. pl. *cesses: v. cess pr. par. cessing;* past, *cessed.*

CESSATION. *s.* Act of ceasing; stop: suspension of action.

CESSION. *s.* Act of ceding; resignation; assignment.

57

CES'TUS. s. The girdle of Venus.
CETA'CEOUS. adj. Of the whale kind.
CHAFE. v. To heat by rubbing; to make angry; to fret. pr. par. *chafing;* past, *chafed:* s. *chafer.*
CHAFF. s. The husks of oats, &c.
CHAF'FINCH. s. A species of bird. pl. *chaffinches.*
CHA'FING-DISH. s. A portable grate for coals. pl. *chafing-dishes.*
CHAGRIN'. s. Ill humour, vexation. v. *chagrin;* pr. par. *chagrining;* past, *chagrined.*
CHAIN. v. To fasten, to link, to unite. pr. par. *chaining;* past, *chained:* s. *chain.*
CHAIN'-SHOT. s. Two balls fastened together by a chain.
CHAIR. s. A moveable seat; a seat of authority; a sedan. v. *chair;* pr. par. *chairing;* past, *chaired.*
CHAIR'MAN. s. The president of an assembly; one whose trade it is to carry a chair.
CHAISE. s. A sort of carriage.
CHAL'DRON, CHAUL'DRON. s. An English measure of coals, containing 36 bushels.
CHAL'ICE. s. A sacramental cup.
CHALK. s. A species of calcareous fossil. pr. par. *chalking;* past, *chalked:* adj. *chalky:* s. *chalkiness.*
CHAL'LENGE. v. To call another to answer for an offence, by combat; to accuse; to object to. pr. par. *challenging;* past, *challenged:* s. *challenge, challenger:* adj. *challengeable.*
CHALYB'EATE. adj. Impregnated with iron or steel.
CHAMA'DE. s. The beat of a drum, indicating a desire for a parley.
CHAM'BER. s. An apartment.
CHAM'BERLAIN. s. An officer of state.
CHAM'BER-MAID. s. A female who attends in a bed-chamber.
CHAME'LEON. s. An animal which is said to assume the colour of those things to which it is applied.

CHAM'OIS. s. A kind of soft leather.
CHAM'OMILE. s. The name of an odoriferous plant.
CHAMP. v. To bite with a frequent action of the teeth. pr. par. *champing;* past, *champed.*
CHAMPAIGN'. s. A kind of wine; a flat open country.
CHAMPAIGN'. adj. Relating to a flat open country.
CHAM'PION. s. A warrior; one who engages in single combat.
CHANCE. s. Fortune, accident. v. *chance;* pr. par. *chancing;* past, *chanced.*
CHAN'CEL. s. The place in a church where the altar stands.
CHAN'CELLOR. s. An officer of the highest power and dignity in the English courts of law; an officer of high rank in universities.
CHAN'CERY. s. A court of equity and conscience. pl. *chanceries.*
CHANDELIE'R. s. A branch for candles.
CHAN'DLER. s. A maker of candles; a seller of corn, and of things required for the use of ships. s. *chandlery,* pl. *chandleries.*
CHANGE. v. To alter; to put one thing in place of another. pr. par. *changing;* past, *changed:* s. *change:* adj. *changeable:* adv. *changeably:* s. *changeableness.*
CHAN'NEL. s. The hollow bed of running waters; a strait or narrow sea; a gutter or furrow. v *channel;* pr. par. *channeling;* past, *channeled.*
CHANT. v. To sing; to sing in the cathedral service. pr. par. *chanting;* past, *chanted.* s. *chant, chanter, chantress,* pl. *chantresses.*
CHAN'TICLEER. s. A name given to the house-cock.
CHANT'RY. s. A chapel endowed with revenue, for priests to sing mass for the souls of the donors. pl. *chantries.*

58

CHA'OS. *s.* A confused mass or mixture. adj. *chaotic:* adv. *chaotically.*

CHAPEAU'. *s.* The French name for *hat.*

CHAPEL. *s.* A species of church.

CHA'PERON. *v.* To attend on a lady, in a public assembly. pr. par. *chaperoning;* past, *chaperoned.*

CHAP'LAIN. *s.* He that attends the king, or other great person, or body of men, to perform divine service. s. *chaplaincy,* the office of a chaplain; pl. *chaplaincies.*

CHAP'LET. *s.* A garland or wreath for the head.

CHAP'MAN. *s.* A petty merchant.

CHAP'TER. *s.* A division of a book; an assembly of the clergy of a cathedral or collegiate church.

CHAR. *s.* A kind of fish.

CHAR. *v.* To burn to a black cinder; to work by the day. pr. par. *charring;* past, *charred:* s. *char.*

CHAR ACTER. *s.* A mark; a stamp; a letter used in writing or printing. adj. *characteristic:* v. *characterise;* pr. par. *characterising;* past, *characterised.*

CHARA'DE. *s.* A species of riddle, usually in verse.

CHAR'COAL. *s.* Coal made by burning wood under turf.

CHARGE. *v.* To entrust; to commission for a certain purpose; to accuse; to censure; to load a gun; to place to account. pr. par. *charging;* past, *charged:* s. *charge:* adj. *chargeable.* adv. *chargeably.*

CHAR'GER. *s.* A large dish; the horse of a cavalry soldier; an instrument used in charging a gun.

CHAR'IOT. *s.* A carriage of pleasure or state. s. *charioteer.*

CHAR'ITY. *s.* Tenderness, kindness, love, benevolence, alms, liberality to the poor. pl. *charities:* adj. *charitable.* adv. *charitably.*

CHARLATAN'. *s.* A quack, or mountebank. adj. *charlatanical:* s. *charlatanry,* pl. *charlatanries.*

CHARM. *s.* Words or philtres imagined to have some occult power; delight, beauty. s. *charmer:* v. *charm;* pr. par. *charming;* past, *charmed:* adv. *charmingly.*

CHAR'NEL-HOUSE. *s.* A reposi tory of human bones.

CHART. *s.* A map for seamen; a delineation of coasts.

CHAR'TER. *s.* Written evidence, legal power of incorporation; exemption. v. *charter;* pr. par. *chartering;* past, *chartered.*

CHASE. *v.* To hunt; to pursue as an enemy; to drive away. pr. par. *chasing;* past, *chased:* s. *chase, chaser.*

CHASM. *s.* A cleft; a place unfilled.

CHASTE. adj. Pure, uncorrupt, undefiled. v. *chasten;* pr. par *chastening;* past, *chastened:* adv. *chastely;* s. *chastity,* pl. *chastities*

CHASTI'SE. *v.* To punish; to reduce to order or obedience. pr par. *chastising;* past, *chastised.* s. *chastisement.*

CHAT. *v.* To prate; to converse at ease. pr. par. *chatting;* past, *chatted:* s. *chat, chatter:* adj. *chatty.*

CHATEAU'. *s.* A castle; a stately mansion.

CHAT'TEL. *s.* Moveable property; real estate not freehold.

CHAT'TER. *v.* To make a noise as a pie, or other unharmonious bird; to talk idly or carelessy. v. pr. par. *chattering;* past, *chattered:* s. *chatter, chatterer.*

CHAUNT. *v.* See CHANT.

CHEAP. adj. To be had at a low rate; easy to be had; not respected. adv. *cheaply:* s. *cheapness.*

CHEAP'EN. *v.* To ask the price to lessen the value. pr. par. *cheapening;* past, *cheapened:* s. *cheapener.*

CHEAT. *v.* To defraud, to impose upon, to trick. pr. par. *cheating* past, *cheated:* s. *cheat, cheater.*

CHECK. *v.* To repress, to curb, to reprove, to chide; to control; to draw upon a bank. pr. par. *checking;* past, *checked.*

CHECK. *s.* Stop; sudden restraint; curb; a reproof; cloth made in squares; a draft on a bank, for the payment of money.

CHECK'ER, CHEQ'UER. *v.* To variegate; to diversify in the manner of a chess-board. pr. par. *checkering;* past, *checkered:* s. *checker, chequer.*

CHECK'MATE. *s.* A term in the game of chess. *v. checkmate;* pr. par. *checkmating;* past, *checkmated.*

CHEEK. *s.* The side of the face below the eye.

CHEER. *v.* To incite; to encourage; to inspirit; to comfort; to gladden. pr. par. *cheering;* past, *cheered:* s. *cheer:* adj. *cheerful, cheerless:* adv. *cheerfully, cheerily.*

CHEESE. *s.* The curd of milk, pressed into a cake.

CHEESE'CAKE. *s.* A cake made of soft curds, sugar, and butter.

CHEESE'MONGER. *s.* One who deals in cheese.

CHEESE'PRESS. *s.* The press in which curds are pressed. pl. *cheesepresses.*

CHEESE'VAT. *s.* The wooden vat in which the curds are confined, in pressing.

CHEMISE'. *s.* A shift.

CHEM'IST, CHYM'IST. *s.* A separater and examiner of matter, and preparer of various compounds. s. *chemistry, chymistry:* adj. *chemical, chymical:* adv. *chemically, chymically.* The latter mode of spelling this word, is the most correct; but the former is the most general.

CHER'ISH. *v.* To support, to shelter, to nurse. pr. par. *cherishing;* past, *cherished* · s. *cherisher, cherishment.*

CHER'RY. *s.* A species of small fruit. pl *cherries.*

CHER'UB. *s.* A celestial spirit. Hebrew pl. *cherubim*· English pl. *cherubs;* adj. *cherubic.*

CHESS. *s.* A sort of game.

CHESS'-BOARD. *s.* The board on which chess is played.

CHESS'-MAN. *s.* A puppet or counter for chess. pl. *chess-men.*

CHEST. *s.* A box made of wood or other materials.

CHES'NUT. *s.* A small nut, of a brown colour.

CHEVAL'IER. *s.* A knight; a title of honour.

CHEVAUX-DE-FRISE'. *s.* A defensive instrument of war, made of timber and iron spikes.

CHEW. *v.* To grind with the teeth; to masticate. pr. par. *chewing,* past, *chewed.*

CHICA'NE. *s.* Artifice, trick, fraud. *v. chicane;* pr. par. *chicaning;* past, *chicaned:* s. *chicanery,* pl. *chicaneries.*

CHICK'EN. *s.* The young of a bird, particularly of a domestic hen.

CHICK'EN-HEARTED. *adj.* Cowardly, timorous.

CHICK'EN-POX. *s.* A species of eruptive disorder.

CHID. *v.* Did chide.

CHIDE. *v.* To reprove, to reproach, to blame. pr. par. *chiding;* past, *chided, chidden:* s. *chider.*

CHIEF. *adj.* Principal, capital, of the first order. s. *chief:* adv. *chiefly.*

CHIEF, CHIEF'TAIN. *s.* A leader; a commander; the head of a clan.

CHIL'BLAIN. *s.* A sore made by frost.

CHILD. *s.* An infant, or very young person. pl. *children:* adj *childish:* adv. *childishly.*

CHILD'HOOD. *s.* The state of a child; infancy.

CHILL. *v.* To make cold; to depress; to deject; to blast with cold. pr. par. *chilling;* past, *chilled:* s. *chill, chillness:* adj. *chilly.*

CHIME. *v.* To sound in harmony; to correspond in relation or proportion; to agree; to jingle. pr. par. *chiming;* past, *chimed:* s. *chime, chimer.*

CHIME'RA. *s.* A vain and wild fancy. adj. *chimerical:* adv. *chimerically.*

CHIM'NEY. *s.* The passage through which the smoke ascends from the fire in a house.

CHIM'NEY-PIECE. *s.* The work round the fire-place; a mantle-piece.

CHIM'NEY-SWEEPER. *s.* One who cleans chimneys.

CHIN. *s.* The part of the face beneath the under lip.

CHI'NA. *s.* China-ware; porcelain.

CHIN'COUGH. *s.* A violent and convulsive cough, to which children are subject.

CHINE. *s.* That part of the back in which the back-bone is.

CHINE'SE. *adj.* Relating to China. *s. Chinese.*

CHINK. *s.* A small aperture. *v. chink,* to fill the spaces between the logs of a cabin.; pr. par. *chinking;* past, *chinked:* s. *chinker.*

CHINK. *v.* To shake, so as to make a sound. pr. par. *chinking;* past, *chinked.*

CHINTZ. *s.* Cotton cloth printed with colours. pl. *chintzes.*

CHIP. *v.* To cut into small pieces. pr. par. *chipping;* past, *chipped:* s. *chip.*

CHIRO'GRAPHY. *s.* The art of writing.

CHIROL'OGY. *s.* Talking by the hand.

CHI'ROMANCY. *s.* The pretended art of foretelling events by inspecting the hand. pl. *chiromancies;* s. *chiromancer.*

CHIRP. *v.* To make a cheerful noise, as birds. pr. par. *chirping;* past, *chirped:* s. *chirp, chirper.*

CHIS'EL. *s.* An instrument with which wood or stone is pared. *v. chisel;* pr. par. *chiseling;* past, *chiseled.*

CHIT'CHAT. *s.* Prattle, idle talk.

CHIV'ALRY. *s.* Knighthood; a military dignity; the qualifications of a knight, as valour and virtue; the general system of knighthood. pl. *chivalries:* adj *chivalrous:* adv. *chivalrously.*

CHOC'OLATE. *s.* A substance made by grinding the kernel of the cocoa-nut.

CHOICE. *adj.* Select, careful. s *choice, choiceness:* adv. *choicely.*

CHOIR. *s.* An assembly or band of singers; the place where they sing. adj. *choral.*

CHOKE. *v.* To suffocate. to stop up, to suppress. pr. par. *choking,* past, *choked.*

CHOL'ER. *s.* The bile; the humour supposed to produce irascibility anger; rage. adj. *choleric.*

CHOLERA-MOR'BUS. *s.* A sudde overflowing of the bile.

CHOOSE. *v.* To select, to elect pr. par. *choosing;* past, *chosen* s. *choice, chooser.*

CHOP. *v.* To cut with a quick blow; to break into small pieces pr. par. *chopping;* past, *chopped* s. *chop, chopper.*

CHOP. *s.* A Chinese word, signify ing *quality.*

CHOPS. *s.* The mouth of a beast the mouth of a man, used in contempt; the mouth of any thing in familiar language.

CHO'RAL. *adj.* Belonging to a choir or concert. s. *chorister.*

CHORD. *s.* The string of a musical instrument; a right line, which joins the two ends of any arc of a circle.

CHORIAM'BIC *s.* The foot of a verse consisting of four syllables, as *anxietas.*

CHO'RUS. *s.* A band of singers; part of a song in which the whole company join. pl. *choruses.*

CHOSE. The preterit of the v. *choose.*

CHOUSE. *v.* To cheat, to trick. pr pr. *chousing;* past, *choused.*

CHRISM. s. Holy ointment. s. *chrismatory*, pl. *chrismatories*.

CHRIS'TEN. v. To baptize; to initiate into Christianity, by water; to name. pr. par. *christening*; past, *christened*: s. *christener*, *christening*.

CHRIS'TENDOM. s. All those regions, taken collectively, in which the inhabitants profess the Christian religion.

CHRIS'TIAN. s. A professor of the religion of Christ. adj. *christian*: s. *christianity*.

CHRIST'MAS. s. The day on which the nativity of Christ is celebrated. pl. *christmases*.

CHROMAT'IC. adj. Relating to the colour of light, and of natural bodies, and to a species of ancient music now unknown.

CHRO'NIC, CHRO'NICAL. adj. Relating to diseases of long continuance. adv. *chronically*.

CHRON'ICLE. s. A brief history, with dates. s. *chronicler*.

CHRONOL'OGY. s. The science of computing relative time. pl. *chronologies*: s. *chronologist*: adj. *chronological*: adv. *chronologically*.

CHRONOM'ETER. s. An instrument for the exact measurement of time.

CHRY'SALIS. s. An insect, such as a butterfly, when changing from its torpid state. pl. *chrysales*.

CHRY'SOLITE. s. A precious stone, of a dusky green, with a shade of yellow.

CHUB'BY, CHUB'-FACED. adj. Having a large or fat face.

CHUCK'LE. v. To utter a smothered laugh. pr. par. *chuckling*; past, *chuckled*.

CHUM. s. A chamber-fellow in the universities.

CHUNK. s. A short, thick block, or bit of wood.

CHURCH. s. The collective body of Christians; the body of Christians adhering to one particular form of worship; the place which Christians consecrate to the worship of God. pl. *churches*: v. *church*; pr. par. *churching*; past, *churched*.

CHURCH'-WARDEN. s. An officer yearly chosen to preserve the property of a church.

CHURL. s. A rustic; a rude, surly, ill-bred man; a miser. adj. *churlish*: adv. *churlishly*: s. *churlishness*.

CHURN. s. A vessel in which butter is, by agitation, coagulated. v. *churn*; pr. par. *churning*; past, *churned*: s. *churner*.

CHYLE. s. A white juice, formed in the intestines, and afterwards converted into blood. adj. *chylaceous*, *chylous*.

CHYM'IST. s. See CHEMIST.

CIC'ATRICE, CIC'ATRIX. s. The scar remaining after a wound.

CIC'ATRIZE. v. To apply such medicines to wounds or ulcers, as will cover them with a skin. pr. par. *cicatrizing*; past, *cicatrized*. s. *cicatrization*.

CICERO'NE. s. An Italian word, used to signify a *guide*. pl. *ciceroni*.

CI'DER. s. The juice of apples, expressed and fermented.

CIMME'RIAN. adj. Extremely dark

CINC'TURE. s. Something worn round the body; a bandage.

CIN'DER. s. A mass of any thing burnt in the fire, but not reduced to ashes; a hot coal, that has ceased to flame.

CINERA'TION. s. The act of reducing to ashes.

CIN'NAMON. s. The fragrant bark of a low tree in the island of Ceylon.

CINQUE. s. A five; a term used in backgammon.

CI'ON. s. A sprout; a shoot from a plant; the shoot engrafted on a stock.

CI'PHER. s. Any arithmetical figure; but in general denoting 0 hence, the appellation to a per of no efficiency, "a mere cipher:" it also means, a secret mode of corresponding. v. *cipher*; pr. par. *ciphering*; past, *ciphered*: s. *cipherer*.

CIRCEN'SIAN. *adj.* Relating to the exhibitions in the amphitheatre of Rome.

CIR'CLE. *s.* A line every where equidistant from a common centre. v. *circle*; pr. par. *circling*; past, *circled*.

CIR'CUIT. *s.* Motion around; comprehensive tour; space; extent. adj. *circuitous*: adv. *circuitously*.

CIR'CULATE. *v.* To move in a circle; to flow around. pr. par. *circulating*; past, *circulated*: s. *circulation*: adj. *circulatory*.

CIR'CULAR. *adj.* Round, like a circle; *Circular letter*, a letter addressed to several persons, on some common affair. adv. *circularly*.

CIRCUMAM'BIENT. *adj.* Surrounding, encompassing, going round. s. *circumambiency*.

CIRCUMAM'BULATE. *v.* To walk around. pr. par. *circumambulating*; past, *circumambulated*: s. *circumambulation*: adj. *circumambulatory*.

CIR'CUMCISE. *v.* To perform a certain religious ceremony, instituted by the Jews. pr. par. *circumcising*; past, *circumcised*: s. *circumcision*.

CIRCUM'FERENCE. *s.* Boundary of a circle; the periphery. adj. *circumferential*: adv. *circumferentially*.

CIRCUMFEREN'TOR. *s.* An instrument used in surveying.

CIR'CUMFLEX. *s.* An accent used to regulate the pronunciation of syllables. pl. *circumflexes*.

CIRCUM'FLUENT. *adj.* Flowing around. s. *circumfluence*.

CIRCUMFORA'NEOUS. *adj.* Wandering from house to house.

CIRCUMFU'SE. *v.* To pour, to spread around. pr. par. *circumfusing*; past, *circumfused*: s. *circumfusion*.

CIRCUMJA'CENT. *adj.* Surrounding, lying round.

CIRCUMLOCU'TION. *s.* Indirect expression of words; a circuit or compass of words. adj. *circumlocutory*.

CIRCUMNAV'IGATE. *v.* To sail around. pr. par. *circumnavigating*; past, *circumnavigated*: adj. *circumnavigable*: s. *circumnavigation*.

CIRCUMSCRI'BE. *v.* To limit, by a real or imaginary circle. pr. par. *circumscribing*; past, *circumscribed*: s. *circumscription*: adj. *circumscriptive*.

CIR'CUMSPECT. *adj.* Cautious, attentive, watchful. s. *circumspection*, *circumspectness*: adv. *circumspectly*.

CIR'CUMSTANCE. *s.* Something relative to a fact; incident; condition; event. part. adj. *circumstanced*: adj. *circumstantial*: adv. *circumstantially*.

CIRCUMVALLA'TION. *s.* A surrounding wall; the fortification thrown up around a place besieged. v. *circumvallate*; pr. par. *circumvallating*; past, *circumvallated*.

CIRCUMVENT'. *v.* To deceive, to cheat, to defeat by stratagem. pr. par. *circumventing*; past, *circumvented*: s. *circumvention*.

CIRCUMVOLA'TION. *s.* The act of flying round.

CIRCUMVOLVE'. *v.* To roll around. pr. par. *circumvolving*; past, *circumvolved*: s. *circumvolution*.

CIR'CUS. *s.* An open place, or theatre, for equestrian exhibitions. pl. *circuses*.

CIS'TERN. *s.* A small reservoir; an enclosed fountain.

CISTER'TIAN. *s.* A monk of the order of reformed Benedictines.

CIT'ADEL. *s.* A fortress, a castle.

CITE. *v.* To summon; to quote as authority. pr. par. *citing;* past, *cited: s. citation:* adj. *citatory.*
CITIZEN. *s.* A freeman of a city; a townsman; an inhabitant. s. *citizenship*
CITRON. *s* A large kind of lemon.
CITY. *s.* An incorporated town, having a mayor; an ancient town claiming this title, by prescription. pl. *cities.*
CIVET. *s.* A perfume from the civet cat.
CIVIC. *adj.* Relating to civil honours; not military.
CIVIL. *adj.* Relating to the community in general, mild; obliging. s. *civility,* pl. *civilities:* adv. *civilly:* v. *civilize;* pr. par. *civilizing;* past, *civilized: s. civilization.*
CIVILIAN. *s.* One who professes a knowledge of the old civil or Roman law, and of general equity.
CLACK. *s.* A lasting and importunate noise.
CLAD. Preterit and past par. of the v. *clothe.*
CLAIM. *v.* To demand as a right; to require authoritatively. pr. par. *claiming;* past, *claimed: s. claim, claimant;* adj. *claimable.*
CLAM. *s.* A species of shell-fish.
CLAMBER. *v.* To climb with difficulty. pr. par. *clambering:* past, *clambered.*
CLAMMY *adj.* Viscous, glutinous. s. *clamminess.*
CLAMOUR, CLAMOR. *s.* Vehement outcry, exclamation, vociferation. adj. *clamorous:* adv. *clamourously:* v. *clamour;* pr. par. *clamouring:* past, *clamoured.*
CLAMP. *s.* A piece of wood joined to another, as an addition of strength; a heap of turf or bricks.
CLAN. *s.* A family; a race; a body or sect of people. adj. *clannish:* s. *clanship.*
CLANDESTINE. *adj.* Secret; done in a manner to elude observation. adj. *clandestinely: s. clandestineness.*
CLANG. *s.* A sharp, shrill noise. v. *clang;* pr. par. *clanging;* past, *clanged.*
CLANGOUR, CLANGOR. *s.* A loud, shrill sound.
CLANK. *v.* To make a loud, rattling noise. pr. par. *clanking;* past, *clanked.*
CLAP. *v.* To strike together, with a quick motion; to applaud. pr par. *clapping;* past, *clapped: s clap, clapper.*
CLAPBOARD. *s.* A narrow board commonly used for the outermost covering of houses in the new settlements of America. v. *clapboard,* pr. par. *clapboarding;* past, *clapboarded.*
CLARE-OBSCURE. *s.* Light and shade in painting.
CLARET. *s.* A species of French wine.
CLARIFY. *v.* To clear from impurities. pr. par. *clarifying;* past, *clarified: s. clarification.*
CLARION. *s.* A trumpet.
CLARIONET. *s.* A kind of wind instrument.
CLASH. *v.* To make a noise, by mutual collision; to oppose. pr. par. *clashing;* past, *clashed:* s. *clash.*
CLASP. *s.* A hook to hold any thing close; an embrace. v. *clasp;* pr. par. *clasping;* past, *clasped.*
CLASS. *s.* A rank or order of persons or things; a number of young persons learning the same lesson. pl. *classes:* v. *class;* pr. par. *classing;* past, *classed.*
CLASSIFY. *v.* To arrange in classes. pr. par. *classifying;* past. *classified:* s. *classifier, classification*
CLASSIC, CLASSICAL. *adj.* Relating to ancient literature, and to architecture; and to modern literature of the highest rank. s. *classics:* adv. *classically.*

CLAT'TER. *v.* To make a noise, by striking two sonorous bodies together. pr. par. *clattering;* past, *clattered* s. *clatter, clatterer, clattering.*

CLAUSE. *s.* A sentence; an article or particular stipulation.

CLAW. *s.* The foot of a beast or bird, armed with sharp nails; the pincers or holders of a shell-fish. *v. claw:* pr. par. *clawing;* past, *clawed.*

CLAY. *s.* Unctuous and tenacious earth; earth in general. *v. clay;* pr. par. *claying;* past, *clayed:* adj. *clayey.*

CLAY'MORE. *s.* A two-handed sword.

CLEAN. *adj.* Free from dirt; neat. *v. clean;* pr. par. *cleaning;* past, *cleaned:* s. *cleanliness, cleanness:* adj. *cleanly.*

CLEANSE. *v.* To free from dirt; to purify; to scour. pr. par. *cleansing;* past, *cleansed:* s. *cleanser.*

CLEAR. *adj.* Bright, transparent, serene, perspicuous, evident. *v. clear;* pr. par. *clearing;* past, *cleared:* s. *clearer, clearance, clearness:* adv. *clearly.*

CLEAR'ING. *s.* In the United States, signifies that part of a forest, which is in a state of preparation for the plough.

CLEAR-SIGHT'ED. *adj.* Perspicacious; discerning. s. *clearsightedness.*

CLEAVE. *v.* To adhere, to stick, to unite aptly. pr. par. *cleaving;* past, *cleaved:* s. *cleaver.*

CLEAVE. *v.* To divide with violence; to split. pr. par. *cleaving;* past, *cloven* or *cleft:* s. *cleever.*

CLEF. *s.* A term in music.

CLEFT. Past par. of the v. *to cleave.*

CLEG. *s.* A horse-fly.

CLEM'ENCY. *s.* Mercy, remission of severity. pl. *clemencies:* adj. *clement:* adv. *clemently.*

CLENCH. *v.* See CLINCH.

CLER'GY. *s.* The body of men, appointed by due ordination, for the service of God.

CLER'GYMAN. *s.* A man in holy orders. pl. *clergymen.*

CLER'ICAL. *adj.* Relating to the clergy. adv. *clerically.*

CLERK. *s.* A clergyman; a man employed under another, as writer; the layman who reads the responses to the congregation in the church, to direct the rest. s. *clerkship.*

CLEV'ER. *adj.* Dexterous, skilful, just, fit, proper. adv. *cleverly:* s. *cleverness.*

CLEW. *s.* Thread wound around something; a guide; a direction. *v. clew;* pr. par. *clewing;* past, *clewed.*

CLICK. *s.* A sharp, small, successive noise. pr. par. *clicking;* past, *clicked.*

CLI'ENT. *s.* One who applies to an advocate for counsel and defence; a dependant.

CLIFF. *s.* A steep rock.

CLIFT. *s.* A large split in a rock. adj. *clifted.*

CLIMAC'TERIC, CLIMAC'TRIC *s.* Relating to a period of life, when some great change is supposed to befal the body.

CLI'MATE. *s.* A space upon the surface of the earth, measured from the equator to the polar circles, in each of which spaces the longest day is half an hour in length; a region or tract of land differing from another by the temperature of the air.

CLI'MAX. *s.* Gradation; ascent; a figure in rhetoric, by which a sentence rises gradually. pl. *climaxes.*

CLIMB. *v.* To ascend with labour; to mount. pr. par. *climbing;* past, *climbed:* s. *climber.*

CLIME. *s.* Climate, region, tract of earth.

CLINCH. *v.* To hold in the hand with the fingers bent; to confine; to fix; to bend the point of a nail pr. par. *clinching;* past, *clinched;* s. *clinch.*

CLING. *v.* To hang upon, by twining around. pr. par. *clinging;* past, *clung:* s. *clinger.*

CLIN'IC, CLIN'ICAL. *adj.* Relating to a person who from sickness is compelled to remain in bed. A "clinical lecture" is delivered by a medical professor at the bedside. adv. *clinically.*

CLINK. *v.* To strike, so as to make a small, sharp noise. pr. par. *clinking;* past, *clinked:* s *clink.*

CLIP. *v.* To curtail, to cut short. pr. par. *clipping;* past, *clipped:* s. *clip, clipper.*

CLOAK. *s.* An outer garment; a concealment. pr. par. *cloaking;* past, *cloaked.*

CLOCK. *s.* The instrument which tells the hour, by striking upon a bell; a sort of beetle.

CLOCK. *v.* To cluck; to call as a hen calls her chickens. pr. par. *clocking;* past, *clocked.*

CLOD. *s.* A lump of earth. v. *clod;* pr. par. *clodding;* past, *clodded.*

CLODHOPPER, }
CLOD'POLL, } *s.* A rustic; a clown.
CLOD'PATE. }

CLOG. *v.* To load with something that may hinder motion; to obstruct; to burthen. pr. par. *clogging;* past, *clogged:* s. *clog.*

CLOG. *s.* A coarse shoe, with a wooden sole.

CLOIS'TER. *s.* A place of religious seclusion. v. *cloister;* pr. par. *cloistering;* past, *cloistered* adj. *cloistral.*

CLOSE. *v.* To shut, to conclude, to end. pr. par. *closing;* past, *closed* adj. *close:* adv. *closely:* s. *closeness.*

CLOS'ET. *s.* A small room for retirement, or for the preservation of valuable things. v. *closet;* pr. par. *closeting;* past, *closeted.*

CLOT. *s.* Concretion, coagulation. v. *clot;* pr. par. *clotting;* past, *clotted:* adj. *clotty*

CLOTH. *s.* Any thing woven for dress or covering.

CLOTHE. *v.* To cover with cloth, to dress. pr. par. *clothing;* past, *clothed:* s. pl. *clothes;* s. *clothier, clothing.*

CLOUD. *s.* An opaque assemblage in the sky; any state of obscurity or darkness. v. *cloud;* pr. par. *clouding;* past, *clouded:* adv. *cloudily.* adj. *cloudy, cloudless:* s. *cloudiness.*

CLOUD'CAPT. *adj.* Topped with clouds.

CLOVE. *s.* A kind of spice.

CLOVE. The preterit of the v. *cleave.*

CLO'VEN. The past par. of the v. *cleave.*

CLOVEN-FOOT'ED. *adj.* Having the hoof divided into two parts.

CLO'VER. *s.* A species of trefoil. adj. *clovered.*

CLOWN. *s.* A rustic; a coarse, ill-bred man; one who makes sport at a theatrical entertainment. adj. *clownish:* adv. *clownishly:* s. *clownishness.*

CLOY. *v.* To satiate, to surfeit. pr. par. *cloying;* past, *cloyed.*

CLUB. *s.* A heavy stick; the name of one of the suits of cards; a society which meets at stated times. v. *club;* pr. par. *clubbing;* past *clubbed.*

CLUB-FOOT'ED. *adj.* Having short or crooked feet.

CLUCK. *v.* To call chickens, as a hen. pr. par. *clucking;* past, *clucked.*

CLUE, CLEW. *s.* Thread wound around something; a guide; a direction.

CLUMP. *s.* A shapeless piece of wood or other matter; a cluster of trees.

CLUM'SY. *adj.* Awkward, heavy, artless, unhandy. adv. *clumsily:* s. *clumsiness.*

CLUNG. The preterit and past par of the v. *cling.*

66

CLUSTER. *s.* A bunch; a number of things of the same kind growing or joined together. *v. cluster;* pr. par. *clustering;* past, *clustered.*

CLUTCH. *v.* To gripe, to grasp. pr. par. *clutching;* past, *clutched* *s. clutch.*

CLUTTER *s.* A noise, a bustle. *v. clutter;* pr. par. *cluttering;* past, *cluttered.*

COACH. *s.* A carriage of pleasure or state.

COADJUTOR. *s.* An assistant; a partner. adj. *coadjutant.*

COAG'ULATE. *v.* To curdle; to form into concretions. pr. par. *coagulating;* past, *coagulated:* s. *coagulation, coagulator:* adj. *coagulative.*

COAL. *s.* The common fossil fuel; the cinder of burnt wood; charcoal.

COALES'CE. *v.* To unite, to grow together, to join. pr. par. *coalescing;* past, *coalesced:* s. *coalescence.*

COALI'TION. *s.* The act of coalescing; persons combined.

COARSE. *adj.* Not refined; rude, gross, unaccomplished. adv. *coarsely:* s. *coarseness.*

COAST. *s.* The edge or margin of the land next the sea. *v. coast;* pr. par. *coasting;* past, *coasted:* s. *coaster.*

COAT. *s.* The upper garment; vesture. *v. coat;* pr. par *coating,* past, *coated*

COAX. *v.* To wheedle, to flatter. pr. par. *coaxing;* past, *coaxed:* s. *coaxer.*

COB. *s.* The spike of an ear of maize; the core, after the corn is taken off.

COB'BLE. *v.* To mend any thing coarsely. pr. par. *cobbling;* past, *cobbled:* s. *cobbler.*

COB'WEB. *s.* The web or net of a spider. adj. *cobwebbed.*

COCH'INEAL. *s.* An insect from which a red colour is extracted

COCKA'DE. *s.* A ribbon worn in the hat.

COCK'LE. *s.* A small shell-fish; a weed that grows in corn.

COCK'NEY. *s.* An ill-bred native of London.

COCK'PIT. *s.* The area where cocks fight · a place on the lower deck of a man of war, where are subdivisions for the purser, surgeon, and his mates.

COCK'SWAIN. *s.* A petty officer on board of a man of war. pronounced *cok'-sn.*

CO'COA. *s.* A kind of plant.

COD. *s.* A kind of fish: *codling*, a young cod.

CODE. *s.* A system of laws or regulations.

COD'ICIL. *s.* A supplement to a will.

COD'DLE. *v.* To parboil. pr. par. *coddling;* past, *coddled.*

CO-EFFI'CIENT. *adj.* Uniting in action. s. *co-efficacy, co-efficiency,* pl. *co-efficacies, co-efficiencies.*

CO-E'QUAL. *adj.* Equal to another. s. *co-equality,* pl. *co-equalities.*

COERCE'. *v.* To force, to restrain. pr. par. *coercing;* past, *coerced:* s. *coercer, coercion:* adj. *coercive:* adv. *coercively.*

CO-ESSEN'TIAL. *adj.* Participating of the same essence. adv. *co-essentially.*

CO-ETER'NAL. *adj.* Equally eternal. adv. *co-eternally:* s. *co-eternity,* pl. *co-eternities.*

COE'VAL. *adj.* Equally ancient; living in the same age.

CO-EXIST'. *v.* To exist at the same time. pr. par. *co-existing;* past, *co-existed:* s. *co-existence:* adj. *co-existent.*

CO-EXTEND'. *v.* To reach to an equal distance. pr. par. *co-extending;* past, *co-extended·* s. *co-extension:* adj. *co-extensive.*

COF'FEE. *s.* The berry of the coffee tree; a drink made by the infusion of the berries in hot water

COF—COI

COF'FER. s. A chest, generally for keeping money.
COF'FIN. s. A chest in which a dead human body is interred.
COG. s. The tooth of a wheel. adj. cogged.
CO'GENT. adj. Forcible, powerful, convincing. adv. cogently: s. cogency, pl. cogencies.
CO'GITATE. v. To think. pr. par. cogitating; past, cogitated: s. cogitation: adj. cogitative.
COGNA'TE. adj. Kindred.
COGNI'TION. s. Knowledge; the power of knowing.
COG'NIZANCE. s. Judicial notice; judicial authority. adj. cognizable.
COHAB'IT. v. To dwell with another; to live together, as husband and wife. pr. par. cohabiting; past, cohabited: s. cohabitant, cohabitation.
COHE'IR. s. One of two or more persons who inherit the same estate. fem. coheiress, pl. coheiresses.
COHE'RE. v. To stick together; to suit. pr. par cohering; past, cohered: s. coherence, coherency: adj. coherent.
COHE'SION. s. Act of cohering. adj. cohesive: adv. cohesively: s. cohesiveness.
CO'HORT. s. A troop of soldiers, in the Roman armies, containing about five hundred foot.
COIF. s. A hood, a cap. adj. coifed.
COIL. v. To gather into a narrow compass. pr. par. coiling; past, coiled: s. coil.
COIN. s. In architecture, a corner; money stamped with a legal impression. v. coin; pr. par. coining; past, coined: s. coinage, coiner.
COINCI'DE. v. To meet in the same point; to agree. pr. par. coinciding; past, coincided: s. coincidence: adj. coincident: adv. coincidently.
COI'TION. s. The act by which two bodies come together.

COK—COL

COKE. s. Pit-coal which has been charred.
COL'ANDER. s. A strainer.
COLD. adj. Wanting heat; having sense of cold; reserved; not cordial. s. cold, coldness: adv. coldly.
COLD-BLOOD'ED. adj. Without feeling; cruel.
COLD-HEART'ED. adj. Indifferent, wanting passion. s. cold-heartedness.
COLE'WORT. s. A species of cabbage.
COLLA'PSE. v. To fall together pr. par. collapsing; past, collapsed: s. collapsion.
COL'LAR. s. A band for the neck. v. collar; pr. par. collaring; past, collared.
COLLA'TE. v. To compare one copy or thing with another of the same kind; to place in an ecclesiastical benefice. pr. par. collating; past, collated: s. collation, collator.
COLLAT'ERAL. adj. Side to side, running parallel; not lineal, as a son is related to his father, but related as uncles, nephews, and cousins. adv. collaterally.
COL'LEAGUE. s. A partner in office; an associate. v. colleague; pr. par. colleaguing; past, colleagued.
COLLECT'. v. To gather, to assemble. pr. par. collecting; past, collected: s. collection, collector: adj. collective: adv. collectively.
COL'LECT. s. A short, compendious prayer.
COL'LEGE. s. A community; a public place of study; a state-assembly. s. collegian; adj. collegiate.
COL'LIER. s. A digger of coals; a dealer in coals; a ship th t carries coals. s. colliery, pl. collieries.
COLLIGA'TION. s. The act o. binding together.
COLLI'SION. s. The act of striking together; a clash. adj. collisive.

63

COL'LOCATE. *v.* To place together; to station. pr. par. *collocating;* past, *collocated:* s. *collocation, collocator.*
COLLOCU'TION. *s.* Conference, conversation.
COL'LOQUY. *s.* Conference; conversation. adj. *colloquial.*
COLLU'DE. *v.* To play in concert, so as to cheat; to conspire in a fraud. pr. par. *colluding;* past, *colluded.*
COLLU'SION. *s.* Act of colluding. adj. *collusive, collusory:* adv. *collusively.*
CO'LON. *s.* A grammatical point (:), used to mark a pause greater than that of a semicolon.
COL'ONEL. *s.* The chief commander of a regiment.
COL'ONY. *s.* A body of people settled in a foreign country; the country where they reside. pl. *colonies:* s. *colonist:* adj. *colonial:* v. *colonize;* pr. par. *colonizing;* past, *colonized:* s. *colonization.*
COLONNA'DE. *s.* A range of insulated columns.
COLOS'SUS. *s.* A statue of enormous magnitude. Latin pl. *colossi:* adj. *colossal.*
COL'OUR. *s.* The appearance of bodies to the eye; hue; die; pretence. s. *colouring:* v. *colour;* pr. par. *colouring;* past, *coloured:* adj. *colourless.*
COL'OURS. *s.* A standard; an ensign of war.
COLT. *s.* A young horse.
COL'TER. *s.* The sharp iron of a plough, that cuts perpendicularly to the share.
COL'UMBARY. *s.* A dove-cot; a pigeon-house. pl. *columbaries.*
COL'UMBINE. *s.* A species of plant; the name of the chief female in a pantomime.
COL'UMN. *s.* A round pillar, by which something is supported; a body of any thing, pressing vertically, upon its base; a body of troops, formed into an oblong; a section of a page, when divided equally, by a perpendicular line.
COLU'RES. *s.* Two great circles, imagined to pass through the poles of the world; one through the equinoctial, the other through the solstitial points.
COMB. *s.* An instrument to separate and adjust the hair; the crest of a cock; the cavities in which bees lodge their honey. v. *comb;* pr. par. *combing;* past, *combed:* s. *comber.*
COM'BAT. *v.* To fight, to oppose. pr. par. *combating;* past, *combated:* s. *combat, combatant.*
COMBI'NE. *v.* To join together; to settle by compact; to coalesce. pr. par. *combining;* past, *combined:* s. *combination.*
COMBUS'TIBLE. adj. Susceptible of ignition. s. *combustibility, combustion.*
COME. *v.* To draw near; to arrive at; to be derived from. pr par. *coming;* past, *come.*
COM'EDY. *s.* A dramatic representation of the lighter faults of mankind; an amusing drama. pl. *comedies:* s. *comedian.* adj. *comic, comical:* adv. *comically.*
COME'LY. adj. Graceful, decent; handsome. adv. *comely:* s. *comeliness.*
COM'ET. *s.* A sort of planet.
COM'FIT. *s.* A kind of sweetmeat.
COM'FORT. *v.* To strengthen, to enliven, to invigorate, to console. pr. par. *comforting;* past, *comforted:* s. *comfort, comforter* adj. *comfortable, comfortless* · adv. *comfortably.*
COM'FREY. *s.* A species of plant.
COM'IC, COM'ICAL. adj. Raising mirth; merry; relating to comedy. adv. *comically.*
COM'ITY. *s.* Courtesy, civility.
COM'MA. *s.* A grammatical point (,) denoting the shortest pause in reading; in music, the ninth part of a tone.
COMMAND'. *v.* To govern, to give

orders, to direct. pr. par. *commanding;* past, *commanded:* s. *command, commander, commandant, commandment:* adj. *commandatory.*

COMMEM'ORATE. *v.* To preserve the memory of, by some public act. pr. par. *commemorating;* past, *commemorated:* s. *commemoration:* adj. *commemorable, commemorative.*

COMMENCE. *v.* To begin; to make a beginning. pr. par. *commencing;* past, *commenced:* s. *commencement.* A *Commencement*, at a college, signifies the day on which degrees are conferred.

COMMEND'. *v.* To recommend, to approve. pr. par. *commending;* past, *commended:* s. *commendation:* adj. *commendable, commendatory:* adv. *commendably.*

COMMEN'DAM. *s.* A church benefice, given in trust.

COMMEN'SURATE. *adj.* Equal, proportionate. adv. *commensurately:* s. *commensuration:* adj. *commensurable;* adv. *commensurably.*

COMMENT'. *v.* To remark, to annotate. pr. par. *commenting;* past, *commented:* s. *com'ment, commentary, commentator,* pl. *commentaries, commentators.*

COM'MERCE. *s.* Trade; traffic with foreign nations; intercourse. adj. *commercial:* adv. *commercially.*

COMMIN'GLE. *v.* To mix, to blend. pr. par. *commingling;* past, *commingled.*

COMMIS'ERATE. *v.* To pity, to compassionate. pr. par. *commiserating;* past, *commiserated:* s. *commiseration, commiserator:* adj. *commiserable.*

COMMISSA'RIAT. *adj.* Relating to the commissary department of an army.

COM'MISSARY. *s.* A delegate, a deputy; an officer who furnishes provisions and ammunition for an army. pl. *commissaries.*

COMMIS'SION. *s.* The act of committing; the act of intrusting; a warrant; a trust; a charge. v. *commission;* pr. par. *commissioning;* past, *commissioned:* v. *commission, commissioner.*

COMMIT'. *v.* To intrust; to perpetrate; to send to prison. pr. par. *committing;* past, *committed* s. *commitment, committal, committee.*

COMMIX'. *v.* To mingle, to blend. pr. par. *commixing;* past, *commixed:* s. *commixture.*

COMMO'DE. *s.* A night-chair.

COMMO'DIOUS. *adj.* Convenient, suitable, useful. adv. *commodiously:* s. *commodiousness.*

COMMOD'ITY. *s.* Wares, merchandise. pl. *commodities.*

COM'MODORE. *s.* The captain who commands a squadron of ships.

COM'MON. *adj.* General, vulgar, public, mean. s. *common, commonalty, commoner, commonness:* adv. *commonly.*

COM'MONPLACE. *adj.* Relating to an ordinary or common topic; trite; vulgar.

COMMONWE'AL. *s.* Public good.

COM'MONWEALTH. *s.* A republic.

COM'MORANCE. *s.* Dwelling, habitation. adj. *commorant.*

COMMO'RIENT. *adj.* Dying at the same time.

COMMO'TION. *s.* Tumult, disturbance, agitation.

COMMO'VE. *v.* To disturb, to agitate. pr. par. *commoving;* past, *commoved.*

COMMU'NE. *v.* To partake in common; to converse; mutually to impart sentiments. pr. par. *communing;* past, *communed:* s. *communion.*

COMMU'NICATE. *v.* To have intercourse; to impart; to reveal; to receive the sacrament. pr. par. *communicating;* past, *communicated:* s. *communication:* adj *communicative communicable.*

70

COMMU'NION. *s.* Intercourse; participation; sacrament. s. *communicant.*

COMMU'NITY. *s.* The state of being common; people united into a society, and having a common interest. pl. *communities.*

COMMU'TE. *v.* To change, to substitute. pr. par. *commuting;* past, *commuted:* adj. *commutable:* s. *commutation.*

COM'PACT. *s.* An agreement, a contract.

COMPACT'. *adj.* Firm, solid, joined. v. *compact;* pr. par. *compacting;* past, *compacted.* adv. *compactly:* s. *compactness.*

COMPA'NION. *s.* An associate; a partner. adj. *companionable.*

COM'PANY. *s.* Persons assembled together; a mercantile association; a band; a subdivision of a regiment; fellowship; state of being together. pl. *companies.*

COMPA'RE. *v.* To judge, or estimate relatively, things which have some resemblance. pr. par. *comparing;* past, *compared:* s. *comparison:* adj. *comparable, comparative:* adv. *comparably, comparatively.*

COMPARTMENT. *s.* An apartment.

COM'PASS. *v.* To encircle, to surround, to effect, to attain. pr. par. *compassing;* past, *compassed:* s. *compass.*

COM'PASS. *s.* Circle, extent, reach; an instrument composed of a magnetic needle and card; an instrument with which circles are drawn. pl. *compasses.*

COMPAS'SION. *s.* Pity, commiseration, painful sympathy. v. *compassionate;* pr. par. *compassionating;* past, *compassionated:* adj. *compassionate:* adv. *compassionately.*

COMPAT'IBLE. *adj.* Suitable, consistent, agreeable. s. *compatibility,* pl. *compatibilities:* adv. *compatibly*

COMPA'TRIOT. *s.* One of the same country; a fellow-patriot.

COMPE'ER. *s.* An equal, a companion.

COMPEL'. *v.* To force, to oblige, to constrain. pr. par. *compelling,* past, *compelled:* adj. *compellable.*

COMPEND'IOUS. *adj.* Short, summary, abridged. adv. *compendiously:* s. *compendiousness.*

COMPEND'IUM. *s.* Abridgment, abstract.

COMPEN'SATE. *v.* To recompense, to counterbalance. pr. par. *compensating;* past, *compensated:* s. *compensation:* adj. *compensative.*

COM'PETENCE, COM'PETENCY *s.* Sufficiency, ability. pl. *competences, competencies* adj. *competent:* adv. *competently.*

COMPETI'TION. *s.* Rivalship, contest. s. *competitor.*

COMPI'LE. *v.* To collect from the works of others; to compose. pr. par. *compiling;* past, *compiled* s. *compilation, compiler.*

COMPLA'CENCE, COMPLA'CENCY. *s.* Tranquillity; ease of mind; satisfaction; civility. adj. *complacent:* adv. *complacently.*

COMPLAI'N. *v.* To mention with sorrow or resentment; to murmur; to lament. pr. par. *complaining;* past, *complained:* s. *complaint.*

COMPLAISA'NCE. *s.* Civility; desire of pleasing. adj. *complaisant* adv. *complaisantly.*

COM'PLEMENT. *s.* Generally signifies a just quantity; complete set.

COMPLE'TE. *adj.* Perfect, full, finished. v. *complete;* pr. par. *completing;* past, *completed:* adv. *completely:* s. *completeness, completion.*

COM'PLEX. *adj.* Of many parts, entangled. s. *complexity,* pl. *complexities:* adv. *complexly.*

COMPLEX'ION. *s.* Appearance, (all the colours, or all the circumstances, being seen in one view,) colour of the face.

COM'PLICATE. *v.* To render complex; to entangle one with another; to join. pr. par. *complicating;* past, *complicated:* s. *complication:* adj. *complicated.*

COM'PLIMENT. *s.* A flattering expression or act of civility. v. *compliment;* pr. par. *complimenting;* past, *complimented:* adj. *complimental, complimentary.*

COM'PLY'. *v.* To yield to; to accord with. pr. par. *complying;* past, *complied:* s. *compliance:* adj. *compliant:* adv. *compliantly.*

COMPO'NENT. *s.* That which constitutes a compound body.

COMPORT'. *v.* To agree, to suit; (followed by with) pr. par. *comporting;* past, *comported:* s. *comportment.*

COMPO'SE. *v.* To put together; to invent; to calm. pr. par. *composing;* past, *composed:* adv. *composedly:* s. *composer, composition, composure.*

COMPOS'ITE. *adj.* Of several kinds.

COMPO'SITOR. *s.* He that ranges and adjusts the types for printing.

COM'POST. *s.* A mixture for manure.

COMPOUND'. *v.* To mix, to combine. pr. par. *compounding;* past, *compounded:* s. *com'pound, compounder:* adj. *compound.*

COMPREHEND'. *v.* To include, to understand, to comprise. pr. par. *comprehending;* past, *comprehended:* s. *comprehension:* adj. *comprehensible, comprehensive:* adv. *comprehensibly, comprehensively.*

COMPRESS'. *v.* To press together, to condense. pr. par. *compressing;* past, *compressed:* adj. *compressible:* s. *compressibility, compressibilities, compression.*

COMPRI'SE. *v.* To contain, to include. pr. par. *comprising;* past, *comprised:* s. *comprisal.*

COM'PROMISE. *s.* Mutual abatement; concession. v. *compromise;* pr. par. *compromising;* past. *compromised:* s. *compromiser.*

COMPROMIS'SION. *s.* Act of compromitting.

COMPROMIT'. *v.* To pledge; to involve, to entangle. pr. par. *compromitting;* past, *compromitted.*

COMPUL'SION. *s.* Act of compelling; force. adj. *compulsory, compulsive:* adv. *compulsively.*

COMPUNC'TION. *s.* Uneasiness of conscience; repentance; contrition. adj. *compunctious.*

COMPU'TE. *v.* To reckon, to calculate, to count. pr. par. *computing;* past, *computed:* s. *computation, computer:* adj. *compute, computable.*

COM'RADE. *s.* A companion, a partner.

CON. *v.* To study; to commit to memory. pr. par. *conning;* past, *conned.*

CONCAT'ENATE. *v.* To link together. pr. par. *concatenating,* past, *concatenated:* s. *concatenation.*

CON'CAVE. *adj.* Hollow; opposed to convex. s. *concavity,* pl. *concavities.*

CONCEAL'. *v.* To hide; to keep secret; not to divulge. pr. par *concealing;* past, *concealed:* s *concealer, concealment:* adj. *concealable.*

CONCE'DE. *v.* To admit, to grant, to yield. pr. par. *conceding;* past, *conceded.*

CONCEIT'. *s.* Thought, opinion pride. v. *conceit;* pr. par. *conceiting;* past, *conceited:* adv. *conceitedly:* s. *conceitedness.*

CONCEI'VE. *v.* To form in the mind; to comprehend; to think, to become pregnant. pr. par. *conceiving;* past, *conceived:* adj. *conceivable.*

72

CONCEN'TRATE. *v.* To bring towards the centre; to bring together. pr. par. *concentrating;* past, *concentrated:* s. *concentration.*

CONCEN'TRIC, CONCEN'TRICAL. *adj.* Having one common centre. adv. *concentrically.*

CONCEP'TION. *s.* Act of conceiving; thing conceived; idea; knowledge.

CONCERN'. *s.* Business, participation, regard. v. *concern;* pr. par. *concerning;* past, *concerned.*

CONCERT'. *v.* To settle any thing in private, by mutual communication; to settle, to contrive. pr. par. *concerting;* past, *concerted.*

CON'CERT. *s.* Communication of designs; an assembly of musicians, performing before an audience.

CONCER'TO. *s.* A piece of music, composed for a concert.

CONCES'SION. *s.* Act of conceding, or yielding; a grant. adj. *concessionary.*

CONCH. *s.* A kind of shell.

CONCHOL'OGY. *s.* A description of shell-fish, or of shells; the science which treats of shell-fish.

CONCIL'IATE. *v.* To gain the favour of; to reconcile. pr. par. *conciliating,* past, *conciliated:* s. *conciliation, conciliator:* adj. *conciliatory.*

CONCI'SE. *adj.* Brief, short. adv. *concisely:* s. *concision, conciseness.*

CON'CLAVE. *s.* A close assembly; a private apartment.

CONCLU'DE. *v.* To finish; to decide; to determine. pr. par. *concluding;* past, *concluded:* s. *conclusion:* adj. *conclusive:* adv. *conclusively.*

CONCOCT'. *v.* To digest, to ripen. pr. par *concocting;* past, *concocted:* s. *concoction:* adj. *concoctive.*

CONCOM'ITANT. *adj.* Accompanying. adv. *concomitantly:* s. *concomitance, concomitancy.*

CON'CORD. *s.* Agreement, union, harmony. s. *concordance, concordancy,* pl. *concordancies:* adj. *concordant:* adv. *concordantly.*

CON'COURSE. *s.* Assemblage.

CONCRE'TE. *v.* To coalesce into one mass; to form by concretion. pr. par. *concreting;* past, *concreted:* s. *concrete, concreteness, concretion:* adj. *con'crete, concretive:* adv. *concretely.*

CONCU'PISCENT. *adj.* Libidinous, lecherous. s. *concupiscence.*

CONCUR'. *v.* To meet in one point, to agree. pr. par. *concurring,* past, *concurred:* s. *concurrence, concurrency,* pl. *concurrences, concurrencies:* adj. *concurrent* adv. *concurrently.*

CONCUS'SION. *s.* Sudden and great agitation. adj. *concussive.*

CONDEMN'. *v.* To pronounce guilty; to censure; to declare unfit for use. pr. par. *condemning;* past, *condemned* s. *condemnation:* adj. *condemnable:* s. *condemner.*

CONDENSE'. *v.* To thicken; to make closer. pr. par. *condensing;* past, *condensed:* adj. *condense* s. *condensation, condensity, condenser.*

CONDESCEND'. *v.* To stoop, to bend, to yield. pr. par. *condescending;* past, *condescended:* s. *condescension:* adv. *condescendingly.*

CONDI'GN. *adj.* Merited; suitable. adv. *condignly.*

CON'DIMENT. *s.* Seasoning, sauce.

CONDI'TION. *s.* Stipulation, state, rank. adj. *conditional, conditionary:* adv. *conditionally.*

CONDI'TION. *v.* To make terms; to stipulate. pr. par. *conditioning,* past, *conditioned.*

CONDO'LE. *v.* To join in grief; to lament with. pr. par. *condoling,* past, *condoled:* s. *condolence, condoler.*

CONDU'CE. *v.* To aid in promoting, to contribute. pr par. *conducing,* past, *conduced* adj. *conducive, conducible.*

CON'DUCT. *s.* Management, behaviour, regular life. *v. conduct'*; pr. par. *conducting*; past, *conducted*: *s. conductor.*

CON'DUIT. *s.* An aqueduct.

CONE. *s.* A solid body, having a circular base, and declining regularly to a point. adj. *conic, conical*: adv. *conically.*

CONFAB'ULATE. *v.* To talk familiarly together; to chat. pr. par. *confabulating*; past, *confabulated*: *s. confabulation*: adj. *confabulatory.*

CONFEC'TIONARY. *s.* The place where sweetmeats are made or sold; sweetmeats. pl. *confectionaries.*

CONFEC'TIONER. *s.* A maker of sweetmeats.

CONFED'ERACY. *s.* League, union, engagement. pl. *confederacies*: *v. confederate*: pr. par. *confederating*; past, *confederated*: *s. confederate, confederation.*

CONFER'. *v.* To consult, to bestow. pr. par. *conferring*; past, *conferred*: *s. conference.*

CONFESS'. *v.* To acknowledge; to avow; to hear the confession of a penitent, as a priest. pr. par. *confessing*; past, *confessed*: *s. confessor, confession*: adv. *confessedly.*

CONFI'DE. *v.* To trust in; to intrust. pr. par. *confiding*; past, *confided*: *s. confidence, confider, confidant*: adj. *confidential*: adv. *confidentially.*

CONFIGURA'TION. *s.* The form of the various parts of any thing, as they are adapted to each other; the face of the horoscope.

CONFI'NE. *v.* To bound, to limit, to imprison, to restrain. pr. par. *confining*; past, *confined*: *s. confiner, confinement.*

CON'FINES. *s.* Common boundary, border, edge. adj. *confineless.*

CONFIRM'. *v.* To strengthen, to establish. pr. par. *confirming*; past, *confirmed*: *s. confirmation*: adj. *confirmable, confirmative.*

CONFIS'CATE. *v.* To seize for public use. pr. par. *confiscating*; past, *confiscated*: *s. confiscation, confiscator.*

CONFLAGRA'TION. *s.* An extensive fire. adj. *conflagrant.*

CON'FLICT. *s.* A violent collision; a combat; strife. *v. conflict'*; pr. par. *conflicting*; past, *conflicted*

CON'FLUENCE. *s.* Meeting of streams; a concourse; a multitude. adj. *confluent.*

CON'FLUX. *s.* Union of several currents; concourse; crowd.

CONFORM'. *v.* To assimilate; to comply with. pr. par. *conforming* past, *conformed*: *s. conformation, conformity*, pl. *conformities*: adj. *conformable*: adv. *conformably*

CONFOUND'. *v.* To perplex, to amaze. pr. par. *confounding*; past, *confounded*: *s. confounder*: adv. *confoundedly.*

CONFRATER'NITY. *s.* A brotherhood, a body of men united for some purpose. pl. *confraternities*

CONFRONT'. *v.* To bring face to face. pr. par. *confronting*; past, *confronted*: *s. confronter.*

CONFU'SE. *v.* To disorder, or perplex. pr. par. *confusing*; past, *confused*: *s. confusion*: adv. *confusedly.*

CONFU'TE. *v.* To convict of error or falsehood; to disprove. pr. par. *confuting*; past, *confuted*: *s. confutation*: adj. *confutable.*

CONGE'E. *s.* Act of reverence, bow; courtesy; leave; farewell.

CONGEAL'. *v.* To become solid, as ice; to concrete. pr. par. *congealing*; past, *congealed*: *s. congealment, congelation*: adj. *congealable.*

CONGE'NIAL. adj. Of the same kind; agreeable. *s. congeniality*, pl. *congenialities*: adv. *congenially.*

CONGLOM'ERATE. *v.* To gather into a ball; to become round. pr. par. *conglomerating*; past, *conglomerated*: *s. conglomeration.*

CONGLU'TINATE. *v.* To cement. pr. par. *conglutinating;* past, *conglutinated:* s. *conglutination, conglutinator:* adj. *conglutinative.*

CONGRATULATE. *v.* To rejoice with a person, on account of his good fortune. pr. par. *congratulating;* past, *congratulated:* s. *congratulator, congratulation:* adj. *congratulatory.*

CON'GREGATE. *v.* To collect; to assemble; to bring into one place. pr. par. *congregating;* past, *congregated:* s. *congregation:* adj. *congregational.*

CON'GRESS. *s.* A meeting; a national assembly. pl. *congresses:* adj. *congressional.*

CONGRU'ITY. *s.* Suitableness, agreeableness, fitness. pl. *congruities:* adj. *congruous:* adv. *congruously.*

CONIF'EROUS. *adj.* Bearing cones, like the pine-tree.

CONJEC'TURE. *s.* Supposition, guess, imperfect knowledge. *v. conjecture;* pr. par. *conjecturing;* past, *conjectured:* adj. *conjectural:* s. *conjecturer.*

CONJOIN'. *v.* To unite; to consolidate into one. pr. par. *conjoining;* past, *conjoined:* adj. *conjoint:* adv. *conjointly.*

CON'JUGAL. *adj.* Matrimonial; belonging to marriage. adv. *conjugally.*

CON'JUGATE. *v.* To decline a verb through its variations. pr. par. *conjugating;* past, *conjugated:* s. *conjugation.*

CONJUNCT'. *adj.* Conjoined, united. adv. *conjunctly.*

CONJUNC'TION. *s.* Union, association, league; a connector of words. adj. *conjunctive:* adv. *conjunctively.*

CONJUNC'TURE. *s.* Combination of many circumstances; occasion; critical time.

CONJU'RE. *v.* To summon in a sacred name; to enjoin with the highest solemnity. pr. par. *conjuring;* past, *conjured:* s. *conjuration.*

CON'JURE. *v.* To enchant; to play slight-of-hand. pr. par. *conjuring,* past, *conjured:* s. *conjurer.*

CONNECT'. *v.* To join, to link, to unite. pr. par. *connecting;* past, *connected:* s. *connexion:* adj. *connective:* adv. *connectively.*

CONNI'VE. *v.* To wink; to pretend blindness or ignorance. pr. par. *conniving;* past, *connived:* s. *connivance, conniver.*

CONNOISSE'UR. *s.* A judge, or critic.

CONNU'BIAL. *adj.* Matrimonial; nuptial; conjugal.

CONOI'DE. *s.* A figure resembling a cone. adj. *conoidal.*

CON'QUER. *v.* To gain by conquest; to overcome. pr. par. *conquering,* past, *conquered:* s. *conqueror, conquest:* adj. *conquerable.*

CONSANGUIN'ITY. *s.* Relation by blood. pl. *consanguinities:* adj. *consanguineous.*

CON'SCIENCE. *s.* Self-knowledge; moral feeling. adj. *conscientious:* adv. *conscientiously:* s. *conscientiousness.*

CON'SCIOUS. *adj.* Knowing any thing from internal judgment, or moral feeling. *s. consciousness:* adv. *consciously.*

CON'SCRIPT. *adj.* Registered, enrolled. *s. conscript, conscription.*

CON'SECRATE. *v.* To make holy, to dedicate. pr. par. *consecrating,* past, *consecrated:* s. *consecration, consecrator.*

CONSEC'UTIVE. *adj.* Uninterrupted; following in train. adv. *consecutively.*

CONSENT'. *s.* Act of yielding or consenting; concord; agreement. *v. consent;* pr. par. *consenting,* past, *consented.*

CONSENTA'NEOUS. *adj.* Agreeable to; consistent with. adv. *consentaneously.*

CON'SEQUENCE. *s.* Effect, deduction, conclusion. adj. *consequent, consequential:* adv. *consequently, consequentially.*

CONSERVA"TOR. *s.* A preserver of the public happiness.

CONSERV'ATORY. *s.* A place for holding delicate things. pl. *conservatories.*

CONSE'RVE. *v.* To preserve. pr. par. *conserving;* past, *conserved:* s. *conservation:* adj. *conservative.*

CONSID'ER. *v.* To think upon with care; to ponder. pr. par. *considering,* past, *considered:* s. *consideration:* adj. *considerable:* adv. *considerably.*

CONSID'ERATE. *adj.* Serious; given to consideration. adv. *considerately.*

CONSIGN'. *v.* To assign; to trust; to give to another in a formal manner. pr. par. *consigning;* past, *consigned:* s. *consignor, consignment.*

CONSIST'. *v.* To agree; to subsist; to be composed. pr. par. *consisting;* past, *consisted:* s. *consistence, consistency,* pl. *consistencies:* adj. *consistent:* adv. *consistently.*

CONSISTO'RIAL. *adj.* Relating to an ecclesiastical court.

CONSO'LE. *v.* To comfort, to cheer. pr. par. *consoling;* past, *consoled:* s. *consoler: consolation:* adv. *consolatory.*

CONSOL'IDATE. *v.* To make firm; to unite. pr. par. *consolidating;* past, *consolidated:* s. *consolidation:* adj. *consolidative.*

CONSO'NANCE. *s.* Accord of sound; consistency; congruence. adj. *consonant:* adv. *consonantly.*

CON'SONANT. *s.* A letter, such as b, c, d; the name of which cannot be articulated without the aid of a vowel; therefore sounded with another letter.

CON'SORT. *s* A companion, a partner; a wife or husband. v. *consort';* pr. par. *consorting;* past, *consorted.*

CONSPICU'ITY. *s.* Brightness, clearness. pl. *conspicuities:* adj *conspicuous:* adv. *conspicuously.*

CONSPI'RE. *v.* To concert a crime; to plot; to agree together. pr. par. *conspiring;* past, *conspired.* s. *conspiracy,* pl. *conspiracies,* *conspirator.*

CON'STABLE. *s.* This officer was originally so called, because his duty was to regulate all matters of chivalry, tilts, tournaments, and feats of arms, that were performed on horseback; the word now mostly signifies a petty civil officer.

CON'STANCY. *s.* Immutability, perpetuity, lasting affection, certainty. pl. *constancies:* adj. *constant:* adv. *constantly.*

CONSTELLA'TION. *s.* A cluster of stars; an assemblage of splendours or excellencies.

CONSTERNA'TION. *s.* Astonishment, amazement, surprise.

CON'STIPATE. *v.* To thicken, to condense. pr. par. *constipating;* past, *constipated:* s. *constipation.*

CONSTIT'UENT. *s.* A necessary part; one who appoints. adj. *constituent.*

CON'STITUTE. *v.* To erect, to establish, to form, to appoint. pr. par. *constituting;* past, *constituted:* s. *constitution:* adj. *constitutional:* adv. *constitutionally.*

CONSTITU'TION. *s.* The act of constituting; corporeal frame, temper of body, or of mind; frame of government. adj. *constitutional:* adv. *constitutionally:* s. *constitutionality.*

CONSTRAIN'. *v.* To compel, to hinder. pr. par. *constraining,* past, *constrained:* s. *constraint* adj. *constrainable:* adv. *constrainedly.*

CONSTRICT'. *v.* To bind, to cramp, to contract. pr. par. *constricting,* past, *constricted:* s. *constriction:* adj. *constrictive.*

CONSTRIN'GENT. *adj.* Binding or compressing. adv. *constringently.*

CONSTRUCT'. *v.* To frame, to build, to form. pr. par. *constructing;* past, *constructed:* s. *construction:* adj. *constructive:* adv. *constructively.*

CONSTRU'E. *v.* To explain, to interpret. pr. par. *construing;* past, *construed.*

CONSUBSTANTIA'TION. *s.* The union of the body of Jesus Christ with the sacramental element, according to the Lutherans.

CON'SUL. *s.* A species of public officer; an officer, commissioned in foreign ports, to judge between the merchants of his own nation, and protect their commerce. adj. *consular:* s. *consulate.*

CONSULT'. *v.* To take counsel together; to ask counsel; to regard. pr. par. *consulting;* past, *consulted:* s. *consultation.*

CONSU'ME. *v.* To waste, to spend, to destroy. pr. par. *consuming;* past, *consumed:* s. *consumer:* adj. *consumable.*

CON'SUMMATE. *v.* To complete, to perfect. pr. par. *consummating;* past, *consummated:* s. *consummation:* adj. *consum'mate:* adv. *consummately.*

CONSUM'PTION. *s.* Act of consuming; waste; the state of wasting or perishing. adj. *consumptive.*

CON'TACT. *s.* Touch, close union.

CONTA'GION. *s.* The emission from body to body, by which diseases are communicated; infection, propagation of mischief, or disease. adj. *contagious:* adv. *contagiously:* s. *contagiousness.*

CONTAIN'. *v.* To hold, to comprise. pr. par. *containing;* past, *contained:* adj. *containable:* s. *container.*

CONTAM'INATE. *v.* To defile, to corrupt, to pollute. pr. par. *contaminating;* past, *contaminated:* s. *contamination, contaminator.*

CONTEMN'. *v.* To despise, to slight. pr. par. *contemning;* past, *contemned:* s. *contemner.*

CONTEM'PLATE. *v.* To consider with continued attention; to study. pr. par. *contemplating;* past, *contemplated:* s. *contemplation, contemplator:* adj. *contemplative:* adv. *contemplatively.*

CONTEM'PORARY, COTEM'PORARY. *adj.* Existing at the same time. s. *cotemporary,* pl. *cotemporaries.*

CONTEMPT'. *s.* Act of despising others; scorn. adj. *contemptible. contemptuous:* adv. *contemptibly, contemptuously.*

CONTEND'. *v.* To strive in opposition; to struggle; to vie. pr. par. *contending;* past, *contended:* s. *contender.*

CONTEN'TION. *s.* Act of contending. adj. *contentious:* adv. *contentiously:* s. *contentiousness.*

CONTENT'. *adj.* Satisfied. v. *content;* pr. par. *contenting;* past, *contented:* s. *content, contentment, contentedness:* adv. *contentedly.*

CONTEST'. *v.* To dispute, to litigate, to strive. pr. par. *contesting;* past, *contested:* s. *con'test:* adj. *contestable.*

CON'TEXT. *s.* General connexion or body of a discourse.

CONTEX'TURE. *s.* The disposition of parts, one amongst others; the system.

CONTIG'UOUS. *adj.* Meeting, so as to touch; bordering upon each other. s. *contiguity,* pl. *contiguities:* adv. *contiguously.*

CON'TINENT. *adj.* Chaste, restrained, moderate. adv. *continently:* s. *continence, continency.*

CON'TINENT. *s.* A vast tract of land. adj. *continental.*

CONTIN'GENT. *adj.* Happening by chance; accidental; unforeseen. adv. *contingently:* s. *contingence, contingency,* pl. *contingencies.*

CONTIN'UE. *v.* To remain, to extend, to protect. pr. par. *continuing;* past, *continued:* s. *continuation, continuance:* adj. *continual.* adv. *continually.*

CONTINU'ITY. *s.* Connexion, continuation. pl. *continuities:* adj. *continuous;* adv. *continuously.*

CONTORT'. *v.* To twist, to writhe. pr. par. *contorting;* past, *contorted: s. contortion.*

CONTOUR. *s.* The outline; the line by which any figure is defined or terminated.

CON'TRA. A Latin proposition, used in composition, which signifies against.

CON'TRABAND. *adj.* Prohibited, illegal.

CONTRACT'. *v.* To draw into less compass; to bargain. pr. par. *contracting;* past, *contracted: s. contract contraction, contractor, contractedness;* adv. *contractedly.*

CONTRACT'IBLE. *adj.* Possible to be contracted. *s. contractibility.*

CONTRADICT'. *v.* To deny; to oppose verbally. pr. par. *contradicting;* past, *contradicted: s. contradiction, contradicter;* adj. *contradictory;* adv. *contradictorily.*

CONTRADISTIN'GUISH. *v.* To distinguish, by qualities, not only different, but opposite. pr. par. *contradistinguishing;* past, *contradistinguished; s. contradistinction;* adj. *contradistinctive.*

CONTRARI'ETY. *s.* Repugnance, opposition. pl. *contrarieties.*

CON'TRARY. *adj.* Opposite, adverse, contradictory, inconsistent. s. pl. *contraries;* adv. *contrarily.*

CON'TRAST. *s.* Opposition and dissimilitude of figures. v. *contrast';* pr. par. *contrasting;* past, *contrasted.*

CONTRAVALLA'TION. *s.* A fortification thrown up by a besieging army, to prevent the sallies of the garrison.

CONTRAVENE. *v.* To oppose, to obstruct, to baffle. pr. par. *contravening;* past, *contravened: s. contravention.*

CONTRAVER'SION. *s.* Act of controverting.

CONTRAVERT'. *v.* See CONTROVERT.

CONTRIB'UTE. *v.* To give aid, in conjunction with one or more persons. pr. par. *contributing;* past, *contributed: s. contribution, contributor;* adj. *contributive, contributory.*

CON'TRITE. *adj.* Penitent. adv. *contritely: s. contrition, contriteness.*

CONTRI'VE. *v.* To plan; to form or design. pr. par. *contriving;* past, *contrived: s. contrivance, contriver.*

CONTROL'. *s.* Check, restraint, power, superintendence. v. *control:* pr. par. *controlling;* past, *controlled:* adj. *controllable: s. controller.*

CONTROVERT'. *v.* To debate, to dispute. pr. par. *controverting;* past, *controverted: s. controverter;* adj. *controvertible.*

CON'TROVERSY. *s.* Debate, dispute. pl. *controversies:* adj. *controversial: s. controversialist.*

CON'TUMACY. *s.* Obstinacy, perverseness, wilful disobedience. pl. *contumacies:* adj. *contumacious:* adv. *contumaciously.*

CON'TUMELY. *s.* Rudeness, contemptuousness, reproach. pl. *contumelies:* adj. *contumelious:* adv. *contumeliously.*

CONTU'SE. *v.* To beat together, to bruise. pr. par. *contusing;* past, *contused: s. contusion.*

CONUN'DRUM. *s.* A low jest; a quibble.

CON'USANCE. *s.* Cognizance, notice, knowledge. (a law term.) adj. *conusable, conusant.*

CONVALES'CENT. *adj.* Recovering strength. *s. convalescence, convalescency.*

CONVE'NE. *v.* To assemble, to come together, to associate. pr. par. *convening;* past, *convened: s. convener.*

CONVE'NIENT. *adj.* Fit, suitable, commodious. adv. *conveniently*

79

s. *convenience, conveniency*, pl. *conveniencies*.

CON'VENT. *s.* A monastery, or nunnery; an assembly of religious persons. adj. *conventual*.

CONVEN'TICLE. *s.* An assembly, a meeting, a secret assembly. s. *conventicler*.

CONVEN'TION. *s.* The act of coming together; an assembly; a contract, previous to a definitive treaty. adj. *conventional, conventionary*.

CONVERGE'. *v.* To tend to one point. pr. par. *converging;* past, *converged:* adj. *convergent*.

CONVERSAZIO'NE. *s.* A meeting of company for literary conversation.

CONVERSE'. *v.* To hold intercourse with; to discourse familiarly upon any subject. pr. par. *conversing;* past, *conversed:* s. *conversation:* adj. *conversant, conversable*.

CON'VERSE. *s.* A term in geometry and logic, signifying opposition. adv. *conversely*.

CONVER'SION. *s.* Act of being converted; state of being converted.

CONVERT'. *v.* To change into another substance; to change from one religion or course of life, to another; to turn from a bad, to a good life; to appropriate. pr. par. *converting;* past, *converted:* s. *con'vert, converter:* adj. *convertible:* s. *convertibility*, pl. *convertibilities*.

CON'VEX. *adj.* Rising in a circular form; opposed to *concave*. s. *convex, convexity*, pl. *convexities:* adv. *convexly*.

CONVEX'O-CON'CAVE. *adj.* Having the hollow on the inside corresponding to the external protuberance.

CONVEY'. *v.* To carry; to impart; to remove secretly; to transmit; to transfer. pr. par. *conveying;* past, *conveyed:* s. *conveyance, conveyer*.

CONVEY'ANCER. *s.* One who draws writings, by which property is transferred. s. *conveyancing*.

CONVICT'. *v.* To prove guilty; to detect in guilt; to confute. pr par. *convicting;* past, *convicted:* s. *conviction, con'vict:* adj. *convictive*.

CONVIN'CE. *v.* To overcome or satisfy by argument. pr. par. *convincing;* past, *convinced:* s. *convincer:* adj. *convincible:* adv. *convincingly*.

CONVIV'IAL. *adj.* Social, cheerful. s. *conviviality*, pl. *convivialities:* adv. *convivially*.

CON'VOCATE. *v.* To call together. pr. par. *convocating;* past, *convocated:* s. *convocation*.

CONVO'KE. *v.* To call together. pr. par. *convoking;* past, *convoked*.

CONVOLVE'. *v.* To roll together pr. par. *convolving;* past, *convolved*.

CONVOLU'TION. *s.* Act of convolving. adj. *convoluted*.

CONVOY'. *v.* To accompany by land or sea, for the sake of defence. pr. par. *convoying;* past *convoyed:* s. *con'voy*.

CONVOL'VULUS. *s.* A genus of plants. pl. *convolvuluses*.

CONVULSE'. *v.* To shake violently into disorder; to give an irregular and involuntary motion. pr. par. *convulsing;* past, *convulsed:* s. *convulsion:* adj. *convulsive:* adv. *convulsively*.

CO'NY. *s.* A rabbit. pl. *conies*.

COO. *v.* To cry as a dove or pigeon. pr. par. *cooing;* past, *cooed:* s. *cooing*.

COOK. *s.* One whose profession is to dress and prepare victuals. v. *cook;* pr. par. *cooking;* past, *cooked:* s. *cookery*, pl. *cookeries*.

COOL. *adj.* Approaching to cold, not zealous, not ardent. v. *cool*. pr. par. *cooling;* past, *cooled:* s. *cool, cooler, coolness:* adv. *coolly*.

COOP. *s.* A cage; a pen for animals. *v. coop;* pr. par. *cooping;* past, *cooped.*

COO'PER. *s.* One that makes barrels. *s. cooperage.*

CO-OP'ERATE. *v.* To labour or act jointly; to concur in the same effect. pr. par. *co-operating;* past, *co-operated:* s. *co-operation, co-operator:* adj. *co-operative.*

CO-OR'DINATE. *adj.* Having the same rank. *s. co-ordination:* adv. *co-ordinately.*

COOT. *s.* A small black water-fowl.

COP. *s.* A quantity of cotton yarn which has been coiled round a spindle.

COPAL'. *s.* The Mexican term for a gum.

COPAR'CENER. *s.* Such as have equal portions in the inheritance of their ancestors.

COPART'MENT. *s.* Compartment.

COPART'NER. *s.* A partner; one that has a share in some common stock or affair. *s. copartnership.*

COPE. *s.* Any thing with which the head is covered; a sacerdotal vestment, worn in sacred ministration.

COPE. *v.* To cover, as with a cope; to be equally eminent or successful with. pr. par. *coping;* past, *coped:* s. *coping.*

COPER'NICAN. *adj.* Relating to the system of Copernicus.

CO'PIOUS. *adj.* Plentiful, abundant; not concise. adv. *copiously:* s. *copiousness.*

COP'PER. *s.* One of the primitive metals. adj. *copperish.*

COP'PERAS. *s.* A name given to sulphate of iron.

COP'PER-PLATE. *s.* A plate of copper on which figures are engraved.

COP'PER-SMITH. *s.* One that manufactures copper utensils.

COP'PICE. *s.* Low woods, cut at stated times, for fuel.

COPSE. *s.* A place overgrown with short wood. (abr. from coppice.)

COP'TIC. *s.* The language of the Copts; the ancient Egyptian language.

CO'PULA. *s.* In logic, signifies the word which unites the subject and predicate of a proposition.

COP'ULATE. *v.* To unite, to conjoin. pr. par. *copulating;* past, *copulated:* s. *copulation:* adj. *copulative.*

COP'Y. *s.* Exact resemblance; a transcript from the original; the autograph. pl. *copies:* v. *copy;* pr. par. *copying;* past, *copied:* s. *copier, copyist.*

COP'Y-RIGHT. *s.* The property which an author, or his assignee, has in a literary work.

COQUET'. *s.* A gay, airy girl; a woman who endeavours to attract notice. v. *coquet;* pr. par. *coquetting;* past, *coquetted:* s. *coquetry.* adj. *coquettish.*

COR'AL. *s.* A subaqueous plant, of a stony nature. adj. *coralline.*

CORD. *s.* A rope; a string composed of several strands or twists certain quantity of wood for fuel, (128 cubic feet) supposed to be measured with a cord v. *cord,* pr. par. *cording;* past, *corded:* s. *corder.*

CORD'AGE. *s.* A quantity of cords; the ropes of a ship; the price paid for measuring cords of wood.

CORDELI'ER. *s.* A Franciscan friar; so named from the cord which serves him for a cincture.

COR'DIAL. *s.* A medicine that increases the force of the heart; any medicine that increases strength.

COR'DIAL. *adj.* Reviving; invigorating; sincere; hearty. s. *cordiality,* pl. *cordialities:* adv. *cordially.*

COR'DON. *s.* An extensive line of soldiers, to prevent communication between different parties.

CORDOVAN'. *s.* Spanish leather.

CORD'WAINER. *s.* A shoemaker.

CORD'WOOD. *s.* Fire-wood piled up for measurement.

CORE. *s.* The heart; the inner part, generally of vegetables.

80

CORIAN'DER. *s.* A plant.
CORIN'THIAN. *adj.* Relating to Corinth; relating to one of the five orders of architecture.
CORK. *s.* A kind of tree; the bark of the cork-tree, used for stoppers. v. *cork;* pr. par. *corking;* past, *corked:* adj. *corky.*
COR'MORANT. *s.* A bird that preys upon fish.
CORN. *s.* A species of farinaceous plant; the fruit of that plant; an excrescence on the feet, hard and painful. v. *corn;* pr. par. *corning;* past, *corned.*
CORN'AGE. *s.* A tenure which obliges the landholder to give notice of an invasion, by blowing a horn.
CORN'-CRAIK. *s.* The land-rail; so called probably from its constant note, *craik, craik.*
COR'NEA. *s.* The horny coat of the eye. adj. *corneous.*
CORNE'LIAN. *s.* A kind of precious stone.
COR'NER. *s.* An angle; a secret or remote place. adj. *cornered.*
COR'NET. *s.* A kind of musical instrument; the officer that bears the standard of a troop of horse.
COR'NETCY. *s.* The commission of a cornet. pl. *cornetcies.*
COR'NICE. *s.* The highest projection of a wall or column.
CORNI'GEROUS, CORNUTED. *adj.* Horned; having horns.
CORNUCO'PIA. *s.* The horn of plenty; a heathenish fiction, referring to the horn said to have been broken off from Achelōus, by Hercules.
COR'OLLARY. *s.* Conclusion; surplus of a train of reasoning. pl. *corollaries.*
CORONA'TION. *s.* The act or solemnity of crowning a king.
COR'ONER. *s.* An officer whose chief duty is to inquire, on the part of a sovereign or state, how any violent or accidental death was caused; for which purpose, a jury is empanneled.
COR'ONET. *s.* An inferior crown, worn by the nobility.
COR'PORAL. *adj.* Relating to the body; material; not spiritual adv. *corporally.*
COR'PORAL. *s.* The lowest officer in a corps of infantry.
COR'PORATE. *adj.* United in a body or community. adv. *corporately:* s. *corporation.*
CORPO'REAL. *adj.* Having a body; not spiritual. adv. *corporeally.*
CORPS. *s.* A body of soldiers; a professional body. pronounced *core.*
CORPSE. *s.* A dead human body.
COR'PULENCE, COR'PULENCY *s.* Bulkiness of body. pl. *corpulences, corpulencies:* adj. *corpulent*
CORPUS'CLE. *s.* A small body; a particle of matter. adj. *corpuscular.*
CORRECT'. *v.* To make right; to remark a fault; to amend; to punish; to chastise. pr. par. *correcting;* past, *corrected:* s. *corrector, correctness, correction:* adj. *correct, corrective:* adv. *correctly.*
CORREL'ATIVE. *adj.* Having reciprocal relation. adv. *correlatively.*
CORRESPOND'. *v.* To communicate by alternate letters; to suit; to fit. pr. par. *corresponding;* past, *corresponded:* s. *correspondence, correspondency,* pl. *correspondencies:* adj. *correspondent:* s. *correspondent:* adv. *correspondingly.*
COR'RIDOR. *s.* A gallery or long aisle round a building.
COR'RIGIBLE. *adj.* Relating to that which can be amended.
CORROB'ORATE. *v.* To strengthen, by additional evidence; to confirm; to establish. pr. par *corroborating;* past, *corroborated.* s. *corroboration, corroborater:* adj. *corroborative.*

CORRO'DE. *v.* To consume slowly; to prey upon. pr. par. *corroding;* past, *corroded.*
CORRO'SION. *s.* Act of corroding. adj. *corrosive:* adv. *corrosively.*
CORRUPT'. *v.* To turn from a sound to a putrescent state; to deprave; to bribe. pr. par. *corrupting;* past, *corrupted:* adj. *corrupt: s. corrupter, corruption, corruptness.*
CORRUPT'IBLE. *adj.* Possible to be corrupted. s. *corruptibility.*
COR'SAIR. *s.* A pirate.
CORSE. *s.* A dead body, a carcass.
CORSE'LET. *s.* A light armour, for the fore part of the body.
COR'SET. *s.* A pair of stays for a woman.
COR'TEGE. *s.* A train of attendants.
COR'TICATED. *adj.* Resembling the bark of a tree.
CORUS'CATE. *v.* To glitter. pr. par. *coruscating;* past, *coruscated:* adj. *coruscant: s. coruscation.*
CORVETT'E. *s.* A small frigate; a sloop of war.
COSMET'IC. *s.* A preparation for improving beauty. adj. *cosmetic.*
COSMOG'ONY. *s.* The formation of the world; the creation. s. *cosmogonist.*
COSMOG'RAPHY. *s.* The science of the general system of the world. s. *cosmographer:* adj. *cosmographical:* adv. *cosmographically.*
COSMOL'OGY. *s.* The science of the general system of the world.
COSMOPOL'ITAN, COSMOPO'LITE. *s.* A citizen of the world; one who is at home in every place.
COS'SACK. *s.* One of the people inhabiting the Ukraine, under the Russian government.
COST. *s.* The price of any thing; sumptuousness; luxury, charge, expense, detriment. v. *cost;* pr. par. *costing;* past. *cost:* adj. *costless, costly·* s. *costliness.*
COS'TAL. *adj.* Belonging to the ribs.
COS'TIVE. *adj.* Bound in body constipated. s. *costiveness.*
COS'TUME. *s.* In painting, the different customs of times and places, to which a painter must conform, with regard to dress.
COT. *s.* A small house; a cottage; a small bed. s. *cotter.*
COT. *s.* A little flat boat.
COTE. *s.* A sheep-fold.
COTEM'PORARY, CONTEM'PORARY. *s.* Existing at the same time. pl. *cotemporaries, contemporaries.*
COTERIE'. *s.* A friendly or fashionable association.
COTILLON', COTIL'LION. *s.* A brisk, lively dance, in which eight or more persons are engaged.
COTT'AGE. *s.* A hut, a cot. s. *cottager, cotter.*
COT'TON. *s.* The down of the cotton-tree; cloth made of cotton v. *cotton;* pr. par. *cottoning;* past, *cottoned:* adj. *cottony.*
COUCH. *v.* To lie down on a place of repose; to lie down in secret, or ambush; to stoop; to bend; to operate in a particular manner upon the eye. pr. par. *couching,* past, *couched:* s. *couch, coucher.*
COUCH'ANT. *adj.* Couching, squatting.
COUGH. *s.* An expressed convulsion of the lungs. v. *cough;* pr. par. *coughing;* past, *coughed:* s *cougher.*
COULD. *v.* The preterit of *can.*
COUL'TER. *s.* The sharp iron of the plough, which cuts the earth
COUN'CIL. *s.* An assembly of persons met together in consultation; act of public deliberation; the body of privy counsellors.
COUN'SEL. *s.* Advice, direction, consultation, interchange of opinions; those that plead a cause. v. *counsel;* pr. par. *counseling;* past, *counseled:* s. *counsellor.*
COUNT. *v.* To number, to tell, to reckon, to esteem, to impute, to charge. pr. par. *counting;* past

counted: s. *count:* adj. *countable, countless.*

COUNT. s. A title of foreign nobility; supposed equivalent to an earl.

COUN'TENANCE s Form of the face; patronage, air, look. v. *countenance;* pr. par. *countenancing;* past, *countenanced:* s. *countenancer.*

COUNT'ER. s. A false piece of money, used as a means of reckoning; the table on which goods are viewed in a shop.

COUNT'ER. adj. Contrary, opposite.

COUNTERACT'. v. To hinder by contrary agency. pr. par. *counteracting;* past, *counteracted:* s. *counteracter, counteraction.*

COUNT'ERBALANCE. v. To weigh against. pr. par. *conterbalancing*, past, *counterbalanced:* s. *counterbalance.*

COUNTER-EVIDENCE. s. Testimony by which the deposition of some former witness is opposed.

COUNTERFEIT. v. To forge, to imitate, to copy. pr. par. *counterfeiting;* past, *counterfeited:* s. *counterfeit, counterfeiter:* adj. *counterfeit.*

COUN I'ERMAND. v. To repeal a command; to prohibit. pr. par. *countermanding;* past, *countermanded:* s. *countermand.*

COUNT'ERMARCH. v. To march back over the same ground. pr. par. *countermarching;* past, *countermarched:* s. *countermarch.*

COUNT'ERMINE. s. A well or hole sunk into the ground, from which a gallery or branch runs out under ground, to seek out the enemy's mine; a stratagem by which any contrivance is defeated. v. *countermine;* pr. par. *countermining;* past, *countermined:* s. *counterminer.*

COUNTERMO'TION. s. Contrary motion.

COUNTERMO'VEMENT. s. Contrary movement.

COUNT'ERPANE. s. A coverlet for a bed.

COUNT'ERPART. s. The corresponding part.

COUNTERPETI'TION. s. A petition against another petition. v *counterpetition;* pr. par. *counterpetitioning;* past, *counterpetitioned*

COUNT'ERPLOT. v. To oppose one machination by another. pr. par. *counterplotting;* past, *counterplotted:* s. *counterplot.*

COUNT'ERPOINT. s. The act of composing harmony; an opposite point or course.

COUNTERPOISE. v. To counter balance; to act against, with equal weight. pr. par. *counterpoising* past, *counterpoised:* s. *counterpoise.*

COUNT'ERPRESSIVE. s. Opposite force.

COUNTER-REVOLU'TION. s. A revolution succeeding another, and opposite to it.

COUNTERSCARF, COUNTER-SCARP. s. (In fortification.) That side of the ditch which is next the camp.

COUNTERSIGN. v. To sign an order or patent of a superior, in quality of secretary, to render it more authentic. pr. par. *countersigning*, past, *countersigned:* s. *countersign.*

COUNTERTEN'OR. s. A term in music.

COUNTERVAIL'. v. To be equivalent to; to have equal force or value. pr. par. *countervailing;* past, *countervailed:* s. *countervail.*

COUNTERVIEW. s. Opposition; a posture in which two persons front each other.

COUNTERVO'TE. v. To oppose, to outvote. pr. par. *countervoting*, past, *countervoted.*

COUNTERWEIGH'. v. To weigh against. pr. par. *counterweighing;* past, *counterweighed.*

83

COUNTERWORK'. *v.* To counteract. pr. par. *counterworking;* past, *counterworked.*

COUNT'ESS. *s.* The lady of an earl or count. pl. *countesses.*

COUNT'ING-HOUSE. *s.* The room appropriated to the books and accounts of a merchant.

COUN'TRY. *s.* A tract of land; a region; the place of one's birth; the native soil. pl. *countries.*

COUN'TRY-DANCE. *s.* A kind of dance.

COUN'TRYMAN. *s.* One born in the same country; a rustic, a husbandman. pl. *countrymen.*

COUN'TY. *s.* A shire; a circuit or portion of a country, under the jurisdiction of a sheriff. pl. *counties.*

COUP-DE-GRACE'. *s.* The stroke which terminated the sufferings of those who had been broken on the wheel.

COUP-DE-MAIN'. *s.* A military expression, denoting an instantaneous, unexpected, and generally desperate attack.

COUP-D'ŒIL. *s.* The first view of any thing; a slight view of it.

COUPE'E. *s.* A motion in dancing.

COUP'LE. *s.* A means of joining two things; two, a male and his female; a brace. *v. couple;* pr. par. *coupling;* past, *coupled.*

COUP'LE-BEGGAR. *s.* One that makes it his business to marry beggars to each other.

COUP'LET. *s.* Two verses; a pair of rhymes; a pair.

COUR'AGE. *s.* Bravery; active fortitude; spirit of enterprise. adj. *courageous.* adv. *courageously.*

COU'RIER. *s.* A messenger sent in haste; an express.

COURSE. *s.* Race: career; passage from place to place; progress; ground on which a race is run. *v. course;* pr. par. *coursing;* past, *coursed:* s. *courser.*

COURT. *s.* The place where a prince resides; a palace; a hall or chamber where justice is administered; open space before a house. adj. *courtlike, courtly, courtliness.*

COURT. *v.* To woo, to solicit, to seek. pr. par. *courting;* past, *courted.*

COURT'EOUS. *adj.* Having the refined manners of a court; polite adv. *courteously:* s. *courteousness.*

COURTESAN', COURTEZAN'. *s.* A woman of the town.

COURT'ESY. *s.* Elegance of manners; civility; a tenure or title derived from another. pl. *courtesies.*

COURT'ESY. *s.* The reverence made by women. (pronounced *curt'se.*) pl. *courtesies:* v. *courtesy,* pr. par. *courtesying;* past, *courtesied.*

COURT'HAND. *s.* The hand or manner of writing used in records and judicial proceedings.

COUR'TIER. *s.* One that frequents the courts of princes; one that courts the favour of others.

COURT-MAR'TIAL. *s.* A court consisting of military officers.

COURT'SHIP. *s.* The solicitation of a woman to marriage.

COUS'IN. *s.* Any one collaterally related more remotely than a brother or sister; a kinsman.

COVE. *s.* A small creek or bay.

COVE. *v.* To arch over. pr. par. *coving;* past, *coved.*

COV'ENANT. *s.* A contract, a stipulation; an agreement on certain terms. *v. covenant;* pr. par. *covenanting;* past, *covenanted:* s. *covenanter.*

COV'ER. *v.* To overspread; to overwhelm; to bury; to shelter, to protect. pr. par. *covering;* past, *covered:* s. *cover. covering, coverer.*

COV'ERLET. *s.* The outermost of the bed-clothes.

COV'ERT. *s.* A shelter, a hiding place. adj. *covert:* adv. *covertly.*

COV'ERTURE. *s.* Shelter, defence; in law, the condition of a woman during her marriage.

COVET. *v.* To desire inordinately. pr. par. *coveting;* past, *coveted:* adj. *covetous:* adv. *covetously:* s. *coveter, covetousness.*

COV'EY. *s.* A brood of partridges; an old bird and her young ones.

COV'ING. *s.* A term in building, used of houses, that project over the ground-plot.

COW. *s.* The female of the bull.

COW. *v.* To depress with fear. pr. par. *cowing;* past, *cowed.*

COW'ARD. *s.* A poltroon, whose predominant passion is fear. *s. cowardice:* adj. *cowardlike:* adj. and adv. *cowardly.*

COW'ER. *v.* To sink by bending the knees; to stoop. pr. par. *cowering;* past, *cowered.*

COW'HERD. *s.* One who attends cows.

COW'-HOUSE. *s.* A house in which cows are kept.

COWL. *s.* A monk's hood. adj. *cowled.*

COW'-POCK. *s.* A disorder, derived from the teats of cows, now called the *vaccine.*

COW'SLIP. *s.* A species of primrose.

COX'COMB. *s.* A fop; a superficial pretender to knowledge or accomplishments. adj. *coxcomical.*

COY. *adj.* Modest, decent, not accessible. adv. *coyly:* s. *coyness.*

COZ'EN. *v.* To cheat, to trick. pr. par. *cozening;* past, *cozened:* s. *cozenage, cozener.*

CRAB. *s.* A crustaceous fish; a wild, sour apple.

CRAB'BED. *adj.* Peevish, morose, harsh. adv. *crabbedly:* s. *crabbedness.*

CRACK. *s.* A narrow breach; the sound of any body bursting; any sudden and quick sound. *v. crack;* pr. par. *cracking;* past, *cracked:* s. *cracker.*

CRACK'BRAINED. *adj.* Crazy.

CRACK'ER. *s.* A small biscuit; a squib; a barbarous wagoner, from the interior of the southern states.

CRACK'LE. *v.* To make slight cracks; to make small and frequent noises. pr. par. *crackling,* past, *crackled:* s. *crackling.*

CRA'DLE. *s.* A movable bed, in which children are rocked; a sort of frame affixed to a scythe. *v. cradle;* pr. par. *cradling;* past, *cradled:* s. *cradler.*

CRAFT. *s.* Manual art; trade; fraud, cunning. adv. *craftily:* s *craftiness:* adj. *crafty.*

CRAFTS'MAN. *s.* An artificer, a mechanic.

CRAG. *s.* A rough, steep rock. adj. *cragged, craggy:* s. *craggedness, cragginess.*

CRAM. *v.* To stuff with more than can conveniently be held; to thrust in by force. pr. par. *cramming,* past, *crammed:* s. *crammer.*

CRAM'BO. *s.* A play at which one gives a word, to which another finds a rhyme.

CRAMP. *s.* A spasm or contraction of the limbs; a restriction; a confinement. *v. cramp;* pr. par. *cramping;* past, *cramped.*

CRAN'BERRY. *s.* The whortleberry or bilberry. pl. *cranberries.*

CRANCH, CRAUNCH. *v.* To crush in the mouth. pr. par. *cranching,* past, *cranched.*

CRANE. *s.* A bird with a long beak an instrument made with ropes pulleys, and hooks, by which great weights are raised.

CRAN'IUM. *s.* The skull.

CRANK. *s.* The end of an iron axis, turned square down, and again turned square to the first turning down.

CRAN'NY. *s.* A chink, a fissure. pl. *crannies:* adj. *crannied.*

CRAPE. *s.* A thin stuff, loosely woven.

CRASH. *v.* To make a loud, complicated noise, as of many things falling or breaking at once. pr.

par. *crashing;* past, *crashed:* s. *crash, crashing.*

CRATE. *s.* A pannier or wicker basket.

CRA'TER. *s.* A vent, or aperture.

CRAUNCH, CRANCH. *v.* To crush in the mouth. pr. par. *craunching,* past, *craunched.*

CRAVAT. *s.* A neckcloth; something worn about the neck.

CRAVE. *v.* To ask with earnestness; to entreat; to long. pr. par. *craving;* past, *craved:* s. *craver.*

CRA'VEN. *s.* A coward, a recreant. adj. *craven.*

CRAW. *s.* The crop or first stomach of birds.

CRAWFISH, CRAY'FISH. *s.* A small crustaceous fish.

CRAWL. *v.* To creep, to move as a worm. pr. par. *crawling;* past, *crawled:* s. *crawler.*

CRAY'ON. *s.* A kind of pencil, used for drawing.

CRAZE. *v.* To break, to crush, to weaken, to impair the intellect. pr. par. *crazing;* past, *crazed:* s. *craziness:* adj. *crazy:* adv. *crazily.*

CREAK. *v.* To make a harsh, protracted noise. pr. par. *creaking;* past, *creaked.*

CREAM. *s.* The unctuous or oily part of milk; the best part of any thing. *v. cream;* pr. par. *creaming;* past, *creamed:* adj. *creamy.*

CREASE. *s.* A mark made by doubling any thing. v. *crease;* pr. par. *creasing;* past, *creased.*

CREA'TE. *v.* To form out of nothing; to cause to exist; to produce; to cause. pr. par. *creating;* past, *created:* s. *creation, creator:* adj. *creative.*

CRE'ATURE. *s.* A being not self-existent, but created by the Supreme Power; an animal, a general term for man.

CRE'DENCE. *s.* Belief, credit. adj. *credent.*

CREDEN'DA. *s.* Things to be believed articles of faith.

CREDEN'TIAL. *s.* That which gives a title to credit; the warrant upon which belief is claimed. adj. *credential.*

CRED'IBLE. *adj.* Worthy of credit s. *credibility,* pl. *credibilities.*

CRED'IT. *s.* Belief, honour, trust, respectability, allowance. v. *credit;* pr. par. *crediting;* past, *credited:* adj. *creditable:* adv. *creditably.*

CRED'ITOR. *s.* He to whom a debt is owed; one who credits.

CRED'ULOUS. *adj.* Apt to believe unsuspecting. adv. *credulously* s. *credulity,* pl. *credulities.*

CREED. *s.* A form of words, in which articles of religious faith are comprehended.

CREEK. *s.* A prominence or jut in a winding coast; a small port; a bay, a cove.

CREEK. *v.* To make a harsh noise. pr. par. *creeking;* past, *creeked.*

CREEP. *v.* To move as a worm; to grow along the ground, or on other supports; to move slowly and feebly. pr. par. *creeping;* past, *crept:* s. *creeper:* adv. *creepingly.*

CRE'OLE. *s.* A native of the southern parts of America and the West Indies, born of white European parents.

CREPT. Preterit of the v. *creep.*

CREPUS'CULE *s* Twilight. adj *crepuscular.*

CRES'CENT. *adj.* Increasing, growing. s. *crescent:* adj. *crescive.*

CRESS. *s.* A species of herb. pl. *cresses.*

CREST. *s.* The plume of feathers on the top of the ancient helmet; the comb of the cock; any ornament or tuft on the head. v. *crest;* pr. par. *cresting;* past, *crested.* adj. *crestless.*

CRESTFALLEN. *adj.* Dejected, sunk; dispirited.

CREV'ICE. *s.* A crack, a cleft.

CREW. *s.* A company of people associated for any purpose; the company of a ship.

CRIB. *s.* The rack or manger of a stable.

CRIB'BAGE. *s.* A game of cards.

CRICK'ET. *s.* An insect that squeaks or chirps about ovens and fire-places; a sport at which the contenders drive a ball with sticks.

CRI'ER. *s* An officer whose business is to cry or make proclamation.

CRIME. *s.* An act contrary to right; an offence; a great fault.

CRIM'INAL. *adj.* Partaking of crime; contrary to right. *s. criminal, criminality,* pl. *criminalities:* adv. *criminally.*

CRIM'INATE. *v.* To accuse, to charge with crime. pr. par. *criminating;* past, *criminated:* s. *crimination:* adj. *criminatory.*

CRIMP. *v.* To curl or crisp the hair. pr. par. *crimping;* past, *crimped:* adj. and s. *crimp.*

CRIM'SON. *s.* Red, in a slight degree darkened with blue. v. *crimson;* pr. par. *crimsoning;* past, *crimsoned.*

CRINGE. *v.* To bow, to fawn, to flatter, to contract. pr. par. *cringing;* past, *cringed:* s. *cringer.*

CRIP'PLE. *s.* One that is lame. v. *cripple;* pr. par. *crippling;* past, *crippled.*

CRI'SIS. *s.* The height, or turn of a disease; critical time. pl. *crises.*

CRISP. *adj.* Indented, brittle, friable, short, brisk, v. *crisp;* pr. par. *crisping;* past, *crisped:* s. *crispness.*

CRITE'RION. *s.* A mark, a sign. pl. *criteria.*

CRIT'IC. *s.* One who is fond of examining and observing; a censurer. adj. *critical:* adv. *critically.*

CRIT'ICISE. *v.* To play the critic; to judge. pr. par. *criticising;* past, *criticised:* s. *criticiser, criticism.*

CRITIQUE. *s.* A critical examination; critical remarks.

CROAK. *v.* To make a hoarse, low noise, like a frog. pr. par. *croaking;* past, *croaked:* s. *croak, croaker.*

CROCK. *s.* A cup: any vessel made of earth. s. *crockery.*

CROC'ODILE. *s.* A kind of amphibious, voracious animal.

CRO'CUS. *s.* A kind of flower. pl *crocuses.*

CRO'NY. *s.* An old acquaintance; a companion of long standing. pl. *cronies.*

CROOK. *s.* Any crooked or bent instrument; a sheep-hook. v. *crook,* pr. par. *crooking;* past, *crooked.*

CROOK'ED. *adj.* Bent, not straight, winding, perverse. adv. *crookedly:* s. *crookedness.*

CROOK'EN. *v.* To make crooked pr. par. *crookening;* past, *crookened.*

CROP. *s.* The craw of a bird; the harvest. v. *crop;* pr. par. *cropping;* past, *cropped.*

CROP'PER. *s.* A kind of pigeon, with a large crop.

CRO'SIER. *s.* A bishop's staff.

CROSS. *s.* One straight body laid at right angles over another.

CROSS. *adj.* Transverse, oblique, adverse, peevish. adv. *crossly* · s. *crossness.*

CROSS. *v.* To lay one body, or draw one line athwart another; to pass over; to thwart. pr. par. *crossing;* past, *crossed.*

CROSS'-BOW. *s.* A missive weapon, formed by placing a bow across a stick.

CROSS'-CUT. *v.* To cut across. pr. par. *cross-cutting;* past, *cross-cut.*

CROSS-EXAM'INE. *v.* To try the faith of evidence, by captious questions of the contrary party. pr. par. *cross-examining;* past, *cross-examined:* s. *cross-examination.*

CROSS'-GRAINED. *adj.* Having the fibres transverse or irregular; perverse.

CROSS'-LEGGED. *adj.* Having the legs crossed.

CROSS-PUR'POSE. *s.* A conceit of conversation, proposing a diffi-

...culty to be solved; a kind of enigma or riddle.

CROSS-QUES'TION. v. To cross-examine. pr. par. *cross-questioning;* past, *cross-questioned.*

CROTCH'ET s. A term in music.

CROUCH. v. To stoop low; to lie close to the ground; to fawn. pr. par. *crouching;* past, *crouched:* s. *croucher.*

CROUP. s. A kind of asthma or catarrh, to which children are subject.

CROW. s. A kind of bird; a bar of iron, used as a lever; the voice of a cock.

CROW. v. To utter the noise which a cock makes in gayety or defiance. pr. par. *crowing;* past, *crowed.*

CROW'-BAR. s. An iron crow.

CROWD. s. A multitude confusedly pressed together. v. *crowd;* pr. par. *crowding;* past, *crowded.*

CROWN. s. The ornament of the head, which denotes imperial or regal dignity; a garland; the top; a piece of money, anciently stamped with a crown. v. *crown:* pr. par. *crowning;* past, *crowned;* s. *crowner.*

CRU'CIBLE. s. A chymist's melting-pot.

CRU'CIFY. v. To put to death by nailing the hands and feet to a cross set upright. pr. par. *crucifying;* past, *crucified:* s. *crucifix, crucifixion, crucifier.*

CRU'CIFORM. adj. Having the form of a cross.

CRUDE. adj. Unfinished, impure, raw, harsh, unripe. adv. *crudely:* s. *crudeness, crudity,* pl. *crudities.*

CRU'EL. adj. Inhuman, hard-hearted, void of pity. adv. *cruelly:* s. *cruelty,* pl. *cruelties.*

CRU'ET. s. A vial for vinegar or oil, with a stopper.

CRUISE. s. A sea-adventure; a voyage in search of plunder. v. *cruise;* pr. par. *cruising;* past, *cruised:* s. *cruiser.*

CRUMB, CRUM. s. The soft part of bread; a small particle or fragment of bread.

CRUM'BLE. v. To break into small pieces. pr. par. *crumbling,* past *crumbled.*

CRUM'PET. s. A soft cake.

CRUM'PLE. v. To draw into wrinkles; to contract. pr. par. *crumpling;* past, *crumpled:* s. *crumpling.*

CRUP'PER. s. That part of the horseman's furniture that reaches from the saddle to the tail.

CRU'RAL. adj. Belonging to the leg.

CRUSA'DE. s. An expedition against infidels. s. *crusader.*

CRUSH. v. To press between two opposite bodies; to squeeze. pr. par. *crushing;* past, *crushed:* s *crush, crusher.*

CRUST. s. A shell or external coat; the covering of a pie; the outer hard part of bread.

CRUSTA'CEOUS. adj. Shelly, with joints; not testaceous; not with one continued, uninterrupted shell.

CRUS'TILY. adv. Peevishly, snappishly. s. *crustiness:* adj. *crusty.*

CRUS'TY. adj. Covered with a crust; morose, snappish. s. *crustiness:* adj. *crusty.*

CRUTCH. s. A support used by cripples. pl. *crutches.*

CRY. v. To speak with vehemence; to call importunately; to proclaim; to weep. pr. par. *crying;* past, *cried:* s. *cry,* pl. *cries, crier, cryer.*

CRYPTOG'RAPHY. s. The science of writing secret characters; ciphers. pl. *crystographies.*

CRYPTOL'OGY. s. Enigmatical language. pl. *cryptologies.*

CRYS'TAL. s. A hard, pellucid, and colourless body. adj. *crystal, crystalline.*

CRYS'TALLIZE. v. To cause to congeal in crystals; to form into crystals. pr. par. *crystallizing;* past, *crystallized:* s. *crystallization.*

CUB. s. The young of a beast, generally of a bear or fox. v. *cub,* pr. par. *cubbing;* past, *cubbed*

CUBA'TION. *s.* The act of lying down. adj. *cubatory.*

CUBE. *s.* A regular, solid body, having six square and equal sides, and all its angles right angles.

CUBE-ROOT. *s.* The origin of a cubic number; or a number by the multiplication of which into itself, and again into the product, any given number is formed. adj. *cubical:* adv. *cubically:* s. *cubicalness.*

CU'BIFORM. *adj.* Of the shape of a cube.

CU'BIT. *s.* An ancient measure, equal to the length of a man's arm from the elbow to the extremity of the fingers; about eighteen inches.

CUCK'OLD. *s.* One that is married to an adultress. v. *cuckold;* pr. par. *cuckolding;* past, *cuckolded:* s. *cuckoldom.*

CUCK'OO. *s.* A species of bird.

CU'CUMBER. *s.* The name of a plant, and the fruit of that plant.

CUD. *s.* The food which is deposited in the first stomach, in order to rumination.

CUD'DLE. *v.* To lie close, to squat. pr. par. *cuddling;* past, *cuddled.*

CUDG'EL. *s.* A stick to strike with. v. *cudgel;* pr. par. *cudgeling;* past, *cudgeled:* s. *cudgeler.*

CUE. *s.* The tail or end of any thing, as, the long curl of a wig; the last words of a speech, which the player who is to answer catches, and regards as an intimation to begin; a hint; an intimation.

CUFF. *s.* A blow with the fist; part of the sleeve. v. *cuff;* pr. par. *cuffing;* past, *cuffed.*

CUI'RASS. *s.* A breastplate. pl. *cuirasses.*

CUI'RASSIER. *s.* A soldier who wears a cuirass.

CULDEE'. *s.* One of the ancient monks in Scotland and Ireland.

CU'LINARY. *adj.* Relating to the kitchen, or cookery

CULL. *v.* To select from others; to pick out of many. pr. par. *culling,* past, *culled:* s. *culler.*

CULLIBIL'ITY. *s.* Credulity; easiness of belief. pl. *cullibilities.*

CULM. *s.* A kind of pit-coal.

CUL'MINATE. *v.* To be vertical; to be in the meridian. pr. par *culminating;* past, *culminated:* s *culmination.*

CUL'PABLE. *adj.* Criminal, blamable, guilty. s. *culpability,* pl. *culpabilities:* adv. *culpably.*

CUL'PRIT. *s.* A man arraigned before his judge; one accused.

CUL'TIVATE. *v.* To forward or improve the product of the earth, by manual industry. pr. par. *cultivating;* past, *cultivated:* s. *cultivation, cultivator.*

CUL'TURE. *s.* The act of cultivation; tillage.

CUM'BER. *v.* To encumber, to embarrass, to entangle, to obstruct. pr. par. *cumbering;* past, *cumbered:* s. *cumbrance:* adj. *cumbrous:* adv. *cumbrously.*

CU'MULATE. *v.* To heap together; to accumulate. pr. par. *cumulating;* past, *cumulated:* s. *cumulation:* adj. *cumulative.*

CU'NEAL. *adj.* Relating to a wedge. adj. *cuneated.*

CU'NIFORM. *adj.* Having the form of a wedge.

CUN'NING. *adj.* Skilful, knowing, artful, sly, designing. s. *cunning, cunningness:* adv. *cunningly.*

CUP. *s.* A small vessel to drink out of; a small hollow vessel.

CUP. *v.* To fix a glass bell or cucurbite upon the skin, for the purpose of drawing the blood by scarification and rare action. pr. par. *cupping;* past, *cupped:* s *cupper*

CUP'BEARER. *s.* An attendant who gives wine at a feast.

CUP'BOARD. *s.* A case with shelves, in which victuals or earthenware are placed.

CUPID'ITY. *s.* Concupiscence; unlawful or unreasonable longing. pl. *cupidities.*

CU'POLA. *s.* A dome; the hemispherical summit of a building.

CU'PREOUS. *adj.* Coppery; consisting of copper.

CUR. *s.* A worthless, degenerate dog. adj. *currish:* adv. *currishly:* s. *currishness.*

CU'RATE. *s.* A clergyman, hired to perform the duties of another; a parish priest.

CU'RACY. *s.* Employment or office of a curate. pl. *curacies.*

CU'RATIVE. *adj.* Relating to the cure of diseases.

CURA'TOR. *s.* One that has the care and superintendence of any thing; a guardian appointed by law.

CURB. *s.* An iron chain, made fast to the upper part of the branches of a bridle, and running over the beard of the horse; restraint; inhibition. v. *curb;* pr. par. *curbing;* past, *curbed.*

CURB'-STONE. *s.* A thick kind of stone, placed at the edge of a footway.

CURD. *s.* The coagulation of milk; the concretion of the thicker parts of any liquor. v. *curd;* pr. par. *curding;* past, *curded:* adj. *curdy.*

CURD'LE. *v.* To coagulate, to concrete. pr. par. *curdling;* past, *curdled.*

CURE. *s.* Remedy, restorative. v. *cure;* pr. par. *curing;* past, *cured:* adj. *curable.*

CUR'FEW. *s.* An evening peal, by which William the Conqueror commanded that every man should cover his fire, and extinguish his light; so that, in many places, at this day, where a bell is customarily rung towards bed-time, it is said to ring *curfew.*

CURIO'SO. *s.* A curious person; a virtuoso.

CU'RIOUS. *adj.* Inquisitive; desirous of information; exact; nice; laboured: worthy of examination; s. *curiosity,* pl. *curiosities:* adv. *curiously.*

CURL. *v.* To turn the hair in ringlets; to writhe; to twist. pr. par. *curling;* past, *curled:* s. *curl, curliness:* adj. *curly.*

CUR'LEW. *s.* A kind of wild fowl

CURMUD'GEON. *s.* An avaricious, churlish fellow; a miser.

CUR'RANT. *s.* A small fruit.

CUR'RENCY. *s.* Circulation, general reception, continuance. pl. *currencies:* adj. and s. *current:* adv. *currently.*

CUR'RICLE. *s.* A chariot; in modern times, an open chaise with two wheels, drawn by two horses abreast.

CUR'RY. *v.* To dress leather; to drub; to rub a horse in order to smooth him. pr. par. *currying,* past, *curried:* s. *currier.*

CUR'RY. *s.* A word imported from the East Indies, denoting a mixture of various eatables.

CUR'RYCOMB. *s.* An iron instrument for currying horses.

CURSE. *v.* To wish evil to; to execrate; to devote; to afflict pr. par. *cursing;* past, *cursed:* s. *curse, cursedness, curser:* adv. *cursedly.*

CUR'SORY. *adj.* Hasty, quick, inattentive. adv. *cursorily:* s. *cursoriness.*

CURTAIL'. *v.* To cut off, to cut short. pr. par. *curtailing;* past, *curtailed:* s. *curtailer, curtailment.*

CUR'TAIN. *s.* A cloth contracted or expanded at pleasure, for the purpose of regulating the admission of light, or of displaying or concealing an object. v. *curtain,* pr. par. *curtaining:* past, *curtained.*

CURT'SY. *s.* See COURTESY.

CU'RULE. *adj.* An epithet applied to the chair in which the Roman magistrates sat.

CURVE. *v.* To bend, to crook. pr. par. *curving:* past, *curved:* s *curve, curvature, curvation.* adj *curvated* · s. *curvity,* pl. *curvities*

90

CURVET'. *v.* To leap, to bound, to frisk. pr. par. *curveting;* past, *curveted:* s. *cur'vet.*

CURVILIN'EAR. *adj.* Consisting of a crooked line.

CUSH'ION. *s.* A pillow for a seat; a soft pad placed upon a chair. *v. cushion;* pr. par. *cushioning;* past, *cushioned.*

CUS'TARD. *s.* A kind of sweetmeat, made by boiling eggs with milk and sugar.

CUS'TODY. *s.* Imprisonment, restraint of liberty, care. pl. *custodies:* adj. *custodial.*

CUS'TOM. *s.* Habit; habitual practice; fashion; established manner; application from buyers. adj. *customary:* adv. *customarily.* s. *customer.*

CUS'TOM-HOUSE. *s.* The house where the taxes upon goods imported or exported, are collected.

CUT. *v.* To penetrate with an edged instrument; to hew; to carve; to separate. pr. par. *cutting;* past, *cut:* s. *cut, cutter, cutting.*

CUTA'NEOUS. *adj.* Relating to the skin.

CU'TICLE. *s.* The first and outermost covering of the body; the scarf-skin.

CUT'LASS. *s.* A broad cutting sword. pl. *cutlasses.*

CUT'LER. *s.* One who makes or sells knives, and other edged instruments. s. *cutlery,* pl. *cutleries.*

CUT'LET. *s.* A steak; properly, a rib.

CUT'PURSE. *s.* A thief.

CUT'TER. *s.* An agent or instrument that cuts; a swift-sailing boat, that *cuts* the water.

CUT'TLE. *s.* A kind of fish.

CY'CLE. *s.* A circle; a periodical space of time.

CY'CLOID. *s.* A species of geometrical curve. adj. *cycloidal.*

CYCLOPÆ'DIA, CYCLOPE'DIA. *s.* A circle of knowledge; a course of the sciences.

CY'CLOPS. *s.* A fabled race of men, of gigantic stature, who inhabited the western part of Sicily, and were said to have only one eye, in the middle of the forehead. adj. *cyclopean.*

CY'DER. *s.* See CIDER.

CYG'NET. *s.* A young swan.

CYL'INDER. *s.* A body having two flat surfaces, and one circular. adj. *cylindrical, cylindric.*

CYL'INDROID. *s.* A solid body, differing from the cylinder, as having its bases elliptical, but parallel and equal.

CYM'BAL. *s.* A musical instrument.

CYN'IC. *s.* A follower of Diogenes, a disagreeable, snarling fellow. adj. *cynic, cynical.*

CY'PHER. *s.* See CIPHER.

CY'PRESS. *s.* A kind of tree. pl. *cypresses.*

CZAR. *s.* The title of the emperor of Russia. fem. *czarina.*

D

DAB. *s.* A small lump of any thing; a blow with something moist or soft.

DAB'BLE. *v.* To smear, to daub, to spatter. pr. par. *dabbling;* past, *dabbled:* s. *dabbler.*

DA CA'PO. *s.* A term in music, signifying that the first part of the tune should be repeated at the conclusion.

DAC'TYLE. *s.* A poetical foot, consisting of one long syllable and two short.

DAD, DAD'DY. *s.* A child's way of expressing father. pl. *daddies.*

DAF'FADIL, DAF'FODIL. *s.* A kind of plant.

DAG—DAN

DAG'GER. *s.* A short sword, a poignard.
DAI'LY. *adj.* Happening every day, or very frequently. *adv. daily.*
DAIN'TY. *s.* Something nice or delicate. pl. *dainties:* s. *daintiness:* adj. *dainty:* adv. *daintily.*
DAI'RY. *s.* A place where milk is kept. pl. *dairies.*
DAI'RY-MAID. *s.* The woman-servant whose business is to manage the milk.
DAI'SY. *s.* A spring-flower. pl. *daisies.*
DALE. *s.* A low place between hills; a vale; a valley.
DAL'LY. *v.* To trifle; to play the fool; to sport; to delay. pr. par. *dallying;* past, *dallied:* s. *dallier, dalliance.*
DAM. *s.* The mother; a term used for beasts.
DAM. *v.* To confine, or shut up water by a bank. pr. par. *damming;* past, *dammed:* s. *dam.*
DAM'AGE. *s.* Mischief, hurt, detriment. *v. damage;* pr. par. *damaging;* past, *damaged:* adj. *damageable.*
DAM'ASK. *s.* Linen or silk invented at Damascus, which, by a various direction of the threads, exhibits flowers or other forms. *v. damask;* pr. par. *damasking;* past, *damasked.*
DAME. *s.* A woman of rank; mistress of a low family; a term applied to women in general.
DAMN. *v.* To condemn, to curse. pr. par. *damning;* past, *damned:* s. *damnation:* adj. *damnable, damnatory.* adv. *damnably.*
DAMP. *adj.* Moist; inclining to wet; foggy. *s. damp, damper, dampness:* v. *damp;* pr. par. *damping;* past, *damped:* adj. *dampish.*
DAM'SEL. *s.* A young gentlewoman; a country lass.
DAM'SON. *s.* A small black plum.
DANCE. *v.* To move in measure, with steps corresponding to the sound of instruments. pr. par.

DAN—DAS

dancing; past, *danced:* s. *dance, dancer, dancing.*
DANDELI'ON. *s.* A species of plant.
DAN'DLE. *v.* To shake a child on the knee, or in the hand. pr. par. *dandling;* past, *dandled:* s. *dandler.*
DANE. *s.* A native of Denmark. adj *Danish.*
DANE'WORT. *s.* A species of elder.
DAN'GER. *s.* Risk, hazard, peril. adj. *dangerous:* adv. *dangerously*
DANG'LE. *v.* To hang loose and quivering; to hang upon any one. pr. par. *dangling;* past, *dangled* s. *dangler.*
DAP'PER. *adj.* Little and active lively, without bulk; pretty; neat
DAP'PLE. *v.* To mark with various colours; to streak. pr. par. *dappling;* past, *dappled:* adj. *dapple.*
DARE. *v.* To have sufficient courage; to challenge; to defy. pr. par *during;* past, *dared:* s. *durer:* adj *daring:* adv. *daringly:* s. *daringness.*
DARK. *adj.* Not light; wanting light; opaque; obscure. *s. dark, darkness:* adv. *darkly.*
DARK'EN. *v.* To make dark; to cloud; to perplex. pr. par. *darkening;* past, *darkened:* s. *darkener:* adj. *darkish.*
DAR'LING. *s.* A favourite; one much beloved. adj. *darling.*
DARN. *v.* To mend holes, by imitating the texture of the stuff. pr. par. *darning;* past, *darned:* s. *darn, darner.*
DART. *s.* A missile weapon, thrown by the hand. v. *dart;* pr. par. *darting;* past, *darted:* s. *darter.*
DASH. *v.* To throw or strike any thing suddenly; to confound. pr. par. *dashing;* past, *dashed:* s. *dash dasher.*
DAS'TARD. *s.* A coward, a poltroon. adv. *dastardly:* s. *dastardness.*
DAS'TARDISE. *v.* To intimidate to deject with cowardice. pr. par *dastardising;* past, *dastardised.*

92

DA'TA. s. Truths admitted; things given, or premises, as grounds of argument. sing. *datum.*

DATE. *s.* The time at which a letter is written; the time at which any event happened. *v. date;* pr. par. *dating;* past, *dated: s. dater.*

DATE *s.* The fruit of the date-tree.

DA'TIVE. *adj.* A case in grammar, denoting to whom given.

DAUB. *v.* To smear with something adhesive; to paint coarsely. pr. par. *daubing;* past, *daubed: s. daub, dauber, daubing.*

DAUGHTER. *s.* The female offspring of a woman; a woman. adj. *daughterly.*

DAUNT. *v.* To discourage, to fright. pr. par. *daunting;* past, *daunted:* adj. *dauntless: s. dauntlessness.*

DAU'PHIN. *s.* The heir-apparent to the crown of France. fem. *dauphiness,* pl. *dauphinesses.*

DAW. *s.* A kind of crow.

DAWD'LER. *s.* A trifler, a dallier.

DAWN. *v.* To grow luminous; to begin to grow light; to glimmer obscurely. pr. par. *dawning;* past, *dawned: s. dawn, dawning.*

DAY. *s.* The time between the rising and setting of the sun, called the *artificial* day; the time occupied in a complete revolution of a planet on its axis, called a *natural* day.

DAYBREAK. *s.* The dawn; the first appearance of light.

DAY'LIGHT. *s.* The light of the day.

DAY'TIME. *s.* The time in which there is light.

DAZ'ZLE *v.* To overpower with light. pr. par. *dazzling;* past, *dazzled· s. dazzler.*

DEA'CON. *s.* One of the lowest of the three orders of the clergy. fem. *deaconess: s. deaconry,* pl. *deaconries: s. deaconship.*

DEAD. *adj.* Deprived of life; inanimate; senseless. *s. dead, deadness:* adj. and adv. *deadly*

DEAD'EN. *v.* To deprive of any kind of force or sensation, to make vapid or spiritless. pr. par. *deadening;* past, *deadened.*

DEAD-LIFT. *s.* A lift without any mechanical aid; hopeless exigence.

DEAD-RECK'ONING. *s.* That estimation or conjecture which the seamen make of the place where a ship is, by keeping an account of her way.

DEAF. *adj.* Wanting the sense of hearing. *v. deafen;* pr. par. *deafening;* past, *deafened:* adv. *deafly: s. deafness.*

DEAL. *s.* Quantity; degree of, more or less; fir-wood, or the wood of the pine.

DEAL. *v.* To distribute cards at a game; to traffic; to behave well or ill in any transaction. pr. par. *dealing;* past, *dealt: s. dealer, dealing.*

DEALT. Pret. and past par. of the *v. deal.*

DEAN. *s.* The second dignitary of a diocese; the name of an officer in some colleges. *s. deanery,* pl. *deaneries.*

DEAR. *adj.* Beloved, favourite, darling; not plentiful; high-priced. *s. dear, dearness, deary:* adv. *dearly.*

DEAR'-BOUGHT. *adj.* Purchased at a high price.

DEARTH. *s.* Scarcity which makes food dear; want; famine.

DEATH. *s.* The extinction of life; mortality; destruction. adj. *deathful, deathless, deathlike.*

DEATH-BED. *s.* The bed to which a person is confined by mortal sickness.

DEATH'S-DOOR'. *s.* A near approach to death.

DEBAR'. *v.* To exclude, to hinder. pr. par. *debarring;* past, *debarred.*

DEBARB'. *v.* To deprive of the beard. pr. par. *debarbing;* past, *debarbed.*

DEBARK'. *v.* To disembark. pr par. *debarking;* past, *debarked:* s *debarkation.*

DEBA'SE. *v.* To reduce from a higher to a lower state; to degrade. pr. par. *debasing;* past, *debased:* s. *debasement, debaser.*

DEBA'TE. *s.* A personal dispute; a controversy. *v. debate;* pr. par. *debating;* past, *debated:* s. *debater:* adj. *debatable.*

DEBAUCH'. *v.* To corrupt; to vitiate; to corrupt by intemperance. pr. par. *debauching;* past, *debauched:* s. *debauch, debauchee', debaucher, debauchery,* pl. *debaucheries.*

DEBEN"TURE. *s.* A writ or note, by which a debt is claimed; (in commerce) allowance, on exportation, of a certain part of a duty which had been paid on goods previously imported.

DEBIL'ITATE. *v.* To weaken, to make faint. pr. par. *debilitating;* past, *debilitated:* s. *debilitation, debility,* pl. *debilities, debilitator.*

DEB'IT. *s.* Money due for goods sold on credit; the debtor side of an account. *v. debit;* pr. par. *debiting;* past, *debited.*

DEBONAI'R. *adj.* Elegant, civil, well-bred. adv. *debonairly.*

DEBOUCH'. *v.* To march out of a wood, or a narrow pass, in order to meet or retire from an enemy. pr. par. *debouching;* past, *debouched.*

DEBT. *s.* That which one man owes to another. s. *debtor.*

DEBU"T. *s.* A French word, denoting the commencement or opening of a discourse, or of any design; first appearance before the public. pronounced *de-bu.*

DEC'ADE. *s.* The sum of ten; a number containing ten.

DECA'DENCE. *s.* Decay, fall.

DEC'AGON. *s.* A plain figure in geometry, having ten sides and angles.

DEC'ALOGUE. *s.* The ten commandments.

DECAL'VATE. *v.* To make bald. pr. par. *decalvating,* past, *decalvated:* s. *decalvation.*

DECAMP'. *v.* To shift the camp; to move off; to depart. pr. par. *decamping;* past, *decamped:* s. *decampment.*

DECANT'. *v.* To pour off gently, by inclination. pr. par. *decanting;* past, *decanted:* s. *decantation, decanter.*

DECAPITATE. *v.* To behead. pr. par. *decapitating;* past, *decapitated:* s. *decapitation, decapitator.*

DECAY'. *v.* To decline from a state of perfection; to fall towards a state of dissolution. pr. par. *decaying;* past, *decayed:* s. *decay, decayer.*

DECEA'SE. *s.* Death; departure from life. par. adj. *deceased.*

DECEIT'. *s.* Fraud, a cheat, stratagem, artifice. adj. *deceitful:* adv. *deceitfully:* s. *deceitfulness.*

DECEI'VE. *v.* To cause one to mistake, to delude by stratagem; to mock. pr. par. *deceiving;* past, *deceived:* s. *deceiver, deceiving:* adj. *deceivable.*

DECEM'BER. *s.* The last month of the year.

DECEM'VIR. *s.* One of the ten governors of Rome. pl. *decemviri.*

DECEM'VIRATE. *s.* The dignity and office of the ten governors of Rome; any body of ten men. adj *decemviral.*

DE'CENCY. *s.* Propriety of form, becoming ceremony; modesty. pl. *decencies:* adj. *decent:* adv. *decently.*

DECEP'TIBLE. *adj.* Liable to be deceived. s. *deceptibility,* pl. *deceptibilities.*

DECEP'TION. *s.* The act or means of deceiving; cheat; fraud. adj. *deceptive, decrptory.*

DECERPT'. *adj.* Cropped, taken off. adj. *decerptible:* s. *decerption.*

DECES'SION. *s.* A departure; going away.

DECI'DE. *v.* To fix the event of; to determine. pr. par. *deciding;* past, *decided:* s. *decider·* adj. *decidable:* adv. *decidedly.*

94

DECID'UOUS. *adj.* Falling; not perennial. *s. deciduousness.*

DE'CIMAL. *adj.* numbered by ten; multiplied by ten; increasing by ten. *adv. decimally.*

DE'CIMATE. *v.* To tithe; to take the tenth. pr. par. *decimating;* past, *decimated: s. decimation, decimator.*

DECI'PHER. *v.* To explain that which is written in ciphers; to write out; to unravel. pr. par. *deciphering;* past, *deciphered.*

DECIS'ION. *s.* Act of deciding; determination. adj. *decisive:* adv. *decisively: s. decisiveness.*

DECK. *s.* The floor of a ship.

DECK. *v.* To cover, to overspread, to dress, to adorn. pr. par. *decking;* past, *decked.*

DECLAIM'. *v.* To harangue; to speak to the passions. pr. par. *declaiming;* past, *declaimed: s. declaimer.*

DECLAMA'TION. *s.* Act of declaiming; a discourse addressed to the passions. adj. *declamatory.*

DECLARA'TION. *s.* A proclamation, or affirmation; (in law) a written statement of the cause of action. adj. *declaratory.*

DECLA'RE. *v.* To free from obscurity; to clear; to make known. pr. par. *declaring;* past, *declared:* adv. *declaredly.*

DECLEN'SION. *s.* Act of declining; declination; decay; inflexion of nouns.

DECLI'NE. *v.* To bend from, to refuse, to decay. pr. par. *declining;* past, *declined: s. decline, declination:* adj. *declinable, declinatory.*

DECLIV'ITY. *s.* Inclination, reckoned downwards. pl. *declivities:* adj. *declivous.*

DECOCT'. *v.* To prepare by boiling; to digest by the heat of the stomach. pr. par. *decocting;* past, *decocted: s. decoction:* adj. *decoctible.*

DECOL'LATE. *v.* To cut through the neck; to behead. pr. par. *decollating;* past, *decollated. s. decollation.*

DECOLORA'TION. *s.* Absence of colour.

DECOMPO'SE. *v.* To decompound, to dissolve. pr. par. *decomposing,* past, *decomposed: s. decomposer, decomposition.*

DEC'ORAMENT. *s.* Ornament.

DEC'ORATE. *v.* To adorn, to embellish. pr. par. *decorating;* past, *decorated: s. decoration, decorater.*

DECOR'TICATE. *v.* To divest of the bark or husk. pr. par. *decorticating;* past, *decorticated: s. decortication.*

DECO'RUM. *s.* Decency, propriety. adj. *decorous:* adv. *decorously.*

DECOY'. *v.* To lure into a cage; to entrap. pr. par. *decoying;* past, *decoyed: s. decoy, decoyer.*

DECREA'SE. *v.* To grow less; to diminish. pr. par. *decreasing;* past, *decreased: s. decrease.*

DECREE'. *v.* To make an edict; to enact; to resolve. pr. par. *decreeing;* past, *decreed: s. decree.*

DE'CREMENT. *s.* Decrease; the quantity lost by decreasing.

DECREP'IT. *adj.* Wasted and worn out with age; infirm. s. *decrepitness, decrepitude.*

DECRE'TAL. *adj.* Appertaining to a decree. s. *decretal:* adj. *decretory.*

DECRUSTA'TION. *s.* Act of taking off the crust.

DECRY'. *v.* To clamour against; to censure. pr. par. *decrying;* past, *decried: s. decryer.*

DEC'UPLE. *adj.* Ten-fold.

DEDEC'ORATE. *v.* To strip of ornament; to disgrace. pr. par. *dedecorating;* past, *dedecorated: s. dedecoration:* adj. *dedecorous.*

DED'ICATE. *v.* To devote to some divine power; to consecrate to sacred uses; to devote to a particular thing. pr. par. *dedicating,* past, *dedicated: s. dedication, dedicator:* adj. *dedicatory.*

95

DEDU'CE. *v.* To draw in a regular, connected series; to subtract; to deduct. pr. par. *deducing;* past, *deduced:* adj. *deducible.*

DEDUCT'. *v.* To subtract, to take away, to separate. pr. par. *deducting;* past, *deducted:* s. *deduction.*

DEED. *s.* Written evidence of any legal act; action, whether good or bad; exploit; performance.

DEEM. *v.* To judge, to think, to estimate. pr. par. *deeming;* past, *deemed.*

DEEP. adj. Having length downwards; descending far; profound, politic; grave. s. *deep:* adv. *deeply:* v. *deepen;* pr. par. *deepening;* past, *deepened.*

DEEP'-MOUTHED. *adj.* Having a hoarse and loud voice.

DEER. *s.* A kind of quadruped. pl. *deer.*

DE'ESS. *s.* A goddess. pl. *deësses.*

DEFA'CE. *v.* To destroy, to raze, to disfigure. pr. par. *defacing;* past, *defaced:* s. *defacement, defacer.*

DEFAL'CATE. *v.* To cut off, to lop, to abate, to deduct. pr. par. *defalcating;* past, *defalcated:* s. *defalcation.*

DEFALK'. *v.* To cut off, to lop, to abate, to deduct. pr. par. *defalkating;* past, *defalkated.*

DEFA'ME. *v.* To make infamous; to censure falsely in public; to calumniate. pr. par. *defaming;* past, *defamed:* s. *defamation, defamer:* adj. *defamatory.*

DEFAULT'. *s.* Omission of that which we ought to do; crime; failure; defect. s. *defaulter.*

DEFEA'SANCE. *s.* The act of annulling or abrogating a contract. adj. *defeasible.*

DEFEAT. *s.* Overthrow; prevention. v. *defeat;* pr. par. *defeating;* past, *defeated*

DE'FECATE. *v.* To purge from lees or foulness; to purify. pr. par. *defecating;* past, *defecated:* s. *defecation.*

DEFECT'. *s.* Want; absence of something necessary; failing; imperfection. adj. *defective:* adv. *defectively:* s. *defectiveness.*

DEFEC'TION. *s.* A falling away; apostasy; revolt.

DEFEN'CE. *s.* Guard, protection, vindication, justification, apology. adj. *defenceless, defensible, defensive:* adv. *defencelessly:* s. *defencelessness.*

DEFEND'. *v.* To stand in defence of; to protect; to vindicate; to uphold. pr. par. *defending;* past, *defended:* s. *defendant, defender* adj. *defendable.*

DEFER'. *v.* To put off, to delay. pr par. *deferring;* past, *deferred* s. *deferment, deferrer.*

DEF'ERENCE. *s.* Regard, respect complaisance, condescension.

DEFI'ANCE. *s.* A challenge. s. *defier.*

DEFI'CIENCY. *s.* Want; something less than is necessary; defect, imperfection. pl. *deficiencies* adj. *deficient:* adv. *deficiently.*

DE'FICIT. *s.* Want, deficiency.

DEFI'LE. *v.* To make foul or impure; to pollute. pr. par. *defiling,* past, *defiled:* s. *defilement, defiler*

DEFI'LE. *v.* To march off in files. pr. par. *defiling;* past, *defiled:* s *defile,* a long narrow pass.

DEFI'NE. *v.* To give the definition to explain. pr. par. *defining;* past *defined:* s. *definer:* adj. *definable.*

DEF'INITE. *adj.* Certain, limited, bounded, exact. adv. *definitely:* s. *definiteness, definition:* adj. *definitive:* adv. *definitively.*

DEFLECT'. *v.* To turn aside; to deviate from a true course. pr. par. *deflecting;* past, *deflected:* s. *deflection, deflexure.*

DE'FLUOUS. *adj.* Flowing downwards.

DEFLUX', DEFLUX'ION. *s.* Downward flow.

DEFORM'. *v.* To disfigure. pr. par. *deforming;* past, *deformed:* s

96

deformation, deformer, deformity, pl. *deformities.*

DEFRAUD'. *v.* To cheat. pr. par. *defrauding;* past, *defrauded:* s. *defrauder.*

DEFRAY'. *v.* To bear the charges. pr. par. *defraying;* past, *defrayed:* s. *defrayer, defrayment.*

DEFUNCT'. *adj.* Dead, deceased. s. *defunct, defunction.*

DEFY'. *v.* To call to combat; to challenge; to slight. pr. par. *defying;* past, *defied:* s. *defiance, defier.*

DEGEN'ERATE. *v.* To fall from the virtue of ancestors; to become of inferior quality. pr. par. *degenerating;* past, *degenerated:* s. *degeneracy,* pl. *degeneracies, degenerateness:* adj. *degenerate:* adv. *degenerately.*

DEGLUTI'TION. *s.* The act of swallowing.

DEGRA'DE. *v.* To put one from his degree; to deprive him of office, dignity, or title. pr. par. *degrading;* past, *degraded:* s. *degradation:* adv. *degradingly.*

DEGREE'. *s.* Quality, rank, station; step, measure, rate, collegiate honour.

DEHOR'TATORY. *adj.* Dissuasive.

DEIFICA'TION. *s.* The heathenish act of deifying, or making a god. s. *deifier.*

DE'IFY. *v.* To make a god of; to adore as a god. pr. par. *deifying;* past, *deified.*

DEIGN. *v.* To vouchsafe, to grant, to consider worth notice. pr. par. *deigning;* past, *deigned.*

DEIN'TEGRATE. *v.* To take from the whole; to spoil. pr. par. *deintegrating;* past, *deintegrated:* s. *deintegration.*

DE'ISM. *s.* The opinion of those who only acknowledge one God, without the reception of any revealed religion. s. *deist:* adj. *deistical.*

DE'ITY. *s.* Divinity; the nature and essence of God. pl. *deities.*

DEJECT'. *v.* To cast down, to afflict. pr. par. *dejecting;* past, *dejected:* s. *dejectedness, dejecter,* d. *jection:* adv. *dejectedly, dejectly.*

DELA'CERATE. *v.* To tear into pieces. pr. par. *delacerating;* past, *delacerated:* s. *delaceration.*

DELACTA'TION. *s.* Act of weaning from the breast.

DELAY'. *v.* To defer, to put off, to hinder, to frustrate, to detain. pr. par. *delaying;* past, *delayed:* s. *delay, delayer.*

DELEC'TABLE. *adj.* Pleasing, delightful. adv. *delectably.*

DEL'EGATE. *v.* To send upon an embassy; to intrust. pr. par. *delegating;* past, *delegated:* s. *delegate delegation.*

DELE'TE. *v.* To blot out. pr. par *deleting;* past, *deleted:* s. *deletion.* adj. *deletory.*

DELETE'RIOUS. *adj.* Deadly, destructive.

DELF, DELFT. *s.* Earthenware first made at Delft.

DELIB'ERATE. *v.* To think, in order to choose; to consider; to hesitate. pr. par. *deliberating,* past, *deliberated:* s. *deliberation, deliberateness, deliberator:* adj. *deliberate, deliberative:* adv. *deliberately.*

DEL'IBLE. *adj.* Capable of being destroyed, or effaced.

DEL'ICACY. *s.* Daintiness; pleasantness to the taste; softness; neatness. pl. *delicacies:* adj. *delicate:* adv *delicately:* s. *delicateness.*

DELI'CIOUS. *adj.* Sweet, delicate, delightful to the palate. adv. *deliciously:* s. *deliciousness.*

DELIGHT'. *v.* To please, to content, to afford pleasure. pr. par. *delighting;* past, *delighted:* s. *delight, delighter.*

DELIGHT'FUL. *adj.* Full of delight; charming. adv. *delightfully:* s. *delightfulness.*

DELIN'EAMENT. *s.* Painting; representation by delineation.

DELIN'EATE. *v.* To make the first draught; to design; to sketch. pr.

par. *delineating;* past, *delineated.* s. *delineation, delineator.*

DELIN'QUENCY. s. A fault, a misdeed. pl. *delinquencies:* s. *delinquent.*

DELIQ'UIDATE. v. To melt; to be dissolved. pr. par. *deliquidating;* past, *deliquidated.*

DELIR'IUM. s. Alienation of mind; dotage. adj. *delirious:* s. *deliriousness.*

DELIV'ER. v. To set free, to rescue, to release, to speak. pr. par. *delivering;* past, *delivered:* s. *deliverance, deliverer, delivery,* pl. *deliveries.*

DELL. s. A little dale.

DELU'DE. v. To beguile, to cheat, to disappoint. pr. par. *deluding;* past, *deluded:* s. *deluder:* adj. *deludable.*

DEL'UGE. s. A general inundation; calamitous state of lying entirely under water. v. *deluge;* pr. par. *deluging;* past, *deluged.*

DELU'SION. s. The act of deluding; state of being deluded; a cheat; guile; deceit. adj. *delusive, delusory.*

DELVE. v. To dig; to open the ground with a spade. pr. par. *delving;* past, *delved:* s. *delve, delver.*

DEM'AGOGUE. s. A ringleader of the rabble; a popular and factious orator.

DEMAND'. v. To claim; to ask with authority. pr. par. *demanding;* past, *demanded:* s. *demand, demander, demandant:* adj. *demandable.*

DEMARCA'TION. s. Division; separation of territory.

DEMEAN'. v. To behave; to lessen, to debase. pr. par. *demeaning;* past, *demeaned:* s. *demeanour.*

DEMEN'TATE. v. To deprive of reason; to make mad. pr. par. *dementating;* past, *dementated:* s. *dementation.*

DEMER'IT. s. The opposite to merit; want of merit.

DEME'SNE. s. That part of an estate which is occupied by the lord himself; the improved land around a mansion.

DEM'I. s. Half; one of two equal parts.

DEM'IGOD. s. In the heathen mythology, signifies the partaking of the divine nature; half a god.

DEMI'SE. v. To grant at one's death, to grant by will. pr. par. *demising,* past, *demised.*

DEMI'SE. s. Death, decease. Used only in relation to a crowned head, or to the crown itself.

DEMOC'RACY. s. Sovereign power lodged in the collective body of the people. pl. *democracies:* s. *democrat:* adj. *democratic, democratical:* adv. *democratically.*

DEMOL'ISH. v. To throw down; to raze; to destroy. pr. par. *demolishing;* past, *demolished:* s. *demolisher.*

DEMOLI'TION. s. The act of demolishing; destruction.

DE'MON. s. A spirit; generally an evil spirit, a devil. s. *demoniac:* adj. *demoniac, demoniacal.*

DEMONOL'ATRY. s. The worship of the devil.

DEMON'STRATE. v. To prove with the highest degree of certainty. pr. par. *demonstrating;* past, *demonstrated:* s. *demonstration, demonstrator:* adj. *demonstrable, demonstrative:* adv. *demonstratively.*

DEMOR'ALIZE. v. To destroy morals and moral feeling. pr. par. *demoralizing:* past, *demoralized:* s. *demoralization, demoralizer.*

DEMUR'. v. To delay a process in law, by formal objections; to hesitate. pr. par. *demurring;* past *demurred:* s. *demur, demurrer.*

DEMU'RE. adj. Sober, decent, grave. adv. *demurely:* s. *demureness.*

DEMUR'RAGE. s. An allowance made by freighters, to owners of ships, for their stay in a port beyond the time appointed.

DEMY'. s. A term relating to the size of paper.

98

DEN. *s.* A cavern or hollow under ground; the cave of a wild beast.

DENA'TIONALIZE. *v.* To take away national rights. pr. par. *denationalizing;* past, *denationalized.*

DENDROL'OGY. *s.* The natural history of trees. pl. *dendrologies.*

DEN'IZEN. *s.* A freeman; an alien invested with the rights of a citizen. s. *denization.*

DENOM'INATE. *v.* To name. pr. par. *denominating;* past, *denominated:* s. *denomination, denominator:* adj. *denominative.*

DENO'TE. *v.* To mark; to be a sign of; to betoken. pr. par. *denoting;* past, *denoted:* s. *denotement:* adj. *denotative.*

DENOU'EMENT. *s.* The discovery of the plot of a drama, or of any other work of the imagination.

DENOU'NCE. *v.* To threaten by proclamation. pr. par. *denouncing;* past, *denounced:* s. *denouncer.*

DENSE. adj. Close, compact, approaching to solidity. s. *density,* pl. *densities.*

DENT. *s.* A mark caused by a stroke or blow. adj. *dented.*

DEN'TAL. *adj.* Belonging to the teeth.

DENTIC'ULATED. *adj.* Set with small teeth, or prominences resembling the teeth of a saw.

DEN'TIFRICE. *s.* A powder made to clean the teeth.

DENT'IST. *s.* One who professes to heal the diseases of the teeth; one who dresses or who draws teeth.

DENU'DATE. *v.* To divest, to strip. pr. par. *denudating;* past, *denudated:* s. *denudation.*

DENU'DE. *v.* To strip; to make naked. pr. par. *denuding;* past, *denuded.*

DENUNCIA'TION. *s.* The act of denouncing. s. *denunciator.*

DENY'. *v.* To contradict, to refuse, to disown, to renounce. pr. par. *denying;* past, *denied:* s. *denial, denier:* adj. *deniable.*

DEOBSTRUCT'. *v.* To clear from obstruction. pr. par. *deobstructing;* past, *deobstructed:* s. *deobstruction.*

DE'ODAND. *s.* A thing given or forfeited to God, in case of any misfortune, by which a human being comes to a violent end, without the fault of any reasonable creature.

DEON'ERATE. *v.* To unload. pr par. *deonerating;* past, *deonerated*

DEPART'. *v.* To go away from a place; to quit; to leave. pr. par. *departing;* past, *departed:* s. *departure.*

DEPART'MENT. *s.* Separate allotment: province or business assigned to a particular person. adj *departmental.*

DEPEND'. *v.* To hang from; to be in a state of dependence. pr. par *depending;* past, *depended:* s. *dependence, dependency,* pl. *dependencies:* adj. and s. *dependent:* s *dependant.*

DEPICT'. *v.* To paint, to portray, to describe. pr. par. *depicting,* past, *depicted:* s. *depicter.*

DEPIC'TURE. *v.* To represent in colours. pr. par. *depicturing;* past, *depictured.*

DE'PILATE. *v.* To pull off hair pr. par. *depilating;* past, *depilated:* s. *depilation:* adj. *depilatory.*

DEPLE'TION. *s.* Act of emptying; state of being empty.

DEFLO'RE. *v.* To lament, to bewail, to mourn. pr. par. *deploring,* past, *deplored:* adj. *deplorable.* adv. *deplorably:* s. *deplorer, deplorableness.*

DEPLOY'. *v.* To display; a column of troops is deployed, when the divisions spread wide, or open out. pr. par. *deploying;* past, *deployed.*

DEPLU'ME. *v.* To strip of its feathers. pr. par. *depluming;* past, *deplumed.* s. *deplumation.*

DEPO'NENT. *s.* One that deposes his testimony; an evidence; a

99

witness; (in grammar) such verbs as have no active voice are called deponents. adj. *deponent.*

DEPOPULATE. *v.* To unpeople; to lay waste. pr. par. *depopulating;* past, *depopulated:* s. *depopulation, depopulator.*

DEPORT. *v.* To carry away; to demean, to behave. pr. par. *deporting;* past, *deported.*

DEPORTATION. *s.* Transportation; act of carrying beyond sea.

DEPORTMENT. *s.* Conduct, demeanour.

DEPOSE. *v.* To degrade from a throne; to testify. pr. par. *deposing;* past, *deposed:* s. *deposer, deposition.*

DEPOSIT. *v.* To lay up; to lodge in any place. pr. par. *depositing;* past, *deposited:* s. *deposit, depositary, depository,* pl. *depositaries, depositories.*

DEPOSITION. *s.* The act of deposing; written evidence.

DEPOT. *s.* A place in which stores are deposited, for the use of an army. pronounced, *de'po.*

DEPRAVE. *v.* To vitiate, to corrupt, to contaminate. pr. par. *depraving;* past, *depraved:* s. *depravation, depravement, depraver, depravedness, depravity,* pl. *depravities:* adv. *depravedly.*

DEPRECATE. *v.* To beg off; to avert by prayer. pr. par. *deprecating;* past, *deprecated:* s. *deprecation, deprecator:* adj. *deprecative, deprecatory.*

DEPRECIATE. *v.* To bring down to a lower price; to fall in value; to undervalue. pr. par. *depreciating;* past, *depreciated:* s. *depreciation.*

DEPREDATE. *v.* To rob, to pillage, to spoil. pr. par. *depredating;* past, *depredated:* s. *depredation, depredator.*

DEPRESS. *v.* To press or thrust down: to humble; to deject. pr. par *depressing;* past, *depressed:* s. *depression, depressor:* adj. *depressive.*

DEPRIVE. *v.* To bereave of a thing; to hinder. pr. par. *depriving;* past, *deprived:* s. *deprivation, depriver:* adj. *deprivable.*

DEPTH. *s.* Deepness; deep place, abstruseness, profundity.

DEPULSION. *s.* A driving or thrusting away. adj. *depulsory.*

DEPUTE. *v.* To send with a special commission. pr. par. *deputing;* past, *deputed:* s. *deputation.*

DEPUTY. *s.* A person deputed by another; a subordinate officer. pl. *deputies.*

DERANGE. *v.* To turn out of the proper course; to disorder. pr. par. *deranging;* past, *deranged:* s. *derangement.*

DERELICTION. *s.* The act of forsaking or leaving.

DERIDE. *v.* To laugh at, to mock. pr. par. *deriding;* past, *derided* s. *derider:* adv. *deridingly.*

DERISION. *s.* Act of deriding; contempt, scorn. adj. *derisive, derisory:* adv. *derisively.*

DERIVE. *v.* To deduce from its original; to descend from; to receive by transmission. pr. par *deriving;* past, *derived:* s. *derivation, deriver:* adj. *derivable, derivative:* adv. *derivatively.*

DEROGATE. *v.* To do an act so far contrary to a law or custom, as to diminish its former extent; to detract; to degenerate. pr. par. *derogating,* past, *derogated:* s. *derogation:* adj *derogative, derogatory:* adv. *derogatorily*

DERVIS. *s.* A Turkish priest or monk. pl. *dervises.*

DESCANT. *v.* To sing in parts; to discourse at large. pr. par. *descanting;* past, *descanted:* s. *descanter.*

DESCEND. *v.* To go downwards; to sink; to fall, in order of inheritance, to a successor. pr. par. *descending;* past, *descended:* s. *descendant, descent:* adj. *descendent.*

100

DESCEND'IBLE. *adj.* Such as may be descended; transmissible by inheritance. *s. descendibility,* pl. *descendibilities.*

DESCEN'SION. *s.* Act of descending. *adj. descensive.*

DESCRI'BE. *v.* To delineate, to mark out, to characterize. pr. par. *describing;* past, *described: s. describer.*

DESCRIP'TION. *s.* Act of describing; a sentence or passage in which any thing is described. *adj. descriptive.*

DESCRY'. *v.* To give notice of any thing suddenly discovered; to spy out at a distance; to detect. pr. par. *descrying;* past, *descried: s. descrier.*

DE'SECRATE. *v.* To divert from the purpose to which any thing was originally consecrated. pr. par. *desecrating;* past, *desecrated: s. desecration.*

DESERT'. *v.* To forsake, to abandon, to leave. pr. par. *deserting;* past, *deserted: s. deserter, desertion.*

DES'ERT. *s.* A wilderness, solitude. *adj. desert.*

DESE'RVE. *v.* To merit; to be worthy of reward. pr. par. *deserving;* past, *deserved: s. deserver:* adv. *deservedly, deservingly.*

DESIC'CATE. *v.* To dry up; to exhaust of moisture. pr. par. *desiccating;* past, *desiccated: s. desiccation: adj. desiccative.*

DESIDERA'TUM. *s.* Something which inquiry has not yet been able to ascertain, or discover; something desired. pl. *desiderata.*

DESIGN'. *v.* To purpose, to intend, to plan. pr. par. *designing;* past, *designed: s. design, designer:* adj. *designable:* adv. *designedly.*

DE'SIGNATE. *v.* To point out, to distinguish. pr. par. *designating;* past, *designated: s. designation:* adj. *designative.*

DESI'RE. *s.* Wish; eagerness to obtain or enjoy. *v. desire.* pr. par. *desiring;* past, *desired: s. desirer:* adj. *desirable, desirous:* adv. *desirously.*

DESIST'. *v.* To cease from; to stop. pr. par. *desisting;* past, *desisted.*

DESK. *s.* An inclining table, for the use of writers or readers.

DE'SOLATE. *v.* To deprive of inhabitants; to lay waste. pr. par. *desolating;* past, *desolated: s. desolation, desolater:* adj. *desolate:* adv. *desolately.*

DESPAI'R. *s.* Hopelessness, despondence. *v. despair;* pr. par. *despairing;* past, *despaired:* adj. *despairable: s. despairer:* adv. *despairingly.*

DESPATCH'. *v.* To send away hastily; to put to death; to perform quickly. pr. par. *despatching*, past, *despatched: s. despatch, despatcher.*

DESPERA'DO. *s.* One who is desperate, without fear of danger. pl. *desperadoes.*

DE'SPERATE. *adj.* Without hope; irretrievable, mad, furious. adv. *desperately: s. desperation.*

DE'SPICABLE. *adj.* Contemptible, vile, worthless. s. *despicableness:* adv. *despicably.*

DESPI'SE. *v.* To scorn, to contemn pr. par. *despising;* past, *despised s. despiser:* adj. *despisable.*

DESPI'TE. *s.* Malice, anger, malignity, defiance. adj. *despiteful:* adv *despitefully: s. despitefulness.*

DESPOIL'. *v.* To rob, to deprive, to strip. pr. par. *despoiling;* past, *despoiled: s. despoiler, despoliation.*

DESPOND'. *v.* To despair, to lose hope. pr. par. *desponding;* past, *desponded: s. despondency,* pl. *despondencies, desponder:* adj. *despondent:* adv. *despondingly.*

DES'POT. *s.* An absolute prince, one that governs with unlimited authority. adj. *despotic, despotical·* adv. *despotically: s. despotism.*

DESSERT', DESERT'. *s.* The fruit or sweetmeats set on the table after the meat. French pronunciation, *dessa'ir*.

DESTINA'TION. *s.* The purpose for which any thing is appointed: the ultimate design.

DES'TINE. *v.* To doom unalterably; to devote. pr. par. *destining;* past, *destined:* s. *destiny,* pl. *destinies.*

DES'TITUTE. *adj.* Forsaken, abandoned, abject. s. *destitution.*

DESTROY'. *v.* To overturn; to ruin; to lay waste; to kill. pr. par. *destroying;* past, *destroyed:* s. *destroyer.*

DESTRUC'TION. *s.* Act of destroying; state of being destroyed. adj. *destructible:* s. *destructibility,* pl. *destructibilities.*

DESTRUC'TIVE. *adj.* Having the quality of destroying; wasteful. adv. *destructively:* s. *destructiveness.*

DESUDA'TION. *s.* A profuse and inordinate sweating.

DE'SUETUDE. *s.* Cessation to be accustomed; discontinuance of practice or habit.

DESUL'TORY. *adj.* Roving from thing to thing; unsettled; wavering. s. *desultoriness.*

DETACH'. *v.* To separate, to disengage, to part from. pr. par. *detaching;* past, *detached;* s. *detachment.*

DETAIL'. *v.* To relate particularly, to display minutely. pr. par *detailing;* past, *detailed:* s. *detail, detailer.*

DETAIN.' *v.* To keep that which belongs to another; to withhold; to keep back. pr. par. *detaining;* past, *detained:* s. *detainer.*

DETECT'. *v.* To discover; to find out any crime or artifice. pr. par. *detecting;* past, *detected:* s. *detector, detection.*

DETEN'TION. *s.* The act of detaining.

DETER'. *v.* To discourage by terror. pr par. *deterring;* past, *deterred.*

DETERGE'. *v.* To cleanse. pr. par. *deterging;* past, *deterged;* adj. and s. *detergent.*

DETE'RIORATE. *v.* To impair, to make worse. pr. par. *deteriorating,* past, *deteriorated:* s. *deterioration*

DETER'MINATE. *adj.* Settled, definite; established; certain. adj *determinable:* adv. *determinately.* s. *determination.*

DETER'MINE. *v.* To fix, to settle, to conclude, to form a resolution. pr. par. *determining;* past, *determined.*

DETER'SION. *s.* The act of cleansing. adj. *detersive.*

DETEST'. *v.* To hate, to abhor. pr. par. *detesting;* past, *detested:* s. *detestation, detester:* adj. *detestable:* adv. *detestably.*

DETHRO'NE. *v.* To divest of regality; to depose. pr. par. *dethroning;* past, *dethroned:* s. *dethronement, dethroner.*

DE'TONATE. *v.* To make a noise like thunder. pr. par. *detonating,* past, *detonated:* s. *detonation.*

DETORT'. *v.* To wrest from the original import, meaning, or design. pr. par. *detorting;* past, *detorted:* s. *detortion.*

DETOU'R. *s.* A turning; a way about. v. *detour;* pr. par. *detouring;* past, *detoured.*

DETRACT'. *v.* To derogate; to take away, by envy, any thing from the reputation of another. pr par. *detracting;* past, *detracted:* s. *detraction, detractor:* adj. *detractive, detractory.*

DE'TRIMENT. *s.* Loss, damage, mischief. adj. *detrimental.*

DETRI'TION. *s.* The act of wearing away.

DETRU'DE. *v.* To thrust down, to force into a lower place. pr. par. *detruding;* past, *detruded:* s. *detrusion.*

DETRUN'CATE. *v.* To lop, to cut. pr. par. *detruncating;* past, *detruncated:* s. *detruncation.*

DEUCE. *s.* Two: a word used for a card or die with two spots.

102

DEUTERONOMY. *s.* The second book of the law; the fifth book of Moses.

DEVAS'TATE. *v.* To lay waste. pr. par. *devastating;* past, *devastated:* s. *devastation, devastator.*

DEVEL'OP. *v.* To disengage, to disentangle. pr. par. *developing;* past, *developed:* s. *development.*

DEVEST, DIVEST. *v.* To deprive of clothes, to strip, to annul. pr. par. *devesting;* past, *devested.*

DEVEX'IVY. *s.* Incurvation downwards, declivity. pl. *devexities.*

DE'VIATE. *v.* To wander from the right or common way; to err; to sin. pr. par. *deviating;* past, *deviated:* s. *deviation.*

DEVI'CE. *s.* A contrivance; a stratagem; a design; the emblem on a shield. adj. *deviceful:* adv. *devicefully.*

DEV'IL. *s.* The prince of hell. adj. *devilish:* adv. *devilishly:* s. *devilishness.*

DE'VIOUS. *adj.* Out of the common track; wandering; roving. adv. *deviously.*

DEVI'SE. *v.* To contrive, to invent, to plan; to grant by will. pr. par. *devising;* past, *devised:* adj. *devisable:* s. *devise, deviser.*

DEVISEE'. *s.* He to whom something is bequeathed by will.

DEVOCA'TION. *s.* A calling away; a seduction.

DEVOID'. *adj.* Empty, vacant, void.

DEVOI'R. *s.* Act of civility or obsequiousness.

DEVOLVE'. *v.* To roll down; to fall in succession, into new hands. pr. par. *devolving;* past, *devolved.*

DEVOLU'TION. *s.* The act of rolling down.

DEVO'TE. *v.* To dedicate, to consecrate, to appropriate by vow. pr. par. *devoting;* past, *devoted:* s. *devotedness, devotee, devoter.*

DEVO'TION. *s.* Act of devoting; the state of being consecrated or dedicated; prayer. adj. *devotional.*

DEVOUR'. *v.* To eat up ravenously, to destroy or consume with rapidity and violence. pr. par. *devouring;* past, *devoured:* s. *devourer:* adv. *devouringly.*

DEVOUT'. *adj.* Pious, religious. s. *devoutness:* adv. *devoutly.*

DEW. *v.* The moisture on the ground. adj. *dewy.*

DEW'BERRY. *s.* A species of fruit, resembling the blackberry. pl. *dewberries.*

DEW'LAP. *s.* The flesh that hangs down from the throats of oxen.

DEX'TER. *s.* The right; not the left: a term used in heraldry. adj. *dextral.*

DEXTER'ITY. *s.* Readiness of limbs; activity; readiness of contrivance. pl. *dexterities:* adj. *dextrous:* adv. *dextrously.*

DEY. *s.* The title of the supreme governor of Algiers, Tunis, and Tripoli.

DIABOL'ICAL, DIABOL'IC. *adj.* Devilish; partaking of the qualities of the devil; impious; atrocious. adv. *diabolically:* s. *diabolicalness.*

DI'ADEM. *s.* A tiara; an ensign of royalty bound about the head of eastern monarchs; a crown. adj. *diademed.*

DIÆ'RESIS. *s.* The separation or disjunction of syllables; the mark (··) of that separation. pl. *diæreses.*

DIA'GONAL. *adj.* Reaching from one angle to another, so as to divide a parallelogram into equal parts. adv. *diagonally.*

DI'AGRAM. *s.* A delineation of a geometrical figure.

DI'AL. *s.* A plate marked with lines, where a hand or shadow shows the hour. s. *dialist, dialing*

DI'ALECT. *s.* The subdivision of a language; style; manner of expression; language.

DIALEC'TICS. *s.* Logic; the art of reasoning. adj. *dialectic:* s. *dialectician.*

DIALOGUE. s. A conference; a conversation between two or more. adj. *dialogistic.*

DIAMETER. s. A right line which divides the area of a circle into two equal parts.

DIAMETRICAL. adj. Describing a diameter; crossing in the manner of a diameter; and hence denoting division or opposition. adv. *diametrically.*

DIAMOND. s. The most valuable and the hardest of all gems; pronounced *di'mund:* adj. *diamonded.*

DIAPA'SON. s. A cord which includes all tones; an octave.

DI'APER. s. Linen cloth, woven in flowers and other figures; the finest species of figured linen after damask.

DI'APHRAGM. s. The midriff, which divides the upper cavity of the body from the lower; any division or partition which divides a hollow body.

DIARRHŒT'IC. adj. Solutive, purgative.

DI'ARY. s. An account of the transactions and observations of every day; a journal. pl. *diaries:* s. *diarist.*

DI'ASTOLE. s. A figure in rhetoric, by which a short syllable is made long; the dilation of the heart.

DI'ASTYLE. s. A sort of edifice, where the pillars stand at so great a distance from one another, that three diameters of their thickness are allowed for intercolumniation.

DI'ATRIBE. s. A disputation, or continued discourse.

DIB'BLE. s. A small spade; a pointed instrument, with which gardeners make holes for planting. v. *dibble;* pr. par. *dibbling;* past, *dibbled.*

DICE. s. The plural of *die.*

DIC'TATE. v. To deliver to another with authority; to declare with confidence. pr. par. *dictating;* past, *dictated:* s. *dictate, dictation.*

DICTATOR. s. A magistrate appointed in time of exigence and danger, and invested with absolute authority; one who dictates. adj. *dictatorial,* adv. *dictatorially.* s. *dictatorship.*

DIC'TION. s. Style, language, expression.

DIC'TIONARY. s. A book containing the words of any language, in alphabetical order, with explanations of their meaning; a lexicon, a vocabulary. pl. *dictionaries.*

DID. v. The preterit of *do:* second person, *didst.*

DIDAC'TIC. adj. Preceptive; giving precepts.

DEDUC'TION. s. Separation, by withdrawing one part from the other.

DIE. v. To lose life, to expire. pr par. *dying;* past, *died.*

DIE. s. A small cube, marked on its faces with numbers from one to six, which gamesters throw in play. pl. *dice.*

DIE. s. The stamp used in coinage. pl. *dies.*

DI'ET. s. Food, provisions, victuals. v *diet;* pr. par. *dieting;* past, *dieted.*

DI'ET. s. An assembly of princes or estates.

DIF'FER. v. To be distinguished from; to contend; to be of a contrary opinion. pr. par. *differing,* past, *differed:* s. *difference:* adj. *different:* s. *differently.*

DIF'FICULT. adj. Hard, not easy, not facile, troublesome, vexatious. adv. *difficultly:* s. *difficulty,* pl. *difficulties.*

DIF'FIDENCE. s. Distrust; want of confidence; doubt. adj. *diffident.* adv. *diffidently.*

DIFFLU'ENCE, DIFFLU'ENCY. s. The quality of falling away on all sides; the effect of fluidity. pl. *diffluences, diffluencies:* adj. *diffluent.*

DIFFRANCH'ISEMENT. s. The act of taking away privileges.

DIFFU'SE. v. To pour out upon a

104

plane, so that the liquor may run every way; to spread; to scatter. pr. par. *diffusing*; past, *diffused*: adj. *diffuse, diffusive*: adv. *diffusely*: s. *diffuseness, diffuser, diffusion*.

DIFFU'SIBLE. *adj.* Capable of being diffused. s. *diffusibility*, pl. *diffusibilities*.

DIG. *v.* To pierce with a spade; to work with a spade. pr. par. *digging*; past, *dug*: s. *digger*.

DIGEST'. *v.* To distribute into various classes; to arrange methodically; to concoct in the stomach. pr. par. *digesting*; past, *digested*: s. *di'gest, digestion, digester*: adj. *digestible, digestive*.

DI'GIT. *s.* Three-fourths of an inch.

DIG'NIFY. *v.* To advance, to prefer, to exalt, to honour. pr. par. *dignifying*; past, *dignified*: s. *dignity*, pl. *dignities, dignification*.

DIG'NITARY. *s.* A clergyman advanced to some rank above that of a parochial priest. pl. *dignitaries*.

DIGRESS'. *v.* To turn aside out of the road; to deviate; to speak of something incidental. pr. par. *digressing*; past, *digressed*: s. *digression*: adj. *digressional, digressive*: adv. *digressively*.

DIKE, DYKE. *s.* A channel to receive water; a mound to hinder inundations. *v. dike*; pr. par. *diking*; past, *diked*.

DILA'CERATE. *v.* To tear, to rend. pr. par. *dilacerating*; past, *dilacerated*: s. *dilaceration*.

DILAP'IDATE. *v.* To go to ruin; to fall by decay. pr. par. *dilapidating*; past, *dilapidated*: s. *dilapidation, dilapidator*.

DILA''TE. *v.* To extend, to spread out, to enlarge. pr. par. *dilating*; past, *dilated*. s. *dilation, dilator*.

DIL'ATORY. *adj.* Tardy; slow; given to procrastination. adv. *dilatorily*: s. *dilatoriness*.

DILEM'MA. *s.* An argument equally conclusive by contrary suppositions; a difficult or doubtful choice.

DILETTA*N*'TE. *s.* One who delights in cultivating or promoting science.

DIL'IGENT. *adj.* Constant, in application; assiduous. s. *diligence*: adv. *diligently*.

DILU'CID. *adj.* Clear, not opaque. *v. dilucidate*; pr. par. *dilucidating*, past, *dilucidated*: s. *dilucidation*.

DILU'ENT. *adj.* Having the power to thin and attenuate other matter.

DILU'TE. *v.* To make thin, to make weak. pr. par. *diluting*; past, *diluted*: s. *diluter, dilution*.

DILU'VIAN. *adj.* Relating to the deluge.

DILU'VIATE. *v.* To run as a flood. pr. par. *diluviating*; past, *diluviated*.

DIM. *adj.* Not having a quick sight; obscure. *v. dim*; pr. par. *dimming*, past, *dimmed*: adv. *dimly*: s. *dimness*.

DIME. *s.* A silver coin of the United States, of the value of ten cents.

DIMEN'SION. *s.* Space contained in any thing; bulk; extent. adj. *dimensionless*.

DIMIN'ISH. *v.* To make less, to impair, to lessen. pr. par. *diminishing*; past, *diminished*.

DIMIN'UTIVE. *adj.* Small, little s. *diminution*: adv. *diminutively* s. *diminutiveness*

DIMIS'SION. *s.* Leave to depart. adj. *dimissory*.

DIM'ITY. *s.* A kind of fustian, or cloth of cotton. pl. *dimities*.

DIM'PLE. *s.* A little hole, as in the cheek. *v. dimple*; pr. par. *dimpling*; past, *dimpled*.

DIN. *s.* A loud noise; a violent and continued sound. *v. din*; pr. par. *dinning*; past, *dinned*.

DINE. *v.* To eat dinner. pr. par. *dining*; past, *dined*: s. *diner*.

DING. *v.* To dash with violence. pr. par. *dinging*; past, *dinged*.

DING'LE. *s.* A hollow between hills a dale.

DIN—DIR

DIN'GY. *adj.* Dark brown; dun; dirty. *s. dinginess.*

DIN'NER. *s.* The chief meal; the meal eaten about the middle of the day.

DINT. *s.* A blow, a stroke, violence, force. *v. dint;* pr. par. *dinting;* past, *dinted.*

DIO'CESAN, DIOCE'SAN. *s.* A bishop as he stands related to his own clergy or flock.

DI'OCESE, DI'OCESS. *s.* The circuit of a bishop's jurisdiction.

DIOP'TRIC. *adj.* Affording a medium for the sight; assisting the sight in the view of distant objects. *s. dioptric.*

DIP. *v.* To immerge; to put into any liquor; to moisten. pr. par. *dipping;* past, *dipped: s. dip, dipper.*

DIPET'ALOUS. *adj.* Having two flower-leaves.

DIPH'THONG. *s.* A coalition of two vowels, to form one sound; as in vain, leaf, Cæsar.

DIPLO'MA. *s.* A letter or writing conferring some privilege. *adj. diplomatic.*

DIPLO'MACY. *s.* A body of envoys or ambassadors. pl. *diplomacies:* adj. *diplomatic:* adv. *diplomatically.*

DIP'TOTE. *s.* A noun consisting only of two cases.

DIRE, DIR'EFUL. *adj.* Dreadful, dismal, mournful. *s. direfulness.*

DIRECT'. *adj.* Straight, not crooked, not oblique; (in astronomy) not retrograde; plain, express. adv. *directly.*

DIRECT'. *v.* To regulate, to adjust, to order, to command. pr. par. *directing;* past, *directed: s. directer, direction, directness, director.* adj. *directive.*

DIRECT'ORY. *s.* A book containing directions; an executive council. pl. *directories:* adj. *directorial.*

DIRGE. *s.* A mournful ditty; a song of lamentation.

DIR—DIS

DIRK. *s.* A kind of dagger, used in the Highlands of Scotland. *v. dirk;* pr. par. *dirking;* past, *dirked.*

DIRT. *s.* Excrement, mud, filth, mire. *v. dirty;* pr. par. *dirtying;* past, *dirtied:* adj. *dirty:* adv. *dirtily: s. dirtiness.*

DIRUP'TION. *s.* Bursting or breaking.

DISABIL'ITY. *s.* Want of power; weakness; legal impediment. pl. *disabilities.*

DISA'BLE. *v.* To deprive of force; to weaken; to impair. pr. par. *disabling;* past, *disabied.*

DISABU'SE. *v.* To set free from a mistake; to set right. pr. par. *disabusing;* past, *disabused.*

DISADVAN'TAGE. *s.* Loss; injury to interest. *v. disadvantage;* pr. par. *disadvantaging;* past, *disadvantaged:* adj. *disadvantageous:* adv. *disadvantageously: s. disadvantageousness.*

DISAFFECT'ED. *adj.* Not disposed to zeal or affection; disloyal. adv. *disaffectedly: s. disaffectedness, disaffection.*

DISAFFIRM'. *v.* To contradict. pr par. *disaffirming;* past, *disaffirmed: s. disaffirmance.*

DISAGREE'. *v.* To differ; to be in a state of opposition. pr. par. *disagreeing;* past, *disagreed: s. disagreement.*

DISAGREE'ABLE. *adj.* Contrary, unsuitable, unpleasing, offensive. *s. disagreeableness:* adv. *disagreeably.*

DISALLOW'. *v.* To deny authority, to consider unlawful; to censure. pr. par. *disallowing;* past, *disallowed: s. disallowance:* adj. *disallowable.*

DISAPPAR'EL. *v.* To disrobe. pr. par. *disappareling;* past, *disappareled.*

DISAPPE'AR. *v.* To be lost to view: to vanish out of sight. pr. par. *disappearing;* past, *disappeared:* s. *disappearance, disappearing.*

DISAPPOINT' *v.* To defeat of ex-

106

pectation; to deprive or bereave of any thing. pr. par. *disappointing;* past, *disappointed:* s. *disappointment.*

DISAPPRO'VE. *v.* To dislike, to censure. pr. par. *disapproving;* past, *disapproved:* s. *disapprobation, disapproval.*

DISARM'. *v.* To spoil or divest of arms. pr. par. *disarming;* past, *disarmed:* s. *disarmer.*

DISARRANGE'. *v.* To disorder, to unsettle. pr. par. *disarranging;* past, *disarranged:* s. *disarrangement.*

DISARRA Y'. *v.* To undress, to discomfit, to overthrow. pr. par. *disarraying;* past, *disarrayed.*

DISAS'TER. *s.* The blast or stroke of an unfavourable planet; misfortune; grief. adj. *disastrous:* adv. *disastrously:* s. *disastrousness.*

DISAVOUCH'. *v.* To retract profession; to disown. pr. par. *disavouching;* past, *disavouched.*

DISAVOW'. *v.* To disown, to deny knowledge of. pr. par. *disavowing;* past, *disavowed:* s. *disavowal, disavowment.*

DISBAND'. *v.* To dismiss from military service; to break up an army. pr. par. *disbanding;* past, *disbanded.*

DISBELIEVE'. *v.* Not to believe. pr. par. *disbelieving;* past, *disbelieved:* s. *disbelief, disbeliever.*

DISBUR'DEN, DISBUR'THEN. *v.* To ease of a burden; to unload. pr. par. *disburdening;* past, *disburdened.*

DISBURSE'. *v.* To spend or lay out money. pr. par. *disbursing;* past, *disbursed:* s. *disburser, disbursement.*

DISCARD'. *v.* To throw out of the hand such cards as are useless; to dismiss from service or employment. pr. par. *discarding:* past, *discarded.*

DISCERN'. *v.* To descry, to see. pr. par. *discerning;* past, *discerned:* s. *discerner, discernment:* adj. *discernable:* adv. *discerningly.*

DISCHARGE'. *v.* To disburden, to exonerate, to unload, to disembark, to dismiss. pr. par. *discharging,* past, *discharged:* s. *discharge, discharger.*

DISCI'PLE. *s.* A scholar; one who professes to receive instruction from another.

DIS'CIPLINE. *s.* Education, instruction, rule of government; military regulation. *v. discipline;* pr. par. *disciplining;* past, *disciplined:* s. *disciplinarian:* adj. *disciplinary.*

DISCLAIM'. *v.* To disown; to deny any knowledge of; to renounce. pr. par. *disclaiming;* past, *disclaimed:* s. *disclaimer.*

DISCLO'SE. *v.* To uncover, to open to reveal. pr. par. *disclosing;* past *disclosed:* s. *discloser, disclosure.*

DISCOL'OUR. *v.* To change from the natural hue; to stain. pr. par. *discolouring;* past, *discoloured:* s. *discoloration.*

DISCOM'FIT. *v.* To defeat, to conquer, to vanquish. pr. par. *discomfiting;* past, *discomfited:* s. *discomfiture.*

DISCOM'FORT. *s.* Uneasiness, sorrow, melancholy. *v. discomfort.* pr. par. *discomforting;* past, *discomforted.*

DISCOMPO'SE. *v.* To disorder, to unsettle, to offend, to fret, to vex. pr. par. *discomposing;* past, *discomposed:* s. *discomposure.*

DISCONCERT'. *v.* To unsettle the mind, to discompose, to defeat a machination. pr. par. *disconcerting;* past, *disconcerted.*

DISCONNECT'. *v.* To break the ties. pr. par. *disconnecting;* past, *disconnected:* s. *disconnection.*

DISCON'SOLATE. adj. Void of comfort; hopeless; sorrowful. adv. *disconsolately:* s. *disconsolateness, disconsolation.*

DISCONTENT'. *s.* Want of content, uneasiness. *v. discontent;* pr. par. *discontenting;* past, *discontented:* adj. *discontented:* adv. *discontent-*

107

edly: *s.* *discontentedness, discontentment.*

DISCONTIN'UE. *v.* To lose the cohesion of parts; to lose an established custom or right. pr. par. *discontinuing;* past, *discontinued: s. discontinuance, discontinuation, discontinuer.*

DISCONTINU'ITY. *s.* Disunity of parts. pl. *discontinuities:* adj. *discontinuous.*

DIS'CORD. *s.* Disagreement, opposition, mutual anger, a combination of disagreeing sounds. *s. discordance, discordancy,* pl. *discordancies:* adj. *discordant:* adv. *discordantly.*

DIS'COUNT. *s.* The sum refunded in a bargain; an allowance made on a bill, or any other debt, not yet due, in order to receive money for the same. *v. discount;* pr. par. *discounting;* past, *discounted.*

DISCOUNT'ENANCE. *v.* To discourage by cold treatment; to abash. pr. par. *discountenancing;* past, *discountenanced:* s. *discountenancer.*

DISCOUR'AGE. *v.* To depress, to deprive of confidence, to deter. pr. par. *discouraging;* past, *discouraged:* s. *discourager, discouragement.*

DISCOURSE'. *s.* Conversation; mutual intercourse of language; speech; a treatise; a dissertation. *v. discourse;* pr. par. *discoursing;* past, *discoursed:* s. *discourser:* adj. *discoursive.*

DISCOUR'TEOUS. *adj.* Uncivil, uncomplaisant. adv. *discourteously.*

DISCOV'ER. *v.* To show, to disclose, to make visible, to detect. pr. par. *discovering;* past, *discovered:* s. *discovery,* pl. *discoveries, discoverer:* adj. *discoverable.*

DISCRED'IT. *s.* Ignominy, reproach, disgrace, want of trust. *v. discredit;* pr. par. *discrediting;* past, *discredited:* adj. *discreditable.*

DISCRE'ET. *adj.* Prudent, circumspect, cautious, modest. adv. *discreetly:* s. *discreetness.*

DISCREP'ANCY. *s.* Difference, contrariety. pl. *discrepancies:* adj *discrepant.*

DISCRE'TION. *s.* Prudence; knowledge to govern or direct one's self; wise management. adj. *discretional.*

DISCRE'TIVE. *adj.* Separate, distinct.

DISCRIM'INATE. *v.* To distinguish by certain tokens; to select; to separate; to sever. pr. par. *discriminating;* past, *discriminated: s. discrimination, discriminator.* adv. *discriminately:* adj. *discriminative.*

DISCUR'SIVE. *adj.* Moving here and there; roving; desultory adj. *discursively:* s. *discursiveness.*

DISCUR'SORY. *adj.* Argumental, rational.

DIS'CUS. *s.* A quoit; a heavy piece of iron, thrown in the ancient sports.

DISCUSS'. *v.* To examine, to clear by disquisition. pr. par. *discussing,* past, *discussed:* s. *discussion, discusser.*

DISCU'TIENT. *s.* A medicine that has the power to repel or drive back the matter of tumours in the blood.

DISDAIN'. *v.* To scorn, to think unworthy. pr. par. *disdaining;* past, *disdained:* s. *disdain, disdainfulness:* adj. *disdainful:* adv. *disdainfully.*

DISEASE'. *s.* Distemper, malady, uneasiness. adj. *diseased.*

DISEMBARK'. *v.* To carry to land; to go on shore. pr. par. *disembarking;* past, *disembarked:* s. *disembarkation.*

DISEMBAR'RASS. *v.* To free from embarrassment. pr. par. *disembarrassing;* past, *disembarrassed* s. *disembarrassment.*

DISEMBAY'. v. To clear from the bay. pr. par. *disembaying;* past, *disembayed.*

DISEMBO'DY. v. To free from the body; to discharge from military incorporation. pr. par. *disembodying;* past, *disembodied.*

DISEMBOGUE'. v. To pour out at the mouth of a river; to vent; to eject. pr. par. *disemboguing;* past, *disembogued.*

DISEMBOW'EL. v. To take out the bowels. pr. par. *disemboweling;* past, *disemboweled.*

DISENCUM'BER. v. To discharge from encumbrances; to disburthen, pr. par. *disencumbring;* past, *disencumbred:* s. *disencumbrance.*

DISENGAGE'. v. To disentangle; to clear from impediments or difficulties; to separate. pr. par. *disengaging;* past, *disengaged:* s. *disengagement.*

DISENNO'BLE. v. To deprive of that which ennobles. pr. par. *disennobling;* past, *disennobled.*

DISENTAN'GLE. v. To set free from impediments; to disengage; to separate. pr. par. *disentangling;* past, *disentangled:* s. *disentanglement.*

DISENTHRAL'. v. To set free; to restore to liberty. pr. par. *disenthralling;* past, *disenthralled:* s. *disenthralment.*

DISENTHRO'NE. v. To depose from sovereignty. pr. par. *disenthroning;* past, *disenthroned.*

DISESTEEM'. s. Slight regard.

DISESTIMA'TION. s. Disrespect, disesteem.

DISFA'VOUR. s. Discountenance, unpropitious regard. v. *disfavour;* pr. par. *disfavouring;* past, *disfavoured:* s. *disfavourer.*

DISFIG'URE. v. To change to a worse form; to deform; to mangle. pr. par. *disfiguring;* past, *disfigured:* s. *disfiguration.*

DISFRANCH'ISE. v. To deprive of privileges or immunities. pr. par. *disfranchising;* past, *disfranchised:* s. *disfranchisement.*

DISGORGE'. v. To discharge by the mouth. pr. par. *disgorging;* past, *disgorged:* s. *disgorgement.*

DISGRA'CE. s. State of being out of favour; dishonour; cause of shame. v. *disgrace;* pr. par. *disgracing;* past, *disgraced:* adj. *disgraceful:* adv. *disgracefully.* s. *disgracer, disgracefulness.*

DISGUI'SE. v. To conceal by an unusual dress; to hide by a counterfeit appearance. pr. par. *disguising;* past, *disguised:* s. *disguise, disguisement, disguiser.*

DISGUST'. s. Aversion of the palate to any thing; ill-humour; malevolence. v. *disgust;* pr. par. *disgusting;* past, *disgusted:* adv. *disgustingly.*

DISH. s. A broad, wide vessel, in which food is served up at the table. pl. *dishes:* v. *dish;* pr. par. *dishing;* past, *dished.*

DISHABILLE'. s. Undress, loose dress.

DISHEART'EN. v. To discourage, to deject, to terrify, to depress. pr. par. *disheartening;* past, *disheartened.*

DISHER'IT. v. To cut off from hereditary succession, to debar from an inheritance. pr. par. *disheriting;* past, *disherited:* s. *disheritance.*

DISHER'ISON. s. The act of debarring from inheritance; disheriting.

DISHEV'EL. v. To spread the hair disorderly. pr. par. *disheveling,* past, *disheveled.*

DISHON'EST. adj. Void of probity; faithless; wicked; fraudulent. adv. *dishonestly:* s. *dishonesty,* pl. *dishonesties.*

DISHON'OUR. s. Reproach, disgrace, ignominy. v. *dishonour;* pr. par. *dishonouring;* past, *dishonoured:* adj. *dishonourable:* adv *dishonourably:* s. *dishonourer.*

DISINCAR'CERATE. *v.* To set at liberty; to free from prison. pr. par. *disincarcerating;* past, *disincarcerated.*

DISINCLI'NE. *v.* To produce dislike to. pr. par. *disinclining;* past, *disinclined:* s. *disinclination.*

DISINGEN'UOUS.*adj.* Unfair; meanly artful; cunning; illiberal. adv. *disingenuously:* s. *disingenuousness.*

DISINHER'IT. *v.* To cut off from an hereditary right; to deprive of an inheritance. pr. par. *disinheriting;* past, *disinherited.*

DISINTER'. *v.* To unbury; to take, as out of the grave. pr. par. *disinterring;* past, *disinterred:* s. *disinterment.*

DISINTEREST'ED. *adj.* Superior to regard of private advantage; without any concern in an affair. adv. *disinterestedly:* s. *disinterestedness.*

DISJOIN'. *v.* To separate; to part from each other; to sunder. pr. par. *disjoining;* past, *disjoined.*

DISJOINT'. *v.* To put out of joint; to break into pieces. pr. par. *disjointing;* past, *disjointed:* adv. *disjointly.*

DISJUNCT'. *adj.* Disjoined, separate. s. *disjunction:* adj. and s. *disjunctive:* adv. *disjuncily.*

DISK. *s.* The face of the sun, or of any planet, as it appears to the eye; a quoit.

DISLI'KE. *v.* To disapprove, to regard without affection. pr. par. *disliking;* past, *disliked:* s. *dislike, disliker.*

DISLI'KEN. *v.* To make unlike. pr. par. *dislikening;* past, *dislikened.*

DIS'LOCATE. *v.* To put out of the proper place; to put out of joint; to disjoint. pr. par. *dislocating;* past, *dislocated:* s. *dislocation.*

DISLODGE'. *v.* To remove from a place, to remove from a habitation. pr. par. *dislodging;* past, *dislodged.*

DISLOY'AL. *adj.* Not true to allegiance; faithless; dishonest. adv. *disloyally:* s. *disloyalty,* pl. *disloyalties.*

DIS'MAL. *adj.* Sorrowful, dire, horrid, melancholy. adv. *dismally:* s. *dismalness.*

DISMAN'TLE. *v.* To deprive of a dress; to strip; to denude. pr. par. *dismantling;* past, *dismantled.*

DISMASK'. *v.* To divest of a mask. pr. par. *dismasking;* past, *dismasked.*

DISMAY'. *v.* To terrify, to discourage, to depress, to deject. pr. par. *dismaying;* past, *dismayed:* s. *dismay.*

DISMEM'BER. *v.* To divide member from member; to cut into pieces. pr. par. *dismembering;* past, *dismembered:* s. *dismemberment.*

DISMISS'. *v.* To send away, to discard, to divest of an office. pr par. *dismissing;* past, *dismissed:* s. *dismissal, dismission:* adj. *dismissive.*

DISMOUNT'. *v.* To throw off a horse; to alight from a horse; to throw from any elevation or place of honour. pr. par. *dismounting,* past, *dismounted.*

DISOBE'DIENCE. *s.* Violation of lawful command or prohibition; breach of duty due to superiors adj. *disobedient:* adv. *disobediently.*

DISOBEY'. *v.* To break commands, or transgress prohibitions. pr. par. *disobeying;* past, *disobeyed.*

DISOBLIGA'TION. *s.* Act of disobliging. adj. *disobligatory.*

DISOBLI'GE. *v.* To refuse an act of convenience; to offend. pr. par. *disobliging;* past, *disobliged:* s. *disobliger, disobligingness:* adv. *disobligingly.*

DISOR'DER. *s.* Want of regular disposition; irregularity; confusion; tumult. v. *disorder;* pr. par. *disordering;* past, *disordered:* adv. *disorderly.*

DISOR'GANIZE. *v.* To break into pieces; to destroy the order of. pr. par. *disorganizing;* past, *disorganized:* s. *disorganization.*

DISOWN'. *v.* To deny, to renounce. pr. par. *disowning;* past, *disowned.*

DISPAR'AGE. *v.* To match unequally; to treat with contempt. pr. par. *disparaging;* past, *disparaged:* s. *disparagement, disparager:* adv. *disparagingly.*

DISPAR'ITY. *s.* Inequality; difference in rank or excellence. pl. *disparities.*

DISPART'. *v.* To divide, to separate. pr. par. *disparting;* past, *disparted.*

DISPAS'SIONATE. *adj.* Cool, calm, impartial. adv. *dispassionately.*

DISPATCH'. *v.* See DESPATCH.

DISPEL'. *v.* To drive, by scattering; to dissipate. pr. par. *dispelling;* past, *dispelled:* s. *dispeller.*

DISPEN'SARY. *s.* The place where medicines are dispensed. pl. *dispensaries.*

DISPENSA'TOR. *s.* One employed in dealing out any thing, a distributer.

DISPENSE'. *v.* To deal out, to distribute, to excuse. pr. par. *dispensing;* past, *dispensed:* s. *dispenser, dispensation:* adj. *dispensative, dispensable* adv. *dispensatively.*

DISPEO'PLE. *v.* To depopulate, to empty of people. pr. par. *dispeopling;* past, *dispeopled.*

DISPERSE'. *v.* To scatter, to dissipate, to distribute. pr. par. *dispersing;* past, *dispersed:* adv. *dispersedly:* s. *dispersedness, disperser, dispersion:* adj. *dispersive.*

DISPIR'IT. *v.* To discourage, to deject, to depress. pr. par. *dispiriting,* past, *dispirited.*

DISPLA'CE. *v.* To put out of place; to disorder. pr. par. *displacing;* past, *displaced.*

DISPLANT'. *v.* To remove a plant; to drive a people from their residence. pr. par. *displanting;* past, *displanted:* s. *displantation.*

DISPLAY'. *v.* To spread wide; to exhibit to the sight or mind; to open. pr. par. *displaying;* past, *displayed:* s. *display, displayer.*

DISPLEA'SE. *v.* To offend, to make angry, to make sad. pr. par *displeasing;* past, *displeased:* s. *displeasingness.*

DISPLEAS'URE. *s.* Uneasiness; pain received; offence; anger; indignation.

DISPLU'ME. *v.* To strip of feathers pr. par. *displuming;* past, *displumed.*

DISPORT'. *v.* To divert. pr. par. *disporting;* past, *disported.*

DISPO'SE. *v.* To give, to place, to bestow, to frame the mind, to appropriate. pr. par. *disposing;* past, *disposed:* s *disposal, disposer:* adj. *disposable.*

DISPOSI'TION. *s.* Act of disposing; order; distribution; method; temper of mind.

DISPOSSESS'. *v.* To put out of possession; to deprive of. pr. par. *dispossessing;* past, *dispossessed:* s. *dispossession.*

DISPRAI'SE. *s.* Blame, censure, dishonour. *v. dispraise;* pr. par. *dispraising;* past, *dispraised:* s. *dispraiser:* adj. *dispraisable:* adv. *dispraisingly.*

DISPROF'IT. *s.* Loss, damage, detriment. *v. disprofit;* pr. par. *disprofiting;* past, *disprofited.*

DISPROOF'. *s.* Confutation.

DISPROPOR'TION. *s.* Want of symmetry; disparity. *v. disproportion,* pr. par. *disproportioning;* past, *disproportioned:* adj. *disproportional, disproportionate:* adv. *disproportionally, disproportionately:* s. *disproportionateness.*

DISPRO'VE. *v.* To confute an assertion; to disapprove; to disallow. pr. par. *disproving;* past, *disproved:* s. *disprover.*

DISPU'TE. *v.* To contend by argument; to debate. pr. par. *disputing;* past, *disputed:* s. *dispute, disputer, disputant:* adj. *disputable.*

111

DISPUTA'TION. *s.* Act of disputing; argumentation. *adj. disputatious, disputative.*

DISQUAL'IFY. *v.* To make unfit; to disable by some natural or legal impediment. pr. par. *disqualifying;* past, *disqualified:* s. *disqualification.*

DISQUI'ET. *s.* Uneasiness, restlessness, vexation, anxiety. *v. disquiet;* pr. par. *disquieting;* past, *disquieted:* s. *disquieter, disquietude.*

DISREGARD'. *s.* Slight notice, neglect, contempt. *v. disregard;* pr. par. *disregarding;* past, *disregarded:* s. *disregarder:* adj. *disregardful:* adv. *disregardfully.*

DISREL'ISH. *s.* Bad taste; dislike of the palate. *v. disrelish;* pr. par. *disrelishing;* past, *disrelished.*

DISREPU'TE. *s.* Ill character; dishonour; want of reputation. *s. disreputation:* adj. *disreputable.*

DISRESPECT'. *s.* Incivility; want of reverence. *v. disrespect;* pr. par. *disrespecting;* past, *disrespected:* adj. *disrespectful:* adv. *disrespectfully.*

DISRO'BE. *v.* To undress, to uncover, to strip. pr. par. *disrobing;* past, *disrobed:* s. *disrober.*

DISRUP'TION. *s.* The act of breaking asunder; breach; rent.

DISSATISFAC'TION. *s.* The state of being dissatisfied; discontent. adj. *dissatisfatory.*

DISSAT'ISFY. *v.* To discontent, to displease. pr par. *dissatisfying;* past, *dissatisfied.*

DISSECT'. *v.* To cut into pieces; to divide and examine minutely. pr. par. *dissecting;* past, *dissected:* s. *dissection, dissector.*

DISSEIZE'. *v.* To dispossess of a freehold; to deprive. pr. par. *disseizing;* past, *disseized:* s. *disseizin, disseizor.*

DISSEM'BLE. *v.* To hide under a false appearance; to pretend that not to be, which is so. pr. par. *dissembling* past, *dissembled:* s. *dissemblance, dissembler:* adv. *dissemblingly.*

DISSEM'INATE. *v.* To scatter as seed; to sow; to spread every way. pr. par. *disseminating;* past, *disseminated:* s. *dissemination, disseminator.*

DISSENT'. *v.* To disagree in opinion; to differ. pr. par. *dissenting;* past, *dissented:* s. *dissent.*

DISSEN'SION. *s.* Act of dissenting; disagreement; strife. adj. *dissentious.*

DISSENTA'NEOUS. *adj.* Disagreeable, contrary. adv. *dissentaneously.*

DISSENT'ER. *s.* One that disagrees from an opinion; one who refuses the communion of the English church. adj. *dissentient.*

DISSERT'. *v.* To discourse, to dispute. pr. par. *disserting;* past, *disserted:* s. *dissertation, dissertator.*

DISSERVE'. *v.* To do injury to; to hurt. pr. par. *disserving;* past, *disserved:* s. *disservice:* adj. *disserviceable.*

DISSEV'ER. *v.* To part in two; to divide. pr. par. *dissevering;* past, *dissevered:* s. *disseverance.*

DISSIM'ILAR. *adj.* Unlike, heterogeneous. s. *dissimilarity,* pl. *dissimilarities.*

DISSIMIL'ITUDE. *s.* Unlikeness, want of resemblance.

DISSIMULA'TION. *s.* The act of dissembling; hypocrisy.

DIS'SIPATE. *v.* To scatter every way; to disperse; to live intemperately. pr. par. *dissipating;* past, *dissipated:* s. *dissipation.*

DISSO'CIATE. *v.* To separate, to disunite. pr. par. *dissociating,* past, *dissociated:* s. *dissociation.*

DISSOL'UBLE. *adj.* Capable of being dissolved. s. *dissolubility,* pl. *dissolubilities.*

DIS'SOLUTE. *adj.* Loose, wanton, unrestrained. adv. *dissolutely:* s. *dissoluteness.*

DISSOLU'TION. *s.* The act of dissolving; destruction, by the separation of parts; death.

DISSOLVE'. *v.* To melt, to liquefy, to break. pr. par. *dissolving;* past, *dissolved:* s. *dissolver:* adj. *dissolvable, dissolvent.*

DIS'SONANCE, DIS'SONANCY. *s.* A mixture of harsh, unpleasing, unharmonious sounds. pl. of *dissonancy, dissonancies.* adj. *dissonant.*

DISSUADE'. *v.* To dehort, to divert by reason or importunity. pr. par. *dissuading;* past, *dissuaded.*

DISSUA'SIVE. *adj.* Dehortatory; tending to dissuade. s. *dissuader, dissuasion.*

DISSYLLA'BIC. *adj.* Consisting of two syllables.

DIS'SYLLABLE. *s.* A word of two syllables.

DIS'TAFF. *s.* The staff from which the material is drawn, in spinning.

DIS'TANCE. *s.* Space, considered barely in length, between any two places; contrariety; opposition; respect. v. *distance;* pr. par. *distancing;* past, *distanced:* adj. *distant:* adv. *distantly.*

DISTASTE'. *s.* Aversion of the palate; disrelish; dislike. adj. *distasteful.*

DISTEM'PER. *s.* A disproportionate mixture of parts; a disease; a disorder; a term used, when colours are worked up with something besides mere water or oil. v. *distemper;* pr. par. *distempering;* past, *distempered:* s. *distemperance, distemperature.*

DISTEND'. *v.* To stretch out in breadth. pr. par. *distending;* past, *distended.*

DISTEN'TION. *s.* The act of distending; breadth. adj. *distent.*

DIS'TICH. *s.* A couplet, a couple of lines.

DISTIL'. *v.* To drop; to fall by drops; to flow gently and silently. pr. par. *distilling;* past, *distilled:* s. *distillation, distiller:* adj. *distillable.*

K 2

DISTIL'LERY. *s.* The place where any thing is distilled. pl. *distilleries.*

DISTINCT'. *adj.* Different, separate, clear, specified. adv. *distinctly.*

DISTINC'TION. *s.* The act of distinguishing; difference; discrimination; honourable note of superiority. adj. *distinctive:* adv. *distinctively:* s. *distinctiveness.*

DISTING'UISH. *v.* To note by the diversity of things; to separate by some mark of honour or preference; to judge; to make known or eminent. pr. par. *distinguishing;* past, *distinguished:* adj. *distinguishable:* s. *distinguisher.*

DISTORT'. *v.* To writhe; to twist; to deform by irregular motions; to wrest from the true meaning. pr. par. *distorting;* past, *distorted:* s. *distortion.*

DISTRACT'. *v.* To pull different ways at once; to divide, to perplex, to derange. pr. par. *distracting;* past, *distracted:* adv. *distractedly:* s. *distractedness, distraction.*

DISTRAIN'. *v.* To seize; to lay hold on, as an indemnification for debt. pr. par. *distraining;* past, *distrained:* s. *distrainer.*

DISTRESS'. *s.* The act of making a legal seizure; calamity; misery; misfortune. v. *distress;* pr. par. *distressing;* past, *distressed:* adj. *distressful:* adv. *distressfully.*

DISTRIB'UTE. *v.* To divide amongst more than two; to deal out. pr. par. *distributing;* past, *distributed:* s. *distributer, distribution:* adj. *distributive:* adv. *distributively.*

DIS'TRICT. *s.* The circuit or territory within which a man may be compelled to appearance; province, region.

DISTRUST'. *v.* To regard with diffidence; not to trust. pr. par. *distrusting;* past, *distrusted:* s. *distrust, distrustfulness:* adj. *distrustful, distrustless:* adv. *distrustfully.*

113

DISTURB'. *v.* To put into irregular motions; to perplex; to disquiet. pr. par. *disturbing;* past, *disturbed:* s. *disturbance, disturber.*

DISU"'ON. *s.* Separation, disjunction, breach of concord.

DISUNI'TE. *v.* To separate, to divide. to fall asunder. pr. par. *disuniting;* past, *disunited:* s. *disuniter.*

DISU SE. *s.* Cessation of use; desuetude. v. *disuse;* pr. par. *disusing;* past, *disused:* s. *disusage.*

DITCH. *s.* A trench cut in the ground, usually between fields; any long, narrow receptacle of water. pl. *ditches:* v. *ditch;* pr. par. *ditching;* past, *ditched:* s. *ditcher.*

DITHYRAM'BIC. *adj.* Wild, enthusiastic.

DIT'TANY. *s.* An herb.

DIT'TO. *s.* A word in the accounts of tradesmen, signifying "the same."

DIT'TY. *s.* A poem to be sung; a song. pl. *ditties.*

DIURET'IC. *adj.* Having the power to provoke urine.

DIUR'NAL. *adj.* Relating to the day; daily; quotidian. adv. *diurnally:* s. *diurnalist.*

DIVAN'. *s.* The council of the oriental princes.

DIVE. *v.* To sink voluntarily under water; to go deep into any question, doctrine, or science. pr. par. *diving;* past, *dived:* s. *diver.*

DIVERGE'. *v.* To tend various ways from one point. pr. par. *diverging;* past, *diverged:* s. *divergence:* adj. *divergent.*

DI'VERS. *adj.* Several, sundry.

DIVERSE'. *adj.* Different from another; various; multiform. adv. *diversely.*

DIVER'SIFY. *v.* To make different; to vary; to variegate. pr. par. *diversifying;* past, *diversified:* s. *diversification.*

DIVER'SION. *s.* The act of turning any thing off from its course; sport; something that unbends the mind by turning it from care.

DIVER'SITY. *s.* Difference, dissimilitude, variety, variegation. pl. *diversities.*

DIVERT'. *v.* To turn off from any direction; to withdraw the mind from; to please. pr. par. *diverting,* past, *diverted:* s. *diverter.*

DIVER'TISEMENT. *s.* Diversion, delight, pleasure, a musical composition.

DIVEST'. *v.* To strip, to make naked. pr. par. *divesting;* past, *divested.*

DIVI'DE. *v.* To separate; to part one whole into different pieces; to give in shares. pr. par. *dividing,* past, *divided:* s. *divider:* adv. *dividedly:* adj. *dividual.*

DIV'IDEND. *s.* The number to be divided; a share; the part allotted in division.

DIVI'NE. *adj.* Partaking of the nature of God; excellent in a supreme degree.

DIVI'NE. *s.* A minister of the Gospel; a priest; a clergyman; a theologian.

DIVI'NE. *v.* To foretel; to utter prognostication. pr. par. *divining,* past, *divined:* adv. *divinely:* s. *divineness, diviner, divination:* adj. *divinatory.*

DIVIN'ITY. *s.* Participation of the nature and excellence of God; deity; godhead; God, the Deity. pl. *divinities.*

DIVIS'ION. *s.* The act of dividing; partition; distinction; disunion. adj. *divisible:* s. *divisor.*

DIVORCE'. *s.* The legal separation of husband and wife. v. *divorce,* pr. par. *divorcing;* past, *divorced.* s. *divorcer.*

DIVULGE'. *v.* To publish; to reveal to the world. pr. par. *divulging;* past, *divulged:* s. *divulger.*

DIVUL'SION. *s.* Plucking away; laceration. adj. *divulsive.*

DIZ'ZY. *adj.* Giddy, vertiginous, whirling. v. *dizzy;* pr. par. *dizzying;* past, *dizzied:* s. *dizziness.*

DO. *v.* To act or behave in any manner, well or ill; to make an end; to conclude. pr. par. *doing;* past, *done:* s. *doer.*

DOAT. *v.* See DOTE.

DO'CILE. *adj.* Teachable; easily instructed. s. *docility,* pl. *docilities.*

DOCK. *s.* A species of weed.

DOCK. *s.* A place where water is let in or out at pleasure, where ships are built, or laid up.

DOCK. *v.* To cut off a tail, to cut any thing short. pr. par. *docking;* past, *docked.*

DOCK'ET. *s.* A direction tied upon goods; a summary of a larger writing; a list of cases in court.

DOCK'-YARD. *s.* A place or yard where ships are built, and naval stores deposited.

DOC'TOR. *s.* One that has taken the highest degree in the faculties of divinity, law, physic, or music; a physician. v. *doctor;* pr. par. *doctoring;* past, *doctored:* s. fem. *doctoress.*

DOC'TRINE. *s.* The principles or positions of any sect or master. adj. *doctrinal:* adv. *doctrinally.*

DOC'UMENT. *s.* Precept, instruction, direction; a written evidence, a record. adj. *documental, documentary.*

DODGE. *v.* To use craft; to shift place, as another approaches. pr. par. *dodging;* past, *dodged:* s. *dodger.*

DOE. *s.* A female deer; the female of a buck.

DOES. *v.* The third person from *do,* synonymous with *doth.*

DOG. *s.* A well known domestic animal. v. *dogging;* past, *dogged.*

DOG'DAYS. *s.* The days in which the dog-star rises and sets with the sun.

DOGE. *s.* The title of the chief magistrate of Venice and Genoa.

DOG'GED. *adj* Sullen, sour, morose. adv. *doggedly:* s. *doggedness.*

DOG'GER. *s.* A small ship, with one mast.

DOG'GREL. *adj.* Loosed from the measures or rules of regular poetry; vile, despicable. s. *doggrel.*

DOG'-KENNEL. *s.* A little hut or house for dogs.

DOG'MA. *s.* Established principle; doctrinal notion. adj. *dogmatic, dogmatical:* adv. *dogmatically:* s. *dogmatism, dogmatist.*

DOG'MATIZE. *v.* To assert positively. pr. par. *dogmatizing;* past, *dogmatized:* s. *dogmatizer.*

DOI'LY. *s.* A species of woollen stuff; the name of a small napkin placed on our tables, after dinner. pl. *doilies.*

DO'INGS. *s.* Things done; events, transactions; feats, actions.

DOIT. *s.* A small piece of money.

DOLE. *v.* To deal, to distribute. pr. par. *doling;* past, *doled:* s. *dole.*

DOLE'FUL. *adj.* Sorrowful, dismal, melancholy. adv. *dolefully:* s *dolefulness.*

DOLL. *s.* A contraction of Dorothy a little girl's puppet or baby.

DOL'LAR. *s.* A silver coin of different value; equal to four shillings and six-pence, British.

DOLORIF'IC. *adj.* Causing grief or pain.

DO'LOROUS. *adj.* Sorrowful, doleful, dismal. adv. *dolorously.*

DOL'PHIN. *s.* A kind of fish.

DOLT. *s.* A heavy, stupid fellow a blockhead. adj. *doltish:* s. *doltishness.*

DOMAIN'. *s.* Dominion, empire possession, estate.

DOME. *s.* A building, a house, a fabric, a cupola

DOMES'DAY. *s.* See DOOMSDAY

DOMES'TIC. *adj.* Belonging to the house; private; not foreign. s. *domestic:* v. *domesticate;* pr. par *domesticating;* past, *domesticated* adv. *domestically.*

DOM'ICILE. *s.* A house; place of residence. adj. *domiciliary.*

DOMICIL'IATE. *v.* To render domestic. pr. par. *domiciliating;* past, *domiciliated.*

DOM'INATE. *v.* To predominate; to govern. pr. par. *dominating;* past, *dominated:* adj. *dominant:* s. *domination, dominator.*

DOMINEER'. *v.* To rule with insolence; to bluster. pr. par. *domineering;* past, *domineered.*

DOMIN'ICAL. *adj.* Noting the Lord's day, or Sunday.

DOMIN'ICAN. *s.* One of the orders of St. Dominick.

DOMIN'ION. *s.* Sovereign authority; unlimited power; territory; region.

DOM'INO. *s.* A kind of hood, worn by canons of cathedral churches in Italy; a masquerade garment.

DON. *s.* The Spanish title for a gentleman.

DONA'TION. *s.* The act of giving any thing; the thing given. s. *donative.*

DONE. The past par. of the v. *to do.*

DO'NOR. *s.* A giver, a bestower.

DOOM. *v.* To judge; to condemn to any punishment; to destine. pr. par. *dooming;* past, *doomed:* s. *doom.*

DOOMS'DAY. *s.* The day of final and universal judgment.

DOOMS'DAY-BOOK. *s.* A book made by order of William the Conqueror, in which the estates of the kingdom were registered.

DOOR. *s.* The gate of a house; entrance, portal, passage.

DOQ'UET. *s.* See DOCKET.

DOR'IC. *adj.* A species of ancient music; an order of architecture.

DOR'MANT. *adj.* Sleeping; in a sleeping posture; private; concealed.

DOR'MITIVE. *s.* A soporific medicine; an opiate.

DOR'MITORY. *s.* A place to sleep in. pl *dormitories.*

DOR'MOUSE. *s.* A small animal which passes a large part of the winter in sleep.

DOR'SAL. *adj.* Belonging to the back.

DOSE. *s.* So much of any medicine as is taken at one time. v. *dose,* pr. par. *dosing;* past, *dosed.*

DOST. *v.* The second person of *do.*

DOT. *s.* A small point or spot, made to mark any place in a writing, usually a period. v. *dot;* pr. par. *dotting;* past, *dotted.*

DOTA'TION. *s.* The act of giving a dowry or portion.

DOTE. *v.* To have the intellect impaired by age or passion; to be delirious; to be in love to extremity. pr. par. *doting;* past, *doted* adv. *dotingly:* s. *dotage, dotard.*

DOTH. *v.* The third person of *do.*

DOUANEE'R. *s.* An officer of customs.

DOUB'LE. *adj.* Two of a sort; one corresponding to the other; in pairs; twice as much; deceitful v. *double;* pr. par. *doubling;* past, *doubled:* s. *double:* adv. *doubly.*

DOUB'LE-DEALER. *s.* A deceitful, subtle, insidious fellow.

DOUBLE-ENTENDRE. s. A double signification of a sentence or expression.

DOUB'LET. *s.* The inner garment of a man; the waistcoat; two; a pair.

DOUBLOON', DOUBLON'. *s.* A Spanish coin, of the value of two pistoles.

DOUBT. *v.* To question; to be in uncertainty; to fear; to suspect; to hesitate. pr. par. *doubting;* past, *doubted:* s. *doubt, doubter.*

DOUBT'FUL. *adj.* Dubious; not settled in opinion; ambiguous, hazardous. adv. *doubtfully:* s. *doubtfulness:* adv. *doubtingly, doubtless, doubtlessly.*

DOUCEUR'. *s.* A lure; a coaxing temptation; a bribe.

DOUGH. *s.* The paste of bread, or of pies, yet unbaked.

DOUGH'TY. *adj.* Brave, noble, illustrious, eminent:—it is now seldom used, except ironically.

116

DOUSE, DOWSE. v. To put over head suddenly in the water. pr. par. *dousing;* past, *doused.*

DOVE. s. A wild pigeon.

DOVE'COT. s. A small building in which pigeons are bred and kept.

DOVE'TAIL. s. A form of joining two bodies together, where that which is inserted has the form of a wedge reversed, and therefore cannot fall out. adj. *dovetailed.*

DOW'ABLE. adj. Capable of being dowered.

DOW'AGER. s. A widow with a jointure; the title given to ladies who survive their husbands.

DOW'DY. s. An awkward, ill dressed, inelegant woman. pl. *dowdies:* adj. *dowdy.*

DOW'ER, DOW'RY. s. That which the wife brings to her husband in marriage; that which a widow possesses. pl. of *dowry, dowries.*

DOW'LAS. s. A coarse kind of linen.

DOWN. s. Soft feathers; soft wool, or tender hair; the soft fibres of plants which wing the seeds; a large, open plain, properly a flat on the top of a hill. adj. *downy.*

DOWN. prep. Along a descent; from a higher place to a lower. adv. *down.*

DOWN'CAST. adj. Bent down; directed to the ground.

DOWN'FAL. s. Ruin, calamity. adj. *downfallen.*

DOWNHEART'ED. adj. Dejected.

DOWN'RIGHT. adj. Plain, open, apparent, undisguised, unceremomonious. adv. *downrightly.*

DOWN'SITTING. s. Rest, repose.

DOWN'WARDS. adv. Towards the centre; from a higher situation to a lower. adj. *downward.*

DOW'RY. s. See Dower.

DOWSE. v. See Douse.

DOXOL'OGY. s. A form of giving glory to God. pl. *doxologies:* adj. *doxological.*

DOX'Y. s. A loose wench. pl. *doxies.*

DOZE. v. To slumber; to sleep lightly. pr. par. *dozing;* past dozed: s. *doze, doziness.*

DOZ'EN. s. The number of twelve.

DRAB. s. A strumpet; a slut; a colour.

DRACHM, DRAM. s. An old Greek coin; the eighth part of an ounce.

DRAFT. s. A corrupt spelling from draught.

DRAFT. s. A check drawn for money; a requisition for part of an army. v. *draft;* pr. par. *drafting;* past, *drafted.*

DRAG. v. To pull along the ground by main force; to pull roughly and forcibly. pr. par. *dragging;* past, *dragged:* s. *drag.*

DRAG'GLE. v. To make dirty by dragging on the ground. pr. par *draggling;* past, *draggled.*

DRAG'OMAN. s. An Asiatic interpreter.

DRAG'ON. s. A kind of winged serpent, perhaps imaginary.

DRAGOON'. s. A soldier that serves on horseback. v. *dragoon;* pr. par. *dragooning;* past, *dragooned.*

DRAIN. v. To draw off gradually; to empty by drawing gradually away. pr. par. *draining;* past, *drained:* s. *drain:* adj. *drainable.*

DRAKE. s. The male of a duck.

DRAM. s. Such a quantity of distilled spirits as is usually drunk at once.

DRA'MA. s. A poem accommodated to action; a poem in which the action is not related, but represented. adj. *dramatic, dramatical:* adv. *dramatically:* s. *dramatist.*

DRA'MATIZE. v. To form into a drama. pr. par. *dramatizing;* past, *dramatized:* s. *dramatizer.*

DRANK. Preterit of the v. *drink.*

DRA'PER. s. One who sells cloth.

DRA'PERY. s. Cloth-work; the dress of a picture or statue. pl. *draperies.*

DRAUGHT, DRAFT. v. To draw out; to call forth. pr. par. *draughting;* past, *draughted.*

117

DRAW. *v.* To pull along; to pull forcibly; to pluck; to practise the art of delineation. pr. par. *drawing;* past, *drawn:* s. *draw, drawing, drawer.*

DRAW'BACK. *s.* Money paid back for ready payment, or any other reason; reduction.

DRAW'BRIDGE. *s.* A bridge made to be lifted up, to hinder or admit communication at pleasure.

DRAW'INGROOM. *s.* The room in which company assembles.

DRAWL. *v.* To utter any thing in a slow manner. pr. par. *drawling;* past, *drawled:* s. *drawl.*

DRAWN. *part.* Collected, pulled, equal, open.

DRAW'-WELL. *s.* A deep well, from which water is drawn with a bucket.

DRAY. *s.* A sort of cart.

DRAY'MAN. *s.* One that attends a dray.

DREAD. *s.* Fear, terror, habitual fear, awe. *v. dread;* pr. par. *dreading;* past, *dreaded:* adj. *dread:* s. *dreader.*

DREAD'FUL. *adj.* Terrible, frightful, awful. adv. *dreadfully:* s. *dreadfulness:* adj. *dreadless:* s. *dreadlessness.*

DREAM. *s.* A phantasm of sleep; an idle fancy; a wild conceit. *v. dream;* pr. par. *dreaming;* past, *dreamed, dreamt:* s. *dreamer.*

DREAR, DREAR'Y. *adj.* Mournful, sorrowful, dismal. adv. *drearily:* s. *dreariness.*

DREDGE. *s.* A kind of net. *v. dredge;* pr. par. *dredging;* past, *dredged:* s. *dredger.*

DREGS. *s.* The sediment of liquors; the lees; the grounds, dross, refuse.

DRENCH. *v.* To wash, to soak, to steep, to physic by violence. pr. par. *drenching;* past, *drenched:* s. *drench, drencher.*

DRESS. *v.* To clothe, to adorn, to embellish; to prepare victuals for the table. pr. par. *dressing;* past, *dressed:* s. *dress, dresser, dressing,* adj. *dressy.*

DREW. Pret. of the *v.* to *draw.*

DRIB'BLE. *v.* To fall in drops; to fall weakly and slowly. pr. par. *dribbling;* past, *dribbled.*

DRIFT. *s.* Force impellent; impulse, course; a storm; a deep body of snow. *v. drift;* pr. par *drifting;* past, *drifted.*

DRIFT'WOOD. *s.* Wood carried by a flood.

DRILL. *v.* To pierce any thing with a drill; to perforate; to bore; to teach the military exercise. pr. par. *drilling;* past, *drilled:* s. *drill.*

DRIL'LING. *s.* A kind of strong, twilled linen, worn by soldiers at the drill.

DRINK. *v.* To swallow liquors; to suck up; to absorb. pr. par. *drinking;* past, *drunk:* s. *drink, drinker:* adj. *drinkable.*

DRIP. *v.* To fall in drops. pr. par. *dripping;* past, *dripped:* s. *drip.*

DRIP'PING-PAN. *s.* A pan in which the fat of roast meat is caught.

DRIVE. *v.* To produce motion by violence; to force along by impetuous pressure; to chase, to hunt, to expel. pr. par. *driving,* past, *driven:* s. *driver.*

DRIV'EL. *v.* To let the spittle fall in drops, like a child, an idiot, or a dotard; to be weak or foolish. pr. par. *driveling;* past, *driveled:* s. *driveler.*

DRIZ'ZLE. *v.* To shed in small, slow drops, as winter rains. pr. par. *drizzling;* past, *drizzled:* s. *drizzle:* adj. *drizzly.*

DROLL. *s.* One whose business is to raise mirth by petty tricks; a jester, a buffoon. adj. *droll:* s. *drollery,* pl. *drolleries.*

DROM'EDARY. *s.* A sort of camel. pl. *dromedaries.*

DRONE. *s.* The bee which makes no honey; the hum, or instrument of humming; an idler. *v. drone,* pr. par. *droning;* past, *droned* adj. *dronish.*

118

DROOP. *v.* To languish with sorrow; to faint; to grow weak. pr. par. *drooping;* past, *drooped.*

DROP. *s.* A globule of moisture; an ornament hanging in the ear. *v. drop;* pr. par. *dropping;* past, *dropped.*

DROP'SY. *s.* A collection of water in the body. pl. *dropsies:* adj. *dropsical, dropsied.*

DROSS. *s.* The recrement or despumation of metals; rust, refuse. adj. *drossy:* s. *drossiness.*

DROUGHT. *s.* Dry weather, want of rain, thirst. s. *droughtiness.*

DROVE. The preterit of the *v. drive.*

DROVE. *s.* A body or number of cattle. s. *drover.*

DROWN. *v.* To suffocate in water; to deluge. pr. par. *drowning;* past, *drowned:* s. *drowner.*

DROW'SY. *adj.* Sleepy, heavy, lazy. adv. *drowsily:* s. *drowsiness.*

DRUB. *v.* To thresh, to beat, to bang. pr. par. *drubbing;* past, *drubbed.*

DRUDGE. *v.* To labour in mean offices; to work hard; to slave. pr. par. *drudging;* past, *drudged:* s. *drudge, drudger, drudgery,* pl. *drudgeries:* adv. *drudgingly.*

DRUDG'ING-BOX. *s.* The box out of which flour is sprinkled.

DRUG. *s.* An ingredient used in physic; a medicinal simple. *v. drug;* pr. par. *drugging;* past, *drugged:* s. *druggist.*

DRUG'GET. *s.* A slight kind of woollen stuff.

DRU'ID. *s.* One of the priests and philosophers of the ancient Britons and Gauls. adj. *druidical:* s. *druidism.*

DRUM. *s.* An instrument of military music; the tympanum of the ear. *v. drum;* pr. par. *drumming;* past, *drummed:* s. *drummer.*

DRUM'FISH. *s.* The name of a fish.

DRUM-MA'JOR. *s.* The chief drummer of a regiment.

DRUM'-STICK. *s.* A stick with which a drum is beaten.

DRUNK *adj.* Intoxicated with strong liquor; inebriated. adj. *drunken:* adv. *drunkenly:* s. *drunkenness, drunkard.*

DRY. *adj.* Arid, not wet, not moist, plain, hard, severe. adv. *drily:* s. *dryness.*

DRY. *v.* To free from moisture; to exhale moisture; to drain. pr. par *drying;* past, *dried:* s. *dryer.*

DRY'AD. *s.* A wood-nymph.

DRY'NURSE. *s.* A woman who brings up and feeds a child without the breast. *v. drynurse;* pr. par. *drynursing;* past, *drynursed.*

DRY'SALTER. *s.* A dealer in salted or dried meats, sauces, oils, pickles, drugs, and various other articles.

DRY'SHOD. *adj.* Without wet feet.

DU'AL. *adj.* Expressing the number two. s. *duality.*

DUB. *v.* To make a man a knight; to confer any kind of dignity or new character. pr. par. *dubbing;* past, *dubbed:* s. *dub.*

DU'BIOUS. *adj.* Doubtful, uncertain, not plain. adv. *dubiously:* s. *dubiousness.*

DU'BITABLE. *adj.* Doubtful, uncertain. s. *dubitancy, dubitation.*

DU'CAL. *adj.* Pertaining to a duke.

DUC'AT. *s.* A coin struck by dukes; in silver, worth four shillings and six-pence; in gold, nine shillings and six-pence.

DUCH'ESS. *s.* The wife of a duke a female who presides over a dutchy. pl. *duchesses.*

DUCH'Y. *s.* See Dutchy.

DUCK. *s.* A species of water-fowl

DUCK. *v.* To dive under water, as a duck; to put under water. pr. par. *ducking;* past, *ducked:* s. *ducker.*

DUCK'ING-STOOL. *s.* A chair in which scolds are tied, and put under water.

DUCK'LING. *s.* A young duck.

DUCT. *s.* Guidance, direction; a passage through which any thing is conducted.

DUCT'ILE. *adj.* Easy to be drawn out into length; flexible; pliable. *s. ductility*, pl. *ductilities*.

DUDG'EON. *s.* A small dagger; sullenness, malignity.

DUE. *adj.* Owed; that which any one has a right to demand; proper, fit. *s. due:* adv. *duly*.

DU'EL. *s.* A combat between two. *s. dueling, duelist*.

DUEN'NA. *s.* An old woman, kept to guard a younger.

DU'ET. *s.* An air for two performers.

DUG. *s.* A pap, a nipple.

DUG. The pret. and past par. of the v. *dig*.

DUKE. *s.* One of the highest order of nobility.

DUKE'DOM. *s.* The seigniory or possession of a duke.

DUL'CET. *adj.* Sweet, luscious, harmonious.

DUL'CIFY. *v.* To sweeten. pr. par. *dulcifying*; past, *dulcified: s. dulcification*.

DUL'CIMER. *s.* A kind of musical instrument.

DULL. *adj.* Stupid, doltish, blunt, obtuse, melancholy. adv. *dully: s. dulness*.

DU'LY. *adv.* Properly, fitly, regularly, exactly.

DUMB. *adj.* Mute; incapable of speech; silent. adv. *dumbly: s. dumbness*.

DUM'PLING. *s.* A sort of pudding.

DUMPS. *s.* In a state of sorrow, melancholy, or sadness. adj. *dumpish:* adv. *dumpishly: s. dumpishness*.

DUN. *adj.* A colour partaking of brown and black; dark, gloomy.

DUN. *s.* A clamorous, importunate creditor; an importunate demand for money. v. *dun*; pr. par. *dunning*; past, *dunned: s. dunner*.

DUN. *s.* An eminence, a mound.

DUNCE. *s.* A dolt; one who is slow in learning.

DUNG. *s.* The excrement of animals. v. *dung;* pr. par. *dunging;* past, *dunged*.

DUN'GEON. *s.* A close prison.

DUODE'CIMO. *s.* A book is said to be in duodecimo, when a sheet is folded into twelve parts.

DUPE. *s.* A credulous man; a man easily tricked. v. *dupe;* pr. par. *duping;* past, *duped: s. duper*.

DU'PLICATE. *v.* To double. pr. par. *duplicating;* past, *duplicated: s. duplication*.

DU'PLICATE. *adj. Duplicate* proportion is the proportion of squares.

DU'PLICATE. *s.* Another, correspondent to the first; a second thing of the same kind.

DUPLI'CITY. *s.* Doubleness, deceit, pl. *duplicities*.

DU'RABLE. *adj.* Lasting. *s. durability*, pl. *durabilities:* adv. *durably*.

DU'RANCE. *s.* Imprisonment, endurance, duration.

DURA'TION. *s.* Power of continuance; length of continuance.

DURESSE'. *s.* Imprisonment, constraint.

DU'RING. *prep.* For the time of the continuance of; while any thing lasts.

DURST. Preterit of the v. *dare*.

DUSK. *adj.* Tending to darkness, dark-coloured. adv. *duskily: s. duskiness:* adj. *duskish, dusky*.

DUST. *s.* Earth or other matter reduced to small particles. v. *dust*, pr. par. *dusting;* past, *dusted: s. duster, dustiness:* adj. *dusty*.

DUST'MAN. *s.* One whose employment is to carry away the dust. pl *dustmen*.

DUTCH. *s.* The people of Holland; the Dutch language.

DUTCH'ESS. *s.* See Duchess.

DUTCH'Y *s.* A territory which gives title to a duke. pl. *dutchies*.

DU'TIFUL. *adj.* Obedient; submissive to natural or legal superiors. adv. *dutifully: s. dutifulness*.

DU'TY. *s.* That to which a man is by any natural or legal obligation bound. pl. *duties:* adj. *duteous*.

DUUM'VIRATE. *s.* A government or jurisdiction among the Romans, exercised by two.

DWARF. *s.* A man below the common size of men; any animal or plant below its natural bulk. *adj. dwarfish:* s. *dwarfishness.*

DWELL. *v.* To remain, to inhabit; to live in a place. pr. par. *dwelling;* past, *dwelt:* s. *dweller, dwelling.*

DWEL'LING-HOUSE. *s.* The house in which a person lives.

DWIN'DLE. *v.* To shrink; to lose bulk; to grow little. pr. par. *dwindling;* past, *dwindled.*

DYE. *v.* To tinge, to colour, to stain. pr. par. *dying;* past, *dyed.* s. *dyer, dying.*

DY'NASTY. *s.* Government, sovereignty; a race or family of rulers. pl. *dynasties.*

DYS'ENTERY. *s.* A looseness of the bowels. pl. *dysenteries.*

DYSPEP'SY. *s.* A difficulty of digestion. pl. *dyspepsies.*

E

EACH. *pron.* Either of two; every one of any number.

EA'GER. *adj.* Struck with desire; ardently wishing. adv. *eagerly:* s. *eagerness.*

EA'GLE. *s.* A bird of prey; the standard of the ancient Romans; a gold coin of the United States, of the value of ten dollars.

EAG'LET. *s.* A young eagle.

EAR. *s.* The whole organ of hearing; that part of the ear which stands prominent; a spike of corn.

EARL. *s.* A title of nobility, next in rank below a marquis. s. *earldom.*

EAR'LY. *adj.* Soon, with respect to something else. adv. *early:* s. *earliness.*

EARN. *v.* To gain as the reward or wages of labour, or any performance; to obtain. pr. par. *earning;* past, *earned:* s. *earner, earning.*

EAR'NEST. *adj.* Ardent in any affection; zealous, importunate. s. *earnest, earnestness:* adv. *earnestly.*

EARTH. *s.* The element distinct from air, fire, or water; the world; soil; terrene matter. v. *earth;* pr. par. *earthing;* past, *earthed:* adj. *earthen:* adv. *earthly.*

EARTH'QUAKE. *s.* Tremor or convulsion of the earth

EAR'-WIG. *s.* A sheath-winged insect, imagined to creep into the ear.

EASE. *s.* Quiet; rest; undisturbed tranquillity; facility. v. *ease;* pr. par. *easing;* past, *eased:* s. *easement, easiness:* adv. *easily:* adj. *easy.*

EA'SEL. *s.* The frame on which painters strain their canvas.

EAST. *s.* The quarter where the sun rises, opposite to the west. adv. *easterly:* adj. *eastern, eastward.*

EAS'TER. *s.* The day on which the Christian church commemorates our Saviour's resurrection.

EAT. *v.* To devour with the mouth; to corrode. pr. par. *eating;* past, *eat, eaten:* adj. *eatable.* s. *eater.*

EAVES. *s.* The edges of the roof which overhang the house.

EAVES'-DROPPER. *s.* An insidious listener. s. *eaves-dropping.*

EBB. *s.* The reflux of the tide towards the sea; decline, decay. v. *ebb;* pr. par. *ebbing;* past, *ebbed.*

EB'ONY. *s.* A kind of black wood. pl. *ebonies.*

EBRI'ETY. *s.* Drunkenness. pl. *ebrieties.*

EBRIOS'ITY. *s.* Habitual drunkenness. pl. *ebriosities.*

L

EBULLI'TION. *s.* The act of boiling up with heat; any intestine motion. adj. *ebullient.*

ECCEN'TRIC. *adj.* Deviating from the centre; not terminating in the same point; irregular; anomalous. *s. eccentricity,* pl. *eccentricities.*

ECCLESIAS'TIC. *s.* A person dedicated to the ministries of religion. adj. *ecclesiastical.*

ECH'O. *s.* The return or repercussion of sound. *v. echo;* pr. par. *echoing;* past, *echoed.*

ECHOM'ETER. *s.* (In music;)—a kind of scale, serving to measure the duration of sounds.

ECCLAIRCIS'SEMENT. s. Explanation; the act of clearing up an affair.

E'CLAT. *s.* Spendour, show, lustre. pronounced *éklaw.*

ECLEC'TIC. *adj.* Selecting.

ECLIPSE'. *s.* An obscuration of the luminaries of heaven; darkness, obscuration. *v. eclipse;* pr. par. *eclipsing;* past, *eclipsed.*

ECLIP'TIC. *s.* A great circle of the sphere, supposed to be drawn through the middle of the zodiac. adj. *ecliptic.*

EC'LOGUE. *s.* A pastoral poem.

ECON'OMIES. *s.* Things which apply to the management of household affairs.

ECON'OMY. *s.* The management of a family; frugality; regulation; system of matter. pl. *economies: v. economize;* pr. par. *economizing;* past, *economized:* adj. *economical:* adv. *economically: s. economist.*

EC'STACY. *s.* Any passion by which the thoughts are absorbed, and in which the mind is for a time lost; rapture. pl. *ecstacies:* adj. *ecstatic.*

EDA'CITY. *s.* Voracity, greediness. pl. *edacities.*

ED'DY. *s.* The water that runs conrary to the main stream. pl. *eddies: v. eddy;* pr. par. *eddying,* past, *eddied.*

E'DEN. *s.* Paradise.

EDGE. *s.* The thin or cutting part of a blade; brink, extremity, keenness. *v. edge;* pr. par. *edging;* past, *edged: s. edging:* adj. *edgeless.*

EDGE'WISE, EDGE'WAYS *adv.* With the edge put into any particular direction

ED'IBLE. *adj.* Fit to be eaten.

E'DICT. *s.* A proclamation, command, or prohibition; a law promulgated.

EDIFICA'TION. *s.* Instruction, improvement. adj. *edificatory.*

ED'IFICE. *s.* A fabric, a building a structure.

ED'IFY. *v.* To instruct, to improve. pr. par. *edifying;* past, *edified.*

E'DILE. *s.* The title of a magistrate in ancient Rome.

ED'IT. *v.* To revise or prepare a work for publication. pr. par. *editing;* past, *edited.*

EDI'TION. *s.* Publication of any thing, particularly of a book; the number of copies of any book, printed with the same types.

ED'ITOR. *s.* He that revises or prepares any literary work for publication. adj. *editorial:* adv. *editorially: s. editorship.*

ED'UCATE. *v.* To bring up; to instruct youth. pr. par. *educating,* past, *educated: s. education, educator.*

EDU'CE. *v.* To bring out, to extract. pr. par. *educing;* past, *educed: s. eduction.*

EEK. *v.* To supply any deficiency; to make larger, by the addition of another piece. pr. par. *eeking,* past, *eeked.*

EEL. *s.* A serpentine, slimy fish, that lurks in the mud.

EF'FABLE. *adj.* Expressive, utterable.

EFFA'CE. *v.* To destroy any thing painted or carved; to destroy pr. par. *effacing;* past, *effaced.*

EFFECT. *s.* That which is produced by an operating cause; consequence; event. *v. effect;* pr. par. *effecting;* past, *effected:* adj. *effectible, effective, effectual:* s. *effectless, effector:* adv. *effectually.*

EFFEC'TUATE. *v.* To bring to pass; to fulfil. pr. par. *effectuating;* past, *effectuated.*

EFFEM'INATE. *adj.* Womanish, voluptuous, tender. s. *effeminacy,* pl. *effeminacies:* v. *effeminate;* pr. par. *effeminating;* past, *effeminated:* adv. *effeminately:* s. *effeminateness, effemination.*

EFFERVESCE'. *v.* To generate heat by intestine motion. pr. par. *effervescing;* past, *effervesced:* s. *effervescence.*

EFFE'TE. *adj.* Barren; worn out with age.

EF'FICACY. *s.* Power to produce effects; production of the consequence intended. pl. *efficacies.* adj. *efficacious:* adv. *efficaciously.*

EFFI'CIENCY. *s.* The act of producing effects; agency. pl. *efficiencies:* adj. and s. *efficient:* adv. *efficiently.*

EF'FIGY. *s.* Resemblance; image, in painting or sculpture. pl. *effigies.*

EFFLORES'CENCE, EFFLORES'CENCY. *s.* Production of flowers; excrescences in the form of flowers; (in physic) the breaking out of some humours in the skin. pl. *efflorescences, efflorescencies:* adj. *efflorescent.*

EF'FLUENCE. *s.* That which issues from some other principle. adj. *effluent.*

EFFLU'VIA. *s.* Those small particles which are continually flying off from bodies.

EF'FLUX, EFFLUX'ION. *s.* The act of flowing out; effusion; emanation: that which flows out.

EF'FORT. *s.* Struggle, strain, vehement action, laborious endeavour.

EFFRON'TERY. *s.* Impudence, shamelessness. pl. *effronteries.*

EFFULGE'. *v.* To send forth lustre or effulgence. pr. par. *effulging,* past, *effulged:* s. *effulgence:* adj. *effulgent.*

EFFU'SION. *s.* The act of pouring out; waste; bounteous donation. adj. *effusive.*

EGG. *s.* That which is laid by feathered and some other animals, from which their young is produced.

EG'LANTINE. *s.* A species of rose, sweet-briar.

E'GOTISM. *s.* Too frequent mention of a man's self. s. *egotist:* adj. *egotistical:* adv. *egotistically.*

EGRE'GIOUS. *adj.* Remarkable, extraordinary, eminently bad. adv *egregiously:* s. *egregiousness.*

E'GRESS. *s.* The power or act of going out of any place; departure.

EGRES'SION. *s.* The act of going out.

EIGHT. *adj.* Twice four. adj. *eighth.* adv. *eighthly.*

EIGHTEEN. *adj.* Twice nine. adj. *eighteenth.*

EIGHTY. *adj.* Eight times ten. adj. *eightieth.*

EI'THER. *pron.* Whichsoever of the two; each; both. conj. *either.*

EJAC'ULATE. *v.* To throw, to shoot, to dart out. pr. par. *ejaculating;* past, *ejaculated:* s. *ejaculation:* adj. *ejaculatory.*

EJECT'. *v.* To throw out; to cast forth; to expel. pr. par. *ejecting,* past, *ejected:* s. *ejection.*

EJECT'MENT. *s.* A legal writ, by which any inhabitant of a house, or tenant of an estate, is commanded to depart.

EKE. *v.* To increase, to supply, to fill up deficiencies. pr. par. *eking;* past, *eked.*

ELAB'ORATE. *v.* To produce with labour; to heighten and improve by successive endeavours or operations. pr. par. *elaborating;* past, *elaborated.* adj. *elaborate* s. *elaborateness, elaboration.*

ELAPSE'. *v.* To pass away; to glide away. pr. par. *elapsing;* past, *elapsed.*

ELAS'TIC. *adj.* Having the power of returning to the form, from which it is distorted or withheld; springy. *s. elasticity,* pl. *elasticities.*

ELA'TE. *adj.* Flushed with success; haughty. *v. elate;* pr. par. *elating;* past, *elated: s. elation.*

EL'BOW. *s.* The next joint or curvature of the arm below the shoulder; any flexure, or angle. *v. elbow;* pr. par. *elbowing;* past, *elbowed.*

EL'DER. *adj.* Surpassing another in years. adv. *elderly.*

EL'DER. *s.* The name of a tree.

EL'DEST. *s.* The oldest; having the right of primogeniture.

ELECT'. *v.* To choose for any office or use. pr. par. *electing;* past, *elected:* adj. *elect, elective: s. election, elector:* adj. *electoral.*

ELEC'TARY, ELEC'TUARY. *s.* A form of medicine made of conserves and powders, of the consistence of honey. pl. *electaries, electuaries.*

ELECTIONEER'. *v.* To be active previous to an election. pr. par. *electioneering;* past, *electioneered.*

ELEC'TORATE. *s.* The territory of an elector.

ELEC'TRESS. *s.* The wife or widow of an elector. pl. *electresses.*

ELEC'TRIC, ELEC'TRICAL. *adj.* Attractive without magnetism; attractive by a peculiar property, supposed once to belong chiefly to amber.

ELECTRI'CITY. *s.* The name of an unknown natural power, which produces a great variety of peculiar and surprising phenomena. pl. *electricities: s. electrician.*

ELEC'TRIFY. *v.* To render electric; to communicate electricity. pr. par. *electrifying;* past, *electrified.*

ELECTROM'ETER *s.* An instrument for measuring the quantity, and determining the quality, of electricity, in any electrified body.

ELEC'TUARY, ELEC'TARY. *s.* A form of medicine made of conserves and powders, of the consistence of honey. pl. *electuaries, electaries.*

ELEEMOS'YNARY. *adj.* Living upon alms; depending upon charity; given in charity.

EL'EGANT. *adj.* Nice; accurate in discerning; pleasing by minuter beauties. adv. *elegantly: s. elegance.*

EL'EGY. *s.* A mournful song; a funeral song. pl. *elegies:* adj. *elegiac, elegiacal: s. eligiast.*

EL'EMENT. *s.* The first or constituent principle of any thing; the proper habitation or sphere of any thing; an ingredient. adj. *elemental, elementary.*

EL'EPHANT. *s.* The largest of quadrupeds. adj. *elephantine.*

EL'EVATE. *v.* To raise, to exalt, to dignify. pr. par. *elevating;* past, *elevated: s. elevation, elevator.*

ELE'VE. *s.* Literally, a scholar or disciple; one who has studied under a particular master; one brought up, or protected by another.

ELEV'EN. *adj.* Ten and one. adj. *eleventh.*

ELF. *s.* A wandering spirit, supposed to be seen in wild, unfrequented places; a fairy. pl. *elves;* adj. *elfish.*

ELF'-LOCK. *s.* Hair twisted by elves, a common superstition.

ELI'CIT. *v.* To strike out; to fetch out by labour or art. pr. par. *eliciting;* past, *elicited: s. elicitation.*

EL'IGIBLE. *adj.* Fit to be chosen; preferable; desirable. *s. eligibility,* pl. *eligibilities.*

ELI'SION. *s.* The act of cutting off; separation of parts.

ELI'TE. *adj.* A military word, denoting the flower or chosen part of an army.

ELIX'IR. *s.* A kind of medicine made by strong infusion; the extract or quintessence of any thing.

ELK. *s.* A large and stately animal of the stag kind.

ELL. *s.* A measure containing, in England, a yard and a quarter.

ELLIP'SIS. *s.* A figure of rhetoric, by which something is left out; in geometry, an oval figure, generated from the section of a cone. pl. *ellipses.*

ELLIP'TIC, ELLIP'TICAL. *adj.* Having the form of an ellipsis; oval. adv. *elliptically.*

ELM. *s.* The name of a tree.

ELOCU'TION. *s.* The power of fluent speech; eloquence; beauty of words. adj. *elocutive.*

ELON'GATE. *v.* To lengthen; to draw out; to put further off. pr. par. *elongating;* past, *elongated:* s. *elongation.*

ELO'PE. *v.* To run away; to break loose. pr. par. *eloping;* past, *eloped:* s. *elopement.*

EL'OQUENCE. *s.* The power of speaking with fluency and elegance; oratory. adj. *eloquent:* adv. *eloquently.*

ELSE. *pron.* Other; one besides. adv. *else.*

ELSEWHE'RE. *adv.* In any other places; in some other place.

ELU'CIDATE. *v.* To explain, to clear, to make plain. pr. par. *elucidating;* past, *elucidated:* s. *elucidation, elucidator:* adj. *elucidative.*

ELU'DE. *v.* To escape by stratagem; to avoid by artifice. pr. par. *eluding;* past, *eluded:* adj. *eludible.*

ELU'SION. *s.* The act of eluding; artifice. adj. *elusive, elusory:* s. *elusoriness.*

ELY'SIUM. *s.* The place assigned by the heathens to happy souls; any place exquisitely pleasant. adj. *elysian.*

EMA'CIATE. *v.* To waste; to deprive of flesh. pr. par. *emaciating;* past, *emaciated:* s. *emaciation.*

EMAC'ULATE. *v.* To make clean; to take out spots. pr. par. *emaculating;* past, *emaculated:* s. *emaculation:* adj. *emaculate.*

EM'ANATE. *v.* To issue or flow from. pr. par. *emanating;* past, *emanated:* s. *emanation:* adj. *emanative.*

EMAN'CIPATE. *v.* To set free from servitude. pr. par. *emancipating* past, *emancipated:* s. *emancipation, emancipator.*

EMAS'CULATE. *v.* To vitiate by unmanly softness; to effeminate. pr. par. *emasculating*, past, *emasculated.*

EMBALM'. *v.* To impregnate a body with aromatics, that it may resist putrefaction. pr. par. *embalming*, past, *embalmed:* s. *embalmer.*

EMBAR'GO. *s.* A prohibition to pass; a stop put to trade. pl. *embargoes:* v. *embargo;* pr. par. *embargoing;* past, *embargoed.*

EMBARK'. *v.* To put on shipboard, to go on shipboard; to engage an other in any affair. pr. par. *embarking;* past, *embarked:* s. *embarkation.*

EMBAR'RASS. *v.* To perplex, to entangle. pr. par. *embarrassing*, past, *embarrassed:* s. *embarrassment.*

EMBAS'SADOR, AMBAS'SADOR *s.* One sent on a public message. adj. *embassadorial, ambassadorial.*

EMBAS'SADRESS, AMBAS'SADRESS. *s.* A woman sent on a public message. pl. *embassadresses, ambassadresses.*

EM'BASSY. *s.* A public message pl. *embassies.*

EMBAT'TLE. *v.* To arrange in order or array of battle. pr. par. *embattling;* past, *embattled.*

EMBED'DED. *adj.* Sunk in another substance.

EMBEL'LISH. *v.* To adorn, to beautify. pr. par. *embellishing;* past, *embellished:* s. *embellishment.*

EM'BERS. *s.* Hot cinders; ashes not yet extinguished.

EMBEZ'ZLE. *v.* To appropriate by breach of trust. pr. par. *embezzling;* past, *embezzled:* s. *embezzlement, embezzler.*

EMBLA'ZON. *v.* To adorn with figures of heraldry; to deck in glaring colours. pr. par. *emblazoning;* past, *emblazoned:* s. *emblazoner, emblazonry,* pl. *emblazonries.*

EM'BLEM. *s.* Inlay; enamel; an allusive picture; a typical designation. adj. *emblematic, emblematical;* adv. *emblematically.*

EMBOD'Y. *v.* See IMBODY.

EMBOSS'. *v.* To form with protuberances; to engrave with relief or rising work; to cover. pr. par. *embossing;* past, *embossed:* s. *embossment.*

EMBOW'EL. *v.* To eviscerate; to deprive of the entrails. pr. par. *emboweling;* past, *emboweled:* s. *emboweler.*

EMBOW'ER. *v.* To lodge, to build, to bower. pr. par. *embowering;* past, *embowered.*

EMBRA'CE. *v.* To hold fondly in the arms; to squeeze in kindness; to include; to seize. pr. par. *embracing;* past, *embraced:* s. *embracement, embracer.*

EMBRASURE'. *s.* An aperture in a wall, through which a cannon is pointed; battlement.

EM'BROCATE. *v.* To rub any part diseased with medicinal liquors. pr. par. *embrocating;* past, *embrocated:* s. *embrocation.*

EMBROI'DER. *v.* To border with ornaments; to decorate with figured work. pr. par. *embroidering;* past, *embroidered:* s. *embroiderer, embroidery,* pl. *embroideries.*

EMBROIL'. *v.* To disturb, to confuse, to distract. pr. par. *embroiling;* past, *embroiled:* s. *embroilment.*

EMBRUE'. *v.* See IMBRUE.

EM'BRYO. *s.* The offspring yet unfinished in the womb; the state of any thing not fit for production. pl. *embryoes.*

EMEND'. *v.* To amend, to correct. pr. par. *emending;* past, *emended:* adj. *emendable:* s. *emendation, emendator:* adj. *emendatory.*

EM'ERALD. *s.* A green, precious stone.

EMERGE'. *v.* To rise out of any thing in which it is covered; to rise into view. pr. par. *emerging* past, *emerged.*

EMER'GENCE, EMER'GENCY. *s.* Any sudden occasion; unexpected casualty. pl. *emergences, emergencies.*

EMER'SION. *s.* The act of rising out of any fluid; the time when a star, having been obscured by its approach to the sun, appears again.

EM'ERY. *s.* An iron ore, useful in cleaning and polishing steel. pl *emeries.*

EMET'IC. *adj.* Having the quality of provoking vomits. adv. *emetically:* s. *emetic.*

EM'IGRATE. *v.* To remove from one place to another pr. par. *emigrating;* past, *emigrated:* s. *emigrant, emigration.*

EM'INENT. *adj.* High, lofty, exalted, conspicuous. adv. *eminently* s. *eminence.*

E'MIR. *s.* A title of dignity among the Turks and Persians.

EM'ISSARY. *s.* One sent on a private message; a spy; a secret agent. pl. *emissaries:* adj. *emissary.*

EMIS'SION. *s.* The act of emitting. adj. *emissive.*

EMIT'. *v.* To send forth; to let go; to dart. pr. par. *emitting;* past, *emitted.*

EM'MET. *s.* An ant, a pismire.

EMOL'LIENT. *adj* Softening, suppling.

EMOL'UMENT. *s* Profit, advantage. adj. *emolumental.*

EMOTION. *s.* Disturbance of mind; vehemence of passion.

EMPA'LE, IMPA'LE. *v.* To fence with a pale; to fortify; to put to death by spitting on a stake fixed upright. pr. par. *empaling;* past, *empaled:* s. *empalement.*

EMPAN'NEL. *v.* To put on the pannel; to summon to serve on a jury. pr. par. *empanneling;* past, *empanneled.*

EMPAR'LANCE, IMPAR'LANCE. *s.* A desire or petition, in court, of a day to consider what is best to do.

EM'PEROR. *s.* A monarch, of title and dignity superior to a king.

EM'PHASIS. *s.* A remarkable stress laid upon a word or sentence; particular force impressed by style or pronunciation. pl. *emphases:* v. *emphasize;* pr. par. *emphasizing;* past, *emphasized.*

EMPHAT'IC, EMPHAT'ICAL. *adj.* With emphasis; forcible, strong, striking. adv. *emphatically.*

EM'PIRE *s.* Imperial power; supreme dominion; command over any thing; dominions of an emperor.

EMPIR'IC. *s.* An experimenter, a quack. adj. *empiric, empirical:* adv. *empirically:* s. *empiricism.*

EMPLOY'. *v.* To busy; to keep at work; to exercise; to use as an instrument. pr. par. *employing;* past, *employed:* s. *employer, employment.*

EMPO'RIUM. *s.* A place of merchandise; a mart, a commercial city.

EMPOV'ERISH, IMPOV'ERISH. *v.* To make poor; to reduce to indigence. pr. par. *empoverishing;* past, *empoverished:* s. *empoverisher, empoverishment.*

EMPOW'ER. *v.* To authorize; to commission; to give power; to enable. pr. par. *empowering;* past, *empowered.*

EM'PRESS. *s.* The wife of an emperor: a female invested with imperial dignity. pl. *empresses.*

EMP'TY. *adj* Void, not full, evacuated, unsatisfactory. v. *empty;* pr. par. *emptying;* past, *emptied:* *s.* *emptier, emptiness.*

EMPUR'PLE, IMPUR'PLE. *v.* To make of a purple colour. pr. par *empurpling;* past, *empurpled.*

EMPY'REAN. *s.* The highest heaven, where the pure element of fire is supposed to subsist. adj. *empyreal.*

EM'ULATE. *v.* To rival; to propose as one to be equalled or excelled; to imitate. pr. par. *emulating;* past, *emulated:* s. *emulation, emulator* adj. *emulative.*

EMULGE'. *v.* To milk out. pr. par. *emulging;* past, *emulged:* adj. *emulgent.*

EM'ULOUS. *adj.* Rivaling; engaged in competition; desirous of superiority.

ENA'BLE. *v.* To make able; to em power. pr. par. *enabling;* past. *enabled.*

ENACT'. *v.* To establish by law; to decree. pr. par. *enacting;* past, *enacted:* s. *enactor.*

ENAM'EL. *v.* To inlay; to variegate with colours, properly with colours fixed by fire. pr. par. *enameling;* past, *enameled:* s. *enamel, enameler.*

ENAM'OUR. *v.* To inflame with love; to make fond. pr. par. *enamouring;* past, *enamoured.*

ENCAMP'. *v.* To pitch tents; to sit down for a time in a march. pr. par. *encamping,* past, *encamped* s. *encampment.*

ENCHAIN'. *v.* To fasten with a chain; to hold in chains; to bind. pr. par. *enchaining;* past, *enchained.*

ENCHANT. *v.* To subdue by charms or spells; to delight in a high degree. pr. par. *enchanting:* past, *enchanted:* s. *enchanter, enchantment:* adv. *enchantingly.*

ENCHANT'RESS. *s.* A sorceress a woman whose beauty and ex cellencies give irresistible influence. pl. *enchantresses.*

ENCHA'SE. *v.* To infix; to enclose in any body, so as to be held fast.

127

but not concealed; to engrave. pr. par. *enchasing;* past, *enchased.*

ENCIRCLE. *v.* To surround, to environ, to enclose in a ring. pr. par. *encircling;* past, *encircled.*

ENCLIT'IC. *s.* A particle which throws back the accent upon the foregoing syllable.

ENCLO'SE, INCLO'SE. *v.* To part from things or grounds common, by a fence; to environ; to encircle. pr. par. *enclosing;* past, *enclosed:* s. *encloser, enclosure.*

ENCO'MIAST. *s.* A panegyrist; a proclaimer of praise. adj. *encomiastic, encomiastical.*

ENCO'MIUM. *s.* Panegyric, praise, eulogy.

ENCOM'PASS. *v.* To enclose, to encircle, to surround. pr. par. *encompassing;* past, *encompassed:* s. *encompassment.*

ENCO'RE. *adv.* In French, signifies again; once more. v. *encore;* pr. par. *encoring;* past, *encored.*

ENCOUN'TER. *v.* To engage, to fight, to come together by chance. pr. par. *encountering;* past, *encountered:* s. *encounter, encounterer.*

ENCOUR'AGE. *v.* To animate; to incite; to embolden. pr. par. *encouraging;* past, *encouraged:* s. *encouragement, encourager:* adv. *encouragingly.*

ENCRIM'SONED. *adj.* Having a crimson colour.

ENCROACH', INCROACH'. *v.* To make invasions upon the right of another; to pass bounds. pr. par. *encroaching;* past, *encroached:* s. *encroacher, encroachment:* adv. *encroachingly.*

ENCYCLOPE'DIA, CYCLOPE'DIA. *s.* The circle of sciences; the round of learning. adj. *encyclopedian:* s. *encyclopedist.*

END. *s.* The extremity of the length of any thing, materially extended; ultimate state; final doom, purpose, intention. v. *end;* pr. par. *ending;* past, *ended.*

ENDAN'GER. *v.* To put into hazard; to bring into peril. pr. par. *endangering;* past, *endangered.*

ENDEAR'. *v.* To make dear; to make beloved. pr. par. *endearing;* past, *endeared:* s. *endearment.*

ENDEA'VOUR. *s.* Labour directed to some certain end. v. *endeavour;* pr. par. *endeavouring;* past, *endeavoured:* s. *endeavourer.*

ENDEM'IC, ENDEM'ICAL. *adj.* Peculiar to a country; used in respect to any disease proceeding from some cause peculiar to the country where it reigns.

EN'DIVE. *s.* A species of plant.

END'LESS. *adj.* Having no end; being without conclusion or termination. adv. *endlessly:* s. *endlessness.*

ENDORSE'. *v.* To register on the back of a writing, to superscribe; to write on the back of a bill of exchange. pr. par. *endorsing;* past, *endorsed:* s. *endorsement, endorser.*

ENDOW'. *v.* To enrich with a portion; to supply with any external goods. pr. par. *endowing;* past, *endowed:* s. *endowment.*

ENDU'E. *v.* To supply with mental excellencies; to invest with other powers and advantages than those of the mind. pr. par. *enduing,* past, *endued.*

ENDU'RE. *v.* To bear, to sustain, to support, to bear with patience. pr. par. *enduring;* past, *endured:* s. *endurance, endurer:* adj. *endurable.*

END'WISE, END'WAYS. *adv.* Erectly, uprightly, on end.

EN'EMY. *s.* A public foe; a private opponent. pl. *enemies.*

EN'ERGY. *s.* Power not exerted in action; force; vigour. pl. *energies:* adj. *energetic:* adv. *energetically.*

EN'ERGIZE. *v.* To give energy; to excite action. pr. par. *energizing,* past, *energized:* s. *energizer.*

ENER'VATE. *v.* To weaken, to deprive of force. pr. par. *enervating,*

128

past, *enervated:* adj. *enervate.* s. *enervater, enervation.*

ENFEE'BLE. *v.* To weaken, to enervate. pr. par. *enfeebling;* past, *enfeebled.*

ENFILA'DE. *v.* To pierce in a right line. pr. par. *enfilading;* past, *enfiladed.*

ENFORCE'. *v.* To strengthen; to put in act by violence; to urge with energy; to compel. pr. par. *enforcing;* past, *enforced:* s. *enforcement, enforcer.*

ENFRANCH'ISE. *v.* To admit to the privileges of a freeman; to set free from slavery; to denizen. pr. par. *enfranchising;* past, *enfranchised:* s. *enfranchisement, enfranchiser.*

ENGAGE'. *v.* To make liable for a debt to a creditor; to embark in an affair; to contract. pr. par. *engaging;* past, *engaged:* s. *engagement, engager:* adv. *engagingly.*

ENGEN'DER. *v.* To produce, to form, to cause. pr. par. *engendering;* past, *engendered:* s. *engenderer.*

EN'GINE. *s.* Any mechanical complication, in which various movements and parts concur to one effect.

ENGINE'ER. *s.* An officer in an army or fortified place, whose business is to contrive and inspect attacks, defences, and works; one who constructs canals, docks, and harbours; one who takes care of an engine.

ENG'LISH. adj. Relating to England.

ENGRAFT'. *v.* To fix deeply; to attach. pr. par. *engrafting;* past, *engrafted.*

ENGRA'VE. *v.* To picture by incisions in any matter. pr. par. *engraving;* past, *engraved:* s. *engraver, engravery, engraving.*

ENGROSS'. *v.* To thicken; to seize the whole of any thing; to purchase any commodity, for the sake of selling it at a high price; to copy in a large hand. pr. par. *en-* *grossing;* past, *engrossed:* s. *engrosser, engrossment.*

ENHANCE'. *v.* To advance; to raise in esteem. pr. par. *enhancing;* past, *enhanced:* s. *enhancement, enhancer.*

ENIG'MA. *s.* A riddle; an obscure question; a position expressed in remote and ambiguous terms. adj. *enigmatic, enigmatical:* adv. *enigmatically:* s. *enigmatist.*

ENJOIN'. *v.* To direct, to order, to prescribe. pr. par. *enjoining;* past, *enjoined:* s. *enjoiner, enjoinment.*

ENJOY'. *v.* To feel or perceive with pleasure; to be pleased with; to obtain possession of. pr. par. *enjoying;* past, *enjoyed:* s. *enjoyer, enjoyment:* adj. *enjoyable.*

ENKIN'DLE. *v.* To set on fire; to inflame. pr. par. *enkindling;* past, *enkindled.*

ENLARGE'. *v.* To make greater in quantity or appearance; to increase in magnitude; to extend. pr. par. *enlarging;* past, *enlarged* s. *enlargement, enlarger.*

ENLIGHT'EN. *v.* To illuminate; to supply with light. pr. par. *enlightening;* past, *enlightened:* s. *enlightener.*

ENLIST, INLIST'. *v.* To enrol or register; to become a soldier. pr. par. *enlisting;* past, *enlisted:* s. *enlistment.*

ENLI'VEN. *v.* To make quick, to animate. pr. par. *enlivening;* past, *enlivened:* s. *enlivener, enlivening.*

EN'MITY. *s.* Unfriendly disposition; malevolence; aversion. pl. *enmities.*

ENNO'BLE. *v.* To raise from commonalty to nobility; to dignify; to exalt. pr. par. *ennobling;* past, *ennobled:* s. *ennoblement.*

EN'NUI. *s.* Weariness, fastidiousness, disgust.

ENOR'MITY. *s.* Deviation from rule; irregularity; depravity; atrocious crime. pl. *enormities:* adj *enormous:* adv. *enormously.*

129

ENOUGH'. *s.* Something sufficient in greatness or excellence. *adv. enough.*

ENQUI'RE. *v.* To ask about; to seek out. pr. par. *enquiring*, past, *enquired:* s. *enquiry*, pl. *enquiries, enquirer.*

ENRAGE'. *v.* To irritate; to make furious. pr. par. *enraging;* past, *enraged.*

ENRAP'TURE. *v.* To transport with pleasure; to delight highly. pr. par. *enrapturing;* past, *enraptured.*

ENRICH'. *v.* To make wealthy; to fertilize. pr. par. *enriching;* past, *enriched:* s. *enrichment.*

ENRO'BE. *v.* To dress, to clothe, pr. par. *enrobing;* past, *enrobed.*

ENROL'. *v.* To insert in a roll, or register; to record. pr. par. *enrolling:* past, *enrolled:* s. *enroller, enrolment.*

ENSANG'UINE. *v.* To smear with gore; to suffuse with blood. pr. par. *ensanguining;* past, *ensanguined.*

ENSCONCE'. *v.* To cover, as with a fort; to secure. pr. par. *esconcing;* past, *ensconced.*

ENSHRI'NE. *v.* To enclose in a chest or cabinet; to preserve as a thing sacred. pr. par. *enshrining;* past, *enshrined.*

EN'SIGN. *s.* The flag or standard of a regiment; badge, or mark of distinction; the officer who carries the flag. s. *ensigncy*, pl. *ensigncies.*

ENSLA'VE. *v.* To reduce to servitude; to deprive of liberty. pr. par. *enslaving;* past, *enslaved:* s. *enslavement, enslaver.*

ENSNA'RE. *v.* See INSNARE.

ENSU'E. *v.* To follow. pr. par. *ensuing;* past, *ensued.*

ENTAB'LATURE. *s.* The architrave, frieze, and cornice, of a pillar.

ENTAIL'. *s.* The estate entailed or settled, with regard to the rule of its descent. *v. entail;* pr. par *entailing;* past, *entailed.*

ENTAN'GLE. *v.* To inwrap or in snare with something not easily extricable; to embarrass. pr. par. *entangling;* past, *entangled:* s *entanglement, entangler.*

EN'TER. *v.* To go or come into any place; to initiate in a business, method, or society. pr. par. *entering;* past, *entered:* s. *entering.*

ENTERLA'CE. *v.* To intermix, to interweave. pr. par. *enterlacing;* past, *enterlaced.*

ENTEROL'OGY. *s.* The anatomical account of the bowels and other internal parts. pl. *enterologies.*

EN'TERPRIZE. *s.* An undertaking of hazard; an arduous attempt. *v. enterprize;* pr. par. *enterprizing,* past, *enterprized:* s. *enterpriser.*

ENTERTAIN'. *v.* To converse with; to talk with; to receive hospitably; to amuse; to reserve in the mind. pr. par. *entertaining;* past, *entertained:* s. *entertainment, entertainer:* adv. *entertainingly.*

ENTHRAL'. *v.* See INTHRAL.

ENTHRO'NE. *v.* To place on a regal seat; to invest with sovereign authority. pr. par. *enthroning;* past, *enthroned.*

ENTHU'SIASM. *s.* A vain belief of private revelation; a vain confidence of divine favour; heat of imagination; elevation of fancy. s. *enthusiast:* adj. *enthusiastic, enthusiastical:* adv. *enthusiastically.*

ENTI'CE. *v.* To allure, to draw by blandishments or hopes. pr. par. *enticing;* past, *enticed:* s. *enticement, enticer:* adv. *enticingly.*

ENTI'RE. *adj.* Whole, undivided, complete in all its parts. adv. *entirely:* s. *entireness.*

ENTI'TLE. *v.* To grace or dignify with a title or honourable appellation; to distinguish by a name. pr. par. *entitling;* past, *entitled.*

EN'TITY. *s.* Something which really is; a real being. pl. *entities.*
ENTOMB'. *v.* To put into a tomb; to bury. pr. par. *entombing;* past, *entombed:* s. *entombment.*
ENTOMOL'OGY. *s.* That part of natural history which treats of insects. pl. *entomologies:* s. *entomologist.*
EN'TRAILS. *s.* The intestines, the bowels.
EN'TRANCE. *s.* The power of entering into a place; the act of entering; avenue.
ENTRA'NCE. *v.* To put into a trance; to put in an ecstacy. pr. par. *entrancing;* past, *entranced.*
ENTRAP'. *v.* To ensnare; to catch in a trap; to entangle. pr. par. *entrapping;* past, *entrapped.*
ENTREAT'. *v.* To petition, to solicit, to importune. pr. par. *entreating;* past, *entreated:* adj. *entreatable:* s. *entreater, entreaty,* pl. *entreaties.*
EN'TREPOT. *s.* A magazine, a warehouse. pronounced *on'-tre-po.*
EN'TRY. *s.* The passage by which any one enters a house; ingress; the act of registering or setting down in writing; the act of entering. pl. *entries.*
ENTWI'NE. *v.* See INTWINE.
ENTWIST. *v.* To wreath around, or together. pr. par. *entwisting;* past, *entwisted.*
ENU'MERATE. *v.* To reckon singly. pr. par. *enumerating;* past, *enumerated:* s. *enumeration;* adj. *enumerative.*
ENUNCIA'TION. *s.* Declaration; public attestation; intelligence. adj. *enunciative:* adv. *enunciatively.*
ENVEL'OP. *v.* To inwrap, to cover, to hide, to surround. pr. par. *enveloping;* past, *enveloped:* s. *envelope, envelopment.*
ENVEN'OM. *v.* To taint with poison; to poison; to enrage. pr. par. *envenoming;* past, *envenomed.*
ENVI'RON. *v.* To surround, to encompass, to besiege. pr. par. *environing;* past, *environed.*
EN'VIRONS. *s.* The neighbourhood or neighbouring places in the country.
EN'VOY. *s.* A public minister sent from one power to another; a messenger.
EN'VY. *v.* To hate another for excellence, happiness, or success; to grudge. pr. par. *envying* past, *envied:* s. *envy,* pl. *envies, envier:* adj. *enviable.*
ENWRAP'. *v.* See INWRAP.
EO'LIAN. *adj.* Denoting one of the five dialects of the Greek tongue; also, a particular kind of verse; and in music, one of the modes of the ancients.
E'PACT. *s.* A number, whereby we note the excess of the common solar year above the lunar; and thereby may find out the age of the moon, every year.
EPAULE'MENT. *s.* In fortification, a side-work, made either of earth thrown up, of bags of earth, gabions, or of fascines and earth.
EP'AULET. *s.* An ornament for the shoulder.
EPHEM'ERON. *s.* An insect that is said to live only one day. pl. *ephemera:* adj. *ephemeral.*
EPHEMER'IDES. *s.* Astronomical tables, showing the present state of the heavens, for every day at noon.
EPHEM'ERIS. *s.* A journal; an account of daily transactions; an account of the daily motions and situations of the planets. pl. *ephemeres.*
EPHE'SIAN. *s.* One of those in Ephesus, to whom St. Paul addressed an epistle.
E'PHOD. *s.* A sort of ornament, worn by the Hebrew priests.
EP'IC. *s.* Narrative; comprising narrations; not acted, but rehearsed.
EP'ICURE. *s.* A follower of Epicurus; a man given wholly to luxury. adj. *epicurean:* s. *epicurism.*

131

EPIDEM'IC, EPIDEM'ICAL. *adj.* Relating to a disease which falls at once upon great numbers of people, as a plague; generally prevailing; affecting great numbers. s. *epidemic.*

EPIGE'UM. *s.* That part of the orbit, in which any planet comes nearest to the earth.

EPIGLOT'TIS. *s.* The thin moveable cartilage, in form of a little tongue, which covers the aperture of the windpipe.

EP'IGRAM. *s.* A short poem, terminating in a point. *adj. epigrammatic, epigrammatical:* s. *epigrammatist.*

EP'IGRAPH. *s.* A title, an inscription.

EP'ILEPSY. *s.* A convulsion, or convulsive motion of the whole body, or of some of its parts, with a loss of sense. pl. *epilepsies:* adj. *epileptic, epileptical.*

EP'ILOGUE. *s.* The poem or speech at the end of a play. adj. *epilogistic.*

EPIPH'ANY. *s.* A church festival, celebrated on the twelfth day after Christmas.

EPIS'COPACY. *s.* The government of bishops. pl. *episcopacies.*

EPIS'COPAL. *adj.* Belonging to a bishop; vested in a bishop. s. and adj. *episcopalian:* adv. *episcopally.*

EP'ISODE. *s.* An incidental narrative, or digression in a poem, separable from the main subject, yet rising naturally from it. adj. *episodic, episodical.*

EPIS'TLE. *s.* A letter. adj. *epistolary.*

EP'ITAPH. *s.* An inscription on a tomb.

EPITHALA'MIUM. *s.* A nuptial song; a compliment upon marriage.

EPITHET. *s.* An adjective denoting any quality, good or bad.

EPI'TOME. *s.* Abridgment; compendious abstract. v. *epitomise;* pr. par. *epitomising;* past, *epitomised:* s. *epitomiser, epitomist.*

EP'OCH, EP'OCHA. *s.* The time at which a new computation is begun; the time from which dates are numbered.

EP'ULARY. *adj.* Belonging to feasts or banquets.

E'QUABLE. *adj.* Equal to itself; even; uniform. adv. *equably:* s. *equability,* pl. *equabilities.*

E'QUAL. *adj.* Like another in bulk, or any quality that admits comparison; adequate to any purpose; even; uniform. s. *equal:* v. *equal;* pr. par. *equaling;* past, *equaled:* s. *equality,* pl. *equalities:* adv. *equally.*

E'QUALISE. *v.* To make even: to be equal to. pr. par. *equalising;* past, *equalised:* s. *equalisation.*

EQUANIM'ITY. *s.* Evenness of mind; neither elated nor depressed. pl. *equanimities.*

EQUA'TION. *s.* The investigation of a mean proportion, collected from the extremities of excess and defect, to be applied to the whole.

EQUA'TOR. *s.* A great circle, the poles of which are the poles of the world: it divides the globe into two equal parts, the northern and southern hemispheres. adj. *equatorial.*

EQUER'Y, EQUER'RY. *s.* A grand lodge or stable for horses; an officer who has the care of horses. pl. *equeries, equerries.*

EQUES'TRIAN. *adj.* Being on horseback; skilled in horsemanship; belonging to the second rank in Rome. s. *equestrian.*

EQUIDIS'TANCE. *s.* Equal distance or remoteness. adj. *equidistant:* adv. *equidistantly.*

EQUILAT'ERAL. *adj.* Having all sides equal.

EQUILI'BRATE. *v.* To balance equally. pr. par. *equilibrating;* past, *equilibrated:* s. *equilibration,* *equilibrity,* pl. *equilibrities.*

EQUILIB'RIUM. *s.* Equipoise equality of weight.

E'QUINOX. *s.* Equinoxes are the precise times at which the sun enters into the first point of Aries and Libra; for then, moving exactly under the equinoctial, he makes our days and nights equal. adj. *equinoctial.*

EQUIP'. *v.* To furnish accoutrements for a horseman; to fi. a ship for sea; to furnish; to accoutre. pr. par. *equiping;* past, *equiped:* s. *equipment.*

EQ'UIPAGE. *s.* Furniture for a horseman; carriage of state; vehicle; attendance; retinue. adj. *equipaged.*

E'QUIPOISE. *s.* Equality of weight; equilibration.

EQUIPON'DERATE. *v.* To weigh equal to any thing. pr. par. *equiponderating;* past, *equiponderated;* s. *equiponderance:* adj. *equiponderant:* adv. *equiponderantly.*

EQ'UITY. *s.* Justice, right, honesty, impartiality. pl. *equities.* adj. *equitable:* adv. *equitably:* s. *equitableness.*

EQUIV'ALENCE. *s.* Equality of power or worth. adj. and s. *equivalent:* adv. *equivalently.*

EQUIV'OCAL. adj. Of doubtful signification; meaning different things; uncertain; doubtful. adv. *equivocally:* s. *equivocalness.*

EQUIV'OCATE. *v.* To use words of double meaning; to use ambiguous expressions. pr. par. *equivocating;* past, *equivocated:* s. *equivocation, equivocator.*

EQ'UIVOKE, EQ'UIVOQUE. *s.* Equivocation; double meaning; an expression where a word has at once different meanings.

E'RA. *s.* The whole time since any particular date or epoch: *epoch* is the commencement of an era.

ERA'DIATE. *v.* To shoot like a ray. pr. par. *eradiating;* past, *eradiated:* s. *eradiation.*

ERAD'ICATE. *v.* To pull up by the root; completely to destroy. pr. par *eradicating;* past, *eradicated:* s. *eradication:* adj *eradicative.*

ERA'SE. *v.* To destroy, to exscind to expunge. pr. par. *erasing,* past. *erased:* s. *erasement, erasure.*

ERE adv. Before, sooner than. prep *ere.*

ERECT'. *v.* To place perpendicularly to the horizon; to raise; to build. pr. par. *erecting;* past, *erected:* s. *erection, erectness, erector:* adj. *erect, erective.*

ERELONG'. adv. Before a long time had elapsed.

ER'EMITE. *s.* One who lives in a wilderness; a hermit. adj. *eremitical.*

ERENOW'. adv. Before this time.

ER'MINE. *s.* An animal which furnishes a valuable fur. adj. *ermined.*

ERR. *v.* To wander; to miss the right way; to stray, to mistake. pr. par. *erring;* past, *erred:* adj. *errable.*

ER'RAND. *s.* A message; something to be told or done by a messenger.

ER'RANT. adj. Wandering, roving, rambling; vile. s. *errantry,* pl. *errantries.*

ERRA'TA. *s.* The faults of the printer, inserted in the beginning or end of a book. sing. *erratum.*

ERRA'TIC. adj. Wandering, uncertain, keeping no certain order adv. *erratically:* s. *erration.*

ER'ROR. *s.* Mistake; involuntary deviation from truth; a blunder; sin. adj. *erroneous:* adv. *errone ously:* s. *erroneousness.*

ERSE, EARSE. *s.* The language of the Highlands of Scotland.

ERST. adv. At first; in the beginning; once; formerly.

ERUBES'CENCE, ERUBES'CENCY. *s.* The act of growing red; redness. pl. *erubuscencis, erubescences:* adj. *erubescent.*

ERUCT'. *v.* To break wind from the stomach. pr. par. *eructing* past, *eructed.*

133

ERUC'TATE. v. To vomit forth. pr. par. *eructating;* past, *eructated:* s. *eructation.*

ERUDI'TE. adj. Learned. s. *erudition.*

ERUP'TION. s. The act of bursting forth; burst. adj. *eruptive.*

ERYSIP'ELAS. s. A disease which affects the skin with a shining pale red, or citron colour.

ESCALA'DE. s. The act of scaling the walls of a fortification.

ESCAL'OP. s. A shellfish, the shell of which is regularly indented; indenture. pronounced *skol'-lup.*

ESCA'PE. v. To obtain exemption from; to obtain security from; to fly; to avoid. pr. par. *escaping;* past, *escaped:* s. *escape, escaper.*

ESCHALOT'. s. A species of plant. pronounced *shal-lot'.*

ESCHEAT'. s. Any lands, or other profits, that fall to a lord within his manor by forfeiture, or by his tenant dying without an heir. v. *escheat;* pr. par. *escheating;* past, *escheated:* adj. *escheatable:* s. *escheator.*

ESCHEW'. v. To fly, to avoid, to shun. pr. par. *eschewing;* past, *eschewed.*

ES'CORT. s. Convoy; guard from place to place. v. *escort';* pr. par. *escorting;* past, *escorted.*

ESCRITOI'RE. s. A box with all the implements necessary for writing.

ESCU'AGE. s. Service of the shield; a species of tenure, by which lands were anciently held.

ESCULA'PIAN. adj. Medical.

ES'CULENT. adj. Proper for food; eatable.

ESCUTCH'EON. s. The shield of a family: the ensigns armorial.

ESPAL'IER. s. A tree planted and cut so as to join others. v. *espalier;* pr. par. *espaliering;* past, *espaliered.*

ESPE'CIAL. adj. Principal, chief. adv. *especially.*

ESPI'ONAGE. s. The act of procuring and giving intelligence.

ESPLANA'DE. s. The empty space between the glacis of a citadel and the first houses of the town; a grass-plot.

ESPOU'SE. v. To contract or betroth to another; to marry; to wed, to embrace. pr. par. *espousing;* past, *espoused:* s. *espousal, espouser.*

ESPY'. v. To see things at a distance; to discover a thing intended to be hidden; to see unexpectedly. pr. par. *espying;* past, *espied.*

ESQUIRE'. s. The armour-bearer or attendant on a knight; a title of dignity, next in degree below a knight. v. *esquire;* pr. par. *esquiring;* past, *esquired.*

ESSAY'. v. To attempt, to try, to endeavour. pr. par. *essaying;* past, *essayed:* s. *essayer.*

ES'SAY. s. Attempt; endeavour; an irregular indigested piece; a trial. s. *essayist.*

ES'SENCE. s. The nature of any being; formal existence; the chief properties or virtues of any simple or composition, collected into a narrow compass; perfume; odour; scent.

ESSEN'TIAL. adj. Partaking of the essence; necessary to the constitution or existence of any thing, important in the highest degree, principal. s. *essential, essentiality,* pl. *essentialities:* adv. *essentially.*

ESTAB'LISH. v. To settle firmly; to fix unalterably; to ratify, to found. pr. par. *establishing;* past, *established:* s. *establisher, establishment.*

ESTA'TE. s. Condition of life; circumstances in general; rank, property. adj. *estated.*

ESTEEM'. v. To set a value, whether high or low, upon any thing; to rate high, to think. pr. par. *esteeming;* past, *esteemed:* s. *esteem, esteemer.*

ES'TIMABLE. adj. Valuable; worth a large price; worthy of esteem.

134

ES'TIMATE. *v.* To rate; to adjust the value of; to judge of any thing by its proportion to something else. pr. par. *estimating;* past, *estimated:* s. *estimate, estimation, estimator:* adj. *estimative.*

ESTRANGE'. *v.* To keep at a distance; to withdraw; to alienate. pr. par. *estranging;* past, *estranged:* s. *estrangement.*

ES'TUARY. *s.* An arm of the sea; the mouth of a lake or river, in which the tide reciprocates; a frith. pl. *estuaries.*

ETCH. *v.* To engrave in a particular manner, by means of nitric acid; to sketch. pr. par. *etching;* past, *etched:* s. *etcher, etching.*

ETER'NAL. *adj.* Without beginning or end; endless; perpetual. adv. *eternally:* s. *eternalist, eternity.*

ETER'NALIZE. *v.* To make eternal. pr. par. *eternalizing;* past, *eternalized.*

ETHER. *s.* An element more fine and subtile than air; the matter of the highest regions above; a volatile distilled spirit. adj. *ethereal.*

ETH'IC, ETH'ICAL. *adj.* Moral, delivering precepts of morality.

ETH'ICS. *s.* The doctrine of morality; a system of morality.

ETH'NIC, ETH'NICAL. *adj.* Heathen, pagan. s. *ethnicism.*

ET'IQUETTE. *s.* Ceremony.

ETYMOL'OGY. *s.* The descent or derivation of a word from its original; the deduction of formations from the radical word. pl. *etymologies:* adj. *etymological:* adv. *etymologically:* s. *etymologist.*

ET'YMON. *s.* Origin; primitive word.

EU'CHARIST. *s.* The act of giving thanks; the sacrament of the Lord's supper. adj. *eucharistic, eucharistical.*

EUDIOM'ETER. *s.* An instrument to determine the salubrity of the air.

EU'LOGIZE. *v.* To commend, to praise. pr. par. *eulogizing;* past, *eulogized.*

EU'LOGY, EULO'GIUM. *s.* Praise. encomium, panegyric. pl. *eulogies, eulogiums.*

EU'NUCH. *s.* One that is castrated.

EU'PHONY. *s.* An agreeable sound: the contrary to harshness. pl. *euphonies:* adj. *euphonical.*

EUROPE'AN. *adj.* Belonging to Europe.

EVAC'UATE. *v.* To make empty, to quit; to void. pr. par. *evacuating;* past, *evacuated:* s. *evacuation, evacuator:* adj. *evacuative.*

EVA'DE. *v.* To elude; to escape by artifice or stratagem. pr. par *evading;* past, *evaded:* s. *evader.*

EVANES'CENCE. *s.* Disappearance; end of appearance. adj. *evanescent.*

EVAN'GELIST. *s.* A writer of the history of our Lord Jesus. s. *evangelism:* adj. *evangelic, evangelical:* adv. *evangelically.*

EVAN'GELIZE. *v.* To instruct in the gospel, or law of Jesus. pr. par. *evangelizing;* past, *evangelized.*

EVAP'ORATE. *v.* To fly away in vapours or fumes; to waste insensibly, as a volatile spirit. pr. par. *evaporating;* past, *evaporated:* adj. *evaporable:* s. *evaporation.*

EVA'SION. *s.* Act of evading; excuse; subterfuge; sophistry. adj *evasive:* adv. *evasively.*

EVE, E'VEN. *s.* The close of th day; the vigil or fast to be observ ed before a holiday.

E'VEN. *adj.* Level; not rugged: not unequal; uniform; capable of being divided into two equal parts. v *even;* pr. par. *evening;* past, *evened:* adv. *evenly:* s. *evenness.*

E'VEN. *adv.* A word of strong assertion; verily; notwithstanding. likewise.

E'VEN-HANDED. *adj.* Impartial, equitable.

E'VENING. *s.* The close of the day; the beginning of night.

EVENT. *s.* An incident; any thing that happens, good or bad; the consequence of an action. adj. *eventful.*

E'VENTIDE. *s.* The time of evening.

EVEN'TUAL. *adj.* Happening in consequence of any thing; consequential. adv. *eventually.*

EVEN'TUATE. *v.* To happen; to result. pr. par. *eventuating;* past, *eventuated.*

EV'ER. *adv.* At any time; at all times; always; without end; eternally.

EV'ERGREEN. *adj.* Verdant throughout the year. *s. evergreen.*

EVERLAST'ING. *adj.* Enduring without end; perpetual; immortal. adv. *everlastingly:* s. *everlastingness.*

EVERMO'RE. *adv.* Always, eternally.

EVER'SION. *s.* Act of everting; overthrow.

EVERT'. *v.* To destroy, to overthrow. pr. par. *everting;* past, *everted.*

EV'ERY. *adj.* Each one of all.

EV'ERY-DAY. *adj.* Common; occurring on any day.

EVES'DROP. *v.* To skulk about a house, in the night, to listen. pr. par. *evesdropping;* past, *evesdropped;* s. *evesdropper.*

EVICT'. *v.* To dispossess by a judicial course; to take away by sentence of law; to prove. pr. par. *evicting;* past, *evicted:* s. *eviction.*

EV'IDENCE. *s.* The state of being evident; clearness; indubitable certainty; testimony; witness. v. *evidence;* pr. par. *evidencing;* past, *evidenced:* adj. *evident:* adv. *evidently.*

E'VIL. *adj.* Having bad qualities; not good; wicked; corrupt s. *evil:* adv. *evilly.*

EVIL-DO'ER. *s.* A malefactor; one that commits crimes.

EVIL-EY'ED. *adj.* Having a malignant look.

E'VIL-FAVOURED. *adj.* Ill countenanced; not having a good aspect.

E'VILMINDED. *adj.* Malicious, mischievous, malignant.

EVINCE'. *v.* To prove, to show, to manifest. pr. par. *evincing;* past, *evinced.*

EVIS'CERATE. *v.* To embowel, to draw, to deprive of the entrails. pr. par. *eviscerating;* past, *eviscerated.*

EV'ITABLE. *adj.* Avoidable; that may be escaped or shunned. s. *evitation.*

EV'OCATE. *v.* To call forth. pr. par. *evocating;* past, *evocated:* s. *evocation.*

EVO'KE. *v.* To call forth. pr. par. *evoking;* past, *evoked.*

EVOLA'TION. *s.* The act of flying away.

EVOL'VE. *v.* To unfold, to disentangle. pr. par. *evolving;* past, *evolved.*

EVUL'SION. *s.* The act of plucking out.

EWE. *s.* The female sheep.

EW'ER. *s.* A vessel in which water is brought, for washing the hands.

EXACT'. *adj.* Nice; not deviating from rule; methodical; careful. adv. *exactly:* s. *exactitude, exactness.*

EXACT'. *v.* To require authoritatively; to enjoin; to extort. pr. par. *exacting;* past, *exacted:* s. *exaction, exacter, exactor.*

EXAG'GERATE. *v.* To heap upon; to accumulate; to heighten by representation. pr. par. *exaggerating;* past, *exaggerated:* s. *exaggeration, exaggerator:* adj. *exaggeratory.*

EXALT'. *v.* To raise on high; to elevate to power, wealth, or dignity. pr. par. *exalting;* past, *exalted:* s. *exaltation, exaltedness, exalter.*

EXAM'INE. *v.* To try a person accused or suspected, by interrogatories; to question, to scrutinize; to try by experiment, or observation; to search into. pr. par. *examining;* past, *examined:* s. *examinant, examination, examiner:* adj. *examinable.*

EXAM'PLE. *s.* Copy or pattern; that which is proposed to be imitated; precedent; instance; matter of illustration.

EXAN'IMATE. *v.* To deprive of life; to dishearten; to weaken. pr. par. *exanimating;* past, *exanimated:* s. *exanimation.*

EX'ARCH. *s.* A viceroy. s. *exarchate.*

EXAS'PERATE. *v.* To provoke, to enrage. pr. par. *exasperating;* past, *exasperated;* s. *exasperator, exasperation.*

EX'CAVATE. *v.* To hollow; to cut out. pr. par. *excavating;* past, *excavated;* s. *excavation, excavator.*

EXCEED'. *v.* To go beyond; to outgo; to excel. pr. par. *exceeding;* past, *exceeded:* s. *exceedingness, exceeder:* adv. *exceedingly.*

EXCEL'. *v.* To surpass, to exceed. pr. par. *excelling;* past, *excelled.*

EX'CELLENCE, EX'CELLENCY. *s.* The state of abounding in any good quality; dignity; purity; goodness; a title of honour. pl. *excellences, excellencies:* adj. *excellent:* adv. *excellently.*

EXCEPT'. *v.* To leave out; to object; to exclude.

EXCEPT'. *prep.* Exclusively of; unless.

EXCEPTION. *s.* Act of excepting; thing excepted; objection. adj. *exceptionable.*

EXCER'PT. *s.* Something gleaned; something selected. s. *excerption, excerptor.*

EXCESS'. *s.* More than enough; superfluity; intemperance. pl. *excesses:* adj. *excessive:* adv. *excessively:* s. *excessiveness.*

EXCHANGE. *v.* To give or quit one thing for the sake of gaining another; to give and take reciprocally. pr. par. *exchanging;* past, *exchanged:* s. *exchange, exchanger:* adj. *exchangeable.*

EXCHEQ'UER. *s.* The court into which are brought all the revenues belonging to the crown of England; and in which all causes touching the revenues of th crown are tried.

EXCIND'. *v.* To cut off. pr. par *excinding;* past, *excinded:* s. *excision.*

EXCI'SE. *s.* A species of tax. v. *excise;* pr. par. *excising;* past, *excised:* adj. *excisable:* s. *exciseman,* pl. *excisemen.*

EXCISION. *s.* Act of cutting off; destruction; ruin.

EXCI'TE. *v.* To rouse, to animate, to stir up, to encourage. pr. par. *exciting;* past, *excited:* s. *excitement, exciter:* adj. *excitable:* s. *excitability,* pl. *excitabilities.*

EXCLAIM'. *v.* To cry out with vehemence; to make an outcry. pr. par. *exclaiming;* past, *exclaimed.* s. *exclamation, exclaimer:* adj. *exclamatory.*

EXCLU'DE. *v.* To shut out; to hinder from entrance or admission; to debar; to prohibit. pr. par. *excluding;* past, *excluded.*

EXCLU'SION. *s.* Act of excluding adj. *exclusive:* adv. *exclusively:* s *exclusionist.*

EXCOMMU'NICATE. *v.* To eject from the communion of the church, by an ecclesiastical censure. pr. par. *excommunicating* past, *excommunicated:* adj. *excommunicable:* s. *excommunicate, excommunication.*

EXCO'RIATE. *v.* To flay; to strip off the skin. pr. par. *excoriating* past, *excoriated:* s. *excoriation.*

EXCORTICA'TION. *s.* Act of stripping off the bark.

EX'CREMENT. *s.* That which is discharged from the natural passages of the body. adj. *excremental, excrementitious.*

EXCRES'CENCE, EXCRES'CENCY. *s.* Something growing out of another, without use, and contrary to the common order of production. pl. *excrescences, excrescencies:* adj. *excrescent.*

EXCRE'TION. *s.* Separation of animal substance; ejecting something out of the body. adj. *excretive.*

EXCRU'CIATE. *v.* To torture, to torment. pr. par. *excruciating;* past, *excruciated:* s. *excruciation.*

EXCUL'PATE. *v.* To clear from the imputation of a fault. pr. par. *exculpating;* past, *exculpated:* s. *exculpation:* adj. *exculpatory.*

EXCUR'SION. *s.* The act of deviating from the stated or settled path; a ramble; a digression. adj. *excursive:* adv. *excursively:* s. *excursiveness.*

EXCU'SE. *v.* To extenuate by apology; to remit; to disengage from an obligation. pr. par. *excusing;* past, *excused:* adj. *excusable, excusatory, excuseless:* s. *excuse, excuser.*

EX'ECRABLE. adj. Hateful, detestable, accursed. adv. *execrably.*

EX'ECRATE. *v.* To curse, to imprecate ill upon. pr. par. *execrating;* past, *execrated:* s. *execration:* adj. *execratory.*

EX'ECUTE. *v.* To put in act; to perform; to practise; to put to death. pr. par. *executing;* past, *executed:* s. *execution, executor.*

EXECU'TIONER. *s.* He that puts in act, or executes; he that inflicts capital punishment. The last is the only sense in which this word is now properly used.

EXEC'UTIVE. adj. Having the quality of executing or performing; active. s. *executive:* adj. *executory.*

EXEC'UTOR. *s.* He that is intrusted to perform the will of a testator. s. *executorship.*

EXEC'UTRIX. *s.* A woman intrusted to perform the will of a testator. pl. *executrices.*

EXEM'PLAR. *s.* A pattern; an example to be imitated.

EXEM'PLARY. adj. Such as may deserve to be proposed to imitation; such as may give warning to others. adv. *exemplarily.*

EXEM'PLIFY. *v.* To illustrate by example; to transcribe; to copy. pr. par. *exemplifying;* past, *exemplified:* s. *exemplifier, exemplification.*

EXEMPT'. *v.* To privilege, to grant immunity from. pr. par. *exempting,* past, *exempted:* adj. *exempt, exemptible:* s. *exemption.*

EX'EQUIES. *s.* Funeral rites; the ceremony of burial; the procession of burial. (without a singular.)

EX'ERCISE. *s.* Labour of the body; labour, considered as conducive to health; use; practice; employment. v. *exercise;* pr. par. *exercising;* past, *exercised:* s. *exerciser.*

EXERCITA'TION. *s.* Exercise, practice, use.

EXER'GUE. *s.* That part of a medal which belongs not to the general device or subject of it, but which contains, in a corner of it, or under a line or figure, the name of the author, or some collateral circumstance.

EXERT'. *v.* To use with an effort; to perform; to enforce, to push to an effort. pr. par. *exerting;* past, *exerted:* s. *exertion.*

EXFO'LIATE. *v.* To shell off, or separate; as a corrupt bone from the sound part. pr. par. *exfoliating,* past, *exfoliated:* s. *exfoliation:* adj. *exfoliative.*

EXHA'LE. *v.* To send or draw out in vapours; to draw out. pr. par. *exhaling;* past, *exhaled:* s. *exhalation, exhalement:* adj. *exhalable*

EXHAUST'. *v.* To drain; to diminish; to draw till nothing is left. pr. par. *exhausting;* past, *exhausted:* s. *exhauster, exhaustion:* adj. *exhaustible, exhaustless.*

EXHIB'IT. *v.* To offer to view or use; to offer or propose in a formal manner; to display. pr. par. *exhibiting;* past, *exhibited:* s. *ex-*

hibit, exhibiter, exhibition, exhibitioner. adj. *exhibitive, exhibitory:* adv. *exhibitively*.

EXHIL'ARATE. *v.* To make cheerful; to cheer; to fill with mirth; to enliven. pr. par. *exhilarating;* past, *exhilarated:* s. *exhilaration*.

EXHORT'. *v.* To incite, by words, to any good action. pr. par. *exhorting;* past, *exhorted:* s. *exhortation, exhorter:* adj. *exhortative, exhortatory*.

EXHUMA'TION. *s.* The act of unburying, or removing out of the grave.

EX'IGENCE, EX'IGENCY. *s.* Demand, want, need. pl. *exigences, exigencies*.

EX'ILE. *s.* Banishment; state of being banished; the person banished. v. *exile;* pr. par. *exiling;* past, *exiled.* s. *exilement*.

EXIST'. *v.* To be; to have a being. pr. par. *existing;* past, *existed:* s. *existence:* adj. *existent*.

EX'IT. *s.* Recess; departure; act of quitting the theatre of life.

EX'ODUS. *s.* Departure; journey from a place: The second book of Moses is so called, because it describes the journey of the Israelites from Egypt.

EXON'ERATE. *v.* To unload, to disburthen. pr. par. *exonerating;* past, *exonerated:* s. *exoneration:* adj. *exonerative*.

EX'ORABLE. *adj.* To be moved by entreaty.

EXOR'BITANCE, EXOR'BITANCY. *s.* The act of going out of the track prescribed; enormity; gross deviation from rule or right. pl. *exorbitances, exorbitancies:* adj. *exorbitant:* adv. *exorbitantly*.

EX'ORCISE. *v.* To abjure by some holy name; to drive away spirits by certain forms of abjuration; to purify from the influence of malignant spirits, by religious ceremonies. pr. par. *exorcising;* past, *exorcised:* s. *exorciser, exorcism, exorcist*.

EXOR'DIUM. *s.* A formal preface; the proemial part of a composition. adj. *exordial*.

EXOT'IC. *adj.* Foreign; not produced in our own country. s. *exotic*.

EXPAND'. *v.* To spread; to lay open as a net or sheet; to dilate; to spread out every way. pr. par. *expanding;* past, *expanded*.

EXPANSE'. *s.* A body widely extended, without inequalities; immense space.

EXPAN'SION. *s.* Act of expanding; state of being expanded into a wider surface or greater space; extent; pure space, as distinct from extension in solid matter. adj. *expansible, expansive:* s. *expansibility*, pl. *expansibilities*.

EXPA'TIATE. *v.* To range at large; to enlarge upon in language. pr. par. *expatiating;* past, *expatiated:* s. *expatiator*.

EXPA'TRIATE. *v.* To banish from one's native country; to quit one's country. pr. par. *expatriating;* past, *expatriated:* s. *expatriation*.

EXPECT'. *v.* To have a previous apprehension of either good or evil; to wait for; to attend the coming. pr. par. *expecting;* past, *expected:* s. *expectation, expecter, expectancy, expectant:* adj. *expectant*.

EXPEC'TORATE. *v.* To eject from the breast. pr. par. *expectorating;* past, *expectorated:* s. *expectoration, expectorant:* adj. *expectorative*.

EXPE'DIENT. *adj.* Proper, fit, convenient, suitable, quick, expeditious. s. *expedience, expediency*, pl. *expediences, expediencies, expedient.* adv. *expediently*.

EXPEDI'TE. *v.* To facilitate; to free from impediment; to hasten; to despatch. pr. par. *expediting;* past, *expedited:* adv. *expeditely*.

EXPEDI'TION. *s.* Haste, speed, activity; a march or voyage, with martial intentions. adj. *expeditious:* adv. *expeditiously*.

139

EXPEL. *v.* To drive out; to force away; to eject; to banish. pr. par. *expelling;* past, *expelled:* s. *expeller.*

EXPEND'. *v.* To lay out, to spend. pr. par. *expending;* past, *expended:* s. *expenditure.*

EXPEN'SIVE. *adj.* Given to expense; extravagant; costly. adv. *expensively:* s. *expensiveness.*

EXPE'RIENCE. *s.* Practice; frequent trial; knowledge gained by practice. *v. experience;* pr. par. *experiencing;* past, *experienced:* s. *experiencer.*

EXPER'IMENT. *s.* Trial of any thing; something done in order to discover an uncertain or unknown effect. adj. *experimental:* adv. *experimentally:* s. *experimenter, experimentalist.*

EXPERT'. *adj.* Skilful, intelligent, ready, dextrous; skilful by practice or experience. adv. *expertly:* s. *expertness.*

EX'PIATE. *v.* To annul the guilt of a crime, by subsequent acts of piety; to atone for; to make reparation for. pr. par. *expiating;* past, *expiated:* s. *expiation:* adj. *expiable, expiatory.*

EXPI'RE. *v.* To breathe out; to exhale; to conclude; to die. pr. par. *expiring;* past, *expired:* s. *expiration.*

EXPLAIN'. *v.* To expound, to illustrate, to clear. pr. par. *explaining;* past, *explained:* s. *explainer, explanation:* adj. *explainable, explanatory.*

EXPLE'TIVE. *s.* Something used only to take up room. adj. *expletory.*

EXPLICA'TION. *s.* The act of opening, unfolding, or expanding; interpretation; explanation. adj. *explicable, explicatory:* s. *explicator.*

EXPLI'CIT. *adj.* Unfolded, plain, clear; not merely implied. adv. *explicitly:* s. *explicitness.*

EXPLO'DE. *v.* To drive out disgracefully, with some noise of contempt; to drive out with noise and violence. pr. par. *exploding;* past, *exploded:* s. *exploder, explosion:* adj. *explosive.*

EXPLO'SION. *s.* Act of exploding noise produced by exploding. adj *explosive.*

EXPLOIT'. *s.* A design accomplished; an achievement; a successfu attempt.

EXPLO'RE. *v.* To try, to search into, to examine by trial. pr. par. *exploring;* past, *explored:* s. *exploration, explorator, explorement:* adj. *exploratory.*

EXPORT'. *v.* To carry or send out of a country, in the way of traffic. pr. par. *exporting,* past, *exported:* s. *ex'port, exportation, exporter:* adj. *exportable.*

EXPO'SE. *v.* To lay open; to make liable; to put in the power of; to make bare; to put in danger. pr. par. *exposing;* past, *exposed:* s *exposer, exposition, exposure.*

EXPOS'ITOR. *s.* Explainer, expounder, interpreter. adj. *expository.*

EXPOS'TULATE. *v.* To canvass with another; to altercate; to debate, without open rupture. pr. par. *expostulating;* past, *expostulated* s. *expostulation, expostulator:* adj *expostulatory.*

EXPOUND'. *v.* To explain, to clear, to interpret, to examine, to lay open. pr. par. *expounding;* past, *expounded:* s. *expounder.*

EXPRESS'. *v.* To represent by any of the imitative arts, as poetry, sculpture, or painting; to exhibit by language; to utter; to declare; to squeeze out. pr. par. *expressing;* past, *expressed:* s. and adj. *express:* adj. *expressible:* adv. *expressly.*

EXPRESS'. *adj.* Copied, resembling, exactly like; plain; in direct terms; on purpose.

EXPRESS'. *s.* A messenger sent on purpose; a message sent.

EXPRES'SION. *s.* The act or power of representing any thing; the form or mode of language in which any thoughts are uttered; a phrase; the act of squeezing or forcing out any thing by a press. adj. *expressive:* adv. *expressively:* s. *expressiveness.*

EXPUL'SION. *s.* The act of expelling; the state of being expelled. adj. *expulsive.*

EXPUNGE'. *v.* To blot out, to rub out, to efface, to annihilate. pr. par. *expunging;* past, *expunged.*

EXPUR'GATE. *v.* To expunge, to purge away. pr. par. *expurgating;* past, *expurgated:* s. *expurgation, expurgator:* adj. *expurgatory.*

EX'QUISITE. *adj.* Far-sought, excellent, consummate. adv. *exquisitely:* s. *exquisiteness.*

EXTANT. *adj.* Standing out to view; standing above the rest; public.

EXTAT'IC, ECSTAT'IC. *adj.* Rapturous.

EX'TASY, EC'STACY. *s.* Rapture. pl. *extasies, ecstacies.*

EXTEM'PORE. *adv.* Without premeditation; suddenly; readily. adj. *extemporaneous, extemporary:* adv. *extemporally.*

EXTEND'. *v.* To stretch out in any direction; to amplify; to expand; to enlarge; to reach to any distance. pr. par. *extending;* past, *extended:* s. *extender, extension, extent.*

EXTEN'SION. *s.* Act of extending; state of being extended. adj. *extensive:* s. *extensiveness:* adv. *extensively.*

EXTEN'SIBLE. *adj.* Capable of being extended. s. *extensibility,* pl. *extensibilities.*

EXTEN'UATE. *v.* To lessen; to make small in bulk. pr. par. *extenuating;* past, *extenuated:* s. *extenuation.*

EXTE'RIOR. *adj.* Outward, external, not intrinsic. s. *exterior:* adv. *exteriorly.*

EXTER'MINATE. *v.* To drive away, to abolish; to destroy. pr. par. *exterminating;* past, *exterminated.* s. *extermination, exterminator:* adj. *exterminatory.*

EXTER'NAL. *adj.* Outward; not proceeding from itself; having the outward appearance. adv. *externally.*

EXTINCT'. *adj.* Extinguished, quenched, put out, abolished. s. *extinction.*

EXTING'UISH. *v.* To put out, to quench, to suppress, to destroy, to obscure. pr. par. *extinguishing;* past, *extinguished:* s. *extinguisher, extinguishment:* adj. *extinguishable.*

EXTIR'PATE. *v.* To root out, to eradicate, totally to destroy. pr. par. *extirpating;* past, *extirpated* s. *extirpation, extirpator:* adj. *extirpable.*

EXTOL'. *v.* To praise, to magnify, to laud, to celebrate. pr. par. *extolling;* past, *extolled:* s. *extoller.*

EXTORT'. *v.* To draw by force; to force away; to wrest; to gain by violence or oppression. pr. par. *extorting;* past, *extorted:* s. *extorter, extortion, extortioner.*

EX'TRA. A word often used in composition, meaning over and above, extraordinary, beyond.

EXTRACT'. *v.* To draw out; to draw by chymical operation; to select and abstract from a larger treatise. pr. par. *extracting;* past, *extracted:* s. *ex'tract, extraction, extractor.*

EXTRAJUDI'CIAL. *adj.* Out of the regular course of legal procedure. adv. *extrajudicially.*

EXTRAMUN'DANE. *adj.* Beyond the verge of the material world.

EXTRA'NEOUS. *adj.* Not belonging to any thing; foreign; of different substance; not intrinsic.

EXTRAOR'DINARY. *adj.* Different from common order and method; not ordinary; eminent; remarkable: pronounced, *extror-di-nary*: adv. *extraordinarily.*

EXTRAPAROCH'IAL. *adj.* Not comprehended within any parish.

EXTRA'VAGANT. *adj.* Wandering out of his bounds; roving beyond just limits or prescribed methods; irregular; wasteful; prodigal. adv. *extravagantly:* s. *extravagance.*

EXTRAV'ASATED. *adj.* Forced out of the proper containing vessels. s. *extravasation.*

EXTRE'ME. *adj.* Greatest, utmost, last; that beyond which there is nothing. s. *extreme:* adv. *extremely:* s. *extremity,* pl. *extremities.*

EX'TRICATE. *v.* To disembarrass; to set free any one in a state of perplexity; to disentangle. pr. par. *extricating;* past, *extricated:* s. *extrication:* adj. *extricable.*

EXTRIN'SIC. *adj.* External, outward, not intimately belonging. adv. *extrinsically.*

EXTRU'DE. *v.* To thrust off, to drive off. pr. par. *extruding,* past, *extruded.*

EXTRU'SION. *s.* Act of extruding.

EXU'BERANT. *adj.* Growing with superfluous shoots; overabundant; luxuriant. s. *exuberance, exuberancy,* pl. *exuberances, exuberancies:* adv. *exuberantly.*

EXU'DE. *v.* To sweat; to issue by sweat. pr. par. *exuding;* past, *exuded:* s. *exudation.*

EXULT'. *v.* To rejoice above measure; to triumph. pr. par. *exulting,* past, *exulted:* s. *exultation:* adj. *exultant.*

EXUVIÆ. *s.* Cast skins; cast shells; whatever is shed by animals.

EY'AS. *s.* A young hawk. pl. *eyases.*

EYE. *s.* The organ of vision; sight; look; a small catch into which a hook goes. v. *eye;* pr. par. *eying,* past, *eyed:* s. *eyer.*

EYE'BALL. *s.* The apple of the eye, the pupil.

EYE'BROW. *s.* The hairy arch over the eye.

EYE'GLASS. *s.* A glass to assist the sight. pl. *eyeglasses.*

EYE'LASH. *s.* The line of hair that edges the eyelid. pl. *eyelashes.*

EYE'LET. *s.* A hole through which light may enter; any small perforation, for a face to go through.

EYE'LID. *s.* The membrane that shuts over the eye.

EYE'SERVANT. *s.* A servant that works only while watched. s. *eyeservice.*

EYE'SIGHT. *s.* Sight of the eye.

EYE'SORE. *s.* Something offensive to the sight.

EYE'TOOTH. *s.* The tooth on the upper jaw, next on each side to the grinders; the fang.

EYE'WITNESS. *s.* An ocular evidence; one who gives testimony to facts seen with his own eyes. pl. *eyewitnesses.*

EY'RY. *s.* The place where birds of prey build their nests, and hatch pl. *eyries.*

F

FA'BLE. *s.* A feigned story, intended to enforce some moral precept; a fiction in general. adj. *fabled:* s. *fabulist.*

FAB'RICATE. *v.* To build, to construct, to forge, to devise falsely.

pr. par. *fabricating;* past, *fabricated:* s. *fabric, fabrication, fabricator.*

FAB'ULOUS. *adj.* Feigned, full of fables. s. *fabulosity,* pl. *fabulosities, fabulousness:* adv. *fabulously*

FACA'DE. *s.* Front. pronounced *fa-sad*, or *fa-sade*.

FACE. *s.* The visage; countenance; surface of any thing: appearance. *v. face*; pr. par. *facing*; past, *faced.*

FACE'TIOUS. *adj.* Gay, cheerful, lively, witty. adv. *facetiously:* s. *facetiousness.*

FACIL'ITATE. *v.* To make easy; to free from difficulty. pr. par. *facilitating*; past, *facilitated:* s *facility*, pl. *facilities.*

FACSIM'ILE. *s.* An exact copy.

FACT. *s.* A thing done; an effect produced; reality.

FAC'TION. *s.* A party in a state; tumult; discord. s. *factionary*, pl. *factionaries, factionist:* adj. *factious:* adv. *factiously:* s. *factiousness.*

FACTI'TIOUS. *adj.* Made by art; in opposition to what is made by nature.

FAC'TOR. *s.* An agent for another; one who transacts business for another; (in arithmetic) the multiplicator and multiplicand. s. *factorage.*

FAC'TORY. *s.* A house or district inhabited by traders in a distant country; a place where any thing is made. pl. *factories.*

FACTO'TUM. *s.* A servant employed alike in all kinds of business; one who can do every thing.

FAC'ULTY. *s.* The power of doing any thing; ability: faculty, in a university, denotes the masters and professors of the several sciences. pl. *faculties.*

FADE. *v.* To disappear instantaneously; to die away gradually; to vanish. pr. par. *fading*; past, *faded.*

FAG. *v.* To grow weary, to faint with weariness. pr. par. *fagging*; past, *fagged:* s. *fag.*

FAG-END'. *s.* The end of a web of cloth; the refuse or meaner part of any thing.

FAG'OT. *s.* A bundle of sticks bound together, for the fire.

FAIL. *v.* To desert, to disappoint, to neglect, to decay. pr. par *failing*; past, *failed:* s. *failure.*

FAIN. *adj.* Glad, merry, fond, forced. adv. *fain.*

FAINT. *v.* To decay; to sink motionless and senseless. pr. par. *fainting*; past, *fainted:* adj. *faint, faintish:* adv. *faintly:* s. *faintishness, faintness.*

FAINT-HEART'ED. *adj.* Cowardly, timorous. adv. *faint-heartedly:* s. *faint-heartedness.*

FAIR. *adj.* Beautiful, clear, pure favourable, equal. adv. *fairly:* s *fairness.*

FAIR. *s.* An annual or stated meeting of buyers and sellers. s. *fairing.*

FAIR'-SPOKEN. *adj.* Bland and civil in language and address.

FAI'RY. *s.* A kind of fabled being supposed to appear in meadows and reward cleanliness in houses an elf. pl. *fairies:* adj. *fairy.*

FAI'SIBLE. *adj.* See FEASIBLE.

FAITH. *s.* Fidelity, honour, veracity, belief. adj. *faithful, faithless* adv. *faithfully:* s. *faithfulness faithlessness.*

FAL'CHION. *s.* A short, crooke sword; a scimetar.

FAL'CON. *s.* A hawk trained fo sport; a sort of cannon. s. *falconer, falconry*, pl. *falconries.*

FAL'CONET. *s.* A sort of cannon.

FALL. *v.* To drop from a higher place; to decrease; to diminish in value. pr. par. *falling*; past, *fallen:* s. *fall.*

FALL. *s.* In the United States, signifies *autumn.*

FAL'LACY. *s.* Sophism, logical artifice. pl. *fallacies:* adj. *fallacious:* s. *fallaciousness:* adv. *fallaciously.*

FAL'LIBLE. *adj.* Liable to error; such as may be deceived. adv. *fallibly:* s *fallibility*, pl. *fallibilities.*

FALLING-SICK'NESS. *s.* The epilepsy.

FAL'LOW. *adj.* Pale red, or yellow; unsown; unoccupied. *v. fallow;* pr. par. *fallowing;* past, *fallowed.*

FALSE. *adj.* Treacherous, perfidious, counterfeit. adv. *false, falsely* · s. *falsehood, falseness, falsity,* pl. *falsities.*

FALSEHEART'ED. *adj.* Treacherous, perfidious, deceitful. s. *falseheartedness.*

FALSET'TO. *s.* A musical term; a feigned voice.

FAL'SIFY. *v.* To counterfeit, to forge, to confute. pr. par. *falsifying;* past, *falsified:* s. *falsification, falsifier:* adj. *falsifiable.*

FAL'TER. *v.* To hesitate, to waver, to fail. pr. par. *faltering;* past, *faltered;* adv. *falteringly.*

FAME. *s.* Celebrity, renown, report. adj. *famed, fameless.*

FAMIL'IAR. *adj.* Domestic; relating to a family; affable; unceremonious; free. s. *familiarity,* pl. *familiarities:* adv. *familiarly:* v. *familiarize;* pr. par. *familiarizing;* past, *familiarized.*

FAM'ILY. *s.* Those who live in the same house; a race; a genealogy. pl. *families.*

FAM'INE. *s.* A scarcity of food; dearth.

FAM'ISH. *v.* To kill with hunger; to starve. pr par. *famishing;* past, *famished.*

FA'MOUS. *adj.* Renowned, celebrated, much spoken of. adv. *famously:* s. *famosity,* pl. *famosities, famousness.*

FAN. *s.* An instrument used by ladies to move the air and cool themselves; any thing by which the air is moved. v. *fan;* pr. par. *fanning;* past, *fanned.*

FANAT'IC. *s.* An enthusiast; a man mad with wild notions of religion. adj. *fanatic, fanatical:* adv. *fanatically:* s. *fanaticism.*

FAN'CY. *s.* Imagination, taste, idea, inclination, caprice. pl. *fancies:* v. *fancy;* pr. par. *fancying:* past,

fancied: adj. *fanciful:* adv. *fancifully:* s. *fancifulness.*

FANDAN'GO. *s.* A kind of very lively dance. pl. *fandangoes.*

FANE. *s.* A temple; a place consecrated to religion.

FANFARONA'DE. *s.* A bluster; a tumour of fictitious dignity.

FANG. *s.* The long tusks of a boar or other animal; the nails, the talons. adj. *fanged.*

FAN'TASM. *s.* See PHANTASM.

FANTAS'TIC, FANTAS'TICAL. *adj.* Irrational; subsisting only in the imagination; unreal. adv. *fantastically, fantastickly.*

FAN'TASY. *s.* Fancy, imagination, idea, humour. pl. *fantasies.*

FA'QUIR. *s.* A sort of dervise, travelling about and collecting alms.

FAR. *adv.* To great extent in length; remotely. adj. *far:* s. *farness.*

FARCE. *s.* A short dramatic representation, written without regularity, and filled with wild and ludicrous conceits. adj. *farcical:* adv. *farcically.*

FAR'CY. *s.* The leprosy of horses. pl. *farcies.*

FAR'DEL. *s.* A bundle, a little pack.

FARE. *v.* To go, to pass, to happen, to feed, to eat. pr. par. *faring,* past, *fared:* s. *fare.*

FAR'-FETCHED. *adj.* Brought from places remote; elaborately strained.

FAREWELL. *int.* The parting compliment; adieu. s. *farewell.*

FARINA'CEOUS. *adj.* Mealy; tasting like meal.

FARM. *s.* Ground let to a tenant; a portion of land tilled by a tenant or the owner. v. *farm;* pr. par. *farming;* past, *farmed:* adj. *farmable:* s. *farmer.*

FARRA'GO. *s.* A mass formed confusedly of several ingredients. pl. *farragoes.*

FAR'RIER. *s.* A shoer of horses; one who professes the medicine of horses. s. *farriery.*

FAR'ROW. s. A litter of pigs. v. *farrow*; pr. par. *farrowing*; past, *farrowed*.

FAR'THER. adv. At a greater distance; beyond. sup. *farthest*.

FARTHERMO'RE. adv. Besides; over and above; likewise.

FAR'THING. s. The fourth of a penny.

FAR'THINGALE. s. A hoop; circles of whalebone, used to spread the petticoat to a wide circumference.

FAS'CES. s. Rods anciently carried before the Roman consuls, as a mark of their authority.

FAS'CINATE. v. To bewitch, to enchant. pr. par. *fascinating*; past, *fascinated*: s. *fascination*.

FAS'CINE. s. A fagot.

FASH'ION. s. Form; make or cut of clothes; manner; custom. v. *fashion*; pr. par. *fashioning*; past, *fashioned*: adj. *fashionable*: s. *fashionableness*: adv. *fashionably*: s. *fashionist*.

FAST. adj. Firm, immovable, strong, speedy. adv. *fast*, *fastly*: s. *fastness*.

FAST. v. To abstain from food; to mortify the body, by religious abstinence. pr. par. *fasting*; past, *fasted*: s. *fast*, *faster*.

FAS'TEN. v. To make fast; to make firm; to cement; to fix itself. pronounced *fas'-n*. pr. par. *fastening*; past, *fastened*: s. *fastener*.

FASTID'IOUS. adj. Disdainful, squeamish, insolently nice. adv. *fastidiously*: s. *fastidiousness*.

FAT. adj. Full-fed, plump, fleshy. s. *fat*, *fatness*, *fatner*, *fattener*.

FA'TALISM. s. The doctrine that all things happen by necessity. s. *fatalist*, *fatality*, pl. *fatalities*.

FATE. s. Destiny; an eternal series of successive causes: death. adj. *fated*, *fatal*: adv. *fatally*.

FA'THER. s. The male parent; the head of a family; the first ancestor. v. *father*; pr. par. *fathering*; past, *fathered*: adj. *fatherly*, *fatherless*.

FA'THOM. s. A measure of length, containing six feet. v. *fathom*, pr. par. *fathoming*; past, *fathomed*: s. *fathomer*: adj. *fathomless*.

FATIGUE'. s. Weariness, lassitude, labour, toil. v. *fatigue*; pr. par. *fatiguing*; past, *fatigued*.

FAT'IGABLE. adj. Easily wearied susceptible of weariness.

FAT'TEN. v. To make fat. pr. par. *fattening*; past, *fattened*. s. *fattener*: adj. *fattish*.

FAT'UOUS. adj. Stupid, foolish, impotent.

FATU'ITY. s. Foolishness, weakness of mind. pl. *fatuities*.

FAU'CET. s. The pipe inserted into a vessel to give vent to the liquor, and stopped up by a peg or spigot.

FAULT. s. Offence, slight crime, defect. v. *fault*; pr. par. *faulting*, past, *faulted*: s. *faultiness*, *faultlessness*: adj. *faulty*, *faultless*. adv. *faultily*.

FAUN. s. A sort of inferior heathen deity, pretended to inhabit the woods.

FA'VOUR. v. To support; to regard with kindness; to countenance to conduce to. pr. par. *favouring* past, *favoured*: s. *favour*, *favourer*: s. and adj. *favourite*: s. *favouritism*.

FA'VOURABLE. adj. Kind, propitious, conducive to; concurrent adv. *favourably*: s. *favourableness*.

FAWN. s. A young deer. v. *fawn*, pr. par. *fawning*; past, *fawned*.

FAWN. v. To court by frisking before one; to court by any means pr. par. *fawning*; past, *fawned*: s. *fawn*, *fawner*: adv. *fawningly*.

FAY. s. A fairy; an elf; faith.

FE'ALTY. s. Duty due to a superior lord; loyalty. pl. *fealties*.

FEAR. s. Dread, terror, awe, anxiety. v. *fear*; pr. par. *fearing* past, *feared*; adj. *fearful*, *fear* *less:* adv. *fearfully, fearlessly:* s. *fearfulness, fearlessness.*

FEA'SIBLE. *adj.* Practicable; possible to be effected. adv. *feasibly:* s. *feasibility,* pl. *feasibilities, feasibleness.*

FEAST *s.* An anniversary day of rejoicing; an entertainment of the table; something delicious to the palate. v. *feast;* pr. par. *feasting;* past, *feasted:* s. *feaster.*

FEAT. *s.* Act, deed, action, exploit.

FEATH'ER. *s.* The plume of a bird; an ornament. v. *feather;* pr. par. *feathering;* past, *feathered:* adj. *featherless, feathery.*

FEA'TURE. *s.* Any lineament or single part of the face.

FEB'RIFUGE. *adj.* Having the power to cure fevers. s. *febrifuge.*

FEB'RILE. *adj.* Constituting a fever; proceeding from a fever. adj. *febrific.*

FEB'RUARY. *s.* The name of the second month in the year.

FEC'ULENCE, FEC'ULENCY. *s.* Muddiness; quality of abounding with lees or sediments; dregs. pl. *feculences, feculencies:* adj. *feculent.*

FE'CUND. *adj.* Fruitful, prolific. v. *fecundify,* pr. par. *fecundifying;* past, *fecundified:* s. *fecundity,* pl. *fecundities.*

FED. Preterit and past par. of *to feed.*

FED'ERAL. *adj.* Relating to a league or contract. adj. *federate, federative:* s. *federation.*

FED'ERALIST. *s.* One of a political party in the United States, opposed to those called *democrats.*

FEE. *s.* Reward, recompense. v. *fee;* pr. par. *feeing;* past, *feed.*

FEE'BLE. *adj.* Weak, debilitated, sickly, infirm. s. *feebleness:* adv. *feebly.*

FEE'BLE-MINDED. *adj.* Weak of mind, defective in resolution.

FEED. *v.* To supply with food; to furnish; to nourish. pr. par. *feeding;* past, *fed:* s. *feeder.*

FEEL. *v.* To have perception of things by the touch; to be affected by; to perceive mentally. pr. par. *feeling;* past, *felt:* s. *feel, feeler, feeling:* adj. *feeling:* adv. *feelingly.*

FEET. *s.* The plural of foot. adj. *feetless.*

FEIGN. *v.* To invent, to dissemble, to conceal. pr. par. *feigning;* past. *feigned:* s. *feignedness, feigned:* adv. *feignedly.*

FEINT. *s.* A false appearance, a mock assault. adj. *feint.*

FELI'CITATE. *v.* To make happy, to congratulate. pr. par. *felicitating;* past, *felicitated:* s. *felicitation, felicity,* pl. *felicities:* adj. *felicitous:* adv. *felicitously.*

FE'LINE. *adj.* Like a cat; pertaining to a cat.

FELL. *adj.* Cruel, barbarous, inhuman.

FELL. *v.* To knock down, to hew down. pr. par. *felling;* past, *felled:* s. *feller.*

FELL. The preterit of *to fall.*

FELLIF'LUOUS. *adj.* Flowing with gall.

FEL'LOE. *s.* The circumference of a wheel; a portion of the rim of a wheel.

FEL'LOW. *s.* A companion; an associate; equal; one of a pair. v. *fellow;* pr. par. *fellowing;* past, *fellowed.*

FELLOW-COM'MONER. *s.* On who has the same right of common, a commoner at the universities of England, of the highest order, who dines with the fellows.

FELLOW-FEEL'ING. *s.* Sympathy, joint interest.

FEL'LOWSHIP. *s.* Companionship, consort, society.

FEL'ON. *s.* One who has committed a great crime; a whitlow. adj. *felonious:* adv. *feloniously:* s. *felony,* pl. *felonies.*

FELT. Pret. and past par. of the v. *feel.*

FELT. *s.* Cloth made of wool, united without weaving; a hide or skin.

146

FELUC'CA. *s.* A small open boat, with six oars.

FE'MALE. *s.* One of the sex which produces young. adj. *female.*

FEM'ININE. *adj.* Of the female sex; soft, tender, delicate. v. *feminize;* pr. par. *feminizing;* past, *feminized.*

FEM'ORAL. *adj.* Belonging to the thigh.

FEN. *s.* A marsh; low and moist ground; a moor, a bog. adj. *fenny.*

FENCE. *s.* Guard, security, defence, enclosure. v. *fence;* pr. par. *fencing;* past, *fenced:* adj. *fenceless, fencible:* s. *fencer.*

FEND. *v.* To keep off; to shut out. pr. par. *fending;* past, *fended:* s. *fender.*

FENES'TRAL. *adj.* Belonging to windows.

FEN'NEL. *s.* A plant of strong scent.

FEO'DAL. *adj.* Held from another; belonging to a feod or tenure. s. *feodality,* pl. *feodalities; feodatary,* pl. *feodataries:* adj. *feodatory.*

FERMENT'. *v.* To exalt or rarefy by intestine motion of parts. pr. par. *fermenting;* past, *fermented:* s. *fer'ment, fermentation:* adj. *fermentable, fermental, fermentative.*

FERN. *s.* A species of plant. adj. *ferny.*

FERO'CIOUS. *adj.* Savage, fierce, ravenous, rapacious. adv. *ferociously:* s. *ferociousness, ferocity,* pl. *ferocities.*

FER'RET. *s.* A kind of rat, with red eyes, used to catch rabbits; a kind of narrow woollen tape. v. *ferret;* pr. par. *ferreting;* past, *ferreted:* s. *ferreter.*

FERRU'GINOUS. *adj.* Partaking of particles and qualities of iron.

FER'RULE. *s.* An iron ring put round any thing, to keep it from cracking.

FER'RY. *v.* To carry over in a boat. pr. par. *ferrying;* past, *ferried:* s. *ferry,* pl. *ferries, ferriage.*

FER'TILE. *adj.* Fruitful, abundant plenteous. s. *fertileness, fertility* pl. *fertilities:* v. *fertilize;* pr. par *fertilizing;* past, *fertilized.*

FER'ULA. *s.* An instrument of correction, with which young scholars are beaten on the hand. v. *ferule,* pr. par. *feruling;* past, *feruled.*

FER'VENCY. *s.* Heat of mind, ardour, eagerness, zeal. pl. *fervencies:* adj. *fervent:* adv. *fervently.*

FER'VID. *adj.* Hot, burning, boiling, vehement. s. *fervidity,* pl. *fervidities, fervidness, fervour.*

FES'TAL. *adj.* Belonging or relating to a feast.

FES'TIVAL. *s.* Time of feast, anniversary-day of civil or religious joy. adj. *festival, festive:* s. *festivity,* pl. *festivities.*

FESTOON'. *s.* An ornament in the form of a wreath. adj. *festooned.*

FETCH. *v.* To go and bring; to derive. pr. par. *fetching;* past, *fetched:* s. *fetch, fetcher.*

FE'TID. *adj.* Stinking; rancid; having a strong and offensive smell. s. *fetidness.*

FET'LOCK. *s.* A tuft of hair, that grows behind the pastern joint of horses.

FET'TER. *s.* Commonly used in the plural. Chains for the feet. v. *fetter;* pr. par. *fettering;* past, *fettered.*

FEU'-DE-JOIE. *s.* A firing of guns on any joyful occasion.

FEUD. *s.* Quarrel, contention, opposition; a conditional allotment of land. adj. *feudal:* s. *feudalism, feudatary,* pl. *feudataries.*

FE'VER. *s.* A disease in which the body is violently heated, and the pulse quickened, or in which heat and cold prevail by turns. adj. *feverish:* s. *feverishness.*

FEW. *adj.* Not in a great number s. *fewness.*

FI'AT. *s.* An order, a decree.

FIB. *s.* A lie, a falsehood. v. *fib* pr. par. *fibbing;* past, *fibbed:* s. *fibber.*

FI'BRE. *s.* A small thread or string; the first constituent part of flowers. adj. *fibrous.*

FICK'LE. *adj.* Changeable, inconstant, irresolute. s. *fickleness:* adv. *fickly.*

FIC'TION. *s.* The act of feigning or inventing; a falsehood.

FICTI'TIOUS. *adj.* Counterfeit, false, feigned, imaginary. adv. *fictitiously:* s. *fictitiousness.*

FID'DLE. *s.* A stringed musical instrument; a violin. v. *fiddle;* pr. par. *fiddling;* past, *fiddled:* s. *fiddler.*

FID'DLESTICK. *s.* The bow which a fiddler draws over the strings of a fiddle.

FID'DLESTRING. *s.* The string of a fiddle.

FIDEL'ITY. *s.* Honesty, veracity, faithful adherence. pl. *fidelities.*

FIDG'ET. *v.* To move nimbly, and irregularly. pr. par. *fidgeting;* past, *fidgeted:* s. *fidget, fidgeter:* adj. *fidgety.*

FIDU'CIAL. *adj.* Confident, undoubting. adv. *fiducially:* adj. *fiduciary:* s. *fiduciary,* pl. *fiduciaries.*

FIE. *int.* A word of blame or indignation.

FIEF. *s.* A fee, a manor, a possession held by some tenure of a superior.

FIELD. *s.* A cultivated tract of ground; ground not inclosed, the open country.

FIELD'FARE. *s.* A bird.

FIELD'MARSHAL. *s.* Commander of an army in a field; the officer of highest military rank in England.

FIELD'OFFICER. *s.* An officer whose command in the field extends to a whole regiment.

FIELD'PIECE *s.* A small cannon used in battle, but not in sieges.

FIEND. *s.* An enemy; the great enemy of mankind. adj. *fiendlike.*

FIERCE. *adj.* Savage, ravenous, violent, angry. adv. *fiercely:* s. *fierceness.*

FI'ERY. *adj.* Consisting of fire; vehement, ardent, passionate. s. *fieriness.*

FIFE. *s.* A pipe blown to the drum. s. *fifer.*

FIF'TEEN. *adj.* Five and ten, ordinal. adj. *fifteenth.*

FIFTH. *adj.* The ordinal of five adv. *fifthly.*

FIF'TY. *adj.* Five tens. pl. *fifties.* adj. *fiftieth.*

FIG. *s.* A tree that bears figs; the fruit of the fig-tree.

FIGHT. *v.* To contend in battle, to combat; to contend. pr. par. *fighting;* past, *fought.* s. *fight, fighter.*

FIG'MENT. *s.* An invention; a fiction; the idea feigned.

FIG'URATIVE. *adj.* Representing something else; typical; representative; not literal. adv. *figuratively.*

FIG'URE. *s.* The form of any thing, as terminated by the outline; shape; form; a statue; type. v. *figure;* pr. par. *figuring;* past, *figured.*

FIL'AMENT. *s.* A slender thread; a body slender and long, like a thread.

FIL'BERT. *s.* A fine hazel-nut, with a thin shell.

FILCH. *v.* To steal, to pilfer. pr par. *filching;* past, *filched:* s. *filcher:* adv. *filchingly.*

FILE. *s.* A thread; a line on which papers are strung, to keep them in order; a line of soldiers, ranged one behind another; a kind of instrument. v. *file;* pr. par. *filing,* past, *filed:* s. *filer, filing.*

FIL'IAL. *adj.* Pertaining to or befitting a son or daughter. s. *filiation.*

FIL'IGREE-WORK. *s.* Work curiously wrought; a kind of wirework.

143

FILL. *v.* To store till no more can be admitted; to satisfy. pr. par. *filling*; past, *filled*: *s. fill, filler*.

FIL'LET. *s.* A band tied round the head or other part; the fleshy part of the thigh, applied commonly to veal. v. *fillet*; pr. par. *filleting*; past, *filleted*.

FIL'LIBEG. *s.* A little plaid; a dress, reaching only to the knees, worn in the Highlands of Scotland, instead of breeches.

FIL'LIP. *v.* To strike with the nail of the finger, by a sudden spring or motion. pr. par. *filliping*; past, *filliped*: *s. fillip*.

FIL'LY. *s.* A young mare. pl. *fillies*.

FILM. *s.* A thin pellicle or skin. adj *filmy*.

FIL'TER. *v.* To strain, to percolate. pr. par. *filtering*; past, *filtered*: *s. filter*.

FILTH. *s.* Dirt, nastiness. adv. *filthily*: *s. filthiness*: adj. *filthy*.

FIL'TRATE. *v.* To strain, to percolate, to filter. pr. par. *filtrating*; past, *filtrated*: *s. filtration*.

FIN. *s.* The wing of a fish; the limb by which he balances his body, and moves in the water. adj. *finned, finny, finless, finlike*.

FI'NAL. *adj.* Ultimate, conclusive, decisive, mortal. adv. *finally*.

FINANCE'. *s.* Revenue, income, profit. adj. *financial*: *s. financier*.

FIND. *v.* To obtain by searching or seeking; to meet with; to detect; to supply, &c. pr. par. *finding*; past, *found*: *s. finder*.

FINE. *adj.* Not coarse, pure, refined, clear, nice. s. *fine, fineness*: v. *fine*; pr. par. *fining*; past, *fined*: adv. *finely*.

FINE *s.* A penalty; a mulct.

FINE'DRAW. *v.* To sew up a rent with so much nicety that it is not perceived. pr. par. *finedrawing*; past, *finedrawn*: *s. finedrawer*.

FI'NERY. *s.* Show, splendour of appearance. pl. *fineries*.

FINE'SPOKEN. *adj.* Using a number of fine phrases.

FINE'SPUN. *adj.* Ingeniously contrived; artfully invented.

FINESSE'. *s.* Artifice, stratagem.

FIN'GER. *s.* The flexible member of the hand, by which men catch and hold. v. *finger*; pr. par. *fingering*; past, *fingered*: *s. fingering*.

FIN'GER-BOARD. *s.* The board at the neck of a fiddle, guitar, or lute where the fingers operate on the strings.

FIN'ICAL. *adj.* Nice, foppish. adv. *finically*: *s. finicalness*.

FIN'ISH. *v.* To complete, to make perfect, to end. pr. par. *finishing*, past, *finished*: *s. finish, finisher, finishing*.

FI'NITE. *adj.* Limited, bounded, terminated. *s. finiteness, finitude*.

FIR. *s.* The tree of which deal-boards are made.

FIRE. *s.* The igneous element; flame; any thing burning. v. *fire*; pr. par. *firing*; past, *fired*: *s. firing*.

FIRE'-ARMS. *s.* Arms which owe their efficacy to fire; guns.

FIRE'BRAND. *s.* A piece of wood kindled; an incendiary.

FIRE'-ENGINE. *s.* A machine for extinguishing accidental fires.

FIRE'LOCK. *s.* A soldier's gun; a gun discharged by striking steel with flint.

FIRE'MAN. *s.* One who is employed to extinguish burning houses.

FIRE'-PLUG. *s.* A stopple which, in the streets of London, covers a cock that conveys water for the fire-engines.

FIRE'-SHOVEL. *s.* The instrument with which coals are thrown upon a fire.

FIRE'SIDE. *s.* The hearth, the chimney.

FIRE'-WOOD. *s.* Wood to burn; fuel.

FIRE'-WORK. *s.* Shows of fire; pyrotechnical performances.

FIR'KIN. *s.* A vessel containing nine gallons.

FIRM. *adj.* Strong, hard, constant, steady. *s. firm, firmness*: adv. *firmly*.

FIRM'AMENT. *s.* The sky, the heavens.

FIR'MAN. *s.* A grant or license given by Asiatic potentates.

FIRST. *adj.* The ordinal of one; earliest in time; great; excellent. *adv. first: s. firstling.*

FIRST'-FRUITS. *s.* What the season earliest produces or matures; the first profits of any thing.

FIRST'-RATE. *adj.* A term adopted from a ship of the first rate or size, for pre-eminent.

FIS'CAL. *adj.* Belonging to the public treasury.

FISH. *s.* An animal that inhabits the water. v. *fish;* pr. par. *fishing;* past, *fished:* s. *fisher, fishing, fishery,* pl. *fisheries:* adj. *fishy.*

FISH'ERMAN. *s.* One whose employment is to catch fish.

FISH'-HOOK. *s.* A hook to catch fish.

FISH'-KETTLE. *s.* A caldron, made long, that fish may be boiled in it without bending.

FISH'MONGER. *s.* A dealer in fish.

FIS'SILE. *adj.* Having the grain in a certain direction, so as to be cleft.

FIS'SURE. *s.* A cleft; a narrow chasm, where a breach has been made.

FIST. *s.* The hand clenched, with the fingers doubled down.

FIS'TICUFFS. *s.* Battle with the fists; blows with the fist.

FIS'TULA. *s.* A sinuous ulcer, callous within. adj. *fistular, fistulous:* v. *fistulate;* pr. par. *fistulating;* past, *fistulated.*

FIT. *s.* A paroxysm or exacerbation of any intermittent distemper; interval; disorder. adj. *fitful.*

FIT. *v.* To accommodate to any thing; to furnish; to become. pr. par. *fitting;* past, *fitted:* adj. *fit:* adv. *fitly, fittingly:* s. *fitness, fitter.*

FIVE *adj.* Four and one.

FIVE'BARRED. *adj.* Having five bars, usually applied to gates.

FIVE'FOLD. *adj.* Having five distinctions; composed of five materials.

FIX. *v.* To make fast; to settle; to pierce. pr. par. *fixing;* past, *fixed:* s. *fixation, fixedness, fixity,* pl. *fixities, fixture:* adv. *fixedly.*

FIZ. *v.* To emit a slight and transient noise. pr. par. *fizzing;* past, *fizzed:* s. *fiz.*

FIZ'GIG. *s.* A kind of dart or harpoon, with which seamen strike fish; a kind of fire-work, which boys make up in paper, and explode.

FLAB'BY. *adj.* Soft, not firm

FLAC'CID. *adj.* Weak, limber, lax. s. *flaccidity,* pl. *flaccidities.*

FLAG. *v.* To hang loose, without stiffness or tension; to grow feeble. pr. par. *flagging;* past, *flagged:* s. *flag, flagginess:* adj. *flaggy.*

FLA'GEOLET. *s.* A kind of musical instrument.

FLAG'-OFFICER. *s.* A commander of a squadron.

FLAG'-SHIP. *s.* The ship in which the commander of a fleet sails.

FLA'GELLATE. *v.* To whip or scourge. pr. par. *flagellating;* past, *flagellated:* s. *flagellation.*

FLAGI'TIOUS. *adj.* Wicked, villanous, atrocious. s. *flagitiousness.*

FLAG'ON. *s.* A vessel of drink, with a narrow mouth.

FLA'GRANT. *adj.* Ardent, burning, eager, notorious. adv. *flagrantly.* s. *flagrance, flagrancy.*

FLAG'-STAFF. *s.* The staff on which a flag is fixed.

FLAIL. *s.* The instrument by which grain is beaten out of the ear.

FLAKE. *s.* Any thing that appears loosely held together, like a flock of wool; a stratum; layer. v. *flake,* pr. par. *flaking;* past, *flaked:* adj. *flaky.*

FLAM. *s.* A freak, a whim, a fancy.

FLAM'BEAU. *s.* A lighted torch. pl. *flambeaux*

FLAME. *s.* Light emitted from fire; fire. v. *flame;* pr. par. *flaming;* past, *flamed:* adv. *flamingly:* adj. *flamy.*
FLA'MEN. *s.* A priest; one that officiates in solemn offices. adj. *flaminical.*
FLAM'MABLE. *adj.* Capable of being set on fire. s. *flammability,* pl. *flammabilities;* s. *flammation:* adj. *flammeous.*
FLAMIN'GO. *s.* The name of a bird, common in many parts of America. pl. *flamingoes.*
FLANK. *s.* That part of the side of a quadruped near the hinder thigh; the side of an army or fleet. v. *flank;* pr. par. *flanking;* past, *flanked:* s. *flanker.*
FLAN'NEL. *s.* A soft, nappy stuff, of wool.
FLAP. *s.* Any thing that hangs broad and loose; a disease in horses. v. *flap;* pr. par. *flapping;* past, *flapped:* s. *flapper.*
FLARE. *v.* To glitter with transient lustre; to glitter offensively. pr. par. *flaring;* past, *flared.*
FLASH. *s.* A sudden, quick, transitory blaze. pl. *flashes:* v. *flash;* pr. par. *flashing;* past, *flashed:* s. *flasher:* adj. *flashy:* adv. *flashily.*
FLASK. *s.* A bottle, a vessel.
FLAT. *adj.* Horizontally level; smooth; not elevated; tasteless; insipid. s. *flat, flatness:* adv. *flatly:* v. *flatten;* pr. par. *flattening;* past, *flattened:* adj. *flattish.*
FLAT'TER. *v.* To soothe with praises; to raise false hopes. pr. par. *flattering;* past, *flattered:* s. *flatterer. flattery,* pl. *flatteries:* adv. *flatteringly.*
FLATULENT. *adj.* Turgid with air; windy; empty. s. *flatulency,* pl. *flatulencies.*
FLAUNT. *v.* To make a fluttering show in apparel; to carry a pert or saucy appearance. pr. par. *flaunting;* past, *flaunted:* s *flaunt.*
FLA'VOUR. *s.* Power of pleasing the taste; odour, fragrance. adj *flavoured.*
FLAW. *s.* A crack or breach; a fault, defect. v. *flaw;* pr. par *flawing;* past, *flawed:* adj. *flawless, flawy.*
FLAX. *s.* The plant of which linen thread is made. adj. *flaxen.*
FLAY. *v.* To strip off the skin. pr. par. *flaying;* past, *flayed:* s. *flayer.*
FLEA. *s.* A small red insect. adj. *fleabitten.*
FLECK'ER. *v.* To spot; to mark with strokes or touches. pr. par. *fleckering,* past, *fleckered.*
FLEC'TION *s.* The act or power of bending.
FLED. Preterit and past par. of the v. *flee.*
FLEDGE. *v.* To furnish with wings; to supply with feathers. pr. par. *fledging;* past, *fledged.*
FLEE. *v.* To run from danger; to have recourse to shelter. pr. par. *fleeing;* past, *fled.*
FLEECE. *s.* As much wool as is shorn from one sheep. s. *fleecer:* adj. *fleecy.*
FLEECE. *v.* To clip the fleece of a sheep; to plunder, as a sheep is stripped of his wool. pr. par. *fleecing;* past, *fleeced.*
FLEET. *adj.* Swift of pace; quick, nimble. adj. *fleeting:* s. *fleetness:* adv. *fleetly.*
FLEET. *s.* A company of ships; a navy.
FLEM'ING. *s.* A native or inhabitant of the Low Countries. adj. *Flemish.*
FLESH. *s.* The body, distinguished from the soul; animal food; carnality. v. *flesh;* pr. par. *fleshing* past, *fleshed:* s. *fleshiness:* adj. *fleshless, fleshly, fleshy.*
FLESH'MEAT. *s.* Animal food; the flesh of animals prepared for food.
FLEUR DE LIS. *s.* A kind of lily, called the iris; the emblem of France.
FLEW. The preterit of the v. *fly.*
FLEX'IBLE. *adj.* Possible to be bent;

pliant, complying, ductile s. *flexibility*, pl. *flexibilities, flexibleness:* adj. *flexile.*

FLEX'ION. s. The act of bending; a double. adj. *flexuous:* s. *flexure.*

FLICK'ER. v. To flutter; to fluctuate; to move with uncertain and hasty motion. pr. par. *flickering;* past, *flickered.*

FLI'ER. s. One that runs away; a fugitive; a part of a machine.

FLIGHT. s. The act of flying or running from danger; a flock of birds flying together; a volley; the space passed by flying. adj. *flighty:* s. *flightiness.*

FLIMSY. adj. Weak, feeble, mean, spiritless. s. *flimsiness.*

FLINCH. v. To shrink from any suffering or undertaking; to fail. pr. par. *flinching;* past, *flinched:* s. *flincher.*

FLING. v. To cast from the hand; to throw; to cast with violence. pr. par. *flinging,* past, *flung:* s. *fling, flinger.*

FLINT. s. A semi-pellucid stone; any thing eminently or proverbially hard. adj. *flinty:* s. *flintiness.*

FLINT-HEART'ED. adj. Having a hard heart; cruel.

FLIP. s. A liquor much used in ships, made by mixing beer with spirits and sugar.

FLIPPANT. adj. Nimble, moveable, pert, petulant. adv. *flippantly:* s. *flippancy,* pl. *flippancies.*

FLIRT. v. To throw any thing with a quick, elastic motion; to be unsteady and fluttering; to coquet. pr. par. *flirting;* past, *flirted:* s. *flirt, flirtation.*

FLIT. v. To fly away, to remove, to flutter. pr. par. *flitting;* past, *flitted:* s. *flitting.*

FLOAT. v. To swim on the surface. pr. par. *floating;* past, *floated:* s. *floater.*

FLOCK. s. A company; usually a company of birds or beasts. v. *flock;* pr. par. *flocking;* past, *flocked*

FLOG. v. To lash, to whip. pr. par *flogging;* past, *flogged:* s. *flogger.*

FLOOD. s. A body of water; the sea; a deluge. v. *flood;* pr. par. *flooding;* past, *flooded.*

FLOOD'GATE. s. A gate or shutter, by which a water-course is closed or opened.

FLOOR. s. The bottom of a room; a story; a flight of rooms. v. *floor;* pr. par. *flooring;* past, *floored:* s. *flooring.*

FLO'RAL. adj. Relating to Flora, or to flowers. s. *florist.*

FLOR'ENTINE. s. A native of Florence.

FLO'RID. adj. Productive of flowers; bright in colour; embellished. s. *floridness:* adv. *floridly.*

FLOR'IN. s. A coin, first made by the Florentines.

FLOTIL'LA. s. Any number of small vessels.

FLOUNCE. v. To move with weight and tumult; to deck with flounces. pr. par. *flouncing;* past, *flounced:* s. *flounce.*

FLOUNCE. s. Something sewed to a garment, and hanging loose, so as to swell and shake.

FLOUN'DER. v. To struggle with violent and irregular motions. pr. par. *floundering;* past, *floundered:* s. *flounder.*

FLOUN'DER. s. A species of flat fish, called fluke.

FLOUR. s. The edible part of corn; the meal. v. *flour;* pr. par. *flouring;* past, *floured.*

FLOUR'ISH. v. To be in a prosperous state; to boast. pr. par. *flourishing;* past, *flourished.* s. *flourish, flourisher:* adv. *flourishingly.*

FLOUT. v. To mock, to insult. pr par. *flouting;* past, *flouted:* s. *flout, flouter:* adv. *floutingly.*

FLOW. v. To run or spread as water; to run; to glide smoothly; to abound. pr. par. *flowing;* past, *flowed:* s. *flow:* adv. *flowingly.*

152

FLOW'ER. *s.* The part of a plant which contains the seeds; an ornament; the prime. *v. flower*; pr. par. *flowering*; past, *flowered*: adj. *flowery*.

FLOWN. The past par. of the v. *to fly*.

FLUC'TUATE. *v.* To float backward and forward; to be irresolute. pr. par. *fluctuating*; past, *fluctuated*: *s. fluctuation*: adj. *fluctuant*.

FLUE. *s.* A small pipe or chimney, to convey air or smoke.

FLU'ENT. *adj.* Liquid, flowing, in motion, copious, voluble. adv. *fluently*: *s. fluency*, pl. *fluencies*.

FLU'ID. *adj.* Having parts easily separable; not solid. *s. fluidity*, pl. *fluidities*.

FLUKE. *s.* A kind of flat fish, called also *flounder*; the broad part of an anchor, which takes hold of the ground.

FLUM'MERY. *s.* A kind of food, made by the coagulation of wheat, flour, or oatmeal.

FLUNG. Pret. and past par. of the v. *to fling*.

FLUR'RY. *s.* A gust or storm of wind; hurry; a violent commotion. pl. *flurries*: *v. flurry*; pr. par. *flurrying*; past, *flurried*.

FLUSH. *v.* To flow with violence; to come in haste; to glow in the skin. pr. par. *flushing*; past, *flushed*: adj. and *s. flush*.

FLUS'TER. *v.* To confound, to hurry. pr. par. *flustering*; past, *flustered*: *s. fluster*.

FLUTE. *s.* A musical pipe; a channel or furrow in a pillar. *v. flute*; pr. par. *fluting*; past, *fluted*.

FLUT'TER. *v.* To take short flights, with great agitation of the wings; to move irregularly. pr. par. *fluttering*; past, *fluttered*: *s. flutter*.

FLUVIAT'IC. *adj.* Belonging to rivers.

FLUX. *s.* The act of flowing; passage, concourse, confluence. *v. flux*, pr par. *fluxing*; past, *fluxed*: *s. fluxation. fluxion, fluxibility*, pl. *fluxibilities*: adj. *fluxible*.

FLUX'IONS. *s.* The arithmetic or analysis of infinitely small, variable quantities. *s. fluxionist*.

FLY. *v.* To move through the air with wings; to move with rapidity, to run away. pr. par. *flying*, past, *flown*: *s. fly*, pl. *flies*, *flyer*.

FLY'-BITTEN. *adj.* Stained by the bites of flies.

FLY'BLOW. *s.* The egg of a fly. v *flyblow*; pr. par. *flyblowing*; past, *flyblown*.

FOAL. *s.* The offspring of a mare; or other beast of burthen. *v. foal*, pr. par. *foaling*; past, *foaled*.

FOAM. *s.* The white substance which agitation or fermentation gathers on the top of liquors; froth, spume. *v. foam*; pr. par *foaming*; past, *foamed*: adj. *foamy* adv. *foamingly*.

FOB. *s.* A small pocket.

FOB. *v.* To cheat, to trick, to defraud. pr. par. *fobbing*; past, *fobbed*.

FO'CUS. *s.* The point of convergence or concourse, where the rays meet and cross the axis after their refraction. Latin pl *foci*, English pl. *focuses*.

FOD'DER. *s.* Dry food, stored up for cattle against winter. *v. fodder*. pr. par. *foddering*; past, *foddered*. *s fodderer*.

FOE. *s.* An enemy in war; a persecutor; an opponent; an ill-wisher. adj. *foelike*: *s. foeman*.

FOE'TUS. *s.* The child in the womb after it is perfectly formed; but before, it is called embryo.

FOG. *s.* A thick mist; a moist dense vapour, near the surface of the land or water. adv. *foggily* s. *fogginess*: adj. *foggy*.

FOI'BLE. *s.* A weak side; a blind side; a failing.

FOIL. *v.* To put to the worst; to defeat; to puzzle. pr. par. *foiling* past, *foiled*: *s. foil*, *foiler*. adj. *foilable*.

FOIST. *v.* To insert by forgery; to falsify; to impose. pr. par. *foisting*; past, *foisted:* s. *foister.*

FOLD. *s.* The ground in which sheep are confined; a limit, a boundary; a double. v. *fold;* pr. par. *folding;* past, *folded:* s. *folder.*

FO'LIAGE. *s.* Leaves; tufts of leaves. v. *foliate;* pr. par. *foliating;* past, *foliated:* s. *foliation.*

FO'LIO. *s.* A leaf or page of a book; a large book, of which the pages are formed by a sheet of paper once doubled.

FOLK. *s.* People; in familiar language, nations, mankind.

FOL'LOW. *v.* To go after; to pursue as an enemy; to chase; to accompany; to imitate; to obey. pr. par. *following;* past, *followed:* s. *follower.*

FOL'LY. *s.* Weakness of intellect; criminal weakness; depravity of mind. pl. *follies.*

FOMENT'. *v.* To cherish with heat; to bathe with warm lotions; to encourage. pr. par. *fomenting;* past, *fomented:* s. *fomentation, fomenter.*

FOND. *adj.* Foolishly tender; injudiciously indulgent; loving. adv. *fondly:* s. *fondness.*

FON'DLE. *v.* To treat with great indulgence; to caress. pr. par. *fondling;* past, *fondled:* s. *fondler, fondling.*

FONT. *s.* A stone vessel, in which the water for holy baptism is contained in the church; an assortment of letters and accents.

FOOD. *s.* Victuals; any thing that nourishes. adj. *foodless.*

FOOL. *s.* One to whom nature has denied reason; an idiot; a buffoon. v. *fool;* pr. par. *fooling;* past, *fooled:* s *foolery,* pl. *fooleries, foolishness:* adj. *foolish:* adv. *foolishly.*

FOOL. *s.* A liquid made of gooseberries, scalded and pounded and used with cream.

FOOL'HARDY. *adj.* Daring, without judgment; madly adventurous. s. *foolhardiness.*

FOOLS'CAP. *s.* A term denoting the size of a sheet of paper.

FOOT. *s.* The part upon which we stand; the support of any thing; the base; infantry; a measure containing twelve inches. v. *foot,* pr. par. *footing;* past, *footed:* s. *footing:* adj. *footless.*

FOOT'BALL. *s.* A ball commonly made of a blown bladder.

FOOT'BOY. *s.* A low menial; an attendant in livery.

FOOT'MAN. *s.* A menial servant in livery. pl. *footmen.*

FOOT'PACE. *s.* A pace no faster than a slow walk.

FOOT'PAD. *s.* A highway-man that robs on foot.

FOOT'PATH. *s.* A narrow way, which will not admit horses or carriages.

FOOT'POST. *s.* A post or messenger that travels on foot.

FOOT'-SOLDIER. *s.* A soldier that marches and fights on foot.

FOOT'STEP. *s.* Trace, track; impression left by the foot.

FOOT'STOOL. *s.* A stool for the feet.

FOP. *s.* A simpleton, a coxcomb, a pretender. s. *fopling, foppery,* pl. *fopperies, foppishness:* adj. *foppish:* adv. *foppishly.*

FOR. *prep.* Because of; with respect to; in the place of, in search of, &c.

FOR'AGE. *v.* To wander in search of provisions. pr. par. *foraging;* past, *foraged:* s. *forage, forager.*

FORBEAR'. *v.* To cease from any thing; to intermit; to pause; to delay; to abstain. pr. par. *forbearing;* past, *forborne:* s. *forbearance, forbearer.*

FORBID'. *v.* To prohibit, to interdict, to oppose, to hinder. pr. par. *forbidding;* past, *forbidden:* s. *forbiddance, forbidder*

FORCE. *s.* Strength, vigour, might, violence, armament. v. *force;* pr. par. *forcing;* past, *forced:* adv. *forcedly, forcefully, forcibly:* s. *forcer, forcibleness:* adj. *forceless, forcible.*

FORCE'MEAT. *s.* A term of cookery.

FOR'CEPS. *s.* A pair of tongs; a surgical instrument. pl. *forcepses.*

FORD. *s.* A shallow part of a river, where it may be passed without swimming. v. *ford;* pr. par. *fording;* past, *forded:* adj. *fordable.*

FORE. *adj.* Anterior; not behind.

FOREADVI'SE. *v.* To counsel early. pr. par. *foreadvising;* past, *foreadvised.*

FOREARM'. *v.* To provide for attack or resistance, before the time of need. pr. par. *forearming;* past, *forearmed.*

FOREBO'DE. *v.* To prognosticate, to foretell. pr. par. *foreboding;* past, *foreboded:* s. *foreboder, forebodement.*

FORECAST'. *v.* To scheme; to plan before execution. pr. par. *forecasting;* past, *forecasted:* s. *fore'cast, forecaster.*

FORE'CASTLE. *s.* In a ship, that part where the foremast stands.

FORECLOSE'. *v.* To shut up, to preclude, to prevent. pr. par. *foreclosing;* past, *foreclosed:* s. *foreclosure.*

FORE'DECK. *s.* That part of the deck which is near the bow of a ship.

FOREDETER'MINE. *v.* To decree beforehand. pr. par. *foredetermining;* past, *foredetermined.*

FOREDOOM'. *v.* To predestinate. pr. par. *foredooming;* past, *foredoomed.*

FORE'END. *s.* The anterior part.

FORE'FATHER. *s.* Ancestor; one who, in any degree of ascending genealogy, precedes another.

FORE'FINGER. *s.* The finger next to the thumb.

FORE'FOOT. *s.* The anterior foot of a quadruped. pl. *forefeet.*

FOREGO'. *v.* To quit, to give up, to resign. pr. par. *foregoing;* past, *foregone:* s. *foregoer.*

FORE'GROUND. *s.* The part of the field or expanse of a picture which seems to lie before the figures.

FORE'HAND. *s.* The part of a horse which is before the rider.

FORE'HEAD. *s.* That part of the face which reaches from the eyes upward to the hair.

FOR'EIGN. *adj.* Not of this country not domestic, alien, extraneous. s *foreigner, foreignness.*

FOREJUDGE. *v.* To judge before hand; to be prepossessed. pr. par *forejudging;* past, *forejudged:* s *forejudgment.*

FOREKNOW'. *v.* To have prescience of; to foresee. pr. par. *foreknowing;* past, *foreknown:* adj. *foreknowable:* s. *foreknower, foreknowledge.*

FORE'LAND. *s.* A promontory, a headland, a cape.

FORE'LOCK. *s.* The hair that grows from the forepart of the head.

FORE'MAN. *s.* The first or chief person. pl. *foremen.*

FORE'MAST. *s.* The first mast of a ship towards the head.

FORE'MOST. *adj.* First in place first in dignity.

FORENOON'. *s.* The time of the day before twelve o'clock.

FOREN'SIC. *adj.* Belonging to courts of judicature.

FOREORDAIN'. *v.* To predestinate, to predetermine, to preordain. p par. *foreordaining;* past, *foreordained:* s. *foreordination.*

FORE'PART. *s.* The part first in time; the part anterior in place.

FORERUN'. *v.* To precede; to have the start of. pr. par. *forerunning* past, *forerun:* s. *forerunner.*

FORE'SAIL. *s.* The sail of the fore mast.

FORESAY'. *v.* To predict, to prophesy, to foretell. pr. par. *foresaying;* past, *foresaid.*

FORESEE'. *v.* To see beforehand; to provide for. pr. par. *foreseeing;* past, *foreseen:* s. *foreseer.*

FORESHORT'EN. *v.* To shorten figures, in order to show those behind. pr. par. *foreshortening;* past, *foreshortened.*

FORESHOW". *v.* To predict, to discover before it happens. pr. par. *foreshowing;* past, *foreshown.*

FORE'SIGHT. *s.* Prescience, prognostication, foreknowledge.

FOR'EST. *s.* A wild, uncultivated tract of ground, interspersed with wood. s. *forester.*

FORE'STAFF. *s.* An instrument used at sea for taking the altitudes of heavenly bodies.

FORESTALL'. *v.* To anticipate; to take up beforehand; to hinder by pre-occupation or prevention. pr. par. *forestalling;* past, *forestalled:* s. *forestaller.*

FORE'TASTE. *s.* Anticipation of. s. *foretaster.*

FORETELL'. *v.* To predict, to prophesy, to foretoken. pr. par. *foretelling;* past, *foretold:* s. *foreteller.*

FORE'THOUGHT. *s.* Prescience, anticipation, provident care.

FORETO'KEN. *s.* Prevenient sign; prognostic. v. *foretoken;* pr. par. *foretokening;* past, *foretokened.*

FORE'TOOTH. *s.* The tooth in the anterior part of the mouth; the incisor.

FORE'WARN. *v.* To admonish beforehand; to inform previously of any future event. pr. par. *forewarning;* past, *forewarned.*

FOR'FEIT. *s.* Something lost by the commission of a crime; a fine, a mulct. v. *forfeit;* pr. par. *forfeiting;* past, *forfeited:* adj. *forfeitable:* s. *forfeiter, forfeiture.*

FORGA'VE. Preterit of *forgive.*

FORGE. *s.* The place where iron is beaten into form. v. *forge;* pr. par. *forging;* past, *forged:* s *forger, forgery,* pl. *forgeries.*

FOR'GERY. *s.* The crime of falsification; smith's work. pl. *forgeries.*

FORGET'. *v.* To lose memory of; not to attend; to neglect. pr. par. *forgetting;* past, *forgot, forgotten.* adj. *forgetful:* s. *forgetfulness, forgetter:* adv. *forgettingly.*

FORGIVE'. *v.* To pardon, not to punish, to remit. pr. par. *forgiving;* past, *forgiven:* adj. *forgivable* s. *forgiveness, forgiver.*

FORGOT', FORGOT'TEN. Past par. of the v. *forget.*

FORK. *s.* An instrument divided at the end into two or more points or prongs. v. *fork;* pr. par. *forking;* past, *forked:* adv. *forkedly* s. *forkedness, forkiness:* adj. *forky.*

FORLORN'. *adj.* Deserted, destitute, forsaken, wretched, solitary. s *forlorn.*

FORLORN-HOPE'. *s.* The soldiers who are sent first to enter a breach, and are therefore doomed or expected to perish.

FORM. *s.* The external appearance of any thing; representation, shape, ceremony; a long seat. v *form;* pr. par. *forming;* past *formed:* s. *formation, former* adj. *formless.*

FOR'MAL. *adj.* Ceremonious, solemn, precise, regular, external. s *formalist, formality,* pl. *formalities:* adv. *formally.*

FOR'MER. *adj.* Before another in time; mentioned before another, past. adv. *formerly.*

FOR'MIDABLE. *adj.* Terrible, dreadful, tremendous, terrific. s *formidableness:* adv. *formidably.*

FORM'ULA. *s.* A prescribed form or order. s. *formulary,* pl. *formularies.*

FORNICA'TION. *s.* Concubinage, or commerce with an unmarried woman. s. *fornicator, fornicatress.*

FORSA'KE. *v.* To leave in resentment or dislike; to leave, to desert. pr. par. *forsaking;* past, *forsaken:* s. *forsaker.*

FORSOOTH'. *adv.* In truth, certainly, very well.

FORSWEAR'. *v.* To renounce upon oath; to deny upon oath; to perjure; to swear falsely. pr. par. *forswearing,* past, *forsworn:* s. *forswearer.*

FORT. *s.* A fortified house; a castle; a strong side. adj. *forted.*

FOR'TE. *adv.* A term in music; loudly, with strength.

FORTH. *adv.* Forward; onward in time; abroad.

FORTH'COMING. *adj.* Ready to appear, not absconding.

FORTHWITH'. *adv.* Immediately; without delay; at once.

FOR'TIETH. *adj.* The fourth tenth, next after the thirty-ninth.

FOR'TIFY. *v.* To strengthen against attacks, by walls or works; to confirm, to encourage. pr. par. *fortifying;* past, *fortified:* adj. *fortifiable:* s. *fortification, fortifier.*

FOR'TITUDE. *s.* Courage, bravery, strength.

FORT'NIGHT. *s.* The space of two weeks.

FOR'TRESS. *s.* A strong hold; a fortified place. pl. *fortresses.*

FORTU'ITOUS. *adj.* Accidental, casual. adv. *fortuitously:* s. *fortuitousness, fortuity,* pl. *fortuities.*

FOR'TUNE. *s.* The power supposed to distribute the lots of life according to her own humour; the good or ill that befals man; success; estate; possessions. adj. *fortunate:* adv. *fortunately:* s. *fortunateness.*

FOR'TUNE-HUNTER. *s.* A man whose employment is to enquire after women with great portions, to enrich himself by marrying one of them.

FOR'TY. *adj.* Four times ten. pl. *forties.*

FO'RUM. *s.* The market-place in Rome; the common place where courts are kept.

FOR'WARD. *adv.* Towards; to a part or place before; onward, progressively. adj. *forward.*

FOR'WARD. *v.* To hasten; to accelerate in growth or improvement; to patronise; to advance pr. par. *forwarding;* past, *forwarded:* s. *forwarder, forwardness.* adv. *forwardly.*

FOR'WARDS. *adv.* Straight before; progressively; not backwards.

FOSS. *s.* A ditch, a moat. pl. *fosses.*

FOS'SIL. *adj.* That may be dug out of the earth. s. *fossil, fossilist.*

FOS'TER. *v.* To nurse, to feed, to support, to cherish, to encourage. pr. par. *fostering;* past, *fostered.* s. *fosterage, fosterer.*

FOS'TER-BROTHER. *s.* One nursed by a mother, at the same time with her own child; the child of that mother, in relation to the other.

FOS'TER-CHILD. *s.* A child nursed by a woman not the mother, or bred by a man not the father. pl. *foster-children.*

FOS'TER-FATHER. *s.* One who gives food in the place of a father.

FOS'TER-MOTHER. *s.* A nurse.

FOUGHT. Pret. and past par. of the v. *fight.*

FOUL. *adj.* Not clean, filthy, impure, polluted, wicked. v. *fo~,* pr. par. *fouling;* past, *fouled:* adv. *foully* s. *foulness.*

FOUL'FACED. *adj.* Having an ugly or hateful visage.

FOUL'MOUTHED. *adj.* Scurrilous; habituated to the use of opprobrious terms or epithets.

FOUL'SPOKEN. *adj.* Contumelious, slanderous.

FOUND. Pret. and past par. of *find.*

FOUND. *v.* To lay the basis of any building; to build; to establish. pr. par. *founding;* past, *founded* s. *foundation, founder, foundress.*

FOUND. *v.* To form by melting and pouring into moulds; to cast. pr par *founding;* past, *founded:* s. *founder, foundery,* pl. *founderies.*

FOUND'ER. *v.* To cause such a soreness and tenderness in a horse's foot, that he is unable to set it to the ground; to sink to the bottom; to fail. pr. par. *foundering;* past, *foundered.*

FOUND'LING. *s.* A child exposed to chance; a child found without any parent or owner.

FOUNT, FOUNT'AIN. *s.* A well, a spring, a jet, a spout of water; a set or quantity of characters or letters.

FOUR. *adj.* Twice two. *adj. fourth:* adv. *fourthly.*

FOUR'-FOLD. *adj.* Four times over.

FOUR'FOOTED. *adj.* Quadruped; having four feet.

FOUR'SCORE. *adj.* Four times twenty; eighty.

FOUR'TEEN. *adj.* Four and ten; twice seven. ordinal adj. *fourteenth.*

FOUR'WHEELED. *adj.* Running upon four wheels.

FOWL. *s.* A winged animal; a bird. *v. fowl;* pr. par. *fowling;* past, *fowled:* s. *fowler.*

FOWL'ING-PIECE. *s.* A gun for the shooting of birds.

FOX. *s.* A wild animal of the canine species. pl. *foxes.*

FOX'GLOVE. *s.* A species of plant.

FOX'TAIL. *s.* A species of plant.

FRAC'TION. *s.* The act of breaking; the state of being broken; a broken part of an integral. adj. *fractional.*

FRAC'TURE. *s.* Breach; separation of continuous parts. v. *fracture;* pr. par. *fracturing;* past, *fractured.*

FRA'GILE. *adj.* Brittle; easily snapped or broken; weak. s. *fragility,* pl. *fragilities.*

FRAG'MENT. *s.* A part broken from the whole; an imperfect piece. adj *fragmentary.*

FRA'GRANT. *adj.* Odorous; sweet of smell. adv. *fragrantly:* s. *fra-* grance, *fragrancy,* pl. *fragrancies.*

FRAIL. *adj.* Weak; easily decaying, easily destroyed. s. *frailness, frailty,* pl. *frailties.*

FRAIL. *s.* A basket made of rushes.

FRAME. *v.* To form or fabricate, by orderly construction; to make; to compose; to regulate. pr. par. *framing;* past, *framed:* s. *frame, framer, framing.*

FRAN'CHISE. *s.* Exemption from any onerous duty; privilege, immunity. s. *franchisement.*

FRANCIS'CAN. *adj.* Relating to the order of St. Francis.

FRANG'IBLE. *adj.* Fragile, brittle, easily broken.

FRANK. *adj.* Liberal, generous, ingenuous, sincere. adv. *frankly:* s. *frankness.*

FRANK. *s.* A privileged letter which pays no postage. v. *frank* pr. par. *franking;* past, *franked.*

FRANK'INCENSE. *s.* A species of aromatic drug.

FRANK'LIN. *s.* A freeholder of considerable property.

FRANK'PLEDGE. *s.* A pledge or surety for freemen.

FRAN'TIC. *adj.* Mad; deprived of understanding by violent madness; outrageous. adv. *frantically:* s. *franticness.*

FRATER'NAL. *adj.* Brotherly, pertaining to brothers. adv. *fraternally:* s. *fraternity,* pl. *fraternities.*

FRA'TERNIZE. *v.* To agree as brothers; to enter into brotherhood. pr. par. *fraternizing;* past. *fraternized.* s. *fraternization.*

FRA'TRICIDE. *s.* The murder of a brother; one who kills a brother.

FRAUD. *s.* Deceit, cheat, artifice. adj. *fraudful:* adv. *fraudfully.*

FRAUD'ULENCE. *s.* Deceitfulness, trickishness, proneness to artifice. pl. *fraudulencies:* adj. *fraudulent* adv. *fraudulently.*

FRAUGHT. *adj.* Laden, charged, filled, stored.

FRAY. *s.* A battle, a fight, a duel, a combat.
FRAY. *v.* To rub, to wear. pr. par. *fraying;* past, *frayed.*
FREAK. *s.* A sudden fancy; a humour; a whim. adj. *freakish:* adv. *freakishly:* s. *freakishness.*
FRECK'LE. *s.* A spot raised in the skin, by nature or the sun. adj. *freckled, freckly:* s. *freckledness.*
FRECK'LEFACED. *adj.* Having the face full of freckles.
FREE. *adj.* At liberty, not enslaved, unrestrained, uncompelled. v. *free;* pr. par. *freeing;* past, *freed:* adv. *freely:* s. *freeness, freer.*
FREE'BOOTER. *s.* A robber, a plunderer, a pillager. s. *freebooting.*
FREE'BORN. *adj.* Not a slave; inheriting liberty.
FREED'MAN. *s.* A slave manumitted. pl. *freedmen.*
FREE'DOM. *s.* Liberty; exemption from servitude; independence.
FREE'HEARTED. *adj.* Liberal, unrestrained.
FREE'HOLD. *s.* That land or tenement which a man holds in fee, fee-tail, or for term of life. s. *freeholder.*
FREE'MAN. *s.* One not a slave; not a vassal; one partaking of rights, privileges, or immunities. pl. *freemen.*
FREEMA'SON. *s.* One of a certain secret order.
FREE'MINDED. *adj* Unperplexed; without a load of care.
FREE'SCHOOL. *s.* A school in which learning is given without pay.
FREE'SPOKEN. *adj.* Accustomed to speak without reserve.
FREE'STONE. *s.* A kind of soft stone.
FREE'THINKER. *s.* One who believes in accordance with his own judgment; one not bigoted.
FREEWILL. *s.* The power of directing our own actions; voluntariness.

FREEZE. *v.* To congeal; to be congealed with cold. pr. par. *freezing* past, *frozen.*
FREIGHT. *v.* To load a ship or vessel with goods for transportation. pr. par. *freighting;* past, *freighted:* s. *freight, freighter.*
FRENCH. *adj.* Belonging to France adj. *Frenchlike.*
FRENCH'IFY. *v.* To infect with the manners of France. pr. par. *frenchifying;* past, *frenchified.*
FREN'ZY. *s.* Madness, distraction of mind. pl. *frenzies:* adj. *frenzied.*
FRE'QUENT. *adj.* Often done, often seen, often occurring. s. *frequency,* pl. *frequencies:* adv. *frequently.*
FREQUENT'. *v.* To visit often; to be much in any place. pr. par. *frequenting;* past, *frequented:* adj. *frequentable:* s. *frequenter.*
FREQUENT'ATIVE. *adj.* A grammatical term, applied to verbs signifying the frequent repetition of an action.
FRES'CO. *s.* Coolness, shade, duskiness; a kind of painting. pl. *frescoes.*
FRESH. *adj.* Cool; not salt; new, recent, florid. v. *freshen;* pr. par. *freshening;* past, *freshened:* adv. *freshly:* s. *freshness.*
FRESH'ET. *s.* A flood of water.
FRESH'MAN. *s.* A novice; one in the rudiments of any knowledge s. *freshmanship.*
FRET. *v.* To wear away by rubbing; to vex. pr. par. *fretting,* past, *fretted:* s. *fret, fretter, fretfulness:* adj. *fretful:* adv. *fretfully.*
FRI ABLE. *adj.* Easily crumbled; easily reduced to powder. s. *friability,* pl. *friabilities.*
FRI'AR. *s.* A brother of some religious order. s. *friary,* pl. *friaries.*
FRICASEE'. *s.* A dish made by cutting chickens or other small things into pieces, and dressing them with strong sauce. v. *fricasee;* pr. par *fricaseeing;* past, *fricaseed.*

159

FRICTION. *s.* The act of rubbing two bodies together.
FRI'DAY. *s.* The sixth day of the week.
FRIEND. *s.* One joined to another in mutual benevolence and intimacy; one propitious. adj. *friendless, friendlike, friendly:* s. *friendliness, friendship:* adv. *friendly.*
FRIEZE. *s.* A coarse, warm cloth. adj. *friezed.*
FRIEZE, FRIZE. *s.* A large flat member which separates the architrave from the cornice.
FRIGATE. *s.* A ship of war, next in size to a vessel of the line.
FRIGHT. *s.* A sudden terror. v. *frighten;* pr. par. *frightening;* past, *frightened:* adj. *frightful:* adv. *frightfully:* s. *frightfulness.*
FRI'GID. *adj.* Cold; wanting warmth; dull. s. *frigidity,* pl. *frigidities, frigidness:* adv. *frigidly.*
FRIGORIF'IC. *adj.* Causing cold.
FRILL. *s.* A sort of ruffle. v. *frill;* pr. par. *frilling;* past, *frilled.*
FRINGE. *s.* Ornamental appendage, added to a dress or to furniture. v. *fringe;* pr. par. *fringing;* past, *fringed:* adj. *fringy.*
FRIP'PERY. *s.* Old clothes, cast dresses, trumpery, trifles. pl. *fripperies.*
FRISEU'R. *s.* A hair-dresser.
FRISK. *v.* To leap, to skip. pr. par. *frisking;* past, *frisked:* s. *frisk, frisker, friskiness:* adj. *friskful, frisky.*
FRITH. *s.* A narrow part of the sea, where the water, being confined, is rough.
FRIT'TER. *s.* A small piece cut to be fried; a fragment. v. *fritter;* pr. par. *frittering;* past, *frittered.*
FRIV'OLOUS. *adj.* Slight, trifling; of no moment. adv. *frivolously:* s. *frivolity,* pl. *frivolities.*
FRIZZ. *v.* To curl, to crisp. pr. par. *frizzing;* past, *frizzed.*
FRIZ'ZLE. *v.* To form into short curls. pr. par. *frizzling;* past, *frizzled:* s. *frizzle, frizzler.*

FRO. *adv.* Backward, regressively.
FROCK. *s.* A dress, a coat; a kind of gown for children.
FROG. *s.* A small amphibious animal, with four feet.
FROL'IC. *s.* A wild prank; a flight of whim and levity. v. *frolic;* pr. par. *frolicking;* past, *frolicked:* adj. *frolicksome:* s. *frolicksomeness:* adv. *frolicksomely.*
FROM. A preposition.
FRONDIF'EROUS. *adj.* Bearing leaves.
FRONT. *s.* The face; the van. v. *front;* pr. par. *fronting;* past, *fronted:* s. *frontal, frontlet:* adj *frontless.*
FRON'TIER. *s.* The marches, the limit, the utmost verge of any territory. adj. *frontier.*
FRONTINIAC'. *s.* A kind of rich wine.
FRONT'ISPIECE. *s.* That part of any building, or other body, that directly meets the eve.
FROST. *s.* The last effect of cold; the power of congelation. adj. *frosted, frosty:* adv. *frostily.* s *frostiness.*
FROST'BITTEN. *adj.* Nipped or withered by frost.
FROST'WORK. *s.* Work in which the substance is laid on with inequalities, like the dew congealed upon shrubs.
FROTH. *s.* Spume, foam. v. *froth;* pr. par. *frothing;* past, *frothed:* adv. *frothily:* s. *frothiness:* adj *frothy.*
FRO'WARD. *adj.* Peevish, ungovernable, angry. adv. *frowardly:* s. *frowardness.*
FROWN. *v.* To express displeasure by contracting the face to wrinkles; to look stern. pr. par. *frowning,* past, *frowned:* s. *frown, frowner* adv. *frowningly.*
FRO'ZEN. *adj.* Congealed with cold void of heat.
FRUC'TIFY. *v.* To make fruitful, to fertilize. pr. par. *fructifying;* past, *fructified:* adj. *fructiferous,*

160

fructuous: s. *fructification, fructuation*.

FRU'GAL. *adj*. Thrifty, sparing, parsimonious. s. *frugality*, pl. *frugalities*: *adv. frugally*.

FRUIT. *s*. The product of a tree or plant; production. s. *fruitage, fruiterer, fruitery*, pl. *fruiteries; fruitfulness*: adj. *fruitful*: adv. *fruitfully*.

FRUI'TION. *s*. Enjoyment, possession.

FRUIT'LESS. *adj*. Barren of fruit; vain, idle, unprofitable. adv. *fruitlessly*: s. *fruitlessness*.

FRUMP. *v*. To mock, to insult. pr. par. *frumping*; past, *frumped*: s. *frump*.

FRUS'TRATE. *v*. To defeat, to disappoint. pr. par. *frustrating*; past, *frustrated*: s. *frustration*; adj. *frustrative, frustratory*.

FRY. *v*. To dress food in a pan on the fire. pr. par. *frying*; past, *fried*: s. *fry*, pl. *fries*.

FUD'DLE. *v*. To make slightly drunk. pr. par. *fuddling*; past, *fuddled*.

FUDGE. *int*. An expression of the utmost contempt.

FU'EL. *s*. The matter or aliment of fire.

FUGA'CIOUS. *adj*. Volatile. s. *fugaciousness, fugacity*, pl. *fugacities*.

FU'GITIVE. *adj*. Not tenable, unsteady, volatile, flying, running from danger. s. *fugitive, fugitiveness*.

FUL'CRUM. *s*. the prop of a lever.

FULFIL'. *v*. To answer any purpose or design; to complete. pr. par. *fulfilling*; past, *fulfilled*. s. *fulfiller, fulfilment*.

FUL'GENT. *adj*. Shining, dazzling, exquisitely bright. s. *fulgency*, pl. *fulgencies; fulgidity*, pl. *fulgidities*.

FULIG'INOUS. *adj*. Sooty, smoky.

FULL. *adj*. Replete; having no space void: large. s. *full, fulness*: adv. *full, fully*.

FULL. *v*. To cleanse cloth from its oil or grease. pr. par. *fulling* past, *fulled*: s. *fullage, fuller, fullery*, pl. *fulleries*.

FULL'-BLOWN *adj* Spread to the utmost extent, as a perfect blossom.

FULL-BOTTOMED. *adj*. Having a large bottom.

FULL'-DRESSED. *adj*. Dressed in form.

FULL-FED'. *adj*. Sated, fat.

FULL-GROWN'. *adj*. Completely grown.

FUL'LING-MILL. *s*. A mill for cleansing cloth.

FUL'MINATE. *v*. To thunder; to make a loud noise. pr. par. *fulminating*; past, *fulminated*: s. *fulmination*: adj. *fulminant, fulminatory*.

FUL'SOME. *adj*. Nauseous, offensive, gross. adv. *fulsomely*: s. *fulsomeness*.

FUM'BLE. *v*. To attempt any thing awkwardly. pr. par. *fumbling*; past, *fumbled*: s. *fumbler*: adv. *fumblingly*.

FUME. *s*. Smoke, vapour. v. *fume*; pr. par. *fuming*; past, *fumed*: adj. *fumid, fumous, fumy*: s. *fumidity*, pl. *fumidities*: adv. *fumingly*.

FU'MIGATE. *v*. To smoke; to perfume by smoke or vapour. pr. par. *fumigating*; past, *fumigated*: s. *fumigation*.

FUN. *s*. Sport, merriment. adj. *funny*: adv. *funnily*.

FUNC'TION. *s*. Discharge, performance, employment, office. s. *functionary*, pl. *functionaries*.

FUND. *s*. Stock, capital; that by which any expense is supported. v. *fund*; pr. par. *funding*; past, *funded*.

FUND'AMENT. *s*. Foundation; the back part of the body. adj. and s *fundamental*: adv. *fundamentally*.

FU'NERAL. *s*. Burial, interment, obsequies. adj. *funeral, funereal*.

FUNG'OUS. *adj*. Excrescent, spongy. s. *fungosity*, pl. *fungosities*.

FUNG'US. *s.* A mushroom.
FUN'NEL. *s.* A sort of pipe, through which liquors are poured into vessels.
FUR. *s.* Skin with soft hair; soft hair of beasts. v. *fur;* pr. par. *furring;* past, *furred:* s. *furrier:* adj. *furry.*
FUR'BELOW. *s.* A kind of trimming. v. *furbelow;* pr. par. *furbelowing;* past, *furbelowed.*
FUR'BISH. *v.* To burnish, to polish. pr. par. *furbishing;* past, *furbished:* s. *furbisher:* adj. *furbishable.*
FU'RIOUS. *adj.* Mad, raging, violent; impetuously agitated. adv. *furiously:* s. *furiousness.*
FURL. *v.* To draw up; to contract. pr. par. *furling;* past, *furled.*
FUR'LONG. *s.* A measure of length.
FUR'LOUGH. *s.* A temporary dismission from military service.
FUR'NACE. *s.* An enclosed fireplace.
FUR'NISH. *v.* To supply with what is necessary; to give, to supply, to equip. pr. par. *furnishing;* past, *furnished:* s. *furnisher.*
FUR'NITURE. *s.* Movables; goods put into a house for use or ornament; appendages.
FUR'RIER. *s.* A dealer in furs.
FUR'ROW. *s.* A small trench, made by the plough for the reception of seed; any long trench or hollow. v. *furrow;* pr. par. *furrowing;* past, *furrowed.*
FUR'THER. *adj.* At a greater distance; beyond this. adv. *further, furthest:* s. *furtherance, furtherer.*

FUR'THER. *v.* To put onward; to forward; to promote. pr. par *furthering;* past, *furthered.*
FUR'THERMORE. *adv.* Moreover, besides.
FUR'TIVE. *adj.* Stolen; gotten by theft. adv. *furtively* s. *furtiveness.*
FU'RY. *s.* Madness, rage, passion of anger, enthusiasm. pl. *furies:* adj. *furylike.*
FURZE. *s.* A kind of prickly bush, sometimes called a *whin.* adj. *furzy.*
FUSE. *v.* To melt; to put into fusion; to liquefy by heat. pr. par *fusing;* past, *fused:* s. *fusion, fusibility,* pl. *fusibilities:* adj. *fusible.*
FUSEE'. *s.* The cylinder around which is wound the cord or chain of a clock or watch; a firelock.
FUSILEER'. *s.* A soldier armed with a fusil; a musketeer.
FUSS. *s.* A tumult, a bustle.
FUS'TIAN. *s.* A kind of cloth
FUS'TIC. *s.* A sort of wood used in dying.
FUSTIGA'TION. *s.* An ancient custom of punishing with a cudgel.
FUS'TY. *adj.* Ill-smelling, mouldy. s. *fustiness.*
FU'TILE. *adj.* Talkative, loquacious, trifling, worthless. s. *futility,* pl. *futilities.*
FU'TURE. *adj.* That which will be hereafter; that which is to come. s. *future, futurity,* pl. *futurities.*
FY. *interj.* A word of blame and disapprobation.

G

GAB'BLE. *v.* To make an inarticulate noise; to prate loudly without meaning. pr par. *gabbling;* past, *gabbled:* s. *gabble, gabbler.*
GAB'ERDINE. *s.* A coarse frock; any mean dress.

GA'BLE. *s.* The triangular part of the end of a house, from the cornice to the top of the roof.
GAD. *v.* To ramble about without any settled purpose. pr. par. *gad-*

162

ding; past, *gadded:* s. *gadder:* adv. *gaddingly.*

GAD'FLY. s. A fly that stings cattle. pl. *gadflies.*

GAE'LIC, GAL'IC. s. A dialect of the Celtic tongue.

GAFF. s. A harpoon or large hook.

GAG. v. To stop the mouth, to prevent speaking. pr. par. *gagging;* past, *gagged:* s. *gag, gagger.*

GAGE. s. A pledge, a pawn, a measure.

GA'IETY. s. See GAYETY.

GAIN. s. Profit, advantage, interest. v. *gain;* pr. par. *gaining;* past, *gained:* adj. *gainable, gainful, gainless:* adv. *gainfully:* s. *gainer, gainfulness.*

GAINSAY. v. To contradict, to oppose. pr. par. *gainsaying;* past, *gainsaid:* s. *gainsayer.*

GAIT. s. A way, march, walk, progress. adj. *gaited.*

GAITERS. s. A kind of spatterdashes.

GA'LA. s. Any show or festivity.

GALA'TIANS. s. Persons descended from the Gauls.

GAL'AXY. s. The milky way. pl. *galaxies.*

GALE. s. A wind not tempestuous, yet stronger than a breeze.

GAL'EATED. adj. Covered as with a helmet.

GALILE'AN. s. A native or inhabitant of Galilee.

GALL. s. The bile; an animal juice remarkable for its supposed bitterness; a slight hurt by fretting off the skin. v. *gall;* pr. par. *galling;* past, *galled.*

GAL'LANT. adj. Gay, well-dressed, showy, splendid, magnificent. adv. *gallantly:* s. *gallantness.*

GALLANT'. v. To pay attention to ladies. pr. par. *gallanting;* past, *gallanted:* s. *gallant, gallantry,* pl. *gallantries:* adj. *gallant'.*

GALLEON'. s. A large ship, with four or five decks.

GAL'LERY. s. A kind of walk along the floor of a house; a part of the theatre. pl. *galleries.*

GAL'LEY. s. A vessel driven by oars.

GAL'LIC, GAL'LICAN. adj. French s. *gallicism.*

GALLIGAS'KINS. s. Large open hose.

GALLIMAU'FRY. s. Any inconsistent or ridiculous medley. pl. *gallimaufries.*

GALLINA'CEOUS. adj. Denoting birds of the pheasant kind.

GAL'LIOT. s. A little galley, built very slight, and fit for the chase.

GAL'LIPOT. s. A pot used for medicines.

GAL'LON. s. A liquid measure, containing four quarts.

GALLOON'. s. A kind of lace.

GAL'LOP. v. To ride very fast. pr. par. *galloping;* past, *galloped:* s. *gallop, galloper.*

GAL'LOWAY. s. A kind of small horse.

GAL'LOWS. s. A beam laid over two posts, on which malefactors are hanged.

GALOCHE'. s. A kind of shoe worn over another, to keep out the wet.

GAL'VANISM. s. The action of metallic substances. v. *galvanize;* pr. par. *galvanizing;* past, *galvanized:* adj. *galvanic:* s. *galvanometer.*

GAM'BLE. v. To play extravagantly for money. pr. par. *gambling,* past, *gambled:* s. *gambler.*

GAMBO'GE. s. A concreted vegetable juice, of a bright yellow colour.

GAM'BOL. v. To dance, to skip, to frisk. pr. par: *gamboling;* past, *gamboled:* s. *gambol.*

GAME. s. Sport of any kind; jest. v. *game;* pr. par. *gaming;* past, *gamed:* s. *gamester.*

GAME'KEEPER. s. A person who takes care of game.

GAM'MON. s. The buttock of a hog, salted and dried; a play with dice

163

GAM'UT. *s.* The scale of musical notes.
GAN'DER. *s.* The male of a goose.
GANG. *s.* A troop, a company, a tribe.
GANG'RENE. *s.* A mortification, a sore. *adj. gangrenous, gangrened.*
GANG'WAY. *s.* A thoroughfare or passage.
GANT'LET. *s.* A military punishment, in which the criminal, running between the ranks, receives a lash from each man.
GAOL, JAIL. *s.* A prison, a place of confinement. *s. gaoler.*
GAP. *s.* An opening, a breach, an avenue.
GAPE. *v.* To open the mouth wide; to yawn. *pr. par. gaping;* past, *gaped: s. gaper.*
GARB. *s.* Dress, clothes, habit, exterior appearance.
GARB'AGE. *s.* The bowels, the offal.
GAR'BLE. *v.* To sift and cleanse spices; to separate the good from the bad. *pr. par. garbling;* past, *garbled: s. garbler.*
GAR'DEN. *s.* A piece of ground, enclosed and planted with herbs or fruits. *v. garden; pr. par. gardening;* past, *gardened: s. gardener, gardening.*
GARG'LE. *v.* To wash the throat with some liquor not suffered immediately to descend. *pr. par. gargling;* past, *gargled: s. gargle.*
GA'RISH. *adj.* Showy, gaudy, splendid, glaring. *adv. garishly: s. garishness.*
GAR'LAND. *s.* A wreath of branches or flowers.
GARLIC *s.* A species of plant.
GAR'MENT. *s.* Any thing by which the body is covered; clothes, dress.
GAR'NER. *s.* A store-house. *v. garner, pr. par. garnering;* past, *garnered.*
GAR'NET. *s.* A gem, a precious stone.
GAR'NISH. *v.* To decorate, to embellish. *pr. par. garnishing;* past,
garnished: *s. garnish, garnisher, garnishment.*
GAR'NITURE. *s.* Furniture, ornament.
GAR'RET. *s.* A room on the highest floor of a house. *adj. garreted.*
GARRETEE'R. *s.* One who lives in a garret.
GAR'RISON. *s.* Soldiers placed in a fortified town or castle to defend it; the town itself. *v. garrison, pr. par. garrisoning;* past, *garrisoned.*
GAR'RON. *s.* A miserable horse, of little power.
GARRU'LITY. *s.* Loquacity, talkativeness. *pl. garrulities: adj. garrulous.*
GAR'TER. *s.* A string or riband, by which the stocking is held upon the leg. *v. garter; pr. par. gartering;* past, *gartered.*
GARTH. *s.* The bulk of the body measured by the girdle; an enclosure.
GAS. *s.* A spirit not capable of being congealed. *pl. gasses.*
GASOM'ETER. *s.* An instrument for measuring or containing gas
GASCONA'DE. *s.* A boast, a bravado. *v. gasconade; pr. par. gasconading;* past, *gasconaded.*
GASH. *v.* To cut into small pieces, to cut deeply. *pr. par. gashing;* past, *gashed: s. gash.*
GASP. *v.* To open the mouth wide; to catch the breath with labour *pr. par. gasping;* past, *gasped: s. gasp.*
GAS'TRIC. *adj.* Belonging to the stomach.
GATE. *s.* A large door, an avenue. *s. gateway.*
GATH'ER. *v.* To collect; to bring into one place; to glean. *pr. par. gathering;* past, *gathered: s. gather, gatherer, gathering.*
GAU'DY. *adj.* Showy, splendid, pompous. *adv. gaudily: s. gaudiness.*
GAUGE. *v.* To measure the capacity of a vessel in which liquors

are contained; to measure with regard to any proportion. pr. par. *gauging;* past, *gauged:* s. *gauge, gauger.*

GAUNT. *adj.* Thin, slender, lean. adv. *gauntly.*

GAUNTLET. *s.* An iron glove, used for defence and thrown down in challenges.

GAUZE. *s.* A kind of thin, transparent silk.

GAVE. The preterit of the v. *to give.*

GAVELKIND. *s.* A custom, whereby the lands of the father are equally divided, at his death, amongst all his sons.

GAVOT. *s.* A kind of dance.

GAWK. *s.* A cuckoo, a foolish fellow. s. *gawky,* pl. *gawkies:* adj. *gawky.*

GAY. *adj.* Airy, cheerful, merry, fine, showy. s. *gayety,* pl. *gayeties:* adv. *gayly.*

GAZE. *v.* To look intently and earnestly. pr. par. *gazing;* past, *gazed;* s. *gaze, gazer.*

GAZETTE. *s.* A news-paper, a paper of public intelligence. v. *gazette;* pr. par. *gazetting;* past, *gazetted:* s. *gazetteer.*

GEAR. *s.* Furniture, accoutrements, dress; the traces by which horses or oxen draw.

GEE. *s.* A word used to horses.

GEESE. *s.* The plural of *goose.*

GELATINOUS. *adj.* Formed into a jelly, viscous.

GELID. *adj.* Extremely cold. s. *gelidity,* pl. *gelidities.*

GEM. *s.* A jewel, a precious stone. v. *gem;* pr. par. *gemming;* past, *gemmed:* adj. *gemmeous, gemmy.*

GEMINI. *s.* The twins; the third sign in the zodiac.

GENDER. *s.* A kind, a sort, a sex.

GENDER. *v.* To beget, to produce. pr. par. *gendering;* past, *gendered.*

GENEALOGY. *s.* History of the succession of families. pl. *genealogies:* adj. *genealogical:* s. *genealogist.*

GENERAL. *adj.* Comprehending many species or individuals; not special; not particular; extensive, common. s. *general, generality,* pl. *generalities, generalness* adv. *generally.*

GENERAL. *s.* One who commands an army. s. *generalship.*

GENERALISSIMO. *s.* The supreme commander.

GENERALIZE. *v.* To reduce to a genus. pr. par. *generalizing;* past, *generalized:* s. *generalization.*

GENERATE. *v.* To beget, to propagate, to produce to life. pr. par *generating;* past, *generated:* s *generation, generator:* adj. *generant, generative.*

GENERIC. *adj.* That which comprehends the genus, or distinguishes from another genus. adv. *generically.*

GENEROUS. *adj.* Not of mean birth; liberal, munificent, strong, vigorous. adv. *generously:* s. *generosity,* pl. *generosities.*

GENESIS. *s.* Generation; the first book of Moses.

GENEVA. *s.* A spirit distilled from the juniper-berry.

GENEVOIS. *s.* People of Geneva.

GENIAL. *adj.* That which contributes to propagation; natural, native. adv. *genially.*

GENITIVE. *adj.* The name of the second case in grammar.

GENIUS. *s.* The protecting or ruling power of men, places, or things. pl. *genii:*—mental power or faculties; a man endowed with superior faculties. pl. *geniuses.*

GENOESE. *s.* The people of Genoa in Italy.

GENTEEL. *adj.* Polite, elegant in behaviour, civil. adv. *genteelly.* s. *genteelness, gentility,* pl. *gentilities.*

GENTIAN. *s.* A kind of medicinal plant.

GENTILE. *adj.* Belonging to a nation.

GEN'TILE. *s.* One of an uncovenanted nation; one who knows not the true God. *adj. gentile: s. gentilism.*

GEN'TLE. *adj.* Well born, soft, bland, mild, tame. *adv. gently: s. gentleness.*

GENT'LEMAN. *s.* A man of birth; a man raised above the vulgar by his character or post. *pl. gentlemen: adj. gentlemanlike, gentlemanly: s. gentlemanliness.*

GEN'TLEWOMAN. *s.* A woman of birth above the vulgar; a woman well descended. *pl. gentlewomen: adj. gentlewomanlike.*

GENTOO'. *s.* An aboriginal inhabitant of Hindostan.

GEN'TRY. *s.* Class of people above the vulgar. *pl. gentries.*

GENUFLEC'TION. *s.* The act of bending the knee; adoration expressed by bending the knee.

GEN'UINE. *adj.* Not spurious; real, natural, true. *adv. genuinely: s. genuineness.*

GE'NUS. *s.* A class of beings or things, comprehending under it many species. *pl. genera.*

GEOCEN'TRIC. *adj.* Applied to a planet or orb having the earth for its centre, or the same centre with the earth.

GEOG'RAPHY. *s.* A description of the earth. *pl. geographies: s. geographer: adj. geographical: adv. geographically.*

GEOL'OGY. *s.* The doctrine of the formation and composition of the earth. *pl. geologies: s. geologer.*

GEOM'ETRY. *s.* The science of quantity, extension, or magnitude, abstractedly considered. *pl. geometries: adj. geometral, geometrical, geometric: adv. geometrically: s. geometrician: v. geometrize; pr. par. geometrizing; past, geometrized.*

GEOR'GIC. *s.* A part of the science of husbandry, put into a pleasing dress, and set off by all the beauties and embellishments of poetry. *adj. georgic, georgical.*

GEORGIUM SI'DUS. *s.* One of the planets.

GERA'NIUM. *s.* A kind of plant.

GERM. *s.* A sprout or shoot; that part which grows and spreads. *adj. germinant: v. germinate; pr. par. germinating; past, germinated: s. germination.*

GER'UND. *s.* A kind of verbal noun.

GESTA'TION. *s.* The act of carrying the young before birth.

GESTIC'ULATE. *v.* To play antic tricks; to show postures. *pr. par. gesticulating; past, gesticulated: s. gesticulation, gesticulator: adj. gesticulatory.*

GES'TURE. *s.* Action or posture expressive of sentiment; movement of the body.

GET. *v.* To procure, to obtain, to have possession of. *pr. par. getting; past, got, gotten: s. getter.*

GEW'GAW. *s.* A showy trifle; a toy, a bauble.

GHAST'LY. *adj.* Like a ghost; pale, dismal, horrible. *s. ghastliness.*

GHER'KIN. *s.* A small pickled cucumber.

GHOST. *s.* The soul of man; a spirit appearing after death. *adj. ghostlike, ghostly: s. ghostliness.*

GI'ANT. *s.* A man of a size above the ordinary rate of men. *adj. giantlike, gigantic.*

GI'ANTESS. *s.* A woman of uncommon size. *pl. giantesses.*

GIB'BER. *v.* To speak inarticulately. *pr. par. gibbering; past, gibbered: s. gibberish.*

GIB'BET. *s.* A gallows; the post on which malefactors are hanged. *v. gibbet; pr. par. gibbeting; past, gibbeted.*

GIB'BOUS. *adj.* Convex, protuberant. *s. gibbosity, pl. gibbosities, gibbousness.*

GIBE. *v.* To sneer; to join censoriousness with contempt *pr. par.*

gibing; past, gibed: s. gibe, giber: adv. gibingly.

GIB'LETS. s. The parts of a goose which are cut off before it is cooked.

GID'DY. adj. Vertiginous; rotary, whirling, inconstant, unsteady. s. giddiness: adv. giddily.

GIFT. s. A thing given or bestowed; offering. v. gift; pr. par. gifting; past, gifted: s. giftedness.

GIG. s. A light vehicle, with two wheels.

GIGAN'TIC. adj. Suitable to a giant; big; very large.

GIG'GLE. v. To laugh idly, to titter. pr. par. giggling; past, giggled: s. giggle, giggler.

GIG'OT. s. The hip joint; a slice.

GILD. v. To overlay with gold. pr. par. gilding; past, gilded, gilt: s. gilder, gilding.

GILL. s. The apertures at each side of a fish's head; a measure of liquids, containing the fourth part of a pint.

GIL'LYFLOWER. s. A kind of plant.

GILT. Pret. and past par. of the v. to gild.

GIM'CRACK. s. A slight or trivial mechanism.

GIM'LET. s. A borer, with a screw at its point.

GIMP. s. A kind of silk twist or lace.

GIN. s. A trap, a snare; a machine for cleaning cotton. v. gin; pr. par. ginning; past, ginned.

GIN. s. A kind of ardent spirits, properly called Geneva.

GIN'GERBREAD. s. A kind of sweet bread, or cake.

GING'LE, JING'LE. v. To make a sharp, clattering noise. pr. par. gingling; past, gingled: s. gingle.

GIN'SENG. s. A kind of aromatic root.

GIP'SY. s. A vagabond who pretends to foretell futurity; a wanderer. pL gipsies.

GIRD. v. To bind around; to fasten by binding. pr. par. girding; past, girded, girt: s. girder, girding.

GIRD'LE. s. Any thing drawn round the waist; enclosure. v. girdle, pr. par. girdling; past, girdled: s. girdler.

GIRL. s. A young woman, or female child. adj. girlish: adv. girlishly.

GIRT. Pret. and past par. of the v. to gird.

GIRTH. s. A band by which a saddle is fixed upon a horse.

GIVE. v. To bestow; to confer, without any price or reward; to deliver. pr. par. giving; past, given; pret. gave.

GIVES. s. Fetters or shackles for the feet.

GIZ'ZARD. s. The strong muscular stomach of a fowl.

GLA'CIAL. adj. Icy; made of ice frozen. v. glaciate; pr. par. glaciating; past, glaciated: s. glaciation: adj. glacious.

GLA'CIS. s. In fortification, a sloping bank.

GLAD. adj. Cheerful; gay; in a state of hilarity; pleased. v. gladden; pr. par. gladdening; past, gladdened: adv. gladly: s. gladness

GLADE. s. A lawn or opening in a wood.

GLA'DIATOR. s. A sword-player a prize-fighter. adj. gladiatory, gladiatorial.

GLANCE. s. A sudden shoot of light or splendour; a quick view. v. glance; pr. par. glancing; past, glanced.

GLAND. s. An organ of the body adj. glandular, glandulous: s glandule.

GLAN'DERS. s. A disease peculiar to horses. adj. glandered.

GLANDIF'EROUS. adj. Bearing mast; bearing acorns, or fruit like acorns.

GLARE. v. To shine so as to dazzle the eyes; to shine ostentatiously pr. par. glaring; past, glared: s glare: adv. glaringly.

GLA'REOUS. adj. Consisting of viscous, transparent matter, like the white of an egg.

167

GLASS. *s.* An artificial, transparent substance; a mirror; a vessel made of glass. pl. *glasses:* s. *glassiness:* adj. *glassy.*

GLAZE. *v.* To furnish with windows of glass; to overlay with something shining and pellucid. pr. par. *glazing;* past, *glazed:* s. *glazier.*

GLEAM. *s.* Sudden shoot of light; lustre, brightness. v. *gleam;* pr. par. *gleaming;* past, *gleamed:* s. *gleaming:* adj. *gleamy.*

GLEAN. *v.* To gather what the harvesters leave behind; to gather any thing thinly scattered. pr. par. *gleaning;* past, *gleaned:* s. *gleaner, gleaning.*

GLEBE. *s.* Turf, soil, ground. adj. *glebous.*

GLEE. *s.* Joy, merriment, gayety; a kind of song.

GLEN. *s.* A valley, a dale; a depression between two hills.

GLIB. *adj.* Smooth, slippery, voluble. adv. *glibly.* s. *glibness.*

GLIDE. *v.* To flow gently and silently; to move swiftly and smoothly along. pr. par. *gliding;* past, *glided:* s. *glider.*

GLIMMER. *v.* To shine faintly; to be perceived imperfectly. pr. par. *glimmering;* past, *glimmered:* s. *glimmer, glimmering.*

GLIMPSE. *s.* A weak, faint light; transitory lustre; a short view.

GLISTEN. *v.* To shine; to sparkle with light. pr. par. *glistening;* past, *glistened.*

GLITTER. *v.* To shine; to exhibit lustre; to gleam. pr. par. *glittering;* past, *glittered:* s. *glitter:* adv. *glitteringly.*

GLOBE. *s.* A sphere, a ball; a round body. adj. *globose, globous, globular:* s. *globosity,* pl. *globosities.*

GLOBULE. *s.* A very small globe. adj. *globulous.*

GLOMERATE. *v.* To gather into a ball or sphere. pr. par. *glomerating;* past, *glomerated:* s. *glomeration:* adj. *glomerous.*

GLOOM. *s.* Imperfect darkness; obscurity; defect of light. adj *gloomy:* adv. *gloomily:* s. *gloominess.*

GLORIFY. *v.* To praise, to honour, to extol. pr. par. *glorifying;* past, *glorified:* s. *glorification.*

GLORY. *s.* Praise paid in adoration; honour, praise, fame, celebrity. pl. *glories:* v. *glory;* pr. par. *glorying;* past, *gloried:* adj. *glorious:* adv. *gloriously:* s. *gloriousness.*

GLOSS. *s.* A comment, an explanation, superficial lustre, a specious representation. v. *gloss;* pr. par. *glossing;* past, *glossed:* adj. *glossy.* s. *glossiness.*

GLOSSARY. *s.* A dictionary of obscure or antiquated words. pl. *glossaries:* adj. *glossarial:* s. *glossarist.*

GLOSSOGRAPHER. *s.* A scholiast, a commentator. s. *glossography,* pl. *glossographies.*

GLOVE. *s.* A cover for the hand. s. *glover.*

GLOW. *v.* To be heated, so as to shine without flame; to exhibit a strong bright colour. pr. par. *glowing;* past, *glowed:* s. *glow:* adv *glowingly.*

GLOWWORM. *s.* A small creeping grub, with a luminous tail.

GLUE. *s.* A kind of cement. v. *glue,* pr. par. *gluing;* past, *glued:* s *gluer, glueyness:* adj. *gluey.*

GLUM. *adj.* Sullen, stubbornly grave, melancholy, dull.

GLUT. *v.* To swallow, to devour, to cloy, to overfill, to load. pr. par *glutting;* past, *glutted:* s. *glut.*

GLUTINATE. *v.* To join with glue; to cement. pr. par. *glutinating;* past, *glutinated:* s. *glutination,* *glutinosity,* pl. *glutinosities:* adj. *glutinative, glutinous.*

GLUTTON. *s.* One who indulges himself too much in eating. v. *gluttonize;* pr. par. *gluttonizing;* past, *gluttonized:* s. *gluttony,* pl.

gluttonies: adj. *gluttonous:* adv. *gluttonously.*

GNASH. *v.* To strike together; to clash; to grind or collide the teeth. pr. par. *gnashing;* past, *gnashed.*

GNAT. *s.* A small insect.

GNAW. *v.* To eat by degrees; to wear away by biting; to corrode. pr. par. *gnawing;* past, *gnawed:* s. *gnawer.*

GNOME. *s.* A brief reflection, worthy to be remembered; one of those invisible people, who are fabled to inhabit the inner parts of the earth, and to fill it to the centre.

GNOMON. *s.* The hand or pin of a dial.

GNOMONICS. *s.* A science which teaches to find the just proportion of shadows for the construction of all kinds of sun and moon dials.

GNOSTIC. *s.* One of a numerous sect of christians, of the first century, who pretended to a high degree of knowledge, and held extravagant notions of religion.

GO. *v.* To proceed, to walk, to move, to travel. pr. par. *going;* past, *gone:* s. *goer, going.*

GOAD. *s.* A pointed instrument, with which oxen are driven forward. *v. goad;* pr. par. *goading;* past, *goaded.*

GOAL. *s.* The landmark set up to bound a race; the point marked out to which racers run.

GOAT. *s.* A ruminating animal.

GOATHERD. *s.* One whose employment is to tend goats.

GOBBET. *s.* A mouthful; as much as can be swallowed at once.

GOBBLE. *v.* To swallow hastily, with tumult and noise. pr. par. *gobbling;* past, *gobbled:* s. *gobbler.*

GO-BETWEEN. *s.* One that transacts business by running between two parties.

GOBLET. *s.* A large cup.

GOBLIN. *s.* An evil spirit; a frightful phantom.

GO-CART. *s.* A machine in which children are enclosed, to teach them to walk.

GOD. *s.* The Supreme Being. adj. *godlike, godly:* adv. *godlily:* s *godhead, godliness.*

GODCHILD. *s.* A child for whom a person became sponsor at baptism, and promised to see educated as a christian.

GODDESS. *s.* A female divinity. pl. *goddesses.*

GODFATHER. *s.* A man who acts as sponsor, at baptism.

GODMOTHER. *s.* A woman who acts as sponsor, at baptism.

GODSON. *s.* A boy for whom a person has been sponsor at the font.

GOGGLES. *s.* Blinds for horses that are apt to take fright: glasses worn to defend the eye from dust.

GOLD. *s.* One of the metals. adj *golden.*

GOLDBEATER. *s.* One whose occupation is to beat or foliate gold.

GOLDFINCH. *s.* A kind of singing bird. pl. *goldfinches.*

GOLDSMITH. *s.* One who manufactures gold.

GONDOLA. *s.* A boat much used in Venice; a small boat.

GONDOLIER. *s.* One that rows a gondola.

GONE. Past par. of the v. *to go.*

GONG. *s.* A sonorous instrument, of a circular form, made of brass, which the Asiatics strike with a large wooden mallet.

GOOD. adj. Not bad, not ill, proper, fit, uncorrupted. s. *good, goodness:* adj. *goodly:* adv. *good*

GOOD-NATURE. *s.* Kindness; habitual benevolence. adj. *goodnatured:* adv. *goodnaturedly.*

GOODS. *s.* Moveables in a house, merchandise.

GOODY. *s.* A low term of civility, used to mean persons. pl. *goodies.*

GOOSE. *s.* A large waterfowl; a tailor's smoothing-iron. pl. *geese.*

GOOSEBERRY. *s.* A kind of small fruit. pl. *gooseberries.*

GOOSECAP. *s.* A silly person.

GORE. *s.* Blood effused from the body, blood clotted or congealed. v. *gore;* pr. par. *goring;* past, *gored.* adj. *gory.*

GORE. *v.* To stab, to pierce; to pierce with a horn. pr. par. *goring;* past, *gored.*

GORGE. *s.* The throat, the swallow. v. *gorge;* pr. par. *gorging;* past, *gorged.*

GOR'GEOUS. *adj.* Fine, splendid, showy, magnificent. adv. *gorgeously:* s. *gorgeousness.*

GOR'GET. *s.* A piece of armour that defends the throat; a small convex ornament, gilt or of silver, worn by the officers of foot, upon their breasts.

GOR'GON. *s.* A monster with snaky hairs, of which the sight turned the beholders to stone. adj. *gorgonian.*

GOR'MAND, GOUR'MAND. *s.* A greedy eater; a ravenous, luxurious feeder. s. *gormandize, gormandizer.*

GOR'MANDIZE. *v.* To play the glutton. pr. par. *gormandizing;* past, *gormandized.*

GOS'HAWK. *s.* A hawk of a large kind.

GOS'LING. *s.* A young goose.

GOS'PEL. *s.* Glad tidings; the holy book of the christian revelation.

GOS'SAMER. *s.* The down of plants; the long white cobwebs which fly in the air in calm, sunny weather.

GOS'SIP. *s.* Mere tattle; trifling talk. v. *gossip;* pr. par. *gossiping;* past, *gossiped.*

GOSSOON'. *s.* A lad; a low attendant formerly in the wealthy families among the Irish.

GOT. Pret. and past par. of the v. *to get.*

GOTH. *s* One of the uncivilized people, who formerly lived in the northern part of Europe; a barbarian. adj. *gothic.*

GOTH'IC *s.* A kind of architecture.

GOT'TEN. *v.* One of the past par. of *get.*

GOUGE. *s.* A kind of concave chisel v. *gouge;* pr. par. *gouging;* past, *gouged.*

GOULARD'. *s.* An infusion of acetate of lead.

GOURD. *s.* A kind of plant.

GOUR'MAND. *s.* A glutton; a greedy feeder.

GOUR'NET. *s.* A kind of fish.

GOUT. *s.* A kind of disease attended with great pain. adj. *gouty:* s. *goutiness.*

GOUT. *s.* A taste. pronounced *goo*

GOV'ERN. *v.* To rule, to regulate, to direct. pr. par. *governing;* past. *governed:* adj. *governable:* s. *governance, government, governor. governess,* pl. *governesses, governante:* adj. *governmental.*

GOWL. *v.* To howl. pr. par. *gowling;* past, *gowled.*

GOWN. *s.* A woman's upper garment; a long upper garment, worn by persons of the learned professions and by students. adj. *gown'd*

GRAB'BLE. *v.* To grope; to feel eagerly with the hands. pr. par *grabbling;* past, *grabbled.*

GRACE. *s.* Favour, kindness, favourable influence of God on the human mind; pardon; a short prayer said before or after meat. adj. *graceless:* adv. *gracelessly.*

GRACE. *v.* To adorn, to dignify, to embellish. pr. par. *gracing*, past, *graced:* adj. *graceful:* adv. *gracefully:* s. *gracefulness.*

GRA'CIOUS. *adj.* Merciful, benevolent, favourable. adv. *graciously* s. *graciousness.*

GRADA'TION. *s.* Regular progress from one degree to another; order, series.

GRADE. *s.* Rank, degree.

GRAD'UAL. *adj.* Proceeding by degrees; advancing step by step. s *graduality,* pl. *gradualities:* adv. *gradually.*

GRAD'UATE. *v.* To dignify with a degree in the university; to obtain a degree; to mark with degrees. pr. par. *graduating:* past *graduated:* s. *graduate, graduation.*

GRAFT. *v.* To insert a cion or branch of one tree into the stock of another; to propagate by insertion or inoculation. pr. par. *grafting;* past, *grafted:* s. *grafter.*

GRAIN. *s.* A single seed of corn; any minute particle; a species of weight; any thing proverbially small; temper; disposition, &c.

GRAINS. *s.* The husks of malt exhausted in brewing.

GRAMIN'EOUS. *adj.* Grassy.

GRAMINIV'OROUS. *adj.* Grass-eating; living upon grass.

GRAM'MAR. *s.* The science of speaking correctly; the book that treats of the various relations of words to one another. s. *grammarian:* adj. *grammatical:* adv. *grammatically.*

GRAM'PUS. *s.* A kind of large fish. pl. *grampuses.*

GRANA'DO. *s.* A grenade. pl. *granadoes.*

GRAN'ARY. *s.* A store-house for threshed corn. pl. *granaries.*

GRAN'ATE, GRAN'ITE. *s.* A kind of mountain stone.

GRAND. *adj.* Great, illustrious, splendid, magnificent, noble. adv. *grandly;* s. *grandness.*

GRAND'CHILD. *s.* The son or daughter of a son or daughter.

GRAND'DAUGHTER. *s.* The daughter of a son or daughter.

GRANDEE'. *s.* A man of great rank, power, or dignity.

GRAN'DEUR. *s.* Magnificence, state, splendour of appearance.

GRAND'FATHER. *s.* The father of a father or mother.

GRANDIL'OQUENCE. *s.* High, lofty, big speaking. adj. *grandiloquous.*

GRAND'MOTHER. *s.* The mother of a father or mother.

GRAND'SIRE. *s.* Grandfather; any ancestor, poetically.

GRAND'SON. *s.* The son of a son or daughter.

GRANGE. *s.* A farm; generally, a farm with a house at a distance from neighbours; a granary.

GRAN'ITE, GRAN'ATE. *s.* A kind of mountain stone.

GRANIV'OROUS. *adj.* Eating grain; living upon grain.

GRANT. *v.* To admit that which is not yet proved; to allow, to yield pr. par. *granting;* past, *granted.* s. *grant, grantee, grantor.*

GRAN'ULATE. *v.* To be formed into small grains. pr. par. *granulating;* past, *granulated:* s. *granulation, granule:* adj. *granulary, granulous.*

GRAPE. *s.* The fruit of the vine, growing in clusters.

GRAPE'-SHOT. *s.* A kind of small shot, discharged from a cannon.

GRAPH'IC, GRAPH'ICAL. *adj.* Relating to engraving; well delineated. adv. *graphically.*

GRAP'NEL. *s.* A small anchor belonging to a little vessel; a grappling iron.

GRAP'PLE. *v.* To contend by seizing; to contest in close fight. pr par. *grappling;* past, *grappled:* s. *grapple.*

GRASS. *s.* The common herbage of the field. pl. *grasses:* adj. *grassy, grassless:* s. *grassiness.*

GRASS'HOPPER. *s.* A small insect.

GRASS'-PLOT. *s.* A small, level piece of ground, covered with grass.

GRASP. *v.* To hold in the hand to gripe, to seize. pr. par. *grasping;* past, *grasped:* s. *grasp grasper.*

GRATE. *s.* A partition made with bars placed near to are another, or crossing each other, the range of bars within which fires are made. v *grate;* pr. par. *grating,* past, *grated:* s. *grating.*

GRATE. *v.* To rub hard, so as to injure or offend; to make a harsh noise. pr. par. *grating;* past, *grated:* s. *grater* adv. *gratingly.*

171

GRATE'FUL. *adj.* Having a due sense of benefits; pleasing, delightful. *adv. gratefully:* s. *gratefulness.*

GRATIFICA'TION. *s.* The act of pleasing; pleasure; delight; reward. *v. gratify;* pr. par. *gratifying;* past, *gratified:* s. *gratifier.*

GRA'TING. *s.* A partition made with bars placed near to one another.

GRA'TIS. *adv.* For nothing; without a recompense.

GRAT'ITUDE. *s.* Duty to benefactors; desire to return benefits.

GRATU'ITOUS. *adj.* Voluntary; granted without claim or reward. *adv. gratuitously:* s. *gratuity,* pl. *gratuities.*

GRATULA'TION. *s.* Salutations made by expressing joy; expression of joy. *adj. gratulatory.*

GRAVE. *s.* A place in the ground in which the dead are deposited.

GRAVE. *v.* To dig; to carve a figure or inscription in any hard substance. pr. par. *graving;* past, *graved:* s. *graver.*

GRAVE. *adj.* Solemn, serious, sober. *adv. gravely:* s. *gravity,* pl. *gravities.*

GRAV'EL. *s.* Hard sand. *v. gravel;* pr. par. *graveling;* past, *graveled:* adj. *gravelly.*

GRAVE'-STONE. *s.* A stone placed over a grave.

GRAV'ITATE. *v.* To tend to the centre of attraction. pr. par. *gravitating;* past, *gravitated:* s. *gravitation, gravity,* pl. *gravities.*

GRAY *adj.* White, with a mixture of black. *adj. grayish:* s. *grayness.*

GRAZE. *v.* To eat grass; to feed on grass; to touch lightly. pr. par. *grazing;* past, *grazed:* s. *grazer, grazier.*

GREASE. *s.* The soft part of the fat. *v. grease;* pr. par. *greasing;* past, *greased:* adj. *greasy:* adv. *greasily:* s. *greasiness.*

GREAT. *adj.* Large in bulk or number; chief, principal. *s. greas, greatness:* adv. *greatly.*

GREAVE. *s.* A groove.

GREAVES. *s.* Armour for the legs a sort of boots.

GRE'CIAN. *adj.* Relating to the country of Greece.

GRE'CISM. *s.* An idiom of the Greek language.

GREE'DY. *adj.* Ravenous, voracious, eager. *adv. greedily:* s. *greediness.*

GREEK. *adj.* Belonging to Greece.

GREEN. *adj.* Having a colour formed commonly by compounding blue and yellow. *v. green;* pr. par. *greening;* past, *greened:* adj *greenish:* s. *green, greenness.*

GREENGA'GE. *s.* A species of plum.

GREENGRO'CER. *s.* A retailer of greens.

GREEN'HORN. *s.* A youth easily imposed upon.

GREEN'HOUSE. *s.* A house in which tender plants are sheltered from the weather.

GREEN'-ROOM. *s.* A room near the stage, to which actors retire, during the intervals of the play.

GREET. *v.* To address at meeting; to salute. pr. par. *greeting;* past, *greeted:* s. *greeter.*

GRE'GAL. *adj.* Belonging to a flock

GREGA'RIAN. *adj.* Of the common sort; ordinary.

GREGA'RIOUS. *adj.* Going in flocks or herds. *adv. gregariously:* s. *gregariousness.*

GREGO'RIAN. *adj.* Belonging to the style or method of computation instituted by Pope Gregory in 1582.

GRENA'DE, GRENA'DO. *s.* A hollow ball of metal, filled with combustibles.

GRENADI'ER. *s.* A tall foot-soldier, whose duty formerly consisted in throwing hand-grenades.

GREW. Preterit of the v. *to grow.*

GREY. *adj.* See GRAY.

172

GREY'HOUND. s: A species of dog, for the chase.
GRID'IRON. s. A portable grate, on which meat is broiled.
GRIEF. s. Sorrow, grievance, pain. adj. *griefless.*
GRIEVE. v. To afflict, to hurt, to lament. pr. par. *grieving;* past, *grieved:* s. *griever, grievance:* adj. *grievous:* adv. *grievingly, grievously.*
GRIF'FIN, GRIF'FON. s. A fabled animal, said to be generated between a lion and an eagle.
GRIG. s. A merry creature; a small eel.
GRILLA'DE. s. Any thing broiled on the gridiron.
GRIM. adj. Having a countenance of terror; horrible, hideous, ugly. adv. *grimly:* s. *grimness.*
GRIMA'CE. s. A distortion of the countenance, from habit, affectation, or insolence.
GRIMAL'KIN. s. The name of a cat.
GRI'MY. adj. Dirty, cloudy.
GRIN. v. To set the teeth together, and withdraw the lips. pr. par. *grinning;* past, *grinned:* s. *grin, grinner:* adv. *grinningly.*
GRIND. v. To reduce to powder by friction; to sharpen or smooth by rubbing on something hard. pr. par. *grinding;* past, *ground:* s. *grinder.*
GRIND'STONE. s. A stone for sharpening e ged instruments.
GRIPE. v. To hold with the fingers closed; to seize; to pinch. pr. par *griping;* past, *griped:* s. *gripe, griper:* adv. *gripingly.*
GRISETTE. s. In France, the wife or daughter of a tradesman.
GRIS'KIN. s. The vertebræ of a hog.
GRIS'LY. adj. Dreadful, hideous, frightful.
GRISONS'. s. Inhabitants of the mountainous parts of the Alps, in Italy.
GRIST. s. Corn to be ground; supply.

GRIST'LE. s. A cartilage. adj. *gristly.*
GRIT. s. The coarse part of meal; sand; rough, hard particles. adj. *gritty:* s. *grittiness.*
GRIZ'ZLE. s. A mixture of white and black; gray. adj. *grizzlea, grizzly.*
GROAN. v. To breathe with a hoarse noise, as in agony or pain. pr. par. *groaning;* past, *groaned:* s. *groan, groaning.*
GROAT. s. A small piece of money, valued at four pence.
GROATS. s. Oats that have the hulls taken off.
GRO'CER. s. One who sells tea, sugar, wine, &c. s. *grocery,* pl. *groceries.*
GROG. s. Gin and water, or any spirit and water. adj. *groggy.*
GROIN. s. The part next above the thigh.
GROOM. s. A boy, a waiter, a servant: a man newly married.
GROOVE. v. To cut hollow. pr. par. *grooving;* past, *grooved:* s. *groove, groover.*
GROPE. v. To feel where one cannot see. pr. par. *groping;* past, *groped:* s. *groper.*
GROSS. adj. Thick, bulky, shameful, enormous, impure, inelegant s. *gross, grossness:* adv. *grossly.*
GROT, GROT'TO. s. A cave; cavern for coolness and pleasure.
GROTESQUE'. adj. Of a distorted figure; unnatural. adv. *grotesquely.*
GROUND. s. The earth, land, country, region, foundation. v. *ground,* pr. par. *grounding;* past, *grounded.*
GROUND'-FLOOR. s. The lower part of a house.
GROUND'-PLOT. s. The ground on which any building is placed.
GROUND'-RENT. s. Rent paid for the privilege of building on another man's ground.
GROUND'LESS. adj. Void of reason; wanting ground. adv. *groundlessly:* s. *groundlessness.*

GROUNDLING. *s.* A fish which keeps at the bottom of the water, —hence, one of the vulgar.

GROUND'SEL. *s.* A species of plant.

GROUND'WORK. *s.* The first stratum; first principle; the first part of an undertaking.

GROUP. *s.* A cluster, a collection, a number thronged together. *v. group;* pr. par. *grouping;* past, *grouped.*

GROUSE. *s.* A kind of fowl; a heathcock.

GROUT. *s.* Coarse meal; pollard; very thin, coarse mortar. *v. grout;* pr. par. *grouting;* past, *grouted.*

GROVE. *s.* A small wood or place, set with trees.

GROV'EL. *v.* To lie prone; to creep low on the ground; to be mean. pr. par. *groveling;* past, *groveled:* s. *groveller.*

GROW. *v.* To vegetate; to increase by vegetation. pr. par. *growing;* past, *grown:* s. *grower.*

GROWL. *v.* To snarl like an angry cur; to murmur; to grumble. pr. par. *growling;* past, *growled:* s. *growl, growler.*

GROWTH. *s.* Vegetation; vegetable life; product.

GRUB. *v.* To dig; to root out of the ground. pr. par. *grubbing;* past, *grubbed:* s. *grub, grubber.*

GRUB. *s.* A kind of small worm.

GRUDGE. *v.* To envy; to give or take unwillingly. pr. par. *grudging;* past, *grudged:* s. *grudge, grudger, grudging:* adv. *grudgingly.*

GRU'EL. *s.* Food made by boiling meal in water.

GRUFF. *adj.* Of sour aspect; of harsh manners. adv. *gruffly:* s. *gruffness.*

GRUM. *adj.* Sour, surly, severe. adv. *grumly.*

GRUM'BLE. *v.* To murmur with discontent; to growl. pr. par. *grumbling;* past, *grumbled:* s. *grumbler, grumbling:* adv. *grumblingly.*

GRUNT. *v.* To murmur like a hog; to groan. pr. par. *grunting,* past, *grunted:* s. *grunt, grunter, grunting:* adv. *gruntingly.*

GRY'PHON. *s.* See GRIFFON.

GUA'IACUM. *s.* A medicinal wood.

GUARANTEE'. *s.* A person who undertakes to see stipulations performed. *v. guarantee;* pr. par. *guaranteeing,* past, *guaranteed.*

GUARD. *v.* To watch by way of defence or security; to protect; to defend. pr. par. *guarding;* past, *guarded:* s. *guard, guarder:* adj. *guardful, guardless:* adv. *guardedly.*

GUAR'DANT. *adj.* Exercising the authority of a guardian; (in heraldry) having the face turned towards the spectator.

GUAR'DIAN. *s.* One that has the care of an orphan; one to whom the care and preservation of any thing are committed. *s. guardianship.*

GUARD'-ROOM. *s.* A room in which those who are appointed to watch, assemble.

GUBERNATO'RIAL. *adj.* Relating or belonging to government.

GUD'GEON. *s.* A small fish.

GUER'DON. *s.* A reward, a recompense.

GUESS. *v.* To conjecture; to judge without any certain principles of judgment. pr. par. *guessing;* past. *guessed:* s. *guess,* pl. *guesses, guesser:* adv. *guessingly.*

GUEST. *s.* One entertained in the house, or at the table of another.

GUG'GLE. *v.* To sound as water running with intermissions out of a narrow-mouthed vessel. pr. par. *guggling;* past, *guggled.*

GUIDE. *v.* To direct, to influence, to instruct. pr. par. *guiding;* past, *guided:* s. *guide, guider, guidance.* adj. *guidable, guideless.*

GUILD. *s.* A society, a corporation, a fraternity, a town-hall.

GUILDHALL'. s. The hall in which a corporation usually assembles; a town-hall.

GUILE. s. Deceitful cunning; insidious artifice. adj. *guileful*, *guileless*: adv. *guilefully*: s. *guilefulness*, *guilelessness*.

GUILLOTINE. s. A machine for separating the head from the body at one stroke. v. *guillotine*; pr. par. *guillotining*; past. *guillotined*.

GUILT. s. Crime, offence, sin. adj. *guilty*, *guiltless*: adv. *guiltily*, *guiltlessly*: s. *guiltiness*, *guiltlessness*.

GUINEA. s. A country in Africa; a gold coin, value 21 shillings sterling.

GUISE. s. Manner, mien, habit.

GUITAR'. s. A stringed musical instrument.

GULF. s. A bay; an opening into land.

GULL. s. A cheat, a fraud, a trick, a kind of sea-bird. v. *gull*; pr. par. *gulling*; past, *gulled*: s. *guller*.

GULLET. s. The throat; the œsophagus.

GULP. v. To swallow eagerly. pr. par. *gulping*; past, *gulped*: s. *gulp*.

GULPH. s. See GULF.

GUM. s. A glutinous vegetable substance; the fleshy covering that contains the teeth. adj. *gummy*. s. *gumminess*, *gummosity*, pl. *gummosities*.

GUN. s. The general name for fire-arms. v. *gun*; pr. par. *gunning*; past, *gunned*: s. *gunner*, *gunnery*, pl. *gunneries*.

GUN'NEL. s. See GUNWALE.

GUN'POWDER. s. The powder put into guns to be fired.

GUN'ROOM. s. The place, on board a ship, where arms are deposited.

GUN'SHOT. s. The reach or range of a gun; the distance to which a shot can be thrown; shot discharged from a gun.

GUN'SMITH. s. A man whose trade is to make guns.

GUN'WALE, GUN'NEL. s. That piece of timber which reaches on each side of a ship, from the half-deck to the forecastle.

GUR'GLE. v. To fall or gush with noise, as water from a bottle. pr. par. *gurgling*; past, *gurgled*.

GUR'NET. s. A kind of fish.

GUSH. v. To flow or rush out with violence. pr. par. *gushing*; past, *gushed*: s. *gush*.

GUS'SET. s. An angular piece of cloth, sewn at the upper end of the sleeve of a shirt or shift.

GUST. s. Sense of tasting; height of perception; a sudden, violent blast of wind. adj. *gusty*.

GUT. s. The stomach; the receptacle of food. v. *gut*; pr. par. *gutting*; past, *gutted*.

GUT'TER. s. A passage for water; a small longitudinal hollow.

GUT'TLE. v. To feed luxuriously; to gormandize. pr. par. *guttling*; past, *guttled*: s. *guttler*.

GUT'TURAL. adj. Pronounced in the throat; belonging to the throat.

GUZ'ZLE. v. To gormandize; to swallow any liquor greedily. pr. par. *guzzling*; past, *guzzled*: s. *guzzler*.

GYMNA'SIUM. s. Formerly a place for athletic exercises; any place of exercise. adj. *gymnastic*: adv. *gymnastically*.

GYMOS'OPHIST. s. One of a sect of Indian philosophers, who went naked.

GYP'SUM. s. The name of a class of fossils: the plaster-stone, called, by chymists, sulphate of lime.

GYP'SY. s. See GIPSY.

GYRA'TION. s. The act of turning any thing about; one revolution.

GYRE. s. A circle described by any thing moving in an orbit.

GY'ROMANCY. s. A sort of divination, performed by walking.

175

H

HA. *int.* An expression of wonder, or surprise.

HAB'ERDASHER. *s.* One who sells small wares. *s. haberdashery,* pl. *haberdasheries.*

HAB'ERGEON. *s.* Armour to cover the neck and breast.

HABIL'IMENT. *s.* Dress, clothes, garment.

HAB'IT. *s.* State of any thing—as a *habit* of body; dress; accoutrement; effect of custom. *v. habit;* pr. par. *habiting;* past, *habited.*

HABITA'TION. *s.* Place of abode; dwelling. *adj. habitable.*

HABIT'UATE. *v.* To accustom; to use one's self by frequent repetition. pr. par. *habituating;* past, *habituated:* adj. *habitual:* adv. *habitually.*

HAB'ITUDE. *s.* Relation, respect, familiarity, long custom.

HACK. *v.* To cut into small pieces; to chop. pr. par. *hacking;* past, *hacked:* s. *hack.*

HACK, HACK'NEY. *s.* A horse let out for hire. *v. hack;* pr. par. *hacking;* past, *hacked.*

HACK'LE. *v.* To dress flax; to separate; to tear asunder. pr. par. *hackling;* past, *hackled:* s. *hackle.*

HACK'LE. *s.* A fly for angling.

HACK'NEY. *s.* A hired horse; a horse for common use. *v. hackney;* pr. par. *hackneying;* past, *hackneyed.*

HAD. Pret. and past par. of the v. *to have.*

HAD'DOCK. *s.* A kind of fish.

HAFT. *s.* A handle; that part of an instrument that is taken into the hand. *v. haft;* pr. par. *hafting;* past, *hafted:* s. *hafter.*

HAG. *s.* A witch; an enchantress; a fury.

HAG'GARD. *adj.* Wild, lean, rugged. adv. *haggardly:* s. *haggardness.*

HAG'GARD. *s.* A stack-yard.

HAG'GESS. *s.* A mass of meat, generally pork chopped, and enclosed in a membrane. pl. *haggesses.*

HAG'GLE. *v.* To cut, to chop, to mangle. pr. par. *haggling;* past, *haggled:* s. *haggler.*

HAGIOG'RAPHER. *s.* A holy writer.

HAIL. *s.* Drops of rain, frozen in their falling. *v. hail;* pr. par. *hailing;* past, *hailed:* s. *hailstone.*

HAIL. *int.* A term of salutation. *v. hail;* pr. par. *hailing;* past, *hailed.*

HAIR. *s.* One of the common teguments; a single hair. adj. *hairy, hairless:* s. *hairiness.*

HAIR'BRAINED. *adj.* Wild, irregular, unsteady.

HAIR'BREADTH. *s.* A very small distance; the diameter of a hair.

HAIR'CLOTH. *s.* Stuff made of hair.

HAKE. *s.* A kind of fish.

HAL'BERD, HAL'BERT. *s.* A battle-axe, fixed to a long pole. *s. halberdier.*

HAL'CYON. *adj.* Placid, quiet, peaceful.

HALE. *adj.* Healthy, sound, hearty, uninjured.

HALF. *s.* A moiety; an equal part. pl. *halves:* adv. *half.*

HALF-BLOOD'. *s.* A person of the half-blood, is one not born of the same father and mother.

HALF-MOON'. *s.* The moon in its appearance, when at half increase, or decrease.

HALF'PENNY. *s.* A copper coin pl. *halfpence, halfpennies.*

HALF-SEAS-O'VER. *adj.* A proverbial expression for any one far advanced; commonly used for one half drunk.

HALF-SIGHT'ED. *adj.* Seeing imperfectly.

HALF-WAY'. *adv.* In the middle

HALF-WITTED. *adj.* Imperfectly furnished with intellect.
HAL'IBUT. *s.* A sort of fish.
HALL. *s.* A court of justice; the public room of a corporation; the first large room of a house.
HALLELU'JAH. *s.* A song of thanksgiving.
HAL'LIARDS, HAL'YARDS. *s.* Ropes or tackle employed to hoist or lower a sail.
HALLOO'. *int.* A word of encouragement, when dogs are let loose on their game. *v. halloo;* pr. par. *nallooing;* past, *hallooed: s. hallooing.*
HAL'LOW. *v.* To consecrate; to make holy. pr. par. *hallowing;* past, *hallowed.*
HALLU'CINATE. *v.* To stumble; to blunder. pr. par. *hallucinating;* past, *hallucinated: s. hallucination.*
HA'LO. *s.* A red circle round the sun or moon.
HALT. *v.* To limp, to hesitate, to falter. pr. par. *halting;* past, *halted:* adj. *halt: s. halt, halter:* adv. *haltingly.*
HAL'TER. *s.* A rope to hang malefactors; a cord. *v. halter;* pr. par. *haltering;* past, *haltered.*
HALVE. *v.* To divide into two parts. pr. par. *halving;* past, *halved.*
HAM. *s.* The hip; the thigh of a hog, salted.
HAM'ADRYAD. *s.* One of those wood-nymphs of antiquity, who were feigned to live and die with the trees to which they were attached.
HAM'ATED. *adj.* Hooked; set with hooks.
HAMES. *s.* The collar by which a horse draws.
HAM'LET. *s.* A small village.
HAM'MER. *s.* An instrument to drive nails, &c. *v. hammer;* pr. par. *hammering;* past, *hammered: s. hammerer.*
HAM'MERCLOTH. *s.* The cloth that covers a coach-box.

HAM'MOCK. *s.* A swinging bed.
HAM'PER. *s.* A large basket.
HAM'PER. *v.* To shackle, to entangle, to ensnare, to complicate. pr par. *hampering;* past, *hampered.*
HAM'STRING. *s.* The tendon of the ham. *v. hamstring;* pr. par *hamstringing;* past, *hamstrung.*
HAND. *s.* The palm, with the fingers; a palm. *v. hand;* pr. par. *handing;* past, *handed.*
HAND'-BARROW. *s.* A frame on which any thing is carried by the hands, without wheeling on the ground.
HAND'CUFF. *s.* A manacle; a fetter for the wrist. *v. handcuff;* pr. par. *handcuffing;* past, *handcuffed.*
HAND'FUL. *s.* As much as the hand can contain.
HAND'GALLOP. *s.* A slow, easy gallop.
HAND-GRENA'DE. *s.* See GRENADO and GRENADE.
HAND'ICRAFT. *s.* Manual occupation; a man who lives by manual labour. *s. handicraftsman.*
HAND'KERCHIEF. *s.* A piece of cloth, used to wipe the face, or cover the neck.
HAND'LE. *v.* To touch; to feel with the hand; to manage. pr. par. *handling;* past, *handled: s. handle:* adj. *handless.*
HAND'MAID. *s.* A maid that waits at hand.
HAND'MILL. *s.* A mill moved by the hand.
HAND'SAW. *s.* A saw managed by the hand.
HAND'SEL. *s.* The first act of using any thing; the first act of sale. *v. handsel;* pr. par. *handseling;* past, *handseled.*
HAND'SOME. *adj.* Beautiful, graceful, elegant. adv. *handsomely: s. handsomeness.*
HAND'SPIKE. *s.* A kind of wooden lever, to move great weights.
HAND'VICE. *s.* A vice for holding small work.

HAND'WRITING. *s.* A cast or form of writing peculiar to each hand; any writing.

HAND'Y. *adj.* Ready, dextrous, skilful. *adv. handily: s. handiness.*

HAND'YWORK. *s.* Work of the hand; product of labour; manufacture.

HANG. *v.* To suspend; to fasten in such a manner as to be sustained not below, but above. *pr. par. hanging; past, hung: s. hanger, hanging.*

HANG'ER. *s.* A short curved sword; a short broad sword.

HANG'MAN. *s.* A public executioner. pl. *hangmen.*

HANK. *s.* A skein of thread, a tie. *v. hank; pr. par. hanking; past, hanked.*

HANK'ER. *v.* To long importunately. *pr. par. hankering; past, hankered: s. hankering.*

HANSEAT'IC. *adj.* Relating to the Hanse-towns.

HAP. *s.* Chance, fortune, accident.

HAP'LESS. *adj.* Unhappy, unfortunate, luckless.

HAP'LY. *adv.* Perhaps, peradventure, by chance.

HAP'PEN. *v.* To chance; to come to pass. *pr. par. happening; past, happened.*

HAP'PY. *adj.* In a state of felicity; lucky; successful. *adv. happily; s. happiness.*

HA'RAM, HA'REM. *s.* A seraglio; the women's apartment in the east.

HARANGUE'. *s.* A speech; a popular oration. *v. harangue; pr. par. haranguing; past, harangued: s. haranguer.*

HARASS'. *v.* To weary, to fatigue. *pr. par. harassing; past, harassed: s. harasser.*

HAR'BINGER. *s.* A forerunner, a precursor.

HAR'BOUR. *s.* A lodging; a place of entertainment; a port or haven for shipping. *v. harbour; pr. par.* harbouring; past, harboured: *s.* harbourage, harbourer.

HARD. *adj.* Firm; resisting penetration or separation; difficult. *adv. hard, hardly: v. harden; pr. par. hardening; past, hardened: s. hardener, hardness.*

HARD'EARNED. *adj.* Earned with difficulty.

HARD'FAVOURED. *adj.* Of coarse features.

HARD'FISTED. *adj.* Covetous, close-handed.

HARD'FOUGHT. *adj.* Vehemently contested.

HARD'GOTTEN. *adj.* Obtained by great labour, and pains.

HARD'HEARTED. *adj.* Cruel, inexorable, merciless. *s. hardheartedness.*

HARD'IHOOD. *s.* Stoutness, bravery.

HARD'LABOURED. *adj.* Elaborate, studied.

HARD'MOUTHED. *adj.* Disobedient to the rein; not sensible of the bit.

HARD'SHIP. *s.* Injury, oppression, fatigue.

HARD'WARE. *s.* Manufactures of metal.

HARD'Y. *adj.* Bold, brave, stout, daring, strong. *s. hardiness.*

HARE. *s.* A kind of small quadruped.

HARE'BELL. *s.* A species of flower.

HARE'BRAINED. *adj.* Volatile, unsettled, wild.

HARE'LIP. *s.* A fissure in the upper lip. *adj. harelipped.*

HAR'ICOT. *s.* A kind of ragout pronounced *har'ico.*

HAR'IER. *s.* A dog for hunting hares.

HARK. *int.* List! hear! listen!

HAR'LEQUIN. *s.* A buffoon who plays tricks to divert the populace.

HAR'LOT. *s.* A whore, a strumpet, a base person. *s. harlotry*, pl. *harlotries.*

HARM. *s.* Injury, crime, mischief.

detriment. adj. *harmful, harmless:* adv. *harmfully, harmlessly:* s. *harmlessness.*

HARMON'IC, HARMON'ICAL. *adj.* Relating to music; concordant; musical. adv. *harmonically.*

HAR'MONY. *s.* The just adaption of one part to another; musical concord; concord. pl. *harmonies:* v. *harmonize;* pr. par. *harmonizing;* past, *harmonized:* s. *harmonist, harmonizer, harmoniousness:* adj. *harmonious:* adv. *harmoniously.*

HAR'NESS. *s.* Armour; the traces &c. of draught horses. v. *harness;* pr. par. *harnessing;* past, *harnessed:* s. *harnesser.*

HARP. *s.* A kind of stringed musical instrument. v. *harp;* pr. par. *harping;* past, *harped:* s. *harper.*

HARPOON'. *s.* A harping iron, used in whalefishing. s. *harpooner, harponier.*

HARP'SICHORD. *s.* A kind of musical instrument.

HAR'PY. *s.* A fabled bird. pl. *harpies.*

HAR'RIDAN. *s.* A decayed strumpet.

HAR'ROW. *s.* An instrument used for fitting the ground for seed, and then covering the seed. v. *harrow;* pr. par. *harrowing;* past, *harrowed:* s. *harrower.*

HAR'RY. *v.* To teaze, to ruffle: in Scotland, it signifies to plunder. pr. par. *harrying;* past, *harried.*

HARSH. *adj.* Austere, rough, unpleasing. adv. *harshly:* s. *harshness.*

HART. *s.* A male deer.

HARTS'HORN. *s.* A drug made of the horns of the deer.

HAR'VEST. *s.* The season of reaping, and gathering in grain. v. *harvest;* pr. par. *harvesting;* past, *harvested:* s. *harvester.*

HAS. *v.* The third person sing. of the v. *have.*

HASH. *v.* To mince; to chop into small pieces. pr. par. *hashing* past, *hashed:* s. *hash,* pl. *hashes.*

HAS'LET. *s.* The heart, liver, and lights, of a hog, with the windpipe, &c.

HASP. *s.* A clasp folded over a staple. v. *hasp;* pr. par. *hasping;* past, *hasped.*

HAST. *v.* The second person sing. of the v. *have.*

HASTE. *s.* Hurry, speed, nimbleness, precipitation. v. *haste, hasten;* pr. par. *hasting, hastening;* past, *hasted, hastened:* s. *hastener, hastiness:* adj. *hasty:* adv. *hastily.*

HAT. *s.* A cover for the head. adj *hatted.*

HAT'BAND. *s.* A string tied round a hat.

HATCH. *v.* To produce young from eggs; to quicken the egg, by incubation. pr. par. *hatching;* past, *hatched:* s. *hatcher.*

HATCH'ES. *s.* The doors or openings in the deck of a ship.

HATCH'ET. s. A small axe.

HATCH'MENT. *s.* An armorial escutcheon, exhibited on the hearse at funerals, and sometimes hung up in churches.

HATCH'WAY. *s.* The way over or through the hatches.

HATE. *v.* To detest, to abhor, t abominate. pr. par. *hating;* past, *hated:* s. *hate, hater:* adj. *hateful.* adv. *hatefully:* s. *hatefulness.*

HA'TRED. *s.* Hate, ill-will, malignity, abhorrence.

HAT'TER. *s.* A manufacturer of hats.

HAU'BERK. *s.* A coat of mail without sleeves.

HAUGH. *s.* A little meadow lying in a valley.

HAUGHT'Y. *adj.* Proud, insolent, arrogant. adv. *haughtily:* s. *haughtiness.*

HAUL. *v.* To pull, to draw, to drag by violence. pr. par. *hauling;* past, *hauled:* s. *haul.*

HAUNCH. *s.* The thigh, the hip, the rear. pl. *haunches.*

179

HAUNT. *v.* To frequent; to be much about any place or person. pr. par. *haunting;* past, *haunted:* s. *haunt, haunter.*

HAU'TBOY. *s.* A kind of wind instrument. pronounced *ho'-boy.*

HAUTE'UR. *s.* Pride, insolence, haughtiness.

HAUT-GOUT. *s.* Any thing with a strong relish, or with a strong scent. pronounced *ho-goo'.*

HAVE. *v.* To possess. pr. par. *having;* past, *had.*

HA'VEN. *s.* A port; a harbour; a station for ships; a shelter.

HAV'ERSACK. *s.* A kind of coarse bag, in which soldiers carry provisions.

HAV'OC. *s.* Waste; wide and general devastation.

HAW. *s.* The seed of the hawthorn; a hedge, or any enclosure.

HAW'HAW. *s.* A defence or bank that interrupts an alley or walk, sunk between two slopes, and not perceived till approached.

HAWK. *s.* A bird of prey. *v. hawk;* pr. par. *hawking;* past, *hawked:* s. *hawker, hawking.*

HAW'SER. *s.* See HALSER.

HAW'THORN. *s.* A thorn that bears haws.

HAY. *s.* Grass dried to fodder cattle in winter. s. *haystack.*

HAY'MAKER. *s.* One employed in drying grass for hay.

HAZ'ARD. *s.* Chance, accident, danger. *v. hazard;* pr. par. *hazarding;* past, *hazarded:* adj. *hazardous:* adv. *hazardously.*

HAZE. *s.* Fog, mist. adj. *hazy:* s. *haziness.*

HA'ZEL. *s.* The nut-tree.

HA'ZEL. *adj.* Light brown.

HE. *pron.* The man that was named before; the person; male.

HEAD. *s.* The part of the animal that contains the brain, or the organ of sensation or thought; a chief; a principal person. adj. *head, headed, headless: v. head;* pr. par. *heading;* past, *headed:* s. *header.*

HEAD'ACHE. *s.* Pain in the head.

HEAD'BAND. *s.* A fillet for the head; a topknot.

HEAD'BOROUGH. *s.* A constable; a subordinate constable.

HEAD'DRESS. *s.* The covering of a woman's head. pl. *head-dresses.*

HEAD'INESS. *s.* Hurry, rashness, precipitation. adj. *heady.*

HEAD'LONG. *adj.* Steep, precipitous, rash, sudden. adv. *headlong.*

HEAD'PIECE. *s.* Armour for the head; a helmet.

HEADQUAR'TERS. *s.* The place of general rendezvous, or lodgment for soldiers.

HEAD'STALL. *s.* Part of a bridle that covers the head.

HEAD'STONE. *s.* The first or capital stone; a grave-stone.

HEADSTRONG. *adj.* Unrestrained, violent, ungovernable.

HEAD'WAY. *s.* The motion of advancing at sea.

HEA'DY. *adj.* Rash, precipitate, hasty.

HEAL. *v.* To cure; to restore from hurt or sickness; to cicatrize. pr. par. *healing;* past, *healed:* s. *healer, healing:* adj. *healable.*

HEALTH. *s.* Freedom from bodily pain or sickness; purity. adj. *healthy, healthful:* s. *healthfulness, healthiness.*

HEAP. *s.* A pile, an accumulation, cluster. *v. heap;* pr. par. *heaping;* past, *heaped:* s. *heaper.*

HEAR. *v.* To enjoy the sense by which sounds are distinguished; to listen. pr. par. *hearing;* past, *heard:* s. *hearer, hearing.*

HEARD. The pret. of the *v. to hear.*

HEARK'EN. *v.* To listen, to attend. pr. par. *hearkening;* past, *hearkened:* s. *hearkener.*

HEAR'SAY. *s.* Report, rumour.

HEARSE. *s.* A carriage in which the dead are conveyed to the grave.

HEART. *s.* That part of an animal which is considered as the source of vital motion; the inner part of any thing; courage; spirit. v *hearten;* pr. par. *heartening;* past, *heartened:* s. *heartener.*

HEART'BURN. s. Pain proceeding from an acrid humour in the stomach. s. *heart-burning.*

HEART'FELT. adj. Felt in the conscience.

HEARTH. s. The pavement of a room, on which a fire is made.

HEART'LESS. adj. Without courage, spiritless. adv. *heartlessly:* s. *heartlessness.*

HEAR'TY. adj. Sincere, warm, zealous; in full health; vigorous. adv. *heartily:* s. *heartiness.*

HEAT. s. The sensation caused by the approach or touch of fire; the cause of the sensation of burning; agitation of sudden or violent passion. v. *heat;* pr. par. *heating;* past, *heated:* s. *heater.*

HEATH. s. A shrub of low stature; a place overgrown with heath. adj. *heathy.*

HEATH'EN. s. A gentile, a pagan. adj. *heathen, heathenish:* adv. *heathenishly:* s. *heathenishness, heathenism.*

HEATH'ER. s. Heath.

HEAVE. v. To lift; to raise from the ground; to carry; to puff. pr. par. *heaving;* past, *heaved:* s. *heave, heaver, heaving.*

HEAV'EN. s. The regions above; the expanse of the sky. adj. and adv. *heavenly:* s. *heavenliness.*

HEAV'Y. adj. Weighty, ponderous, sorrowful, grievous. com. *heavier;* sup. *heaviest:* adv. *heavily:* s. *heaviness.*

HEBDOM'ADAL. HEBDOM'ADARY. adj. Weekly.

HE'BRAISM. s. A Hebrew idiom. s. *Hebraist.*

HE'BREW. s. An Israelite; one of the children of Israel; the Hebrew tongue. adj. *Hebrew.*

HEBRID'IAN. adj. Respecting the Western Islands of Scotland.

HEC'ATOMB. s. A sacrifice of a hundred cattle.

HEC'TIC, HEC'TICAL. adj Habitual, constitutional. s. *hectic:* adv. *hectically.*

HEC'TOR. s. A bully; a blustering, turbulent, noisy fellow. v. *hector,* pr. par. *hectoring;* past, *hectored.*

HEDGE. s. A fence made round grounds or a garden. v. *hedge,* pr. par. *hedging;* past, *hedged* s. *hedger.*

HEDGE'-HOG. s. An animal set with prickles.

HEED. v. To mind, to regard, to attend. pr. par. *heeding;* past, *heeded:* s. *heed:* adj. *heedful, heedless:* adv. *heedfully, heedlessly* · s. *heedfulness, heedlessness.*

HEEL. s. The part of the foot that projects behind. v. *heel;* pr. par *heeling;* past, *heeled.*

HEGI'RA. s. A term in chronology, signifying the epoch, or account of time, used by the Arabians, who begin from the day that Mahomet was forced to make his escape from Mecca, July 16, A. D. 622.

HEIF'ER. s. A young cow, that has not had a calf.

HEIGH'-HO. int. An expression o. slight languor and uneasiness.

HEIGHT. s. Elevation above the ground; altitude; summit; space measured upwards. v. *heighten,* pr. par. *heightening;* past, *heightened.*

HEI'NOUS. adj. Atrocious; wicked in a high degree. adv. *heinously:* s. *heinousness.*

HEIR. s. One who inherits after the present possessor. adj. *heirless.*

HEIR'ESS. s. A woman who inherits. pl. *heiresses.*

HEIR'LOOM. s. Any furniture or movable, that descends by inheritance, and is therefore inseparable from the freehold.

HELD. Pret. and past par. of the v. *to hold.*

HELIOCEN'TRIC. adj. The heliocentric place of a planet is said to be such as it would appear to us from the sun, if our eye were fixed in its centre.

HELIOM'ETER. s. An instrument for measuring the diameters of the sun and moon.

HE'LIOSCOPE. s. A sort of telescope, fitted so as to look on the body of the sun, without offence to the eyes.

HE'LIOTROPE. s. A plant that turns towards the sun.

HELL. s. The place of the devil and wicked souls. adj. *hellish:* adv. *hellishly:* s. *hellishness.*

HEL'LEBORE. s. Christmas flower.

HELLEN'IC. *adj.* Grecian. s. *Hellenism, Hellenist.*

HELM. s. A covering for the head in war; a rudder.

HEL'MET. s. A helm; a headpiece. adj. *helmeted.*

HELMS'MAN. s. He who manages the rudder of a vessel.

HEL'OT. s. A slave.

HELP. v. To assist, to support, to aid, to remedy. pr. par. *helping;* past, *helped:* s. *help, helper, helplessness:* adj. *helpful, helpless:* adv. *helplessly.*

HELP'MATE. s. A companion; an assistant.

HEL'TER-SKEL'TER. *adv.* In a hurry; without order; tumultuously.

HEM. s. The edge of a garment, doubled and sewed, to keep the threads from spreading; the noise uttered by a sudden and violent expiration of the breath. v. *hem,* pr. par. *hemming;* past, *hemmed.*

HEM'I. s. A word often used in composition, signifying *half.*

HEM'ICYCLE. s. A half round.

HEM'ISPHERE. s. The half of a globe, when it is supposed to be cut through its centre, in the plane of one of its greatest circles. adj. *hemispheric, hemispherical.*

HEM'ISTIC, HEM'ISTICH. s. Half a verse.

HEM'LOCK. s. A species of herb.

HEM'ORRHAGE. s. A violent flux of blood.

HEM'ORRHOIDS. s. The piles, the emerods.

HEMP. s. A fibrous plant, of which coarse linen and ropes are made. adj. *hempen.*

HEN. s. The female of a house cock; the female of any landfowl.

HENCE. adv. and *int.* From this place to another; away to a distance; from this time; in the future; for this reason.

HENCE'FORTH. *adv.* From this time forward.

HENCEFOR'WARD. *adv.* From this time to futurity.

HENCH'MAN. s. A page, an attendant. pl. *henchmen.*

HEN'-COOP. s. A cage in which poultry are kept.

HEN'-PECKED. *adj.* Governed by the wife.

HEPAT'IC, HEPAT'ICAL. *adj.* Belonging to the liver.

HEP'TACHORD. s. Anciently, a musical instrument of seven strings.

HEP'TAGON. s. A figure with seven sides or angles. adv. *heptagonal.*

HEP'TARCHY. s. A sevenfold government. pl. *heptarchies.*

HER. *pron.* Belonging to a female of a woman; the objective case of *she.* emphatic pron. *herself.*

HER'ALD. s. A precursor, a forerunner, a public messenger, a proclaimer; one who registers genealogies. s. *heraldry,* pl. *heraldries:* adj. *heraldic.*

HERB. s. Plants whose stalks are soft, and have nothing woody in them. s. *herbage, herbist:* adj. *herbous.*

HERBA'CEOUS. *adj.* Belonging to herbs; feeding on vegetables.

HER'BAL. s. A book containing the names and description of plants.

HERBES'CENT. *adj.* Growing into herbs.

HERCU'LEAN. *adj.* Of extraordinary strength, like Hercules; large; massy.

HERD. *s.* A number of beasts together; a keeper of cattle. *v. herd;* pr. par. *herding;* past, *herded.*

HERDS'MAN. *s.* One employed in tending herds. pl. *herdsmen.*

HERE. *adv.* In this place; in the present state.

HERE'ABOUTS. *adv.* About this place.

HEREAF'TER. *adv.* In time to come; in futurity. *s. hereafter.*

HEREAT'. *adv.* At this.

HEREBY'. *adv.* By this.

HERED'ITARY. *adj.* Possessed or claimed by right of inheritance; descending by inheritance. adv. *hereditarily:* adj. *hereditable.*

HEREIN'. *adv.* In this.

HEREINTO'. *adv.* Into this.

HEREOF'. *adv.* From this; of this.

HEREON'. *adv.* Upon this.

HEREOUT'. *adv.* Out of this place.

HER'EMITE. *s.* A hermit. adj. *heremitical.*

HERE'SIARCH. *s.* A leader in heresy.

HER'ESY. *s.* An opinion different from that of the catholic church. pl. *heresies.*

HER'ETIC. *s.* One charged with heresy. adj. *heretical:* adv. *heretically.*

HERETO'. *adv.* To this; add to this.

HERE'TOFORE. *adv.* Formerly, anciently.

HEREUNTO'. *adv.* To this.

HEREUPON'. *adv.* Upon this.

HEREWITH'. *adv.* With this.

HER'IOT. *s.* A fine paid to the lord at the death of a landholder.

HER'ITABLE. *adj.* Capable to inherit; whatever may be inherited.

HER'ITAGE. *s.* Inheritance; estate devolved by succession.

HERMA'PHRODITE. *s.* An animal uniting two sexes.

HERMET'IC, HERMET'ICAL. *adj.* Chymical. adv. *hermetically.*

HER'MIT. *s.* An anchoret; one who retires from society, to contemplation or devotion. adj. *hermitical* s. *hermitage.*

HER'NIA. *s.* Any kind of rupture.

HE'RO. *s.* A man eminent for bravery. pl. *heroes:* adj. *heroic, heroical:* adv. *heroically:* s. *heroism* · s. fem. *heroine.*

HERO'IC. *s.* An heroic verse consists, in our poetry, of ten feet.

HER'ON. *s.* A kind of bird that preys upon fish; a crane. *s. heronry,* pl. *heronries.*

HER'PES. *s.* A cutaneous inflammation. adj. *herpetic.*

HER'RING. *s.* A small fish.

HES'ITANCY. *s.* Dubiousness, uncertainty, suspense. pl. *hesitancies.*

HES'ITATE. *v.* To be doubtful; to delay; to pause. pr. par. *hesitating;* past, *hesitated:* s. *hesitation.*

HET'EROCLITE. *s.* Such nouns as vary from the common forms of declension.

HET'ERODOX. *adj.* Deviating from the established opinion; not orthodox. s. *heterodoxy,* pl. *heterodoxies.*

HETEROGE'NEOUS, HETEROGE'NEAL. *adj.* Not of the same kind; dissimilar. s. *heterogeneity,* pl. *heterogeneities, heterogeneousness.*

HEW. *v.* To cut, by blows, with an edged instrument; to chop; to cut. pr. par. *hewing;* past, *hewed:* s. *hewer.*

HEX'ACHORD. *s.* A concord, commonly called a sixth.

HEX'AEDRON. *s.* A cube.

HEX'AGON. *s.* A figure of six sides or angles. adj. *hexagonal.*

HEXAM'ETER. *s.* A verse of six feet. adj. *hexameter, hexametric, hexametrical.*

HEXANG'ULAR. *adj.* Having six angles.

HEX'APOD. *s.* An animal with six feet.

HEX'ASTILE. *s.* A building with six columns in front.

HEY. *int* An expression of joy, or mutual exhortation.

HEY'DAY. *int.* An expression of frolic and exultation.

HIA'TION. *s.* The act of gaping.

HIA'TUS. *s.* An aperture; a gaping breach; the opening of the mouth by the succession of an initial to a final vowel.

HIBER'NAL. *adj.* Belonging to winter.

HIBER'NIAN. *adj.* Relating to Ireland. *s. Hibernicism.*

HICK'UP. *v.* To sob with a convulsed stomach. pr. par. *hickuping;* past, *hickuped: s. hickup.*

HID, HID'DEN. Past par. of the v. *to hide.*

HIDAL'GO. *s.* In Spain, one of noble birth. pl. *hidalgoes.*

HIDE. *v.* To conceal; to withhold or withdraw from sight or knowledge. pr. par. *hiding;* past, *hid, hidden.*

HIDE. *s.* The skin of an animal, either raw or dressed.

HIDE'BOUND. *adj.* A horse is said to be *hide-bound,* when his skin sticks closely to his ribs and back.

HID'EOUS. *adj.* Horrible, dreadful, shocking. adv. *hideously: s. hideousness.*

HIE. *v.* To hasten; to go in haste. pr. par. *hying;* past, *hied.*

HI'ERARCH. *s.* The chief of a sacred order; the chief of any establishment. adj. *hierarchal: s. hierarchy,* pl. *hierarchies.*

HI'EROGLYPH, HIEROGLYPH'IC. *s.* An emblem; a figure by which a word was implied, and used before the alphabet was invented. adj. *hieroglyphic:* adv. *hieroglyphically.*

HIEROG'RAPHY. *s.* Holy writing. pl. *hierographies:* adj. *hierographic, hierographical.*

HIEROL'OGY. *s.* Discourse on sacred things. pl. *hierologies.*

HI'EROMANCY. *s.* Divination by sacrifices pl. *hieromancies.*

HIG'GLE. *v.* To chaffer; to be penurious in a bargain. pr. par. *higgling;* past, *higgled: s. higgler.*

HIGH. *adj.* Elevated in place; raised aloft; rising above from the surface, or from the centre. adv. *high, highly: s. highness.*

HIGH'-FLIER. *s.* One that carries his opinions to extravagance. adj *high-flying.*

HIGH'LAND. *s.* Mountainous region. *s. highlander.*

HIGH'-METTLED. *adj.* Of proud or ardent spirit.

HIGH'NESS. *s.* A title given to princes. pl. *highnesses.*

HIGH-WA'TER. *s.* The utmost flow of the tide.

HIGHWAY'. *s.* A great road, a public path.

HIGH'WAYMAN. *s.* A robber tha plunders on the public roads. pL *highwaymen.*

HILAR'ITY. *s.* Merriment, gayety.

HILL. *s.* An elevation of ground, less than a mountain. adj. *hilly: s. hilliness.*

HIL'LOCK. *s.* A little hill.

HILT. *s.* The handle of any thing, particularly of a sword. adj. *hilted*

HIM. *pron.* The objective case of *he.*

HIMSELF'. *pron.* A compound pronoun.

HIND. *adj.* Backward; contrary in position to the face.

HIND. *s.* The female to a stag; a servant; a peasant.

HIND'ER. *v.* To obstruct, to stop; to impede. pr. par. *hindering;* past, *hindered: s. hinderer, hindrance.*

HIN'DER. *adj.* In a position contrary to that of the face.

HIND'ERMOST. *adj.* Hindmost, last.

HIND'MOST. *adj.* The last; that which comes in the rear.

HINDOO'. *s.* An aboriginal inhabitant of Hindostan.

HIN'DRANCE. *s.* Impediment, obstruction.

HINGE. *s.* A joint upon which a

184

gate or door turns. v. *hinge;* pr. par. *hinging;* past, *hinged.*
HINT. *v.* To bring to mind, by a slight mention or remote allusion; to mention imperfectly. pr. par. *hinting;* past, *hinted:* s. *hint.*
HIP. *s.* The joint of the thigh; the haunch.
HIP. *s.* The fruit of the brier or the dog-rose.
HIP'PISH, HIP'PED. *adj.* Melancholy.
HIPPOCEN'TAUR. *s.* A fabulous monster, half horse and half man.
HIP'PODROME. *s.* A course for chariot and horse races, or exercises.
HIP'POGRIFF. *s.* A winged horse.
HIPPOPOT'AMUS. *s.* The river horse.
HIP'SHOT. *adj.* Sprained or dislocated in the hip.
HIRE. *v.* To procure for temporary use, at a certain price; to bribe; to engage for pay. pr. par. *hiring;* past, *hired:* s. *hire, hirer.*
HIRE'LING. *s.* One who serves for wages; a mercenary. adj. *hireling.*
HIS. *pron.* Belonging to him that was before mentioned.
HISS. *v.* To utter a noise like that of a serpent, and some other animals; to condemn at a public exhibition. pr. par. *hissing;* past, *hissed:* s. *hiss,* pl. *hisses, hissing:* adv. *hissingly.*
HIST. *int.* An exclamation commanding silence.
HISTO'RIAN. *s.* A writer of history.
HISTORIOG'RAPHER. *s.* An historian; a writer of history. s. *historiography,* pl. *historiographies.*
HISTORIOL'OGY. *s.* Knowledge of history; explanation of history. pl. *historiologies.*
HIS'TORY. *s.* A narration of facts and events; narration; relation. pl. *histories:* adj. *historic, historical:* adv. *historically.*
HISTRION'IC. *adj.* Befitting the stage. adv. *histrionically.*
HIT. *v.* To strike; to touch with a blow; to attain; to clash; to agree. pr. par. *hitting;* past, *hit:* s. *hit.*
HITCH. *v.* To become entangled, or hooked together; to be caught. pr. par. *hitching;* past, *hitched:* s. *hitch.*
HITH'ER. *adv.* To this place, from some other; to this end; to this design. adj. *hither.*
HITH'ERMOST. *adj.* Nearest on this side.
HITH'ERTO. *adv.* In any time till now, at every time till now.
HITH'ERWARD, HITH'ERWARDS. *adv.* This way; towards this place.
HIVE. *s.* The habitation or artificial receptacle of bees. v. *hive;* pr. par. *hiving;* past, *hived.*
HO. *int.* A call; a command to stop; cease.
HOAR. *adj.* White; gray with age. adj. *hoary:* s. *hoariness.*
HOARD. *s.* A store laid up in secret; a hidden stock; a treasure. v. *hoard;* pr. par. *hoarding;* past, *hoarded:* s. *hoarder.*
HOAR'-FROST. *s.* The congelations of dew, in frosty mornings, on the grass.
HOAR'HOUND. *s.* A species of plant.
HOARSE. *adj.* Having the voice rough, as with a cold; having a rough sound. adv. *hoarsely:* s *hoarseness.*
HOAX. *s.* An imposition, a deception.
HOB, HUB. *s.* The nave of a wheel.
HOB'BLE. *v.* To walk lamely or awkwardly upon one leg more than the other; to move roughly or unevenly. pr. par. *hobbling;* past, *hobbled:* s. *hobble, hobbler:* adv. *hobblingly.*
HOB'BY. *s.* A pacing horse; a nag. pl. *hobbies.*
HOB'BY-HORSE. *s.* A wooden horse, on which children ride.
HOBGOB'LIN. *s.* A fairy; vulgarly, a frightful one.

HOB'NAIL. *s.* A nail with a large head.
HOB NOB. *s.* A familiar call to reciprocal drinking.
HO'BOY, HAUT'BOY. *s.* A sort of wind instrument.
HOCK. *s.* Strong old Rhenish wine.
HOD. *s.* A kind of trough, in which a labourer carries mortar. *s. hodman*, pl. *hodmen*.
HODGE'-PODGE. *s.* A medley of ingredients, boiled together.
HOE. *s.* An instrument to cut up the earth. *v. hoe;* pr. par. *hoeing;* past, *hoed*.
HOG. *s.* The general name of swine. *v. hog;* pr. par. *hogging;* past, *hogged:* adj. *hoggish:* adv. *hoggishly:* s. *hoggishness*.
HO'GO. *s.* High flavour; strong scent.
HOGS'HEAD. *s.* A cask containing sixty-three gallons.
HOG'STY. *s.* A place in which swine are kept. pl. *hogsties*.
HOG'WASH. *s.* Liquid food given to swine.
HOI'DEN. *s.* An awkward, rude, ill-behaved man; an ill-taught, awkward, country girl. adj. *hoiden, hoidenish*.
HOIST. *v.* To raise up on high. pr. par. *hoisting;* past, *hoisted:* s. *hoist*.
HOIT'Y-TOIT'Y. *adj.* Thoughtless, giddy.
HOLD. *v.* To grasp in the hand; to gripe; to keep; to retain. pr. par. *holding;* past, *held:* s. *hold, holder, holding*.
HOLD'FAST. *s.* A catch, a hook, a support, a hold.
HOLE. *s.* A cavity, a perforation, a hollow place.
HOL'IDAY. *s.* See HOLYDAY.
HOLLA'. *int.* A word used in calling to any one at a distance. *v. holla;* pr. par. *hollaing;* past, *hollaed*.
HOL'LAND. *s.* Fine linen made in Holland.
HOL'LANDER. *s.* A man of Holland.
HOL'LOW. *adj.* Excavated; having a void space within; not solid. *s. hollow, hollowness:* v. *hollow;* pr. par. *hollowing;* past, *hollowed*.
HOL'LY. *s.* A kind of ever-green tree.
HOL'LYHOCK. *s.* A species of flowering plant.
HOLM. *s.* A river-island; an islet the ilex; the ever-green oak.
HOL'STER. *s.* A case for a horseman's pistol.
HO'LY. *adj.*-Hallowed, pious, religious. adv. *holily:* s. *holiness*.
HOL'YDAY. *s.* The day of some ecclesiastical festival; anniversary feast; a day of rest from ordinary occupation.
HOM'AGE. *s.* Obeisance; respect paid by external action.
HOME. *s.* Private dwelling; the place of constant residence.
HOME'LY. *adj.* Plain, homespun, not elegant. *s. homeliness*.
HO'MER. *s.* A Hebrew measure, of about three pints.
HOME'SPUN. *adj.* Spun or wrought at home; coarse. *s. homespun*.
HOME'STEAD. *s.* The place of the house, including sometimes a small portion of land adjoining.
HOME'WARD, HOME'WARDS. *adv.* Towards home.
HOM'ICIDE. *s.* Murder; a manslayer. adj. *homicidal*.
HOM'ILY. *s.* A discourse read to a congregation. pl. *homilies*.
HOM'INY, HOM'MONY. *s.* Maize pounded or ground into very coarse meal.
HOMOGE'NEAL, HOMOGE'NEOUS. *adj.* Having the same nature or principles; suitable to each other. *s. homogenealness, homogeneity,* pl. *homogeneities, homogeneousness*.
HONE. *s.* A whetstone. *v. hone* pr. par. *honing;* past, *honed*.
HON'EST. *adj.* Upright, true, sincere, chaste, just. adv *honestly* *s. honesty,* pl. *honesties*.

186

HON'EY. *s.* The elaborate produce of bees, extracted from flowers. adj. *honied.*

HON'EY-COMB. *s.* The cells of wax in which the bee stores its honey. adj. *honey-combed.*

HON'EY-MOON. *s.* The first month after marriage.

HON'EYSUCKLE. *s.* Woodbine.

HON'ORARY. *adj.* Done in honour; made in honour; conferring honour, without gain.

HON'OUR. *s.* Dignity, high rank, reputation, fame, magnanimity. v. *honour;* pr. par. *honouring;* past, *honoured:* s. *honourer, honourableness:* adj. *honourable, honourless:* adv. *honourably.*

HOOD. *s.* The upper covering of a woman's head. v. *hood;* pr. par. *hooding;* past, *hooded.*

HOOD'WINK. *v.* To blind with something bound over the eyes; to deceive. pr. par. *hoodwinking;* past, *hoodwinked.*

HOOF. *s.* The hard, horny substance on the feet of animals. adj. *hoofed.*

HOOK. *s.* Any thing bent, so as to catch hold. v. *hook;* pr. par. *hooking;* past, *hooked:* s. *hooker, hookedness.*

HOOK'ER. *s.* A kind of small ship.

HOOP. *s.* Any thing circular, by which something else is bound; any thing circular. v. *hoop;* pr. par. *hooping;* past, *hooped.*

HOOP. *s.* A shout, a measure.

HOOPING-COUGH. *s.* A convulsive cough, so called from its noise.

HOOT. *v.* To shout in contempt; to cry as an owl. pr. par *hooting;* past, *hooted:* s. *hoot, hooting.*

HOP. *v.* To dance; to jump; to leap on one leg; to limp. pr. par. *hopping;* past, *hopped:* s. *hop, hopper.*

HOP. *s.* A kind of plant.

HOPE. *s.* Expectation of some good. v. *hope;* pr. par. *hoping;* past, *hoped:* s. *hoper:* adj. *hopeful, hopeless:* adv. *hopefully, hopelessly, hopingly:* s. *hopefulness.*

HOP'PER. *s.* The box or open frame of wood into which corn is put to be ground.

HO'RAL. *adj.* Relating to the hours. adj. *horary.*

HORDE. *s.* A clan; a migratory crew of people.

HORI'ZON. *s.* The line that terminates the view.

HORIZON'TAL. *adj.* Near the horizon; parallel to the horizon. adv. *horizontally.*

HORN. *s.* The hard body, which grows on the heads of some graminivorous quadrupeds, and serves them for weapons; a kind of wind instrument. v. *horn;* pr. par. *horning;* past, *horned:* adj. *horny, horned, hornless:* s. *hornedness.*

HORN'BEAM. *s.* A kind of tree.

HORN'BOOK. *s.* The first book of children, covered with horn, to keep it unsoiled.

HOR'NET. *s.* A large, stinging fly.

HORN'PIPE. *s.* A kind of dance; a wind instrument.

HORN'WORK. *s.* A kind of angular fortification.

HO'ROSCOPE. *s.* The configuration of the planets, at the hour of birth.

HOR'RIBLE. *adj.* Dreadful, terrible, shocking, hideous. adv. *horribly.* s. *horribleness.*

HOR'RID. *adj.* Hideous, dreadful, shocking. adv. *horridly:* s. *horridness.*

HORRIF'IC. *adj.* Causing horror.

HOR'ROR. *s.* Terror, mixed with detestation; gloom; dreariness.

HORSE. *s.* A species of quadruped. v. *horse;* pr. par. *horsing;* past, *horsed.*

HORSE'BACK. *s.* Riding posture; the state of being on a horse.

HORSE'BREAKER. *s.* One whose employment is to tame horses to the saddle.

HORSE'-CHESNUT. *s.* A kind of tree.

HORSE'-GUARDS. *s.* Regiments of horse of the King's Guard.

HORSE'LEECH. *s.* A leech that bites horses; a farrier.

HORSE'MAN. *s.* One skilled in riding; a rider; a man on horseback. pl. *horsemen:* s. *horsemanship.*

HORSE'PLAY *s.* Coarse, rough play.

HORSE'POND. *s.* A pond for horses.

HORSE'RACE. *s.* A match of horses in running.

HORSE'RADISH. *s.* An acrid biting root.

HORSE'SHOE. *s.* A plate of iron, nailed to the foot of a horse.

HORSE'WHIP. *s.* A whip to strike a horse with. v. *horsewhip;* pr. par. *horsewhipping;* past, *horsewhipped.*

HORTA'TION. *s.* The act of exhorting; a hortatory precept. adj. *hortative, hortatory.*

HORTICUL'TURE. *s.* The art of cultivating gardens. adj. *horticultural:* s. *horticulturist.*

HOSAN'NA. *s.* A form of exclamation; an exclamation of praise to God.

HOSE. *s.* Breeches; stockings; coverings for the feet.

HO'SIER. *s.* One who makes or sells stockings.

HOS'PITABLE. *adj.* Giving entertainment to strangers; kind to strangers. adv. *hospitably:* s. *hospitality,* pl. *hospitalities.*

HOS'PITAL. *s.* A place built for the reception of the sick, or support of the poor; a place for shelter or entertainment pronounced *os'petal.*

HOS'PITALLER. *s.* One of a religious community, whose office it was to relieve the poor; a knight of a religious order.

HOST. *s.* One who gives entertainment to another; the landlord of an inn; an army; any great number; the consecrated wafer.

HOS'TAGE. *s.* One given in pledge for security of performance of conditions.

HOS'TESS. *s.* A female host; a woman that keeps a house of public entertainment. pl. *hostesses.*

HOS'TILE. *adj.* Inimical, adverse opposite; suitable to an enemy. adv. *hostilely:* s *hostility,* pl. *hostilities.*

HOST'LER. *s.* One who has the care of horses at an inn. pronounced *os'-ler.*

HOT. *adj.* Having the power to excite the sense of heat; fiery; ardent. adv. *hotly.*

HOT'BED. *s.* A bed of earth, made hot by the fermentation of manure

HOTCH'POTCH. *s.* A mingled hash; a mixture.

HOTCOCK'LES. *s.* A kind of play.

HOTEL'. *s.* A lodging-house; a public boarding-house.

HOT'HEADED. *adj.* Vehement, violent, passionate.

HOT'HOUSE. *s.* A place for rearing tender plants.

HOT'TENTOT. *s.* A savage inhabitant of the southern extremity of Africa.

HOUGH. *s.* The joint of the hinder leg of a beast. v. *hough;* pr. par. *houghing;* past, *houghed.*

HOUND. *s.* A dog used in the chase.

HOUR. *s.* The twenty-fourth part of a natural day; a particular time. adj. *hourly:* adv. *hourly.*

HOUR'GLASS. *s.* A sand-glass which marks one hour. pl. *hourglasses.*

HOU'RI. *s.* A Mahometan nymph of paradise. pl. *houries.*

HOUSE. *s.* A place of human abode; any place of abode. v. *house;* pr. par. *housing;* past, *housed:* adj *houseless.*

HOUSE'HOLD. *s.* A family living together; domestic management. s. *householder.*

HOUSE KEEPER. *s.* A householder; a woman who has the care of a family, and superintends the other servants. s. *housekeeping.*

HOUSE'LEEK. *s.* A species of plant.

HOUSE'MAID. *s.* A maid servant

HOUSE'WARMING. *s.* A feast or

188

merrymaking, on going into a new house.

HOUSE'WIFE. *s.* The mistress of a family; a little case or bag, for articles of female work. pl. *housewives:* s. *housewifery.*

HOUS'ING. *s.* Cloth added to a saddle, for ornament.

HOVE. The pret of the *v. heave.*

HOV'EL. *s.* A mean habitation; a cottage.

HOV'ER. *v.* To hang in the air, over head, without flying one way or another. pr. par. *hovering;* past, *hovered:* s. *hover.*

HOW. *adv.* To what degree; in what manner; for what reason.

HOWBE'IT. *adv.* Nevertheless.

HOWEV'ER. *adv.* In whatsoever manner; in whatsoever degree; nevertheless.

HOW'ITZER. *s.* A kind of mortar, or cannon.

HOWL. *v.* To cry as a wolf or dog; to utter cries of distress. pr. par. *howling;* past, *howled:* s. *howl, howling.*

HOWSOEV'ER. *adv.* In what manner soever; although.

HOY. *s.* A large boat, sometimes with one deck.

HOY. *int.* An exclamation: begone; stop; halt.

HUB'BUB. *s.* A shout, a shriek, a tumult, a riot.

HUCK'ABACK. *s.* A kind of coarse table linen.

HUCKS'TER. *s.* One who sells common goods in very small quantities. v. *huckster;* pr. par. *huckstering;* past, *huckstered.*

HUD'DLE. *v.* To put on carelessly, in a hurry; to cover up in haste; to throw together, in confusion. pr. par. *huddling;* past, *huddled:* s. *huddle, huddler.*

HUE. *s* Colour, die; a clamour.

HUFF. *s.* Swell of sudden anger or arrogance. v. *huff;* pr. par. *huffing;* past, *huffed:* adj. *huffish:* adv. *huffishly:* s. *huffishness.*

HUG. *v.* To press close in an embrace; to fondle; to hold fast. pr par. *hugging;* past, *hugged:* s *hug.*

HUGE. *adj.* Vast, immense, very great. adv. *hugely:* s. *hugeness.*

HU'GUENOT, HU'GONOT. *s.* One of the reformed religion in France; a French Calvinist.

HULK. *s.* A ship; a vessel of burthen; the body of a ship.

HULL. *s.* The husk, or integument, the outer covering; the body of a ship; the hulk. v. *hull;* pr. par *hulling;* past, *hulled.*

HUM. *v.* To make the noise of bees; to murmur. pr. par. *humming,* past, *hummed:* s. *hum, hummer, humming.*

HU'MAN. *adj.* Having the qualities of a man; belonging to man. v. *humanize;* pr. par. *humanizing,* past, *humanized:* adv. *humanly.*

HUMA'NE. *adj.* Kind, civil, benevolent, good-natured. adv. *humanely:* s. *humaneness, humanity.*

HUMANKIND'. *s.* The race of man; mankind.

HUMA'TION. *s.* Interment.

HUM'BLE. *adj.* Low; not proud, modest. pronounced *um'-ble.* v. *humble;* pr. par. *humbling;* past, *humbled:* s. *humbler:* adv. *humo y.*

HUM'BUG. *s.* An imposition; a very low word.

HUM'DRUM *adj.* Dull, dronish, stupid.

HU'MID. *adj.* Wet, moist, watery. s. *humidity,* pl. *humidities.*

HUMIL'ITY. *s.* Freedom from pride; modesty; act of submission. pl. *humilities:* s. *humiliation.*

HU'MOUR. *s.* Moisture; the different kinds of moisture in man's body; general turn or temper of mind; jocularity; merriment; petulance; caprice. pronounced *u'-mur.* v. *humour;* pr. par. *humouring;* past, *humoured:* s. *humorist:* adj. *numorous, humorsome* adv. *humorously.*

189

HUMP. *s.* The protuberance formed by a crooked back.
HUMP'BACK. *s.* Crooked back; high shoulders. *adj. humpbacked.*
HUNCH'BACKED. *adj.* Having a crooked back.
HUN'DRED. *adj.* The number consisting of ten multiplied by ten; a district, supposed to contain one hundred families. *s. hundred: adj. hundredth.*
HUNG. Pret. and past par. of the *v. to hang.*
HUNGA'RIAN. *adj.* Relating or belonging to Hungary.
HUNG'ER. *s.* Desire of food; the pain felt from fasting. *v. hunger; pr. par. hungering; past, hungered: adj. hungry: adv. hungrily.*
HUNT. *v.* To chase wild animals; to pursue; to search for. *pr. par. hunting;* past, *hunted: s. hunt, hunter.*
HUNT'RESS. *s.* A woman that follows the chase. pl. *huntresses.*
HUNTS'MAN. *s.* One who delights in the chase; the servant whose office it is to manage the chase. pl. *huntsmen.*
HUR'DLE. *s.* A texture of sticks woven together.
HUR'DY-GUR'DY. *s.* A kind of stringed instrument.
HURL. *v.* To throw with violence. *pr. par. hurling;* past. *hurled: s. hurl, hurler.*
HUR'LY, HUR'LEY-BUR'LEY. *s.* Tumult, commotion, bustle.
HURRA', HURRAH'. *int.* A shout of joy, triumph, applause, or encouragement.
HUR'RICANE. *s.* A violent storm.
HUR'RY. *v.* To hasten confusedly; to put into precipitation or confusion. *pr. par. hurrying;* past, *hurried: s. hurry, hurrier.*
HURT. *v.* To harm, to wound, to damage. *pr. par. hurting;* past, *hurt: s. hurt, hurter, hurtfulness: adj. hurtful: adv. hurtfully.*
HURT'LEBERRY. *s.* The bilberry. pl. *hurtleberries.*

HURT'LESS. *adj* Innocent, harmless, innoxious. *adv. hurtlessly. s. hurtlessness.*
HUS'BAND. *s.* A man married to a woman.
HUS'BAND. *v.* To manage with economy. *pr. par. husbanding;* past, *husbanded: s. husbander.*
HUS'BANDMAN. *s.* One who works in tillage; a farmer. pl. *husbandmen.*
HUS'BANDRY. *s.* Tillage; manner of cultivating land; thrift; frugality.
HUSH. *int.* Silence! be still! *v. hush; pr. par. hushing,* past, *hushed.*
HUSH'-MONEY. *s.* A bribe, to hinder information.
HUSK. *s.* The outer integument of fruits. *v. husk;* pr. par. *husking;* past, *husked: adj. husky: s. huskiness.*
HUSSAR'. *s.* Originally, a Hungarian horse-soldier, light-armed.
HUS'SITE. *s.* One of the followers of John Huss, of Prague.
HUS'SY. *s.* A worthless wench. pl. *hussies.*
HUS'TINGS. *s.* A council; a court held; the place of meeting, to choose a member of parliament.
HUS'TLE. *v.* To shake together in confusion. *pr. par. hustling;* past, *hustled.*
HUT. *s.* A poor cottage; a temporary building, to lodge soldiers. *v hut;* pr. par. *hutting,* past, *hutted*
HUZZA'. *int.* An exclamation of joy, or triumph. *v. huzza;* pr. par. *huzzaing;* past, *huzzaed.*
HY'ACINTH. *s.* A kind of flower; a gem.
HY'ADES, HY'ADS. *s.* A watery constellation.
HY'DRA. *s.* A monster with many heads, slain by Hercules.
HYDRAU'LICS. *s.* The science of conveying water through pipes *adj. hydraulic.*

HYDROCE'PHALUS. *s.* A dropsy in the head.
HY'DROGEN. *s.* One of the principles of water; a kind of gas.
HYDROG'RAPHY. *s.* Description of the watery part of the terraqueous globe. pl *hydrographies:* s. *hydrographer:* adj. *hydrographical.*
HYDROL'OGY. *s.* Description of the nature and properties of water in general. pl. *hydrologies.*
HY'DROMEL. *s.* Honey and water.
HYDROM'ETER. *s.* An instrument for ascertaining the weight of liquids. adj. *hydrometrical.*
HYDROPHO'BIA. *s.* Dread of water; canine madness.
HYDROP'IC, HYDROP'ICAL. *adj.* Dropsical.
HYDROSTA'TICS. *s.* The science of the weight and pressure of water. adj. *hydrostatical:* adv. *hydrostatically.*
HYE'MAL. *adj.* Belonging to winter. v. *hyemate;* pr. par. *hyemating;* past, *hyemated:* s. *hyemation.*
HYE'NA. *s.* A species of quadruped.
HYGROM'ETER. *s.* An instrument to measure the degrees of moisture.
HYMENE'AL, HYMENE'AN. *adj.* Relating to marriage.
HYMN. *s.* An encomiastic song, or song of adoration. v. *hymn;* pr. par. *hymning;* past, *hymned.*
HYP. *v.* To make melancholy; to dispirit. pr. par. *hypping;* past, *hypped.*

HYPER'BOLA. *s.* A term in geometry.
HYPER'BOLE. *s.* A figure in rhetoric, by which any thing is increased or diminished beyond the exact truth. adj. *hyperbolic, hyperbolical,* adv. *hyperbolically:* v. *hyperbolize,* pr. par. *hyperbolizing;* past, *hyperbolized:* s. *hyperbolist.*
HYPERBO'REAN. *adj.* Northern.
HYPERCRIT'IC. *s.* A person who criticises with too much severity. adj. *hypercritical.*
HY'PHEN. *s.* A note of conjunction, as, vir-tue.
HYPOCHON'DRIA. *s.* Melancholy. adj. *hypochondriac, hypochondriacal:* s. *hypochondriac.*
HYP'OCRITE. *s.* A dissembler in morality or religion. adj. *hypocritical:* adv. *hypocritically:* s. *hypocrisy,* pl. *hypocrisies.*
HYPOT'ENUSE. *s.* The line that subtends the right angle of a right-angled triangle; the subtense.
HYPOTH'ECATE. *v.* To pawn; to give in pledge. pr. par. *hypothecating;* past, *hypothecated.*
HYPOTH'ESIS. *s.* A supposition; a system formed upon some principle not proved. pl. *hypotheses* adj. *hypothetic, hypothetical:* adv *hypothetically.*
HYS'SOP. *s.* A species of plant.
HYSTER'IC, HYSTER'ICAL *adj* Troubled with fits; disordered in the regions of the womb. s. *hysterics.*

I

IAMBUS *s.* A poetical foot, consisting of a short syllable, followed by a long one. adj. *iam'bic.*
I'BIS. *s.* The name of an Egyptian bird, of the stork kind.
ICE. *s.* Water or other liquid, made solid by congelation. adj. *icy.*
ICE'-HOUSE. *s.* A house in which ice is stored.

ICHNEU'MON. *s.* A small animal that breaks the eggs of the crocodile.
I'CHOR. *s.* A thin watery humour. adj. *ichorous.*
ICHTHYOL'OGY. *s.* The science of the nature of fishes.
ICHTHYOPH'AGY. *s.* Diet of fish; the practice of eating fish.

I'CICLE. s. A shoot of ice, hanging down.
ICON'OCLAST. s. A breaker of images. adj. *iconoclastic.*
ICONOG'RAPHY. s. A history or description of images. pl. *iconographies:* adj. *inconographical.*
ICTER'ICAL. *adj.* Afflicted with jaundice.
IDE'A. s. A mental conception. adj. *ideal:* adv. *ideally.*
IDEN'TIFY. v. To prove sameness; to make the same. pr. par. *identifying;* past, *identified:* s. *identification, identifier.*
IDEN'TITY. s. Sameness. pl. *identities:* adj. *identical:* adv. *identically.*
IDES. s. A term in the Roman kalendar, denoting the 13th day of each month, except of March, May, July, and October; in which, it relates to the 15th.
ID'IOM. s. A mode of speech peculiar to a language. adj. *idiomatic, idiomatical:* adv. *idiomatically.*
ID'IOT. s. One born a fool. s. *idiocy,* pl. *idiocies, idiotism:* adj. *idiotic,* adv. *idiotically.*
I'DLE. adj. Lazy; averse to labour; not engaged. v. *idle;* pr. par. *idling;* past, *idled:* s. *idleness, idler:* adv. *idly.*
I'DOL. s. An image worshiped as God. v. *idolize;* (the v. is used only *figuratively.*) pr. par. *idolizing;* past, *idolized:* s. *idolizer.*
IDOL'ATRY. s. The worship of images. pl. *idolatries:* pr. par. *idolatrizing;* past, *idolatrized:* adj. *idolatrous:* adv. *idolatrously.*
IDO'NEOUS. adj. Fit, proper, convenient.
IF. One of the conjunctions.
IG'NEOUS. adj. containing fire.
IGNIF'LUOUS. adj. Flowing with fire.
IGNIP'OTENT. *adj.* Presiding over fire.
IG'NIS-FAT'UUS. s. Will with the wisp; ignited vapour arising from putrefied water.
IGNI'TE. v. To kindle. pr par. *igniting;* past, *ignited:* s. *ignition:* adj. *ignitible.*
IGNIV'OMOUS. adj. Vomiting fire
IGNO'BLE. adj. Of mean birth; not noble; worthless; not deserving honour. adv. *ignobly.*
IG'NOMINY. s. Shame, disgrace. pl *ignominies:* adj. *ignominious:* adv. *ignominiously.*
IG'NORANCE. s. Want of knowledge. adj. *ignorant:* adv. *ignorantly.*
IGNO'RE. v. To quash a bill of indictment, by writing on it the word *ignoramus.*
ILL. adj. Bad, evil, sick. adv. and s. *ill · s. illness.*
ILLA'QUEATE. v. To entangle, to entrap, to ensnare. pr. par. *illaqueating;* past, *illaqueated:* s. *illaqueation.*
ILLA'TION. s. Inference; conclusion drawn from premises. adj. *illative:* adv. *illatively.*
ILLAUD'ABLE. adj. Unworthy of praise or commendation. adv. *illaudably.*
ILLE'GAL. adj. Contrary to law. s *illegality,* pl. *illegalities:* v. *illegalize;* pr. par. *illegalizing;* past, *illegalized:* adv. *illegally.*
ILLEG'IBLE. adj. What cannot be read. s. *illegibility,* pl. *illegibilities* adv. *illegibly.*
ILLEGIT'IMATE. adj. Unlawful not born in wedlock. adv. *illegitimately:* s. *illegitimacy,* pl. *illegitimacies:* v. *illegitimate;* pr. par *illegitimating;* past, *illegitimated.*
ILL-FA'VOURED. adj. Deformed; ugly. s. *ill-favouredness.*
ILLIB'ERAL. adj. Not liberal; not ingenuous. s. *illiberality:* adv. *illiberally.*
ILLI'CIT. adj. Unlawful; criminal. adv. *illicitly:* s. *illicitness.*
ILLIM'ITABLE. adj. That cannot be bounded or limited. adv. *illimitably:* s. *illimitedness.*
ILLIT'ERATE. adj. Unlettered, unlearned. s. *illiteracy,* pl. *illiteracies, illiterateness.*

192

ILLNA'TURE. *s.* Habitual malevolence; want of humanity. adj. *illnatured:* adv. *illnaturedly:* s. *illnaturedness.*

ILLO'GICAL. *adj.* Ignorant or negligent of the rules of reasoning; contrary to the rules of reason. adv. *illogically:* s. *illogicalness.*

ILL-STAR'RED. *adj.* Unlucky.

ILLU'DE. *v.* To deceive or mock. pr. par. *illuding;* past, *illuded.*

ILLU'ME. *v.* To enlighten. pr. par. *illuming;* past, *illumed.*

ILLU'MINE. *v.* To supply with light. pr. par. *illumining;* past, *illumined.*

ILLU'MINATE. *v.* To enlighten; to adorn with festal lamps, or bonfires. pr. par. *illuminating;* past, *illuminated:* s. *illumination:* adj. *illuminative.*

ILLUMINA'TI. *s.* One of those who pretend to be enlightened with superior knowledge, as certain persons of the 16th century, and certain mock philosophers on the continent of Europe, in our own time.

ILLU'SION. *s.* The act of illuding; mockery; false appearance. adj. *illusive, illusory:* adv. *illusively.*

ILLUS'TRATE. *v.* To brighten with light; to explain. pr. par. *illustrating;* past, *illustrated:* s. *illustration:* adj. *illustrative:* adv. *illustratively.*

ILLUS'TRIOUS. *adj.* Bright; conspicuously noble for good qualities. s. *illustriousness:* adv. *illustriously.*

IM'AGE. *s.* Any corporeal representation; generally, a statue; a copy; semblance; an idea. v. *image;* pr. par. *imaging;* past, *imaged.*

IM'AGERY. *s.* Sensible representations; show. pl. *imageries.*

IMA'GINE. *v.* To fancy; to paint in the mind; to contrive. pr. par. *imagining;* past, *imagined:* s. *imagination:* adj. *imaginable, imaginary, imaginative.*

IMBALM'. *v.* See EMBALM.

IMBE'CILE. *adj.* Weak, feeble; wanting strength, either of mind or body. s. *imbecility,* pl. *imbecilities.*

IMBED'DED. *adj.* See EMBEDDED.

IMBI'BE. *v.* To drink in. pr. par *imbibing;* past, *imbibed:* s. *imbibition.*

IMBIT'TER. *v.* To make bitter. pr. par. *imbittering;* past, *imbittered.*

IMBOD'Y. *v.* To invest with matter; to make corporeal; to bring together into one mass or body. pr. par. *imbodying;* past, *imbodied.*

IM'BRICATED. *adj.* Indented with cavities; hollowed like a guttertile. s. *imbrication.*

IMBROWN'. *v.* To make brown. pr. par. *imbrowning;* past, *imbrowned.*

IMBRU'E. *v.* To steep, to soak. pr. par. *imbruing;* past, *imbrued.*

IMBU'E. *v.* To tincture deeply; to soak with a liquor or die. pr. par. *imbuing;* past, *imbued.*

IM'ITABLE. *adj.* Capable of being imitated. s. *imitation, imitator:* adj. *imitative:* v. *imitate;* pr. par. *imitating;* past, *imitated.*

IMMAC'ULATE. *adj.* Spotless, pure. s. *immaculateness:* adv. *immaculately.*

IMMATE'RIAL. *adj.* Incorporeal; distinct from matter. s. *immateriality,* pl. *immaterialities:* adv. *immaterially.*

IMMATU'RE. *adj.* Not ripe, not perfect. s. *immaturity,* pl. *immaturities:* adv. *immaturely.*

IMMEAS'URABLE. *adj.* Not to be measured; immense. s. *immeasurableness:* adv. *immeasurably.*

IMME'DIATE. *adj.* Proximate; having nothing between; instant. s. *immediateness:* adv. *immediately.*

IMMED'ICABLE. *adj.* Not possible to be healed; incurable.

IMMELO'DIOUS. *adj.* Not melodious; unmusical.

IMMEMO'RIAL. *adj.* Past time of memory.

IMMENSE'. *adj.* Immeasurable, unlimited. *adv. immensely: s. immensity,* pl. *immensities.*

IMMERGE'. *v.* To put under water; to keep in a state of intellectual depression. pr. par. *immerging;* past, *immerged.*

IMMERSE'. *v.* To dip; to put under water. pr. par. *immersing,* past, *immersed: s. immersion.*

IMMETHOD'ICAL. *adj.* Confused; without regularity. *s. immethodicalness:* adv. *immethodically.*

IM'MIGRATE. *v.* To enter or pass into; to migrate into. pr. par. *immigrating;* past, *immigrated: s. immigrant, immigration, immigrator.*

IM'MINENT. *adj.* Impending; threatening. *s. imminence.*

IMMIS'CIBLE. *adj.* Not capable of being mingled. *s. immiscibility,* pl. *immiscibilities.*

IMMIS'SION. *s.* Act of immitting.

IMMIT'. *v.* To send in, to inject. pr. par. *immitting;* past, *immitted.*

IMMOBIL'ITY. *s.* Unmovableness. pl. *immobilities.*

IMMOD'ERATE. *adj.* Excessive. *s. immoderateness, immoderation:* adv. *immoderately.*

IMMOD'EST. *adj.* Wanting shame; indelicate; unchaste. *s. immodesty:* adv. *immodestly.*

IM'MOLATE. *v.* To sacrifice. pr. par. *immolating;* past, *immolated: s. immolation.*

IMMOR'AL. *adj.* Wanting regard to the laws of natural religion; dishonest. *s. immorality,* pl. *immoralities.*

IMMOR'TAL. *adj.* Exempt from death; perpetual. *v. immortalize;* pr. par. *immortalizing;* past, *immortalized: s. immortality,* pl. *immortalities:* adv. *immortally.*

IMMO'VABLE. *adj.* Not to be removed from its place; unshaken. *s. immovability,* pl. *immovabilities, immovableness:* adv. *immovably.*

IMMU'NITY. *s.* Discharge from any obligation; privilege, pl. *immunities*

IMMU'RE. *v.* To enclose within walls; to confine. pr. par. *immuring,* past, *immured.*

IMMU'TABLE. *adj.* Unchangeable, unalterable. *s. immutability:* adv. *immutably.*

IMP. *s.* A son; the offspring; progeny:—always used in a bad sense.

IMPA'IR. *v.* To injure, to diminish. pr. par. *impairing;* past, *impaired: s. impairer, impairment.*

IMPA'LE. *v.* See EMPALE.

IMPAL'PABLE. *adj.* Not to be perceived by touch. *s. impalpability:* adv. *impalpably.*

IMPAN'NEL, EMPAN'NEL. *v.* To summon to serve on a jury. pr. par. *impanneling;* past, *impanneled.*

IMPART'. *v.* To make known, to communicate. pr. par. *imparting;* past, *imparted.*

IMPAR'TIAL. *adj.* equitable, disinterested. *s. impartiality,* pl. *impartialities:* adv. *impartially.*

IMPART'IBLE. *adj.* Communicable; capable of being conferred or bestowed. *s. impartibility,* pl. *impartibilities.*

IMPAS'SABLE. *adj.* Not to be passed. *s. impassableness:* adv. *impassably.*

IMPAS'SION. *v.* To move with passion; to affect strongly. pr. par *impassioning;* past, *impassioned.*

IMPA'TIENCE. *s.* Inability to suffer pain, or delay; vehemence of temper. *adj. impatient:* adv. *impatiently.*

IMPEACH *v.* To accuse by public authority. pr. par. *impeaching;* past, *impeached: s. impeachment:* adj. *impeachably.*

IMPEARL'. *v.* To form in resemblance of pearls; to decorate as with pearls. pr. par. *impearling,* past, *impearled.*

IMPEC'CABLE. *adj.* Exempt from possibility of sin. *s. impeccability,* pl. *impeccabilities.*

IMPE'DE. *v.* To hinder, to obstruct, to delay. pr. par. *impeding;* past,

194

impeded: s. *impediment:* adj. *impedimental.*
IMPEL'. *v.* To drive on towards a point. pr. par. *impelling;* past, *impelled:* adj. *impellent:* s. *impeller.*
IMPEND'. *v.* To hang over. pr. par. *impending;* past, *impended:* s. *impendence:* adj. *impendent.*
IMPEN'ETRABLE. *adj.* Impervious; not to be pierced. s. *impenetrability,* pl. *impenetrabilities:* adv. *impenetrably.*
IMPEN'ITENCE. *s.* Obduracy; want of remorse for crimes. adj. *impenitent:* adv. *impenitently.*
IMPER'ATIVE. *adj.* Commanding; expressive of command. adv. *imperatively:* adj. *imperatorial.*
IMPERCEP'TIBLE. *adj.* Not to be discovered or perceived. s. *imperceptibleness:* adv. *imperceptibly.*
IMPER'FECT. *adj.* Not complete, defective. s. *imperfection:* adv. *imperfectly.*
IMPE'RIAL. *adj.* Relating or belonging to an empire; royal. s. *imperialist:* adv. *imperially.*
IMPE'RIOUS. *adj.* Commanding, authoritative. s. *imperiousness:* adv. *imperiously.*
IMPER'ISHABLE. *adj.* Not to be destroyed. s. *imperishability,* pl. *imperishabilities:* adv. *imperishably.*
IMPER'MEABLE. *adj.* Not possible to be passed through.
IMPER'SONAL. *adj.* Not varied according to the persons. s. *impersonality,* pl. *impersonalities:* adv. *impersonally.*
IMPERSPIC'UOUS. *adj.* Not perspicuous, not clear. s. *imperspicuity,* pl. *imperspicuities:* adv. *imperspicuously.*
IMPER'TINENCE, IMPER'TINENCY. *s.* That which has no relation to the matter in question; troublesomeness, intrusion; sauciness, rudeness. pl. *impertinences, impertinencies:* adj. *impertinent:* adv. *impertinently.*
IMPERTUR'BABLE. *adj.* Impossible to be disturbed. s. *imperturbation:* adv. *imperturbably:* adj. *imperturbed.*
IMPER'VIOUS. *adj.* Impassable, impenetrable. adv. *imperviously:* s. *imperviousness.*
IM'PETRATE. *v.* To obtain by application or entreaty. pr. par. *impetrating;* past, *impetrated:* adj. *impetrative.*
IMPET'UOUS. *adj.* Vehement, violent, fierce, passionate. s. *impetuosity,* pl. *impetuosities:* adv. *impetuously.*
IM'PETUS. *s.* Violent tendency to any point; violent effort.
IMPI'ETY. *s.* Irreverence to the Supreme Being; contempt of the duties of religion; wickedness. pl. *impieties:* adj. *impious:* adv. *impiously.*
IMPINGE'. *v.* To fall or strike against. pr. par. *impinging;* past, *impinged.*
IMPLAC'ABLE. *adj.* Not to be pacified; inexorable; irreconcilable adv. *implacably:* s. *implacability,* pl. *implacabilities.*
IMPLANT'. *v.* To insert, to infix. pr. par. *implanting;* past, *implanted:* s. *implantation.*
IMPLEAD'. *v.* To accuse, to indict. pr. par. *impleading;* past, *impleaded:* s. *impleader.*
IM'PLEMENT. *s.* A tool; an instrument of manufacture. adj. *implemental:* adv. *implementally.*
IM'PLICATE. *v.* To entangle, to involve. pr. par. *implicating;* past, *implicated:* s. *implication:* adj. *implicative:* adv. *implicatively.*
IMPLICA'TION. *s.* Involution; entanglement; inference not expressed, but tacitly inculcated
IMPLI'CIT. *adj.* Trusting without reserve or examination. s. *implicitness:* adv. *implicitly.*
IMPLO'RE. *v.* To solicit, to ask, to beg. pr. par. *imploring;* past, *implored:* s. *implorer.*
IMPLY'. *v.* To involve or comprise as a consequence. pr. par. *implying;* past, *implied* s. *implication.*

IMPOL'ICY. s. Imprudence, indiscretion. adj. *impolitic:* adv. *impolitically.*

IMPOLI'TE. adj. Not polite. s. *impoliteness:* adv. *impolitely.*

IMPORT'. v. To carry into any country, from abroad; to infer, to imply. pr. par. *importing;* past, *imported:* s. *importation:* adj. *importable.*

IMPOR'TANT. adj. Momentous; of great consequence. s. *importance:* adv. *importantly.*

IMPORTU'NE. v. To tease; to harass with slight vexation, perpetually recurring; to solicit earnestly. pr. par. *importuning;* past, *importuned:* adj. *importunate:* adv. *importunately:* s. *importunity,* pl. *importunities.*

IMPO'SE. v. To lay on as a burthen or penalty; to obtrude fallaciously; to put a cheat on. pr. par. *imposing;* past, *imposed:* s. *imposition.*

IMPOS'SIBLE. adj. Not to be done; impracticable. s. *impossibility,* pl. *impossibilities:* adv. *impossibly.*

IM POST. s. A tax, a toll.

IMPOS'TOR. s. One who cheats, by a fictitious character. s. *imposture.*

IM'POTENCE, IM'POTENCY. s. Want of power, imbecility. pl. *impotences, impotencies:* adj. *impotent:* adv. *impotently.*

IMPOV'ERISH. v. To make poor; to reduce to indigence. pr. par. *impoverishing;* past, *impoverished.*

IMPOW'ER. v. To give power; to authorize. pr. par. *impowering;* past, *impowered.*

IMPRAC'TICABLE. adj. Impossible; not to be performed; untractable. s. *impracticability,* pl. *impracticabilities.*

IM'PRECATE. v. To curse; to call for evil upon one's-self or another. s. *imprecation:* adj. *imprecatory, imprecative.*

IMPREG'NABLE. adj. Not to be taken; not to be moved. adv. *impregnably.*

IMPREG'NATE v. To fill, to saturate. pr. par. *impregnating;* past, *impregnated:* s. *impregnation.*

IMPRESCRIP'TIBLE. adj. Without the compass of prescription; by no length of time, to be alienated or lost. s. *imprescriptibility.*

IMPRESS'. v. To print by pressure; to stamp; to take by force. pr. par. *impressing;* past, *impressed:* s. *impress, impression:* adj. *impressible.*

IMPRES'SIVE. adj. Capable of being impressed; susceptible; capable of making impression. adj. *impressively:* s. *impressiveness.*

IMPRIMA'TUR. s. A license to print; a word formerly at the beginning of books, signifying "let it be printed."

IMPRINT'. v. To print upon; to mark upon any substance, by press. pr. par. *imprinting:* past, *imprinted.* s. *im'print.*

IMPRIS'ON. v. To shut up, to confine. pr. par. *imprisoning,* past, *imprisoned:* s. *imprisonment.*

IMPROB'ABLE. adj. Unlikely, incredible. s. *improbability,* pl. *improbabilities:* adv. *improbably.*

IMPROMP'TU. s. A brief, extemporaneous, and often witty or merry composition.

IMPROP'ER. adj. Not well adapted, unqualified. adv. *improperly:* s. *impropriety,* pl. *improprieties.*

IMPROV'ABLE. adj. Capable of improvement. s. *improvability:* adv. *improvably.*

IMPRO'VE. v. To advance nearer to perfection. pr. par. *improving,* past, *improved:* s. *improvement:* adj. *improvable:* s. *improvability.*

IMPROV'IDENT. adj. Wanting care to provide. adv. *improvidently:* s. *improvidence.*

IMPRU'DENCE. s. Want of prudence; indiscretion. adj. *imprudently.*

IMPUGN'. v. To attack by law or argument; to oppose. pr. par. *impugning;* past, *impugned:* s. *impugner.*

IMPUIS'SANCE. s. Importance, in

ability. adj. *impuissant:* adv. *impuissantly.*

IM'PULSE. s. Communicated force. adj. *impulsive:* adv. *impulsively.*

IMPU'NITY. s. Freedom from punishment. pl. *impunities.*

IMPU'RE. adj. Not pure, unholy, foul. s. *impurity,* pl. *impurities:* adv. *impurely.*

IMPUR'PLE. v. To colour as with purple. pr. par. *impurpling;* past, *impurpled.*

IMPU'TE. v. To charge upon; to attribute. pr. par. *imputing;* past, *imputed:* s. *imputation:* adj. *imputative:* adv. *imputatively:* adj. *imputable.*

IN. One of the prepositions. adv. *in.*

INABIL'ITY. s. Impotence; want of power. pl. *inabilities.*

INACCES'SIBLE. adj. Not to be reached; not to be approached. s. *inaccessibility:* adv. *inaccessibly.*

INAC'CURATE. adj. Not accurate; not exact. adv. *inaccurately:* s. *inaccuracy,* pl. *inaccuracies.*

INAC'TIVE. adj. Not busy, idle, indolent. adv. *inactively:* s. *inactivity,* pl. *inactivities, inaction.*

INADE'QUATE. adj. Not equal to the purpose; defective. s. *inadequacy:* adv. *inadequately.*

INADMIS'SIBLE. adj. Not to be admitted. adv. *inadmissibly:* s. *inadmissibility,* pl. *inadmissibilities.*

INADVER'TENCE, INADVER'TENCY. s. Negligence, inattention. pl. *inadvertences, inadvertencies:* adj. *inadvertent:* adv. *inadvertently.*

INAMORA'TO. s. One in love; one loved by another.

INA'NE. adj. Empty, void. s. *inanity,* pl. *inanities, inanition.*

INAN'IMATE. adj. Void of life; without animation. s. *inanimation:* adj. *inanimately.*

INAPPETENCE, INAPPETENCY. s. Want of appetite. pl. *inappetences, inappetencies.*

INAP'PLICABLE. adj. Not applicable. s. *inapplicability,* pl. *inapplicabilities:* adv. *inapplicably:* s. *inapplication.*

INAP'POSITE. adj. Not apposite, ill-placed; not to the purpose. s. *inappositeness:* adv. *inappositely.*

INAPT'. adj. Unfit. s. *inaptness, inaptitude.*

INARTIC'ULATE. adj. Not uttered with distinctness. s. *inarticulateness, inarticulation:* adv. *inarticulately.*

INARTIFI'CIAL. adj. Contrary to art; artless; rude. adv. *inartificially.*

INATTEN'TION. s. Want of attention; disregard. adj. *inattentive:* adv. *inattentively.*

INAUD'IBLE. adj. Not to be heard. adv. *inaudibly.*

INAUG'URATE. v. To invest with a new office, by solemn rites. pr. par. *inaugurating;* past, *inaugurated:* s. *inauguration:* adj. *inauguratory.*

INAUSPI'CIOUS. adj. Ill-omened, betokening ill. adv. *inauspiciously:* s. *inauspiciousness.*

IN'BORN. adj. Innate; implanted by nature.

IN'BRED. adj. Produced within; hatched or generated within.

INCAL'CULABLE. adj. Beyond calculation. s. *incalculability:* adv *incalculably.*

INCANTA'TION. s. Charms uttered by singing. adj. *incantatory.*

INCA'PABLE. adj. Wanting power; unable to comprehend, learn, or understand. s. *incapability,* pl *incapabilities.*

INCAPA'CIOUS. adj. Not capacious; narrow; wanting power to contain. s. *incapaciousness.*

INCAPA'CITATE. v. To disable; to weaken. pr. par. *incapacitating,* past, *incapacitated:* s. *incapacity,* pl. *incapacities.*

INCAR'CERATE. v. To imprison. pr. par. *incarcerating;* past, *incarcerated:* s. *incarceration.*

INCAR'NATE. v. To clothe with flesh. adj. *incarnate, incarnative:* s. *incarnation.*

INCASE'. v. To cover, to enclose, to enwrap. pr. par. *incasing;* past, *incased.*

INCAU'TIOUS. adj. Unwary, negligent, heedless. adv. *incautiously:* s. *incautiousness.*

INCEN'DIARY. s. One who sets houses, or towns, or any other valuable thing, on fire, in malice, or with a design of committing robbery. pl. *incendiaries:* adj. *incendiary.*

IN'CENSE. s. Perfumes exhaled by fire, in honour of some god or goddess.

INCENSE'. v. To enkindle to rage; to inflame with anger. pr. par. *incensing;* past, *incensed:* adj. *incensive:* s. *incensement.*

INCEN'TIVE. adj. Provocative, encouraging, inciting. s. *incentive.*

INCEP'TION. s. Beginning. adj. *inceptive:* adv. *inceptively.*

INCERA'TION. s. The act of covering with wax. adj. *incerative.*

INCER'TITUDE. s. Uncertainty.

INCES'SANT. adj. Unceasing. adv. *incessantly.*

IN'CEST. s. Criminal conjunction of persons within degrees prohibited. adj. *incestuous:* adv. *incestuously.*

INCH. s. The twelfth part of a foot. pl. *inches.*

INCHASE'. v. See ENCHASE.

IN'CHOATE. adj. In an incipient state; just begun; imperfect. s. *inchoateness.*

IN'CIDENT. s. Something happening besides the main design; casualty. adj. *incidental:* adv. *incidentally.*

INCIN'ERATE. v. To burn to ashes. pr. par. *incinerating;* past, *incinerated:* s. *incineration.*

INCIP'IENT. adj. Beginning, commencing. s. *incipience, incipiency,* pl. *incipiences, incipiencies.*

INCIS'ION. s. A cut; a wound made with a sharp instrument. adj. *incisive.*

INCI'TE. v. To push forward in a purpose; to animate or encourage. pr. par. *inciting;* past, *incited:* s. *incitement.*

INCIVIL'ITY. s. Want of courtesy; rudeness. pl. *incivilities.*

INCLASP'. v. To hold fast; to clasp. pr. par. *inclasping;* past, *inclasped.*

INCLEM'ENCY. s. Severity, roughness, unmercifulness. adj *inclement:* adv. *inclemently.*

INCLINA'TION. s. Natural aptness, favourable disposition. adj. *inclinatory;* adv. *inclinatorily.*

INCLI'NE. v. To bend, to lean, to bend towards any part; to be favourably disposed to. pr. par. *inclining;* past, *inclined:* adj. *inclinable:* s. *inclination.*

INCLO'SE, ENCLO'SE. v. To shut in; to encircle; to surround. pr. par. *inclosing;* past, *inclosed:* s. *incloser, inclosure.*

INCLU'DE. v. To shut in, to inclose, to embrace. pr. par. *including,* past, *included.*

INCLU'SION. s. Act of including adj. *inclusive:* adv. *inclusively.*

INCOAG'ULABLE. adj. Incapable of coagulation.

INCOG'NITO. adj. In a state of concealment.

INCOHE'RENCE, INCOHE'RENCY. s. Want of cohesion; irregularity. pl. *incoherences, incoherencies:* adj. *incoherent:* adv. *incoherently.*

INCOMBUS'TIBLE. adj. Not to be consumed by fire. s. *incombustibility,* pl. *incombustibilities:* adv. *incombustibly.*

IN'COME. s. Revenue; produce of any thing.

INCOMMEN'SURABLE. adj. Not to be reduced to any measure common to both. s. *incommensurability:* adj. *incommensurate.*

INCOMMO'DE. v. To be inconvenient to; to hinder, or slightly to embarrass. pr. par. *incommoding;*

past, *incommoded:* adj. *incommodious:* adv. *incommodiously:* s. *incommodiousness.*
INCOMMU'NICABLE. *adj.* Not impartible; not to be told. s. *incommunicability:* adv. *incommunicably.*
INCOMMU'TABLE. *adj.* Not possible to be changed. s. *incommutability:* adv. *incommutably.*
INCOM'PARABLE. *adj.* Excellent; above all competition. s. *incomparableness:* adv. *incomparably.*
INCOMPAT'IBLE. *adj.* Inconsistent with something else. adv. *incompatibly:* s. *incompatibility*, pl. *incompatibilities.*
INCOM'PETENT. *adj.* Not suitable; not adequate. adv. *incompetently:* s. *incompetence, incompetency,* pl. *incompetences, incompetencies.*
INCOMPLETE. *adj.* Not perfect. adv. *incompletely:* s. *incompleteness.*
INCO' 'PREHE.N'SIBLE. *adj.* Not to be fully understood. adv. *incomprehensibl* s. *incomprehensibility.*
INCOMPREHEN'SIVE. *adj.* Not comprehensive. adv. *incomprehensively:* s. *incomprehension.*
INCOMPRES'SIBLE. *adj.* Not capable of being compressed. adv. *incompressibly:* s. *incompressibility,* pl. *incompressibilities.*
INCONCEIV'ABLE. *adj.* Incomprehensible: not to be conceived by the mind. adv. *inconceivably:* s. *inconceivableness.*
INCONCLU'SIVE. *adj.* Not conclusive. adv. *inconclusively:* s. *inconclusiveness.*
INCON'GRUENCE. *s.* Unsuitableness; want of adaptation. adj. *incongruent, incongruous:* adv. *incongruously:* s. *incongruity,* pl. *incongruities.*
INCON'SEQUENT. *adj.* Without just conclusion; without regular inference.
INCONSID'ERABLE. *adj.* Unworthy of notice; unimportant. adv. *inconsiderably.* s. *inconsiderableness.*

INCONSID'ERATE. *adj.* Careless, thoughtless. adv. *inconsiderately:* s. *inconsiderateness.*
INCONSIS'TENCE, INCONSIS'TENCY. *s.* Incongruity, unsteadiness, pl. *inconsistences, inconsistencies:* adj. *inconsistent:* adv. *inconsistently.*
INCONSO'LABLE. *adj.* Not to be comforted. adv. *inconsolably.*
INCONSO'NANT. *adj.* Disagreeing with itself; discordant. s. *inconsonance, inconsonancy,* pl. *inconsonancies.*
INCON'STANT. *adj.* Not firm in resolution; not steady in affection; variable. adv. *inconstantly:* s. *inconstancy,* pl. *inconstancies.*
INCONTES'TABLE. *adj.* Not to be disputed. adv. *incontestably.*
INCON'TINENT. *adj.* Unchaste; indulging unlawful pleasure. s. *incontinence.*
INCONTROVER'TIBLE. *adj.* Indisputable. adv. *incontrovertibly:* s. *incontrovertibility,* pl. *incontrovertibilities.*
INCONVE'NIENCE. *s.* Unfitness; disadvantage; difficulty. v. *inconvenience;* pr. par. *inconveniencing;* past, *inconvenienced:* adj. *inconvenient:* adv. *inconveniently.*
INCOR'PORATE. *v.* To mingle different ingredients, so as to make one mass; to form into a corporation. pr. par. *incorporating;* past, *incorporated:* s. *incorporation.*
INCORPO'REAL. *adj.* Immaterial; distinct from matter; distinct from body. adv. *incorporeally.*
INCORRECT'. *adj.* Not exact, inaccurate. s. *incorrectness:* adv. *incorrectly.*
INCOR'RIGIBLE. *adj.* Bad beyond correction. adv. *incorrigibly:* s. *incorrigibleness, incorrigibility,* pl. *incorrigibilities.*
INCORRUPT', INCORRUPTED *adj.* Not corrupt; not corrupted, honest. adv. *incorruptly:* s. *incorruption, incorruptness.*
INCORRUPT'IBLE. *adj.* Not capa-

ble of corruption. adv. *incorruptibly:* s. *incorruptibility.*

INCREASE'. v. To grow more in number, or greater in bulk; to advance in quantity or value. pr. par. *increasing;* past, *increased:* adj. *increasible:* s. *in'crease, increaser.*

INCRED'IBLE. adj. Surpassing belief. adv. *incredibly:* s. *incredibility.*

INCRED'ULOUS. adj. Sceptical; not readily believing. adv. *incredulously:* s. *incredulity,* pl. *incredulities.*

IN'CREMENT. s. Act of growing greater; increase; matter added; produce.

INCROACH', ENCROACH'. v. To invade another's right; to creep on gradually, without right. pr. par. *incroaching;* past, *incroached:* s. *incroacher, incroachment:* adv. *incroachingly.*

INCRUS'TATE. v. To cover with a crust; to cover with an additional coat. pr. par. *incrustating;* past, *incrustated:* adj. *incrustate:* s. *incrustation.*

IN'CUBATE. v. To sit upon eggs. pr. par. *incubating;* past, *incubated:* s. *incubation.*

IN'CUBUS. s. The night-mare.

INCUL'CATE. v. To impress by frequent repetition. pr. par. *inculcating;* past, *inculcated:* s. *inculcation.*

INCUM'BENT. adj. Resting or lying upon; imposed as a duty. adv. *incumbently:* s. *incumbency.*

INCUM'BER, ENCUM'BER. v. To press upon; to embarrass. pr. par. *incumbering;* past, *incumbered:* s. *incumbrance.*

INCUR'. v. To become liable to a punishment or reprehension, &c. pr. par. *incurring;* past, *incurred.*

INCU'RABLE. adj. Not admitting remedy. adv. *incurably:* s. *incurability,* pl. *incurabilities.*

INCU'RIOUS. adj. Negligent, inattentive. adv. *incuriously.* s. *incuriousness.*

INCUR'SION. s. Invasion, without conquest; inroad. adj. *incursive.*

INDEBT'ED. adj. Having incurred a debt; obliged by something received.

INDE'CENT. adj. Unbecoming, indecorous. adv. *indecently:* s. *indecency,* pl. *indecencies.*

INDECIS'ION. s. Want of determination. adj. *indecisive:* adv. *indecisively.*

INDECLI'NABLE. adj. Not variable; not varied by terminations. adv. *indeclinably.*

INDEC'OROUS. adj. Indecent; unbecoming. adv. *indecorously.*

INDECO'RUM. s. Indecency; something unbecoming.

INDEFAT'IGABLE. adj. Not to be wearied; unwearied. adv. *indefatigably:* s. *indefatigableness.*

INDEFEAS'IBLE. adj. Not defeasible. adv. *indefeasibly:* s. *indefeasibleness, indefeasibility.*

INDEFEN'SIBLE. adj. Not defensible. s. *indefensibility.*

INDEFI'NABLE. adj. Not to be defined. adv. *indefinably.*

INDEF'INITE. adj. Not determined; not limited; large, beyond the comprehension of man. adv. *indefinitely:* s. *indefiniteness.*

INDEL'IBLE. adj. Not to be blotted out or defaced. adv. *indelibly:* s. *indelibility,* pl. *indelibilities.*

INDEL'ICATE. adj. Wanting delicacy; indecent. adv. *indelicately:* s. *indelicacy,* pl. *indelicacies.*

INDEM'NIFY. v. To secure against loss or penalty. pr. par. *indemnifying;* past, *indemnified:* s. *indemnification.*

INDEM'NITY. s. Security from loss or punishment. pl. *indemnities.*

INDENT'. v. To mark with inequalities, like a row of teeth. pr. par *indenting;* past, *indented:* s. *indentment, indenture.*

INDEN'TURE. s. A covenant, so named because the counter-parts

200

are indented or cut one by the other. v. *indention.*

INDEPEN'DENT. *adj.* Not supported by another; not controlled; not relating to any thing else. *adv. independently: s. independence, independency,* pl. *independences, independencies.*

INDEPRI'VABLE. *adj.* Not to be taken away.

INDESCRI'BABLE. *adj.* Not to be described. *adv. indescribably.*

INDESTRUC'TIBLE. *adj.* Not to be destroyed.

INDETER'MINATE. *adj.* Not defined; indefinite, uncertain. *adv. indeterminately: s. indetermination.*

IN'DEX. *s.* A discoverer; the hand that points to any thing, as to the hour or way; a table of contents. pl. *indexes.*

IN'DIAN. *adj.* Belonging to India. *s. Indian,* one of the aborigines of America.

IN'DICATE. *v.* To show; to point out. pr. par. *indicating;* past, *indicated: s. indication, indicator:* adj. *indicative, indicatory:* adv. *indicatively.*

INDICT'. *v.* To charge any person by a written accusation, before a court of justice. pronounced *indi'te.* pr. par. *indicting;* past, *indicted:* adj. *indictable: s. indictment.*

INDIF'FERENT. *adj.* Neutral, regardless, of a middling state. *adv. indifferently: s. indifference.*

INDIG'ENOUS. *adj.* Natural to a country; not foreign or exotic.

IN'DIGENT. *adj.* Poor, needy. *s. indigence.*

INDIGES'TION. *s.* Weakness of stomach; want of concoctive powers. adj. *indigestible, indigested.*

INDIG'NANT. *adj.* Angry; inflamed at once with anger and disdain. *adv. indignantly: s. indignance, indignancy, indignation.*

INDIG'NITY. *s.* Contumely pl. *indignities.*

IN'DIGO. *s.* A plant which produces a blue die. pl. *indigoes.*

INDIRECT'. *adj.* Not straight, not tending otherwise than obliquely or consequentially to a purpose, not fair. *adv. indirectly: s. indirectness.*

INDISCREET'. *adj.* Imprudent, injudicious. *adv. indiscreetly: s. indiscretion.*

INDISCRIM'INATE. *adj.* Undistinguishable, undistinguished. *adv. indiscriminately: s. indiscrimination:* adj. *indiscriminating.*

INDISPEN'SABLE. *adj.* Not to be dispensed with; necessary. *adv indispensably: s. indispensability.*

INDISPO'SE. *v.* To make unfit; to disincline. pr. par. *indisposing,* past, *indisposed: s. indisposition.*

INDISPU'TABLE. *adj.* Incontestable. *adv. indisputably: s. indisputability.*

INDISSOL'UBLE. *adj.* Not soluble. *adv. indissolubly: s. indissolubility,* pl. *indissolubilities.*

INDISTINCT'. *adj.* Not distinct; not plainly marked. *adv. indistinctly: s. indistinctness.*

INDI'TE. *v.* See INDICT.

INDIVID'UAL. *s.* A single thing, or single person. adj. *individual:* adv. *individually: s. individuality,* pl. *individualities.*

INDIVIS'IBLE. *adj.* Not possible to be divided. *adv. indivisibly: s. indivisibility,* pl. *indivisibilities.*

INDO'CILE. *adj.* Unteachable. *s. indocility,* pl. *indocilities.*

IN'DOLENT. *adj.* Lazy, listless. *adv. indolently: s. indolence.*

INDOM'ITABLE. *adj.* Untameable.

INDORSE', ENDORSE'. *v.* To write on the back of any written paper. pr. par. *indorsing;* past, *indorsed s. indorser, indorsement.*

INDOW'. *v.* See ENDOW.

INDU'BITABLE. *adj.* Undoubted unquestionable. *adv. indubitably s. indubitableness.*

INDU'CE. *v.* To offer by way of induction, to influence to any thing

201

pr. par. *inducing;* past, *induced. s. inducement.*

INDUCT'. *v.* To bring in; to put into actual possession of a benefice. pr. par. *inducting;* past, *inducted.*

INDUC'TION. *s.* Act of inducing; introduction; inferring one general proposition, from several particulars. adj. *inductive:* adv. *inductively.*

INDUE'. *v.* To invest. pr. par. *induing;* past, *indued:* s. *induement.*

INDULGE'. *v.* To encourage by compliance; to fondle. pr. par. *indulging;* past, *indulged:* s. *indulgence:* adj. *indulgent:* adv. *indulgently.*

IN'DURATE. *v.* To grow hard; to harden. pr. par. *indurating;* past, *indurated:* adj. *indurate:* s. *induration.*

IN'DUSTRY. *s.* Diligence, assiduity. adj. *industrious:* adv. *industriously.*

INEB'RIATE. *v.* To intoxicate. pr. par. *inebriating;* past, *inebriated: s. inebriation, inebriety:* adj. *inebriate.*

INEF'FABLE. *adj.* Unspeakable, unutterable. adv. *ineffably:* s. *ineffability.*

INEFFEC'TIVE. *adj.* Not effective. adv. *ineffectively.*

INEFFEC'TUAL. *adj.* Not effectual. adv. *ineffectually:* s. *ineffectualness.*

INEF'FICACY. *s.* Want of power; want of effect. pl. *inefficacies:* adj. *inefficacious:* adv. *inefficaciously.*

INEFFI'CIENT. *adj.* Unactive, ineffective. s. *inefficiency,* pl. *inefficiencies:* adv. *inefficiently.*

INEL'EGANCE, INEL'IGANCY. *s.* Want of elegance. adj. *inelegant:* adv. *inelegantly.*

INEPT'. *adj.* Trifling, foolish, useless. adv. *ineptly:* s. *ineptitude, ineptness.*

INEQUAL'ITY. *s.* Difference of comparative quantity; unevenness; disproportion to any office or purpose. pl. *inequalities.*

INEQ'UITABLE. *adj.* Unjust. adv *inequitably.*

INERT'. *adj.* Dull, sluggish. adv. *inertly:* s. *inertness.*

INES'TIMABLE. *adj.* Too valuable to be rated. adv. *inestimably:* s. *inestimableness.*

INEV'ITABLE. *adj.* Unavoidable, adv. *inevitably:* s. *inevitableness.*

INEXCU'SABLE. *adj.* Not to be excused. adv. *inexcusably:* s. *inexcusableness.*

INEXHAUS'TIBLE. *adj.* Not to be exhausted. adv. *inexhaustibly:* s. *inexhaustibility:* adj. *inexhaustive.*

INEX'ORABLE. *adj.* Not to be moved by intreaty. adv. *inexorably:* s. *inexorability.*

INEXPE'DIENT. *adj.* Not expedient adv. *inexpediently:* s. *inexpedience inexpediency,* pl. *inexpediences, in expediencies.*

INEXPE'RIENCE. *s.* Want of experimental knowledge. part. adj *inexperienced.*

INEXPERT'. *adj.* Unskilful. adv *inexpertly.*

INEX'PIABLE. *adj.* Not to be atoned. adv. *inexpiably.*

INEX'PLICABLE. *adj.* Incapable o being explained. adv. *inexplicably:* s. *inexplicability.*

INEXPRES'SIBLE. *adj.* Not to be told. adv. *inexpressibly.*

INEXTIN'GUISHABLE. *adj.* Not to be extinguished; unquenchable. adv. *inextinguishably.*

INEX'TRICABLE. *adj.* Not to be disentangled. adv. *inextricably.* s. *inextricability.*

INFAL'LIBLE. *adj.* Not fallible. adv. *infallibly:* s. *infallibility,* pl. *infallibilities.*

IN'FAMOUS. *adj.* Publicly branded with guilt; disgraced. s. *infamy,* pl. *infamies:* adv. *infamously.*

IN'FANCY. *s.* The first part of life-non-age; beginning. pl. *infancies.*

202

INFANT. *s.* A young child; a minor; the title of a Spanish prince. (fem. *infanta:*) adj. *infantile.*

INFAN'TICIDE. *s.* Act of killing an infant; one who has killed an infant. adj. *infanticidal.*

IN'FANTRY. *s.* The foot-soldiers of an army. pl. *infantries.*

INFAT'UATE. *v.* To strike with folly. pr. par. *infatuating;* past, *infatuated:* s. *infatuation.*

INFECT'. *v.* To hurt by contagion. pr. par. *infecting;* past, *infected:* s. *infection:* adj. *infectious:* adv. *infectiously.*

INFECUN'DITY. *s.* Want of fertility; barrenness. pl. *infecundities.*

INFEE'BLE. *v.* See ENFEEBLE.

INFELIC'ITY. *s.* Unhappiness.

INFER'. *v.* To deduce. pr. par. *inferring;* past, *inferred:* adj. *inferrible:* s. *inference.*

INFE'RIOR. *adj.* Lower in place; lower in value or excellence. s. *inferiority,* pl. *inferiorities.*

INFER'NAL. *adj.* Hellish, detestable.

INFEST'. *v.* To harass, to disturb. pr. par. *infesting;* past, *infested:* adj. *infestuous:* s. *infestation.*

IN'FIDEL. *s.* An unbeliever. adj. *infidel:* s. *infidelity,* pl. *infidelities.*

IN'FINITE. *adj.* Unbounded, unlimited, immense. adv. *infinitely:* s. *infinity,* pl. *infinities, infinitude.*

INFIN'ITIVE. *adj.* In grammar, the infinitive mood affirms or intimates the intention of affirming, but not absolutely.

INFIRM'. *adj.* Weak, feeble. s. *infirmity,* pl. *infirmities.*

INFIRM'ARY. *s.* A lodging for the weak or sick. pl. *infirmaries.*

INFIX'. *v.* To drive in; to fasten. pr. par. *infixing;* past, *infixed.*

INFLAME'. *v.* To kindle; to set on fire. pr. par. *inflaming;* past, *inflamed.*

INFLAM'MATORY. *adj.* Having the power of inflaming. s. *inflammation.*

INFLA'TE. *v.* To swell with wind.
pr. par. *inflating;* past, *inflated* s. *inflation.*

INFLECT'. *v.* To bend, to turn. pr par. *inflecting;* past, *inflected:* adj. *inflective:* s. *inflection.*

INFLEX'IBLE. *adj.* Not to be bent or incurvated. adv. *inflexibly* s. *inflexibility,* pl. *inflexibilities.*

INFLICT'. *v.* To put in act, or impose as a punishment. pr. par *inflicting;* past, *inflicted* adj. *in flictive:* s. *infliction.*

IN'FLUENCE. *s.* Ascendant power, power of directing or modifying. v. *influence;* pr. par. *influencing,* past, *influenced:* adj. *influential:* adv. *influentially.*

IN'FLUX. *s.* Act of flowing into any thing.

INFOLD'. *v.* To inwrap. pr. par. *infolding;* past, *infolded.*

INFO'LIATE. *v.* To cover with leaves. pr. par. *infoliating;* past, *infoliated:* s. *infoliation.*

INFORM'. *v.* To instruct; to supply with new knowledge; to acquaint. pr. par. *informing;* past, *informed:* s. *informant, information, informer.*

INFORM'AL. *adj.* Irregular; contrary to established forms. adv. *informally:* s. *informality,* pl. *informalities.*

INFRACT'. *v.* To break. pr. par. *infracting;* past, *infracted:* s. *infraction.*

INFRAN'CHISE, ENFRAN'CHISE. *v.* To admit to the privilege of a freeman. pr par. *infranchising;* past, *infranchised:* s. *infranchisement.*

INFRAN'GIBLE. *adj.* Not to be broken. s. *infrangibility:* adv. *infrangibly.*

INFRE'QUENT. *adj.* Not frequent, rare; uncommon. adv. *infrequently:* s. *infrequence, infrequency,* pl *infrequencies.*

INFRINGE'. *v.* To violate; to break laws or contracts. pr. par. *infringing;* past, *infringed.* s. *infringement.*

INFU'RIATE. *v.* To fill with rage

or fury pr. par. *infuriating*, past, *infuriated.*

INFU'SE. *v.* To pour in, to instil. pr. par. *infusing;* past, *infused:* adj. *infusive, infusible:* s. *infusion.*

IN'GATHERING. *s.* The act of getting in a harvest.

INGEN'DER, ENGEN'DER. *v.* To beget, to produce. pr. par. *ingendering;* past, *ingendered.*

INGE'NIOUS. *adj.* Witty, inventive. adv. *ingeniously:* s. *ingenuity,* pl. *ingenuities.*

INGEN'UOUS. *adj.* Open, fair, candid. adv. *ingenuously:* s. *ingenuousness.*

INGLO'RIOUS. *adj.* Without glory; void of honour. adv. *ingloriously.*

IN'GOT. *s.* A mass of metal.

INGRAFT', ENGRAFT'. *v.* To propagate trees by incision. pr. par. *ingrafting;* past, *ingrafted:* s. *ingraftment.*

IN'GRAINED. *part. adj.* Dyed in grain; deeply fixed.

IN'GRATE. *adj.* Ungrateful. s. *ingrate.*

INGRA'TIATE. *v.* To put in favour; to recommend to kindness. pr. par. *ingratiating;* past, *ingratiated:* s. *ingratiation.*

INGRAT'ITUDE. *s.* Retribution of evil for good.

INGRE'DIENT. *s.* Component part of a body, consisting of several materials.

IN'GRESS. *s.* Entrance; power of entrance. s. *ingression:* adj. *ingressive.*

IN'GUINAL. *adj.* Belonging to the groin.

INGULF'. *v.* To swallow up, in a vast profundity; to cast into a gulf. pr. par. *ingulfing;* past, *ingulfed.*

INGUR'GITATE. *v.* To swallow down. pr. par. *ingurgitating;* past, *ingurgitated:* s. *ingurgitation.*

INHAB'IT. *v.* To dwell in. pr. par. *inhabiting;* past, *inhabited:* adj. *inhabitable:* s. *inhabitation, inhabitant, inhabitancy.*

INHANCE'. *v.* To raise, to advance to heighten in price. pr. par. *inhancing;* past, *inhanced.*

INHA'LE. *v.* To draw in with air. pr. par. *inhaling;* past, *inhaled:* s. *inhaler.*

INHARMO'NIOUS, INHARMONI'CAL. *adj.* Discordant, unmusical. adv. *inharmoniously:* s. *inharmoniousness.*

INHE'RE. *v.* To exist in something else. s. *inherence, inherency:* adj. *inherent:* adv. *inherently.*

INHER'IT. *v.* To receive or possess as an heir; to derive from an ancestor. pr. par. *inheriting;* past, *inherited:* adj. *inheritable:* adv. *inheritably:* s. *inheritance, inheritor, inheritress,* pl. *inheritresses.*

INHIB'IT. *v.* To restrain, to hinder, to prohibit, to forbid. pr. par. *inhibiting;* past, *inhibited:* s. *inhibition.*

INHOS'PITABLE. *adj.* Affording no kindness or entertainment to strangers. adv. *inhospitably:* s. *hospitality,* pl. *inhospitalities.*

INHU'MAN. *adj.* Barbarous, savage, cruel. adv. *inhumanly:* s. *inhumanity,* pl. *inhumanities.*

INHU'ME. *v.* To bury in the earth pr. par. *inhuming;* past, *inhumed* adj. *inhumative:* s. *inhumation.*

INIM'ICAL. *adj.* Unfriendly, hostile, adverse. adv. *inimically.*

INIM'ITABLE. *adj.* That cannot be imitated. adv. *inimitably:* s. *inimitableness.*

INIQ'UITY. *s.* Injustice, wickedness, crime. adj. *iniquitous:* adv. *iniquitously.*

INI'TIAL. *adj.* Placed at the beginning. s. *initial:* adv. *initially.*

INI'TIATE. *v.* To enter; to instruct in the rudiments of any art. pr. par. *initiating;* past, *initiated:* s. *initiation:* adj. *initiatory.*

INJECT'. *v.* To throw into. pr. par. *injecting;* past, *injected:* s. *injection.*

INJOIN', ENJOIN'. *v.* To direct, to order, to prescribe pr. par. *in-*

joining; past, *injoined:* s. *injoiner, injoinment.*
INJUDI'CIOUS. *adj.* Without judgment. *adv. injudiciously:* s. *injudiciousness.*
INJUNC'TION. *s.* Act of injoining; command. *adj. injunctive.*
IN'JURE. *v.* To hurt unjustly; to wrong. pr. par. *injuring;* past, *injured:* s. *injury,* pl. *injuries, injuriousness:* adj. *injurious:* adv. *injuriously.*
INJUS'TICE. *s.* Iniquity, wrong.
INK. *s.* A liquid, used for writing and printing. v. *ink;* pr. par. *inking;* past, *inked:* adj. *inky:* s. *inkiness.*
INK'STAND. *s.* A utensil for holding the instruments of writing.
IN'LAND. *adj.* Interior; lying remote from the sea. s. *inlander.*
INLAY'. *v.* To diversify with different bodies, inserted into the ground or substratum. pr. par. *inlaying;* past, *inlaid.*
IN'MATE. *s.* One who dwells in the same house with another.
IN'MOST. *adj.* Deepest within; remotest from the surface.
INN. *s.* A chamber, a lodging; a house of entertainment, for travellers.
IN'NATE. *adj.* Inborn. adv. *innately:* s. *innateness.*
INNAV'IGABLE. *adj.* Not possible to be navigated.
IN'NER. *adj.* Interior. superlative, *innermost.*
INN'KEEPER. *s.* One who keeps an inn.
IN'NOCENCE. *s.* Harmlessness; freedom from guilt. adj. *innocent:* adv. *innocently.*
INNOC'UOUS. *adj.* Harmless. adv. *innocuously:* s. *innocuousness.*
IN'NOVATE. *v.* To introduce a novelty. pr. par. *innovating;* past, *innovated:* s. *innovation, innovator.*
INNOX'IOUS. *adj.* Free from mischievous effects. adv. *innoxiously:* s. *innoxiousness.*

INNUEN'DO. *s.* An oblique hint. pl. *innuendoes.*
INNU'MERABLE. *adj.* Not to be counted. adv. *innumerably:* s. *innumerableness.*
INOC'ULATE. *v.* To propagate any plant, by inserting its bud into another stock; to infect by inoculation. pr. par. *inoculating;* past, *inoculated:* s. *inoculation, inoculator.*
INO'DOROUS. *adj.* Wanting scent. adv. *inodorously.*
INOFFEN'SIVE. *adj.* Harmless, innocent. adv. *inoffensively:* s. *inoffensiveness.*
INOPPORTU'NE. *adj.* Unseasonable, inconvenient. adv. *inopportunely.*
INOR'DINATE. *adj.* Irregular, unlawful. adv. *inordinately:* s. *inordinateness.*
IN'QUEST. *s.* Judicial inquiry or examination.
INQUI'ET. *adj.* Disquiet. s. *inquietude.*
INQUI'RE, ENQUI'RE. *v.* To ask questions; to make search. p: par. *inquiring;* past, *inquired:* s. *inquiry,* pl. *inquiries, inquirer.*
INQUISI'TION. *s.* Judicial inquiry. s. *inquisitor:* adj. *inquisitorial* adv. *inquisitorially.*
INQUIS'ITIVE. *adj.* Curious; busy in search. adv. *inquisitively* s. *inquisitiveness.*
IN'ROAD. *s.* Incursion.
INSALU'BRITY. *s.* Unwholesomeness. adj. *insalubrious.*
INSA'NE. *adj.* Disordered in mind. s. *insanity,* pl. *insanities.*
INSA'TIABLE. *adj.* Greedy beyond measure. adv. *insatiably:* s. *insatiableness.*
INSA'TIATE. *adj.* Greedy, so as not to be satisfied. adv. *insatiately:* s. *insatiety.*
INSCRI'BE. *v.* To write on any thing; to dedicate. pr. par. *inscribing;* past, *inscribed:* s *inscriber.*
INSCRIP'TION. *s.* Act of inscrib-

ing; thing inscribed. adj. *inscriptive*.

INSCRU'TABLE. *adj.* Incapable of being discovered. *adv. inscrutably*: *s. inscrutability*.

IN'SECT. *s.* A small animal, having a separation in the middle, or between the extremities of its body, joined by a ligature, as a common fly. *v. insect*; pr. par. *insecting*; past, *insected*: *adj. insectile*.

INSECTOL'OGER. *s.* One who studies or describes insects. *s. insectology*.

INSECU'RE. *adj.* Not secure. *adv. insecurely*: *s. insecurity*, pl. *insecurities*.

INSEN'SATE. *adj.* Wanting sensibility; wanting feeling. *adj. insensitive*: *s. insensation*.

INSEN'SIBLE. *adj.* Imperceptible; void of feeling; void of meaning. *adv. insensibly*: *s. insensibility*, pl. *insensibilities*.

INSEP'ARABLE. *adj.* Not to be separated. *adv. inseparably*: *s. inseparability*.

INSERT'. *v.* To place in or amongst other things. pr. par. *inserting*; past, *inserted*: *s. insertion*.

INSHRI'NE, ENSHRI'NE. *v.* To enclose in a shrine. pr. par. *inshrining*; past, *inshrined*.

INSID'IOUS. *adj.* Sly, treacherous. *adv. insidiously*: *s. insidiousness*.

IN'SIGHT. *s.* Deep view; thorough skill in any thing.

INSIG'NIA. *s.* Distinguishing marks of office or honour.

INSIGNIF'ICANT. *adj.* Wanting meaning; void of signification; mean. *adv. insignificantly*: *s. insignificance, insignificancy*.

INSINCE'RE. *adj.* Wanting sincerity. *adv. insincerely*. *s. insincerity*, pl. *insincerities*.

INSIN'UATE. *v.* To push gently into favour or regard. pr. par. *insinuating*; past, *insinuated*: *adj. insinuative*: *s. insinuation, insinuator*.

INSIP'ID *adj.* Wanting taste. *adv. insipidly*: *s. insipidity*, pl. *insipidities*.

INSIST'. *v.* To stand or rest upon; to persist in. pr. par. *insisting*; past, *insisted*.

INSNA'RE. *v.* To entrap. pr. par *insnaring*; past, *insnared*: *s. insnarer*.

INSO'CIABLE. *adj.* Not sociable. *adv. insociably*: *s. insociability*.

IN'SOLENT. *adj.* Haughty, overbearing. *adv. insolently*: *s. insolence*.

INSOL'ID. *adj.* Not solid. *s. insolidity*, pl. *insolidities*.

INSOL'UBLE. *adj.* Not to be dissolved or separated. *adv. insolubly*: *s. insolubility*, pl. *insolubilities*.

INSOL'VABLE. *adj.* Not to be explained. *adv. insolvably*.

INSOL'VENCY. *s.* Inability to pay debts. pl. *insolvencies*: *adj. insol vent*.

INSPECT'. *v.* To look into, by way of examination. pr. par. *inspecting*, past, *inspected*: *s. inspection, inspector*: *adj. inspectorial*.

INSPER'SION. *s.* Act of sprinkling upon.

INSPI'RE. *v.* To draw in the breath, to breath into; to infuse into the mind; to impress upon the fancy. pr. par. *inspiring*; past, *inspired*: *s. inspiration, inspirer*: *adj. inspirable*.

INSPIR'IT. *v.* To enliven. pr. par *inspiriting*; past, *inspirited*: *s. inspiration*: *adj. inspiritive*.

INSPIS'SATE. *v.* To thicken. pr. par *inspissating*; past, *inspissated*: s *inspissation*.

INSTA'BLE. *adj.* Inconstant. adv *instably*. *s. instability*, pl. *instabilities*.

INSTALL. *v.* To advance to any rank or office, by placing in an official seat, or stall. pr. par. *installing*, past, *installed*: *s. installation, in stalment*.

INSTAL'MENT. *s.* Act of installing; in commercial language, a certain

206

portion of a debt to be paid at stated times.

IN'STANT. *adj.* Pressing, urgent, earnest, immediate.

IN'STANT. *s.* Such a part of duration wherein we perceive no succession; a particular time.

INSTANTA'NEOUS. *adj.* Done in an instant. adv. *instantaneously:* s. *instantaneousness.*

INSTAURA'TION. *s.* Reparation, renewal. s. *instaurator.*

INSTEAD'. *adv.* In the room or place

IN'STEP. *s.* The upper part of the foot, which joins the leg.

IN'STIGATE. *v.* To urge to ill. pr. par. *instigating;* past, *instigated:* adj. *instigative:* s. *instigation, instigator.*

INSTIL'. *v.* To infuse by drops; to insinuate any thing imperceptibly into the mind. pr. par. *instilling;* past, *instilled:* s. *instillation, instiller, instilment.*

IN'STINCT. *s.* The power determining the will of brutes; desire or aversion acting in the mind, without the intervention of reason. adj. *instinctive:* adv. *instinctively.*

IN'STITUTE. *v.* To fix, to establish, to commence, to prescribe. pr. par. *instituting;* past, *instituted:* s. *institution, institute, institutor:* adj. *institutive, institutionary.*

INSTRUCT'. *v.* To teach, to direct. pr. par. *instructing;* past, *instructed:* adj. *instructive:* adv. *instructively:* s. *instruction, instructer, instructiveness, instructress.*

IN'STRUMENT. *s.* A tool used for any work, or purpose; a frame constructed so as to yield harmonious sounds. adj. *instrumental:* s. *instrumentality:* adv. *instrumentally.*

INSUBJEC'TION. *s.* State of disobedience.

INSUBOR'DINATE. *adj.* In a state of disorder or disobedience. s. *insubordination.*

INSUF'FERABLE. *adj.* Intolerable. adv. *insufferably:* s. *insufferableness.*

INSUFFI'CIENT. *adj.* Not sufficient. adv. *insufficiently:* s. *insufficience, insufficiency,* pl. *insufficiencies.*

IN'SULAR. *adj.* Belonging to an island; having the quality of an island. s. *insularity.*

IN'SULATE. *v.* To form into an island; to separate. pr. par. *insulating;* past, *insulated.*

INSULT'. *v.* To treat with insolence or contempt. pr. par. *insulting,* past, *insulted:* adj. *insulting:* adv *insultingly:* s. *in'sult, insulter.*

INSU'PERABLE. *adj.* Invincible; insurmountable. adv. *insuperably:* s. *insuperability.*

INSUPPORT'ABLE. *adj.* Intolerable, insufferable. adv. *insupportably:* s. *insupportableness.*

INSU'RE. *v.* To exempt from hazard, by the payment of a certain sum; to make sure. pr. par. *insuring,* past, *insured:* s. *insurance, insurer.*

INSUR'GENT. *s.* One who rebels against the established government of a country.

INSURMOUNT'ABLE. *adj.* Insuperable. adv. *insurmountably:* s *insurmountability.*

INSURREC'TION. *s.* A seditious rising. adj. *insurrectional, insurrectionary.*

INSUSCEP'TIBLE. *adj.* Not susceptible. s. *insusceptibility:* adv. *insusceptibly.*

INTAG'LIO. *s.* Any thing that has figures engraved upon it, so as to rise above the ground.

INTAIL'. See ENTAIL.

INTAN'GIBLE. *adj.* Not to be touched. adv. *intangibly:* s. *intangibility,* pl. *intangibilities.*

IN'TEGER. *s.* The whole of any thing. adj. *integral:* adv. *integrally:* s. *integrality.*

IN'TEGRATE. *v.* To form one whole; to contain all the parts of. pr. par. *integrating;* past, *integrated.*

INTEG'RITY. *s.* Entireness, incorruptibility, honesty. pl. *integrities.*

INTEG'UMENT. *s.* Any thing that covers or envelops another thing. adj. *integumental.*

INTELLECT. *s.* The intelligent mind. adj. *intellectual:* adv. *intellectually:* s. *intellectualist, intellectuality.*

INTEL'LIGENT. *adj.* Knowing, instructed, skilful. s. *intelligence, intelligencer.*

INTEL'LIGIBLE. *adj.* Possible to be understood. adv. *intelligibly:* s. *intelligibility.*

INTEM'PERATE. *adj.* Immoderate in appetite; drunken; ungovernable; exceeding the just or convenient mean. adv. *intemperately:* s. *intemperance.*

INTEND'. *v.* To mean or design. pr. par. *intending;* past, *intended:* s. *intender, intention, intendment.*

INTEND'ANT. *s.* An officer of the highest class, who oversees any particular allotment of public business.

INTENSE'. *adj.* Raised to a high degree; vehement, ardent. adv. *intensely:* s. *intenseness, intension, intensity,* pl. *intensities.*

INTENT'. *adj.* Anxiously diligent. s. *intent, intentness:* adv. *intently.*

INTEN'TION. *s.* Design, purpose. adj. *intentional:* adv. *intentionally.*

INTER'. *v.* To bury. pr. par. *interring;* past, *interred:* s. *interment.*

INTER'CALAR, INTER'CALARY. *adj.* Inserted out of the common order, to preserve the equation of time. v. *intercalate;* pr. par. *intercalating;* past, *intercalated:* s. *intercalation.*

INTERCE'DE. *v.* To pass between; to mediate. pr. par. *interceding;* past, *interceded.*

INTERCEPT'. *v.* To stop and seize in the way; to obstruct. pr. par. *intercepting;* past, *intercepted:* s. *interception, intercepter:* adj. *interceptive:* adv *interceptively.*

INTERCES'SION. *s* Act of interceding; mediation. s. *intercessor:* adj. *intercessory.*

INTERCHAIN'. *v.* To chain or link together. pr. par. *interchaining,* past, *interchained.*

INTERCHANGE'. *v.* To give and take mutually; to put each in the place of the other. pr. par. *interchanging;* past, *interchanged* adj. *interchangeable:* adv. *interchangeably:* s. *interchangement.*

IN'TERCOURSE. *s.* Commerce communication.

INTERDICT'. *v.* To forbid, to prohibit. pr. par. *interdicting;* past *interdicted:* s. *in'terdict, interdiction:* adj. *interdictive, interdictory*

INTEREST'. *v.* To concern, to effect. pr. par. *interesting;* past, *in terested.*

IN'TEREST. *s.* Concern, advantage, influence over others; money paid for the use of money.

INTERFE'RE. *v.* To interpose; to intermeddle. pr. par. *interfering,* past, *interfered:* s. *interference.*

IN'TERIM. *s.* Intervening time.

INTE'RIOR. *adj.* Internal, not out ward. s. *interior.*

INTERJEC'TION. *s.* Intervention; one of the parts of speech. v. *interject;* pr. par. *interjecting;* past, *interjected.*

INTERLA'CE. *v.* To intermix; to put one thing within another. pr. par. *interlacing;* past, *interlaced.*

INTERLARD'. *v.* To insert between. pr. par. *interlarding;* past, *interlarded.*

INTERLE'AVE. *v.* To insert blank leaves into a book. pr. par. *inter leaving;* past, *interleaved.*

INTERLI'NE. *v.* To write in alternate lines; to write between two lines. pr. par. *interlining;* past, *interlined:* adj. *interlinear, interlineary:* s. *interlineation.*

INTERLO'PE. *v.* To intrude; to run between parties, and intercept the advantage one should gain from the other. pr. par. *interloping* past, *interloped:* s. *interloper.*

INTERLUDE. *s.* Something played at the intervals of a festival or play.

INTERMAR'RY. *v.* To marry some of each family with another. pr. par. *intermarrying;* past, *intermarried:* s. *intermarriage.*

INTERMED'DLE. *v.* To interpose officiously. pr. par. *intermeddling;* past, *intermeddled:* s. *intermeddler.*

INTERME'DIATE. *adj.* Intervening. adv. *intermediately.*

INTER'MINABLE. *adj.* Immense: without limit. adv. *interminably:* adj. *interminate.*

INTERMIN'GLE. *v.* To mix. pr. par. *intermingling;* past, *intermingled.*

INTERMIS'SION. *s.* Act of intermitting; cessation for a time. adj. *intermissive.*

INTERMIT'. *v.* To cease or forbear for a time. pr. par. *intermitting;* past, *intermitted:* adj. *intermittent:* adv. *intermittingly.*

INTERMIX'. *v.* To mingle; to mix. pr. par. *intermixing;* past, *intermixed:* s. *intermixture.*

INTER'NAL. *adj.* Inward. adv. *internally.*

INTER'POLATE. *v.* To put any thing into a place to which it does not belong. pr. par. *interpolating;* past, *interpolated:* s. *interpolation, interpolater.*

INTERPO'SE. *v.* To place between; to thrust in, as an obstruction, interruption, or inconvenience. pr. par. *interposing;* past, *interposed:* s. *interposition.*

INTER'PRET. *v.* To explain. pr. par. *interpreting;* past, *interpreted:* s. *interpretation, interpreter:* adj. *interpretative, interpretable:* adv. *interpretatively.*

INTERREG'NUM. *s.* The time in which a throne is vacant between the death of one prince, and the accession of another.

INTER'ROGATE. *v.* To question. pr. par. *interrogating;* past, *interrogated:* s. *interrogation, interrogator:* adj. *interrogative, interrogatory:* adv. *interrogatively.*

INTERRUPT'. *v.* To hinder from proceeding, by interposition. pr. par. *interrupting;* past, *interrupted:* s. *interruption, interrupter* adv. *interruptedly.*

INTERSECT'. *v.* To cut; to divide each other mutually. pr. par. *intersecting;* past, *intersected:* s. *intersection.*

INTERSPERSE'. *v.* To scatter amongst other things. pr. par. *interspersing;* past, *interspersed:* s. *interspersion.*

INTER'STICE. *s.* Intervening space. adj. *interstitial.*

INTERTWI'NE. *v.* To unite, by twisting one in another. pr. par *intertwining;* past, *intertwined.*

IN'TERVAL. *s.* Intervening space or time.

INTERVE'NE. *v.* To come between. pr. par. *intervening;* past, *intervened:* s. *intervention:* adj. *intervenient.*

IN'TERVIEW. *s.* Mutual sight; meeting of persons generally by appointment.

INTERWEAVE'. *v.* To mix one with another, in a regular texture. pr. par. *interweaving;* past, *interwoven.*

INTES'TATE. *adj.* Dying without a will. s. *intestate, intestacy.*

INTES'TINE. *adj.* Internal. s. *intestine.*

INTHRAL', ENTHRAL'. *v.* To enslave. pr. par. *inthralling;* past, *inthralled:* s. *inthralment, inthraller.*

INTHRO'NE. *v.* To raise to royalty. pr. par. *inthroning;* past, *inthroned:* s. *inthronement.*

INTI'CE. *v.* See ENTICE.

IN'TIMATE. *adj.* Familiar; closely acquainted. adv. *intimately:* s. *intimacy, intimacies.*

IN'TIMATE. *v.* To point out indirectly. pr. par. *intimating;* past,

INT—INT

intimated: s. *intimation:* adv. *intimately.*
INTIM'IDATE. *v.* To make fearful. pr. par. *intimidating;* past, *intimidated:* s. *intimidation.*
INTI'RE, ENTI'RE. *adj.* Whole, unbroken. adv. *intirely:* s. *intireness.*
INTI'TLE, ENTI'TLE. *v.* To give a claim to; to have a title. pr. par. *intitling;* past, *intitled.*
INTOL'ERABLE. *adj.* Insufferable. adv. *intolerably.*
INTOL'ERANCE. *s.* Want of patience to bear the opinion of others. adj. *intolerant.*
INTOMB. *v.* To enclose in a tomb. pr. par. *intombing;* past, *intombed.*
IN'TONATE. *v.* To thunder. pr. par. *intonating;* past, *intonated:* s. *intonation.*
INTOX'ICATE. *v.* To make drunk. pr. par. *intoxicating;* past, *intoxicated:* s. *intoxication.*
INTRAC'TABLE. *adj.* Ungovernable, obstinate. adv. *intractably:* s. *intractability, intractableness.*
IN'TRANCE', ENTRANCE'. *v.* To put into a trance. pr. par. *intrancing;* past, *intranced.*
INTRANQUIL'ITY. *s.* Unquietness; want of rest.
INTRAN'SITIVE. *adj.* Not transitive. adv. *intransitively.*
INTRAP', ENTRAP'. *v.* To ensnare, to entangle. pr. par. *intrapping;* past, *intrapped.*
INTREAT', ENTREAT'. *v.* To petition; to solicit. pr. par. *intreating;* past, *intreated.*
INTRENCH'. *v.* To fortify with a trench; to encroach. pr. par. *intrenching;* past, *intrenched:* s. *intrenchment.*
INTREP'ID. *adj.* Fearless, daring. adv. *intrepidly:* s. *intrepidity.*
IN'TRICATE. *adj.* Entangled, complicated. adv. *intricately:* s. *intricacy.*
IN'TRIGUE. *s.* A plot; a private transaction in which many parties are engaged. *v.* intrigue'; pr. par.

INT—INV

intriguing; past, *intrigued:* s. *intriguer:* adv. *intriguingly.*
INTRIN'SIC. *adj.* Inward; internal real; true. adv. *intrinsically.*
INTRODU'CE. *v.* To conduct another to a place or person; to bring any thing into notice or practice. pr. par. *introducing;* past, *introduced:* s. *introduction:* adj. *introductive, introductory.*
INTROMIT'. *v.* To send in; to let in; to admit; to intermeddle. pr. par. *intromitting;* past, *intromitted:* s. *intromission.*
INTRU'DE. *v.* To enter without invitation or permission; to encroach pr. par. *intruding;* past, *intruded:* s. *intruder.*
INTRU'SION. *s.* Act of intruding. adj. *intrusive:* adv. *intrusively.*
INTRUST'. *v.* To treat with confidence; to confide. pr. par. *intrusting;* past, *intrusted.*
INTU'ITIVE. *adj.* Immediately perceived by the mind, without the intervention of argument or testimony. s. *intuition:* adv. *intuitively.*
INTWI'NE. *v.* To twist or wreath together. pr. par. *intwining;* past, *intwined.*
INUEN'DO. *s.* See INNUENDO.
INUM'BRATE. *v.* To shade; to cover with shades. pr. par. *inumbrating;* past, *inumbrated:* s. *inumbration.*
IN'UNDATE. *v.* To overflow with water. pr. par. *inundating;* past, *inundated:* s. *inundation.*
INURBAN'ITY. *s.* Want of courteousness; rudeness; unkindness.
INU'RE. *v.* To habituate; to accustom. pr. par. *inuring;* past, *inured:* s. *inurement.*
INURN'. *v.* To entomb; to bury pr. par. *inurning;* past, *inurned.*
INUTIL'ITY. *s.* Uselessness.
INVA'DE. *v.* To make a hostile entrance; to infringe. pr. par. *invading;* past, *invaded:* s. *invader*
INVA'SION. *s.* Act of invading. adj. *invasive.*

210

INVAL'ID. *adj.* Weak; of no weight or cogency; null. *v. invalidate;* pr. par. *invalidating;* past, *invalidated:* s. *invalidation, invalidity.*

INVAL'UABLE. *adj.* Inestimable. adv. *invaluably.*

INVARIABLE. *adj.* Unchangeable. adv. *invariably:* s. *invariableness.*

INVEC'TIVE. *s.* Censure; satirical or reproachful accusation. adj. *invective:* adv. *invectively.*

INVEIGH'. *v.* To utter censure or reproach. pr. par. *inveighing;* past, *inveighed:* s. *inveigher.*

INVEI'GLE. *v.* To persuade to something bad or hurtful; to allure. pr. par. *inveigling;* past, *inveigled:* s. *inveiglement, inveigler.*

INVEN'OM. *v.* See ENVENOM.

INVENT. *v.* To find out; to produce something not made before; to fabricate. pr. par. *inventing;* past, *invented:* s. *inventer, invention:* adj. *inventive.*

IN'VENTORY. *s.* An account or catalogue. pl. *inventories:* v. *inventory.*

INVERT'. *v.* To turn upside down; to place the last first. pr. par. *inverting;* past, *inverted:* s. *inversion:* adj. *inverse:* adv. *invertedly.*

INVEST'. *v.* To place in possession of a rank or office; to confer; to enclose. pr. par. *investing;* past, *invested:* s. *investment, investiture.*

INVES'TIGATE. *v.* To search out; to examine. pr. par. *investigating;* past, *investigated:* s. *investigation, investigator:* adj. *investigative.*

INVET'ERATE. *adj.* Old; obstinate by long continuance. s. *inveterateness:* adv. *inveterately.*

INVID'IOUS. *adj.* Envious, malignant. s. *invidiousness:* adv. *invidiously.*

INVIG'ORATE. *v.* To endue with vigour. pr. par. *invigorating;* past, *invigorated:* s. *invigoration.*

INVIN'CIBLE. *adj.* Insuperable, unconquerable. adv. *invincibly:* s. *invincibility*

INVI'OLABLE. *adj.* Not to be profaned; not to be broken. adv. *inviolably:* s. *inviolability:* adv. *inviolably:* adj. *inviolate.*

INVIS'IBLE. *adj.* Not to be seen. adv. *invisibly:* s. *invisibility.*

INVI'TE. *v.* To ask to any place with entreaty and complaisance; to allure. pr. par. *inviting;* past, *invited:* s. *inviter, invitation:* adv. *invitingly.*

INVOCA'TION. *s.* Act of invoking; entreaty.

IN'VOICE. *s.* A catalogue of the freight of a ship; or of the articles and price of goods sent by or to a factor. adj. *invoiced.*

INVO'KE. *v.* To call upon, to implore. pr. par. *invoking;* past, *invoked.*

INVOL'UNTARY. *adj.* Not having the power of choice; not done willingly. adv. *involuntarily.*

INVOLVE'. *v.* To inwrap, to imply, to comprise. pr. par. *involving,* past, *involved.*

INVOLU'TION. *s.* Act of involving.

INVUL'NERABLE. *adj.* Not to be wounded. adv. *invulnerably.*

IN'WARD. *adj.* Internal, within. adv. *inwardly.*

INWRAP'. *v.* To cover by involution; to involve. pr. par. *inwrapping;* past, *inwrapped.*

INWREATH'. *v.* To surround as with a wreath. pr. par. *inwreathing;* past, *inwreathed.*

INWROUGHT'. *adj.* Adorned with work.

ION'IC. *adj.* Relating to or belonging to one of the orders of architecture.

IO'TA. *s.* A tittle; the smallest letter in the Greek alphabet.

IPECACUAN'HA. *s.* An Indian plant of emetic virtues.

IRAS'CIBLE. *adj.* Easily provoked. s. *irascibility:* adj. *irascibly.*

IRE. *s.* Anger, rage. adv. *irefully*

I'RIS. *s.* The rainbow, the circle round the pupil of the eye; the fleur de lis

I'RISH. *adj.* Belonging to Ireland. *s. Irishism.*
IRK'SOME. *adj.* Wearisome, tedious, troublesome. *s. irksomeness:* adv. *irksomely.*
I'RON. *s.* The hardest and most useful of the metals. *adj. iron.*
IRON. *v* To smooth with an iron; to shackle with irons. pr. par. *ironing;* past, *ironed.*
I'RONMONGER. *s.* A dealer in iron. *s. ironmongery.*
I'RONMOULD. *s.* A stain caused by oxydated iron. adj. *ironmoulded.*
I'RONY. *s.* A mode of speech, in which the meaning is contrary to the words. pl. *ironies:* adj. *ironical:* adv. *ironically:* s. *ironist.*
IRRA'DIATE. *v.* To shine upon; to emit beams of light. pr. par. *irradiating;* past, *irradiated:* s. *irradiance, irradiation.*
IRRA'TIONAL. *adj.* Void of reason; absurd. *s. irrationality:* adv. *irrationally.*
IRRECLAIM'ABLE. *adj.* Not to be reclaimed. adv. *irreclaimably.*
IRRECONCI'LABLE. *adj.* Not to be reconciled. adv. *irreconcilably.*
IRRECOV'ERABLE. *adj.* Not to be regained, not to be remedied. adv. *irrecoverably.*
IRREDU'CIBLE. *adj.* Not to be reduced. adv. *irreducibly.*
IRREF'RAGABLE. *adj.* Not to be confuted. adv. *irrefragably.*
IRREFU'TABLE. *adj.* Not to be refuted. adv. *irrefutably.*
IRREG'ULAR. *adj.* Deviating from rule, custom, or nature; immethodical. s. *irregularity:* adv. *irregularly.*
IRREL'ATIVE. *adj.* Having no reference to. adv. *irrelatively.*
IRREL'EVANT. *adj.* Not applicable; not to the purpose. adv. *irrelevantly:* s. *irrelevancy.*
IRRELIEV'ABLE. *adj.* Not admitting relief.
IRRELI'GION. *s.* Want of religion; contempt of religion. adj. *irreligious:* adv. *irreligiously.*

IRREME'DIABLE. *adj.* Admitting no cure. adv. *irremediably.*
IRREMO'VABLE. *adj.* Not to be removed or changed. adv. *irremovably.*
IRREMU'NERABLE. *adj.* Not to be rewarded.
IRREP'ARABLE. *adj.* Not to be recovered or repaired. adv. *irreparably.*
IRREPREHEN'SIBLE. *adj.* Exempt from blame. adv. *irreprehensibly.*
IRREPRES'SIBLE. *adj.* Not to be repressed. adv. *irrepressibly.*
IRREPROACH'ABLE. *adj.* Free from reproach. adv. *irreproachably.*
IRRESIS'TIBLE. *adj.* Superior to opposition. s. *irresistibility:* adv. *irresistibly.*
IRRES'OLUTE. *adj.* Not constant in purpose; not determined. adv. *irresolutely:* s. *irresolution.*
IRRESPON'SIBLE. *adj.* Not responsible. s. *irresponsibility.*
IRRETRIEV'ABLE. *adj.* Not to be repaired; irrecoverable. adv. *irretrievably.*
IRREV'ERENCE. *s.* Want of reverence; want of respect. adj. *irreverent:* adv. *irreverently.*
IRREVER'SIBLE. *adj.* Not to be reversed. adv. *irreversibly.*
IRREV'OCABLE. *adj.* Not to be revoked. s. *irrevocability:* adv. *irrevocably.*
IR'RIGATE. *v.* To moisten, to water. pr. par. *irrigating;* past, *irrigated:* s. *irrigation:* adj. *irriguous.*
IR'RITATE. *v.* To provoke, to teaze, to stimulate. pr. par. *irritating,* past, *irritated:* adj. *irritable:* s. *irritation, irritability.*
IRRUP'TION. *s.* The act of forcing an entrance; inroad. adj. *irruptive.*
I'SINGLASS. *s.* A glue prepared from the intestines of a fish.
I'SLAND. *s.* A tract of land surrounded by water. s. *islander.*
ISLE. *s.* An island; a long walk in a church. pronounced *ile.*

ISO—ITA

ISOLATE. *v.* To detach, to separate. pr. par. *isolating;* past, *isolated.*

IS'SUE. *v.* To come out; to make an irruption. pr. par. *issuing;* past, *issued:* s. *issue.*

ISTH'MUS. *s.* A neck of land, joining a peninsula to a continent. pl. *isthmuses.*

IT. One of the pronouns.

ITAL'IAN. *adj.* Relating or belonging to Italy.

ITAL'IC. *adj.* Denoting a species of type.

ITE—IVY

I'TEM. *s.* A new article; a hint.

IT'ERATE. *v.* To repeat; to utter again; to inculcate by frequent mention. pr. par. *iterating;* past, *iterated:* s. *iteration:* adj. *iterative.*

ITIN'ERANT. *adj.* Traveling, wandering. adj. *itinerary.*

ITIN'ERARY. *s.* A book of travels. pl. *itineraries.*

I'VORY. *s.* The tusk of the elephant.

I'VY. *s.* A species of creeping plant adj. *ivied.*

J

JAB—JAD

JAB'BER. *v.* To talk idly; to chatter. pr. par. *jabbering;* past, *jabbered:* s. *jabber, jabberer.*

JACK'AL. *s.* A small animal, supposed to start prey for the lion.

JACK'ANAPES. *s.* A monkey; a coxcomb.

JACK'ASS. *s.* A male ass. pl. *jackasses.*

JACK'DAW. *s.* A species of crow.

JACK'ET. *s.* A short coat. adj. *jacketed.*

JAC'OBIN. *s.* A friar of the order of St. Dominic; the name of a faction in the French revolution, so called from their assembling in the monastery of the Jacobin friars. s. *jacobinism.*

JACK-PUD'DING. *s.* A zany; a merry andrew.

JAC'OBITE. *s.* One attached to the person and family of James the Second of England, after his abdication. s. *jacobitism.*

JACTITA'TION. *s.* Tossing; restlessness; vain-boasting; a term in the canon law, denoting a false pretension to marriage.

JACULA'TION. *s.* The act of throwing a missive weapon.

JADE. *s.* A horse of no spirit; a worthless nag; an impudent woman.

JAD—JAR

JADE. *v.* To tire, to harass, to dispirit. pr. par. *jading;* past, *jaded.*

JAG. *v.* To cut into teeth, like those of a saw; to stick, as with a pin. pr. par. *jagging;* past, *jagged:* adj. *jaggy:* s. *jaggedness.*

JAIL, GAOL. *s.* A prison. s. *jailer.*

JAL'AP. *s.* A medicinal drug.

JAM. *s.* A conserve of fruit, boiled with sugar and water.

JAM. *v.* To squeeze closely; to enclose an object between two bodies, so as to render it immovable. pr. par. *jamming;* past, *jammed.*

JANE. *s.* A kind of fustian.

JAN'ITOR. *s.* A door-keeper.

JAN'IZARY. *s.* One of the guards of the Turkish emperor. adj. *janizarian.*

JAN'SENIST. *s.* One who espouses the religious opinions of Jansen, bishop of Ypres. s. *jansenism.*

JAN'TY, JAUN'TY. *adj.* Showy, fluttering, finical. s. *jantiness.*

JAN'UARY. *s.* The first month of the year.

JAPAN'. *v.* To varnish and embellish with gold and raised figures. pr. par. *japanning;* past, *japanned:* s. *japan, japanner.*

JAR. *v.* To strike or vibrate irregularly; to clash; to act in opposi-

213

tion. pr. par. *jarring;* past, *jarred: s. jar.*
JAR. *s.* A kind of earthen vessel.
JAR'GON. *s.* Unintelligible talk.
JARGONELL'E. *s.* A species of pear.
JAS'PER. *s.* A hard stone, of a bright green colour.
JAUN'DICE. *s.* A disease, which makes the skin yellow. adj. *jaundiced.*
JAUNT. *s.* A short drive. v. *jaunt;* pr. par. *jaunting;* past, *jaunted.*
JAUN'TY. adj. See JANTY.
JAV'ELIN. *s.* A kind of lance.
JAW. *s.* The bone of the mouth, in which the teeth are fixed; in low language, "gross abuse."
JAY. *s.* A kind of bird.
JEAL'OUS. adj. Suspicious in love; emulous. s. *jealousy:* adv. *jealously.*
JEER. *v.* To scoff, to mock. pr. par. *jeering;* past, *jeered: s. jeerer:* adv. *jeeringly.*
JEHO'VAH. *s.* God, in the Hebrew language.
JEJU'NE. adj. Empty, vacant, hungry, not saturated, unaffecting. s. *jejuneness, jejunity.*
JEL'LY. *s.* Any thing brought to a glutinous and viscous state. pl. *jellies.* adj. *jellied.*
JEN'NET. *s.* A Spanish horse.
JEOP'ARDY. *s.* Hazard, danger, peril. v. *jeopardize;* pr. par. *jeopardizing;* past, *jeopardized.*
JERK. *v.* To strike with a quick, smart blow; to pull suddenly. pr. par. *jerking;* past, *jerked: s. jerk, jerker.*
JER'KIN. *s.* A jacket; a close waistcoat.
JESS. *s.* A short strap of leather, tied about the legs of a hawk, with which it is held on the hand. pl. *jesses:* part. adj. *jessed.*
JES'SAMINE. *s.* A fragrant flower.
JEST. *v.* To joke; to make merry by words or actions. pr. par. *jesting;* past, *jested: s. jest, jester:* adv. *jestingly.*
JES'UIT. *s.* One of a religious and learned order. s. *jesuitism:* adj. *jesuitic, jesuitical:* adv. *jesuitically*

JET. *s.* A beautiful fossil, of a fine, deep black colour; a spout or shoot of water. v. *jet;* pr. par. *jetting,* past, *jetted.*
JEW. *s.* A Hebrew, an Israelite. fem. *Jewess,* pl. *Jewesses:* adj. *Jewish.*
JEW'EL. *s.* Any ornament of great value; commonly, such as are adorned with precious stones; a precious stone. v. *jewel:* s. *jeweller.*
JEWS'-HARP. *s.* A trump; a kind of musical instrument, held between the teeth.
JIF'FY. *s.* An instant.
JIG. *s.* A light, careless dance; a song. v. *jig;* pr. par. *jigging,* past, *jigged.*
JILT. *s.* A woman who gives her lover hopes, and deceives him. v. *jilt;* pr. par. *jilting;* past, *jilted.*
JIN'GLE. *v.* To clink; to sound with a kind of sharp rattle. pr. par. *jingling;* past, *jingled: s. jingle.*
JOB. *s.* Trifling work; a piece of chance work; a piece of labour undertaken at a stated price; a low, mean, lucrative affair; a sudden stab with a sharp instrument. v. *job;* pr. par. *jobbing;* past, *jobbed:* s. *jobber.*
JOCK'EY. *s.* One who rides horses in a race; one who deals in horses; a cheat. v. *jockey;* pr. par. *jockeying;* past, *jockeyed.*
JOCOSE'. adj. Merry, jocular. s. *jocoseness:* adv. *jocosely.*
JOC'ULAR. adj. Used in jest: merry. s. *jocularity:* adv. *jocularly.*
JO'CUND. adj. Merry, gay. adv. *jocundly:* s *jocundity.*
JOG. *v.* To push; to shake by a sudden impulse; to give notice by a sudden push; to travel slowly. pr. par. *jogging;* past, *jogged:* s. *jogger.*
JOHN-DO'RY. *s.* A kind of fish.
JOIN. *v.* To grow to; to unite; to close. pr. par. *joining;* past, *joined*

214

JOIN'ER. *s.* One whose trade is to make utensils of wood compacted. *s. joiner, joinery.*

JOINT. *s.* Articulation of limbs; hinge. *v. joint;* pr. par. *jointing;* past, *jointed.*

JOINT. *adj.* Shared amongst many; united in the same possessions. adv. *jointly.*

JOIN'TURE. *s.* The wife's estate.

JOIST. *s.* The secondary beam of a floor. *v. joist;* pr. par. *joisting;* past, *joisted.*

JOKE. *s.* A jest. *v. joke;* pr. par. *joking;* past, *joked:* adv. *jokingly.*

JOL'LY. *adj.* Gay, merry, plump, handsome. *s. jollity:* adv. *jollily.*

JOL'LY-BOAT. *s.* The small boat of a ship.

JOLT. *v.* To shake as a carriage on rough ground. pr. par. *jolting;* past, *jolted:* s. *jolt, jolter.*

JONQUILLE. *s.* A species of daffodil.

JOS'TLE. *v.* To justle; to rush against. pr. par. *jostling;* past, *jostled:* s. *jostler.*

JOT. *s.* A point, a tittle; the least quantity assignable.

JOUR'NAL. *s.* A diary; an account of daily transactions. *s. journalist:* v. *journalize;* pr. par. *journalizing;* past, *journalized.*

JOUR'NEY. *s.* The travel of a day; passage from place to place. *v. journey;* past, *journeyed.*

JOUR'NEYMAN. *s.* A hired workman; formerly a workman hired by the day. pl. *journeymen.*

JOUR'NEYWORK. *s.* Work done by the day.

JOUST. *s.* Jilt; tournament, mock fight. *v. joust;* pr. par. *jousting;* past, *jousted.*

JO'VIAL. *adj.* Gay, merry, cheerful. *s. jovialty:* adv. *jovially.*

JOWL. *s.* The face or cheek; the head of a fish.

JOY. *s.* Gayety, merriment; the passion, produced by any happy occurrence. *v. joy:* s. *joyfulness:* adj. *joyful, joyous.* adv. *joyfully,* *joyously:* adj. *joyless:* adv. *joylessly.*

JU'BILEE. *s.* A public festivity; a time of rejoicing. adj. *jubilant.*

JUDA'ICAL. *adj.* Jewish; belonging to the Jews. adv. *judaically.* *s. judaism.*

JUDGE. *v.* To decide; to form or give an opinion. pr. par. *judging;* past, *judged:* s. *judgment, judger.* adj. *judicatory, judicial:* adv. *judicially.*

JU'DICATURE. *s.* Power of distributing justice; court of justice.

JUDI'CIAL. *adj.* Practised in the distributing of public justice. ad*v. judicially: s. judiciary,* pl. *judiciaries.*

JUDI'CIOUS. *adj.* Prudent, wise skilful. *s. judiciousness:* adv. *judiciously.*

JUG. *s.* A large drinking vessel.

JUG'GLE. *v.* To play tricks, by sleight of hand. pr. par. *juggling,* past, *juggled:* s. *juggler:* adv. *jugglingly.*

JUG'ULAR. *adj.* Belonging to the throat.

JUICE. *s.* The liquor, sap, or water, of plants and fruits; the fluid in animal bodies. adj. *juicy, juiceless* *s. juiciness.*

JU'LAP. *s.* A kind of medicine.

JULY'. *s.* The seventh month o the year, so called from Julius Cæsar.

JUM'BLE. *v.* To mix violently and confusedly together. pr. par. *jumbling;* past, *jumbled:* s. *jumble, jumbler.*

JUMP. *v.* To leap, to skip. pr. par. *jumping;* past, *jumped:* s. *jump, jumper.*

JUNC'TION. *s.* Act of joining; union; coalition.

JUNC'TURE. *s.* The line at which two things are joined together, critical point or article of time.

JUNE. *s.* The sixth month of the year.

JU'NIOR. *s.* One younger than another. s. *juniority.*

JUN—JUR

JU'NIPER. s. A kind of tree.
JUNK'ET. s. A sweetmeat; a stolen entertainment.
JUN'TA, JUN'TO. s. A cabal; a congress of statesmen; a council.
JU'PITER. s. The chief amongst the heathen Gods; one of the planets.
JURID'ICAL. adj. Acting in the distribution of justice. adv. *juridically.*
JURISDIC'TION. s. Legal authority; extent of power; district to which any authority extends. adj. *jurisdictive.*
JURISPRU'DENCE. s. The science of law. adj. *jurisprudent.*
JU'RIST. s. One skilled in the science of law.
U'RY. s. A company of men, sworn to deliver a true verdict. pl. *juries:* s. *juror, juryman,* pl. *jurymen.*

JUS—JUX

JUST. adj. Equitable; honest, exact, true. s. *justice, justness:* adv. *justly.*
JUSTI'CIARY. s. An administrator of justice; the bench of judges. pl. *justiciaries.*
JUS'TIFY. v. To clear from imputed guilt; to defend. pr. par. *justifying;* past, *justified:* s. *justifier, justificator.*
JUS'TLE, JOS'TLE. v. To encounter, to clash. pr. par. *justling* past, *justled:* s. *justler.*
JUT. v. To push or shoot into prominences; to come beyond the main bulk; to run against. pr. par. *jutting;* past, *jutted.*
JU'VENILE. adj. Youthful, young s. *juvenility,* pl. *juvenilities.*
JUXTAPOSI'TION. s. Apposition: act of placing together; state of being placed by each other.

K

KAI—KEG

KAIL. s. A kind of cabbage.
KAL'ENDAR. s. An account of time.
KANGAROO'. s. An animal of South Wales.
KEDGE. v. To bring a ship up or down a narrow river, against the wind, by means of an anchor ahead. pr. par. *kedging;* past, *kedged.*
KEEL. s. The bottom of a ship. s. *keelage.*
KEEL'SON. s. The piece of timber in a ship next to her keel.
KEEN. adj. Sharp, severe, piercing. s. *keenness;* adv. *keenly.*
KEEP. v. To retain; to preserve; to tend; to have care of. pr. par. *keeping;* past, *kept:* s. *keep, keeper.*
KEEP'SAKE. s. A gift, in token of remembrance.
KEEVE. s. A large tub, used chiefly by bleachers.
KEG s. A small barrel. part. adj. *kegged.*

KEL—KET

KELP. s. A kind of sea-plant.
KEL'PY, KEL'PIE. s. A supposed spirit of the waters. pl. *kelpies, kelpies.*
KEN. v. To see at a distance; to descry; to know. pr. par. *kenning;* past, *kenned:* s. *ken.*
KEN'NEL. s. A place for dogs; the hole of a fox, or other beast; the water-course of a street. v. *kennel;* pr. par. *kenneling;* past, *kenneled.*
KEPT. Pret. and past par. of the v. *to keep.*
KER'NEL. s. The edible substance contained in a shell; any thing included in a husk or integument.
KER'SEY. s. Coarse stuff.
KETCH. s. A heavy ship, as a bomb-ketch; a vessel with two masts, usually from 100 to 250 tons burthen. pl. *ketches.*
KET'TLE. s. A vessel for boiling liquids.

KETTLE-DRUM. s. A drum, of which the head is spread over a body of brass or copper.

KEY. s. An instrument used to open a lock; the parts of a musical instrument which are struck with the fingers; a certain tone, to which every composition of music ought to be adapted.

KEY'-STONE. s. The middle stone of an arch.

KIBE. s. An ulcerated chilblain.

KICK. v. To strike with the foot. pr. par. *kicking;* past, *kicked:* s. *kick, kicker.*

KICK'-SHAW. s. Something uncommon, fantastical, or ridiculous.

KID. s. The young of a goat. v. *kid;* pr. par. *kidding;* past, *kidded.*

KID'NAP. v. To steal human beings. pr. par. *kidnapping;* past, *kidnapped:* s *kidnapper.*

KID'NEY. s. One of the intestines.

KID'NEYBEAN. s. A kind of leguminous plant.

KILL. v. To deprive of life. pr. par. *killing;* past, *killed:* s. *killer.*

KILN. s. A kind of stove. v. *kilndry;* pr. par. *kilndrying;* past, *kilndried.*

KIM'BO. s. The arms are said to be *a-kimbo,* when the hands are placed upon the hips.

KIN. s. Relation, either of consanguinity or affinity; a relation. s. *kindred.*

KIND. s. Race; generical class; particular nature; sort.

KIND. adj. Benevolent; favourable; beneficent. s. *kindness:* adv. *kindly.*

KIND'HEARTED. adj. Having great benevolence.

KIN'DLE. v. To set on fire; to inflame. pr. par. *kindling;* past, *kindled:* s. *kindler.*

KINE. s. An old plural for cow.

KING. s. A monarch; a supreme governor. adj. *kinglike:* adv. *kingly:* s. *kingdom.*

KING'CRAFT. s. The art of governing.

KING'FISHER. s. A species of bird.

KING'S-E'VIL. s. A disorder, called also scrofula

KINS'MAN. s. A man of the same race or family. pl. *kinsmen.*

KINS'WOMAN. s. A woman of the same race or family. pl. *kinswomen.*

KIRK. s. An old Scotch word for church.

KIR'TLE. s. A garment. part. adj *kirtled.*

KISS. s. Salute given by joining lips, pl. *kisses:* v. *kiss;* pr. par. *kissing;* past, *kissed:* s. *kisser.*

KIT. s. A large bottle; a diminutive fiddle; a small wooden vessel; a milking-pail, like a churn.

KITCH'EN. s. The room where provisions are cooked. s. *kitchen-garden, kitchen-maid, kitchen-stuff, kitchen-work.*

KITE. s. A bird of prey; a fictitious bird made of paper.

KITES'FOOT. s. A kind of plant.

KITH. s. Acquaintance, (used by the Scotch.)

KIT'TEN. s. A young cat. v. *kitten,* pr. par. *kittening;* past, *kittened.*

KNACK. s. A petty contrivance; a toy; a readiness; an habitual facility.

KNAP'SACK. s. The bag which a soldier carries on his back; a bag of provisions.

KNARL'ED. adj. Knotted.

KNAVE. s. A petty rascal; a scoundrel; a card with a knave painted on it. s. *knavery, knavishness:* adj. *knavish:* adv. *knavishly.*

KNEAD. v. To beat or mingle an stuff or substance,—as dough. pr. par. *kneading;* past, *kneaded:* s. *kneader.*

KNEE. s. The joint of the leg, where it is joined to the thigh.

KNEEL. v. To perform the act of genuflection; to rest on the knee. pr. par. *kneeling;* past, *kneeled.*

KNELL. s. The sound of a bell, rung at a funeral.

KNICK'-KNACK. *s.* Any trifle or toy.
KNIFE. *s.* An edged instrument used for cutting. pl. *knives.*
KNIGHT. *s.* A man advanced to a certain degree of military rank. In England, knighthood confers the title of Sir. v. *knight;* pr. par. *knighting;* past, *knighted:* adv. *knightly:* s. *knighthood.*
KNIGHT-ER'RANT. *s.* A wandering knight; one who went about, in quest of adventures. s. *knight-errantry.*
KNIT. *v.* To weave without a loom; to unite. pr. par. *knitting;* past, *knitted:* adj. *knit:* s. *knitter.*
KNOB. *s.* A protuberance; any part bluntly arising above the rest. adj. *knubbed, knobby.*
KNOCK. *v.* To clash; to be driven suddenly together; to beat, as at a door, for admittance. pr. par. *knocking;* past, *knocked:* s. *knocker.*
KNOLL. *s.* A little round hill; the top or cope of a mountain or hill.
KNOP. *s.* The bud of a flower; any protuberance or bunch. adj. *knopped.*
KNOT. *s.* A complication of a cord or string, &c. v. *knot;* pr. par. *knotting;* past, *knotted:* s. *knottiness:* adj. *knotty.*
KNOW. *v.* To perceive with certainty; to be informed of; to distinguish; to recognise. pr. par. *knowing;* past, *known:* adv. *knowingly.*
KNOWL'EDGE. *s.* Certain perception; learning; illumination of the mind.
KNUCK'LE. *s.* The joints of the fingers, protuberant when the fingers close; the knee-joint of a calf. v. *knuckle;* pr. par. *knuckling;* past, *knuckled.*
KO'RAN, AL'CO'RAN. *s.* The book containing the precepts of Mahomet.

L

LAB'DANUM. *s.* A kind of resin.
LA'BEL. *s.* A small slip; a small slip of writing; any thing appendant to a larger writing. v. *label;* pr. par. *labeling;* past, *labeled.*
LA'BIAL. *adj.* Uttered by the lips. part. adj. *labiated.*
LABOR'ATORY. *s.* A chymist's work-room. pl. *laboratories.*
LABO'RIOUS. *adj.* Diligent in work; requiring labour. s. *laboriousness:* adv. *laboriously.*
LA'BOUR. *s.* The act of doing what requires a painful exertion of strength; pains; toil. v. *labour;* pr. par. *labouring;* past, *laboured:* s. *labourer.*
LAB'YRINTH. *s.* A maze; a place formed with inextricable windings. adj. *labyrinthian.*
LABUR'NUM. *s.* A shrub of the cytisus kind.

LACE. *s.* A string; a cord; ornaments of fine thread, curiously woven; textures of thread, with gold or silver. v. *lace;* pr. par. *lacing;* past, *laced.*
LA'CERATE. *v.* To tear, to rend pr. par. *lacerating;* past, *lacerated.* s. *laceration:* adj. *lacerable, lacerative.*
LA'CHRYMAL. *adj.* Generating tears.
LACHRYM'ATORY. *s.* A vessel in which tears were gathered, in honour of the dead. pl. *lachrymatories.*
LACK. *v.* To want. pr. par. *lacking;* past, *lacked:* s. *lack, lacker,* (little used.)
LACK'BRAIN. *s.* A person that wants wit.
LACK'ER. *s.* A kind of varnish. v

lacker; pr. par. *lackering;* past, *lackered.*
LACK'EY. *s.* An attending servant; a foot-boy.
LACON'IC. *adj.* Short, concise. adv. *laconically:* s. *laconism.*
LAC"TEAL, LAC"TEOUS. *adj.* Milky.
LACTIF'EROUS. *adj.* Conveying or bringing milk.
LAD. *s.* A boy; a stripling, in familiar language.
LAD'DER. *s.* A frame made with steps placed between two upright pieces.
LADE. *v.* To load, to freight. pr. par. *lading;* past, *laded:* s. *lading.*
LA'DLE. *s.* A large spoon.
LA'DY. *s.* A woman of high rank: —the title of lady properly belongs to the wives of knights, and all titled personages of every superior rank; to the daughters of earls, and of nobles of higher rank. pl. *ladies:* adj. *ladylike:* s. *ladyship.*
LA'DY-DAY. *s.* The day on which the annunciation of the blessed Virgin is celebrated.
LA'DYSLIPPER. *s.* A kind of plant.
LAG. *v.* To loiter; to move slowly. pr. par. *lagging;* past, *lagged:* s. *lagger.*
LA'IC. *s.* One of the people, distinct from the clergy. adj. *laical.*
LAIR. *s.* The couch of a boar, or wild beast.
LAIRD. *s.* The lord of a manor, in the Scottish dialect.
LA'ITY. *s.* The people, as distinguished from the clergy. pl. *laities.*
LAKE. *s.* A large diffusion of inland water; a middle colour, between ultramarine and vermilion. adj. *laky.*
LAMB. *s.* A young sheep. adj. *lamblike:* v. *lamb;* pr. par. *lambing;* past, *lambed.*
LAM'BENT. *adj.* Playing about; gliding over without harm.
LAMB'KIN. *s.* A little lamb.

LAME. *adj.* Crippled; disabled in the limbs; imperfect; unsatisfactory. v. *lame;* pr. par. *laming;* past, *lamed:* s. *lameness:* adv. *lamely.*
LAMENT'. *v.* To bewail; to mourn; to bemoan. pr. par. *lamenting,* past, *lamented;* s. *lament, lamentation:* adj. *lamentable:* adv. *lamentably.*
LAM'INA. *s.* A thin plate; one coat laid over another. adj. *laminated.*
LAM'MAS. *s.* A festival which occurs on the first of August.
LAMP. *s.* A light made with oil and a wick; the vessel in which the light is contained.
LAMP'BLACK. *s.* A kind of black substance, made from smoke.
LAMPOON'. *s.* Personal satire, written for the purpose of vexing. v. *lampoon;* pr. par. *lampooning;* past, *lampooned:* s. *lampooner.*
LAM'PREY. *s.* A fish like the eel.
LANCE. *s.* A long spear. s. *lancer.*
LANCE. *v.* To pierce; to cut; to open with a lancet. pr. par. *lancing;* past, *lanced.*
LAN'CET. *s.* A small, pointed, surgical instrument.
LAND. *s.* A country; a region, distinct from other countries; earth, distinct from water. v. *land;* pr par. *landing;* past, *landed.*
LANDAU'. *s.* A coach, of which the top may be occasionally opened.
LAND'FALL. *s.* In naval language, the first land discovered after a voyage.
LAND'GRAVE. *s.* A German title of dominion. fem. *landgravine.*
LAND'HOLDER. *s.* One who holds lands.
LAND'LADY. *s.* A woman who has lands or houses, and has tenants under her; the mistress of an inn. pl. *landladies.*
LAND'LORD. *s.* One who owns lands or houses, and has tenants under him, the master of an inn
LAND'MARK. *s.* Any thing set up to preserve the boundaries of lands.

LAND'SCAPE. *s.* The prospect of a country; a picture representing that prospect.

LANE. *s.* A narrow way between hedges; a narrow street.

LANG'UAGE. *s.* Human speech; the tongue of one nation as distinct from others. adj. *languaged.*

LANG'UISH. *v.* To grow feeble; to pine away; to look with softness or tenderness. pr. par. *languishing;* past, *languished:* adv. *languishingly:* adj. *languid:* s. *languor.*

LANIG'EROUS. *adj.* Bearing wool.

LANK. *adj.* Loose; not filled up; not fat, not plump. s. *lankness:* adv. *lankly.*

LANSQUENET. *s.* A common foot-soldier; a game at cards.

LAN'TERN. *s.* A transparent case for a candle; a kind of little dome, raised over the roof of a building.

LANU'GINOUS. *adj.* Downy; covered with a soft hair.

LAN'YARDS. *s.* Short pieces of cord, fastened to several machines in a ship.

LAP. *v.* To wrap or twist around; to fold; to lick up. pr. par. *lapping;* past, *lapped:* s. *lap.*

LAP. *s.* The part of the clothes that is spread over the knees. s. *lapdog, lapful.*

LAPEL'. *s.* That part of the coat which laps over.

LAP'IDARY, LAP'IDIST. *s.* One who finishes or deals in stones or gems. pl. *lapidaries.*

LAPIDES'CENT. *adj.* Growing or turning to stone. s. *lapidescence.*

LA PIS. *s.* A stone.

LA PIS-LAZU'LI. *s.* The azure stone; a copper ore.

LAP'PET. *s.* The parts of a head-dress which hang loose.

LAPSE. *s.* Flow, fall, slip, failure of a bequest. *v. lapse;* pr. par. *lapsing;* past, *lapsed.*

LAP'WING. *s.* A clamorous bird with long wings.

LAR'BOARD. *adj.* The left hand side of a ship, when you stand with your face to the head; opposed to starboard.

LAR'CENY. *s.* Theft, without violence. pl. *larcenies.*

LARCH. *s.* A species of coniferous tree, of the pine genus. pl. *larches.*

LARD. *s.* The grease of swine. v *lard;* pr. par. *larding;* past, *larded.*

LAR'DER. *s.* The room where meat is kept.

LARGE. *adj.* Wide, extensive, plentiful, diffuse, without restraint. s. *largeness:* adv. *largely.*

LAR'GESS. *s.* A present, a gift, a bounty. pl. *largesses.*

LAR'GO, LARGHET'TO. *s.* Musical terms, denoting a slow movement.

LARK. *s.* A small singing bird.

LARK'SPUR. *s.* A kind of plant.

LA'RUM. *s.* Alarm; an instrument that makes a noise at a certain hour.

LAR'VATED. *adj.* Masked.

LAR'YNX. *s.* The upper part of the trachea.

LASCAR. *s.* A native seaman or gunner, of India.

LASCI'VIOUS. *adj.* Lewd; lustful; wanton. s. *lasciviousness:* adv. *lasciviously.*

LASH. *s.* A stroke with any thing pliant and tough; the thong or point of a whip. v. *lash;* pr. par. *lashing;* past, *lashed:* s. *lasher.*

LASS. *s.* A girl; a maid. pl. *lasses.*

LAS'SITUDE. *s.* Weariness, fatigue.

LAST. *adj.* Latest; that which follows all the rest in time; hindmost; lowest. adv. *lastly.*

LAST. *v.* To endure; to continue. pr. par. *lasting;* past, *lasted:* s. *lastingness:* adv. *lastingly.*

LAST. *s.* The mould on which shoes are formed.

LATCH. *s.* A catch of a door. pl. *latches:* v. *latch;* pr. par. *latching;* past, *latched.*

LATCH'ET. *s.* The string that fastens a shoe.
LATE. *adj.* Contrary to early; slow; tardy, &c. *s. lateness:* adv. *lately.*
LA'TENT. *adj.* Hidden; concealed; secret. *s. latency:* adv. *latently.*
LATERAL. *adj.* Relating or belonging to the side. *s. laterality:* adv. *laterally.*
LATH. *s.* A long thin piece of wood. *v. lath;* pr. par. *lathing;* past, *lathed:* adj. *lathy.*
LATHE. *s.* The revolving tool of a turner.
LATH'ER. *v.* To make a foam; to cover with foam of water or soap. pr. par. *lathering;* past, *lathered: s. lather.*
LAT'IN. *s.* The Latin language. *s. Latinism, Latinist, Latinity:* v. *Latinize;* pr. par. *Latinizing;* past, *Latinized.*
LAT'ITANT. *adj.* Concealed; lying hid. *s. latitancy, latitation.*
LAT'ITUDE. *s.* Breadth; width; room; space, the extent of the earth or heavens, reckoning from the equator to either pole; freedom from settled rules; laxity.
LATITUDINA'RIAN. *adj.* Not restrained; not confined.
LAT'TER. *adj.* Happening after something else; modern; lately done or past. adv. *latterly.*
LAT'TICE. *s.* A reticulated window; a window formed of gratework. *v. lattice;* pr. par. *latticing;* past, *latticed.*
LAUD. *v.* To praise. pr. par. *lauding;* past, *lauded: s. laud, lauder, laudation:* adj. *laudative, laudatory.*
LAUD'ABLE. *adj.* Praiseworthy; commendable. *s. laudability:* adv. *laudably.*
LAUD'ANUM. *s.* A soporific tincture.
LAUGH. *v.* To make that noise which sudden merriment excites. pr. par. *laughing;* past, *laughed: s. laugh, laugher, laughter:* adj. *laughable:* adv. *laughingly.*

LAUGH'INGSTOCK. *s.* An object of ridicule.
LAUNCH. *v.* To force a vessel into the sea; to rove at large. pr par. *launching;* past, *launched: s. launch.*
LAUN'DRY. *s.* The room in which clothes are washed; the act or state of washing. pl. *laundries: s. laundress,* pl. *laundresses.*
LAU'REATE. *adj.* Decked or invested with laurel. *v. laureate;* pr. par *laureating;* past, *laureated: s. laureation.*
LAU'REL. *s.* A species of shrub. adj. *laureled.*
LAURUSTI'NUS. *s.* A species of flowering shrub.
LA'VA. *s.* Liquid and vitrified matter discharged from a volcano.
LA'VATORY. *s.* A wash. pl. *lavatories.*
LAVE. *v.* To wash. pr. par. *laving,* past, *laved. s. laver.*
LAV'ENDER. *s.* A species of aromatic plant.
LAV'ISH. *v.* To scatter with profusion; to waste. pr. par. *lavishing,* past, *lavished: s. lavisher, lavishment, lavishness:* adj. *lavish:* adv *lavishly.*
LAW. *s.* A rule of action; a decree a statute or custom publicly established; judicial process. adj *lawful: s. lawyer, lawfulness, lawgiver:* adv. *lawfully:* adj. *lawless s. lawlessness:* adv. *lawlessly.*
LAWN. *s.* An open space between woods; fine linen. adj. *lawny.*
LAX. *adj.* Loose; not confined. *s. lax, laxation, laxity:* adj. *laxative.*
LAY. Pret of the v. *to lie.*
LAY. *v.* To place, to put, to wager, &c. pr. par. *laying;* past, *laid.*
LAY. *s.* Grassy ground; meadow; ground unploughed, more properly written *lea;* a song, a poem.
LAY. *adj.* Not clerical; regarding or belonging to the people. *s layman,* pl. *laymen.*
LAY'ER. *s.* A stratum or row; a bed
LA'ZAR. *s.* One deformed and nau-

seous with filthy and pestilential diseases.

LAZARET,TO. *s.* A house for the reception of the diseased.

LA'ZY. *adj.* Idle, sluggish, slow. *s. laziness;* adv. *lazily.*

LEA. *s.* An extensive plain.

LEAD. *v.* To guide by the hand; to conduct; to introduce by going first; to induce. pr. par. *leading;* past, *led: s. leader.*

LEAD. *s.* One of the metals.

LEAF. *s.* The green deciduous part of plants and flowers; a part of a book, containing two pages; any thing foliated or thinly beaten. pl. *leaves:* adj. *leafed, leafless, leafy.*

LEAGUE. *s.* A confederacy. v. *league;* pr. par. *leaguing;* past, *leagued: s. leaguer.*

LEAGUE. *s.* A measure of length, containing three miles.

LEAK. *s.* A breach or hole which lets in or emits water. v. *leak;* pr. par. *leaking;* past, *leaked: s. leakage, leakiness:* adj. *leaky.*

LEAN. *v.* To incline; to bend; to rest against. pr. par. *leaning;* past, *leaned.*

LEAN. *adj.* Not fat; meagre; wanting flesh. *s. leanness:* adv. *leanly.*

LEAP. *v.* To jump, to bound, to spring. pr. par. *leaping;* past, *leaped: s. leap, leaper.*

LEAP-FROG. *s.* A play of children, in which they imitate the jump of frogs.

LEAP-YEAR or BISSEX'TILE. *s.* Every fourth year. A common year has 365 days; leap-year, 366. In leap-year, February has 29 days, but in other years, only 28.

LEARN. *v.* To gain the knowledge or skill of. pr. par. *learning;* past, *learned: s. learner, learning:* adv. *learnedly.*

LEASE. *s.* A contract, by which a temporary possession is granted of houses, lands, &c. v. *lease;* pr. par. *leasing;* past, *leased: s. leasehold.*

LEASH. *s.* A leather thong; a band wherewith to tie any thing; a brace and a half. pl. *leashes.*

LEAST. *adj.* The superlative of *little.*

LEATH'ER. *s.* Dressed hides of animals. adj. *leathern.*

LEAVE. *s.* Grant of permission; allowance; farewell.

LEAVE. *v.* To quit, to forsake, to depart from; to have remaining at death; not to deprive of; to bequeath. pr. par. *leaving;* past, *left.*

LEAV'EN. *s.* Ferment mixed with any body, to make it light; any mixture which makes a general change in the mass. v. *leaven;* pr. par. *leavening;* past, *leavened.*

LEAVES. *s.* The plural of *leaf.*

LEAV'INGS. *s.* Remnant; relics, refuse :—it has no singular.

LECH'EROUS. *adj.* Provoking lust; lewd. *s. lechery:* adv. *lecherously.*

LEC'TURE. *s.* A discourse pronounced upon any subject; the act or practice of reading. v. *lecture;* pr. par. *lecturing;* past, *lectured: s. lecturer, lectureship.*

LED. Pret. and past par. of the v. *to lead.*

LEDGE. *s.* A layer; a stratum; a ridge rising above, or projecting beyond the rest.

LEDG'ER. *s.* An account-book. See LEGER.

LEE. *s.* That side which is opposite to the wind. adj. *leeward.*

LEECH. *s.* A mean professor of the art of healing; a kind of small water serpent. v. *leech;* pr. par *leeching;* past, *leeched.*

LEEK. *s.* A kind of plant.

LEER. *s.* Oblique view; a laboured cast of countenance. v. *leer;* pr. par. *leering;* past, *leered:* adv. *leeringly.*

LEES. *s.* Dregs; sediment.

LEET. *s.* A law-day; a minor court of jurisdiction.

LEFT. Pret. and past par. of the v *to leave.*

LEFT. *adj.* Sinistrous; not right.

LEG. *s.* The limb between the knee and the foot. adj. *legged.*

LEG'ACY. *s.* A bequest made by will. pl. *legacies.*

LE'GAL. *adj.* Done or conceived according to law; lawful. s. *legality*, pl. *legalities:* v. *legalize;* pr. par. *legalizing;* past, *legalized:* adv. *legally.*

LEG ATE. *s.* An ambassador; ambassador from the pope. s. *legation* · adj. *legatine.*

LEGATEE'. *s.* One who has a legacy left him.

LEGA'TION. *s.* Deputation, commission, embassy.

LE'GEND. *s.* A chronicle or register; any memorial or relation; any inscription, particularly on medals or coins. adj. *legendary.*

LE'GER. *s.* In commercial language, the book into which accounts are finally posted.

LEGERDEMAIN' *s* Sleight of hand; juggle.

LEGER'ITY. *s.* Lightness; nimbleness. pl. *legerities.*

LE GIBLE. *adj.* Such as can be read. s. *legibility:* adv. *legibly.*

LE'GION. *s.* A body of Roman soldiers, consisting of about five thousand; any great number. adj. *legionary.*

LE'GISLATE. *v.* To make laws. pr. par. *legislating;* past, *legislated:* s. *legislation, legislator, legislature;* adj. *legislative:* adv. *legislatively.*

LEGIT'IMATE. *adj.* Lawful; regular; born in wedlock. v. *legitimate;* pr. par. *legitimating;* past, *legitimated:* s. *legitimacy,* pl. *legitimacies, legitimation:* adv. *legitimately.*

LEGU MINOUS. *adj.* Belonging to pulse; consisting of pulse.

LEIS'URE. *s.* Freedom from business or hurry. adj. *leisure:* adv. *leisurely.*

LEM'ON. *s.* A species of fruit.

LEMONA'DE. *s.* A liquor made of water, sugar, and the juice of lemons.

LEND. *v.* To afford or supply, on condition of repayment or return pr. par. *lending;* past, *lent:* s. *lender.*

LENGTH. *s.* The extent of any thing material, from end to end; horizontal extension; extent of duration or space. v. *lengthen;* pr. par. *lengthening;* past, *lengthened:* adv. *lengthways, lengthwise:* adj. *lengthy,* tediously long: s. *lengthiness.*

LE'NIENT. *adj.* Assuasive; softening; mild. adv. *leniently.*

LEN'ITY. *s.* Mildness, mercy, tenderness. adj. *lenitive:* v. *lenify,* pr. par. *lenifying;* past, *lenified.*

LENS. *s.* A glass spherically convex on both sides. pl. *lenses.*

LENT. Pret. and past par. of the v. *to lend.*

LENT. *s.* The quadragesimal fast; a time of abstinence. adj. *lenten.*

LENTIC'ULAR, LEN'TIFORM. *adj.* Doubly convex; of the form of a lens.

LENTI'GINOUS. *adj.* Scurfy; furfuraceous.

LEN'TIL. *s.* A kind of plant.

LE'O. *s.* The fifth sign of the zodiac.

LEOP'ARD. *adj.* A spotted beast of prey.

LE'PER. *s.* One infected with a leprosy. s. *leprosy:* adj. *leprous.*

LEP'ORINE. *adj.* Belonging or relating to a hare.

LESS. *adj.* The comparative of little. v. *lessen;* pr. par. *lessening;* past, *lessened.*

LESSEE'. *s.* The person to whom a lease is given.

LES'SON. *s.* Any thing read or repeated to or by a teacher; precept

LES'SOR. *s.* One who grants a lease.

LEST. One of the conjunctions.

LET. *v.* To allow; to permit; to put to hire; to grant to a tenant. pr. par. *letting;* past, *let.*

LET. *s.* Hindrance, impediment.

LETH'ARGY. *s.* A morbid drowsiness. pl. *lethargies;* adj. *lethargic* adv. *lethargically.*

LE'THEAN. *adj.* Oblivious; causing oblivion.

LET'TER *s.* A character in the alphabet; a written message; an epistle; the literal meaning. v. *letter;* pr. par. *lettering;* past, *lettered.*

LET'TER-PRESS. *s.* Print; what is given in types from a written copy.

LET'TUCE. *s.* A kind of plant.

LEVANT'. *s.* The east, particularly those coasts of the Mediterranean east of Italy. adj. *levantine.*

LEV'EE. *s.* The concourse of those who crowd round a man of power.

LEV'EL. *adj.* Even, plane, flat, smooth, horizontal. v. *level;* pr. par. *leveling;* past, *leveled:* s. *level, leveler, levelness.*

LE'VER. *s.* The second mechanical power.

LEV'ERET. *s.* A young hare.

LEV'EROCK. *s.* In Scotland, denotes the lark.

LEVI'ATHAN. *s.* Some very large fish.

LEV'IGATE. *v.* To polish; to smooth; to rub or grind to an impalpable powder. pr. par. *levigating;* past, *levigated:* s. *levigation.*

LE'VITE. *s.* One of the tribe of Levi; a Jewish priest. adj. *levitical.*

LEV'ITY. *s.* Lightness; inconstancy; idle pleasure. pl. *levities.*

LEV'Y. *v.* To raise; to raise supplies of money or men. pr. par. *levying;* past, *levied:* s. *levy,* pl. *levies.*

LEWD. *adj.* Wicked, dissolute, libidinous. s. *lewdness:* adv. *lewdly.*

LEXICOG'RAPHER. *s.* A writer of dictionaries. s. *lexicography,* pl. *lexicographies.*

LEX'ICON. *s.* A dictionary.

LI'ABLE. *adj.* Subject to; not exempt. s. *liability,* pl. *liabilities.*

LI'AR. *s.* One who tells a falsehood.

LIBA'TION. *s.* The act of pouring wine on the ground, in honour of some deity; the wine so poured.

LI'BEL. *s.* A defamatory writing; a lampoon; a declaration exhibited in a civil court. v. *libel;* pr. par. *libeling;* past, *libeled:* s. *libeler* adj. *libelous:* adv. *libelously.*

LIB'ERAL. *adj.* Generous; bountiful; free to excess. s. *liberality,* pl. *liberalities:* adv. *liberally.*

LIB'ERATE. *v.* To free; to set free. pr. par. *liberating;* past, *liberated.* s. *liberation, liberator.*

LIB'ERTINE. *s.* One who lives without restraint or law; a rake. adj. *libertine:* s. *libertinism.*

LIB'ERTY. *s.* Freedom; exemption from tyranny; immunity; permission; part of a town, without the bounds of the corporate jurisdiction. pl. *liberties.*

LIBID'INOUS. *adj.* Lewd, lustful. s. *libidinist:* adv. *libidinously.*

LI'BRA. *s.* The seventh sign in the zodiac.

LI'BRARY. *s.* A large collection of books. pl. *libraries:* s. *librarian.*

LI'BRATE. *v.* To poise; to balance. pr. par. *librating;* past, *librated.* s. *libration:* adj. *libratory.*

LICE. *s.* The plural of *louse.*

LI'CENSE. *s.* Exorbitant liberty; contempt of legal and necessary restraint; leave, permission. v. *license;* pr. par. *licensing;* past, *licensed:* s. *licenser.*

LICEN'TIATE. *s.* One who has a license to practise any faculty or art.

LICEN'TIOUS. *adj.* Unrestrained by law or morality; presumptuous; unconfined. s. *licentiousness* adv. *licentiously.*

LICHEN. *s.* Liverwort.

LICK. *v.* To pass over with the tongue; to lap. pr. par. *licking,* past, *licked;* s. *lick, licker*

LICK. *s.* In the United States, means a place impregnated with salt, so as to attract quadrupeds to enjoy its savour.

LICK'ERISH, LICK'OROUS. *adj* Nice in the choice of food. s. *lickerishness.*

LIC'ORICE. *s.* A root of sweet taste.

LIC—LIG

LIC'TOR. *s.* A beadle who attended the Roman consuls.
LID. *s.* A cover for a pan, box, &c.
LIE. *s.* Any thing impregnated with some other body, as soap or salt.
LIE. *s.* A criminal falsehood; a charge of falsehood; a fiction. v. *lie;* pr. par. *lying;* past, *lied:* s. *liar.*
LIE. *v.* To rest horizontally; to lean upon, &c. pr. par. *lying;* past, *lain.*
LIEGE. *s.* A sovereign; superior lord. adj. *liege.*
LIEUTEN'ANT. *s.* A deputy; a second in rank. s. *lieutenancy,* pl. *lieutenancies.*
LIFE. *s* Union and co-operation of soul and body; vitality; animation. pl. *lives:* adj. *lifeless:* adv. *lifelessly:* s. *lifetime.*
LIFE'-GUARD. *s.* The guard of a king's person.
LIFT. *v.* To raise from the ground; to heave: to elevate. pr. par. *lifting;* past, *lifted:* s. *lift, lifter.*
LIG'AMENT. *s.* A band to tie parts together. adj. *ligamental.*
LIG'ATURE. *s.* Any thing tied round another; bandage. s. *ligation.*
LIGHT. *s.* The material medium of sight; that body by which we see. v. *light;* pr. par. *lighting;* past, *lit.*
LIGHT. *adj.* Not heavy; not burthensome; active; slight; gay; airy; bright; clear. s. *lightness:* adv. *lightly:* adj. *light-headed, light-hearted, light-minded.*
LIGHT'EN. *v.* To make light; to flash with thunder; to shine like lightning. pr. par. *lightning;* past, *lightened.*
LIGHT'ER. *s.* A large boat for unloading ships.
LIGHT'-HOUSE. *s.* A high building, at the top of which lights are hung, to guide ships at sea.
LIGHT'NING. *s.* The flash that attends thunder.
LIGHTS. *s.* The lungs; the organs of breathing: we say *lights* of other animals, and *lungs* of men.

LIG—LIM

LIG'NEOUS. *adj.* Made of wood, resembling wood.
LIG'NOUS. *adj.* Of a woody substance.
LIGNUM-VI'TÆ. *s.* Guaiacum; a very hard wood.
LIKE. *adj.* Resembling; having resemblance; equal. s. *likeness, likeliness:* adj. and adv. *likely.*
LIKE. *v.* To choose; to approve; to be agreeable to. pr. par. *liking* past, *liked:* s. *liking.*
LIKE'LIHOOD, LIKE'LINESS. *s* Appearance, show, probability.
LI'KEN. *v.* To represent as having resemblance; to compare. pr. par. *likening;* past, *likened.*
LIKE'WISE. *adj.* In like manner; also; moreover; too.
LI'LACH. *s.* A kind of tree.
LIL'Y. *s.* A plant, and also its flower. pl. *lilies:* adj. *lillied.*
LIMB. *s.* A member; a jointed or articulated part of animals; a bough. adj. *limbed.*
LIM'BER. *adj.* Flexible; easily bent. s. *limberness.*
LIM'BERS. *s.* In military language, two wheel carriages, having boxes for ammunition: and, in naval language, little square apertures cut in the timbers of a ship, to convey the bilge water to the pump.
LIM'BO. *s.* A feigned region bordering upon hell, in which there is neither pleasure nor pain; any place of misery or restraint. pl. *limboes.*
LIME. *s.* A viscous substance, for catching birds; matter of which mortar is made. v. *lime;* pr. par *liming;* past, *limed:* adj. *limy.*
LIME. *s.* A species of small lemon
LIME'-KILN. *s.* A kiln in which stones are burnt to lime.
LIME'-STONE. *s.* The stone of which lime is made.
LIM'IT. *s.* Bound; border; utmost reach. v. *limit;* pr. par. *limiting,* past, *limited:* s. *limitation.*

225

LIMN. *v.* To draw; to paint any thing. pr. par. *limning*. past, *limned:* s. *limner.*
LI'MOUS. *adj.* Muddy, slimy.
LIMP. *v.* To halt; to walk lamely. pr. par. *limping;* past, *limped:* s. *limp, limper:* adv. *limpingly.*
LIM'PID. *adj.* Clear; transparent. s. *limpidness, limpitude.*
LIN'DEN. *s.* The lime-tree.
LINE. *s.* Longitudinal extension; a slender string; that which has length without breadth, &c. &c. adj. *lineal:* adv. *lineally:* adj. *linear:* s. *lineation.*
LINE. *v.* To cover on the inside; to strengthen. pr. par. *lining;* past, *lined:* s. *lining.*
LIN'EAGE. *s.* Race; progeny; family, ascending or descending.
LIN'EAMENT. *s.* Feature; discriminating mark in the form.
LIN'EN. *s.* Cloth made of hemp or flax. s. *linendraper.*
LING. *s.* A kind of sea-fish.
LING'ER. *v.* To remain long in languor or pain; to hesitate; to be in suspense. pr par. *lingering;* past, *lingered:* s. *lingerer:* adv. *lingeringly.*
LINGUADEN'TAL. *adj.* Uttered by the joint action of the tongue and teeth.
LING'UIST. *s.* A person skilful in languages.
LIN'IMENT. *s.* Ointment, balsam.
LINK. *s.* A single ring of a chain; any thing doubled and closed together; a torch made of pitch and boards. v. *link;* pr. par. *linking;* past, *linked.*
LINK'-BOY. *s.* A boy that carries a torch, to accommodate passengers with light.
LIN'NET. *s.* A kind of small bird.
LIN'SEED. *s.* The seed of flax.
LIN'SEY-WOOL'SEY. *s.* Stuff made of linen and wool mixed.
LIN'STOCK. *s.* A kind of match, used in firing cannon.
LINT. *s.* Flax; linen scraped into a soft woolly substance.

LIN'TEL. *s.* That part of a doorframe which lies across the door posts, over head.
LI'ON. *s.* The most magnanimous of beasts. fem. *lioness*, pl. *lionesses.*
LIP. *s.* The outer part of the mouth; the edge of any thing. adj. *lipped.*
LIPOTH'YMY. *s.* A swoon; a fainting fit. adj. *lypothymous.*
LI'QUATE. *v.* To melt; to liquefy. pr. par. *liquating;* past, *liquated.* s. *liquation:* adj. *liquable.*
LI'QUEFY. *v.* To melt; to dissolve. pr. par. *liquefying;* past, *liquefied:* s. *liquefaction:* adj. *liquefiable.*
LIQUES'CENT. *adj.* Melting. s. *liquescency.*
LIQUEUR'. *s.* A cordial.
LI'QUID. *adj.* Fluid; dissolved. s. *liquid, liquidity.*
LI'QUIDATE. *v.* To clear away; to lessen debts. pr. par. *liquidating;* past, *liquidated:* s. *liquidation.*
LI'QUOR. *s.* Any thing liquid; any strong drink.
LI'QUORICE. *s.* See LICORICE.
LISP. *v.* To speak with too frequent appulses of the tongue to the teeth or palate. pr. par. *lisping;* past, *lisped;* s. *lisp, lisper:* adv. *lispingly.*
LIST. *s.* A roll; a catalogue; enclosed ground, in which tilts are run, and combats fought; a strip of cloth, next to the selvage.
LIST. *v.* To desire; to choose; to be pleased.
LIST. *v.* To enlist; to enrol or register; to retain and enrol soldiers; to enclose for combats; to hearken to; to listen. pr. par. *listing;* past, *listed*
LIS'TEN. *v.* To hear; to attend; to give attention. pr. par. *listening,* past, *listened:* s. *listener.*
LIST'LESS. *adj.* Without any determination to do one thing more than another; careless; heedless. s. *listlessness:* adv. *listlessly.*
LIT. Pret. of the v. *to light.*
LIT'ANY. *s* A form of supplicatory prayer. pl. *litanies.*

226

LIT'ERAL. *adj.* According to the primitive meaning; not figurative; following the letter or exact words. *s. literalist, literality:* adv. *literally.*

LIT'ERARY. *adj.* Respecting letters; appertaining to literature. *s. literature.*

LIT'ERATE. *adj.* Learned.

LITERA'TI. *s.* The learned.

LITH'ARGE. *s.* Lead vitrified, either alone or with a mixture of copper.

LITHOG'RAPHY. *s.* The art or practice of engraving upon stone.

LIT'IGATE. *v.* To contest in law. pr. par. *litigating;* past, *litigated: s. litigant, litigation:* adj. *litigant, litigious.*

LIT'TER. *s.* A kind of vehiculary bed; the straw laid under animals, or on plants; a brood of young; any number of things thrown sluttishly about. v. *litter;* pr. par. *littering;* past, *littered.*

LIT'TLE. *adj.* Small in quantity or extent; diminutive; unimportant. *s. littleness.*

LIT'URGY. *s.* Form of public prayers. adj. *liturgic, liturgical.*

LIVE. *v.* To be in a state of life; to exist; to be nourished, &c. pr. par. *living;* past, *lived: s. liver:* adj. *living.*

LIVE'LIHOOD. *s.* Support of life; maintenance.

LIVE'LY. *adj.* Brisk; vivacious; gay; airy; energetic. *s. liveliness.*

LIV'ER. *s.* One of the entrails.

LIV'ERY. *s.* The act of giving possession; state of being kept at a certain rate; the clothes given to servants; a particular dress. pl. *liveries.*

LIV'ID. *adj.* Discoloured, as with a blow; black and blue. *s. lividness, lividity.*

LI'VRE. *s.* A French coin, value about 18 cents.

LIXIV'IUM. *s.* Lie; water impregnated with alkaline salt, &c. adj. *lixivial, lixiviate, lixiviated.*

LIZ'ARD *s.* An animal resembling a serpent, with legs.

LO. *int.* Look, behold.

LOAD. *v.* To burthen; to freight; to encumber; to charge a gun. pr. par. *loading;* past, *loaded:* s. *loader.*

LOAD'-STAR. *s.* The pole-star; the cynosure.

LOAD'STONE. *s.* The magnet.

LOAF. *s.* A mass of bread; a mass of refined sugar. pl. *loaves.*

LOAM. *s.* Fat, unctuous, tenacious earth. adj. *loamy.*

LOATH. *adj.* Unwilling, not inclined, disliking. *s. loather, loathing.* adj. *loathsome: s. loathsomeness.*

LOATHE. *v.* To hate, to abhor, to consider with the disgust of satiety. pr. par. *loathing;* past, *loathed.*

LOAVES. *s.* The plural of *loaf.*

LOB'BY. *s.* A narrow passage in a house. pl. *lobbies.*

LOBE. *s.* A distinct part:—commonly used for a part of the lungs.

LOB'STER. *s.* A kind of crustaceous fish.

LO'CAL. *adj.* Having the properties of place; relating to place; confined to a particular place. *s. locality,* pl. *localities:* adv. *locally.*

LOCA'TE. *v.* To place; to fix in a particular place. pr. par. *locating,* past, *located: s. location.*

LOCH. *s.* A lake.

LOCK. *s.* An instrument used to fasten doors, &c. the part of a gun by which fire is struck; a chamber in a canal, for raising and lowering boats; a tuft. v. *lock;* pr. par *locking;* past, *locked.*

LOCOMO'TION. *s.* Act or power of changing place. adj. *locomotive*

LO'CUST. *s.* A devouring insect; a kind of tree.

LODGE. *v.* To place in a temporary habitation; to afford a temporary dwelling; to place; to fix; to lie flat. pr. par. *lodging;* past, *lodged. s. lodge, lodger, lodging.*

LODGE'MENT. *s.* Disposition or

227

coLocation in a certain place; possession of the enemy's work.

LOFT. *s.* The highest floor; rooms on high.

LOF'TY. *adj.* High; elevated; sublime; proud; haughty. *s. loftiness:* adv. *loftily.*

LOG. *s.* A shapeless bulky piece of wood; a piece of wood, which, with its line, serves to measure the course of a ship at sea.

LOG'ARITHMS. *s* The index of the ratios of numbers, one to another. adj. *logarithmic, logarithmical.*

LOG'-BOOK. *s.* A register of a ship's way, and other naval incidents.

LOG'GERHEAD. *s.* A dolt; a blockhead. adj. *loggerheaded.*

LO'GIC. *s.* The art of reasoning. adj. *logical:* adv. *logically:* s. *logician.*

LOGOM'ACHY. *s.* A contention in words; a contention about words.

LOG WOOD. *s.* A species of diewood.

LOIN. *s.* The back of an animal, carved out by the butcher.

LOI'TER. *v.* To linger; to lounge; to idle. pr. par. *loitering;* past, *loitered:* s. *loiterer.*

LOLL. *v.* To lean idly; to rest lazily against any thing; to hang out —used of the tongue. pr. par. *lolling;* past. *lolled:* s. *loller.*

LOL'LARD. *s.* A name given to the first religious reformers in England; one of the followers of Wicliffe.

LONE. *adj.* Solitary; unfrequented; single. s. *loneliness:* adv. *lonely.*

LONG. *adj.* Not short; extended; tedious. adj. *long-lived, long-suffering, long-tongued:* adv. *longways, longwise.*

LONG. *v.* To desire earnestly; to wish with eagerness continued. pr. par. *longing;* past, *longed:* s. *longing:* adv. *longingly.*

LONG'BOAT. *s.* The largest boat belonging to a ship.

LONGE. *s.* A thrust with a sword.

LONGEV'ITY. *s.* Length of life. pl. *longevities.*

LONGIM'ETRY. *s.* The art or practice of measuring distances.

LON'GITUDE. *s.* Length; the greatest dimension; the circumference of the earth, measured from any meridian; the distance of any part of the earth to the east or west of any place. adj. *longitudinal:* adv. *longitudinally.*

LONG'-WINDED. *adj.* Long-breathed; tedious.

LOO. *s.* A kind of game at cards. v. *loo;* pr. par. *looing;* past, *looed.*

LOOK. *v.* To direct the eye to or from any object; to expect; to seem. pr. par. *looking;* past, *looked:* s. *looker.*

LOOK'ING-GLASS. *s.* A reflecting mirror.

LOOM. *s.* The frame in which weavers work their cloth.

LOOM. *v.* To appear unnaturally large at sea. pr. par. *looming;* past, *loomed.*

LOON. *s.* A mean lazy fellow

LOOP. *s.* A double, through which a string or lace is drawn. v. *loop* pr. par. *looping;* past, *looped:* s. *loop-hole.*

LOOSE. *v.* To unbind; to untie; to relax. pr. par. *loosing;* past, *loosed.* s. *looseness:* adj. *loose:* adv. *loosely.*

LOOS'EN. *v.* To untie; to part; to separate. pr. par. *loosening;* past, *loosened.*

LOP. *v.* To cut or chop short. pr. par. *lopping;* past, *lopped* s. *lopper, loppings.*

LOQUA'CIOUS. *adj.* Talkative. s. *loquacity:* adv. *loquaciously.*

LORD. *s.* A monarch; a ruler; a master; a nobleman; a general name for a peer of England. v *lord;* pr. par. *lording;* past, *lorded:* s. *lordliness:* adj. *lord-like.* adv. *lordly:* s. *lordship.*

LORE. *s.* Instruction; knowledge

LOR'ICATE. *v.* To plate over. pr par. *loricating;* past, *loricated:* s *lorication.*

228

LOSE. *v.* To forfeit by unsuccessful contest; to forfeit as a penalty; to miss so as not to find. pr. par. *losing;* past, *lost:* s. *loss,* pl. *losses,* *loser.*

LOT. *s.* Fortune; state assigned; any thing used in determining chances; a portion.

LO'TION. *s.* A kind of medicinal wash.

LOT'TERY. *s.* A game of chance. pl. *lotteries.*

LOUD. *adj.* Noisy; clamorous. s. *loudness:* adv. *loudly.*

LOUGH. *s.* A lake; a large inland standing water.

LOUIS D'OR. *s.* A golden coin of France, valued at about twenty shillings sterling.

LOUNGE. *v.* To idle; to live lazily. pr. par. *lounging;* past, *lounged:* s. *lounger.*

LOUSE. *s.* A species of insect. pl. *lice:* adj. *lousy:* adv. *lousily:* s. *lousiness.*

LOUT'ISH. *adj.* Clownish. adv. *loutishly.*

LOVE. *v.* To regard with passionate affection; to delight in. pr. par. *loving;* past, *loved:* s. *love, lover, lovingness:* adj. *lovely:* adv. *lovely, lovingly:* s. *love-favour, love-knot, love-letter, love-shaft, love-song, love-token:* adj. *love-sick.*

LOW. *adj.* Not high; not deep; not elevated; mean. v. *lower;* pr. par. *lowering;* past, *lowered:* s. *lowness, lowerer:* adv. *lowly:* s. *lowliness.*

LOW. *v.* To bellow as a cow. pr. par. *lowing;* past, *lowed:* s. *lowing.*

LOW'ER. *v.* To appear dark, stormy and gloomy; to frown. pr. par. *lowering;* past, *lowered:* s. *lower:* adj. *lowering:* adv. *loweringly.*

LOW'ERMOST. *adj.* Lowest.

LOW'LAND. *s.* A low country.

LOWSPIR'ITED. *adj.* Dejected; not lively; cowardly. s. *lowspiritedness.*

LOY'AL. *adj.* Obedient; true to the prince; faithful in love. s. *loyalist, loyalty:* adv. *loyally.*

LOZ'ENGE. *s.* A form of medicine to be held in the mouth till melted; a cake of preserved fruits.

LUB'BER. *s.* A sturdy drone; a booby. adv. *lubberly.*

LU'BRICATE. *v.* To make smooth or slippery. pr. par. *lubricating,* past, *lubricated:* s. *lubricator, lubricity:* adj. *lubricous.*

LU'CENT. *adj.* Shining; splendid.

LU'CERNE. *s.* A species of plant.

LU'CID. *adj.* Shining; pellucid sane. s. *lucidity, lucidness:* adv *lucidly.*

LUCIF'EROUS, LUCIF'IC. *adj.* Giving light. adv. *luciferously.*

LU'CIFORM. *adj.* Having the nature of light.

LUCK. *s.* Chance; fortune. adj *lucky:* s. *luckiness:* adv. *luckily:* adj. *luckless.*

LU'CRATIVE. *adj.* Gainful, profitable. s. *lucrativeness:* adv. *lucratively.*

LU'CRE. *s.* Gain, profit.

LU'CUBRATE. *v.* To study by candle-light. pr. par. *lucubrating;* past, *lucubrated:* s *lucubration.*

LU'CULENT. *adj.* Clear, certain. adv. *luculently.*

LU'DICROUS, LUDIC'ROUS. *adj.* Burlesque; merry. s. *ludicrousness:* adv. *ludicrously.*

LUFF. *v.* To keep close to the wind. pr. par. *luffing;* past, *luffed:* s. *luff.*

LUG. *s.* The ear; a kind of small fish.

LUG. *v.* To drag by the ear; to pull with violence. pr. par. *lugging* past, *lugged.*

LUG'GAGE. *s.* Any thing cumbrous and unwieldy; baggage.

LUGU'BRIOUS. *adj.* Mournful.

LUKE'WARM. *adj.* Moderately or mildly warm; indifferent. s. *lukewarmness:* adv. *lukewarmly.*

LULL. *v.* To compose to sleep, to quiet. pr. par. *lulling;* past, *lulled.*

LUL'LABY. *s.* A song to still babes, pl. *lullabies.*

LUMBA'GO. *s.* Pain about the loins.
LUM'BAL. *adj.* Pertaining to the loins.
LUM'BER. *s.* Any thing useless or cumbersome; any thing very bulky in proportion to its value. v. *lumber;* pr. par. *lumbering;* past, *lumbered.*
LU'MINARY. *s.* A body which gives light. pl. *luminaries:* adj. *luminous:* adv. *luminously:* s. *luminousness.*
LUMP. *s.* A shapeless mass; the whole together. v. *lump;* pr. par. *lumping;* past, *lumped:* adj. *lumpy:* s. *lumpiness, lumpishness.*
LU'NACY. *s.* A kind of madness supposed to be influenced by the moon; madness in general. s. *lunatic.*
LU'NAR. *adj.* Relating to the moon.
LU'NATED. *adj.* Formed like a half-moon.
LUNA'TION. *s.* A revolution of the moon.
LUNCH, LUNCH'EON. *s.* As much food as one's hand can hold; a meal between breakfast and dinner.
LUNETTE'. *s.* A small half-moon.
LUNGS. *s.* The part by which breath is inspired and expired.
LUNT. *s.* The match-cord with which guns are fired.
LU'PINE. *s.* A kind of pulse.
LURCH. *s.* A forlorn or deserted state.
LURE. *s.* An enticement. v. *lure;* pr. par. *luring;* past, *lured.*
LU'RID. *adj.* Gloomy, dismal. s. *luridness:* adv. *luridly.*
LURK. *v.* To lie in wait; to lie hidden. pr. par. *lurking;* past, *lurked:* s. *lurker.*
LUS'CIOUS. *adj.* Sweet, pleasing, cloying. s. *lusciousness:* adv. *lusciously.*

LU'SORY. *adj.* Used in play; sportive
LUST. *s.* Inordinate desire. v. *lust;* pr. par. *lusting,* past, *lusted:* adj. *lustful:* s. *lustfulness:* adv. *lustfully.*
LUS'TRATE. *v.* To purify. pr. par. *lustrating;* past, *lustrated:* s. *lustration.*
LUS'TRE. *s.* Brightness, splendour.
LUS'TRING. *s.* A shining silk.
LUS'TRUM. *s.* A space of five years.
LUS'TY. *adj.* Stout; vigorous. s. *lustiness:* adv. *lustily.*
LUTA'RIOUS. *adj.* Living in mud; of the colour of mud.
LUTE. *s.* A stringed instrument of music.
LUTE. *s.* A composition with which chymists close their vessels. v. *lute;* pr. par. *luting;* past, *luted:* s. *lutation.*
LUTE'STRING. *s.* The string of a lute; a kind of silk.
LU'THERAN. *adj.* Denoting the doctrine and discipline of Luther. s. *lutheranism.*
LU'TULENT. *adj.* Muddy.
LUXU'RIANT. *adj.* Exuberant; superfluously plenteous. s. *luxuriance, luxuriancy:* adv. *luxuriantly.* v. *luxuriate;* pr. par. *luxuriating,* past, *luxuriated.*
LUX'URY. *s.* Voluptuousness; addictedness to pleasure; delicious fare. pl. *luxuries:* adj. *luxurious:* s. *luxuriousness:* adv. *luxuriously.*
LY'DIAN. *adj.* A species of ancien music; a soft and slow air.
LYE. *v.* See LIE.
LYMPH. *s.* Water; transparent, colourless liquor. adj. and s. *lymphatic:* s. *lympheduct.*
LYRE. *s.* A harp. adj. *lyric, lyrical:* s. *lyrist.*

M

MACARO'NI. *s.* A kind of paste meat, boiled in broth; a sort of droll or fool; a fop.

MACAW'. *s.* A large species of parrot.
MACE. *s.* An ensign of authority,

borne before magistrates; a kind of spice. s. *mace-bearer.*

MA'CERATE. *v.* To make lean; to wear away; to steep almost to solution. pr. par. *macerating;* past, *macerated:* s. *maceration.*

MACHIAVE'LIAN. *s.* A follower of the opinions of Machiavel. adj. *machiavelian:* s. *machiavelism.*

MACHINA'TION. *s.* Artifice, contrivance.

MACHI'NE. *s.* Any complicated work, in which one part contributes to the motion of another; an engine. s. *machinery,* pl. *machineries, machinist.*

MACK'AREL. *s.* A kind of sea-fish.

MAD. *adj.* Disordered in the mind; furious. s. *madness:* adv. *madly:* adj. *mad-brained:* s. *mad-cap, madhouse.*

MAD'AM. *s.* The term of compliment, used in addressing a lady.

MAD'DEN. *v.* To become mad; to make mad. pr. par. *maddening;* past, *maddened.*

MAD'DER. *s.* A plant used in dying.

MADE. Pret. and past par. of the v. *to make.*

MADEI'RA. *s.* A rich wine, made at the island of Madeira. pronounced *Mu-da'-ra.*

MADON'NA. *s.* A name given to pictures of the Virgin Mary.

MAD'RIGAL. *s.* A pastoral song; any light, airy, short song.

MAGAZI'NE. *s.* A store-house; commonly an arsenal or armory, or repository for provisions; a miscellaneous pamphlet.

MAG'GOT. *s.* A small grub. adj. *maggotty.*

MA'GIC. *s.* Sorcery; enchantment. adj. *magical:* adv. *magically:* s. *magician.*

MAGISTE'RIAL. *adj.* Such as suits a magistrate or a master; lofty; arrogant; despotic. adv. *magisterially.*

MA'GISTRATE. *s.* A man invested with authority; a governor. s. *magistracy,* pl. *magistracies.*

MAG'NA CHAR'TA. *s.* The great charter of liberties, signed in England, by King John.

MAGNANIM'ITY. *s.* Greatness of mind. adj. *magnanimous.* adv *magnanimously.*

MAGNE'SIA. *s.* A white alkaline earth, used in medicine.

MAG'NET. *s.* The loadstone; the stone that attracts iron. adj. *magnetic, magnetical:* adv. *magnetically:* s. *magnetism.*

MAGNIF'ICENCE. *s.* Grandeur of appearance; splendour. adj. *magnificent:* adv. *magnificently.*

MAG'NIFY. *v.* To make great; to exaggerate; to exalt. pr. par. *magnifying;* past, *magnified:* s. *magnifier.*

MAG'NITUDE. *s.* Greatness; comparative bulk.

MAGNO'LIA. *s.* A kind of flowering tree.

MAG'PIE. *s.* A kind of bird.

MAHOG'ANY. *s.* A kind of reddish wood. pl. *mahoganies.*

MAHOM'ETAN, MAHOM'EDAN. *s.* A mussulman; a professor of the religion of Mahomet. s. *Mahometanism:* adj. *Mahometan.*

MAID, MAID'EN. *s.* A woman unmarried; a virgin. adj. *maiden, maidenly, maidenlike.*

MAIL. *s.* A coat of steel network, worn for defence; any armour; a postman's bundle; the conveyance by which the bag of letters is sent. v. *mail;* pr. par. *mailing;* past, *mailed.*

MAIM. *v.* To deprive of any necessary part; to cripple, by loss of a limb. pr. par. *maiming;* past, *maimed.*

MAIN. *adj.* Principal; chief. adv. *mainly.*

MAIN. *s.* The ocean.

MAIN'LAND. *s.* The continent.

MAIN'MAST. *s.* The chief or middle mast.

MAIN'SAIL. *s.* The sail of the main mast.

231

MAIN'SHEET. s. The sheet or sail of the mainmast.
MAINTAIN'. v. To preserve; to defend; to vindicate; to support with the necessaries of life. pr. par. *maintaining;* past, *maintained:* s. *maintainer, maintenance.*
MAIN'TOP. s The top of the mainmast.
MAIN'YARD. s. The yard of the mainmast.
MAIZE. s. Indian corn.
MA'JESTY. s. Dignity; grandeur; elevation of appearance; the title of kings and queens. pl. *majesties:* adj. *majestic:* adv. *majestically.*
MA'JOR. adj. Greater, senior, elder. s. *majority,* pl. *majorities.*
MA'JOR. s. The officer next above a captain.
MAJOR'ITY. s. State of being of full age; office of a major. pl. *majorities.*
MAKE. v. To form, to create; to compel; to raise as profit, &c. pr. par. *making;* past, *made:* s. *make, maker.*
MAKE'WEIGHT. s. Any small thing thrown in to make up a weight.
MAL'ADY. s. A disease; a distemper. pl. *maladies.*
MAL'AGA. s. A kind of wine, imported from Malaga.
MAL'APERT. adj. Saucy; quick, with impudence. s. *malapertness:* adv. *malapertly.*
MALE. s. The he of any species. adj. *male.*
MAL'CONTENT. s. One who is dissatisfied. adj. *malcontent:* s. *malcontentedness.*
MALEDIC'TION. s. A curse; denunciation of evil.
MALEFAC'TOR. s. An offender against law; a criminal.
MALEF'IC. adj. Mischievous; hurtful.
MALEV'OLENCE. s. Ill-will; inclination to hurt others. adj. *malevolent:* adv. *malevolently.*
MAL'ICE. s. Badness of design; deliberate mischief. s. *maliciousness:* adj. *malicious:* adv. *maliciously*
MALIGN'. adj. Unfavourable; malicious; infectious. s. *malignancy;* adv. *malignly.*
MALIG'NANT. adj. Malign; envious; hostile to life. s. *malignity.* adv. *malignantly.*
MALL. s. A kind of beater or hammer; a public walk.
MAL'LARD. s. The drake of the wild duck.
MAL'LEABLE. adj. Capable of being spread by beating with a hammer. s. *malleability,* pl. *malleabilities.*
MAL'LET. s. A wooden hammer.
MAL'LOWS. s. A kind of plant.
MALM'SEY. s. A sort of grape; a kind of wine.
MALPRAC'TICE. s. Practice contrary to rules; evil-doing.
MALT. s. Grain steeped in water, and dried. v *malt;* pr. par. *malting;* past, *malted:* s. *maltster.*
MALTREAT'. v. To use with roughness or unkindness. pr. par. *maltreating;* past, *maltreated:* s. *maltreater, maltreatment.*
MALVERSA'TION. s. Misbehaviour in office; mean artifices.
MAM'ELUKE. s. A cavalry soldier of Egypt.
MAMMA'. s. The fond word for mother.
MAN. s. A human being; the male of the human species. pl. *men:* adj. *manful, manlike:* adv. *manfully.*
MAN. v. To furnish with men; to guard with men. pr. par. *manning,* past, *manned.*
MAN'ACLE. s. A chain for the hands; shackles. v. *manacle;* pr. par. *manacling;* past, *manacled.*
MAN'AGE. v. To conduct; to carry on; to govern; to wield. pr. par. *managing;* past, *managed:* s. *management, manager:* adj. *manageable:* adv. *manageably.*
MANCH'ET. s. A small loaf of fine bread.

MAN—MAN

MANDARIN'. *s.* A Chinese nobleman or magistrate.
MAN'DATE. *s.* Command; precept; commission sent or transmitted. adj. *mandatory.*
MAN'DRAKE. *s.* A kind of plant.
MAN'DREL. *s.* An instrument used in a lathe.
MANE. *s.* The hair which hangs from the neck of horses or other animals.
MANE'GE. *s.* A place where horses are trained, or horsemanship taught. pronounced *ma-nĕ'je.*
MA'NES. *s.* Ghost, shade. pronounced *ma'-nes.*
MAN'GANESE. *s.* A kind of mineral.
MANGE. *s.* The itch or scab in cattle. adj. *mangy.*
MAN'GER. *s.* The trough or vessel in which animals are fed with corn.
MANG'LE. *v.* To lacerate; to cut or hack to pieces; to press with a mangle. pr. par. *mangling;* past, *mangled:* s. *mangler.*
MANG'LE. *s.* A rolling press for smoothing linen; a calender.
MANG'O. *s.* A kind of Indian fruit, used for pickling.
MAN'GROVE. *s.* A species of plant.
MAN'HOOD. *s.* Human nature.
MA'NIA. *s.* Madness, rage.
MA'NIAC. *s.* A mad person.
MAN'IFEST. *adj.* Plain, open. v. *manifest:* pr. par. *manifesting;* past, *manifested:* s. *manifestation, manifestness:* adv. *manifestly.*
MAN'IFEST. *s.* The written particulars of a ship's cargo.
MANIFES'TO. *s.* Public protestation. pl. *manifestoes.*
MAN'IFOLD. *adj.* Of different kinds; many; complicated. adv. *manifoldly.*
MAN'IKIN, MAN'NIKEN. *s.* A little man.
MAN'IPLE. *s.* A handful; a small band of soldiers. adj. *manipular:* s. *manipulation.*
MAN'KIND. *s.* The race or species of human beings.

MAN—MAN

MAN'NA. *s.* A gum, or honey-like juice, collected into a solid form.
MAN'NER. *s.* Form; method; custom; mien; sort. s. *mannerliness* adj. and adv. *mannerly.*
MAN'NERIST. *s.* A person who performs all his works in one unvaried manner.
MANŒU'VRE, MANEU'VRE. *s.* An operation of military tactics a stratagem; any kind of management. v. *manœuvre;* pr. par. *manœuvring;* past, *manœuvred:* s. *manœuvrer.*
MAN'OR. *s.* A certain district of land. adj. *manorial.*
MANSE. *s.* A parsonage-house.
MAN'SION. *s.* The house erected on a manor; a house adapted for a permanent residence; place of abode.
MAN'SLAUGHTER. *s.* Murder; the act of killing a human being, not wholly without fault, though without malice.
MAN'SLAYER. *s.* One that has killed another.
MAN'SUETUDE. *s.* Mildness, gentleness, tameness.
MANTELET'. *s.* A small cloak: in fortification, a kind of movable pent-house, driven before the pioneers to shelter them from the enemy's shot.
MAN'TLE. *s.* A kind of cloak. v. *mantle;* pr. par. *mantling;* past, *mantled.*
MAN'TLE. *v.* To be expanded; to spread luxuriantly; to froth; t ferment. pr. par. *mantling;* past *mantled.*
MAN'TUAMAKER. *s.* One who makes gowns for women.
MAN'UAL. *adj.* Performed or used by the hand. adv. *manually:* s. *manual.*
MANUFAC'TORY. *s.* The practice of making any piece of workmanship; the place where manufacture is carried on. pl. *manufactories.*

MANUFAC'TURE. *s.* The practice of making any piece of workmanship; any thing made by art. *v. manufacture;* pr. par. *manufacturing;* past, *manufactured: s. manufacturer.*
MANUMIT'. *v.* To release from slavery. pr. par. *manumitting;* past, *manumitted.*
MANUMIS'SION. *s.* Act of manumitting.
MANU'RE. *v.* To enrich with some fertilizing matter. pr. par. *manuring;* past, *manured: s. manure.*
MAN'USCRIPT. *s.* Hand-writing; a written book.
MAN'Y. *adj.* Numerous; not few.
MAN'Y-COLOURED. *adj.* Having various colours.
MAP. *s.* A delineation of countries.
MA'PLE. *s.* A kind of tree.
MAR. *v.* To injure; to spoil. pr. par. *marring;* past, *marred.*
MARAU'DE. *v.* To plunder. pr. par. *marauding;* past, *marauded: s. marauder.*
MAR'BLE. *s.* A kind of stone; a little ball, supposed to be made of marble, with which children play.
MAR'BLE. *v.* To variegate or vein like marble. pr. par. *marbling;* past, *marbled.*
MARCH. *s.* The third month of the year.
MARCH. *v.* To move in military form; to walk in a grave, deliberate, or stately manner. pr. par. *marching;* past, *marched: s. march,* pl. *marches.*
MARCH'IONESS. *s.* The wife of a marquis: a lady raised to the rank of marquis. pl. *marchionesses.*
MARE. *s.* The female of a horse.
MARES'CHAL. *s* A marshal.
MAR'GIN. *s.* The verge; the border; the edge of a page, left blank. *adj. marginal.*
MAR'GRAVE. *s.* A title of sovereignty, in Germany. fem. *margravine.*
MA'RIGOLD. *s.* A kind of yellow flower.

MARI'NE. *adj.* Belonging to the sea.
MARI'NE. *s.* A soldier taken on shipboard, to be employed in descents upon the land, &c.
MAR'INER. *s.* A seaman; a sailor.
MAR'ITAL. *adj.* Pertaining to a husband.
MAR'ITIME. *adj.* Performed on the sea; naval; bordering on the sea.
MAR'JORAM. *s.* A species of fragrant plant.
MARK. *s.* A token; a stamp; notice taken; any thing at which a missile weapon is directed; a sum of thirteen shillings and four pence. *v. mark;* pr. par. *marking;* past, *marked: s. marker.*
MAR'KET. *s.* A public time, and appointed place, for buying and selling; purchase and sale. *v. market;* pr. par. *marketing;* past, *marketed: s. marketer:* adj. *marketable: s. market-town.*
MARKS'MAN. *s.* One skilful in hitting a mark. pl. *marksmen.*
MARL. *s.* A kind of fertilizing clay adj. *marly: s. marl-pit.*
MAR'LINE. *s.* Long wreaths of un twisted hemp, dipped in pitch.
MAR'LINESPIKE. *s.* A small piece of iron, for fastening ropes together.
MAR'MALADE. *s.* The pulp of quinces or of oranges, boiled with sugar.
MARMOSET'. *s.* A small monkey.
MAR'MOT. *s.* A small animal, called *mus alpinus.*
MAROON'. *s.* A free, or a runaway negro, living in the mountains in the West Indies.
MAR'QUIS, MAR'QUESS. *s.* One of the second order of nobility. pl. *marquises, marquesses: s. marquisate.*
MAR'RIAGE. *s.* The act of uniting a man and woman for life. adj. *marriageable.*
MAR'ROW. *s.* An oleaginous substance, contained within the bones.
MAR'ROWFAT. *s.* A kind of pea.
MAR'RY. *v.* To take for husband or

wife; to dispose of in marriage; to perform the marriage ceremony. pr. par. *marrying;* past, *married.*

MARSH. *s.* A fen; a bog; a swamp. pl. *marshes:* adj. *marshy.*

MARSH-MAL'LOW. *s.* A kind of plant.

MAR'SHAL. *s.* The chief officer of arms; any one who regulates rank or order at a feast, or any other assembly.

MAR'SHAL. *v.* To arrange; to rank in order. pr. par. *marshaling;* past, *marshaled:* s. *marshaler.*

MART. *s.* A market; a place of public traffic.

MAR'TIAL. *adj.* Warlike, given to war.

MARTINET'. *s.* A strict military disciplinarian.

MAR'TINGAL. *s.* A broad strap, made fast to the girths under the belly of a horse.

MAR'TINMAS. *s.* The feast of St. Martin; the 11th of November.

MAR'TYR. *s.* One who, by his death, bears witness to what he considers the truth. v. *martyr;* pr. par. *martyring;* past, *martyred:* s. *martyrdom.*

MARTYROL'OGY. *s.* A register of martyrs. pl. *martyrologies.*

MAR'VEL. *s.* A wonder; any thing astonishing. pr. par. *marveling;* past, *marveled:* adj. *marvellous:* adv. *marvellously:* s. *marvellousness.*

MAS'CULINE. *adj.* Male; resembling man; robust. adv. *masculinely:* s. *masculineness.*

MASH. *s.* Any thing mingled or beaten together into an undistinguished or confused body. v. *mash;* pr. par. *mashing;* past, *mashed.*

MASK. *s.* A cover to disguise the face; a visor; a dramatic performance, written in a tragic style, without attention to rules or probability. pr. par. *masking;* past, *masked:* s. *masker.*

MA'SON. *s.* A builder with stone; one of a society bearing the epithet of free and accepted. adj. *masonic* s. *masonry.*

MASQUERA'DE. *s.* A diversion in which the company is masked; state of disguise. v. *masquerade;* pr. par. *masquerading;* past, *masqueraded:* s. *masquerader.*

MASS. *s.* A body; a lump; a large quantity; assemblage; the service of the Romish church. pl. *masses.*

MAS'SACRE. *s.* Butchery; indiscriminate destruction. v. *massacre,* pr. par. *massacring;* past, *massacred.*

MAS'SIVE. *adj.* Heavy; ponderous. s. *massiveness:* adv. *massively.*

MAST. *s.* The beam raised above a vessel, to which the sail is fixed; the fruit of the oak and beech.

MAS'TER. *s.* One who has servants; a director; a governor; an owner; a young gentleman; one who teaches; a man eminently skilful in practice or science. v. *master;* pr. par. *mastering;* past, *mastered:* adv. *masterly:* s. *mastery.*

MAS'TER-KEY. *s.* A key which opens many locks.

MAS'TERPIECE. *s.* Any thing done or made with extraordinary skill.

MAS'TER-STROKE. *s.* Capital performance; an able act of policy.

MAS'TIC. *s.* A kind of gum; a kind of cement.

MASTICA'TION. *s.* The act of chewing. v. *masticate;* pr. par. *masticating;* past, *masticated.*

MAS'TIFF. *s.* A dog of the largest size.

MAT. *s.* A texture of sedge, flags, or rushes. s. *matting:* v. *mat;* pr. par. *matting;* past, *matted.*

MATADORE. *s.* One of the three principal cards in the games of ombre and quadrille.

MATCH. *s.* Any thing that catches fire, generally a card. rope, or small chip of wood, dipped in melted sulphur. pl. *matches.*

MATCH. *s.* One equal to another; one equal to contend with another; a contest; a game. *v.* match; pr. par. *matching;* past, *matched:* s. *match,* pl. *matches* adj. *matchless:* s. *matchlessness, match-maker.*

MATCH'LOCK. *s.* The lock of a musket, to which a match is applied.

MATE. *s.* A companion; the second officer in a merchant-ship.

MATE. *v.* To match, to marry. pr. par. *mating;* past, *mated.*

MATE'RIAL. *adj.* Consisting of matter; corporeal; not spiritual; important. adv. *materially.*

MATE'RIALIST. *s.* One who denies the existence of spiritual substances.

MATER'NAL. *adj.* Motherly; befitting or pertaining to a mother. s. *maternity.*

MATHEMA'TICS. *s.* The science which contemplates whatever is capable of being numbered or measured. adj. *mathematic, mathematical:* adv. *mathematically.*

MAT'IN. *s.* Morning; used in the morning. s. *matins,* morning worship.

MA'TRICE, MA'TRIX. *s.* The womb; a mould. pl. *matrices.*

MA'TRICIDE. *s.* Slaughter of a mother; one who has killed his mother. adj. *matricidal.*

MATRIC'ULATE. *v.* To enter or admit to a membership of a university; to enlist. pr. par. *matriculating;* past, *matriculated:* s. *matriculation.*

MAT'RIMONY. *s.* Marriage; nuptials. adj. *matrimonial:* adv. *matrimonially.*

MA'TRON. *s.* A wife; an elderly lady v. *matronize;* pr. par. *matronizing;* past, *matronized:* adj. *matronal, matronly.*

MATROSS'. *s.* A soldier in the artillery. pl. *matrosses.*

MAT'TER. *s.* Body, substance, materials; subject; affair; that which is formed by suppuration.

MAT'TER. *v.* To be of importance. pr. par. *mattering;* past, *mattered.*

MAT'TRASS. *s.* A kind of bed. pl. *mattrasses.*

MATURE'. *adj.* Ripe; perfected by time; brought near to completion. s. *maturity,* pl. *maturities:* adv. *maturely:* v. *mature;* pr. par. *maturing;* past, *matured.*

MAUL. *v.* To beat; to bruise. pr par. *mauling;* past, *mauled.*

MAUSOLE'UM. *s.* A pompous funeral monument.

MAW. *s.* The stomach of an animal; the craw of a bird.

MAWK'ISH. *adj.* Apt to cause loathing. s. *mawkishness.*

MAX'ILARY. *adj.* Belonging to the jaw-bone.

MAX'IM. *s.* A general principle; an axiom.

MAX'IMUM. *s.* The greatest quantity attainable in any given case.

MAY. *v.* To be at liberty; to be permitted; to be possible. pret. *might.*

MAY. *s.* The fifth month of the year. s. *may-day,* the first day of May: s. *may-pole.*

MAY. *v.* To gather flowers on May day. pr. par. *maying;* past, *mayed.*

MAY'OR. *s.* The chief magistrate of a city. fem. *mayoress,* pl. *mayoresses; mayoralty,* pl. *mayoralties.*

MAZE. *s.* A labyrinth; confusion of thought. adj. *mazy.*

ME. *pron.* The objective case of *I.*

MEAD. *s.* A kind of drink, made of water and honey.

MEAD, MEAD'OW. *s.* Pasture or grass-land, annually mowed for hay.

MEA'GRE. *adj.* Lean, poor. s. *meagreness:* adv. *meagrely.*

MEAL. *s.* A repast; the flour or edible part of corn. adj. *mealy:* s *mealiness.*

MEAL'Y-MOUTH'ED. *adj.* Using soft words; concealing the real intention. s. *mealy-mouthedness.*

MEAN. *adj.* Wanting dignity; of

low rank or birth; low-minded; base; middle. s. *meanness*: adv. *meanly*.

MEAN. s. Mediocrity; middle rate; measure; instrument; that which is used in order to any end: more generally used in the plural;—as, a *means*.

MEAN. v. To have in the mind; to purpose; to understand. pr. par. *meaning*; past, *meant*: s. *meaning*.

MEAN'DER. s. Serpentine winding; winding course. v. *meander*; pr. par. *meandering*; past, *meandered*.

MEAS'LES. s. An eruption of the skin, attended with fever. adj. *measled, measly*.

MEA'SURE. s. That by which any thing is measured; proportion; sufficient quantity; limit; means of action. v. *measure*; pr. par. *measuring*; past, *measured*: s. *measurer, measurement*: adj. *measurable*.

MEAT. s. Flesh to be eaten; food in general.

MECHAN'ICS. s. A mathematical science, which shows the effects of powers or moving forces. adj. *mechanic, mechanical*: adv. *mechanically*: s. *mechanic, mechanism, mechanician, mechanist*.

MED'AL. s. A piece of metal, stamped in honour of some remarkable performance. adj. *medallic*: s. *medalist*.

MEDAL'LION. s. A kind of large medal.

MED'DLE. v. To interpose, to act in. pr. par. *meddling*; past, *meddled*: s. *meddler*: adj. *meddlesome*.

ME'DIATE. v. To interpose, as an equal friend to both parties; to intercede. pr. par. *mediating*; past, *mediated*: s. *mediation, mediator*; fem. *mediatress, mediatrix*: adj. *mediatorial, mediatory*.

MED'ICABLE. adj. That may be healed.

MED'ICAL. adj. Physical; relating to the art of healing. adv. *medically*.

MEDIC'AMENT. s. Any thing used in healing; generally, a topical application.

MED'ICATE. v. To tincture or impregnate with any thing medicinal pr. par. *medicating*; past, *medicated*: s. *medication*.

MED'ICINE. s. Physic; any remedy administered by a physician. adj *medicinal*: adv. *medicinally*.

MEDIOC'RITY. s. Moderate degree, middle rate. pl. *mediocrities*.

MED'ITATE. v. To think on; to plan; to contrive. pr. par. *meditating*; past, *meditated*: s. *meditation*: adj. *meditative*.

MEDITERRA'NEAN. adj. Encircled with land.

ME'DIUM. s. Any thing intervening; middle place or degree. pl. *media, mediums*.

MED'LAR. s. A kind of fruit.

MED'LEY. s. A mixture; a miscellany.

MEDUL'LARY. adj. Pertaining to the marrow.

MEED. s. Recompense; reward.

MEEK. adj. Mild in temper; gentle. s. *meekness*: adv. *meekly*: v. *meeken*; pr. par. *meekening*; past, *meekened*.

MEET. adj. Fit; proper. s. *meetness*. adv. *meetly*.

MEET. v. To come face to face; to encounter; to join another in the same place. pr. par. *meeting*; past, *met*: s. *meeting*.

ME'GRIM. s. Disorder of the head.

MEL'ANCHOLY. s. Sadness, pensiveness, gloom. adj. *melancholy, melancholic*.

MELANGE'. s. A mixture.

ME'LIORATE. v. To make better to improve. pr. par. *meliorating* past, *meliorated*: s. *melioration*.

MELLIF'EROUS. adj. Producing honey.

MELLIFAC'TION. s. The art or practice of making honey.

MELLIF'LUENCE. s. A honied flow; a flow of sweetness. adj *mellifluent, mellifluous*.

237

MEL'LOW. *adj.* Soft with ripeness; fully ripe. v. *mellow;* pr. par. *mellowing;* past, *mellowed:* s. *mellowness.*

MEL'ODRAME. *s.* A dramatic performance, in which songs are intermixed.

MEL'ODY. *s* Sweetness of sound. adj. *melodious:* adv. *melodiously:* s. *melodiousness.*

MEL'ON. *s.* A kind of fruit.

MELT. *v.* To make liquid; to dissolve. pr. par. *melting;* past, *melted:* s. *melter:* adv. *meltingly.*

MEM'BER. *s.* A limb; a part of a discourse or period; one of a community. s. *membership.*

MEM'BRANE. *s.* A web of several sorts of fibres, interwoven for the covering of some parts of the body. adj. *membraneous, membranous.*

MEMEN'TO *s.* A memorial notice; a hint to awaken the memory.

MEM'OIR. *s.* An account of transactions, familiarly written.

MEM'ORABLE. *adj.* Worthy of being remembered. adv. *memorably.*

MEMORAN'DUM. *s.* A note to help the memory. pl. *memoranda, memorandums.*

MEMO'RIAL. *s.* A monument; something to preserve the memory; an address, reminding of services, and soliciting reward. s. *memorialist.*

MEM'ORY. *s.* The power of retaining or recollecting things past; exemption from oblivion. pl. *memories.*

MEN. *s.* The plural of *man.*

MEN ACE. *v.* To threaten. pr. par. *menacing;* past, *menaced:* s. *menace.*

MENA'GERIE. *s.* A collection of foreign animals; the place in which they are kept.

MEND. *v.* To repair, to correct, to improve. pr. par. *mending;* past, *mended:* s. *mender.*

MENDA'CIOUS. *adj.* False; lying. s. *mendacity.*

MEN'DICANT. *s.* A beggar; one of some begging fraternity. adj. *mendicant:* s. *mendicity.*

ME'NIAL. *adj.* Belonging to the retinue or train of servants. s. *menial.*

MEN'SAL. *adj.* Belonging or relating to the table.

MEN'STRUUM. *s.* Any liquid used as a dissolvent, or to extract the virtues of ingredients by infusion and decoction.

MEN'SURABLE. *adj.* Measurable; that may be measured. adv. *measurably:* s. *measurability.*

MENSURA'TION. *s.* The art or act of measuring.

MEN'TAL. *adj.* Intellectual; existing in the mind. adv. *mentally.*

MEN'TION. *s.* Oral or written expression, or recital of any thing pr. par. *mentioning;* past, *mentioned.*

MEPHIT'IC, MEPHIT'ICAL. *adj.* Ill-savoured.

MERCAN'TILE. *adj.* Trading, commercial.

MER'CENARY. *adj.* Venal; hired; too studious of profit. s. *mercenary,* pl. *mercenaries.*

MER'CER. *s.* One who sells cloths. s. *mercery.*

MER'CHANDISE. *s.* Traffic; commerce; wares. v. *merchandise;* pr. par. *merchandising;* past, *merchandised.*

MER'CHANT. *s.* One who traffics to remote countries. adj. *merchantable.*

MER'CILESS. *adj.* Void of mercy, pitiless. s. *mercilessness:* adv. *mercilessly.*

MERCU'RIAL. *adj.* Formed under the influence of Mercury; sprightly; consisting of quicksilver.

MER'CURY. *s.* One of the planets; the chymist's name for quicksilver

MER'CY. *s.* Clemency, pardon. pl. *mercies:* adj. *merciful:* adv. *mercifully.*

MERE. *adj.* That or this only; such and nothing else; absolute. adv *merely.*

238

MERETRI'CIOUS. *adj.* Such as is practised by prostitutes; alluring by false show. *adv. meretriciously: s. meretriciousness.*

MERGE. *v.* To immerse; to be swallowed up; to be sunk. pr. par. *merging;* past, *merged.*

MERID'IAN. *s.* Mid-day; the line drawn from north to south, which the sun crosses at noon; the highest point of glory or power. *adj. meridian, meridional: adv. meridionally.*

MER'IT *s.* Desert; excellence deserving honour or reward. *v. merit;* pr. par. *meriting;* past, *merited: adj. meritorious: adv. meritoriously: s. meritoriousness.*

MER'LIN. *s.* A kind of hawk.

MER'MAID. *s.* A sea woman; an animal with a woman's head and a fish's tail.

MER'RY. *adj.* Pleasant; cheerful; gay. *s. merriment: adv. merrily.*

MERRY-AN'DREW. *s.* A buffoon; a jack-pudding.

MER'RY-THOUGHT. *s.* A forked bone, in the body of fowls.

MER'SION. *s.* The act of sinking or dipping.

MESH. *s.* The interstice of a net. pl. *meshes:* adj. *meshy.*

MES'LIN. *s.* Mixed corn, as wheat and rye.

MESS. *s.* A dish or portion of food; the ordinary of military men. pl. *messes:* v. *mess;* pr. par. *messing;* past, *messed.*

MES'SAGE *s.* An errand; advice sent.

MES'SENGER. *s.* One who carries an errand.

MESSI'AH. *s.* The Anointed; the Christ.

MESSIEURS. *s.* Sirs; gentlemen.

MESS'MATE. *s.* One who eats at the same table with another.

MES'SUAGE. *s.* The house and ground set apart for household uses. pronounced *mess'-wage.*

MET'AL. *s.* A firm, heavy, and hard substance, fusible by fire, malleable and ductile. adj. *metallic: s. metallist:* adj. *metalline.*

MET'ALLURGY. *s.* The art of working in metals. *s. metallurgist.*

METAMOR'PHOSE. *v.* To change the form or shape. pr. par. *metamorphosing;* past, *metamorphosed: s. metamorphoser, metamorphosis,* pl. *metamorphoses.*

MET'APHOR. *s.* A figure of speech. adj. *metaphoric, metaphorical:* adv. *metaphorically.*

MET'APHRASE. *s.* A mere verbal translation from one language into another. *s. metaphrast:* adj. *metaphrastic.*

METAPHYS'ICS. *s.* The doctrine of the general affections of substances existing. *s. metaphysician* adj. *metaphysic, metaphysical:* adv. *metaphysically.*

METE. *v.* To measure. pr. par. *meting;* past, *meted: s. meter.*

METEMPSYCHO'SIS. *s.* The transmigration of souls from body to body. pl. *metempsychoses.*

ME'TEOR. *s.* Any body in the air or sky, of a flux and transitory nature.

METEOROL'OGY. *s.* The doctrine of meteors. adj. *meteorological: s. meteorologist.*

METH'OD. *s.* Convenient order; regularity. adj. *methodical:* adv. *methodically:* v. *methodize;* pr. par. *methodizing;* past, *methodized.*

METH'ODISTS. *s.* One of the religious sects. adj. *methodistical.* s. *methodism.*

METON'YMY. *s.* A rhetorical figure, founded on the several relations of cause and effect, container and contained, sign and thing signified. pl. *metonymies.*

ME'TRE. *s.* Speech confined to a certain number and harmonic disposition of syllables; verse; measure. adj. *metrical.*

METROP'OLIS. *s.* The chief city of any country or district. pl. *metropolises:* adj. *metropolitan.*

METROPOL'ITAN. *s.* A bishop of

the mother church; an archbishop. adj. *metropolitan*, belonging to a metropolis.

MET'TLE. *s.* Spirit, courage, substance. adj. *mettled, mettlesome.*

MEW. *s.* A cage for hawks; an enclosure; a sea-fowl. v. *mew;* pr. par. *mewing;* past, *mewed.*

MEZZOTIN'TO. *s.* A kind of engraving, so named as nearly resembling paint; the word importing, "half painted."

MIAS'MA. *s.* Such particles or atoms, as are supposed to arise from distempered, putrefying, or poisonous bodies.

MICE. *s.* The plural of *mouse.*

MICH'AELMAS. *s.* The feast of the archangel Michael, celebrated on the 29th of September.

MICHE. *v.* To lie hid; to absent one's-self, as a boy from school. pr. par. *miching;* past, *miched:* s. *micher.*

MI'CROCOSM. *s.* The little world: the body of man is so called.

MICROM'ETER. *s.* An instrument for measuring small spaces.

MI'CROSCOPE. *s.* An optic for viewing and magnifying small objects. adj. *microscopic, microscopical.*

MID'-DAY. *adj.* Meridional; being at noon. s. *mid-day.*

MID'DLE. *adj.* Equally distant from two extremes; intermediate. adj. *middlemost:* s. *middle.*

MID'DLING. *adj.* Of middle rank; of moderate size; having moderate qualities of any kind. adv. *middlingly.*

MIDGE. *s.* A gnat.

MID'LAND. *adj.* Surrounded by land.

MID'NIGHT. *s.* The depth of night; twelve o'clock.

MID'RIFF. *s.* The diaphragm.

MID'SHIPMAN. *s.* A naval officer, next in rank below a lieutenant. pl. *midshipmen.*

MIDST. *s.* Middle.

MID'SUMMER. *s.* The summer solstice, reckoned to fall on the 21st of June.

MID'WAY. *adj.* In the middle of a passage. s. *midway.*

MID'WIFE. *s.* A woman who assists women in childbirth. pl. *midwives* s. *midwifery.*

MIEN. *s.* Look, manner, air.

MIFF. *s.* Displeasure; ill-humour.

MIGHT. *v.* Pret. of *may.*

MIGHT. *s.* Power, strength, force adj. *mighty:* adv. *mightily:* s. *mightiness.*

MIGNONETTE. *s.* A kind of annual flower.

MI'GRATE. *v.* To remove from one place to another. pr. par. *migrating;* past, *migrated:* s. *migration:* adj. *migratory.*

MILD. *adj.* Kind; soft; tender; compassionate. s. *mildness:* adv. *mildly.*

MIL'DEW. *s.* A disease in plants. v. *mildew;* pr. par. *mildewing;* past, *mildewed.*

MILE. *s.* The usual measure of roads; in England, 1760 yards. s. *milestone.*

MIL'IARY. *adj.* Small; resembling a millet-seed.

MIL'ITANT. *adj.* Fighting; a term applied to the church of Christ.

MIL'ITARY. *adj.* Engaged in the life of a soldier; suiting a soldier warlike; effected by soldiers. s *military.*

MIL'ITATE. *v.* To oppose; to operate against. pr. par. *militating* past, *militated.*

MILI'TIA. *s.* The people in arms the popular force of a nation.

MILK. *s.* The liquor with which animals feed their young from the breast. v. *milk;* pr. par. *milking* past, *milked:* s. *milker, milkiness:* adj. *milky:* s. *milkmaid, milkman, milkpail, milkpan, milksop.*

MILL. *s.* An engine for grinding corn, &c. v. *mill;* pr. par. *milling,* past, *milled:* s. *miller, mill-dam, millstone.*

MILLENA'RIAN. *s.* One who expects the millennium.

240

MIL'LENARY. *adj* Consisting of a thousand.

MILLEN'IUM. *s.* A thousand years; generally taken for the thousand years, during which some imagine Christ will reign on earth, after the resurrection.

MIL'LEPED. *s.* A species of insect, so called from its numerous feet.

MILLEN'NIAL. *adj.* Thousandth; consisting of thousandth parts.

MIL'LET. *s.* A kind of plant; a kind of fish.

MIL'LINER. *s.* One who makes ladies' head-dresses, and sells ribands, &c.

MIL'LION. *s.* The number of a hundred myriads, or ten hundred thousand.

MILT. *s.* The sperm of the male fish; the spleen. *v. milt;* pr. par. *milting;* past, *milted:* s. *milter.*

MIMET'IC, MIMET'ICAL. *adj.* Imitative. adv. *mimetrically.*

MIM'IC. *s.* A ludicrous imitator; a mean or servile imitator. v. *mimic;* pr. par. *mimicking;* past, *mimicked:* adv. *mimically:* s. *mimicry,* pl. *mimicries.*

MINA'CIOUS. *adj.* Full of threats. s. *minacity.*

MIN'ARET. *s.* A kind of spire.

MI'NATORY. *adj.* Threatening.

MINCE. *v.* To cut into very small parts. pr. par. *mincing;* past, *minced:* adv. *mincingly.*

MIND. *s.* The intelligent power; intellectual capacity; choice; memory. v. *mind;* pr. par. *minding;* past, *minded:* adj. *mindful:* adv. *mindfully:* s. *mindfulness.*

MINE. *pron.* Belonging to me.

MINE. *s.* A place or cavern in the earth, which contains metals or minerals; a cavern dug under any fortification, that it may sink for want of support; or, in modern war, that powder may be lodged in it, which, being fired, may blow up whatever is over it. v. *mine;* pr. par. *mining;* past, *mined:* s. *miner.*

MIN'ERAL. *s.* A fossil body matter dug out of mines. adj. *mineral.* s. *mineralist.*

MINERAL'OGY. *s.* The doctrine of minerals. s. *mineralogist.* adj *mineralogical.*

MIN'GLE. *v.* To mix; to compound. pr. par. *mingling;* past, *mingled* s. *mingler.*

MIN'IATURE. *s.* A painting in water colours, very small and delicate; a representation in a small compass.

MIN'IKEN. *adj.* Small, diminutive.

MIN'IM. *s.* A dwarf; a note in music.

MIN'IMUM. *s.* The smallest quantity possible.

MIN'ION. *s.* A favourite; a low unprincipled dependant.

MIN'ISTER. *s.* An agent; one wl o acts under another; one who serves at the altar; a delegate. v. *minister;* pr. par. *ministering;* past, *ministered:* s. *ministration:* adj *ministerial:* adv. *ministerially.*

MIN'ISTRY. *s.* Office; service; ecclesiastical function; agency; body of ministers. pl. *ministries.*

MIN'NOW. *s.* A very small fish.

MI'NOR. *adj.* Less; smaller; inconsiderable.

MI'NOR. *s.* One under age; the second or particular proposition in a syllogism. s. *minority,* pl. *minorities.*

MIN'OTAUR. *s.* A monster, invented by the poets, half man and half bull.

MIN'STER. *s.* A monastery; an ecclesiastical fraternity; a cathedral church.

MIN'STREL. *s.* A musician; a singer. s. *minstrelsy,* pl. *minstrelsies.*

MINT. *s.* A kind of plant.

MINT. *s.* The place where money is coined. v. *mint;* pr. par. *minting;* past, *minted:* s. *mintage.* *minter.*

MIN'UET. *s.* A stately regular dance generally performed by two persons.

MINU′TE. *adj.* Small, little, slender. *s. minuteness;* adv. *minutely.*

MIN′UTE. *s.* The sixtieth part of an hour; a short note. *v. minute;* pr. par. *minuting;* past, *minuted;* s. *minute-book.*

MINU′TIÆ. *s.* The smallest particular.

MINX. *s.* A kind of small quadruped; a pert, wanton girl. pl. *minxes.*

MIR′ACLE. *s.* A wonder; something above human power. adj. *miraculous;* s. *miraculousness;* adv. *miraculously.*

MIRE. *s.* Mud. adj. *miry;* s. *miriness.*

MIRK′Y. *adj.* Dark. s. *mirkiness.*

MIR′ROR. *s.* A looking-glass; a pattern.

MIRTH. *s.* Merriment, laughter. adj. *mirthful, mirthless;* adv. *mirthfully.*

MISADVEN′TURE. *s.* Mischance; ill-luck.

MISAN′THROPE, MISAN′THROPIST. *s.* A hater of mankind. s. *misanthropy;* adj. *misanthropic, misanthropical;* adv. *misanthropically.*

MISAPPLY′. *v.* To apply to wrong purposes. pr. par. *misapplying;* past, *misapplied;* s. *misapplication.*

MISAPPREHEND′. *v.* Not to understand rightly. pr. par. *misapprehending;* past, *misapprehended;* s. *misapprehension.*

MISBECO′ME. *v.* To be unseemly. pr. par. *misbecoming;* past, *misbecome.*

MISBEHA′VE. *v.* To behave improperly. pr. par. *misbehaving;* past, *misbehaved;* s. *misbehaviour.*

MISCAL′CULATE. *v.* To reckon wrong. pr. par. *miscalculating;* past, *miscalculated;* s. *miscalculation.*

MISCAL′. *v.* To name improperly. pr. par. *miscalling;* past, *miscalled.*

MISCAR′RY. *v.* To be lost on the way; to fail; not to have the intended event. pr. par. *miscarrying,* past, *miscarried;* s. *miscarriage.*

MISCEL′LANY. *s.* A mixed variety pl. *miscellanies;* adj. *miscellaneous.*

MISCHANCE′. *s.* Ill-luck; misfortune.

MIS′CHIEF. *s.* Harm; hurt; injury. adj. *mischievous;* s. *mischievousness;* adv. *mischievously.*

MIS′CIBLE. *adj.* Possible to be mingled. s. *miscibility,* pl. *miscibilities.*

MISCI′TE. *v.* To quote wrong. pr par. *misciting;* past, *miscited;* s *miscitation.*

MISCOMPUTA′TION. *s.* False reckoning.

MISCONCEIVE′. *v.* To entertain a mistaken notion. pr. par. *misconceiving;* past, *misconceived;* s *misconception.*

MISCONDUCT′. *v.* To manage amiss; to carry on wrong. pr. par *misconducting;* past, *misconducted;* s. *miscon′duct.*

MISCONJEC′TURE. *v.* To conjecture wrong. pr. par. *misconjecturing;* past, *misconjectured;* s. *misconjecture, misconjecturer.*

MISCONSTRUE′. *v.* To interpret wrong. pr. par. *misconstruing;* past, *misconstrued;* s. *misconstruction.*

MISCOUNT′. *v.* To reckon wrong. pr. par. *miscounting;* past, *miscounted.*

MIS′CREANT. *s.* A vile wretch.

MISDA′TE. *v.* To mark with untrue time. pr. par. *misdating;* past, *misdated.*

MISDEED′. *s.* Evil action.

MISDEMEAN′. *v.* To behave ill. pr. par. *misdemeaning;* past, *misdemeaned;* s. *misdemeanour.*

MISDO′. *v.* To do wrong. pr. par. *misdoing;* past, *misdone;* s. *misdoer, misdoing.*

MISEMPLOY′. *v.* To use to wrong purposes. pr. par. *misemploying,* past, *misemployed;* s *misemployment.*

MI'SER. *s.* A wretch covetous to extremity.
MIS'ERY. *s.* Wretchedness; unhappiness; misfortune. pl. *miseries:* adj. *miserable:* adv. *miserably.*
MISFOR'TUNE. *s.* Calamity; ill-luck.
MISGIVE'. *v.* To fill with doubt. pr. par. *misgiving;* past, *misgiven:* s. *misgiving.*
MISGOV'ERN. *v.* To govern ill. pr. par. *misgoverning;* past, *misgoverned:* s. *misgovernment.*
MISGUIDE'. *v.* To direct ill. pr. par. *misguiding;* past, *misguided:* s. *misguidance.*
MISHAP'. *s.* Ill chance.
MISINFORM'. *v.* To deceive by false accounts. pr. par. *misinforming;* past, *misinformed:* s. *misinformation, misinformer.*
MISINTER'PRET. *v.* To explain in a wrong sense. pr. par. *misinterpreting;* past, *misinterpreted:* s. *misinterpretation, misinterpreter.*
MISJOIN'. *v.* To join unfitly or improperly. pr. par. *misjoining;* past, *misjoined.*
MISJUDGE'. *v.* To mistake; to judge wrong. pr. par. *misjudging;* past, *misjudged:* s. *misjudgment.*
MISLAY'. *v.* To lay in a wrong place. pr. par. *mislaying;* past, *mislaid.*
MISLEAD'. *v.* To guide a wrong way. pr. par. *misleading;* past, *misled:* s. *misleader.*
MIS'LETOE. *s.* A kind of plant, which grows on trees.
MISMAN'AGE. *v.* To manage ill. pr. par. *mismanaging;* past, *mismanaged:* s. *mismanager, mismanagement.*
MISMATCH'. *v.* To match unsuitably. pr. par. *mismatching;* past, *mismatched.*
MISNA'ME. *v.* To call by a wrong name. pr. par. *misnaming;* past, *misnamed.*
MISNO'MER. *s.* A wrong name.

MISOG'AMIST. *s.* A marriage-hate
MIS-SPEND'. *v.* To spend ill, to waste. pr. par. *mis-spending;* past, *mis-spent:* s. *mis-spender.*
MISPLA'CE. *v.* To put in a wrong place. pr. par. *misplacing;* past *misplaced.*
MISPRINT'. *v.* To print wrong. pr. par. *misprinting;* past, *misprinted:* s. *misprint.*
MISPRI'SION. *s.* Mistake, scorn, neglect, concealment.
MISPRONOUNCE'. *v.* To pronounce improperly. pr. par. *mispronouncing;* past, *mispronounced:* s. *mispronunciation.*
MISPROPOR'TION. *v.* To join without due proportion. pr. par. *misproportioning;* past, *misproportioned:* s. *misproportion.*
MISQUOTE'. *v.* To quote falsely. pr. par. *misquoting;* past, *misquoted:* s. *misquotation.*
MISRECI'TE. *v.* To recite wrong. pr. par. *misreciting;* past, *misrecited:* s. *misrecital.*
MISRECK'ON. *v.* To reckon wrong. pr. par. *misreckoning;* past, *misreckoned:* s. *misreckoning.*
MISREPORT'. *v.* To give a false account of. pr. par. *misreporting;* past, *misreported.*
MISREPRESENT'. *v.* To represent not as it is. pr. par. *misrepresenting;* past, *misrepresented:* s. *misrepresentation, misrepresenter.*
MISRU'LE. *s.* Tumult; confusion.
MISS. *s.* The term of honour to a young girl. pl. *misses.*
MISS. *v.* To mistake; not to hit to fail of obtaining. pr. par. *missing;* past, *missed:* s. *miss,* pl. *misses*
MIS'SAL. *s* The mass-book.
MISSHA'PE' *v.* To shape ill; to deform. pr par. *misshaping;* past *misshaped:* adj. *misshapen.*
MIS'SILE. *adj.* Thrown by the hand. s. *missile.*
MIS'SION. *s.* Commission; legation
MIS'SIONARY. *s.* One sent to propagate religion. pl. *missionaries:* adj. *missionary.*

243

MIS'SIVE. *adj.* Such as is sent, or thrown. *s. missive.*

MIST. *s.* A low, thin cloud; a small, thin rain; dimness. adj. *misty:* s. *mistiness:* adv. *mistily.*

MISTA'KE. *v.* To conceive wrong; to take something for that which it is not. pr. par. *mistaking;* past, *mistaken:* pret. *mistook:* s. *mistake.*

MISSTA'TE. *v.* To state wrong. pr. par. *misstating;* past, *misstated:* s. *misstatement.*

MISTEACH'. *v.* To teach wrong. pr. par. *misteaching;* past, *mistaught.*

MISTI'ME. *v.* Not to time right. pr. par. *mistiming;* past, *mistimed.*

MISTOLD'. *par.* Erroneously narrated.

MISTRANSLA'TE. *v.* To translate incorrectly. pr. par. *mistranslating;* past, *mistranslated:* s. *mistranslation.*

MIS'TRESS. *s.* A woman who governs or teaches; a woman who has something in possession. pl. *mistresses.*

MISTRUST'. *s.* Diffidence; suspicion. v. *mistrust;* pr. par. *mistrusting;* past, *mistrusted:* adj. *mistrustful, mistrustless:* s. *mistrustfulness:* adv. *mistrustfully.*

MISTU'NE. *v.* To tune badly. pr. par. *mistuning;* past, *mistuned.*

MISUNDERSTAND'. *v.* To misconceive. pr. par. *misunderstanding;* past, *misunderstood.*

MISU'SE. *v.* To treat or use improperly. pr. par. *misusing;* past, *misused:* s. *misusage.*

MITE. *s.* A small insect; a small particle.

MIT'IGATE. *v.* To alleviate; to mollify. pr. par. *mitigating;* past, *mitigated:* s. *mitigation, mitigator:* adj. *mitigable, mitigant, mitigative.*

MI'TRE. *s.* A kind of episcopal crown. adj. *mitred.*

MIT'TENS. *s.* Gloves without fingers.

MIT'TIMUS. *s.* A warrant by which a justice commits an offender to prison.

MIX. *v.* To unite, to mingle. pr. par. *mixing;* past, *mixed:* s. *mixer, mixture.*

MIXTILIN'EAR. *adj.* Consisting of a line, or lines, part straight, and part curved.

MIZ'ZEN. *s.* The mast in the stern or hinder part of a ship.

MIZ'ZLE. *v.* To rain small drops, like mist. pr. par. *mizzling;* past, *mizzled.*

MNEMON'ICS. *s.* The art of assisting memory. adj. *mnemonic, mnemonical:* adv. *mnemonically.*

MOAN. *v.* To lament; to deplore. pr. par. *moaning;* past, *moaned:* s. *moan, moaner:* adj. *moanful.* adv. *moanfully.*

MOAT. *s.* A canal of water, round a castle. v. *moat;* pr. par. *moating,* past, *moated.*

MOB. *s.* A crowd; a tumultuous rout. v. *mob;* pr. par. *mobbing,* past, *mobbed.*

MOB. *s.* A kind of female undress, for the head.

MOBIL'ITY. *s.* The power of being moved; nimbleness; in cant language, the populace. pl. *mobilities.*

MOC'CASON. *s.* An Indian shoe.

MOCK. *v.* To deride; to laugh at. pr. par. *mocking;* past, *mocked:* s. *mocker, mockery:* adv. *mockingly.*

MOCK. *adj.* False; not real.

MOCK'ING-BIRD. *s.* A bird which imitates the notes of other birds.

MODE. *s.* Manner; form; method; a kind of silk. adj. *modish:* adv *modishly:* s. *modishness.*

MOD'EL. *s.* A small representation a copy to be imitated. v. *model,* pr. par. *modeling;* past, *modeled:* s. *modeler.*

MOD'ERATE. *adj.* Temperate; not excessive. v. *moderate;* pr. par. *moderating;* past, *moderated:* s. *moderation, moderator·* adv *moderately.*

244

MOD'ERN. *adj.* According to the present mode; recent; not ancient. *s. moderns:* v. *modernize;* pr. par. *modernizing;* past, *modernized:* s. *modernizer.*

MOD'EST. *adj.* Diffident; not impudent; chaste. s. *modesty:* adv. *modestly.*

MOD'ICUM. *s.* A small portion.

MOD'IFY. *v.* To alter the form or appearance, so as to accommodate something. pr. par. *modifying;* past, *modified:* s. *modification:* adj. *modifiable.*

MOD'ULATE. *v.* To form sound to a certain key, or to certain notes. pr. par. *modulating;* past, *modulated:* s. *modulation, modulator.*

MO'DUS. *s.* Compensation for tythes.

MOGUL'. *s.* An emperor of India.

MO'HAIR. *s.* Thread or stuff made of camel's, or other hair.

MOI'DER. *v.* To puzzle, to perplex, to confound. pr. par. *moidering;* past, *moidered.*

MOI'DORE. *s.* A Portuguese coin, rated at twenty-seven shillings sterling.

MOI'ETY. *s.* A half. pl. *moieties.*

MOIST. *adj.* Wet in a small degree; juicy. v. *moisten;* pr. par. *moistening;* past, *moistened:* s. *moistener, moistness, moisture.*

MOLAS'SES. *s.* Treacle; the spume or scum of the juice of the sugarcane.

MOLE. *s.* A natural spot on the body; a mound; a little animal, that works under ground. s. *molehill.*

MO'LECULE. *s.* A small mass, or portion.

MOLEST'. *v.* To disturb; to vex. pr. par. *molesting;* past, *molested:* s. *molester, molestation.*

MOL'LIENT. *adj.* Softening. s. pl. *mollients.*

MOL'LIFY. *v.* To soften; to appease. pr. par. *mollifying;* past, *mollified:* s. *mollifier, mollification:* adj. *mollifiable.*

MOLT'EN. Past par. of the v. *to melt.*

MO'MENT. *s.* Impulsive weight, force; importance; an indivisible particle of time. adj. *momentous, momentary, momentaneous:* adv. *momentarily.*

MOMEN'TUM. *s.* Impetus; force.

MON'ACHISM. *s.* The monastic life.

MON'ARCH. *s.* A king. s. *monarchy,* pl. *monarchies, monarchist* adj. *monarchal, monarchial.*

MON'ASTERY. *s.* A house of religious retirement. pl. *monasteries:* adj. *monastic:* adv. *monastically.*

MON'DAY. *s.* The second day of the week.

MON'EY. *s.* Metal coined for the purpose of commerce. adj. *monied,* or properly, *moneyed, moneyless.*

MON'EY'S-WORTH. *s.* Something valuable; worth its cost.

MONG'ER. *s.* A dealer, a seller.

MONG'REL. *adj.* Of a mixed breed.

MON'ITOR. *s.* One who warns of faults, or informs of duty. fem. *monitress,* pl. *monitresses:* adj. *monitory, monitorial:* s. *monition.*

MONK. *s.* One of a religious fraternity. adj. *monkish.*

MON'KEY. *s.* An ape, a baboon.

MON'OCHORD. *s.* An instrument of one string.

MON'ODY. *s.* A poem sung by one person. pl. *monodies.*

MON'OGRAM. *s.* A cipher; a character compounded of several letters.

MON'OLOGUE. *s.* A soliloquy.

MONOM'ACHY. *s.* A duel. pl. *monomachies.*

MONOPET'ALOUS. *adj.* Having one leaf.

MONOP'OLIZE. *v.* To obtain the whole; to engross exclusively pr. par. *monopolizing,* past, *monopolized:* s. *monopolizer, monopoly,* pl. *monopolies, monopolist.*

MON'OPTOTE. *s.* A noun used only in some oblique case.

MONOSYL'LABLE. *s.* A word of one syllable. adj. *monosyllabic.*

MONOT'ONOUS. *adj.* Wanting va

riety in cadence. *s. monotony:* adv. *monotonously.*

MONSOON'. *s.* The trade wind.

MON'STER. *s.* Something out of the common order of nature. adj. *monstrous:* s. *monstrousness:* adv. *monstrously.*

MONTH. *s.* A division of time, either by the sun or moon. adj. and adv. *monthly.*

MON'UMENT. *s.* Anything by which remembrance is preserved; a tomb. adj. *monumental.*

MOOD. *s.* A variation of a verb; temper of mind.

MOOD'Y. *adj.* Angry; out of humour; sad. s. *moodiness:* adv. *moodily.*

MOON. *s.* The changing luminary of the night; the satellite of the earth. s. *moon-beams, moonlight, moonshine.*

MOON'-EYED. *adj.* Dim-eyed; purblind.

MOOR. *s.* A marsh; a fen. s. *moorcock, moor-game, moor-hen.*

MOOR. *s.* A native of Morocco.

MOOR. *v.* To fasten by anchors. pr. par. *mooring;* past, *moored:* s. *moorings.*

MOOSE. *s.* The large American deer.

MOOT. *v.* To plead a mock cause. pr. par. *mooting;* past, *mooted:* s. *mooter.*

MOP. *s.* A utensil for cleaning a floor, &c. v. *mop;* pr. par. *mopping;* past, *mopped.*

MOPE. *v.* To be stupid; to make spiritless. pr. par. *moping;* past, *moped:* adj. *mopish:* s. *mopishness.*

MOR'AL. *adj.* Relating to the practice of men towards each other, as it may be virtuous or criminal; known and admitted in the general business of life. s. pl. *morals:* s. *morality, moralist:* adv. *morally.*

MOR'ALIZE. *v.* To make moral; to explain in a moral sense. pr. par. *moralizing;* past, *moralized:* s. *moralizer.*

MORASS'. *s.* A fen, a bog; a moor. pl. *morasses.*

MORA'VIAN. *s.* One of a religious sect, founded in Moravia.

MOR'BID. *adj.* Diseased. s. *morbidness:* adv. *morbidly.*

MORBIF'IC. *adj.* Causing disease.

MORBO'SE. *adj.* Proceeding from disease. s. *morbosity.*

MORDA'CIOUS. *adj.* Biting. s. *mordacity.*

MOR'DICANT. *adj.* Biting, acrid. s. *mordication.*

MORE. *adj.* In greater quantity or quality. s. *more:* adv. *more.*

MOREEN'. *s.* A kind of stuff.

MOREL'LO. *s.* A kind of cherry. pl. *morelloes.*

MOREO'VER. *adv.* Besides; likewise.

MORN, MORN'ING. *s.* The first part of the day.

MOROC'CO. *s.* A fine sort of leather.

MORO'SE. *adj.* Of sour temper; peevish. s *moroseness*. adv. *morosely.*

MOR'RIS-DANCE. *s.* A kind of dance. s. *morris-dancer.*

MOR'ROW. *s.* The day after the present day.

MOR'SEL. *s.* A small piece, a mouthful.

MOR'TAL. *adj.* Doomed to death; deadly; human. s. *mortality,* pl. *mortalities:* adv. *mortally.*

MOR'TAR. *s.* A vessel in which things are pounded; a wide cannon; a kind of cement.

MORT'GAGE. *s.* A thing put into the hands of a creditor, &c. v. *mortgage;* pr. par. *mortgaging,* past, *mortgaged.*

MORTGAGEE' *s.* He that receives a mortgage.

MORTGAGOR'. *s.* He that gives a mortgage.

MORTIF'EROUS. *adj.* Deadly, fatal.

MOR'TIFY. *v.* To destroy vital qualities; to vex; to depress. pr. par. *mortifying;* past, *mortified:* s. *mortification, mortifier.*

MOR'TISE. *s.* A hole cut in wood, that another piece may be put in to form a joint. v. *mortise;* pr. par. *mortising;* past, *mortised.*

MORT'MAIN. *s.* Such a state of possession as makes it unalienable.

MORT'UARY. *s.* A burial place; a gift left by a man, at his death, to his parish church, for the recompense of his personal tithes and offerings not duly paid in his lifetime. pl. *mortuaries.*

MOSA'IC. *s.* A kind of painting in pebbles and shells, of sundry colours.

MOSA'IC. *adj.* Denoting the writings or laws of Moses.

MOSQUE. *s.* A Mahometan temple.

MOSS. *s.* A kind of plant; a morass. pl. *mosses:* adj. *mossy:* s. *mossiness:* adj. *moss-grown.*

MOST. *adj.* The superlative of *more.* adv. *mostly:* s. *most.*

MOTE. *s.* A small particle of matter.

MOTH. *s.* A kind of small insect. adj. *mothy, moth-eaten.*

MOTH'ER. *s.* A woman that has borne a child; a thick substance concreting in liquors. adj. *motherless, motherly.*

MOTH'ER-IN-LAW. *s.* The mother of a husband or wife.

MOTH'ER-OF-PEARL. *s.* A kind of coarse pearl: the shell in which pearls are generated.

MO'TION. *s.* The act of moving: impulse communicated; proposal made. v. *motion;* pr. par. *motioning;* past, *motioned:* adj. *motionless, motive.*

MOTIVE. *s.* That which incites to an action.

MOT'LEY. *adj.* Mingled; of various colours.

MOT'TO. *s.* A sentence or word added to a device, or prefixed to any thing. pl. *mottoes.*

MOULD. *s.* A kind of concretion on things kept motionless and damp: earth, the matrix in which any thing is cast, or receives its form. v. *mould;* pr. par. *moulding;* past,

moulded: s. *moulder:* adj. *mouldy* s. *mouldiness.*

MOULD'ER. *v.* To turn to dust; to crumble. pr. par. *mouldering,* past, *mouldered.*

MOULD'ING. *s.* Ornamental cavities in wood or stone.

MOULT. *v.* To shed or change the feathers. pr. par. *moulting;* past, *moulted.*

MOUND. *s.* A rampart; a fence.

MOUNT. *s.* A mountain; a hill.

MOUNT. *v.* To rise on high; to get on horseback; to attain in value; to embellish. pr. par. *mounting,* past, *mounted:* s. *mounter, mounting.*

MOUNT'AIN. *s.* A large hill. adj. *mountain, mountainous:* s. *mountaineer.*

MOUNT'EBANK. *s.* Any boastful and false pretender.

MOURN. *v.* To grieve; to be sorrowful. pr. par. *mourning;* past, *mourned:* s. *mourner, mourning* adj. *mournful:* adv. *mournfully, mourningly:* s. *mournfulness.*

MOUSE. *s.* A kind of small quadruped. pl. *mice:* v. *mouse;* pr. par. *mousing;* past, *moused:* s. *mouser.*

MOUTH. *s.* The aperture in the head, at which food is received; an entrance. adj. *mouthless:* s. *mouthful.*

MOUTH. *v.* To speak big; to vociferate. pr. par. *mouthing;* past, *mouthed:* s. *mouther.*

MOUTH'-PIECE. *s.* The piece of a trumpet, or other wind instrument, to which the mouth is applied.

MOV'ABLES. *s.* Chattels, goods, furniture.

MOVE. *v.* To put out of one place into another; to put in motion; to propose. pr. par. *moving;* past, *moved:* s. *move, movement, mover:* adj. *moving, movable:* adv. *movingly.*

MOW. *s.* A heap of corn or hay, laid up in a barn.

MOW. *v.* To cut with a scythe. pr par. *mowing;* past, *mowed:* s. *mower*

MUCH. *adj.* Large in quantity; long in time; many in number. *s. much.*

MU'CID. *adj.* Slimy; musty. *s. mucidity.*

MU'CILAGE. *s.* A slimy or viscous body. *adj. mucilaginous.*

MU'COUS. *adj.* Slimy, viscous. *s. mucousness:* adj. *muculent.*

MU'CUS. *s.* A slimy liquor, separated by the mucilaginous glands.

MUD. *s.* The slimy matter at the bottom of still water. *v. muddy;* pr. par. *muddying;* past, *muddied:* adj. *muddy:* s. *muddiness:* adv. *muddily.*

MUD'DLE. *v.* To make turbid; to foul. pr. par. *muddling;* past, *muddled.*

MUFF. *s.* A soft warm cover for the hands.

MUF'FIN. *s.* A kind of light cake.

MUF'FLE. *v.* To wrap; to cover. pr. par. *muffling;* past, *muffled:* s. *muffler.*

MUF'TI. *s.* The high priest of the Mahometans.

MUG. *s.* A cup to drink out of.

MUGGLETO'NIAN. *s.* One of a sect of enthusiasts, followers of Lodowick Muggleton.

MULAT'TO. *s.* One begot between a white and a black. pl. *mulattoes.*

MUL'BERRY. *s.* A kind of fruit. pl. *mulberries.*

MULCT. *s.* A fine; a penalty. *v. mulct;* pr. par. *mulcting;* past, *mulcted.*

MULE. *s.* An animal generated between an ass and a mare; an animal of a mixed breed. adj. *mulish:* s. *mulishness.*

MULETEE'R. *s.* A mule-driver.

MULL. *v.* To heat any liquor, and sweeten and spice it. pr. par. *mulling,* past, *mulled.*

MULL-MUS'LIN. *s.* A kind of soft thin muslin.

MUL'LEIN. *s.* A kind of plant.

MUL'LET. *s.* A species of sea-fish.

MULTANG'ULAR. *adj.* Many-cornered.

MULTIFA'RIOUS. *adj.* Having great diversity in itself. s. *multifariousness;* adv. *multifariously.*

MUL'TIFORM. *adj.* Having various shapes. s. *multiformity.*

MULTILAT'ERAL. *adj.* Having many sides.

MULTILIN'EAL. *adj.* Having many lines.

MULTIL'OQUOUS. *adj.* Very talkative.

MULTINO'MIAL, MULTINOM'INAL, MULTINOM'INOUS. *adj.* Having many names.

MULTIP'AROUS. *adj.* Bringing many at a birth.

MUL'TIPEDE. *s.* An insect with many feet.

MUL'TIPLE. *s.* A term in arithmetic, when one number contains another several times.

MULTIPLICAND'. *s.* The number to be multiplied.

MUL'TIPLY. *v.* To increase in number. pr. par. *multiplying;* past, *multiplied:* s. *multiplier, multiplicator, multiplication:* adj. *multiplicable, multiplyable.*

MULTIPLI'CITY. *s.* More than one of the same kind; state of being many.

MULTIPRES'ENCE. *s.* The power or act of being present in many places at the same time. adj. *multipresent.*

MULTIS'ONOUS. *adj.* Having many sounds.

MUL'TITUDE. *s.* The state of being many; a crowd or throng; the vulgar. adj. *multitudinous.*

MUM. *int.* Silence; hush.

MUM. *s.* Ale brewed with wheat.

MUM'BLE. *v.* To speak inwardly; to grumble; to chew. pr. par. *mumbling;* past, *mumbled:* s. *mumbler.* adv. *mumblingly.*

MUM'MER. *s.* A masker; one who performs frolics in a personated dress. s. *mummery,* pl. *mummeries.*

MUM'MY. *s.* A dead body, preserved by embalming. pl. *mummies.*

MUMP. *v.* To nibble; to talk low and quick. pr. par. *mumping;* past, *mumped:* s. *mumper.*

MUMPS. *s.* Sullenness; a swelling of the glands, about the throat and jaws.

MUNCH. *v.* To chew by great mouthfuls. pr. par. *munching;* past, *munched:* s. *muncher.*

MUN'DANE. *adj.* Belonging to the world. s. *mundanity.*

MU'NERARY. *adj.* Having the nature of a gift.

MUNG'REL. *s.* See MONGREL.

MUNI'CIPAL. *adj.* Belonging to a corporation. s. *municipality,* pl. *municipalities.*

MUNIF'ICENCE. *s.* Liberality. adj. *munificent:* adv. *munificently.*

MU'NIMENT. *s.* Fortification; support; record; evidences; charters.

MUNI'TION. *s.* Ammunition; materials for war.

MU'RAGE. *s.* Money paid to keep walls in repair.

MU'RAL. *adj.* Pertaining to a wall.

MUR'DER. *s.* The act of killing a human being unlawfully. *v. murder;* pr. par. *murdering;* past, *murdered:* s. *murderer:* adj. *murderous:* adv. *murderously.*

MURIAT'IC. *adj.* Partaking of the taste or nature of sea-salt.

MURK'Y. *adj.* Dark; cloudy. s. *murkiness.*

MUR'MUR. *s.* A complaint half suppressed. v. *murmur;* pr. par. *murmuring;* past, *murmured:* s. *murmuring, murmurer:* adj. *murmuring:* adv. *murmuringly.*

MUR'RAIN. *s.* The plague in cattle.

MUSCADEL', MUS'CADINE. *s.* A kind of sweet grape, sweet wine, and sweet pear.

MUS'CLE. *s.* A fleshy fibre; a bivalve shell-fish. adj. *muscular, musculous.*

MUSE. *v.* To ponder; to study; pr. par. *musing;* past, *mused:* s. *muser.*

MUSE. *s.* One of the nine sister goddesses, who are supposed to preside over the liberal arts.

MUSE'UM. *s.* A repository of curiosities.

MUSH. *s.* Food of maize-flour and water, boiled.

MUSH'ROOM. *s.* A kind of plant.

MU'SIC. *s.* The science of harmonical sounds; instrumental or vocal harmony. adj. *musical:* adv *musically:* s. *musician.*

MUSK. *s.* An animal perfume.

MUSK'ET. *s.* A soldier's hand-gun. s. *musketeer.*

MUSQUI'TO. *s.* A stinging fly or gnat. pl. *musquitoes.*

MUSK'-MELON. *s.* A kind of fragrant melon.

MUSK'-ROSE. *s.* A kind of rose.

MUS'LIN. *s.* A fine stuff, made of cotton.

MUS'SULMAN. *s.* A follower of Mahomet. regular pl. *mussulmans.*

MUST. *v.* To be obliged: an imperfect verb.

MUST. *v.* To mould. pr. par. *musting;* past, *musted:* s. *must, mustiness:* adj. *musty.*

MUSTA'CHIO. *s.* A whisker; hair on the upper lip. pl. *mustachioes.*

MUS'TARD. *s.* A kind of plant.

MUS'TER. *v.* To bring together; to form into an army. pr. par. *mustering;* past, *mustered:* s. *muster, muster-master, muster-roll.*

MU'TABLE. *adj.* Subject to change; inconstant. s. *mutability:* adv. *mutably:* s. *mutation.*

MUTA'TION. *s.* Change; alteration.

MUTE. *adj.* Silent; dumb; not vocal. s. *mute, muteness:* adv. *mutely.*

MU'TILATE. *v.* To deprive of some essential part. pr. par. *mutilating,* past, *mutilated:* s. *mutilation, mutilator.*

MU'TINY. *v.* To rise against authority; to move sedition. pr. par. *mutinying;* past, *mutinied:* s. *mutiny,* pl. *mutinies:* adj. *mutinous:* adv. *mutinously:* s. *mutineer.*

MUT'TER. *v.* To grumble; to murmur. pr par. *muttering;* past,

MUT—MYR

muttered; s. *mutter,* *mutterer:* adv. *mutteringly.*

MUT'TON. s. The flesh of sheep.

MU'TUAL. *adj.* Reciprocal. adv. *mutually:* s. *mutuality.*

MUZ'ZLE. s. The mouth; a fastening for the mouth. v. *muzzle;* pr. par. *muzzling;* past, *muzzled.*

MY. *pron.* Belonging to me.

MYNHEE'R. s. Sir, my lord or master—among the Dutch.

MYR'IAD. s. The number of ten thousand; proverbially, any great number.

MYR'MIDON. s. Any rude ruffian.

MYRRH. s. A kind of gum.

MYR'TLE. s. A kind of fragrant tree. adj. *myrtled.*

MYS—MYT

MYSELF'. s. An emphatical word added to *I.*

MYS'TERY. s. Something above human intelligence; any thing artfully made difficult; a trade. pl. *mysteries:* adj. *mysterious:* adv. *mysteriously:* s. *mysteriousness.*

MYS'TICAL. *adj.* Containing a mystery. adv. *mystically:* s. *mysticism.*

MYTHOL'OGIZE. *v.* To relate or explain the fabulous history of the heathens. pr. par. *mythologizing;* past, *mythologized:* s. *mythologist.*

MYTHOL'OGY. s. System of fables. adj. *mythologic, mythological;* adv. *mythologically.*

N

NAB—NAM

NAB. *v.* To catch unexpectedly. pr. par. *nabbing;* past, *nabbed:* s. *nabber.*

NA'BOB. s. The title of an Indian prince.

NA'DIR. s. The point under foot, directly opposite the zenith.

NAG. s. A small horse.

NAI'AD. s. A water-nymph.

NAIL. s. The horny substance at the ends of the fingers and toes; a spike of metal; the 16th part of a yard. s. *nailer, nailery,* pl. *naileries.*

NAIL. *v.* To fasten with nails. pr. par. *nailing;* past, *nailed.*

NAIVETE'. s. Simplicity; ingenuousness.

NA'KED. *adj.* Wanting clothes; uncovered; unarmed; simple. s. *nakedness:* adv. *nakedly.*

NAM'BY-PAM'BY. *adj.* Having little affected prettiness.

NAME. s. Appellation; reputation; renown. v. *name;* pr. par. *naming;* past, *named:* s. *namer:* adj. *nameless:* adv. *namely.*

NAM—NAS

NAME'SAKE. s. One that has the same name.

NANKEEN'. s. A kind of cotton cloth.

NAP. s. A short sleep; down. v. *nap,* pr. par. *napping;* past, *napped:* s. *napper.*

NAPE. s. The joint of the neck behind.

NAPH'THA. s. A pure, clear, thin, mineral fluid.

NAP'PY. *adj.* Hairy; full of down. s. *nappiness.*

NARCIS'SUS. s. The daffodil.

NARCOT'IC, NARCOTICAL. *adj* Producing torpor or stupefaction s. *narcotic.*

NARRA'TION. s. Act of narrating; history. v. *narrate;* pr. par. *narrating;* past, *narrated:* s. *narrator:* adj. *narratory.*

NAR'RATIVE. s. A relation; a story. adj. *narrative.*

NAR'ROW. *adj.* Not broad or wide; covetous; contracted. v. *narrow,* pr. par. *narrowing;* past, *narrowed:* adv. *narrowly:* s. *narrowness.*

NA'SAL. *adj.* Belonging to the nose

NAS'CENT. *adj.* Growing; increasing.
NAS'TY. *adj.* Dirty; filthy. *adv. nastily:* s. *nastiness.*
NA'TAL. *adj.* Native; relating to nativity.
NA'TION. *s.* A people distinguished from another people.
NA'TIONAL. *adj.* Public; general; attached to one's own country. *adv. nationally:* s. *nationality:* v. *nationalize;* pr. par. *nationalizing;* past, *nationalized.*
NA'TIVE. *adj.* Produced by nature; natural; pertaining to the time or place of birth. s. *native, nativity,* pl. *nativities.*
NAT'URAL. *adj.* Produced or effected by nature; not born in wedlock; following the stated course of things; unaffected. *adv. naturally:* s. *naturalness, naturality, naturalist.*
NAT'URALIZE. *v.* To invest with the privileges of a native subject; to make natural. pr. par. *naturalizing;* past, *naturalized:* s. *naturalization.*
NA'TURE. *s.* An imaginary being, supposed to preside over the material and animal world; the native state or properties of any thing; disposition of mind.
NAUGHT. *s.* Nothing.
NAUGH'TY. *adj.* Bad; wicked. *adv. naughtily:* s. *naughtiness.*
NAU'SEA. *s.* Sickness. v. *nauseate;* pr. par. *nauseating;* past, *nauseated:* adj. *nauseous.*
NAUT'IC, NAUT'ICAL. *adj.* Pertaining to sailors.
NAUT'ILUS. *s.* A small shell-fish. pl. *nautiluses.*
NAVE. *s.* The middle part of a wheel, in which the axle moves; the middle part of a church, distinct from the aisles or wings.
NA'VEL. *s.* The point in the middle of the belly.
NAV'IGATE. *v.* To sail; to pass by water. pr. par. *navigating;* past, *navigated:* s. *navigation, navigator:* adj. *navigable.*
NA'VY. *s.* An assemblage of ships of war; a fleet. pl. *navies:* adj. *naval.*
NAY. *adv.* No; not only so, but more.
NAZARE'NE. *s.* One of Nazareth.
NAZ'ARITE. *s.* One separated from others, by a profession of some extraordinary and special acts of religion.
NEAP. *adj.* Low, decrescent: used in relation to the tide. adj. *neaped.*
NEAPOL'ITAN. *adj.* Belonging to Naples.
NEAR. *adj.* Close to; nigh; almost; not distant. *adv. nearly:* s. *nearness.*
NEAR. *v.* To approach. pr. par *nearing,* past, *neared.*
NEAR-SIGHT'ED. *adj.* Short-sighted.
NEAT. *adj.* Elegant, but without dignity; clean. *adv. neatly:* s. *neatness.*
NEB. *s.* Nose; beak; mouth.
NEB'ULOUS. *adj.* Misty, cloudy.
NE'CESSARY. *adj.* Needful; indispensably requisite. *adv. necessarily:* s. *necessaries.*
NECES'SITY. *s.* Cogency; indispensableness; want; poverty; compulsion. pl. *necessities.* v. *necessitate;* pr. par. *necessitating;* past *necessitated:* s. *necessitation:* adj *necessitous.*
NECK. *s.* That part between th head and the body; a long narrow part. s. *neckcloth, necklace.*
NEC'ROMANCER. *s.* A conjurer an enchanter. s. *necromancy,* pl. *necromancies:* adj. *necromantic: adv. necromantically.*
NEC'TAR. *s.* The supposed drink of the gods; any pleasant drink. adj. *nectarean, nectareous, nectared.*
NEC'TARINE. *s.* A fruit of the plum kind.
NEED. *s.* Exigency; pressing difficulty; want. v. *need;* pr. par. *needing;* past, *needed:* s. *needer, neediness:* adj. *needy, needful · adv. needily, needfully:* s. *needfulness.*
NEED'LE. *s.* A small instrument used in sewing; the small steel

251

NEE—NEO

bar, which, in the mariner's compass, points north and south. s. *needlework.*

NEED'LEFUL. *s.* As much thread as is put at one time into a needle.

NEED'LESS. *adj.* Unnecessary. adv. *needlessly:* s. *needlessness.*

NEFA'RIOUS. *adj.* Wicked; abominable. adv. *nefariously:* s. *nefariousness.*

NEGA'TION. *s.* Denial; argument drawn from denial.

NEG'ATIVE. *s.* A proposition, by which something is denied ; a particle of denial. v. *negative;* pr. par. *negativing;* past, *negatived:* adj. *negative:* adv. *negatively.*

NEGLECT'. *v.* To omit by carelessness; to slight. pr. par. *neglecting;* past, *neglected:* s. *neglect, neglecter:* adj. *neglectful:* adv. *neglectfully, neglectingly.*

NEGLIGEE'. *s.* A sort of gown, worn by ladies in the morning.

NEG'LIGENCE. *s.* Habit of omitting by heedlessness, or of acting carelessly. adj. *negligent:* adv. *negligently.*

NEGO'TIATE. *v.* To have intercourse of business; to treat; to traffic. pr. par. *negotiating;* past, *negotiated:* s. *negotiation, negotiator:* adj. *negotiable.*

NE'GRO. *s.* A black person. pl. *negroes.*

NE'GUS. *s.* A mixture of wine, water, sugar, lemon, and nutmeg.

NEIGH. *v.* To make a noise like a horse. pr. par. *neighing;* past, *neighed:* s. *neigh, neighing.*

NEIGH'BOUR. *s.* One who lives near another. v. *neighbour;* pr. par. *neighbouring;* past, *neighboured:* s. *neighbourhood:* adj. and adv. *neighbourly.*

NEITHER. *conj. and pron.* Not either.

NEOL'OGY. *s.* Invention or use of new words and phrases. adj. *neological:* s. *neologism.*

NE'OPHYTE. *s.* One regenerated; a convert.

NEP—NEW

NEPH'EW. *s.* The son of a brother or sister.

NEP'OTISM. *s.* Fondness for nephews.

NE'REID. *s.* A sea-nymph.

NERVE. *s.* An organ of sensation, force; strength. v. *nerve;* pr. par. *nerving;* past, *nerved:* adj. *nervous, nerveless:* adv. *nervously:* s. *nervousness.*

NES'CIENCE. *s.* Ignorance. adj. *nescient.*

NEST. *s.* The bed formed by a bird; boxes or drawers. v. *nest;* pr. par. *nesting;* past, *nested:* s. *nest-egg.*

NEST'LE. *v.* To lie close and snug, as a bird in her nest. pr. par. *nestling;* past, *nestled:* s. *nestler.*

NEST'LING. *s.* A young bird.

NET. *s.* A texture interwoven with large interstices or meshes. v. *net;* pr. par. *netting;* past, *netted:* s. *netter, netting, network.*

NET. *adj.* Pure, clear, genuine, &c.

NETH'ER. *adj.* Lower, infernal. sup. *nethermost.*

NET'TLE. *s.* A stinging herb.

NET'TLE. *v.* To sting; to irritate; to provoke. pr. par. *nettling;* past, *nettled:* s. *nettler.*

NEUROL'OGY. *s.* A description of the nerves.

NEUROT'OMY. *s.* The anatomy of the nerves.

NEU'TER. *adj.* Indifferent; not engaged on either side; implying no ex. adj. *neutral:* s. *neutrality*, pl. *neutralities, neutralist:* adv. *neutrally:* v. *neutralize;* pr. par. *neutralizing;* past, *neutralized.*

NEV'ER. *adv.* At no time; in no degree. adv. *nevertheless.*

NEW. *adj.* Not old; fresh, modern. s. *newness:* adv. *newly.*

NEWFANG'LED. *adj.* Affected by vain or foolish love of novelty. v. *newfangle;* pr. par. *newfangling;* past, *newfangled:* s. *newfangledness.*

NEWS. *s.* Fresh account of any thing; something not heard before.

NEXT. *adj.* Nearest; immediately after.

NIB. *s.* The point of any thing, generally of a pen.

NIB'BLE. *v.* To bite by little at a time. pr. par. *nibbling;* past, *nibbled:* s. *nibble, nibbler.*

NICE. *adj.* Accurate, scrupulous; delicate; trivial. adv. *nicely:* s. *niceness, nicety,* pl. *niceties.*

NICHE. *s.* A hollow, in which a statue may be placed. adj. *niched.*

NICK. *s.* A notch; a winning throw; exact point of time. v. *nick;* pr. par. *nicking;* past, *nicked.*

NICK'EL. *s.* One of the semi-metals.

NICK'NAME. *s.* A name given in scoff or contempt. v. *nickname;* pr. par. *nicknaming;* past, *nicknamed.*

NIDIFICA'TION. *s.* The act of building nests.

NIDULA'TION. *s.* The time of remaining in the nest.

NIECE. *s.* The daughter of a brother or sister.

NIG'GARD. *s.* A miser; a sordid fellow. adj. *niggard:* adv. *niggardly:* s. *niggardliness.*

NIGH. *adj.* Near. adv. *nigh.*

NIGHT. *s.* The time of darkness. adv. *nightly:* adj. *nightborn:* s. *nightcap, nightdew, nightdress, nightfall, nightgown.*

NIGHT'INGALE. *s.* A small bird that sings in the night.

NIGHT'MARE. *s.* A morbid oppression, in the night, resembling the pressure of weight upon the breast.

NIGHT'PIECE. *s.* A picture so coloured as to be supposed seen by candle or moonlight.

NIGHT'SHADE. *s.* The darkness of the night; a poisonous plant.

NIGHT'WALKER. *s.* One who roves in the night, upon ill designs. s. *nightwalking.*

NIGHT'WATCH. *s.* A period of the night, as distinguished by change of watch. s. *nightwatcher, nightwatching.*

NIGRES'CENT. *adj.* Growing black, approaching to blackness.

NIM'BLE. *adj.* Quick, active, ready. adv. *nimbly:* s. *nimbleness:* adj. *nimblewitted.*

NIN'COMPOOP. *s.* A fool; a trifler

NINE. *adj.* One more than eight. s. *ninth:* adv. *ninthly:* adj. *ninefold.* s. *nineholes, ninepins.*

NINE'TEEN. *adj.* Nine and ten: ordinal adj. *nineteenth.*

NINE'TY. *adj.* Nine times ten: ordinal adj. *ninetieth.*

NIN'NY. *s.* A fool; a simpleton. pl. *ninnies.*

NIN'NYHAMMER. *s.* A simpleton

NIP. *v.* To pinch, to blast. pr. par *nipping;* past, *nipped:* s. *nip, nipper:* adv. *nippingly.*

NIP'PERKIN. *s.* A little cup, a small tankard.

NIP'PERS. *s.* Small pincers.

NIP'PLE. *s.* The teat; the dug.

NIT. *s.* The egg of a louse. adj *nitty.*

NI'TRE. *s.* Saltpetre. adj. *nitrous* s. *nitrosity.*

NIV'EOUS. *adj.* Snowy; resembling snow.

NO. *adv.* The word of denial; the word of refusal. adj. *no:* s. *no* pl. *noes.*

NOBIL'ITATE. *v.* To ennoble. pr par. *nobilitating;* past, *nobilitated* s. *nobilitation.*

NOBIL'ITY. *s.* The class of nobles. pl. *nobilities.*

NO'BLE. *adj.* Of an ancient and splendid family; worthy; sublime; magnificent. s. *noble, nobleman,* pl. *noblemen.*

NOBLESSE'. *s.* Nobility, collectively; dignity.

NO'BODY. *s.* No one; not any one. pl. *nobodies.*

NO'CENT. *adj.* Hurtful.

NOCTAMBULA'TION. *s.* The act of walking in sleep.

NOCTIF'EROUS. *adj.* Bringing night.

NOC'TUARY. *s.* An account of

what passes by night. pl. *noctuaries.*
NOCTUR'NAL. *adj.* Nightly. *adv. nocturnally.*
NOC'UOUS. *adj.* Noxious; hurtful.
NOD. *v.* To decline the head with a quick motion; to be drowsy; to shake. pr. par. *nodding;* past, *nodded:* s. *nod, nodder.*
NODA'TION. *s.* The state of being knotted, or the act of making knots.
NOD'DLE. *s.* The head, in contempt.
NOD'DY. *s.* A simpleton; a species of carriage. pl. *noddies.*
NO'DOUS. *adj.* Full of knots.
NOD'ULE. *s.* A small lump.
NOG'GIN. *s.* A small mug.
NOISE. *s.* Any kind of sound; outcry. *adj. noisy, noiseless:* s. *noisiness.*
NOISE. *v.* To spread by rumour. pr. par. *noising;* past, *noised.*
NOI'SOME. *adj.* Noxious; unwholesome; offensive. *adv. noisomely:* s. *noisomeness.*
NOLI'TION. *s.* Unwillingness.
NOLL. *s.* A head; a noddle.
NOMENCLA'TURE. *s.* The act of naming; a vocabulary.
NOM'INAL. *adj.* Referring to names, rather than things; not real. *adv. nominally.*
NOM'INATE. *v.* To name; to appoint. pr. par. *nominating;* past, *nominated:* s. *nomination, nominator.*
NOM INATIVE. *s.* The name of the case that designates the name of any thing.
NON AGE. *s.* Minority.
NONATTEND'ANCE. *s.* The not giving personal attendance.
NONCOMPLI'ANCE. *s.* Refusal or omission to comply.
NONCONFORM'ITY. *s.* Refusal of compliance; refusal to join in the established religion. *s. nonconformist: adj. nonconforming.*
NONE. *adj.* Not any; not other.
NONEN'TITY. *s.* Non-existence; a thing not existing. pl. *nonentities.*

NONE'SUCH. *s.* Something unique, something superior.
NONEXIS'TENCE. *s.* Negation of being; a thing not existing. *adj. nonexistent.*
NONJU'RING. *adj.* Belonging to those who will not swear allegiance to the Hanoverian family. *s. nonjuror.*
NONPAREIL'. *s.* Excellence unequalled; a kind of apple; printers' letters of a small size; a kind of bird.
NON'PLUS. *s.* Puzzle; inability to say or do more. *v. nonplus;* pr. par. *nonplusing;* past, *nonplused.*
NON-RES'IDENT. *s.* One who does not reside at the proper place. *adj. non-resident:* s. *non-residence.*
NON-RESIST'ANCE. *s.* Passive obedience. *adj.* and *s. non-resistant.*
NON'SENSE. *s.* Unmeaning language; trifles. *adj. nonsensical:* adv. *nonsensically:* s. *nonsensicalness.*
NON'SUIT. *s.* Stoppage of a suit at law. *v. nonsuit;* pr. par. *nonsuiting;* past, *nonsuited.*
NOO'DLE. *s.* A fool; a simpleton.
NOOK. *s.* A corner.
NOON. *s.* The middle of the day; twelve. *s. noonday, noontide.*
NOOSE. *s.* A running knot. *v. noose* pr. par. *noosing;* past, *noosed.*
NOR. One of the conjunctions.
NOR'MAN. *adj.* Relating or belonging to Normandy.
NORTH. *s.* The point opposite to the south. *adj. north, northern:* adv. *northerly:* s. *north-star, north-wind.*
NORTH-EAST'. *s.* The point midway between the north and east. *adj. north-eastern:* adv. *north-easterly.*
NORTH'WARD, NORTH'WARDS *adv.* Towards the north.
NORTH-WEST'. *s.* The point midway between the north and west. *adj. north-western:* adv. *north-westerly.*
NORWE'GIAN. *adj.* Belonging to Norway.

NOSE. *s.* The prominence on the face which is the organ of scent. *v. nose;* pr. par. *nosing;* past, *nosed:* adj. *noseless.*

NOSE'GAY. *s.* A posy; a bunch of flowers.

NOSOL'OGY. *s.* Doctrine of diseases.

NOS'TRIL. *s.* The cavity in the nose.

NOS'TRUM. *s.* A medicine not yet made public.

NOT. *adv.* The particle of negation, or refusal.

NO'TABLE. *adj.* Remarkable; memorable; careful; bustling. adv. *notably.*

NO'TARY. *s.* An officer whose business it is to take notes of any thing which may concern the public. adj. *notarial.*

NOTA'TION. *s.* The act or practice of recording by marks, as by figures or letters.

NOTCH. *s.* A nick; a hollow cut in any thing. v. *notch;* pr. par. *notching;* past, *notched:* s. *notcher.*

NOTE. *s.* Mark; token; notice; reputation; account; tune; single sound in music; short hint; a short letter. v. *note;* pr. par. *noting;* past, *noted:* s. *noter:* adj. *noteworthy.*

NOTHING. *s.* Negation of being; nonentity; nonexistence; no importance. s. *nothingness.*

NOTICE. *s.* Remark; heed; information. v. *notice,* pr. par. *noticing;* past, *noticed.*

NO'TIFY. *v.* To declare; to make known. pr. par. *notifying;* past, *notified:* s. *notification.*

NO'TION. *s.* Thought; representation formed in the mind.

NOTO'RIOUS. *adj.* Publicly known; apparent; not hidden; infamous. s. *notoriety,* pl. *notorieties.*

NOTWITHSTANDING. *con.* Without hindrance or obstruction from; although; nevertheless; however.

NOUGHT. *s.* Not any thing; nothing.

NOUN. *s.* In grammar, the name of any thing.

NOUR'ISH. *v.* To increase or support by food; to maintain; to encourage. pr. par. *nourishing;* past, *nourished:* s. *nourisher, nourishment:* adj. *nourishable.*

NOV'EL. *adj.* New; not ancient. s. *novelty,* pl. *novelties:* v. *novelize,* pr. par. *novelizing;* past, *novelized*

NOV'EL. *s.* A tale; an amusing book, chiefly of fiction. s. *novelist.*

NOVEM'BER. *s.* The eleventh month of the year.

NOVER'CAL. *adj.* Relating or belonging to a stepmother.

NOV'ICE. *s.* One not acquainted with any thing; a freshman; one who has entered a religious house, but not yet taken the vow. s. *noviitate.*

NOW. *adv.* At this time; at the time present.

NO'WAY, NO'WAYS, NO'WISE. *adv.* Not in any manner or degree.

NO'WHERE. *adv.* Not in any place.

NOX'IOUS. *adj.* Hurtful, baneful. adv. *noxiously:* s. *noxiousness.*

NUBIF'EROUS. *adj.* Bringing clouds.

NU'BILATE. *v.* To cloud. pr. par. *nubilating;* past, *nubilated:* s. *nubilation.*

NU'BILE. *adj.* Marriageable.

NUCIF'EROUS. *adj.* Nut-bearing.

NU'CLEUS. *s.* A kernel; any thing about which matter is gathered or conglomerated. Latin pl. *nuclei.*

NUDA'TION. *s.* The act of making bare or naked.

NU'DITY. *s.* Nakedness.

NU'GATORY. *adj.* Trifling; futile; ineffectual.

NU'ISANCE. *s.* Something noxious or offensive.

NULL. *adj.* Void; of no force. v. *nullify;* pr. par. *nullifying;* past, *nullified:* s. *nullity,* pl. *nullities.*

NUMB. *adj.* Torpid; chill. v. *numb.* pr. par. *numbing;* past, *numbed.* s. *numbness.*

NUM'BER. *v.* To count; to tell, to reckon. pr. par. *numbering,* past, *numbered:* adj. *numberless*

255

NUM—NUR

NUM'BERS. s. The title of the fourth book in the Old Testament.
NU'MERAL. adj. Relating to number. s. numeral: adv. numerally.
NU'MERARY. adj. Belonging to a certain number.
NU'MERATE. v. To reckon; to calculate. pr. par. numerating; past, numerated: s. numeration, numerator: adj. numerical: adv. numerically.
NU'MEROUS. adj. Containing many; consisting of many. s. numerousness: adv. numerously.
NUM'SKULL. s. A dunce; a blockhead. adj. numskulled.
NUN. s. A woman secluded in a cloister, and dedicated to religion. s. nunnery, pl. nunneries.
NUN'CIO. s. A messenger; a kind of spiritual envoy from the pope.
NUNCU'PATIVE, NUNCU'PATORY. adj. Publicly or solemnly declaratory; verbally pronounced; not written.
NUP'TIAL. adj. Pertaining or relating to marriage. s. nuptials.
NURSE. s. A woman who has the care of another's child, or of a sick

NUR—NYM

person; one who breeds, educates, or protects. v. nurse; pr. par. nursing; past, nursed: s. nurser.
NUR'SERY. s. The chamber of a nurse; the place where young children are nursed; a plantation of young trees. pl. nurseries.
NURS'LING. s. One nursed; a fondling.
NUR'TURE. s. Food; diet; education. v. nurture; pr. par. nurturing; past, nurtured: s. nurturer.
NUT. s. The fruit of certain trees, &c. s. nutcrackers, nutshell.
NUTA'TION. s. A kind of tremulous motion.
NUT'BROWN. adj. Brown like a ripe nut.
NUT'GALL. s. Hard excrescence of an oak.
NUT'MEG. s. The kernel of a large aromatic fruit.
NU'TRIMENT. s. Food; aliment. adj. nutrimental.
NUTRI'TION. s. The act or quality of nourishing. adj. nutritious, nutritive.
NYMPH. s. A goddess of the woods, meadows, or waters. adj. nymphish, nymphlike.

O

OAF—OBD

OAF. s. A changeling; a dolt; an idiot. adj. oafish: s. oafishness.
OAK. s. A species of tree. adj. oaken.
OAK'UM. s. Cords untwisted and reduced to hemp.
OAR. s. An instrument to row with. v. oar; pr. par. oaring; past, oared.
OA'SIS. s. A fertile spot, surrounded by an arid desert. pl. oases.
OAT. s. A kind of grain. adj. oaten: s. oatcake, oatmeal.
OATH. s. A solemn affirmation, corroborated by the attestation of the Divine Being.
OB'DURATE. adj. Inflexibly obsti-

OBE—OBJ

nate in ill; impenitent: stubborn. adv. obdurately: s. obduracy.
OBE'DIENCE. s. Submission, obsequiousness. adj. obedient: adv. obediently.
OBEI'SANCE. s. A bow; a courtesy.
OB'ELISK. s. A pyramid of stone; a marginal mark (†).
OBE'SE. adj. Fat. s. obesity.
OBEY'. v. To pay submission to; to comply with. pr. par. obeying, past, obeyed: s. obeyer.
OBIT'UARY. s. A list of the dead; a register of burials. pl. obituaries: adj. obituary.
OB'JECT. s. That about which any power or faculty is employed; any

256

thing influenced by something else. s. *objector:* adj. *objective.*

OBJECT. *v.* To urge against; to oppose. pr. par. *objecting;* past, *objected:* s. *objection:* adj. *objectionable:* adv. *objectionably.*

OBJUR'GATE. *v.* To chide; to reprove. pr. par. *objurgating;* past, *objurgated:* s. *objurgation:* adj. *objurgatory.*

OBLA'TE. *adj.* Flat at the poles: used of a spheroid.

OBLA'TION. *s.* An offering; a sacrifice.

OB'LIGATE. *v.* To bind by contract or duty. pr. par. *obligating;* past, *obligated:* s. *obligation:* adj. *obligatory.*

OBLIGA'TO. *adj.* A musical term, signifying necessary, on purpose, for the instrument named.

OBLI'GE. *v.* To bind; to impose obligation; to indebt. pr. par. *obliging;* past, *obliged:* s. *obliger,* adj. *obliging:* s. *obligingness.*

OBLIGEE'. *s.* The person to whom another, called the obligor, is bound by a legal contract.

OBLIGOR'. *s.* The person bound to the obligee.

OBLI'QUE. *adj.* Not direct; not perpendicular. adv. *obliquely:* s. *obliqueness, obliquity.*

OBLIT'ERATE. *v.* To efface any thing written; to destroy. pr. par. *obliterating;* past, *obliterated:* s. *obliteration.*

OBLIV'ION. *s.* Forgetfulness; amnesty. adj. *oblivious.*

OB'LONG. *adj.* Longer than broad. s. *oblongness.*

OB'LOQUY. *s.* Censorious speech; blame; disgrace.

OBNOX'IOUS. *adj.* Liable to punishment; reprehensible. adv. *obnoxiously:* s. *obnoxiousness.*

OBSCE'NE. *adj.* Immodest, disgusting, offensive. adv. *obscenely:* s. *obsceneness, obscenity,* pl. *obscenities.*

OBSCU'RE. *adj.* Dark; not easily intelligible; difficult; unknown.

adv. *obscurely:* s. *obscurity:* pl. *obscurities.*

OB'SEQUIES. *s.* Funeral rites.

OBSE'QUIOUS. *adj.* Obedient; meanly compliant. adv. *obsequiously:* s. *obsequiousness.*

OBSER'VANCE. *s.* Respect; ceremonial reverence; attention. adj. *observant:* adv. *observantly, observably.*

OBSERVAN'DA. *s.* Things to b observed.

OBSER'VATORY. *s.* A place built for astronomical observation. pl. *observatories.*

OBSERVE'. *v.* To watch; to regard attentively; to note; to obey. pr. par. *observing;* past, *observed:* s. *observation, observer:* adv. *observingly.*

OBSOLES'CENT. *adj.* Growing obsolete.

OB'SOLETE. *adj.* Worn out of use; disused. s. *obsoleteness.*

OB'STACLE. *s.* Something opposed; hindrance.

OBSTET'RIC. *adj.* Relating or belonging to midwifery.

OB'STINATE. *adj.* Stubborn; contumacious. s. *obstinacy.* adv. *obstinately.*

OBSTREP'EROUS. *adj.* Loud; clamorous; noisy. adv. *obstreperously.* s. *obstreperousness.*

OBSTRUCT'. *v.* To block up; to bar; to hinder. pr. par. *obstructing;* past, *obstructed:* s. *obstruction:* adj. *obstructive.*

OBTAIN'. *v.* To gain; to acquire. pr. par. *obtaining;* past, *obtained:* s. *obtainer, obtainment:* adj. *obtainable.*

OBTRU'DE. *v.* To thrust in by force or imposture; to offer with unreasonable importunity. pr. par. *obtruding;* past, *obtruded:* s. *obtruder, obtrusion:* adj. *obtrusive:* adv. *obtrusively.*

OBTU'SE. *adj.* Not pointed; not acute; dull. adv. *obtusely:* s. *obtuseness.*

OB'VIATE. *v.* To prevent by interception. pr. par. *obviating;* past, *obviated.*

OB'VIOUS. *adj.* Easily seen; plain; open. adv. *obviously:* s. *obviousness.*

OCCA'SION. *s.* Occurrence; casualty; opportunity; accidental cause. *v. occasion;* pr. par. *occasioning;* past, *occasioned:* adj. *occasional:* adv. *occasionally.*

OCCIDEN'TAL. *adj.* Western.

OCCLU'DE. *v.* To shut up. pr. par. *occluding;* past, *occluded:* s. *occlusion.*

OCCULT'. *adj.* Hidden; secret. s. *occultness:* adv. *occultly.*

OC'CUPANCY. *s.* The act of taking possession; state of being in possession. s. *occupant.*

OC'CUPY. *v.* To possess; to keep; to busy; to use; to follow as business. pr. par. *occupying;* past, *occupied:* s. *occupier, occupation.*

OCCUR'. *v.* To be presented to the memory or attention; to appear; to happen. pr. par. *occurring;* past, *occurred:* s. *occurrence:* adj. *occurrent.*

O'CEAN. *s.* The main; the great sea. adj. *oceanic.*

OCEL'LATED. *adj.* Resembling the eye.

O'CHRE. *s.* A species of earth, of various colours. adj. *ochreous.*

OC'TAGON. *s.* A figure consisting of eight sides and angles. adj. *octagonal.*

OCTANG'ULAR. *adj.* Having eight angles.

OC'TAVE, *s.* The eighth day after some festival; an eighth, or an interval of eight sounds.

OCTA'VO. *s.* A book is said to be in *octavo,* when a sheet is folded into eight leaves.

OCTEN'NIAL. *adj.* Happening every eighth year.

OCTO'BER. *s.* The tenth month of the year.

OCTOGEN'ARY. *adj.* Of eighty years of age.

OC'TUPLE. *adj.* Eightfold.

OC'ULAR. *adj.* Depending on the eye; known by the eye. adv. *ocularly.*

OC'ULIST. *s.* One who professes to cure distempers of the eye.

ODD. *adj.* Not even; particular; strange. adv. *oddly:* s. *odds, oddness, oddity,* pl. *oddities.*

ODE. *s.* A poem to be sung to music.

O'DIOUS. *adj.* Hateful; detestable · causing hate. adv. *odiously:* s *odium, odiousness.*

ODORIF'EROUS. *adj.* Giving scent; fragrant. adv. *odoriferously:* s. *odoriferousness.*

O'DOUR. *s.* Scent; fragrance. adj. *odorous.*

ŒCONOM'ICS. *s.* Management of household affairs. See ECONOMY.

OF. One of the prepositions.

OFF. One of the adverbs.

OF'FAL. *s.* Waste meat; refuse; carrion.

OFFENCE'. *s.* Transgression; displeasure given; anger. adj. *offenceless:* v. *offend;* pr. par. *offending;* past, *offended:* s. *offender.* adj. *offensive:* adv. *offensively:* s. *offensiveness.*

OF'FER. *v.* To present; to sacrifice; to attempt. pr. par. *offering,* past, *offered:* s. *offer, offering, offerer.*

OF'FICE. *s.* A public employment, agency, &c. adj. *official:* adv. *officially:* s. *officer.*

OFFI'CIATE. *v.* To discharge the duties of an office. pr. par. *officiating;* past, *officiated.*

OFFICI'NAL. *adj.* Belonging to, or used in a shop.

OFFI'CIOUS. *adj.* Importunately forward; intrusive. adv. *officiously:* s. *officiousness.*

OF'FING. *s.* Out at sea, or at a sufficient distance from the shore.

OFF'SCOURING. *s.* Recrement; part rubbed away in cleaning any thing.

OFF'SET. *s.* A sprout; a shoot of a plant.

OFF—OMI

OFF'SPRING. *s.* Propagation; children; production.

OF'TEN. *adv.* Oft; frequently; many times. pronounced *of-n.* comp. *oftener;* sup. *oftenest:* adv. *oftentimes.*

O'GLE. *v.* To view with side glances. pr. par. *ogling;* past, *ogled:* s. *ogler.*

O'GRE. *s.* An imaginary monster of the east. fem. *ogress,* pl. *ogresses.*

OH. *int.* An exclamation denoting pain, sorrow, or surprise.

OIL. *s.* Any fat, greasy, unctuous matter. v. *oil;* pr. par. *oiling;* past, *oiled:* adj. *oily:* s. *oiliness.*

OIL'COLOUR. *s.* Paint made by grinding coloured substances with oil.

OINT'MENT. *s.* Unguent; a salve.

OLD. *adj.* Past the middle of life; decayed by time; of long continuance. s. *oldness:* adj. *oldfashioned.*

OLEA'GINOUS. *adj.* Oily; unctuous s. *oleaginousness.*

OLFAC'TORY. *adj.* Having the sense of smelling.

OL'IGARCHY. *s.* A form of government which places the supreme power in a small number; aristocracy. pl. *oligarchies:* adj. *oligarchical.*

O'LIO. *s.* A mixture; a medley.

OL'IVE. *s.* A plant producing oil; the emblem of peace.

OLYM'PIAD. *s.* A Grecian epoch; the space of four years.

OM'BRE *s.* A game at cards.

OM'ELET. *s.* A kind of pancake made with eggs.

O'MEN. *s.* A sign; a prognostic. adj. *omened.*

O'MER. *s.* A Hebrew measure.

OM'INOUS *adj.* Exhibiting bad tokens of futurity; inauspicious; exhibiting tokens good or ill. adv. *ominously:* s. *ominousness.*

OMIS'SION. *s.* Act of omitting. adj. *omissive.*

OMIT'. *v.* To leave out; not to mention. pr. par. *omitting;* past, *omitted.*

OMN—OPE

OMNIP'OTENT. *adj.* All-powerful s. *omnipotence.*

OMNIPRES'ENCE. *s.* Ubiquity; unbounded presence. adj. *omnipresent.*

OMNIS'CIENCE. *s.* Boundless knowledge; infinite wisdom. adj. *omniscient.*

OMNIV'OROUS. *adj.* All-devouring

ON. One of the prepositions. adv. *on*

ONE. *adj.* Single; denoted by a unit some one. s. *one, oneness:* adv. *once.*

ONE'-EYED. *adj.* Having only one eye.

ON'ERARY. *adj.* Fitted for carriage or burthens; comprising a burthen.

ONERA'TION. *s.* The act of loading.

ON'EROUS. *adj.* Burthensome.

ON'ION. *s.* A species of bulbous plant.

ON'LY. *adv.* Single; simply; one and no more; this and no other.

ON'OMANCY. *s.* Divination by a name. pl. *onomancies.*

ON'SET. *s.* Attack; assault; a beginning.

ONTOL'OGY. *s.* The science of the affections of being in general; metaphysics. s. *ontologist.*

ON'WARDS. *adv.* Forward; in a state of advanced progression. adj. *onward.*

ON'YX. *s.* A semi-pellucid gem. pl. *onyxes.*

OOZE. *s.* Soft mud; slime; soft flow. v. *ooze;* pr. par. *oozing,* past, *oozed:* adj. *oozy.*

OPA'CITY. *s.* Cloudiness; want of transparency. pl. *opacities.*

OPAQUE'. *adj.* Dark; not transparent. adv. *opaquely.*

O'PEN. *v.* To unclose; to unlock to explain; to begin. pr. par. *opening;* past, *opened:* adj. *open:* adv *openly:* s. *opener, openness, opening:* adj. *openeyed, openhanded openhearted, openmouthed.*

OP'ERA. *s.* A musical drama.

OP'ERATE. *v.* To act; to produce effects pr. par. *operating;* past, *operated:* s. *operation, operator:* adj. *operative.*

OP'EROSE. *adj.* Laborious; full of trouble and tediousness. s. *operoseness, operosity.*

OPHTHAL'MIA. *s.* A disease of the eyes. adj. *ophthalmic.*

O'PIATE. *s.* A medicine that causes sleep. adj. *opiate.*

OPIF'ICER. *s.* One that performs any work; an artist.

OPIN'ION. *s.* Persuasion of the mind, without proof or certain knowledge; sentiments; judgment. adj. *opinioned.*

O'PIUM. *s.* A soporific drug.

OPODEL'DOC. *s.* The name of a plaster, and of a popular ointment.

OPOS'SUM. *s.* A kind of American quadruped.

OPPO'NENT. *adj.* Opposite; adverse. s. *opponent.*

OPPORTU'NE. *adj.* Seasonable; convenient; well-timed. adv. *opportunely.*

OPPORTU'NITY. *s.* Fit time; convenience; fit place. pl. *opportunities.*

OPPO'SE. *v.* To act against; to resist; to put in opposition. pr. par. *opposing;* past, *opposed:* s. *opposer, opposition.*

OP'POSITE. *adj.* Placed in front; adverse; repugnant. s. *opposite:* adv. *oppositely.*

OPPRESS'. *v.* To crush by hardship; to overpower. pr. par. *oppressing;* past, *oppressed:* s. *oppression, oppressor:* adj. *oppressive:* adv. *oppressively.*

OPPRO'BRIOUS. *adj.* Reproachful; causing infamy; scurrilous. adv. *opprobriously:* s. *opprobrium.*

OPPUGN'. *v.* To oppose; to attack; to refute. pr. par. *oppugning;* past, *oppugned:* s. *oppugner.*

OP'TATIVE. *adj.* Expressive of desire.

OP'TIC, OP'TICAL. *adj.* Visual; relating to the science of vision. adj. *optical:* s. *optics, optician.*

OP'TIMISM. *s.* The doctrine that every thing in nature is ordered for the best.

OP'TION. *s.* Choice, election; wish adj. *optional.*

OP'ULENCE. *s.* Wealth; riches. adj. *opulent:* adv. *opulently.*

OR. One of the conjunctions.

OR'ACLE. *s* Something delivered by supernatural wisdom; one famed for wisdom. adj. *oracular:* adv. *oracularly.*

O'RAL. *adj.* Delivered by mouth: not written. adv. *orally.*

OR'ANGE. *s.* A kind of fruit. s *orangery,* pl. *orangeries.*

ORA'TION. *s.* A speech made according to the laws of rhetoric; an harangue.

OR'ATOR. *s.* A public speaker; a man of eloquence. adj. *oratorical.* adv. *oratorically:* s. *oratory.*

ORATO'RIO. *s.* A kind of sacred drama, the subject being generally taken from the scriptures, and set to music. adj. *oratorical.*

ORB. *s.* A sphere; a circular body; a celestial body. adj. *orbed.*

ORBA'TION. *s.* Privation of parents or children; any privation.

ORBIC'ULAR. *adj.* Spherical.

ORB'IT. *s.* The line described by the revolution of a planet.

ORCH'ARD. *s.* A garden of fruit trees.

ORCH'ESTRE, ORCH'ESTRA. *s.* The place where musicians sit; the band of musicians.

ORDAIN'. *v.* To appoint; to decree; to establish; to invest. pr. par. *ordaining;* past, *ordained:* s. *ordination, ordainer:* adj. *ordainable.*

ORDE'AL. *s.* A trial by fire or water.

OR'DER. *s.* Method; regularity; command; a rank; a religious fraternity; a class. v. *order;* pr. par. *ordering;* past, *ordered:* s. *orderer, orderliness:* adv. *orderly.*

OR'DINABLE. *adj.* Such as may be appointed.

OR'DINAL. *adj.* Denoting order, as second, third, fourth.

OR'DINANCE. *s.* Law; rule; appointment. adj. *ordinant.*

OR'DINARY. *adj.* Established; regular; common; mean; ugly. adv. *ordinarily.*

OR'DINARY. *s.* A place of eating, where the meal is established at a certain price. pl. *ordinaries.*

OR'DINATE. *adj.* Regular; methodical.

ORD'NANCE *s.* Cannon; great guns.

OR'DURE. *s.* Excrement; filth.

ORE. *s.* Metal unrefined.

OR'GAN. *s.* A natural instrument; an instrument of music. adj. *organic, organical:* adv. *organically:* s. *organism, organist.*

OR'GANIZE. *v.* To construct so that one part co-operates with another; to form organically. pr. par. *organizing;* past, *organized:* s. *organization.*

O'RIENT. *adj.* Rising, as the sun; eastern; bright. adj. *oriental:* s. *orientalism.*

OR'IFICE. *s.* An opening or perforation.

OR'IFLAMB. *s.* The ancient golden standard of France.

OR'IGIN. *s.* Beginning; source. adj. *original:* adv. *originally:* s. *originality:* pl. *originalities:* v. *originate;* pr. par. *originating;* past, *originated:* s. *origination.*

ORIG'INAL. *s.* First thing of the kind

OR'ISON. *s.* A prayer; a supplication.

OR'NAMENT. *s.* Embellishment; honour. adj. *ornamental:* adv. *ornamentally.*

ORNITHOL'OGY. *s.* A discourse on birds. pl. *ornithologies:* s. *ornithologist.*

OR'PHAN. *s.* A child who has lost its father or mother, or both. adj. *orphan.*

OR'PIMENT. *s.* A fossil of a yellow colour.

OR'RERY. *s.* An instrument, representing the motions of the heavenly bodies. pl. *orreries.*

OR'THODOX. *adj.* Right in opinion and doctrine. s. *orthodoxy.*

ORTHO'EPY. *s.* The art of pronouncing words properly. s. *orthoepist.*

ORTHOG'RAPHY. *s.* The art or practice of spelling. adj. *orthographical:* adv. *orthographically.*

OR'TOLAN. *s.* A kind of bird.

OS'CILLATE. *v.* To move backward and forward. pr. par. *oscillating;* past, *oscillated:* s. *oscillation:* adj. *oscillatory.*

O'SIER. *s.* A tree of the willow kind.

OS'NABURG. *s.* A kind of coarse linen cloth.

OS'PREY. *s.* A large blackish hawk.

OS'SEOUS. *adj.* Bony; resembling a bone.

OS'SIFY. *v.* To change to bone. pr. par. *ossifying;* past, *ossified:* s. *ossification:* adj. *ossific.*

OSTEN'SIBLE. *adj.* Such as is proper or intended to be shown; colourable; pretended. adv. *ostensibly.*

OSTENTA'TION. *s.* Outward show; ambitious display; vain show. adj. *ostentatious:* adv. *ostentatiously:* s. *ostentatiousness.*

OS'TLER, HOS'TLER. *s.* The man who takes care of horses at an inn. pronounced, *os'-lur.*

OS'TRACISM. *s.* An ancient manner of passing sentence, in which each vote was marked on a shell. v. *ostracize;* pr. par. *ostracizing,* past, *ostracized.*

OS'TRICH. *s.* A kind of bird. pl. *ostriches.*

OTH'ER. *pron.* Not the same; not the one; something besides. adv *otherwise.*

OT'TER. *s.* A kind of small quadruped.

OUGHT. *v.* Had a right to; to be obliged by duty; to be fit.

OUNCE. *s.* A weight; a kind of animal. pl. *ounces.*

261

OUR. *pron.* Belonging to us.
OURSEL'VES. *pron.* Plural of myself: *ourself*, is used, in the regal style, for *myself*.
OUT. *adv.* One of the adverbs.
OUTBAL'ANCE. *v.* To overweigh; to preponderate. pr. par. *outbalancing;* past, *outbalanced.*
OUTBID'. *v.* To bid a higher price. pr. par. *outbidding;* past, *outbidden:* s. *outbidder.*
OUTBOUND. *adj.* Destined on a distant voyage.
OUT'CAST. *adj.* Thrown away as refuse; banished. s. *outcast.*
OUT'CRY. *s.* Cry of vehemence; cry of distress; clamour of detestation. pl. *outcries.*
OUTDO'. *v.* To excel; to surpass. pr. par. *outdoing;* past, *outdone:* s. *outdoer.*
OU'T'ER. *adj.* That which is without: sup. *outermost.*
OUTFA'CE. *v.* To brave. pr. par. *outfacing:* past, *outfaced.* s. *outfacer.*
OUTFIT. *s.* The equipment of a ship for her voyage; necessaries for a person going abroad. v. *outfit;* pr. par. *outfitting;* past, *outfitted.*
OUTGEN'ERAL. *v.* To exceed in military skill. pr. par. *outgeneraling;* past, *outgeneraled.*
OUTGO'. *v.* To surpass; to excel; to circumvent. pr. par. *outgoing;* past, *outgone.*
OUTGROW'. *v.* To surpass in growth; to grow too large. pr. par. *outgrowing;* past, *outgrown.*
OUT'HOUSE. *s.* A building attached or belonging to a dwelling-house. pl. *outhouses.*
OUTLAND'ISH. *adj.* Not native; foreign. adv. *outlandishly.*
OUTLAST'. *v.* To surpass in duration. pr. par. *outlasting;* past, *outlasted.*
OUT'LAW. *s.* One excluded from the benefit of the law. v. *outlaw;* pr. par. *outlawing;* past, *outlawed:* s. *outlawry*

OUTLEAP'. *v.* To surpass in leaping. pr. par. *outleaping;* past, *outleaped.*
OUT'LET. *s.* Passage outwards; egress.
OUT'LINE. *s.* A line by which any figure is defined; contour; extremity. v. *outline;* pr. par. *outlining;* past, *outlined.*
OUTLI'VE. *v.* To live beyond; to survive. pr. par. *outliving;* past, *outlived:* s. *outliver.*
OUTMARCH'. *v.* To leave behind in a march. pr. par. *outmarching,* past, *outmarched.*
OUTMEAS'URE. *v.* To exceed in measure. pr. par. *outmeasuring,* past, *outmeasured.*
OUTMOST. *adj.* The most outward.
OUTNUM'BER. *v.* To exceed in number. pr. par. *outnumbering;* past, *outnumbered.*
OUTPOST. *s.* A military station, at a distance from the camp or the main body of the army. v. *outpost,* pr. par. *outposting;* past, *outposted.*
OUTPOUR'. *v.* To emit; to send forth in a stream. pr. par. *outpouring;* past, *outpoured.*
OUT'RAGE. *s.* Open violence; tumultuous mischief. v. *outrage;* pr. par. *outraging;* past, *outraged:* s. *outrager:* adj. *outrageous:* adv *outrageously:* s. *outrageousness.*
OUTREACH'. *v.* To reach beyond; to extend. pr. par. *outreaching;* past, *outreached.*
OUTRECK'ON. *v.* To exceed in number. pr. par. *outreckoning;* past, *outreckoned.*
OUTREIGN'. *v.* To reign through the whole of; to reign longer than another. pr. par. *outreigning,* past, *outreigned.*
OUTRI'DE. *v.* To pass by riding. pr. par. *outriding;* past, *outridden*
OUTRI'DER. *s.* One who precedes, or follows as an attendant, on horseback.
OUTRIGHT'. *adj.* Immediately without delay.

OUTRUN'. *v.* To leave behind in running. pr. par. *outrunning;* past, *outrun:* pret. *outran.*

OUTSAIL'. *v.* To leave behind in sailing. pr. par. *outsailing;* past, *outsailed.*

OUTSELL'. *v.* To sell for a higher price. pr. par. *outselling;* past, *outsold.*

OUT'SET. *s.* Opening; beginning.

OUTSHI'NE. *v.* To emit lustre; to excel in lustre. pr. par. *outshining;* past, *outshone.*

OUT'SIDE. *s.* External part; outer part; show. adj. *outside.*

OUTSIT'. *v.* To sit beyond the due time; to sit longer than another. pr. par. *outsitting;* past, *outsat.*

OUT'SKIRT. *s.* Suburb; edge.

OUTSLEEP'. *v.* To sleep beyond. pr. par. *outsleeping;* past, *outslept.*

OUTSPREAD'. *v.* To extend; to diffuse. pr. par. *outspreading;* past, *outspread.*

OUTSTAND'. *v.* To support; to resist; to stand beyond the proper time. pr. par. *outstanding;* past, *outstood.*

OUTSTA'RE. *v.* To outface with effrontery. pr. par. *outstaring;* past, *outstared.*

OUTSTRETCH'. *v.* To extend; to spread out. pr. par. *outstretching;* past, *outstretched.*

OUTSTRI'DE. *v.* To surpass in striding. pr. par. *outstriding;* past, *outstridden:* pret. *outstrode.*

OUTSTRIP'. *v.* To outgo; to leave behind in a race. pr. par. *outstripping;* past, *outstripped.*

OUTSWEAR'. *v.* To overpower by swearing. pr. par. *outswearing;* past, *outsworn:* pret. *outswore.*

OUTSWELL. *v.* To overflow. pr. par. *outswelling;* past, *outswelled.*

OUTTOP'. *v.* To overtop; to make of less importance. pr. par. *outtopping;* past, *outtopped.*

OUTVEN'OM. *v.* To exceed in poison. pr. par. *outvenoming;* past, *outvenomed.*

OUTVI'E. *v.* To exceed; to surpass. pr. par. *outvying;* past, *outvied:* s. *outvier.*

OUTVO'TE. *v.* To conquer by plurality of votes. pr. par. *outvoting,* past, *outvoted.*

OUTWALK'. *v.* To pass in walking. pr. par. *outwalking;* past, *outwalked.*

OUT'WARD. *adj.* External; towards a foreign port. adv. *outward, outwardly, outwards.*

OUTWATCH'. *v.* To surpass in watchfulness. pr. par. *outwatching;* past, *outwatched.*

OUTWE'AR. *v.* To wear out; to last longer than something else. pr. par. *outwearing;* past, *outworn.*

OUTWEIGH'. *v.* To exceed in weight, &c. pr. par. *outweighing* past, *outweighed.*

OUTWIT'. *v.* To cheat; to overcome by stratagem. pr. par. *outwitting;* past, *outwitted.*

OUT'WORK. *s.* Parts of a fortification next an enemy.

O'VAL. *adj.* Oblong; shaped like an egg.

OVA'TION. *s.* A lesser triumph, among the Romans.

OV'EN. *s.* An arched cavity to bake in.

O'VER. One of the prepositions. adv. *over.*

OVERACT'. *v.* To act more than enough. pr. par. *overacting;* past *overacted.*

OVERARCH'. *v.* To cover with an arch. pr. par. *overarching;* past *overarched.*

OVERAWE'. *v.* To keep in awe by superior influence. pr. par *overawing;* past, *overawed.*

OVERBAL'ANCE. *v.* To weigh down; to preponderate. pr. par *overbalancing;* past, *overbalanced.*

OVERBEAR'. *v.* To repress; to subdue; to bear down. pr. par. *overbearing;* past, *overborne:* adj *overbearing.*

O'VERBOARD. *adv.* Off the ship; out of the ship.

OVERBUR'DEN, OVERBURTH'-EN. *v.* To load with too great weight. pr. par. *overburdening;* past, *overburdened.*

OVERCAST'. *v.* To cloud; to darken. pr. par. *overcasting;* past, *overcast.*

OVERCHARGE'. *v.* To charge too much; to overload. pr. par. *overcharging;* past, *overcharged:* s. *overcharge.*

OVERCLOUD'. *v.* To cover with clouds. pr. par. *overclouding;* past, *overclouded.*

OVERCOME. *v.* To subdue; to conquer; to surmount. pr. par. *overcoming;* past, *overcome.*

OVERCOUNT'. *v.* To rate above the true value. pr. par. *overcounting;* past, *overcounted.*

OVERDO'. *v.* To do more than enough. pr. par. *overdoing;* past, *overdone.*

OVERDRIVE'. *v.* To drive too fast, or beyond strength. pr. par. *overdriving;* past, *overdriven.*

OVERDRY'. *v.* To dry too much. pr. par. *overdrying;* past, *overdried:* adj. *overdry.*

OVEREA'GER. *adj.* Too vehement in desire. s. *overeagerness.*

O'VERFAL. *s.* Cataract.

OVERFLOW'. *v.* To flow over; to deluge; to abound. pr. par. *overflowing;* past, *overflowed:* s. *overflow.*

OVERFRUIT'FUL. *adj.* Too fruitful; too luxuriant. s. *overfruitfulness.*

OVERGO'. *v.* To surpass; to excel. pr. par. *overgoing;* past, *overgone.*

OVERGREAT'. *adj.* Too great. s. *overgreatness.*

OVERGROW'. *v.* To cover with growth. pr. par. *overgrowing;* past, *overgrown:* s. *overgrowth.*

OVERHANG'. *v.* To jut over; to impend over. pr. par. *overhanging;* past, *overhung.*

OVERHAS'TY. *adj.* Too quick; in too great haste. s. *overhastiness:* adv. *overhastily.*

OVERHAUL'. *v.* To unfold or loosen an assemblage of the tackle; to examine over again. pr. par. *overhauling;* past, *overhauled.*

OVERHEAD'. *adv.* Aloft; in the zenith; above.

OVERHEAR'. *v.* To hear those who do not mean to be heard. pr. par. *overhearing;* past, *overheard.*

OVERHEAT'. *v.* To heat too much. pr. par. *overheating;* past, *overheated.*

OVERJOY'. *v.* To enrapture. pr. par. *overjoying;* past, *overjoyed.*

OVERLA'DE. *v.* To overburthen. pr. par. *overlading;* past, *overladen.*

OVERLARGE'. *adj.* Larger than enough.

OVERLAY'. *v.* To smother, to cover over. pr. par. *overlaying;* past, *overlayed.*

OVERLEAP'. *v.* To pass by a jump. pr. par. *overleaping;* past, *overleaped.*

OVERLOAD'. *v.* To burthen with too much. pr. par. *overloading;* past, *overloaded.*

OVERLOOK'. *v.* To view from a higher place; to superintend; to pass by indulgently; to neglect. pr. par. *overlooking,* past, *overlooked:* s. *overlooker.*

OVERMATCH'. *v.* To be too powerful. pr. par. *overmatching;* past, *overmatched:* s. *overmatch.*

OVERMEAS'URE. *s.* Something given over the due measure.

OVERMUCH'. *adv.* In too great a degree. s. *overmuch.*

OVERNIGHT'. *adv.* Night before bed-time.

OVERPASS'. *v.* To pass over; to cross. pr. par. *overpassing;* past, *overpassed.*

OVERPAY'. *v.* To pay more than the price. pr. par. *overpaying,* past, *overpaid:* s. *overpayment.*

O'VERPLUS. *s.* Surplus; what remains more than sufficient.

OVERPOW'ER. *v.* To oppress, by power; to subdue. pr. par. *over-*

264

powering; past, *overpowered*: s. *overpowerer*: adj. *overpowering*.

OVERRA'TE. v. To rate at too much. pr. par. *overrating*, past, *overrated*.

OVERREACH'. v. To go beyond; to deceive. pr. par. *overreaching*; past, *overreached*: s. *overreacher*.

OVERRI'DE. v. To ride too much. pr.par.*overriding*; past, *overridden*.

OVERROAST'. v. To roast too much. pr. par. *overroasting*; past, *overroasted*.

OVERRU'LF v. To superintend; to supersede. pr. par. *overruling*; past, *overruled*.

OVERRUN'. v. To harass by incursions; to ravage; to outrun; to overspread. pr. par. *overrunning*; past, *overrun*: s. *overrunner*: pret. *overran*.

OVERSEE'. v. To superintend; to overlook. pr. par. *overseeing*; past, *overseen*: s. *overseer*: pret. *oversaw*.

OVERSET'. v. To turn bottom upwards; to subvert. pr. par. *oversetting*; past, *overset*.

OVERSHA'DE. v. To cover with any thing that causes darkness. pr. par. *overshading*; past, *overshaded*.

OVERSHADOW. v. To throw a shadow over; to shelter. pr. par. *overshadowing*; past, *overshadowed*.

OVERSHOOT'. v. To shoot beyond the mark. pr. par. *overshooting*; past, *overshot*.

O'VERSIGHT. s. Superintendence; omission: mistake.

OVERSLEEP'. v. To sleep too long. pr. par. *oversleeping*; past, *overslept*.

OVERSOON'. adv. Too soon.

OVERSPREAD'. v. To cover over; to scatter about. pr.par.*overspreading*; past, *overspread*.

OVERSTOCK'. v. To fill too full; to crowd. pr. par. *overstocking*; past, *overstocked*.

O'VERT. adj. Open; public; apparent. adv. *overtly*.

OVERTAKE. v. To come up with in a pursuit; to take by surprise. pr. par. *overtaking*; past, *overtaken*: pret. *overtook*: s. *overtaker*.

OVERTAX'. v. To tax too heavily. pr. par. *overtaxing*; past, *overtaxed*: s. *overtax*.

OVERTHROW'. v. To turn upside down; to throw down; to defeat; to conquer. pr. par. *overthrowing*. past, *overthrown*: s. *overthrow*, *overthrower*.

OVERTOP'. v. To rise above; to raise the head above; to excel. pr. par. *overtopping*; past, *overtopped*.

O'VERTURE. s. An opening; a proposal; a musical composition, played at the beginning of an oratorio, concert, or opera.

OVERTURN'. v. To throw down, to subvert. pr. par. *overturning*, past, *overturned*: s. *overturn*, *overturner*: adj. *overturnable*.

OVERVAL'UE. v. To rate at too high a price. pr. par. *overvaluing*: past, *overvalued*.

O'VERWEIGHT. s. Preponderance; extra weight.

OVERWHELM'. v. To crush; to fill too much. pr. par. *overwhelming*; past, *overwhelmed*: adv. *overwhelmingly*.

OVERWI'SE. adj. Wise to affectation.

OVERWORK'. v. To tire; to work beyond one's strength. pr. par. *overworking*; past, *overworked* s. *o'verwork*, work done after the usual hours.

OVERWROUGHT'. part. adj. Laboured too much; compelled to work beyond one's strength.

OVERZEALOUS. adj. Too zealous.

O'VIFORM. adj. Having the shape of an egg.

OVIP'AROUS. adj. Bringing forth eggs.

OWE. v. To be indebted; to be obliged to. pr. par. *owing*; past, *owed*.

OWL. s. A species of bird.

OWN. One of the pronouns.

OWN. v. To acknowledge; to avow for one's own; to possess; to con-

OX—OXY

fess. pr. par. *owning;* past, *owned:* s. *owner, ownership.*
OX. s. A castrated bull. pl. *oxen.*
OX'YGEN. s. The principle of acids, and of combustions, and a necessary agent in the support of human life. adj. *oxygenated.*

OYS—OYS

OYS'TER. s A bivalve, testaceous fish.

P

PAB—PAD

PAB'ULAR, PAB'ULOUS. adj. Affording aliment or provender.
PACE. s. Step; gait; manner of walk. v. *pace;* pr. par. *pacing;* past, *paced:* s. *pacer.*
PACIF'IC. adj. Peace-making; mild; gentle. s. *pacification, pacificator:* adj. *pacificatory.*
PA'CIFY. v. To appease; to quiet. pr. par. *pacifying;* past, *pacified:* s. *pacifier, pacification.*
PACK. s. A large bundle, tied up for carriage; a set of cards; a number of hounds, &c. v. *pack;* pr. par. *packing;* past, *packed:* s. *packer, package.*
PACK'CLOTH. s. A cloth in which goods are packed.
PACK'ET. s. A small pack; a mail of letters; a ship that carries letters periodically. v. *packet;* pr. par. *packeting;* past, *packeted.*
PACK'HORSE. s. A horse of burthen.
PACK'SADDLE. s. A saddle on which burthens are laid.
PACK'THREAD. s. Strong thread used in tying parcels.
PACT. s. A contract; a bargain.
PAC'TION. s. A bargain; a covenant. adj. *pactional.*
PAD. s. A footpath; an easy paced horse; a robber that infests the roads on foot; a low, soft saddle. v *pad;* pr. par. *padding;* past, *padded.*
PAD'DLE. v. To row; to play in the water. pr. par. *paddling;* past, *paddled:* s. *paddle, paddler.*
PAD'DOCK. s. A small enclosure; a toad or frog.
PAD'LOCK. s. A lock hung on a staple. v. *padlock;* pr. par. *padlocking;* past, *padlocked.*

PÆA—PAL

PÆ'AN. s. A song of triumph or praise.
PA'GAN. s. A heathen; one not a Christian. adj. *pagan:* s. *paganism.*
PAGE. s. One side of the leaf of a book; a boy attending, rather in formality than in servitude, on a great person. v. *page;* pr. par. *paging;* past, *paged.*
PA'GEANT. s. Any show; a spectacle of entertainment. adj. *pageant:* s. *pageantry,* pl. *pageantries*
PA'GOD. s. An Indian idol.
PAGO'DA. s. The temple of an Indian idol; the name of an Indian coin.
PAIL. s. A wooden vessel, for water, &c.
PAIN. s. Sensation of uneasiness; punishment. v. *pain;* pr. par. *paining;* past, *pained:* s. *painer:* adj. *painful:* adv. *painfully:* s. *painfulness.*
PAINS'TAKING. adj. Laborious, industrious. s. *painstaker.*
PAINT. v. To represent by delineation and colours; to colour. pr. par. *painting;* past, *painted:* s. *painting, painter.*
PAIR. s. Two things suiting one another; a man and wife; two of a sort; a couple. v. *pair;* pr. par. *pairing;* past, *paired:* s. *pairer*
PAL'ACE. s. A royal house; a house eminently splendid.
PALANQUIN'. s. A kind of covered carriage, borne on men's shoulders.
PAL'ATE. s. The instrument of taste; the upper part or roof of

the mouth; mental relish. adj. *palatable:* s. *palatableness:* adv. *palatably.*

PALAT'INATE. s. The county in which is the seat of a count palatine.

PAL'ATINE. s. One invested with regal rights and prerogatives. adj. *palatine.*

PALAV'ER. s. Superfluous talk; deceitful conversation.

PALE. adj. Wan, whitish. s. *paleness:* adj. *palish.*

PALE. s. A narrow piece of wood, joined above and below to a rail; any enclosure; a district or territory. v. *pale;* pr. par. *paling;* past, *paled:* s. *paling.*

PAL'FREY. s. A small horse, fit for ladies.

PAL'INDROME. s. A word or sentence which is the same read backwards or forward.

PAL'INODE. s. A recantation.

PALISA'DE, PALISA'DO. s. A pale set by way of enclosure or defence. pl. *palisades, palisadoes:* v. *palisade;* pr. par. *palisading;* past, *palisaded.*

PALL. s. A cloak or mantle of state; the covering thrown over the dead.

PALL. v. To grow vapid; to become insipid; to be weakened. pr. par. *palling;* past, *palled.*

PALLA'DIUM. s. A statue of Pallas, pretended to be the guardian of Troy—thence any security or protection.

PAL'LET. s. A small bed; a mean bed.

PAL'LIATE. v. To cover with excuse; to extenuate. pr. par. *palliating;* past, *palliated:* s. *palliation:* adj. *palliative.*

PAL'LID. adj. Pale; not bright. s. *pallidness.*

PALM. s. A kind of tree; victory; the inner part of the hand; a measure of length. adj. *palmy.*

PALM. v. To conceal in the palm of the hand, as jugglers; to impose by fraud. pr. par. *palming,* past, *palmed.*

PAL'MATED. adj. Having the feet broad; also applied, by naturalists, to certain roots and stones having the appearance of hands or fingers.

PALM'ER. s. A pilgrim.

PALMET'TO. s. A species of palm-tree. pl. *palmettoes.*

PALMIF'EROUS. adj. Bearing palms.

PALM'ISTRY. s. The pretended science or practice of foretelling fortunes by the lines of the palm. s. *palmister.*

PAL'PABLE. adj. Perceptible by the touch; easily detected; plain. adv. *palpably:* s. *palpableness, palpability.*

PAL'PITATE. v. To beat as the heart; to flutter. pr. par. *palpitating;* past, *palpitated:* s. *palpitation.*

PAL'SY. s. A privation of motion or feeling, or both. v. *palsy;* pr. par. *palsying;* past, *palsied.*

PAL'TRY. adj. Worthless; despicable; contemptible. s. *paltriness.*

PAM. s. The knave of clubs.

PAM'PER. v. To feed luxuriously; to glut. pr. par. *pampering;* past, *pampered:* s. *pamperer.*

PAM'PHLET. s. A small book; properly a book sold unbound, and only stitched. s. *pamphleteer.*

PAN. s. A vessel broad and shallow; the part of the lock of a gun that holds the powder.

PANACE'A. s. A universal medicine.

PANA'DO. s. Food made by boiling bread in water. pl. *panadoes.*

PAN'CAKE. s. Thin pudding, baked in a frying-pan.

PAN'DECT. s. A treatise that comprehends the whole of any science, the digest of the civil law.

PAN'DER. s. A pimp; a procurer. v. *pander;* pr. par. *pandering;* past, *pandered.*

PANE. s. A square of glass, wainscot, &c. adj. *paned, paneless.*

PANEGYR'IC. s. A eulogy; encomium; praise. adj. *panegyric, panegyrical:* s. *panegyrist:* v. *pane gyrize;* pr. par. *panegyrizing;* past, *panegyrized.*

PANG. *s.* Extreme pain; sudden paroxysm of torment.

PAN'IC. *s.* A sudden fright without cause.

PAN'NIER. *s.* A basket; a wicker vessel, in which things are carried on a horse.

PAN'OPLY. *s.* Complete armour. pl. *panoplies:* adj. *panoplied.*

PANORA'MA. *s.* A large circular painting, from the centre of which the beholder views the objects of representation.

PAN'SY. *s* A kind of flower. pl. *pansies:* adj. *pansied.*

PANT. *v.* To palpitate; to long; to wish earnestly. pr. par. *panting,* past, *panted:* s. *panter:* adv. *pantingly.*

PANTALOON'. *s.* A man's garment; a character in the Italian comedy; a buffoon in the pantomime of modern times.

PANTHE'ON. *s.* A temple of all the gods.

PAN'THER. *s.* A spotted wild beast; a pard.

PAN'TOMIME. *s.* A tale exhibited only in gestures and dumb show. adj. *pantomimic, pantomimical.*

PAN'TOGRAPH. *s.* A mathematical instrument, contrived to copy drawings and designs.

PANTOM'ETER. *s.* An instrument for measuring all sorts of angles, elevations, and distances.

PAN'TRY. *s.* The room in which provisions are deposited. pl. *pantries.*

PAP. *s.* The nipple; food made for infants; the pulp of fruit.

PA'PA. *s.* A fond name for father.

PA'PACY. *s.* Popedom; office and dignity of bishops of Rome. pl. *papacies.*

PA'PAL. adj. Popish; belonging to the pope; annexed to the bishopric of Rome.

PAPAV'EROUS. *adj.* Resembling poppies.

PA'PER. *s.* A substance made from rags. adj. *paper:* v. *paper;* pr. par. *papering;* past, *papered:* s. *paperer.*

PAPERMON'EY. *s.* Bills of exchange; bank and promissory notes.

PAPIL'LARY. *adj.* Having emulgent vessels or resemblances of paps.

PA'PISM. *s.* Popery. s. *papist·* adj. *papistic, papistical:* s. *papistry.*

PAPPOOS', PAPPOOSE'. *s.* The Indian name for a child.

PAP'PY. *adj.* Soft; succulent; easily divided.

PAR. *s.* State of equality; equivalence.

PAR'ABLE. *s.* A similitude; a relation under which something else is figured. adj. *parabolic, parabolical:* adv. *parabolically.*

PARAB'OLA. *s.* One of the conic sections.

PA'RACLETE. *s.* The title of the Holy Ghost.

PARA'DE. *s.* Show; ostentation; procession; military order; place where troops are exercised; a public walk. v. *parade;* pr. par. *parading;* past, *paraded.*

PAR'ADISE. *s.* Any place of felicity. adj. *paradisaical.*

PAR'ADOX. *s.* A tenet contrary to received opinion; an assertion contrary to appearance. pl. *paradoxes:* adj. *paradoxical:* adv. *paradoxically:* s. *paradoxicalness.*

PARAGO'GE. *s.* A figure whereby a letter or syllable is added to a word.

PAR'AGON. *s.* A model; a pattern: something supremely excellent.

PAR'AGRAM. *s.* A kind of play upon words.

PAR'AGRAPH. *s.* A distinct part of a discourse. v. *paragraph;* pr. par. *paragraphing;* past, *paragraphed.* adj. *paragraphic.*

PAR'ALLAX. *s.* The distance between the true and apparent place of the sun or a star. pl. *parallaxes.*

PAR'ALLEL. *adj.* Extended in the same direction, and always preserving the same distance; equal; like. *s. parallel: v. parallel;* pr. par. *paralleling;* past, *paralleled: s. parallelism.*

PARALLEL'OGRAM. *s.* A right-lined, quadrilateral figure, the opposite sides of which are parallel and equal.

PARAL'OGY. *s.* False reasoning. pl. *paralogies: s. paralogism.*

PAR'ALYSE. *v.* To strike with the palsy; to render useless. pr. par. *paralysing;* past, *paralysed: s. paralysis, paralyser.*

PARALYT'IC, PARALYTICAL. *adj.* Palsied; inclined to palsy.

PAR'AMOUNT. *adj.* Superior; chief.

PAR AMOUR. *s.* A lover; a mistress.

PARAPHERNA'LIA. *s.* Goods in the wife's disposal, besides her fixed dowry.

PAR'APHRASE. *s.* A loose interpretation; an explanation in many words. *v. paraphrase;* pr. par. *paraphrasing;* past, *paraphrased: s. paraphrast: adj. paraphrastical;* adv. *paraphrastically.*

PAR'ASITE. *s.* One who frequents rich tables, and earns his welcome by flattery. adj. *parasitic, parasitical:* adv. *parasitically: s. parasitism.*

PARASOL'. *s.* A small umbrella.

PAR'BOIL. *v.* To half boil. pr. par. *parboiling;* past, *parboiled.*

PAR'CEL. *s.* A small bundle; a part of the whole. *v. parcel;* pr. par. *parceling;* past, *parceled.*

PAR'CENER. *s.* A coheiress. adj. *parcenary.*

PARCH. *v.* To burn slightly; to scorch; to dry up. pr. par. *parching;* past, *parched: s. parcher, parchedness.*

PARCH'MENT. *s.* A skin dressed for writing on.

PAR'DON. *v.* To forgive; to remit a penalt v. pr. par. *pardoning;* past, *pardoned: s. pardon, pardoner:* adj. *pardonable:* adv. *pardonably.*

PARE. *v.* To cut off the surface; to diminish. pr. par. *paring;* past, *pared: s. parer.*

PAREGOR'IC. *s.* A medical preparation, for comforting and assuaging.

PA'RENT. *s.* A father or mother adj. *parental, parentless:* adv. *parentally.*

PAR'ENTAGE. *s.* Extraction; birth.

PAREN'THESIS. *s.* A sentence, so included in another sentence, that it may be omitted, without injuring the sense of that by which it is enclosed: being commonly marked thus, ( ). pl. *parentheses:* adj. *parenthetic, parenthetical.*

PAR'GET. *s.* A kind of plaster. v, *parget;* pr. par. *pargeting;* past, *pargeted.*

PARHE'LION. *s.* A mock sun.

PARIE'TAL. *adj.* Constituting the sides or walls.

PAR'ISH. *s.* The particular charge of a secular priest. pl. *parishes: s. parishioner.*

PAR'ITY. *s.* Equality; resemblance. pl. *parities.*

PARK. *s.* A piece of ground, enclosed and stored with beasts of chase. *v. park;* pr. par. *parking,* past, *parked.*

PAR'LANCE. *s.* Conversation; talk.

PAR'LEY. *v.* To treat by word of mouth; to talk. pr. par. *parleying,* past, *parleyed: s. parley.*

PAR'LIAMENT. *s.* The assembly of the king, lords, and commons of England. adj. *parliamentary.*

PAR'LOUR. *s.* A room in a house furnished for reception.

PARMESAN'. *s.* A sort of cheese.

PAROCH'IAL. *adj.* Belonging to a parish. adv. *parochially.*

PAR'ODY. *s.* A kind of writing. in which the words of an author, or his thoughts, are taken, and, by a slight change, adapted to some new purpose. pl. *parodies: v. parody;* pr. par. *parodying;* past, *parodied:* adj. *parodical.*

PARO'LE. *s.* Spoken language; word given as an assurance; promise given by a prisoner, when liberated as a man of honour.

PAROQUET'. *s.* A species of small parrot.

PAR'OXYSM. *s.* A fit; periodical return of a disease.

PAR'RICIDE. *s.* One who has murdered his father; the murder committed. adj. *parricidal.*

PAR'ROT. *s.* A kind of bird, that can be taught to speak.

PAR'RY. *v.* To put aside; to fence. pr. par. *parrying;* past, *parried.*

PARSE. *v.* To resolve a sentence into parts of speech. pr. par. *parsing;* past, *parsed.*

PAR'SIMONY. *s.* Niggardliness; avarice. adj. *parsimonious:* adv. *parsimoniously:* s. *parsimoniousness.*

PARS'LEY. *s.* A kind of herb.

PARS'NIP. *s.* A kind of plant.

PAR'SON. *s.* The rector or vicar of a parish; a clergyman.

PART. *s.* Something less than the whole; a portion. *v. part;* pr. par. *parting;* past, *parted:* adv. *partly:* adj. *partable:* s. *parter.*

PARTA'KE. *v.* To have share of; to participate. pr. par. *partaking;* past, *partaken:* s. *partaker.*

PARTERR'E. *s.* A level division of ground, planted with shrubs and flowers.

PAR'TIAL. adj. Inclined to favour one party more than another. s. *partiality,* pl. *partialities:* adv. *partially.*

PAR'TIBLE. adj. Divisible. s. *partibility.*

PARTI'CIPATE. *v.* To partake; to have share. pr. par. *participating;* past, *participated:* s. *participant, participation, participator:* adj. *participant.*

PAR'TICIPLE. *s.* A word partaking the nature of both noun and verb. adj. *participial:* adv. *participially.*

PAR'TICLE. *s.* Any small portion of a greater substance.

PARTIC'ULAR. adj. Relating to single persons or things; not general; individual. *s. particular, particularity,* pl. *particularities:* adv. *particularly:* v. *particularize;* pr. par. *particularizing;* past, *particularized.*

PARTISAN'. *s.* An adherent to a party; a pike.

PARTI'TION. *s.* The act of dividing; state of being divided; thing that divides. v. *partition;* pr. par. *partitioning;* past, *partitioned.*

PART'NER. *s.* Partaker; sharer; associate. s. *partnership.*

PARTOOK'. Pret. of the v. *to partake.*

PAR'TRIDGE. *s.* A bird of game.

PARTU'RIENT. adj. About to bring forth. s. *parturition.*

PAR'TY. *s.* A faction; one concerned in any affair; cause. pl. *parties.*

PAR'TY-COLOURED. adj. Having diversity of colours.

PAR'TY-WALL. *s.* A wall that separates one house from another.

PAR'VITUDE, PAR'VITY. *s.* Littleness; minuteness.

PAS'CHAL. adj. Relating to the passover; relating to Easter.

PASQUINA'DE. *s.* A lampoon.

PASS. *v.* To go; to move from one place to another; to be progressive; to thrust. pr. par. *passing,* past, *passed:* adj. *passable:* s. *passer.*

PASS. *s.* Passage; road; a permission to go or come any where; push; state. pl. *passes.*

PASS'ABLY. adv. Tolerably.

PAS'SANT. adj. In heraldry, standing on all its legs.

PAS'SENGER. *s.* A traveller; one who is upon the road.

PASS'ING-BELL. *s.* The death-bell.

PAS'SION. *s.* Any effect caused by external agency; violent commotion of the mind. adj. *passionate, passionless:* adv. *passionately:* s. *passionateness.*

PAS'SION-WEEK. *s.* The week immediately preceding Easter.

PAS'SIVE. *adj.* Receiving impression from some external agent; unresisting. *adv. passively: s. passiveness.*

PASS'OVER. *s.* One of the Jewish feasts.

PASS'PORT. *s.* Permission of passage.

PAST. *adj.* Not present; gone through. *s. past: prep. past.*

PASTE. *s.* Any viscous, tenacious mixture; a mixture, in imitation of precious stones. *v. paste;* pr. par. *pasting;* past, *pasted.*

PASTE'BOARD. *s.* A kind of coarse, stiff, thick paper.

PAS'TERN. *s.* That part of the leg of a horse between the joint next the foot and the hoof.

PAS'TIME. *s.* Sport; amusement.

PAS'TOR. *s.* A shepherd; a clergyman. *adj. pastoral.*

AS'TORAL. *adj.* Rural; rustic; relating or belonging to shepherds.

PAS'TORAL. *s.* A rural poem; a bucolic.

PAS'TRY. *s.* Pies or baked paste. pl. *pastries.*

PAS'TURE. *s.* Food; the act of feeding; ground on which cattle feed. *v. pasture;* pr. par. *pasturing;* past, *pastured: s. pasturage:* adj. *pasturable.*

PAS'TY. *s.* A pie of crust, raised without a dish. pl. *pasties.*

PAT. *adj.* Fit; convenient; exactly suitable. *adv. pat, patly: s. patness.*

PAT. *s.* A light quick blow. *v. pat;* pr. par. *patting;* past, *patted.*

PATCH. *s.* A piece sewed on, to cover a hole; a small particle or piece. pl. *patches: v. patch;* pr. par. *patching;* past, *patched: s. patcher, patchwork.*

PATE. *s.* The head. *adj. pated.*

PATEFAC'TION. *s.* Act or state of opening.

PAT'ENT. *adj.* Open to the perusal of all, as letters patent; appropriated exclusively to the inventor; apparent. *s. patent, patentee.*

PAT'ER-NOS'TER. *s.* The Lord's Prayer.

PATER'NAL. *adj.* Fatherly, pertaining to a father. *s. paternity,* pl. *paternities.*

PATH. *s.* Way; road. *adj. pathless: s. pathway.*

PATHET'IC. *adj.* Affecting the passions. *adv. pathetically.*

PATHOL'OGY. *s.* That part of medicine which relates to distempers, with their differences, causes, and effects.

PATH'OS. *s.* Passion; affection of mind.

PA'TIENCE. *s.* The power of suffering; calm endurance of pain or labour. *adj. patient: s. patient. adv. patiently.*

PA'TRIARCH. *s.* One who governs by paternal right; a bishop superior to archbishops. *adj. patriarchal.*

PATRI'CIAN. *adj.* Senatorial, noble; not plebeian. *s. patrician.*

PA'TRIMONY. *s.* An estate possessed by inheritance. pl. *patrimonies:* adj. *patrimonial:* adv. *patrimonially.*

PA'TRIOT. *s.* One whose ruling passion is love of his country. *adj. patriot, patriotic: adv. patriotically: s. patriotism.*

PATROL'. *s.* The act of going the rounds, to observe how orders are kept; those that go the rounds. *v. patrol;* pr. par. *patrolling;* past, *patrolled.*

PA'TRON. *s.* One who countenances, supports or protects. fem. *patroness,* pl. *patronesses: s. patronage.* adj. *patronal:* v. *patronise;* pr. par. *patronising;* past, *patronised: s. patroniser.*

PATRONYM'IC. *s.* A name expressing the name of the father or ancestor.

PAT'TEN. *s.* A shoe of wood, with an iron ring, worn under the common shoe, by women.

PAT'TER. *v.* To make a noise like

271

the quick steps of many feet. pr. par. *pattering;* past, *pattered.*
PAT'TERN. *s.* The original proposed for imitation; a specimen.
PAT'TY. *s.* A little pie. pl. *patties:* s. *pattypan.*
PAU'CITY. *s.* Fewness; smallness of quantity.
PAUNCH. *s.* The belly. pl. *paunches.*
PAU'PER. *s.* A poor person, who receives alms. s. *pauperism.*
PAUSE. *s.* A stop; an intermission; suspense. v. *pause;* pr. par. *pausing;* past, *paused:* s. *pauser.*
PAVE *v.* To lay with brick or stone. pr. par. *paving;* past, *paved:* s. *paver, pavement.*
PAVIL'ION. *s.* A tent; a temporary or movable house. v. *pavilion;* pr. par. *pavilioning;* past, *pavilioned.*
PAW. *s.* The foot of a beast of prey. v. *paw;* pr. par. *pawing;* past, *pawed:* s. *pawer.*
PAWN. *s.* Something given as a pledge; the state of being pawned; a common man at chess. v. *pawn;* pr. par. *pawning;* past, *pawned:* s. *pawner.*
PAWN'BROKER. *s.* One who lends money upon pledge.
PAY. *v.* To discharge a debt; to reward. pr. par. *paying;* past, *paid:* s. *pay, payer, payment:* adj. *payable:* s. *payday, paymaster.*
PEA. *s.* A kind of pulse.
PEACE. *s.* Respite from war; quiet. adj. *peaceable, peaceful, peaceless:* s. *peaceableness, peacefulness:* adv. *peaceably:* s. *peacemaker.*
PEACH. *s.* A kind of fruit. pl. *peaches.*
PEA'COCK. *s.* A sort of fowl. fem. *peahen.*
PEAK. *s.* The top of a hill; any thing pointed.
PEAL. *s.* A succession of loud sounds. v. *peal;* pr. par. *pealing;* past, *pealed.*
PEAR. *s.* A kind of fruit.
PEARL. *s.* A precious gem; a white speck or film growing on the eye. adj. *pearly, pearled.*

PEAR'MAIN. *s.* A kind of apple.
PEAS'ANT. *s.* A hind; one whose business is rural labour. s. *peasantry.*
PEAT. *s.* A species of turf.
PEB'BLE, PEB'BLESTONE. *s.* A small stone. adj. *pebbled, pebbly.*
PEC'CABLE. *adj.* Liable to sin. s. *peccability.*
PECCADIL'LO. *s.* A petty fault; a venial offence. pl. *peccadilloes.*
PEC'CANT. *adj.* Guilty; ill disposed; injurious to health. s. *peccancy.*
PECK. *s.* The fourth part of a bushel.
PECK. *v.* To strike with the beak, as a bird; to pick up food with the beak. pr. par. *pecking;* past, *pecked:* s. *peck.*
PEC'TORAL. *adj.* Belonging to the breast.
PECULA'TION. *s.* Theft of the public money. v. *peculate;* pr. pr. *peculating;* past, *peculated:* s. *peculation.*
PECU'LIAR. *adj.* Appropriate; belonging exclusively. s. *peculiarity,* pl. *peculiarities:* adv. *peculiarly.*
PECU'NIARY. *adj.* Relating to money.
PED'AGOGUE. *s.* A schoolmaster; a pedant.
PE'DAL. *adj.* Belonging to a foot. s. *pedals.*
PED'ANT. *s.* A schoolmaster; a man vain of low knowledge. adj. *pedantic:* adv. *pedantically:* s. *pedantry.*
PED'DLE. *v.* To be busy about trifles, to sell as a pedler. pr. par. *peddling;* past, *peddled:* s. *pedler, pedlery.*
PED'ESTAL. *s.* The lower member of a pillar; the basis of a statue.
PEDES'TRIAN. *s.* One who makes a journey on foot. adj. *pedestrian.*
PED'ICLE. *s.* The footstalk.
PEDIC'ULAR. *adj.* Having the phthirisis or lousy distemper.
PED'IGREE. *s.* Genealogy, lineage.
PED'IMENT. *s.* In architecture, an ornamental projection, &c.

272

PEDOBAPTISM. s. Infant baptism. s. *pedobaptist.*

PEDOM'ETER. s. A mathematical instrument, by the management of the wheels of which, paces are numbered, and distances measured.

PEEL. v. To decorticate; to flay. pr. par. *peeling*; past, *peeled*: s. *peel, peeler.*

PEEL. s. A board used by bakers; the rind.

PEEP. v. To make the first appearance; to look slily or closely. pr. par. *peeping*; past, *peeped*: s. *peep, peeper.*

PEER. s. One of the same rank; an equal; a nobleman. fem. *peeress*, pl. *peeresses*: s. *peerage.*

PEER. v. To come just in sight; to look narrowly. pr. par. *peering*; past, *peered*: s. *peerer.*

PEER'LESS. adj. Unequalled; having no peer. adv. *peerlessly*: s. *peerlessness.*

PEEV'ISH. adj. Petulant; easily offended. adv. *peevishly*: s. *peevishness.*

PEG. s. A wooden pin. v. *peg*; pr. par. *pegging*; past, *pegged.*

PELF. s. Money, riches.

PEL'ICAN. s. A kind of bird.

PELISSE'. s. A kind of coat or robe.

PEL'LET. s. A little ball. v. *pellet*; pr. par. *pelleting*; past, *pelleted.*

PEL'LICLE. s. A thin skin.

ELLMELL'. adv. Confusedly; tumultuously.

PELLU'CID. adj. Clear; not opaque. s. *pellucidity, pellucidness.*

PELT. s. A skin; a hide; a blow from something thrown. v. *pelt*; pr. par. *pelting*; past, *pelted*: s. *pelter.*

PEL'TRY. s. Furs or skins. pl. *peltries.*

PEN. s. An instrument for writing; a small enclosure. v. *pen*; pr. par. *penning*; past, *penned*. s. *penner, penman*, pl. *penmen, penmanship*

PE'NAL. adj. Denouncing a penalty. adv. *penally.*

PEN'ALTY. s. Punishment; censure; fine. pl. *penalties.*

PEN'ANCE. s. Infliction suffered as an expression of repentance for sin; repentance.

PENCE. s. Plural of *penny.*

PEN'CIL. s. A small brush of hair; a black lead pen. v. *pencil*; pr. par. *penciling*; past, *penciled*: s. *penciler.*

PEN'DANT. s. Something hanging; a flag. adj. *pendant.*

PEN'DENCE. s. State of hanging; inclination. s. *pendency*: adj. *pendent.*

PEN'DULOUS. adj. Hanging. s. *pendulosity.*

PEN'DULUM. s. A weight hung so that it may easily swing backwards and forwards.

PEN'ETRABLE. adj. Such as may be pierced. s. *penetrability.*

PEN'ETRATE. v. To pierce; to enter beyond the surface. pr. par *penetrating*; past, *penetrated*: s. *penetration*: adj. *penetrative, penetrant.*

PEN'GUIN. s. A kind of bird.

PENIN'SULA. s. A piece of land almost surrounded with water adj. *peninsulated, peninsular.*

PEN'ITENCE. s. Repentance; sorrow for crime. adj. *penitent, penitential*: s. *penitent*: adv. *penitently, penitentially.*

PENITEN'TIARY. adj. Relating to the rules and measures of penance. s. *penitentiary*, pl. *penitentiaries.*

PEN'KNIFE. s. A knife used to cut pens. pl. *penknives.*

PEN'NANT. s. A small flag.

PEN'NATED. adj. Winged.

PEN'NILESS. adj. Poor.

PEN'NON. s. A small flag.

PEN'NY. s. A small coin. pl. *pennies, pence*: adj. *pennywise*: s. *pennyworth.*

PENNYROY'AL. s. A species of plant.

PEN'NYWEIGHT. s. A weight containing 24 grains, troy.

273

PEN'SILE. *adj.* Hanging.
PEN'SION. *s.* A payment made annually, for services performed. v. *pension;* pr. par. *pensioning;* past, *pensioned:* s. *pensioner:* adj. *pensionary.*
PEN'SIVE. *adj.* Sorrowfully thoughtful. adv. *pensively:* s. *pensiveness.*
PENT. *adj.* Shut up.
PEN'TACHORD. *s.* An instrument with five strings.
PEN"TAGON. *s.* A figure with five angles. adj. *pentagonal.*
PENTAM'ETER. *s.* A verse of five feet. adj. *pentameter.*
PENTANG'ULAR. *adj.* Five cornered.
PENTAPET'ALOUS. *adj.* Having five leaves.
PEN'TASTYLE. *s.* A building in which are five rows of columns.
PEN'TATEUCH. *s.* The five books of Moses. pronounced *pen'-ta-tuke.*
PEN"TECOST. *s.* Whitsuntide.
PENT'HOUSE. *s.* A shed sloping from the main wall.
PENUL'TIMA. *s.* The last syllable but one. adj. *penultimate.*
PENUM'BRA. *s.* An imperfect shadow.
PENU'RIOUS. *adj.* Niggardly; sparing. adv. *penuriously:* s. *penuriousness.*
PEN'URY. *s.* Poverty.
PE'ONY. *s.* A kind of flower. pl. *peonies.*
PE'OPLE. *s.* A nation; the vulgar. v. *people;* pr. par. *peopling;* past, *peopled.*
PEP'PER. *s.* A kind of spice. v. *pepper;* pr. par. *peppering;* past, *peppered.*
PEP'PERCORN. *s.* Something of only nominal value.
PEP'PERMINT. *s.* A kind of aromatic herb.
PEP'TIC. *adj.* Helping digestion.
PERADVEN'TURE. *adv.* Perhaps; may be.
PERAM'BULATE. *v.* To walk through; to survey. pr. par. *perambulating;* past, *perambulated.* s. *perambulation, perambulator.*
PERCEI'VE. *v.* To discover by some sensible effects. pr. par. *perceiving;* past, *perceived:* s. *perceiver:* adj. *perceivable:* adv. *perceivably.*
PERCEP'TIBLE. *adj.* Such as may be known or observed. s. *perception:* adj. *perceptive:* adv. *perceptibly:* s. *perceptibility.*
PERCH. *s.* A kind of fish; a measure of five yards and a half; a pole; something on which birds sit. v. *perch;* pr. par. *perching;* past, *perched:* s. *percher.*
PERCHANCE'. *adv.* Perhaps.
PERCIP'IENT. *adj.* Perceiving. s. *percipient.*
PER'COLATE. *v.* To strain through. pr. par. *percolating;* past, *percolated:* s. *percolation.*
PERCUSS'. *v.* To strike. pr. par. *percussing;* past, *percussed:* s. *percussion.*
PERCU'TIENT. *adj.* Striking.
PERDI'TION. *s.* Destruction; ruin.
PER'EGRINATE. *v.* To travel. pr. par. *peregrinating;* past, *peregrinated:* s. *peregrination, peregrinator.*
PEREMP'TORY, PER'EMPTORY *adj.* Dogmatical; absolute. adv. *peremptorily:* s. *peremptoriness.*
PEREN'NIAL. *adj.* Lasting through the year; perpetual. s. *perennial, perennity.*
PERERRA'TION. *s.* Travel.
PER'FECT. *adj.* Complete; finished. v. *perfect';* pr. par. *perfecting;* past, *perfected:* s. *perfection, perfectness, perfecter:* adj. *perfective.* adv. *perfectly, perfectively.*
PERFID'IOUS. *adj.* Treacherous. s. *perfidy:* adv. *perfidiously.*
PERFLA'TE. *v.* To blow through. pr. par. *perflating;* past, *perflated:* s. *perflation.*
PER'FORATE. *v.* To pierce through; to bore. pr. par. *perforating;* past, *perforated:* s. *perforation, perforator:* adj. *perforative.*
PERFORCE'. *adv.* By violence.

PERFORM. *v.* To do; to accomplish. pr. par. *performing;* past, *performed:* s. *performance, performer:* adj. *performable.*

PERFU'ME. *s.* Strong odour; fragrance. *v. perfume;* pr. par. *perfuming;* past, *perfumed:* s. *perfumer, perfumery:* adj. *perfumatory.*

PERFU'SE. *v.* To overspread; to tincture. pr. par. *perfusing;* past, *perfused:* s. *perfusion.*

PERHAPS'. *adv.* Peradventure.

PERICAR'DIUM. *s.* A thin membrane, that encloses the heart.

PERICAR'PIUM. *s.* A membrane enclosing the fruit of a plant.

PERICRA'NIUM. *s.* The membrane that covers the skull.

PER'IGEE, PERIGE'UM. *s.* The nearest possible distance of a planet from the earth.

PERIHE'LIUM. *s.* That point of a planet's orbit, wherein it is nearest the sun.

PER'IL. *s.* Danger; hazard. *v. peril;* pr. par. *periling;* past, *periled:* adj. *perilous:* adv. *perilously.*

PERIM'ETER. *s.* The compass or sum of all the sides which bound a figure.

PE'RIOD. *s.* A circuit; era, epocha; length of duration; a full stop. adj. *periodical:* adv. *periodically.*

PERIPH'ERY. *s.* Circumference. pl. *peripheries.*

PERIPH'RASIS. *s.* Circumlocution. pl. *periphrases:* v. *periphrase;* pr. par. *periphrasing;* past, *periphrased:* adj. *periphrastical:* adv. *periphrastically.*

PER'ISH. *v.* To die; to be destroyed. pr. par. *perishing;* past, *perished:* adj. *perishable:* s. *perishableness.*

PER'IWIG. *s.* A wig.

PER'IWINKLE. *s.* A small shellfish; a kind of plant.

PER'JURE. *v.* To swear falsely and corruptly. pr. par. *perjuring:* past, *perjured:* s. *perjurer, perjury,* pl. *perjuries.*

PER'MANENT. *adj.* Durable; unchanged. adv. *permanently:* s. *permanence.*

PER'MEATE. *v.* To pass through pr. par. *permeating;* past, *permeated:* s. *permeation:* adj. *permeable.*

PERMIS'CIBLE. *s.* Such as may be mingled. s. *permistion, permixtion*

PERMIT'. *v.* To allow, without command; to suffer. pr. par. *permitting;* past, *permitted:* s. *per'mit, permission:* adj. *permissible, permissive:* adv. *permissively.*

PERMU'TE. *v.* To exchange. pr par. *permuting;* past, *permuted:* s. *permuter, permutation.*

PERNI'CIOUS. *adj.* Destructive; very hurtful. s. *perniciousness:* adv. *perniciously.*

PERNOCTA'TION. *s.* Act of staying or watching all night.

PERORA'TION. *s.* The conclusion of an oration.

PERPENDIC'ULAR. *adj.* Hanging at a right angle with the horizon; crossing any other line at right angles. s. *perpendicular, perpendicularity:* adv. *perpendicularly.*

PER'PETRATE. *v.* To commit; to act. pr. par. *perpetrating;* past, *perpetrated:* s. *perpetration, perpetrator.*

PERPET'UAL. *adj.* Never ceasing; eternal. adv. *perpetually.*

PERPET'UATE. *v.* To make perpetual. pr. par. *perpetuating;* past, *perpetuated:* s. *perpetuation, perpetuity,* pl. *perpetuities.*

PERPLEX'. *v.* To disturb with doubts, to entangle; to vex. pr. par. *perplexing;* past, *perplexed:* s. *perplexedness, perplexity,* pl. *perplexities:* adv. *perplexedly.*

PER'QUISITE. *s.* Something gained, by a place, over and above the settled wages.

PER'RY. *s.* A drink made of pears

PER'SECUTE. *v.* To pursue with malignity; to oppress. pr. par *persecuting;* past, *persecuted:* s. *persecution, persecutor.*

275

PERSEVE'RANCE. *s.* Steadiness in pursuits; constancy in progress. *v. persevere;* pr. par. *persevering;* past, *persevered:* s. *perseverer:* adv. *perseveringly.*

PERSIST'. *v.* To persevere; to continue firm. pr. par. *persisting;* past, *persisted:* s. *persistence, persistency.*

PER'SON. *s.* An individual; a particular man or woman; exterior appearance. adj. *personal:* s. *personality,* pl. *personalities:* adv. *personally.*

PER'SONABLE. *adj.* Handsome; graceful.

PER'SONATE. *v.* To represent by a fictitious or assumed character; to act; to feign. pr. par. *personating;* past, *personated:* s. *personation, personator.*

PERSON'IFY. *v.* To change from a thing to a person. pr. par. *personifying;* past, *personified:* s. *personification.*

PERSPEC'TIVE. *s.* Forward view; view of futurity; the science by which things are ranged in a picture according to their real appearance. adj. *perspective:* adv. *perspectively.*

PERSPICA'CIOUS. *adj.* Quick sighted. s. *perspicacity.*

PERSPIC'UOUS. *adj.* Transparent; clear to the understanding. s. *perspicuity:* adv. *perspicuously.*

PERSPI'RE. *v.* To sweat. pr. par. *perspiring;* past, *perspired:* s. *perspiration:* adj. *perspiratory, perspirative.*

PERSUA'DE. *v.* To bring to any particular opinion; to inculcate by argument or expostulation. pr. par. *persuading;* past, *persuaded:* s. *persuader.*

PERSUA'SION. *s.* Act of persuading. adj. *persuasive, persuasory:* adv. *persuasively.*

PERT. *adj.* Smart; saucy. s. *pertness:* adv *pertly.*

PERTAIN'. *v.* To belong; to relate. pr. par. *pertaining;* past, *pertained.*

PERTINA'CIOUS. *adj.* Obstinate, stubborn. adv. *pertinaciously:* s. *pertinacity.*

PER'TINENCE, PER'TINENCY. *s.* Fitness to the purpose. adj. *pertinent:* adv. *pertinently.*

PERTURBA'TION. *s.* Disquiet of mind; disturbance; disorder.

PERTU'SED. *adj.* Pierced with holes. s. *pertusion.*

PER'UKE. *s.* A periwig.

PERU'SE. *v.* To read through; to examine. pr. par. *perusing;* past. *perused:* s. *perusal, peruser.*

PERVA'DE. *v.* To pass through; to be general. pr. par. *pervading,* past, *pervaded:* s. *pervasion:* adj *pervasive.*

PERVERSE'. *adj.* Obstinate, stubborn, untractable. s. *perverseness perversity:* adv. *perversely.*

PERVERT'. *v.* To distort from the true end or purpose; to corrupt; to mislead. pr. par. *perverting,* past, *perverted:* s. *perverter:* adj. *pervertible.*

PERVER'SION. *s.* Act of perverting adj. *perversive.*

PER'VIOUS. *adj.* Admitting passage. s. *perviousness.*

PEST. *s.* Plague; pestilence.

PESTIF'EROUS. *adj.* Pestilential. infectious.

PES'TER. *v.* To disturb; to perplex; pr. par. *pestering;* past, *pestered.* s. *pesterer:* adj. *pesterous.*

PEST'HOUSE. *s.* An hospital for persons infected with the plague.

PEST'ILENCE. *s.* Plague; pest. adj. *pestilent, pestilential:* adv. *pestilently, pestilentially.*

PES'TLE. *s.* An instrument with which any thing is broken in a mortar. s. *pestillation.*

PET. *s.* A slight passion; a fit of peevishness; any creature fondled and indulged. v. *pet;* pr. par. *petting;* past, *petted:* adj. *pettish:* s. *pettishness:* adv. *pettishly.*

PE'TAL. *s.* The leaf of a flower. adj. *petalous.*

276

PETARD'. *s.* An explosive engine, used to break down gates or barriers.

PET'EREL. *s.* A kind of sea-bird.

PETI'TION. *s.* Request; entreaty. *v. petition;* pr. par. *petitioning;* past, *petitioned: s. petitioner:* adj. *petitionary.*

PETRES'CENT. *adj.* Growing to stone.

PET'RIFY. *v.* To change to stone. pr. par. *petrifying;* past, *petrified: s. petrifaction, petrification:* adj. *petrifactive.*

PET'TICOAT. *s.* Part of a woman's dress.

PET'TIFOGGER. *s.* A petty lawyer.

PET'TITOES. *s.* The feet of a sucking pig.

PET'TO. *s.* The breast; figuratively, privacy as "*in petto,*" i. e. in reserve.

PET'TY. *adj.* Small; inconsiderable. *s. pettiness.*

PET'ULANT. *adj.* Saucy; perverse. *s. petulance, petulancy:* adv. *petulantly.*

PEW. *s.* A seat enclosed in a church.

PEW'TER. *s.* A compound metal. *s. pewterer.*

PHÆNOM'ENON. *s.* See PHENOMONON.

PHA'ETON. *s.* A kind of lofty, open, four-wheeled chaise.

PHAL'ANX. *s.* A troop of men, closely imbodied. pl. *phalanxes.*

PHAN'TASM, PHANTAS'MA. *s.* Vain and airy appearance.

PHAN'TASY. *s.* See FANTASY.

PHAN'TOM. *s.* A spectre; a fancied vision.

PHARISA IC, PHARISA'ICAL. *adj.* Externally religious. *s. pharisaism, pharisaicalness.*

PHAR'ISEE. *s.* One of a religious sect amongst the Jews.

PHARMACEU'TIC, PHARMACEU'TICAL. *adj.* Relating to the art of preparing medicines.

PHARMACOL'OGY. *s.* The knowledge of drugs and medicines.

PHARMACO'PŒIA. *s.* A book of rules for the composition of medicines.

PHARMACOP'OLIST. *s.* An apothecary.

PHAR'MACY. *s* The trade of an apothecary.

PHA'RO, PHA'ROS. *s.* A light-house

PHARYNGOT'OMY. *s.* The act of making an incision into the wind pipe.

PHEA'SANT. *s.* A species of game bird.

PHE'NIX, PHŒ'NIX. *s.* A fabulous bird. pl. *phenixes.*

PHENOM'ENON. *s.* Appearance; visible quality. pl. *phenomena.*

PHI'AL. *s.* A small bottle.

PHILAN'THROPY. *s.* Love of man kind. adj. *philanthropic, philanthropical:* s. *philanthropist.*

PHIL'IBEG. *s.* See FILIBEG.

PHILIP'PIC. *s.* Any invective declamation. v. *philippize;* pr. par *philippizing;* past, *philippized.*

PHILOL'OGY. *s.* Criticism; grammatical learning. adj. *philologic, philological:* s. *philologist.*

PHIL'OMATH. *s.* A lover of learning.

PHIL'OMEL, PHILOME'LA. *s.* The nightingale.

PHILOS'OPHY. *s.* Desire of acquiring wisdom; knowledge, natural or moral; reasoning. adj. *philosophic, philosophical: s. philosopher:* adv. *philosophically* v. *philosophize;* pr. par. *philosophizing* past, *philosophized.*

PHIL'TER. *s.* A charm to cause love. v. *philter;* pr. par. *philtering,* past, *philtered.*

PHIZ. *s.* The face, in contempt.

PHLEBOT'OMY. *s.* Blood-letting. *s. phlebotomist:* v. *phlebotomize* pr. par. *phlebotomizing;* past, *phlebotomized.*

PHLEGM. *s.* The watery humour of the body; coolness; indifference. adj. *phlegmatic:* adv. *phlegmatically*

PHLEG'MONOUS. *adj.* Inflammatory.

PHLEME. *s.* An instrument to bleed with, particularly used for horses.

PHLOGIS'TON. *s.* An exploded chymical name for an imaginary substance, thought to be a constituent part of all inflammable bodies.

PHO'NICS. *s.* The doctrine of sounds.

PHOS'PHORUS. *s.* The morning star; a chymical substance, which, when exposed to the air, takes fire. *adj. phosphorated.*

PHRASE. *s.* An idiom; style; expression.

PHRASEOL'OGY. *s.* Style; diction.

PHRENET'IC. *adj.* Mad.

PHRENOL'OGY. *s.* The science of cerebral pathology; craniology. *s. phrenologist.*

PHREN'SY. *s.* Madness. pl. *phrensies:* adj. *phrensied.*

PHRY'GIAN. *adj.* Denoting, amongst the ancients, a sprightly and animating kind of music.

PHTHIS'IC, PHTHIS'IS. *s.* A consumption. adj. *phthisical.*

PHYS'ICAL. *adj.* Relating to nature, or to natural philosophy; medicinal. adv. *physically.*

PHYS'IC. *s.* The science of healing; medicine. v. *physic;* pr. par. *physicking;* past, *physicked:* s. *physician.*

PHYSIOG'NOMY. *s.* The art of discovering the temper, and foreknowing the fortune, by the features of the face; the face. pl. *physiognomies:* s. *physiognomist.*

PHYSIOL'OGY. *s.* The doctrine of the constitution of the works of nature. adj. *physiologic, physiological:* s. *physiologist.*

PIAC'ULAR, PIAC'ULOUS. *adj.* Expiatory; such as requires expiation.

PI'ANET. *s.* A kind of bird.

PIAN'O-FOR'TE. *s.* A kind of musical instrument.

PIAS'TER. *s.* An Italian coin.

PIAZ'ZA. *s.* A walk under a roof, supported by pillars.

PI'BRACH or PI'BROCH. *s.* A kind of martial music, amongst the highlanders of Scotland.

PI'CA. *s.* A particular sized type.

PICAROON'. *s.* A robber.

PICK. *v.* To choose; to select; to gather; to open a lock, &c. pr. par. *picking;* past, *picked:* s. *pick, picker.*

PICK'ET. *s.* A sharp stake; a guard posted before an army v. *picket.* pr. par. *picketing;* past, *picketed.*

PICK'LE. *s.* A salt liquor; thing pickled. v. *pickle;* pr. par. *pickling;* past, *pickled.*

PICK'NIC. *s.* An assembly where each person contributes provisions to the general entertainment.

PICK'POCKET. *s.* A thief, who steals from the pocket.

PICK'THANK. *s.* A talebearer; a flatterer.

PICT. *s.* A painted person; one of the ancient inhabitants of Scotland.

PICTO'RIAL. *adj.* Produced by a painter.

PIC'TURE. *s.* A resemblance of persons or things in colours. v. *picture;* pr. par. *picturing;* past, *pictured.*

PICTURESQUE'. *adj.* Expressing that peculiar kind of beauty which is agreeable in a picture. s. *picturesqueness.*

PIE. *s.* Any crust baked, with something in it; a magpie.

PIE'BALD. *adj.* Of various colours.

PIECE. *s.* A part of the whole; a fragment; a picture; a perform ance; a gun; a coin.

PIECE. *v.* To enlarge by the addition of a piece; to join. pr. par *piecing;* past, *pieced:* s. *piecer.*

PIED. *adj.* Variegated. s. *piedness.*

PIER. *s.* A column on which the arch of a bridge is raised.

PIERCE. *v.* To penetrate; to enter. pr. par. *piercing;* past, *pierced:* s. *piercingness, piercer:* adj. *piercing, pierceable:* adv. *piercingly.*

PI'ETY. *s.* Discharge of duty to God.

278

PIG. *s.* A sow or boar; a mass of unforged lead, &c. v. *pig;* pr. par. *pigging;* past, *pigged.*

PI'GEON. *s.* A kind of bird.

PI'GEONHEARTED. *adj.* Timid.

PI'GEONHOLES. *s.* An old English game; cavities or divisions in which papers are deposited.

PIG'GIN. *s.* A small wooden vessel.

PIG'MENT. *s.* Paint.

PIG'MY, PYG'MY. *s.* A dwarf. pl. *pigmies, pygmies.*

PIGNORA'TION. *s.* The act of pledging. adj. *pignorative.*

PIG'NUT. *s.* A kind of nut that grows in the earth.

PIG'TAIL. *s.* A cue; a kind of twisted tobacco.

PIKE. *s* A fish; a lance used by foot-soldiers. adj. *piked.*

PIKE'LET. *s.* A light cake.

PIKE'MAN. *s.* A soldier armed with a pike. pl. *pikemen.*

PIKE'STAFF. *s.* The wooden staff of a pike.

PILAS'TER. *s.* A small square column.

PILCH'ARD. *s.* A kind of fish.

PILE. *s.* A heap; a strong piece of wood driven into the ground, to make a firm foundation. v. *pile;* pr. par. *piling;* past, *piled:* s. *piler.*

PIL'FER. *v.* To steal. pr. par. *pilfering:* past, *pilfered:* s. *pilferer;* adv. *pilferingly.*

PIL'GRIM. *s.* A traveller; a wanderer; one who travels to sacred places, for devotion. s. *pilgrimage.*

PILL. *s.* Medicine made into a small ball.

PIL'LAGE. *v.* To plunder; to spoil. pr. par. *pillaging;* past, *pillaged;* s. *pillager.*

PIL'LAR. *s.* A column; a supporter. adj. *pillared.*

PIL'LION. *s.* A low soft saddle, placed behind another, on which a woman rides.

PIL'LORY. *s.* A kind of punishment. pl. *pillories.* pr. par. *pillorying;* past, *pillored.*

PIL'LOW. *s.* A support for the head v. *pillow;* pr. par. *pillowing;* past, *pillowed:* s. *pillow-case.*

PILOS'ITY. *s.* Hairiness. adj. *pilous.*

PI'LOT. *s.* He whose office is to steer a ship. v. *pilot;* pr. par. *piloting;* past, *piloted:* s. *pilotage.*

PIMEN'TO. *s.* A kind of spice, pl *pimentoes.*

PIMP. *v.* To pander. pr. par. *pimping;* past, *pimped.*

PIM'PLE. *s.* A small red pustule. adj. *pimpled.*

PIN. *s.* A short wire, used to fasten clothes; any thing driven to hold parts together. v. *pin;* pr. par. *pinning;* past, *pinned:* s. *pincase, pincushion, pinhole.*

PINAS'TER. *s.* The wild pine.

PIN'CERS. *s.* An instrument for drawing nails, &c.

PINCH. *v.* To squeeze, to gripe, to be frugal. pr. par. *pinching;* past, *pinched:* s. *pinch,* pl. *pinches, pincher.*

PINCH'BECK. *s.* Mixed gold-coloured metal.

PINDAR'IC. *s.* An ode, in the manner of Pindar. adj. *pindaric.*

PINE. *s.* A species of tree. adj. *piny*

PINE. *v.* To languish; to wear away with misery or pain. pr. par *pining;* past, *pined.*

PINE'APPLE. *s.* A kind of fruit.

PI'NEAL. *adj.* Resembling a pine apple.

PI'NERY. *s.* A place where pineapples are raised. pl. *pineries.*

PIN'FOLD. *s.* A place in which beasts are confined.

PIN'GUID. *adj.* Fat.

PIN'ION. *s.* A joint of the wing fetters. v. *pinion;* pr. par. *pinioning;* past, *pinioned.*

PINK. *s.* A flower; a colour; a kind of heavy, narrow-sterned ship.

PINK. *v.* To work in eyelet holes to stab; to pierce. pr. par. *pinking;* past, *pinked.*

PINK'EYED. *adj.* Having small eyes.

279

PINK'STERNED. *adj.* Having a narrow stern.
PIN'MONEY. *s.* An annual sum, settled on a wife, to defray her own charges.
PIN'NACE. *s.* A boat belonging to a ship of war.
PIN'NACLE. *s.* A turret, or high spiring point. adj. *pinnacled.*
PIN'NER. *s.* The lappet of a head-dress, which flies loose.
PINT. *s.* Half a quart.
PIONEE'R. *s.* One who opens the road for an army.
PI'ONY. *s.* A kind of flower. pl. *pionies.*
PI'OUS. *adj.* Devout; godly; religious; careful of the duties of a near relation. adv. *piously.*
PIP. *s.* A disorder of fowls.
PIPE. *s.* A tube; a musical instrument; a liquid measure, containing two hogsheads.
PIPE. *v.* To play on the pipe; to emit a shrill sound. pr. par. *piping;* past, *piped:* s. *piper.*
PI'PING. *adj.* Weak; hot; boiling.
PIP'KIN. *s.* A small earthen vessel.
PIP'PIN. *s.* A kind of apple.
PI'QUANT. *adj.* Pricking; stimulating to the taste; sharp. adv. *piquantly:* s. *piquancy.*
PIQUE. *s.* Ill-will; petty malice; grudge. v. *pique;* pr. pa.. *piquing;* past, *piqued.*
PIQUET'. *s.* A game at cards.
PI'RACY. *s.* The act of robbing on the sea. pl. *piracies:* s. *pirate:* adj. *piratical:* adv. *piratically.*
PIS'CARY. *s.* A privilege of fishing. s. *piscation:* adj. *piscatory.*
PIS'CES. *s.* A sign of the zodiac; the fishes.
PISCIV'OROUS. *adj.* Fish-eating.
PISH. *int.* A contemptuous exclamation.
PIS'MIRE. *s.* An ant.
PISTILLA'TION. *s.* The act of pounding in a mortar.
PIS'TOL. *s.* A small hand-gun. v. *pistol:* pr. par. *pistoling;* past, *pistoled*

PISTO'LE. *s.* A coin of many countries, and many degrees of value.
PIS'TON. *s.* A rod moving within a cylinder.
PIT. *s.* A hole; an abyss; the middle part of a theatre. v. *pit;* pr. par. *pitting;* past, *pitted.*
PIT'APAT. *s.* A flutter; a light, quick step.
PITCH. *s.* The resin of the pine, any degree of elevation; degree; rate. pl. *pitches.*
PITCH. *v.* To fix; to throw head long ; to smear with pitch. pr. par. *pitching;* past, *pitched:* s. *pitch, pitchiness:* adj. *pitchy.*
PI'TCH'ER. *s.* An earthen vessel; a water-pot.
PITCH'FORK. *s.* An instrument with which hay or corn is pitched upon a wagon.
PITCH'PIPE. *s.* An instrument to regulate the voice.
PIT'COAL. *s.* Fossil coal.
PIT'EOUS. *adj.* Sorrowful; mournful; compassionate. s. *piteousness* adv. *piteously.*
PIT'FALL. *s.* A covered pit.
PITH. *s.* The marrow of a plant, energy; strength. adj. *pithless, pithy:* s. *pithiness:* adv. *pithily.*
PIT'SAW. *s.* A large saw, used by two men.
PIT'TANCE. *s.* An allowance; a small portion.
PIT'Y. *s.* Compassion; sympathy for misery. v. *pity;* pr. par. *pitying,* past, *pitied:* adj. *pitiable, pitiful, pitiless:* s. *pitifulness:* adv. *pitifully.*
PIV'OT. *s.* A pin on which any thing turns.
PIX. *s* A box for the consecrated host.
PLAC'ABLE. *adj.* Possible to be appeased. s. *placability:* adv *placably.*
PLACARD'. *s.* An edict; a manifesto; an advertisement or public notification. v. *placard;* pr. par. *placarding;* past, *placarded.*
PLACE. *s.* Particular portion of

280

space; locality; office. v. *place;* pr. par. *placing;* past, *placed:* s. *placer.*

PLACE'MAN. s. One who exercises a public employment. pl. *placemen.*

PLA'CID. adj. Gentle; quiet; soft. s. *placidness, placidity:* adv. *placidly.*

PLA'GIARY. s. A thief in literature; literary theft. s. *plagiarism, plagiarist:* adj. *plagiary.*

PLAGUE. s. Pestilence; any thing troublesome or vexatious. v. *plague;* pr. par. *plaguing;* past, *plagued:* s. *plaguer:* adj. *plaguy:* adv. *plaguily.*

PLAICE. s. A kind of flat fish.

PLAID. s. A variegated cloth; a cloak made of plaid.

PLAIN. adj. Smooth; level; open; clear; simple. s. *plain, plainness:* adv. *plainly:* adj. *plaindealing, plainhearted, plainspoken.*

PLAINT. s. Lamentation; complaint. adj. *plaintful, plaintless, plaintive:* n. *plaintiveness:* adv. *plaintively.*

PLAIN'TIFF. s. One that brings a suit.

PLAIN'WORK. s. Needlework, as distinguished from embroidery.

PLAIT. s. A fold; a double. pronounced *plate.* v. *plait;* pr. par. *plaiting;* past, *plaited:* s. *plaiter.*

PLAN. s. A scheme; a model. v. *plan;* pr. par. *planning;* past, *planned:* s. *planner.*

PLANE. s. A level surface; an instrument for smoothing boards. pr. par. *planing;* past, *planed:* s. *planer.*

PLAN'ET. s. One of the erratic stars. adj. *planetary.*

PLANE-TREE. s. A kind of tree.

PLANIM'ETRY. s. The mensuration of plane surfaces. adj. *planimetrical.*

PLANISPHERE. s. A sphere projected on a plane.

PLANK. s. A thick, strong board. v. *plank;* pr. par. *planking;* past, *planked.*

PLA'NO-CON'VEX. adj. Flat on one side, and convex on the other a *plano-convexity.*

PLANT. s. Any vegetable production. v. *plant;* pr. par. *planting,* past, *planted:* s. *plantation, planter.*

PLAN'TAIN. s. A kind of tree, and its fruit.

PLAS'TER. s. A glutinous or adhesive mixture. v. *plaster;* pr. par. *plastering;* past, *plastered:* s. *plastering, plasterer.*

PLAS'TIC. adj. Having the power to give form.

PLAT. v. To weave. pr. par. *platting;* past, *platted:* s. *platter.*

PLAT. s. A small piece of ground.

PLATE. s. A piece of metal, beat out into breadth; wrought silver, a dish to eat off. v. *plate;* pr. par. *plating;* past, *plated.*

PLAT'FORM. s. A level place before a fortification; an elevated stage; a scheme.

PLATI'NA. s. A recently discovered metal, of the colour of silver; heavier than gold; and, next to iron, the hardest of metals.

PLATON'IC. adj. Relating to the philosophy, opinions, or school of Plato. s. *platonism, platonist:* adv *platonically.*

PLATOON'. s. A small square body of musketeers.

PLAT'TER. s. A large dish, generally of earth or wood.

PLAU'DIT. s. Applause.

PLAU'SIBLE. adj. Superficially pleasing; specious. adj. *plausive:* adv. *plausibly:* s. *plausibility.*

PLAY. v. To sport; to game; to touch a musical instrument; to operate; to personate a drama pr. par. *playing;* past, *played.* s. *play, player:* adj. *playful:* s. *playfulness:* adv. *playfully:* s. *playbook, playday, playdebt, playfellow, playhouse, playmate, plaything.*

PLEA. s. The act or form of pleading; an apology.

PLEAD v. To enter a plea; to argue before a court of justice; to reason with another. pr. par. *plead*

PLE—PLI

ing; past, *pleaded;* s. *pleader;* adj. *pleadable.*

PLEAS'ANT. *adj.* Delightful; good-humoured; gay. s. *pleasantness, pleasantry,* pl. *pleasantries:* adv. *pleasantly.*

PLEASE. *v.* To gain approbation; to like. pr. par. *pleasing;* past, *pleased:* s. *pleaser, pleasingness:* adv. *pleasingly.*

PLEAS'URE. *s.* Delight; gratification; choice. adj. *pleasurable:* s. *pleasurableness:* adv. *pleasurably.*

PLEBE'IAN. *s.* One of the lower people. adj. *plebeian.*

PLEDGE. *s.* A pawn; a gage; a surety, &c. v. *pledge;* pr. par. *pledging;* past, *pledged:* s. *pledger.*

PLEI'ADES, PLEI'ADS. *s.* A northern constellation.

PLEN'ARY. *adj.* Full; complete. adv. *plenarily.*

PLENIP'OTENCE. *s.* Fulness of power. adj. *plenipotent.*

PLENIPOTEN'TIARY. *s.* A negotiator invested with full power. pl. *plenipotentiaries:* adj. *plenipotentiary.*

PLE'NIST. *s.* One that holds all space to be full of matter.

PLEN'ITUDE. *s.* Fulness; repletion.

PLEN'TEOUS. *adj.* Copious; abundant. s. *plenteousness:* adv. *plenteously.*

PLEN'TY. *s.* Abundance; fruitfulness. adj. *plentiful:* s. *plentifulness;* adv. *plentifully.*

PLE'ONASM. *s.* A figure of rhetoric, by which more words are used than are necessary.

PLETH'ORA. *s.* The state in which the vessels are fuller of humours than is agreeable to a natural state of health.

PLEU'RISY *s.* An inflammation of the pleura. pl. *pleurisies;* adj. *pleuritic, pleuritical*

PLI'ABLE. *adj.* Easy to be bent; flexible. s. *pliability,* pl. *pliabilities:* adv. *pliably.*

PLI—PLU

PLI'ANT. *adj.* Bending, flexible; easy to take a form. *s. pliancy.*

PLICA'TION, PLIC'ATURE. *s.* Fold; double.

PLI'ERS. *s.* An instrument by which any thing is laid hold of, to bend it.

PLIGHT. *v.* To pledge. pr. par. *plighting;* past, *plighted:* s. *plighter.*

PLIGHT. *s.* Condition; state.

PLINTH. *s.* The lowermost part of a pillar.

PLOD. *v.* To toil; to travel laboriously; to study dully. pr. par. *plodding;* past, *plodded:* s. *plodder.*

PLOT. *s.* A small extent of ground; a scheme; a stratagem v. *plot;* pr. par. *plotting;* past, *plotted;* s. *plotter.*

PLOUGH. *s.* An instrument of agriculture. v. *plough;* pr. par. *ploughing;* past, *ploughed:* s. *plougher, ploughboy, ploughland, ploughman, ploughshare.*

PLOV'ER. *s.* A kind of bird.

PLUCK. *v.* To pull with nimbleness or force; to snatch. pr. par. *plucking,* past, *plucked.* s. *pluck, plucker.*

PLUCK. *s.* The heart, liver, and lights of an animal; courage.

PLUG. *s.* Any thing driven in, to stop a hole. v. *plug;* pr. par. *plugging;* past, *plugged.*

PLUM. *s.* A kind of fruit. s. *plumcake.*

PLU'MAGE. *s.* Feathers.

PLUMB. *s.* A plummet. v. *plumb,* pr. par. *plumbing;* past, *plumbed.*

PLUMB. *adj.* Perpendicular to the horizon.

PLUM'BEAN. *adj.* Consisting of lead.

PLUM'BEOUS. *adj.* Resembling lead.

PLUMB'ER. *s.* One who makes things of lead.

PLUME. *s.* A feather of birds; a feather worn as an ornament. v *plume;* pr. par. *pluming:* past, *plumed.* adj. *plumeless.*

PLUMIG'EROUS. *adj.* Feathered.

PLU—POE

PLU'MIPEDE. *s.* A fowl that has feathers on the foot.
PLUM'MET. *s.* A leaden weight, hung to a string, used for measuring depths.
PLU'MOUS, PLU'MY.*adj.* Feathery; resembling feathers. s. *plumosity.*
PLUMP. *adj.* Inclining to fatness; sleek; full and smooth. s. *plumpness:* adv. *plumply.*
PLUMP. *v.* To fall like a stone into water. pr. par. *plumping;* past, *plumped:* adv. *plump.*
PLUN'DER. *v.* To pillage. pr. par. *plundering;* past, *plundered:* s. *plunder, plunderer.*
PLUNGE. *v.* To put or immerse suddenly under water, &c. pr. par. *plunging;* past, *plunged:* s. *plunge, plunger.*
PLU'RAL. *adj.* Implying more than one. s. *plurality:* adv. *plurally.*
PLUSH. *s.* A kind of cloth.
PLU'VIAL, PLU'VIOUS. *adj.* Relating to rain.
PLY. *v.* To work diligently; to solicit. pr. par. *plying;* past, *plied:* s. *ply, plier.*
PLY'ERS. *s.* See PLIERS.
PNEUMAT'ICS. *s.* The science of the density and pressure of the atmosphere. adj. *pneumatic.*
POACH. *v.* To boil slightly; to plunder by stealth. pr. par. *poaching;* past, *poached:* s. *poacher.*
POCK. *s.* A pustule.
POCK'ET. *s.* The small bag inserted into clothes. pr. par. *pocketing;* past, *pocketed.*
POC'ULENT. *adj.* Fit for drink.
POD. *s.* The case of leguminous seeds.
PODA'GRAL. *adj.* Afflicted with the gout; relating to the gout.
PO'EM. *s.* A metrical composition.
PO'ESY. *s.* The art of writing poems; a poem; a short conceit, engraved on a ring or other things.
PO'ET. *s.* A writer of poems. fem. *poetess,* pl. *poetesses:* adj. *poetic, poetical:* adv. *poetically:* s. *poetics,* poetry: v *poetize;* pr. par. *poetizing;* past, *poetized.*
POE—POL

PO'ETASTER. *s.* A vile, petty poet
POI'GNANT. *adj.* Sharp, penetrating; severe. s. *poignancy:* adv. *poignantly.*
POINT. *s.* A sharp end; a moment, particular place, &c. v. *point;* pr. par. *pointing;* past, *pointed:* s. *pointer, pointedness:* adj. *pointless* adv. *pointedly.*
POINT'ER. *s.* Any thing that points. a setting-dog.
POI'SON. *s.* Venom; any thing malignant. v. *poison;* pr. par. *poisoning;* past, *poisoned* s. *poisoner* adj. *poisonous:* s. *poisonousness:* adv. *poisonously.*
POIZE. *s.* Weight; balance; a regulating power. v. *poize;* pr. par. *poizing;* past, *poized.*
POKE. *s.* A bag; a sack; a kind of berry.
POKE. *v.* To feel in the dark; to search any thing with a long instrument. pr. par. *poking;* past, *poked:* s. *poker.*
PO'LAR. *adj.* Relating or belonging to the poles. s. *polarity,* tendency towards the poles.
POLE. *s.* The extremity of the axis of the earth; a long staff; a measure of length containing five yards and a half, &c. adj. *polar:* s. *polarity.*
POLE'AXE. *s.* An axe fixed to a long pole.
POLE'CAT. *s.* A kind of animal.
POLEM'IC, POLEM'ICAL *adj.* Controversial.
POLE'STAR. *s.* A star near the pole.
POLI'CE. *s.* The regulation of a city or country; officers employed in preserving the peace.
POL'ICY. *s.* The art of government; prudence, &c. pl. *policies.*
POL'ISH. *v.* To smooth; to brighten. to refine. pr. par. *polishing;* past, *polished:* s. *polish, polisher:* adj. *polishable.*
POLI'TE. *adj.* Po..snea; refined

283

of elegant manners. *s. politeness:* adv. *politely.*

POL'ITIC. *adj.* Political; civil; prudent; artful. adv. *politically.*

POL'ITICS. *s.* The science of government. adj. *political:* adv. *politically:* s. *politician.*

POL'ITY. *s.* A form of government; policy; art. pl. *polities.*

POLL. *s.* The head; a catalogue or list of those who vote. v. *poll;* pr. par. *polling;* past, *polled.*

POL'LARD. *s.* A tree lopped; the chub-fish; a mixture of bran and meal. v. *pollard.*

POL'LEN. *s.* A sort of fine bran.

POLL-E'VIL. *s.* A disorder in a horse's neck.

POLLU'TE. *v.* To make unclean; to defile; to corrupt. pr. par. *polluting;* past, *polluted:* s. *pollution, polluter, pollutedness.*

POLTROON'. *s.* A coward. s. *poltroonry.*

POLYAN"THUS. *s.* A kind of plant. pl. *polyanthuses.*

POLYE'DRON. *s.* A multiplying glass.

POLYG'AMY. *s.* The act of having more than one wife. s. *polygamist.*

POL'YGLOT. *adj.* Containing many languages. s. *polyglot.*

POL'YGON. *s.* A figure of many angles. adj. *polygonal.*

POL'YGRAM. *s.* A figure of many lines.

POL'YPUS. *s.* A sea animal with many feet; any thing with many roots or feet. pl. *polypuses:* adj. *polypous.*

POLYSYL'LABLE. *s.* A word of many syllables; a word of more than three syllables. adj. *polysyllabic, polysyllabical.*

POLY'THEISM. *s.* The doctrine of a plurality of gods. s. *polytheist:* adj. *polytheistic, polytheistical.*

POM'ACE. *s.* The dross of cider-pressings.

POMA'CEOUS. *adj.* Consisting of apples.

POMA'DE. *s.* A fragrant ointment.

POMAN'DER. *s.* A perfumed ball or powder.

POMA'TUM. *s.* An ointment for the hair. v. *pomatum;* pr. par *pomatuming;* past, *pomatumed.*

POME'GRANATE. *s.* A kind of tree, and its fruit.

POM'MEL. *s.* A round ball or knob; the knob that balances the blade of a sword; the protuberant part of a saddle, before.

POM'MEL. *v.* To beat with any thing thick and bulky; to bruise. pr. par. *pommeling;* past, *pomeled.*

POMP. *s.* Splendour, pride, ostentation. adj. *pompous:* s. *pomposity:* adv. *pompously.*

POMP'ION. *s.* See PUMPKIN.

POND. *s.* A small pool of water; a lake.

PON'DER. *v.* To consider; to muse. pr. par. *pondering;* past, *pondered:* s. *ponderer.*

PONDERA'TION. *s.* The act of weighing. adj. *ponderable, ponderal.*

PON'DEROUS. *adj.* Heavy, weighty s. *ponderousness:* adv. *ponderously.*

PON'IARD. *s.* A dagger. v. *poniard* pr. par. *poniarding;* past, *poniarded.*

PONT'AGE. *s.* Duty paid to repair bridges.

PONT'IFF. *s.* A high priest; the pope. adj. *pontific, pontifical:* s. *pontificate:* adv. *pontifically.*

PONTON'. *s.* A floating bridge of boats. pronounced *pon-toon'.*

PO'NY. *s.* A small horse. pl. *ponies.*

POOL. *s.* A lake of standing water.

POOP. *s.* The hindmost part of a ship.

POOP. *v.* A ship is said to be pooped, when she receives on her poop the shock of a high and heavy sea.

POOR. *adj.* Not rich; necessitous; paltry; lean. s. *poorness:* adv. *poorly:* adj. *poorspirited:* s. *poorspiritedness.*

POP. *s.* A small, smart, quick sound. s. *popgun.*

POP. *v.* To move or enter with a quick, sudden, and unexpected motion. pr. par. *popping;* past, *popped.*

POPE. *s.* The bishop of Rome; a small fish. adj. *popish:* s. *popedom, popery:* adv. *popishly.*

POPE-JOAN'. *s.* A game at cards.

POPES-EYE'. *s.* The gland surrounded with fat, in the middle of the thigh.

POP'INJAY. *s.* A parrot; a woodpecker; a trifling fop.

POP'LAR. *s.* A kind of tree.

POP'LIN. *s.* A kind of stuff, made of silk and worsted.

POP'PET. *s.* See PUPPET.

POP'PY. *s.* A kind of flower. pl. *poppies.*

POP'ULACE. *s.* The vulgar; the multitude.

POP'ULAR. *adj.* Vulgar; pleasing to the people. s. *popularity:* adv. *popularly.*

POP'ULATE. *v.* To breed people; to fill with inhabitants. pr. par. *populating;* past, *populated:* s. *population:* adj. *populous:* s. *populousness:* adv. *populously.*

PORCELAIN. *s.* China ware.

PORCH. *s.* A portico; a covered walk. pl. *porches.*

POR'CUPINE. *s.* A kind of animal.

PORE. *s.* Spiracle of the skin. adj. *porous:* s. *porousness.*

PORE. *v.* To look with great intenseness and care. pr. par. *poring;* past, *pored.*

PORK. *s.* Swine's flesh. s. *porker, porket, porkling.*

POR'PHYRY. *s.* Marble of a particular kind.

POR'POISE, POR'PUS. *s.* The sea-hog. pl. *porpoises, porpuses.*

PORREC'TION. *s.* The act of reaching forth.

POR'RIDGE. *s.* A kind of broth.

POR RINGER. *s.* A vessel to eat out of.

PORT. *s.* A harbour; a gate; the aperture in a ship, out of which the gun is projected; mien; a kind of wine.

PORT. *v.* To carry. pr. par. *porting;* past, *ported:* adj. *portable:* s. *portableness.*

PORT'AGE. *s.* Carriage; price of carrying; land-road between two navigable waters.

POR'TAL. *s.* A gate; the arch of a gate.

PORTCUL'LIS. *s.* A sort of machine hung over the gates of a city. pl. *portcullises:* adj. *portcullised.*

PORTEND'. *v.* To foretoken; to foreshow. pr. par. *portending;* past, *portended:* s. *portension, portent.*

POR'TER. *s.* One who has the charge of a gate; a carrier; a kind of strong beer. fem. *portress,* pl. *portresses:* s. *porterage.*

PORTFO'LIO. *s.* A case for keeping loose papers.

PORT'HOLE. *s.* A hole in a ship's side, where the guns are placed.

POR'TICO. *s.* A covered walk, in front of a house. pl. *porticoes.*

POR'TION. *s.* A part assigned. *v. portion;* pr. par. *portioning;* past, *portioned:* s. *portioner:* adj. *portionless.*

PORT'LY. *adj.* Of stately mien; bulky. s. *portliness.*

PORTMAN'TEAU. *s.* A chest or bag in which clothes are carried.

PORT'MOTE. *s.* A court held in port towns.

POR'TRAIT. *s.* A picture drawn from life. s. *portraiture.*

PORTRAY'. *v.* To paint; to describe by picture. pr. par. *portraying,* past, *portrayed.*

POR'TREVE. *s.* The bailiff of a port town.

POSE. *v.* To puzzle. pr. par. *posing;* past, *posed:* s. *poser.*

POSI'TION. *s.* State of being placed; situation. adj. *positional.*

POS'ITIVE. *adj.* Not negative; real, absolute; direct. s. *positiveness:* adv. *positively.*

POS'SE. *s.* An armed power; a low

word, from *posse comitatus,* the power of the shire.

POSSESS'. *v.* To have as an owner; to seize; to make master of. pr. par. *possessing;* past, *possessed:* s. *possession, possessor:* adj. *possessive, possessory.*

POS'SET. *s.* Milk curdled.

POS SIBLE. *adj.* Having the power to be, or to be done. adv. *possibly:* s. *possibility,* pl. *possibilities.*

POST *s.* A messenger; quick course or manner of travelling; situation; military station; a piece of timber set erect, &c. v. *post;* pr. par. *posting;* past, *posted:* s. *postage, poster, postboy, postchaise, posthaste, posthorse, posthouse, postman, postmaster, post-office, post-town.*

POST'DATE. *v.* To date later than the real time. pr. par. *postdating;* past, *postdated.*

POSTDILU'VIAN. *adj.* Posterior to the flood.

POSTE'RIOR. *adj.* Happening after; placed after. s. *posteriors, posteriority.*

POSTER'ITY. *s.* Succeeding generations. pl. *posterities.*

POS'TERN. *s.* A small gate.

POSTEXIS'TENCE. *s.* Future existence.

POST'HUMOUS. *adj.* Done, had, or published, after a person's death. adv. *posthumously.*

POSTIL'ION. *s.* A driver of a coach or postchaise.

POSTLIMIN'IAR, POSTLIMIN'IOUS. *adj.* Done or contrived subsequently.

POSTMERID'IAN. *adj.* Being in the afternoon. P. M.

POSTPO'NE. *v.* To put off; to delay. pr. par. *postponing;* past, *postponed.* s. *postponement.*

POST'SCRIPT. *s.* Something added to the end of a letter.

POS'TULATE. *v.* To assume without proof. pr. par. *postulating;* past, *postulated:* s. *postulate, pos-* *tulatum, postulation:* adj. *postulatory.*

POS'TURE. *s.* Position, disposition

POS'TUREMASTER. *s.* One who teaches or practises artificial contortions of the body.

PO'SY. *s.* A motto on a ring; a bunch of flowers. pl. *posies.*

POT. *s.* A vessel to hold liquids, &c. v. *pot;* pr. par. *potting;* past, *potted:* s. *potherb, pothook.*

PO'TABLE. *adj.* Drinkable. s. *potableness.*

POT'ASH. *s.* An alkaline salt. pl *potashes.*

POTA'TION. *s.* Drinking bout; drink.

POTA'TO. *s.* A kind of esculent root. pl. *potatoes.*

POT'COMPANION. *s.* A fellow-drinker.

PO'TENT. *adj.* Powerful; strong. s. *potent, potency,* pl. *potencies.*

PO'TENTATE. *s.* A monarch, a prince, a sovereign.

POTEN'TIAL. *adj.* Existing in possibility, not in act; powerful. adv *potentially:* s. *potentiality.*

POTH'ER. *s.* Bustle; tumult.

POT'HOUSE. *s.* An ale-house.

PO'TION. *s.* A draught; commonly a medicinal draught.

POT'TAGE. *s.* Any thing boiled for food.

POT'TER. *s.* A maker of earthen vessels. s. *pottery,* pl. *potteries.*

POT'TLE. *s.* A measure containing two quarts.

POT'VALIANT. *adj.* Heated to courage by strong drink.

POUCH. *s.* A small bag; a pocket. pl. *pouches:* v. *pouch;* pr. par. *pouching;* past, *pouched.*

POUL'TERER. *s.* One who sells fowls.

POUL'TICE. *s.* A soft, mollifying application. v. *poultice;* pr. par. *poulticing;* past, *poulticed.*

POUL'TRY. *s.* Domestic fowls. pl *poultries.*

POUNCE. *s.* The talon of a bird o prey; the powder of gum sands

286

lach or rosin. v. *pounce;* pr. par. *pouncing;* past, *pounced.*

POUN'CETBOX. *s.* A small box, perforated. pl. *pouncetboxes.*

POUND. *s.* A weight; twenty shillings; an enclosure.

POUND. *v.* To beat; to shut up. pr. par. *pounding;* past, *pounded:* s. *pounder.*

POUND'AGE. *s.* A certain sum deducted from a pound; confinement of cattle in a pound.

POUR. *v.* To empty liquid out of a vessel; to flow. pr. par. *pouring;* past, *poured:* s. *pourer*

POURTRAY'. *v.* See PORTRAY.

POUT. *v.* To look sullen, by thrusting out the lips; to frown. pr. par. *pouting;* past, *pouted:* s. *pout, pouter.*

POV'ERTY. *s.* Indigence, meanness, defect.

POW'DER. *s.* Dust; any body comminuted. v. *powder;* pr. par. *powdering;* past, *powdered:* s. *powderer, powderhorn, powdermill.*

POW'DERING-TUB. *s.* A vessel in which meat is salted.

POW'ER. *s.* Authority; influence; ability; strength. adj. *powerful, powerless:* s. *powerfulness:* adv. *powerfully.*

POX. *s.* Pustules.

POZE. *v.* To puzzle. pr. par. *pozing;* past, *pozed.*

PRAC'TICABLE. *adj.* Performable; possible to be accomplished. s. *practicability,* pl. *practicabilities:* adv. *practicably.*

PRAC'TICE. *s.* Frequent repetition of an act; use; actual performance. adj. *practical:* s. *practicalness.* adv. *practically.*

PRAC'TISE. *v.* To repeat an act frequently; to do; to exercise. pr. par. *practising;* past, *practised:* s. *practiser, practitioner.*

PRAGMAT'IC, PRAGMAT'ICAL. *adj.* Meddling; impertinently busy. s. *pragmaticalness:* adv. *pragmatically*

PRA'IRIE. *s.* A tract of land, in the valley of the Mississippi, and other parts of the west, destitute of trees, and covered with long, coarse grass.

PRAISE. *s.* Commendation; applause; honour. v. *praise;* pr. par. *praising;* past, *praised:* s. *praiser.*

PRAISE'WORTHY. *adj.* Commendable. s. *praiseworthiness:* adv. *praiseworthily.*

PRAME. *s.* A flat-bottomed boat.

PRANCE. *v.* To spring and bound. pr. par. *prancing;* past, *pranced* s. *prancer.*

PRANK. *s.* A frolic; a mischievous trick.

PRATE. *v.* To talk idly; to chatter. pr. par. *prating;* past, *prated* s. *prate, prater:* adv. *pratingly.*

PRAT'TLE. *v.* To talk lightly. pr par. *prattling;* past, *prattled:* s. *prattle, prattler.*

PRAV'ITY. *s.* Corruption, badness.

PRAWN. *s.* A small crustaceous fish.

PRAY. *v.* To petition; to entreat. pr. par. *praying;* past, *prayed:* s. *prayer:* adv. *prayingly:* s. *prayerbook.*

PREACH. *v.* To pronounce a public discourse, upon sacred subjects. pr. par. *preaching;* past, *preached* s. *preacher.*

PREADMON'ISH. *v.* To caution o advise beforehand. pr. par. *preadmonishing;* past, *preadmonished* s. *preadmonition.*

PREAM'BLE. *s.* Something previous; introduction. v. *preamble;* pr. par. *preambling;* past, *preambled.*

PREAM'BULATE. *v.* To walk before. pr. par. *preambulating;* past, *preambulated:* s. *preambulation:* adj. *preambulatory.*

PREAU'DIENCE. *s.* The right or state of being heard before another.

PREBEND. *s.* A stipend granted in cathedral churches. adj. *prebendal* s. *prebendary,* pl. *preben laries.*

PRECA'RIOUS. *adj.* Dependent, uncertain. s. *precariousness:* adv *precariously.*

287

PRE—PRE

PREC'ATORY. *adj.* Suppliant.
PRECAU'TION. *s.* Preservative caution. *adj. precautional.*
PRECE'DE. *v.* To go before, in rank or time. pr. par. *preceding;* past, *preceded:* s. *precedence, pre'cedent:* adj. *prece'dent.*
PRECES'SION. *s.* Act of preceding.
PRECEN'TOR. *s.* He that leads a choir.
PRE'CEPT. *s.* A command, injunction, mandate. s. *preceptor:* adj. *preceptive, preceptory.*
PRE'CINCT. *s.* Outward limit, boundary.
PRE'CIOUS. *adj.* Valuable; costly. s. *preciousness:* adv. *preciously.*
PRE'CIPICE. *s.* A headlong steep.
PRECIP'ITATE. *v.* To throw headlong; to hasten unexpectedly. pr. par. *precipitating;* past, *precipitated:* s. *precipitation, precipitance, precipitancy:* adj. *precipitate, precipitant:* adv. *precipitately.*
PRECIP'ITATE. *s.* A corrosive medicine, made by precipitating mercury.
PRECI'SE. *adj.* Exact; strict; nice. s. *precisian, precision, preciseness:* adv. *precisely.*
PRECLU'DE. *v.* To shut out or hinder, by some anticipation. pr. par. *precluding;* past, *precluded.*
PRECLU'SION. *s.* Act of precluding. adj. *preclusive:* adv. *preclusively.*
PRECO'CIOUS. *adj.* Ripe before the usual time. s. *precocity,* pl. *precocities.*
PRECO'GITATE. *v.* To consider or scheme beforehand. pr. par. *precogitating;* past, *precogitated.*
PRECOGNI'TION. *s.* Previous knowledge.
PRECOMPO'SE. *v.* To compose beforehand. pr. par. *precomposing;* past, *precomposed.*
PRECONCEIT'. *s.* An opinion previously formed.
PRECONCEI'VE. *v.* To form an opinion beforehand. pr. par. *preconceiving;* past, *preconceived.*

PRECONCEP'TION. *s.* Act of preconceiving; notion preconceived.
PRECON'TRACT. *s.* A previous contract. *v. precontract'; precontracting;* past, *precontracted.*
PRECUR'SOR. *s.* Forerunner; harbinger. adj. *precursory.*
PREDA'CEOUS. *adj.* Living by prey
PRE'DAL. *adj.* Practising plunder
PRE'DATORY. *adj.* Plundering; tapacious.
PREDECES'SOR. *s.* One who preceded in time; an ancestor.
PREDES'TINATE. *v.* To appoint by irreversible decree. pr. par. *predestinating;* past, *predestinated:* s. *predestination, predestinarian, predestinator.*
PREDES'TINE. *v.* To decree beforehand. pr. par. *predestining;* past, *predestined.*
PREDETER'MINE. *v.* To determine beforehand. pr. par. *predetermining;* past, *predetermined:* adj. *predeterminate:* s. *predetermination.*
PRE'DIAL. *adj.* Consisting of farms; belonging to a farm.
PREDIC'AMENT. *s.* A class or arrangement of beings or substances, ranked according to their natures adj. *predicamental.*
PRED'ICATE. *v.* To affirm any thing of a subject. pr. par. *predicating;* past, *predicated:* adj. *predicable, predicatory:* s. *predicate, predication, predicability.*
PREDICT'. *v.* To foretel; to foreshow. pr. par. *predicting;* past, *predicted:* s. *prediction, predictor.*
PREDILEC'TION. *s.* Prepossession in favour of any particular person or thing.
PREDISPO'SE. *v.* To adapt previously to any certain purpose. pr par. *predisposing;* past, *predisposed:* s. *predisposition.*
PREDOM'INATE. *v.* To prevail; to be ascendant. pr. par. *predominating;* past, *predominated:* s. *predominance, predomination:* adj *predominant:* adv. *predominantly*

288

PRE-ELECT'. *v.* To choose by previous decision. pr. par. *preelecting;* past, *preelected:* s. *preelection:* adj. *preelective.*

PREEM'INENCE. *s.* Superiority of excellence; precedence. adj. *preeminent:* adv. *preeminently.*

PREEM'PTION. *s.* The right of purchasing before another.

PREENGA'GE. *v.* To engage by precedent ties or contracts. pr. par. *preengaging;* past, *preengaged:* s. *preengagement.*

PREEXIS'TENCE. *s.* Existence before. adj. *preexistent.*

PREF'ACE. *s.* An introduction to a book, &c. v. *preface;* pr. par. *prefacing;* past, *prefaced.*

PREF'ATORY. adj. Introductory.

PRE'FECT. *s.* A governor, a commander. s. *prefecture.*

PREFER'. *v.* To regard more; to exalt; to present ceremoniously. pr. par. *preferring;* past, *preferred:* s. *preference, preferment, preferrer:* adj. *preferable:* adv. *preferably.*

PREFIG'URE. *v.* To exhibit by antecedent representation. pr. par. *prefiguring;* past, *prefigured:* s. *prefiguration:* adj. *prefigurative.*

PREFIX'. *v.* To appoint beforehand; to put before another thing. pr. par. *prefixing;* past, *prefixed:* s. *prefix, prefixion.*

PREG'NABLE. adj. That may be won by force.

PREG'NANT. adj. Teeming, breeding, fruitful, full. s. *pregnancy:* adv. *pregnantly.*

PREJUDGE'. *v.* To determine without due testimony. pr. par. *prejudging;* past, *prejudged:* s. *prejudgment.*

PREJUDICA'TION. *s.* The act of prejudging. adj. *prejudicative.*

PRE'JUDICE. *s.* Judgment formed without examination; prepossession of mind. v. *prejudice;* pr. par. *prejudicing;* past, *prejudiced.*

PREJUDI'CIAL. adj. Exciting prejudice; injurious, hurtful. adv. *prejudicially.*

2 B

PRE'LATE. *s.* An ecclesiastic of the highest order. adj. *prelatic, prelatical:* s. *prelacy,* pl. *prelacies* adj. *prelatically.*

PRELA'TION. *s.* Preference; the setting of one before another.

PRELEC'TION. *s.* Reading; lecture. s. *prelector.*

PRELIBA'TION. *s.* Taste beforehand.

PRELIM'INARY. adj. Previous; introductory. s. *preliminary,* pl. *preliminaries.*

PRE'LUDE. *s.* Some short flight of music, played before a full concert; something introductory. v. *prelude;* pr. par. *preluding;* past, *preluded.*

PRELU'SIVE. adj. Previous, introductory, proemial. adj. *prelusory*

PREMATU'RE. adj. Ripe too soon too early. s. *prematureness, prematurity:* adv. *prematurely.*

PREMED'ITATE. *v.* To think or contrive beforehand. pr. par. *premeditating;* past, *premeditated:* s. *premeditation:* adj. *premeditate* adv. *premeditately.*

PRE'MIER. *s.* A principal minister of state.

PREMI'SE. *v.* To explain previously. pr. par. *premising;* past, *premised:* s. *premises.* (in law language) houses or lands; previous expressions.

PRE'MIUM. *s.* Something given to invite a loan or bargain; a reward proposed.

PREMON'ISH. *v.* To admonish beforehand. pr. par. *premonishing* past, *premonished:* s. *premonition* adj. *premonitory.*

PREMONSTRA'TION. *s.* Act of showing beforehand

PRENOM'INATE. *v.* To forename. pr. par. *prenominating;* past, *prenominated:* s. *prenomination.*

PREOC'CUPY. *v.* To take previous possession of; to prepossess. pr par. *preoccupying;* past, *preoccupied:* s. *preoccupation.*

289

PREOPIN'ION. *s.* Opinion antecedently formed.

PREOP'TION. *s.* Right of first choice.

PREORDAIN'. *v.* To ordain beforehand. pr. par. *preordaining;* past, *preordained:* s. *preordinance, preordination:* adj. *preordinate.*

PREPA'RE. *v.* To take previous measures; to fit for; to adjust to. pr. par. *preparing;* past, *prepared:* s. *preparation, preparer, preparedness:* adj. *preparatory, preparative:* adv. *preparedly, preparatively.*

PREPENSE'. *adj.* Forethought; preconceived: as malice *prepense.*

PREPON'DERATE. *v.* To outweigh; to overpower by weight. pr. par. *preponderating;* past, *preponderated:* s. *preponderance, preponderation:* adj. *preponderant.*

PREPOSI'TION. (In grammar) a particle governing a case.

PREPOSSESS'. *v.* To preoccupy; to prejudice. pr. par. *prepossessing;* past, *prepossessed:* s. *prepossession.*

PREPOS'TEROUS. *adj.* Absurd; perverted. s. *preposterousness:* adv. *preposterously.*

PREREQ'UISITE. *adj.* Previously necessary. s. *prerequisite.*

PREROG'ATIVE. *s.* Exclusive privilege or right. adj. *prerogatived.*

PRE'SAGE. *s.* Prognostic; perception of futurity. v. *presa'ge;* pr. par. *presaging;* past, *presaged:* adj. *presageful:* s. *presager.*

PRES'BYTER. *s.* A priest; a presbyterian. s. *presbytery,* pl. *presbyteries.*

PRESBYTE'RIAN. *adj.* Consisting of elders; governed by elders. s. *presbyterian, presbyterianism.*

PRES'CIENT. *adj.* Foreknowing; prophetic. s. *prescience.*

PRESCRI'BE. *v.* To influence by long custom; to give law; to write medical directions. pr. par. *prescribing;* past, *prescribed:* s. *prescriber:* adj. *prescriptive.*

PRESCRIP'TION. *s.* Act of prescribing; written direction. adj. *prescriptive.*

PRES'ENCE-CHAMBER. *s.* The room, in which a great person receives company.

PRES'ENT. *adj.* Not absent; not past; not future. s. *presence:* adv. *presently.*

PRES'ENT. *s.* A gift; something ceremoniously given. v. *present';* pr. par. *presenting;* past, *presented:* adj. *presentable.*

PRESENTA'TION. *s.* Act of presenting; exhibition.

PRESEN'TIMENT. *s.* Previous idea; notion previously formed.

PRESERVE'. *v.* To save; to defend from evil; to keep; to season fruits and other vegetables with sugar. pr. par. *preserving* part, *preserved:* s. *preserve, preserver*

PRESI'DE. *v.* To be set over; to have authority over; to act as chairman or governor. pr. pas. *presiding;* past, *presided.*

PRES'IDENT. *s.* One placed with authority over others; a chairman; a governor. adj. *presidential:* s. *presidency,* pl. *presidencies.*

PRESS. *v.* To squeeze; to crush; to distress; to constrain. pr. pa. *pressing;* past, *pressed:* s. *press, presser, pressure:* adv. *pressingly.*

PRESS'-BED. *s.* A bed, so formed as to be shut up in a case.

PRESS'GANG. *s.* A crew employed to force men into the naval service.

PRESS'MAN. *s.* One who makes the impression of print by the press. pl. *pressmen.*

PRES'TO. *adv.* Gayly; with quickness: a musical term.

PRESU'ME. *v.* To suppose; to believe previously, without examination; to make confident or arrogant attempts. pr. par. *presuming,* past, *presumed.*

PRESUMP'TION. *s.* Act of presuming; supposition previously formed.

290

PRESUMPTUOUS. *adj.* Arrogant; confident; irreverent. *adv. presumptuously.*

PRESUPPOSE. *v.* To suppose previously. pr. par. *presupposing;* past, *presupposed:* s. *presupposal, presupposition.*

PRETEND. *v.* To hold out; to make false appearances or representations; to claim. pr. par. *pretending;* past, *pretended:* s. *pretence, pretension, pretender:* adv. *pretendedly, pretendingly.*

PRETERIT. *adj.* Past.

PRETERNATURAL. *adj.* Not natural; irregular. adv. *preternaturally.*

PRETEXT. *s.* Pretence; false allegation.

PRETEXTA. *s.* The robe that was worn by the Roman youths under seventeen years of age.

PRETOR. *s.* A Roman judge. adj. *pretorial, pretorian.*

PRETTY. *adj.* Neat; elegant; beautiful without grandeur. s. *prettiness:* adv. *prettily.*

PREVAIL. *v.* To be in force; to have effect; to overcome. pr. par. *prevailing;* past, *prevailed:* s. *prevalence:* adj. *prevalent:* adv. *prevalently.*

PREVARICATE. *v.* To evade by some quibble; to cavil. pr. par. *prevaricating;* past, *prevaricated:* s. *prevarication, prevaricator.*

PREVENT. *v.* To obstruct; to hinder; to obviate. pr. par. *preventing;* past, *prevented:* s. *prevention, preventive:* adj. *preventable, preventive.*

PREVIOUS. *adj.* Antecedent; going before. adv. *previously.*

PREY. *s.* Something to be devoured or seized; plunder. v. *prey;* pr. par. *preying;* past, *preyed:* s. *preyer.*

PRICE. *s.* Equivalent paid; value. v. *price;* pr. par. *pricing;* past, *priced.*

PRICK. *v.* To pierce with a small puncture; to spur. pr. par. *pricking;* past, *pricked:* s. *prick, pricker.*

PRICKLE. *s.* A small, sharp point s. *prickliness:* adv. *prickly.*

PRICKLEBACK. *s.* A small fish.

PRIDE. *s.* Inordinate self-esteem. dignity of manner; generous elation of heart. v. *pride;* pr. par. *priding;* past, *prided:* adj. *prideless.*

PRIEST. *s.* One who officiates in sacred offices. fem. *priestess,* pl *priestesses:* s. *priesthood, priestliness:* adj. *priestlike, priestly:* s. *priestcraft.*

PRIESTRIDDEN. *adj.* Managed or governed by priests.

PRIG. *s.* A pert, conceited little fellow.

PRIM. *adj.* Formal; affectedly nice.

PRIMARY. *adj.* First in order; chief; principal. adv. *primarily.*

PRIMATE. *s.* The chief ecclesiastic. s. *primacy.*

PRIME. *s.* The first part of the day; the beginning; the best part; the height of perfection. adj. *prime:* s. *primeness, primer:* adv. *primely.*

PRIME. *v.* To put powder into the pan of a gun; to lay the ground on a canvas, to be painted. pr. par. *priming;* past, *primed.*

PRIMEVAL. *adj.* Original.

PRIMITIVE. *adj.* Original; established from the beginning; ancient. s. *primitive, primitiveness:* adv. *primitively.*

PRIMOGENITURE. *s.* Seniority; state of being first born. s. *primogenitor:* adj. *primogeneal.*

PRIMORDEAL. *adj.* Original.

PRIMROSE. *s.* A flower that appears early in the year.

PRINCE. *s.* A sovereign; a chief ruler; a king's son. fem. *princess,* pl. *princesses:* adj. and adv. *princely:* s. *princeliness.*

PRINCIPAL. *adj.* Chief; of the first rate; important. s. *principal:* adv *principally.*

PRINCIPALITY. *s.* Sovereignty; the country which gives title to a prince. pl. *principalities.*

PRIN'CIPLE. *s.* Element; constituent part; motive.

PRINT. *v.* To mark by pressing; to form by impression. pr. par. *printing;* past, *printed: s. print, printing, printer.*

PRI'OR. *adj.* Former; antecedent. *s. priority* adv. *priorly.*

PRI'OR. *s.* The head of a convent of monks. fem. *prioress,* pl. *prioresses: s. priory,* pl. *priories.*

PRISM. *s.* A kind of mathematical glass. adj. *prismatic.*

PRIS'MOID. *s.* A body approaching to the form of a prism.

PRIS'ON. *s.* A jail. *s. prisoner.*

PRIS'TINE. *adj.* First; ancient.

PRITH'EE. A familiar corruption of "pray thee."

PRIV'ACY. *s.* Secrecy; retirement. pl. *privacies.*

PRI'VATE. *adj.* Secret; alone; particular; not public; sequestered. *s. privateness:* adv. *privately.*

PRIVATEE'R. *s.* A private ship of war. *v. privateer;* pr. par. *privateering;* past, *privateered.*

PRIV'ATIVE. *adj.* Causing privation; negative. *s. privation, privative.*

PRIV'ILEGE. *s.* Peculiar advantage; immunity. *v. privilege;* pr. par. *privileging;* past, *privileged.*

PRIV'Y. *adj.* Private; secret; clandestine. *s. privity:* adv. *privily.*

PRIZE. *s.* A reward gained; plunder. *s. prizefighter.*

PRIZE. *v.* To rate; to value highly; to act upon, as a lever. pr. par. *prizing;* past, *prized.*

PRO. For; in defence of.

PROB'ABLE. *adj.* Likely; capable of being proved. adv. *probably: s. probability,* pl. *probabilities.*

PRO'BATE. *s.* The proof of a will.

PROBA'TION. *s.* Proof; trial; novitiate. adj. *probational, probationary: s. probationer.*

PROBE. *s.* An instrument with which surgeons search the depth of wounds. *v. probe;* pr. par. *probing;* past, *probed.*

PROB'ITY. *s.* Honesty, sincerity. pl. *probities.*

PROB'LEM. *s.* A question proposed for solution. adj. *problematical:* adv. *problematically.*

PROBOS'CIS. *s.* A snout; the trunk of an elephant. pl. *proboscides.*

PROCEED'. *v.* To go forward; to tend to the end designed; to issue; to advance. pr. par. *proceeding,* past, *proceeded: s. proceeds, procedure.*

PROCER'ITY. *s.* Tallness; height of stature.

PRO'CESS. *s.* Progressive course; course of law; methodical management. pl. *processes.*

PROCES'SION. *s.* A train, marching in solemnity. adj. *processionary.*

PROCLAIM'. *v.* To publish solemnly; to tell openly. pr. par. *proclaiming;* past, *proclaimed: s. proclamation, proclaimer.*

PROCLIV'ITY. *s.* Tendency; natural inclination; readiness. adj. *proclivous.*

PROCON'SUL. *s.* A Roman governor. adj. *proconsular: s. proconsulship.*

PROCRAS'TINATE. *v.* To defer; to delay. pr. par. *procrastinating;* past, *procrastinated: s. procrastination, procrastinator.*

PRO'CREATE. *v.* To generate; to produce. pr. par. *procreating;* past, *procreated: s. procreation, procreator:* adj. *procreative.*

PROC'TOR. *s.* A manager of another man's affairs; an attorney in the spiritual court.

PROCU'RE. *v.* To manage; to obtain; to pimp. pr. par. *procuring,* past, *procured: s. procuration, procurer, procuress,* pl. *procuresses, procurator:* adj. *procurable.*

PROD'IGAL. *adj.* Profuse, wasteful, lavish. *s. prodigal, prodigality,* pl. *prodigalities:* adv. *prodigally.*

PRODI'GIOUS. *adj.* Amazing; astonishing; enormous. adv. *prodigiously.*

292

PRO—PRO

PRODIGY. *s.* A preternatural thing; a monster. pl. *prodigies.*

PRODUCE. *v.* To offer to the view or notice; to bring forth; to cause. pr. par. *producing;* past, *produced·* s. *produce, producer:* adj. *producible.*

PRODUCT. *s.* Thing produced; work; effect. s. *production:* adj. *productive:* s. *productiveness.*

PROEM. *s.* Preface, introduction. adj. *proemial.*

PROFANE. *adj.* Not sacred; irreverent; secular; polluted. v. *profane;* pr. par. *profaning;* past, *profaned:* s. *profanation, profaner, profaneness, profanity:* adv. *profanely.*

PROFESS'. *v.* To declare openly; to follow as a profession. pr. par. *professing;* past, *professed :* s. *profession, professor:* adj. *professional, professorial:* adv. *professedly, professionally.*

PROFFER. *v.* To propose; to offer to acceptance. pr. par. *proffering;* past, *proffered:* s. *proffer, profferer.*

PROFICIENT. *s.* One who has made advancement in any study or business. s. *proficience, proficiency,* pl. *proficiencies.*

PROFILE. *s.* The side face.

PROFIT. *s.* Gain; pecuniary advantage; accession of good. v. *profit;* pr. par. *profiting;* past, *profited:* adj. *profitable:* adv. *profitably.*

PROFLIGATE. *adj.* Wicked; abandoned; shameless. s. *profligate, profligacy:* adv. *profligately.*

PROFLUENT. *adj.* Flowing forward. s. *profluence.*

PROFOUND'. *adj.* Deep; descending far below the surface; lowly. s. *profound, profoundness:* adv. *profoundly.*

PROFUNDITY. *s.* Depth.

PROFUSE. *adj.* Lavish; prodigal; exuberant. s. *profusion, profuseness:* adv. *profusely.*

PROGENITOR. *s.* A forefather.

PROGENY. *s.* Offspring; race. pl. *progenies.*

PROGNOSTIC. *adj.* Foretokening, foreshowing. v. *prognosticate;* pr. par. *prognosticating;* past, *prognosticated:* s. *prognostic, prognostication, prognosticator.*

PROGRESS. *s.* Course, procession, advancement. v. *progress;* pr. par. *progressing;* past, *progressed:* s. *progression:* adj. *progressional, progressive:* adv. *progressively.*

PROHIBIT. *v.* To forbid; to interdict; to debar. pr. par. *prohibiting;* past, *prohibited:* s. *prohibition, prohibiter:* adj. *prohibitive, prohibitory.*

PROJECT'. *v.* To throw forward; to jut out; to contrive. pr. par. *projecting;* past, *projected:* s. *projection, projectment, projector:* adj. *projectile.*

PROLATE. *adj.* Extended beyond an exact round. s. *prolation.*

PROLEPSIS. *s.* A form of rhetoric, in which objections are anticipated; an error in chronology, by which events are dated too early.

PROLIFIC. *adj.* Fruitful; productive. s. *prolificness:* adv. *prolifically.*

PROLIX'. *adj.* Long; tedious; not concise. adv. *prolixly:* s. *prolixity.*

PROLOCUTOR. *s.* The speaker of a convocation.

PROLOGUE. *s.* Preface; introduction.

PROLONG'. *v.* To lengthen; to continue. s. *prolongation, prolonger.*

PROMENADE. *s.* A walk. v. *promenade;* pr. par. *promenading;* past, *promenaded.*

PROMINENCE. *s.* A jutting out; protuberance. part. adj. *prominent:* adv. *prominently.*

PROMISCUOUS. *adj.* Mingled; confused. s. *promiscuousness:* adv. *promiscuously.*

PROMISE. *s.* Declaration of design; hopes; expectation. v. *promise,* pr. par. *promising;* past, *promised:* s. *promiser:* adj. *promissory.*

PROM'ONTORY. *s.* A headland; a cape. pl. *promontories.*

PROMOTE. *v.* To forward; to advance. pr. par. *promoting;* past, *promoted: s. promoter, promotion:* adj. *promotive.*

PROMPT. *adj.* Quick; ready. *s. promptitude, promptness:* adv. *promptly.*

PROMPT. *v.* To assist by private instruction; to help when at a loss; to incite. pr. par. *prompting;* past, *prompted: s. prompter.*

PROMUL'GATE. *v.* To publish; to make known by open declaration. pr. par. *promulgating;* past, *promulgated: s. promulgation, promulgator.*

PRONE. *adj.* Bending downward; not erect; lying with the face downwards; inclined. *s. proneness:* adv. *pronely.*

PRONG. *s.* A fork; a pitch-fork.

PRONOM'INAL. *adj.* Having the nature of a pronoun.

PRO'NOUN. *s.* A word used instead of a noun.

PRONOUNCE'. *v.* To speak; to utter; to declare. pr. par. *pronouncing;* past, *pronounced:* adj. *pronounceable: s. pronunciation, pronouncer.*

PROOF. *s.* Evidence; testimony; trial; test. adj. *proof,* impenetrable, able to resist.

PROP. *v.* To support, to sustain. pr. par. *propping;* past, *propped: s. prop.*

PROP'AGATE. *v.* To generate; to increase; to extend. pr. par. *propagating;* past, *propagated:* s. *propagation, propagator.*

PROPEL'. *v.* To drive forward. pr. par. *propelling;* past, *propelled: s. propeller.*

PROPEN'SITY. *s.* Moral inclination; natural tendency. pl. *propensities.*

PROP'ER. *adj.* Peculiar; not common; natural; fit; suitable. adv. *properly.*

PROP'ERTY. *s.* Peculiar quality; right of possession; thing possessed. pl. *properties.*

PROPH'ECY. *s.* A declaration of something to come; prediction. pl. *prophecies.*

PROPH'ESY. *v.* To predict; to foretell. pr. par. *prophesying;* past, *prophesied: s. prophesier.*

PROPH'ET. *s.* One who predicts; a foreteller. fem. *prophetess,* pl. *prophetesses:* adj. *prophetic, prophetical:* adv. *prophetically.*

PROPIN'QUATE. *v.* To approach; to draw near. pr. par. *propinquating;* past, *propinquated: s. propinquity.*

PROPI'TIATE. *v.* To induce to favour; to conciliate. pr. par. *propitiating;* past, *propitiated: s. propitiation, propitiator:* adj. *propitiatory, propitious: s. propitiousness:* adv. *propitiously.*

PROPOR'TION. *s.* Comparative relation of one thing to another; ratio; size. *v. proportion;* pr. par. *proportioning;* past, *proportioned:* adj. *proportionable, proportional, proportionate:* adv. *proportionably, proportionally, proportionately:* s. *proportionality.*

PROPO'SE. *v.* To offer to consideration. pr. par. *proposing;* past, *proposed: s. proposal, proposition, proposer:* adj. *propositional.*

PROPOUND'. *v.* To offer to consideration; to propose. pr. par. *propounding;* past, *propounded: s. propounder.*

PROPRI'ETARY. *s.* Possessor in his own right. pl. *proprietaries.*

PROPRI'ETOR. *s.* One to whom property belongs; owner.

PROPRI'ETY. *s.* Fitness; accuracy; justness.

PROPUGN'. *v.* To defend; to vindicate. *s. propugner.*

PROPUL'SION. *s.* The act of propelling.

PROROGUE'. *v.* To protract; to put off; to delay. pr. par. *proroguing,* past, *prorogued.*

PROSCRI'BE. *v.* To censure capitally; to doom to destruction. pr. par. *proscribing;* past, *proscribed:* s. *proscription:* adj. *proscriptive.*

PROSE. *s.* Language written or spoken in the usual way; opposed to verse; not restrained to harmonic sounds. adj. *prosaic.*

PROSE. *v.* To write prose; to make a tedious relation. pr. par. *prosing;* past, *prosed:* s. *proser.*

PROS'ECUTE. *v.* To pursue; to continue; to sue at law. pr. par. *prosecuting;* past, *prosecuted:* s. *prosecution, prosecutor.*

PROS'ELYTE. *s.* One brought over to any new opinion. s. *proselytism.*

PROS'ODY. *s.* That part of grammar, which teaches the just sound and quantity of syllables, and the measure of verse. adj. *prosodiacal, prosodical:* s. *prosodian, prosodist.*

PROSOPOPŒIA. *s.* Personification.

PROS'PECT. *s.* View of something distant; series of objects open to the eye. s. *prospection:* adj. *prospective:* adv. *prospectively.*

PROSPEC'TUS. *s.* Plan, generally of a proposed literary work. pl. *prospectuses.*

PROS'PER. *v.* To make happy; to favour; to be successful. pr. par. *prospering;* past, *prospered:* adj. *prosperous:* s. *prosperity:* adv. *prosperously.*

PROSPI'CIENCE. *s.* The act of looking forward. adj. *prospicient.*

PROSTERNA'TION. *s.* Dejection; depression.

PROS'TITUTE. *v.* To sell to wickedness; to expose upon vile terms. pr. par. *prostituting;* past, *prostituted:* s. *prostitute, prostitution, prostitutor.*

PROS'TRATE. *adj.* Lying at length; lying at mercy. v. *prostrate;* pr. par. *prostrating;* past, *prostrated:* s. *prostration.*

PROTECT'. *v.* To defend: to cover from evil. pr. par. *protecting;* past, *protected:* s. *protection, protector,*

fem. *protectress,* pl. *protectresses* adj. *protective.*

PROTECT'ORATE. *s.* Government by a protector.

PROTEND'. *v.* To hold out; to stretch forth. pr. par. *protending* past, *protended.*

PROTER'VITY. *s.* Peevishness.

PROTEST'. *v.* To give a solemn declaration of opinion or resolution; to show; to call as a witness; to object. pr. par. *protesting;* past, *protested:* s. *pro'test, protestation, protester.*

PROT'ESTANT. *s.* An adherent of those, who, at the beginning of the Reformation, protested against the doctrines of the church of Rome. adj. *protestant:* s. *protestantism.*

PROTHON'OTARY. *s.* The head register. pl. *prothonotaries.*

PRO'TOCOL. *s.* The original copy of a writing.

PROTOMAR'TYR. *s.* The first martyr.

PRO'TOTYPE. *s.* The original of a copy.

PROTRACT'. *v.* To draw out, to delay. pr. par. *protracting;* past, *protracted:* s. *protraction, protracter, protractor:* adj. *protractive.* adv. *protractively.*

PROTRU'DE. *v.* To thrust forward. pr. par. *protruding;* past, *protruded:* s. *protrusion:* adj. *protrusive:* adv. *protrusively.*

PROTU'BERANCE. *s.* Something swelling above the rest; prominence. adj. *protuberant.*

PROUD. *adj.* Too much pleased with one's-self; elated; haughty. adv *proudly:* s. *pride.*

PROVE. *v.* To evince; to show by argument or testimony; to try; to experience. pr. par. *proving;* past, *proved:* adj. *provable, proveable.*

PROVE'DORE. *s.* One who undertakes to procure supplies or provisions.

PROV'ENDER. *s.* Dry food for cattle.

PROV'ERB. *s.* An adage; a short

moral sentence. adj. *proverbial:* adv. *proverbially.*

PROVI'DE. *v.* To procure beforehand; to get ready; to supply. pr. par. *providing;* past, *provided:* s. *provider.*

PROV'IDENCE. *s.* Foresight; timely care; divine superintendence. adj. *provident, providential:* adv. *providently, providentially.*

PROV'INCE. *s.* A conquered country; a district; the proper office or business of any one. adj. *provincial:* s. *provinciality, provincialism.*

PROVISION. *s.* The act of providing; measures taken; stock collected; food. v. *provision;* pr. par. *provisioning;* past, *provisioned:* adj. *provisional, provisionary:* adv. *provisionally.*

PROVI'SO. *s.* Stipulation; caution. adj. *provisory.*

PROVO'KE. *v.* To rouse; to excite by something offensive; to anger; to incite. pr. par. *provoking;* past, *provoked:* s. *provocation, provocative:* adj. *provocative:* adv. *provokingly.*

PROV'OST. *s.* The chief of any corporate body; the executioner of an army. pronounced *pro-vo'.*

PROW. *s.* The head or fore-part of a ship.

PROWL. *v.* To rove over; to wander for prey. pr. par. *prowling,* past, *prowled:* s. *prowler.*

PROX'IMATE. *adj.* Next; near and immediate. adv. *proximately:* s. *proximity.*

PROX'Y. *s.* The agency or substitution of another; the person substituted. pl. *proxies.*

PRUDE. *s.* A woman over-nice and scrupulous. s. *prudery:* adj. *prudish:* adv. *prudishly.*

PRU'DENT *adj.* Practically wise; provident: discreet. s. *prudence:* adj. *prudential:* s. *prudentials:* adv. *prudently, prudentially.*

PRUNE. *v.* To lop; to divest of superfluities. pr. par. *pruning;* past, *pruned:* s. *pruner, pruninghook, pruningknife,* pl. *pruningknives.*

PRUNE. *s.* A dried plum. adj. *pruniferous.*

PRUNEL'LO, PRUNELLE'. *s.* A kind of stuff.

PRU'RIENCE, PRU'RIENCY. *s.* An itching or great desire. adj. *prurient.*

PRY. *v.* To peep narrowly; to inspect curiously or impertinently. pr. par. *prying;* past, *pried:* s. *prier:* adv. *pryingly.*

PSALM. *s.* A holy song. adj. *psalmodic, psalmodical:* s. *psalmist, psalmodist, psalmody.*

PSAL'TER. *s.* A psalm-book; the volume of psalms.

PSAL'TERY. *s.* A kind of harp. pl. *psalteries.*

PSEU'DO. *adj.* False, counterfeit, pretended.

PSHAW. *int.* An expression of contempt.

PTOLEMA'IC. *adj.* Belonging to the system of Ptolemy.

PU'BERTY. *s.* Sexual maturity. pl. *puberties:* s. *pubescence:* adj. *pubescent.*

PUB'LICAN. *s.* A toll-gatherer; a man that keeps a public house.

PUB'LIC. *adj.* Belonging to a state or nation; not private; generally known. s. *public, publication, publicity:* adv. *publicly:* adj. *public-spirited.*

PUB'LISH. *v.* To make public; to sell, after being printed. pr. par *publishing;* past, *published:* s. *publisher.*

PUCE. *adj.* Of a dark brown colour

PU'CELAGE. *s.* State of virginity.

PUCK. *s.* A supposed sprite or fairy

PUCK'ER. *v.* To gather into plaits or folds. pr. par. *puckering;* past, *puckered:* s. *pucker.*

PUD'DER. *s.* Noise, tumult.

PUD'DING. *s.* A kind of food; the gut of an animal.

PUD'DLE. *s.* A small muddy lake; a dirty plash. v. *puddle;* pr. par. *puddling;* past, *puddled:* adj. *puddly.*

PU'ERILE. *adj.* Childish; boyish. *s. puerility,* pl. *puerilities.*

PUER'PERAL. *adj.* Relating to childbirth.

PUFF. *s.* A small breath or blast of wind; any thing light and porous; something to sprinkle powder on the hair; an exaggerated statement or recommendation. *v. puff;* pr. par. *puffing;* past, *puffed:* adj. *puffy.*

PUF'FIN. *s.* A water-fowl; a kind of fish; a fungus filled with dust.

PUG. *s.* A kind name of a monkey.

PUGH. *int.* A word of contempt.

PU'GILISM. *s.* The practice of boxing. *s. pugilist:* adj. *pugilistic.*

PUGNA'CIOUS. *adj.* Quarrelsome; fighting. *s. pugnacity.*

PU'ISNE. *adj.* Young; inferior; petty; inconsiderable. *pu'ny.*

PUIS'SANT. *adj.* Powerful; strong. *s. puissance:* adv. *puissantly.*

PUKE. *s.* Vomit; medicine causing vomit. *v. puke;* pr. par. *puking;* past, *puked.*

PUL'CHRITUDE. *s.* Beauty.

PULE. *v.* To whine, to cry. pr. par. *puling;* past, *puled:* s. *puling.*

PULL. *v.* To draw violently; to pluck; to tear. pr. par. *pulling;* past, *pulled:* s. *pull, puller.*

PUL'LET. *s.* A young hen.

PUL'LEY. *s.* A small wheel with a furrow on its outside, in which a rope runs.

PUL'MONARY. *adj.* Belonging to the lungs.

PULP. *s.* Any soft mass; the soft part of fruit. adj. *pulpous, pulpy.*

PUL'PIT. *s.* A place raised on high, where a speaker stands.

PULSE. *s.* Motion of the blood; vibration; leguminous plants. s. *pulsation:* adj. *pulsatory.*

PUL'VERIZE. *v.* To reduce to powder. pr. par. *pulverizing,* past, *pulverized:* s *pulverization.*

PUM'ICE. *s.* A cinder of some fossil, formed by fire.

PUM'MEL. *s.* See POMMEL.

PUMP. *s.* An engine by which water is drawn up from wells; a shoe with a thin sole. *v. pump;* pr. par. *pumping;* past, *pumped:* s. *pumper.*

PUM'PION, PUMP'KIN. *s.* A kind of plant, and also its fruit.

PUN. *s.* An equivocation; a quibble; an expression in which a word has at once different meanings. *v. pun,* pr. par. *punning;* past, *punned* s. *punster.*

PUNCH. *v.* To bore or perforate with a punch; to push or strike with the fist. pr. par. *punching,* past, *punched:* s. *puncher.*

PUNCH. *s.* A kind of pointed instrument; a blow, a drink made by mixing spirits with water, sugar, and lemon-juice; the harlequin of a puppet-show. pl. *punches.*

PUNCH'EON. *s.* A cask containing 84 gallons.

PUNCHINEL'LO. *s.* A sort of buffoon.

PUNCTIL'IO. *s.* A small nicety of behaviour. adj. *punctilious:* s *punctiliousness:* adv. *punctiliously*

PUNC'TUAL. *adj.* Exact, nice, in strict time. s. *punctualist, punctuality:* adv. *punctually.*

PUNC'TUATE. *v.* To distinguish by pointing. pr. par. *punctuating,* past, *punctuated:* s. *punctuation.*

PUNC'TURE. *s.* A small prick; a hole made with a very sharp point. *v. puncture;* pr. par. *puncturing,* past, *punctured.*

PUN'GENT. *adj.* Sharp on the tongue; acrid; piercing. s. *pungency:* adv. *pungently.*

PUN'ISH. *v.* To chastise; to afflict with penalty for a crime. pr. par. *punishing;* past, *punished:* adj. *punishable:* s. *punisher, punishment.*

PUNK. *s.* A common prostitute.

PUNT. *s.* A flat-bottomed boat.

PU'NY. *adj.* Young; inferior; petty. s. *puniness.*

PUP. *v.* To produce whelps. pr par. *pupping:* past, *pupped:* s *pup.*

297

PU'PIL. *s.* The apple of the eye; a scholar. *s. pupilage.*
PUP'PET. *s.* A small image, moved by wire, in a mock drama.
PUP'PY. *s.* A whelp; a name of contemptuous reproach to a man. pl. *puppies: s. puppyism.*
PUR. *s.* A gentle noise, made by a cat. *v. pur;* pr. par. *purring;* past, *purred.*
PURBLIND. *adj.* Near-sighted; dimsighted.
PUR'CHASE. *s.* Any thing bought or obtained for a price. *v. purchase;* pr. par. *purchasing;* past, *purchased: s. purchaser.*
PURE. *adj.* Not sullied; unmingled; chaste. *s. pureness, purity:* adv. *purely.*
PURGA'TION. *s.* The act of cleansing or purifying. adj. *purgative: s. purgative.*
PUR'GATORY. *s.* A place in which souls are supposed to be purged from carnal impurities, before they are received into heaven.
PURGE. *v.* To cleanse; to purify, &c. pr. par. *purging;* past, *purged: s. purge.*
PU'RIFY. *v.* To make pure. pr. par. *purifying;* past, *purified: s. purification, purifier:* adj. *purificative, purificatory.*
PU'RITAN. *s.* A sectary pretending to eminent purity of religion. adj. *puritan, puritanic, puritanical: s. puritanism:* adv. *puritanically.*
PURL. *v.* To murmur; to flow with a gentle noise; to rise or appear in undulations. pr. par. *purling;* past, *purled: s. purl.*
PUR'LIEU. *s.* The grounds on the borders of a forest; border; enclosure.
PURLOIN. *v.* To steal any thing intrusted. pr. par. *purloining;* past, *purloined: s. purloiner.*
PUR'PLE. *adj.* Red tinctured with blue. *v. purple;* pr. par. *purpling;* past, *purpled: s. purple:* adj. *purplish.*

PUR'PORT. *s.* Design, tendency, meaning. *v. purport;* pr. par. *purporting;* past, *purported.*
PUR'POSE. *s.* Intention; design; the end desired. *v. purpose;* pr. par. *purposing;* past, *purposed:* adv. *purposely.*
PURR. *v.* See PUR.
PURSE. *s.* A small bag in which money is kept. adj. *purseproud.*
PURSE. *v.* To put into a purse; to contract as a purse. pr. par. *pursing;* past, *pursed:* adj. *pursy.*
PUR'SER. *s.* The paymaster of a ship.
PURS'LAIN. *s.* A kind of plant.
PURSUE'. *v.* To chase; to follow in hostility; to continue; to imitate. pr. par. *pursuing;* past, *pursued: s. pursuance, pursuer, pursuit:* adj. *pursuable, pursuant.*
PUR'SUIVANT. *s.* An attendant on a herald.
PUR'ULENT. *adj.* Consisting of corrupt matter or pus. *s. purulence, purulency.*
PURVEY'. *v.* To provide with conveniences; to buy provisions. pr. par. *purveying;* past, *purveyed. s. purveyance, purveyor.*
PUR'VIEW. *s.* Proviso; providing clause.
PUS. *s.* The matter of a sore.
PUSH. *v.* To strike with a thrust, to force or drive by impulse; to press forward. pr. par. *pushing,* past, *pushed: s. push, pusher.*
PUSILLAN'IMOUS. *adj.* Meanspirited; cowardly. *s. pusillanimity:* adv. *pusillanimously.*
PUSS. *s.* The fondling name of a cat; the sportsman's term for a hare.
PUS'TULE. *s.* A small swelling; a pimple. *v. pustulate;* pr. par. *pustulating;* past, *pustulated: s. pustulation:* adj. *pustulous.*
PUT. *v.* To lay; to place; to propose; to throw off the hand, &c. pr. par. *putting;* past, *put: s. putter, puttingstone.*
PU'TREFY. *v.* To make rotten; to

298

corrupt. pr. par. *putrefying:* past, *putrefied:* s. *putrefaction:* adj. *putrefactive.*
PUTRES'CENT. *adj.* Growing rotten. s. *putrescence:* adj. *putrescible.*
PU'TRID. *adj.* Rotten; corrupt. s. *putridity.*
PUT'TY. *s.* A kind of cement, used by glaziers. v. *putty;* pr. par. *puttying;* past, *puttied.*
PUZ'ZLE. *v.* To perplex; to embarrass. pr. par. *puzzling;* past, *puzzled:* s. *puzzle, puzzler.*
PYE. *s.* See PIE.
PYE'BALD. *adj.* See PIEBALD.
PYG'MY. *s.* A dwarf. pl. *pygmies:* adj. *pygmy, pygmean.*
PYR'AMID. *s.* A solid figure, the base of which is a polygon, and the sides plain triangles. adj. *pyramidal, pyramidic, pyramidical.*
PYRE. *s.* A pile to be burned.
PY'RITES. *s.* Firestone.
PYR'OMANCY. *s.* Divination by fire
PYROM'ETER. *s.* An instrument to measure the heat of ovens, furnaces, and intense fires.
PYROTECH'NICS. *s.* The art of making fire-works. adj. *pyrotechnic.*
PYR'RHONISM. *s.* Scepticism; universal doubt. s. *pyrrhonist.*
PYTHAGO'REAN. *s.* A follower of Pythagoras. adj. *pythagorean.*
PYX. *s.* The box in which the Romanists keep the host.

Q

QUACK. *v.* To cry like a duck. pr. par. *quacking;* past, *quacked:* s. *quack,* a boastful pretender: s. *quackery.*
QUADRAGES'IMAL. *adj.* Lenten; belonging to Lent.
QUAD'RANGLE. *s.* A square; a figure with four right angles. adj. *quadrangular.*
QUAD'RANT. *s.* The fourth part; the quarter of a circle; an instrument with which altitudes are taken. adj. *quadrantal.*
QUAD'RATE. *adj.* Square; having four equal and parallel sides; divided into four equal parts. s. *quadrate:* v. *quadrate;* pr. par. *quadrating;* past, *quadrated.*
QUADRAT'IC. *adj.* Square; belonging to a square.
QUAD'RATURE. *s.* The act of squaring; the first and last quarter of the moon; state of being square.
QUADREN'NIAL. *adj.* Comprising four years; happening once in four years.
QUAD'RIBLE. *adj.* Capable of being squared.
QUADRILAT'ERAL. *adj.* Having four sides.
QUADRILLE'. *s.* A game, or a dance, in which four persons are engaged.
QUADRIPART'ITE. *adj.* Having four parts; divided into four parts.
QUAD'RIREME. *s.* A galley with four banks of oars.
QUAD'RUPED. *s.* An animal tha has four legs.
QUAD'RUPLE. *adj.* Fourfold.
QUADRU'PLICATE. *v.* To double twice; to make fourfold. pr. par *quadruplicating;* past, *quadruplicated:* s. *quadruplication:* adv *quadruply.*
QUÆ'RE, QUE'RE. *s.* A word used when any thing is questioned. pl. *quæries, queries.*
QUAFF. *v.* To drink; to swallow in large drafts. pr. par. *quaffing.* past, *quaffed:* s. *quaffer.*
QUAG'GY. *adj.* Boggy; soft.
QUAG'MIRE. *s.* A shaking marsh.
QUAIL. *s.* A species of bird of game
QUAIL. *v.* To languish; to de-

press. pr. par. *quailing;* past, *quailed.*

QUAINT. *adj.* Nice; strange; unusual; affected. *s. quaintness:* adv. *quaintly.*

QUAKE. *v.* To shake with cold or fear; to tremble. pr. par. *quaking;* past, *quaked: s. quake, quaker, quakerism:* adv. *quakerly.*

QUAL'IFY. *v.* To furnish with qualifications; to soften; to modify. pr. par. *qualifying;* past, *qualified:* adj. *qualifiable: s. qualification.*

QUAL'ITY. *s.* Property; accidental adjunct; temper. pl. *qualities.*

QUALM. *s.* A sudden fit of sickness. adj. *qualmish.*

QUANDA'RY. *s.* A doubt, a difficulty, an uncertainty: a low word. pl. *quandaries.*

QUAN'TITY. *s.* That property in any thing which may be increased or diminished; any indeterminate weight or measure. pl. *quantities.*

QUAR'ANTINE. *s.* The space of forty days. *v. quarantine;* pr. par. *quarantining;* past, *quarantined.*

QUAR'REL. *s.* A breach of concord; a brawl; a petty fight. *v. quarrel;* pr. par. *quarreling;* past, *quarreled: s. quarreller:* adj. *quarrelsome: s. quarrelsomeness*

QUAR'RY. *s.* Game flown at by a hawk; a stone mine. pl. *quarries: v. quarry;* pr. par. *quarrying;* past, *quarried.*

QUART. *s.* The fourth part of a gallon; a sequence of four cards, at the game of piquet.

QUAR'TAN. *s.* The fourth day ague.

QUARTA'TION. *s.* A kind of chymical operation.

QUAR'TER. *s.* A fourth part; a region of the skies, as referred to the seaman's card; a particular region of a town or country; (pl. *quarters,*) the place where soldiers are lodged; proper station; mercy shown by an enemy; a measure of eight bushels. *v. quarter;* pr. par. *quartering;* past, *quartered:* adj. and adv. *quarterly.*

QUAR'TERDECK. *s.* The short upper deck.

QUAR'TERMASTER. *s.* One who regulates the quarters of soldiers.

QUAR'TERSTAFF. *s.* A staff of defence. pl. *quarterstaves.*

QUAR'TILE. *s.* An aspect of the planets, when they are three signs, or ninety degrees, distant from each other.

QUAR'TO. *s.* A book, in which every leaf, being twice doubled, makes four leaves. pl. *quartoes.*

QUARTZ. *s.* A kind of stone.

QUASH. *v.* To crush; to subdue suddenly; to annul. pr. par. *quashing;* past, *quashed.*

QUAS'SIA. *s.* A kind of medicinal bitter.

QUA'TERCOUSINS. *s.* Those with in the first four degrees of kindred pronounced *ka'-ter-cousins.*

QUATER'NARY, QUATER'NION, QUATER'NITY. *s.* The number four.

QUAT'RAIN. *s.* A stanza of four lines, rhyming alternately.

QUAV'ER. *v.* To shake the voice; to produce a shake on a musical instrument. pr. par. *quavering,* past, *quavered.*

QUAV'ER. *s.* A shake; a musical note, equal in time to half a crotchet.

QUAY. *s.* An artificial bank to the sea, or to a river, on which goods are unladen; a wharf. pronounced *kay.*

QUEA'SY. *adj.* Sick with nausea; fastidious. *s. queasiness.*

QUEEN. *s.* The wife of a king; a woman who is sovereign of a kingdom. adv. *queenly.*

QUEER. *adj.* Odd, strange. adv. *queerly: s. queerness.*

QUELL. *v.* To crush, to subdue. pr. par. *quelling;* past, *quelled: s. queller.*

QUENCH. *v.* To extinguish fire; to allay. pr. par. *quenching;* past, *quenched:* adj. *quenchable:* s *quencher* · adj. *quenchless.*

300

QUE'RENT. s. The complainant; the plaintiff; an enquirer.
QUERIMO'NIOUS. adj. Querulous, complaining. adv. querimoniously: s. querimoniousness.
QUE'RIST. s. An enquirer.
QUERN. s. A handmill, for grinding corn.
QUERULOUS. adj. Mourning; whining; habitually complaining. adv. querulously· s. querulousness.
QUE'RY. s. See QUÆRY.
QUEST. s. Search; act of seeking.
QUES'TION. s. Interrogatory; any thing inquired; inquiry; disquisition. pr. par. questioning; past, questioned: adj. questionable: adv. questionably: s. questioner.
QUES'TOR. s. A Roman public treasurer.
QUIB'BLE. s. A slight cavil; a sort of pun. pr. par. quibbling; past, quibbled: s. quibbler.
QUICK. adj. Living; not dead; swift; ready. adv. quickly: s. quickness, adj. quickeyed, quickscented, quicksighted, quickwitted: s. quicklime, quicksand.
QUICK'EN. v. To make alive; to hasten. pr. par. quickening; past, quickened: s. quickener.
QUICK'SET. s. A living plant, set to grow.
QUICK'SILVER. s. A fluid metal, called mercury, by chymists. adj. quicksilvered.
QUID'DITY. s. A trifling nicety; a cavil. pl. quiddities.
QUIES'CENCE. s. Rest, repose. adj. quiescent.
QUI'ET. adj. Still; free from disturbance; peaceable. adv. quietly: s. quiet, quietness, quietude.
QUIE'TUS. s. Final discharge; complete acquittance.
QUILL. s. The strong feather of a wing, &c.
QUILL. v. To plait; to form in plaits or folds, like quills. pr. par. quilling; past, quilled.
QUILT. s. The covering of a bed.
v. quilt; pr. par. quilting; past, quilted.
QUI'NARY. adj. Consisting of five.
QUINCE. s. A species of fruit.
QUIN'CUNX. s. A plantation of trees, disposed originally in squares, consisting of five trees, one at each corner, and a fifth in the middle. adj. quincuncial.
QUINQUAGES'IMA. s. Quinquagesima Sunday; Shrove Sunday.
QUINQUANG'ULAR. adj. Having five corners.
QUINQUEN'NIAL. adj. Lasting five years; happening once in five years.
QUIN'SY. s. A tumid inflammation in the throat.
QUIN'TAL. s. A hundred weight.
QUINTES'SENCE. s. A fifth being; an extract from any thing, containing all its virtues, in a small quantity. adj. quintessential.
QUIN'TUPLE. adj. Fivefold.
QUIP. s. A sharp jest; a taunt.
QUIRE. s. A body of singers; a choir; the part of the church where the service is chanted; a bundle of paper, consisting of twenty-four sheets.
QUIR'ISTER. s. A chorister.
QUIRK. s. A taunt, jest, subtility.
QUIT. v. To discharge an obligation; to clear one's-self of an affair; to repay; to requite: to acquit; to resign; to depart from. v. quit; pr. par. quitting; past, quitted: s. quittance.
QUIV'ER. s. A case for arrows. adj quivered.
QUIV'ER. v. To quake; to shiver pr. par. quivering; past, quivered.
QUIX'OTISM. s. Romantic or absurd notions or actions.
QUOIT. s. A kind of discus, to throw at a mark.
QUO'RUM. s. A bench of justices, such a number of any officers as is sufficient to do business.
QUO'TA. s. Share; proportion assigned to each.
QUOTE. v. To cite an author; to adduce the words of another. pr

QUO—QUO

par. *quoting*; past, *quoted*: s. *quotation, quoter*.

QUOTH. *v.* *Quoth I*, say I, or said I; *quoth he*, says he, or said he.

QUOTID'IEN. *adj.* Daily; happening every day.

QUO'TIENT. *s.* The number produced by dividing two given numbers, the one by the other.

R

RAB—RAD

RABA'TE. *v.* To recover a hawk to the hand. pr. par. *rabating*; past, *rabated*.

RAB'BET. *v.* To pare pieces of wood so as to fit each other. pr. par. *rabbeting*; past, *rabbeted*: s. *rabbet*.

RAB'BI, RAB'BIN. *s.* A Jewish doctor. adj. *rabbinical*.

RAB'BIT. *s.* A species of furry quadruped.

RAB'BLE. *s.* An assemblage of low people.

RAB'ID. *adj.* Fierce, furious, mad. s. *rabidness*.

RACE. *s.* A family, ascending or descending; a generation; a particular breed; a water-course; *race ginger*, ginger in the root; contest in running; course. v. *race*; pr. par. *racing*; past, *raced*: s. *racer*.

RACK. *s.* An engine of torture; torture; a neck of mutton; a grate; a wooden grate, in which hay is placed, for cattle; arrack.

RACK. *v.* To torment by the rack; to torment; to draw from the lees. pr. par. *racking*; past, *racked*.

RACK'ET. *s.* An irregular clattering noise; an instrument to strike a ball. v. *racket*; pr. par. *racketing*; past, *racketed* · adj. *rackety*.

RACK'RENT *s.* Annual rent, raised to the uttermost.

RACOON'. *s.* A species of small quadruped.

RA'CY. *adj.* Strong, flavorous; tasting of the soil. s. *raciness*.

RA'DIANT. *adj.* Emitting rays;

RAD—RAI

shining; brightly sparkling. adv. *radiantly*: s. *radiance*.

RA'DIATE. *v.* To emit rays; to shine. pr. par. *radiating*; past, *radiated*: s. *radiation*.

RAD'ICAL. *adj.* Affecting the root; primitive; implanted by nature. s. *radicality*: adv. *radically*.

RAD'ICATE. *v.* To take root; to plant firmly and deeply. s. *radication*.

RAD'ICLE. *s.* That part of the seed of a plant, which, upon its vegetation, becomes its root.

RAD'ISH. *s.* A species of esculent root. pl. *radishes*.

RA'DIUS. *s.* The semi-diameter of a circle. Latin pl. *radii*.

RAF'FLE. *s.* A species of lottery v. *raffle*; pr. par. *raffling*; past, *raffled*: s. *raffler*.

RAFT. *s.* A float of timber. v. *raft*, pr. par. *rafting*; past, *rafted*.

RAF'TER. *s.* The secondary timbers of a house. adj. *raftered*.

RAG. *s.* A piece of cloth, torn from the rest; a tatter. adj. *ragged*: s. *raggedness*.

RAG'AMUFFIN. *s.* A paltry, mean fellow.

RAGE. *s.* Violent anger; fury; enthusiasm; newest fashion. v. *rage*, pr. par. *raging*; past, *raged*: adv. *ragingly*.

RAG'MAN. *s.* One who deals in rags pl. *ragmen*.

RAGOU'T. *s.* Meat stewed and highly seasoned. pronounced *ra-goo'*.

RAIL. *s.* A cross beam, fixed at the ends, in two upright posts; a kind of bird. v. *rail;* pr. par. *railing;* past, *railed.*

RAIL. v. To use insolent and reproachful language. pr. par. *railing;* past, *railed:* s. *railer, raillery,* pl. *railleries.*

RAI'MENT. s. Vesture, garment, dress.

RAIN. v. To fall in drops, from the clouds. pr. par. *raining;* past, *rained:* s. *rain:* adj. *rainy:* s. *rainbow.*

RAIN'DEER. s. A large northern deer.

RAISE. v. To lift, to elevate. pr. par. *raising;* past, *raised.*

RAI'SIN. s. The fruit of the vine dried. pronounced *raz'n.*

RA'JAH. s. A Hindoo prince.

RAKE. s. An agricultural instrument, with teeth; a man addicted to pleasure. pr. par. *raking;* past, *raked:* s. *raker:* adj. *rakish:* adv. *rakishly.*

RAL'LY. v. To put disordered or dispersed forces into order; to treat with satirical merriment. pr. par. *rallying;* past, *rallied.*

RAM. s. A male sheep; Aries, the vernal sign; an instrument for battering walls. adj. *rammish,* strong scented.

RAM. v. To drive by violence; to stuff hard. pr. par. *ramming;* past, *rammed:* s. *rammer.*

RAM'BLE. v. To rove loosely and irregular.y; to wander. pr. par. *rambling;* past, *rambled:* s. *ramble, rambler.*

RAM'IFY. v. To separate into branches. pr. par. *ramifying;* past, *ramified:* s. *ramification.*

RAM'OUS. adj. Branchy.

RAM'PANT. adj. Exuberant; overgrowing restraint. In heraldry, reared up, as if ready to combat an enemy. s. *rampancy.*

RAM'PART. s. The platform of the wall behind the parapet.

RAN'CID. adj. Ill scented. s. *rancidness, rancidity.*

RAN'COROUS. adj. Malignant; malicious in the highest degree. s. *rancour:* adv. *rancorously.*

RAN'DOM. s. Want of direction, want of rule or method; chance adj. *random.*

RANG. Pret. of the v. *to ring.*

RANGE. v. To place in order; to put in ranks; to rove: to lie in a particular direction. pr. par. *ranging;* past, *ranged:* s. *range, ranger.*

RANK. adj. High growing; luxuriant; strong scented; gross. s. *rankness.*

RANK. s. A class; an order; dignity; a line of men placed abreast pr. par. *ranking;* past, *runked.*

RANK'LE. v. To fester; to be inflamed in body or mind. pr. par *rankling;* past, *rankled.*

RAN'SACK. v. To pillage; to search narrowly. pr. par. *ransacking* past, *ransacked.*

RAN'SOM. s. Price paid for liberty v. *ransom;* pr. par. *ransoming* past, *ransomed:* s. *ransomer*

RANT. v. To rave in violent or high-sounding language, without proportionable dignity of thought. pr. par. *ranting;* past, *ranted:* s. *ranter, rant.*

RANUN'CULUS. s. A kind of garden plant. pl. *ranunculuses.*

RAP. s. A quick, smart blow; counterfeit coin. pr. par. *rapping;* past, *rapped.*

RAPA'CIOUS. adj. Addicted to plunder; seizing by violence. adv. *rapaciously:* s. *rapacity.*

RAPE. s. Act of taking away; violent defloration of chastity; a kind of plant.

RAP'ID. adj. Quick, swift. s. *rapidity:* adv. *rapidly:* s. *rapids,* a part of a river where the water is rapid over a moderate descent.

RA'PIER. s. A kind of sword, used only in thrusting.

RAP'INE. s. Act of plundering

RAPAREE'. s. A wild Irish plunderer.

303

RAP'TURE. *s.* Ecstacy; transport; enthusiasm. adj. *rapturous.*
RARE. *adj.* Scarce; uncommon; not frequent; thin; raw. *s. rareness, rarely,* pl. *rareties:* adv. *rarely.*
RA'REESHOW. *s.* A show carried in a box.
RAREFY. *v.* To make thin; contrary to *condense.* pr. par. *rarefying;* past, *rarefied:* s. *rarefaction:* adj. *rarefiable.*
RAS'CAL. *s.* A mean fellow; a scoundrel. *s. rascality.* adv. *rascally.*
RASH. *adj.* Hasty; violent; acting without caution or reflection. adv. *rashly:* s. *rashness.*
RASH. *s.* An eruption on the body.
RASH'ER. *s.* A thin slice of bacon.
RASP. *v.* To rub to powder, with a very rough file. pr. par. *rasping;* past, *rasped:* s. *rasp, rasper.*
RASP'BERRY. *s.* A kind of fruit. pl. *raspberries.*
RA'SURE. *s.* Act of scraping or shaving; a mark in writing, where something has been scraped out.
RAT. *s.* An animal of the mouse kind.
RATAFI'A, RATIFI'A. *s.* A kind of cordial.
RATAN'. *s.* An Indian cane.
RATE. *s.* Fixed price; settled allowance; degree. v. *rate;* pr. par. *rating;* past, *rated:* adj. *ratable:* adv. *ratably.*
RATE. *v.* To chide. pr. par. *rating;* past, *rated.*
RATH. *s.* A mound.
RATH'ER. *adv.* More willingly; with better liking; with better reason.
RATIFY. *v.* To confirm. pr. par. *ratifying;* past, *ratified:* s. *ratification, ratifier.*
RA'TIO. *s.* The relation which one thing has to another of the same kind, in respect to magnitude or quantity; rule of proportion.
RATIO'CINATE. *v.* To reason, to argue. pr. par. *ratiocinating;* past, *ratiocinated:* s. *ratiocination:* adj. *ratiocinative.*
RA'TION. *s.* A certain allowance or share of provisions.
RA'TIONAL. *adj.* Having the power of reasoning; agreeable to reason; judicious. s. *rationality:* adv. *rationally.*
RATS'BANE. *s.* Poison for rats; arsenic.
RATEEN'. *s.* A kind of stuff.
RAT'TLE. *v.* To make a quick, sharp noise, with bodies not very sonorous. pr. par. *rattling;* past, *rattled:* s. *rattle.*
RATTLEHEADED. *adj.* Giddy; not steady.
RAT'TLESNAKE. *s.* A kind of serpent.
RAU'CITY. *s.* Hoarseness.
RAV'AGE. *v.* To lay waste; to plunder. pr. par. *ravaging;* past, *ravaged:* s. *ravage, ravager.*
RAVE. *v.* To be delirious; to talk irrationally; to be unreasonably fond. pr. par. *raving;* past, *raved* adv. *ravingly.*
RAV'EL. *v.* To entangle. pr par *raveling;* past, *raveled.*
RAV'ELIN. *s.* In fortification, a work consisting of two faces, that make a salient angle, commonly called a *half-moon,* by soldiers.
RA'VEN. *s.* A species of crow.
RA'VEN. *v.* To obtain by violence to devour with great rapacity; to prey with rapacity. pr. par. *ravening;* past, *ravened:* adj. *ravenous* adv. *ravenously:* s. *ravenousness.*
RAVI'NE. *s.* A deep hollow, usually formed by a flood; any hollow pass.
RAV'ISH. *v.* To take away by violence; to constuprate by force; to delight; to transport. pr. par. *ravishing;* past, *ravished:* s. *ravisher, ravishment.*
RAW. *adj.* Immature; unripe; not fully cooked; new; bleak. cold; not spun; not covered with the skin. adv. *rawly:* s. *rawness.*
RAY. *s.* A beam of light; lustre; a kind of flat fish.

RAZE. *v.* To efface; to extirpate; to overthrow. pr. par. *razing;* past, *razed:* s. *razure.*

RA'ZOR. *s.* A knife used in shaving the beard.

RE-ACCESS'. *s.* Visit renewed.

REACH. *v.* To touch with the hand extended; to arrive at; to stretch forth; to extend to. pr. par. *reaching;* past, *reached:* s. *reach.*

REACT'. *v.* To return the impulse or impression. pr. par. *reacting;* past, *reacted:* s. *reaction.*

READ. *v.* To peruse any thing written or printed. pr. par. *reading;* past, *read:* s. *reader, reading.*

READMIS'SION. *s.* Act of admitting again.

READMIT'. *v.* To admit again. pr. par. *readmitting;* past, *readmitted:* s. *readmittance.*

READ'Y. *adj.* Prompt; prepared; eager; near; easy; expedite. adv. *readily:* s. *readiness.*

REAL. *adj.* Relating to things, not persons; not personal; not fictitious; genuine; consisting of things immovable, as land. s. *reality*, pl. *realities, realty:* adv. *really.*

RE'ALIZE. *v.* To bring into being or act; to make real. pr. par. *realizing;* past, *realized:* s. *realization.*

REALM. *s.* A kingdom; a king's dominion.

REAM. *s.* A bundle of paper, containing 20 quires.

REAN'IMATE. *v.* To revive; to restore to life. pr. par. *reanimating;* past, *reanimated.*

REAP. *v.* To cut corn; to obtain. pr. par. *reaping;* past, *reaped:* s. *reaper, reapinghook.*

REAPPEAR'. *v.* To appear again. pr. par. *reappearing;* past, *reappeared:* s. *reappearance.*

REAPPLICA'TION. *s.* Act of applying anew.

REAR. *s.* The hinder part; the last in order.

REAR. *adj.* Raw; half-roasted.

REAR *v* To raise up; to move upwards; to bring to maturity; to breed. pr. par. *rearing;* past, *reared.*

REASCEND'. *v.* To climb again; to mount again. pr. par. *reascending,* past, *reascended:* s. *reascension.*

REA'SON. *s.* The rational faculty; cause; argument; moderation. v *reason;* pr. par. *reasoning;* past, *reasoned:* adj. *reasonable:* s. *reasonableness:* adv. *reasonably:* s. *reasoner.*

REASSEM'BLE. *v.* To collect anew pr. par. *reassembling;* past, *reassembled.*

REASSERT'. *v.* To assert anew. pr. par. *reasserting;* past, *reasserted.*

REASSU'ME. *v.* To resume; to take again. pr. par. *reassuming*, past, *reassumed.*

REBAPTI'ZE. *v.* To baptize again. pr. par. *rebaptizing;* past, *rebaptized.*

REBA'TE. *v.* To blunt; to beat to obtuseness. pr. par. *rebating;* past, *rebated.*

REB'EL. *s.* One who opposes lawful authority by violence. v. *rebel*, pr. par. *rebelling;* past, *rebelled.* s. *rebellion:* adj. *rebellious:* adv *rebelliously.*

REBOUND'. *v.* To spring back; to be reverberated. pr. par. *rebounding;* past, *rebounded:* s. *rebound.*

REBUFF'. *s.* Quick and sudden resistance.

REBUILD'. *v.* To build anew. pr. par. *rebuilding;* past, *rebuilt.*

REBU'KE. *v.* To chide; to reprehend. pr. par. *rebuking;* past, *rebuked:* s. *rebuke, rebuker.*

RE'BUS. *s.* A word or name represented by things; a sort of riddle. pl. *rebuses.*

REBUT'. *v.* To retire back; to return an answer to a rejoinder. pr par. *rebutting;* past, *rebutted:* s *rebutter.*

RECALL'. *v.* To call back, to revoke pr. par. *recalling;* past, *recalled* s. *recall.*

RECANT'. *v.* To retract; to recall; to contradict what one has said or done. pr. par. *recanting;* past, *recanted:* s. *recantation, recanter.*

RECAPIT'ULATE. *v.* To repeat the sum of a former discourse. pr. par. *recapitulating;* past, *recapitulated:* s. *recapitulation·* adj. *recapitulatory*

RECAP'TURE. *v.* To retake a prize. pr. par. *recapturing;* past, *recaptured:* s. *recapture.*

RECAST'. *v.* To throw again; to cast anew. pr. par. *recasting;* past, *recast.*

RECE'DE. *v.* To fall back; to retreat; to desist. pr. par. *receding;* past, *receded.*

RECEIPT'. *s.* Act of receiving; a written acknowledgment of something paid or received; prescription.

RECEI'VE. *v.* To take or obtain; to embrace intellectually; to admit; to entertain as a guest. pr. par. *receiving;* past, *received:* s. *receiver.*

RE'CENT. *adj.* New, late, fresh. s. *recentness:* adv. *recently.*

RECEP'TACLE. *s.* A vessel or place into which any thing is received.

RECEP'TION. *s.* Act of receiving; state of being received. s. *receptibility:* adj. *receptive.*

RECESS'. *s.* Retirement; retreat; place of retirement; remission or suspension. pl. *recesses; recession.*

RECHARGE'. *v.* To accuse in return; to charge again. pr. par. *recharging;* past, *recharged.*

RE'CIPE. *s.* A prescription.

RECIP'IENT. *s.* A receiver; that to which any thing is communicated.

RECIPROCAL. *adj.* Acting in vicissitude; alternate; done by each to each; mutually interchangeable. adv. *reciprocally:* s. *reciprocity.*

RECI'TATIVE, RECITATI'VO. *s.* A kind of tuneful pronunciation, more musical than common speech, and less musical than song; chant adv. *recitatively.*

RECI'TE. *v.* To rehearse; to repeat, to enumerate. pr. par. *reciting,* past, *recited:* s. *recital, recitation.*

RECK'LESS. *adj.* Careless; heedless; untouched. s. *recklessness.*

RECK'ON. *v.* To number; to count; to esteem. pr. par. *reckoning;* past, *reckoned:* s. *reckoner, reckoning.*

RECLAIM'. *v.* To reform; to correct; to recall. pr. par. *reclaiming.* past, *reclaimed:* adj. *reclaimable* s. *reclamation.*

RECLI'NE. *v.* To lean back; to rest pr. par. *reclining;* past, *reclined* s. *reclination.*

RECLO'SE. *v.* To close again. pr par. *reclosing;* past, *reclosed.*

RECLU'SE. *s.* One shut up; a retired person. adj. *recluse:* s. *recluseness.*

REC'OGNISE. *v.* To acknowledge; to recover and avow knowledge of; to review. pr. par. *recognising;* past, *recognised:* s. *recognisance, recognition:* adj. *recognizable.*

RECOIL'. *v.* To rush or fall back; to slink. pr. par. *recoiling;* past, *recoiled:* s. *recoil.*

RECOIN'. *v.* To coin over again pr. par. *recoining;* past, *recoined:* s. *recoinage.*

RECOLLECT'. *v.* To recover to memory; to recover reason or resolution; to gather again. pr. par. *recollecting;* past, *recollected:* s. *recollection.*

RECOMBI'NE. *v.* To join again. pr. par. *recombining;* past, *recombined:* s. *recombination.*

RECOMMENCE'. *v.* To begin anew. pr. par. *recommencing;* past, *recommenced.*

RECOMMEND'. *v.* To praise to another; to make acceptable. pr. par. *recommending;* past, *recommended:* adj. *recommendable:* s. *recommendation, recommender:* adj. *recommendatory.*

306

RECOMMIT'. *v.* To commit anew; to send back. pr. par. *recommitting;* past, *recommitted.*

RECOMPENSE. *v.* To repay, to requite. pr. par. *recompensing;* past, *recompensed:* s. *recompense.*

RECONCILE. *v.* To restore to favour; to make consistent. pr. par. *reconciling;* past, *reconciled:* s. *reconcilement, reconciliation:* adj. *reconciliatory.*

RECON'DITE. *adj.* Hidden, profound, abstruse.

RECONDUCT'. *v.* To conduct back again. pr. par. *reconducting;* past, *reconducted.*

RECONQ'UER *v.* To conquer again. pr. par. *reconquering;* past, *reconquered.*

RECONNOI'TRE. *v.* To examine; to view. pr. par. *reconnoitring;* past, *reconnoitred.*

RECONSID'ER. *v.* To consider anew. pr. par. *reconsidering;* past, *reconsidered.*

RECONVEY'. *v.* To convey again; to reassign. pr. par. *reconveying;* past, *reconveyed.*

RECORD. *v.* To register; to cause to be remembered. pr. par. *recording;* past, *recorded:* s. *rec'ord, recorder.*

RECOUNT'. *v.* To relate in detail; to tell distinctly. pr. par. *recounting;* past, *recounted.*

RECOURSE'. *s.* Frequent passage; return: recurrence, &c.

RECOV'ER. *v.* To restore from sickness or disorder; to grow well from a disease; to regain. pr. par. *recovering;* past, *recovered:* adj. *recoverable:* s. *recovery.*

RECREANT. *adj.* Subdued; false; cowardly.

RECREA'TE. *v.* To refresh after toil; to amuse. pr. par. *recreating;* past, *recreated:* s. *recreation:* adv. *recreative.*

RECREMENT. *s.* Dross; superfluous or useless parts. adj. *recremental. recrementitious.*

RECRIM'INATE. *v.* To return one accusation with another. pr. par. *recriminating,* past, *recriminated.* s. *recrimination, recriminator:* adj. *recriminatory.*

RECRUIT. *v.* To repair with new supplies. pr. par. *recruiting;* past, *recruited:* s. *recruit.*

RECT'ANGLE. *s.* A figure having four sides, of which the opposite sides are equal, and all its angles right angles. adj. *rectangled, rectangular.*

RECTIFY. *v.* To make right; to reform; to improve by repeated distillation. pr. par. *rectifying;* past, *rectified:* adj. *rectifiable:* s. *rectification, rectifier.*

RECTILIN'EAR. *adj.* Consisting of right lines.

REC'TITUDE. *s.* Straightness; justness; uprightness.

REC'TOR. *s.* A ruler; a governor; a parson of an unappropriated parish. adj. *rectorial:* s. *rectory,* pl. *rectories.*

RECUBA'TION. *s.* Act of lying and leaning.

RECUM'BENCE, RECUM'BENCY *s.* Act of reposing, or resting in confidence.

RECUR'. *v.* To come back to the thought; to have recourse to. pr. par. *recurring;* past, *recurred:* s. *recurrence:* adj. *recurrent.*

RECUR'SION. *s.* Return.

RECUR'VATE. *v.* To bend back. pr. par. *recurvating;* past, *recurvated:* s. *recurvation, recurvity:* adj. *recurvous.*

RECU'SANT. *adj.* Refusing to conform. s. *recusant, recusancy.*

RED. *adj.* Of the colour of blood. s. *red, redness:* v. *redden;* pr. par. *reddening;* past, *reddened:* adj. *reddish:* s. *reddishness.*

RED'BREAST. *s.* A kind of bird.

RED'DLE. *s.* A sort of red mineral earth.

REDEEM'. *v.* To ransom; to relieve from forfeiture or captivity, by paying a price. pr. par. *redeem* *ing;* past, *redeemed:* adj. *redeemable:* s. *redeemer.*

REDEMP'TION. *s.* Act of redeeming; state of being redeemed. adj. *redemptory:* s. *redemptioner,* a foreigner who pays his passage to the United States by service for a certain time.

RED'HOT. *adj.* Heated to redness.

REDIN"TEGRATE. *v.* To restore; to make new. pr. par. *redintegrating;* past, *redintegrated:* s. *redintegration.*

RE'DOLENT. *adj.* Of sweet scent. s. *redolence, redolency.*

REDOUB'LE. *v.* To become twice as much; to increase in a twofold degree. pr. par. *redoubling;* past, *redoubled.*

REDOUBT'. *s.* The outwork of a fortification.

REDOUBT"ABLE. *adj.* Formidable; terrible to foes.

REDOUND'. *v.* To be sent back, by reaction; to conduce in the consequence. pr. par. *redounding;* past, *redounded.*

REDRESS'. *v.* To set right; to amend; to remedy. pr. par. *redressing;* past, *redressed:* s. *redress, redresser:* adj. *redressive.*

RED'SHANK. *s.* A kind of bird.

REDU'CE. *v.* To bring back; to make less; to degrade; to impoverish; to subdue. pr. par. *reducing;* past, *reduced:* adj. *reducible.*

REDUC'TION. *s.* Act of reducing; state of being reduced. adj. *reductive.*

REDUN'DANT. *adj.* Superabundant, exuberant. s. *redundance, redundancy:* adv. *redundantly.*

REDU'PLICATE. *v.* To double. pr. par. *reduplicating;* past, *reduplicated* · s. *reduplication:* adj. *reduplicative.*

RED'WING. *s.* A kind of bird.

REED. *s.* A species of small cane; an instrument through which the threads are drawn, in a loom. adj. *reedy.*

REEF. *s.* A certain portion of sail, contracted by being tied up; a chain of rocks. v. *reef;* pr. par. *reefing;* past, *reefed.*

REEK. *s.* Smoke, steam. pr. par. *reeking;* past, *reeked:* adj. *reeky.*

REEL. *s.* A turning frame, upon which yarn is wound; a kind of dance. pr. par. *reeling;* past, *reeled*

REEL. *v.* To stagger. pr. par. *reeling;* past, *reeled.*

RE-ELECT'. *v.* To elect again. pr. par. *re-electing;* past, *re-elected;* s *re-election.*

RE-ENACT'. *v.* To enact again. pr par. *re-enacting;* past, *re-enacted;* s. *re-enactment.*

RE-ENFORCE', REINFORCE'. *v.* To strengthen with new assistance or support. pr. par. *re-enforcing;* past, *re-enforced:* s. *re-enforcement, reinforcement.*

RE-ESTAB'LISH. *v.* To establish anew. pr. par. *re-establishing;* past, *re-established:* s. *re-establishment.*

RE-EXAM'INE. *v.* To examine anew. pr. par. *re-examining;* past, *re-examined:* s. *re-examination.*

REFEC'TION. *s.* Refreshment. s *refectory,* a room of refreshment; pl. *refectories.*

REFER'. *v.* To dismiss for information or judgment; to betake to, for decision; to reduce to, as to the ultimate end. pr. par. *referring;* past, *referred:* adj. *referable, referrible:* s. *referee, reference.*

REFI'NE. *v.* To purify; to polish; to affect nicety. pr. par. *refining:* past, *refined:* adv. *refinedly:* s. *refinement, refiner.*

REFIT'. *v.* To repair; to equip again. pr. par. *refitting;* past, *re fitted.*

REFLECT'. *v.* To throw or bend back; to consider attentively; to throw reproach or censure; to bring reproach pr. par. *reflecting,* past, *reflected:* adj. *reflectent, reflective:* s. *reflection, reflector.*

RE'FLEX. *adj.* Bent or directed backwards. adj. *reflexible:* s. *reflexibility.*

308

RE'FLUENT. *adj.* Flowing back. s. *refluence.*
RE'FLUX. *s.* Backward course of water.
REFORM'. *v.* To form again; to amend. pr. par. *reforming;* past, *reformed:* s. *reform, reformation, reformer, reformist.*
REFRACT'. *v.* To break the natural course of rays. pr. par. *refracting;* past, *refracted:* s. *refraction:* adj. *refractive.*
REFRAC'TORY. *adj.* Obstinate, contumacious. s. *refractoriness.*
REFRAIN'. *v.* To hold back; to forbear. pr. par. *refraining;* past, *refrained.*
REFRAN'GIBLE. *adj.* Capable of being refracted. s. *refrangibility.*
REFRESH'. *v.* To recreate; to relieve after pain, fatigue, or want; to freshen; to cool. pr. par. *refreshing;* past, *refreshed:* s. *refresher, refreshment.*
REFRI'GERATE. *v.* To cool. pr. par. *refrigerating;* past, *refrigerated:* adj. *refrigerant:* s. *refrigeration, refrigerator.*
REF'UGE. *s.* Shelter from danger or distress. s. *refugee.*
REFUL'GENT. *adj.* Bright, shining, splendid. s. *refulgence:* adv. *refulgently.*
REFUND'. *v.* To pour back; to repay. pr. par. *refunding;* past, *refunded.*
REFU'SE. *v.* To deny what is solicited or required; to reject. pr. par. *refusing;* past, *refused:* s. *refusal, ref'use.*
REFU'TE. *v.* To prove false or erroneous. pr. par. *refuting;* past, *refuted:* adj. *refutable:* s. *refutation.*
REGAIN'. *v.* To recover, to gain anew. pr. par. *regaining;* past, *regained.*
RE'GAL. *adj.* Royal, kingly. s. *regality:* adv. *regally.*
REGA'LE. *v.* To refresh; to gratify. pr. par. *regaling;* past, *regaled:* s. *regalement.*
REGAL'IA. *s.* Ensigns of royalty.

REGARD'. *v.* To respect; to look towards; to observe; to value. pr. par. *regarding;* past, *regarded:* adj. *regardful, regardless:* adv. *regardfully, regardlessly.*
RE'GENT. *adj.* Governing; exercising vicarious authority. s. *regent, regency,* pl. *regencies.*
REGERMINA'TION. *s.* Act of sprouting again.
RE'GICIDE. *s.* A murderer of his king; the murder of one's king adj. *regicidal.*
RE'GIMEN. *s.* That care in diet and living, that is suitable to every particular course of medicine, or state of body.
RE'GIMENT. *s.* A body of soldiers, commanded by a colonel. adj. *regimental:* s. *regimentals,* the uniform dress.
RE'GION. *s.* Tract of land; country; tract of space.
RE'GISTER. *s.* An account of any thing, regularly kept; the officer who registers, &c. v. *register;* pr. par. *registering;* past, *registered:* s. *registry, registration.*
RE'GISTRAR. *s.* The officer who keeps the register.
REG'NANT. *adj.* Reigning; reigning in one's own right; not reigning as a regent.
REGRA'TE. *v.* To engross; to forestall. pr. par. *regrating;* past, *regrated:* s. *regrater.*
REGRESS'. *s.* Passage back. v. *regress;* pr. par. *regressing;* past, *regressed:* s. *regression.*
REGRET'. *s.* Vexation at something past; grief; sorrow. v. *regret;* pr. par *regretting;* past, *regretted.*
REG'ULAR. *adj.* Agreeable to rule; consistent with the mode prescribed: governed by strict regulations; orderly. s. *regular, regularity:* adv. *regularly.*
REG'ULATE. *v.* To adjust by rule or method; to direct. pr. par. *regulating;* past, *regulated:* s. *regulation, regulator.*

REGURGITATE. *v.* To throw back; to pour back. pr. par. *regurgitating;* past, *regurgitated:* s. *regurgitation.*

REHEAR'. *v.* To hear again. pr. par. *rehearing;* past, *reheard:* s. *rehearing.*

REHEARSE'. *v.* To repeat; to recite; to recite previously to exhibition. pr. par. *rehearsing;* past, *rehearsed:* s. *rehearsal.*

REIGN. *v.* To enjoy or exercise sovereign authority; to be predominant. pr. par. *reigning;* past, *reigned:* s. *reign.*

REIMBOD'Y. *v.* To embody again. pr. par. *reimbodying;* past, *reimbodied.*

REIMBURSE'. *v.* To repay; to repair loss or expense by an equivalent. pr. par. *reimbursing;* past, *reimbursed:* s *reimbursement.*

REIN. *s.* The part of the bridle which is held in the driver's hand. pr. par. *reining;* past, *reined.*

REINS. *s.* The kidneys; the lower part of the back.

REINSERT'. *v.* To insert a second time. pr. par. *reinserting;* past, *reinserted:* s. *reinsertion.*

REINSPI'RE. *v.* To inspire anew. pr. par. *reinspiring;* past, *reinspired.*

REINSTAL'. *v.* To seat again; to put again in possession. pr. par. *reinstalling;* past, *reinstalled.*

REINSTA'TE. *v.* To put into the same state or condition as before. pr. par. *reinstating;* past, *reinstated.*

REIN'TEGRATE. *v.* To renew with regard to any state or quality; to repair; to restore. pr. par. *reintegrating;* past, *reintegrated:* s. *reintegration.*

REINVEST'. *v.* To invest anew. pr. par. *reinvesting;* past, *reinvested.*

REIT'ERATE. *v.* To repeat again and again. pr par. *reiterating;* past, *reiterated:* s. *reiteration.*

REJECT'. *v.* To dismiss without compliance; to cast off; to refuse; to throw aside. pr. par. *rejecting,* past, *rejected:* s. *rejection.*

REJOI'CE. *v.* To be glad; to exult; to exhilarate; to gladden. pr. par. *rejoicing;* past, *rejoiced:* s. *rejoicer:* adv. *rejoicingly.*

REJOIN'. *v.* To join again ; to meet again; to answer to an answer. pr. par. *rejoining;* past, *rejoined.* s. *rejoiner.*

REJUDGE'. *v.* To re-examine; to review. pr. par. *rejudging;* past, *rejudged.*

REJUVENES'CENCE. *s.* State of being young again.

RELAPSE'. *v.* To slide or fall back, to fall back from a state of recovery to sickness. pr. par. *relapsing;* past, *relapsed:* s. *relapse.*

RELA'TE. *v.* To tell; to recite; to ally by kindred; to have relation to. pr. par. *relating;* past, *related:* s. *relater, relation.*

REL'ATIVE. *adj.* Having relation; considered not absolutely, but as belonging to, or respecting something else. s. *relative:* adv. *relatively.*

RELAX'. *v.* To slacken; to remit, to make less secure or rigorous; to ease. pr. par. *relaxing;* past, *relaxed:* s. *relaxation, relaxative.*

RELAY'. *s.* Dogs held in reserve, horses on the road, to relieve others, on a journey.

RELEA'SE. *v.* To set free; to free from obligation or penalty. pr. par. *releasing;* past, *released:* s. *release.*

RELENT'. *v.* To soften; to grow tender; to feel compassion. pr. par. *relenting;* past, *relented:* adj. *relentless.*

REL'EVANT. *adj.* Relieving; if fording something to the purpose; having relation to. s. *relevancy.*

REL'IC. *s.* That which is left, after the loss or decay of the rest; something held in superstitious veneration.

REL'ICT. *s.* A widow.

RELIEF'. *s.* Aid, help, alleviation, mitigation.

RELIE'VE. *v.* To afford relief. pr. par. *relieving;* past, *relieved:* adj. *relievable:* s. *reliever.*
RELIEV'O. *s.* The prominence of a figure or picture.
RELI'GION. *s.* Reverence of a Supreme Being; a particular system of divine faith and worship. adj. *religious:* adv. *religiously:* s. *religiousness.*
RELIN'QUISH. *v.* To forsake; to abandon; to leave; to quit. pr. par. *relinquishing;* past, *relinquished:* s. *relinquishment.*
REL'ISH. *s.* Taste; effect on the palate; liking; delight. v. *relish;* pr. par. *relishing;* past, *relished:* adj. *relishable.*
RELU'CENT. *adj.* Shining; transparent. s. *relucency.*
RELUC'TANT. *adj.* Struggling against; unwilling. adv. *reluctantly:* s. *reluctance.*
RELU'ME. *v.* To light anew; to rekindle. pr. par. *reluming;* past, *relumed.*
RELY'. *v.* To lean upon with confidence; to trust in. pr. par. *relying;* past, *relied:* s. *reliance.*
REMAIN'. *v.* To be left; to stay behind. pr. par. *remaining;* past, *remained:* s. *remainder, remains.*
REMAND'. *v.* To send back; to call back. pr. par. *remanding;* past, *remanded.*
REMARK'. *s.* Observation; note; notice taken. v. *remark;* pr. par. *remarking;* past, *remarked:* adj. *remarkable:* adv. *remarkably.*
REM'EDY. *s.* A medicine by which any illness is cured; that which counteracts any evil; reparation. v. *remedy;* pr. par. *remedying;* past, *remedied:* adj. *remediable, remedial, remediless.*
REMEM'BER. *v.* To bear in mind; to put in mind. pr. par. *remembering;* past, *remembered:* s. *remembrance, remembrancer.*
REMIND'. *v.* To put in mind. pr. par. *reminding,* past, *reminded.*
REMINIS'CENCE. *s.* Recollection.

REMISS'. *adj.* Not careful; slothful. adv. *remissly:* s. *remissness*
REMIS'SION. *s.* Act of remitting
REMIT'. *v.* To relax; to forgive; to abate; to send money to a distant place. pr. par. *remitting;* past, *remitted:* s. *remittance, remitter.*
REM'NANT. *s.* Residue.
REMOD'EL. *v.* To model anew. pr. par. *remodeling;* past, *remodeled.*
REMON'STRATE. *v.* To show rea son against. pr. par. *remonstrating,* past, *remonstrated:* s. *remonstrance:* adj. *remonstrant.*
REMORSE'. *s.* Pain of guilt; pity adj. *remorseless.*
REMO'TE. *adj.* Distant; far removed; alien; not agreeing. adv. *remotely:* s. *remoteness.*
REMOUNT'. *v.* To mount agai 1. pr. par. *remounting;* past, *re mounted.*
REMO'VE. *v.* To put from its place, to place at a distance; to go from one place to another. pr. par. *removing;* past, *removed:* adj. *removable:* s. *removal.*
REMU'NERATE. *v.* To repay; to reward; to compensate. pr. par. *remunerating;* past, *remunerated.* s. *remuneration, remunerator:* adj. *remunerative.*
RENAS'CENCE. *s.* State of being produced again. adj. *renascent.*
RENCOUN'TER. *s.* Clash; collision; personal opposition; sudden combat.
REND. *v.* To tear with violence. pr. par. *rending;* past, *rent.*
REN'DER. *v.* To return; to pay back; to invest with qualities; to yield; to show. pr. par. *rendering;* past, *rendered.*
REN'DEZVOUS. *s.* Assembly: meeting appointed; place appointed for assembling. v. *rendezvous;* pr. par. *rendezvousing:* past, *rendezvoused.*
REN'EGADE, RENEGA'DO. *s.* An apostate; a deserter. pl. *renegades, renegadoes.*
RENEW'. *v.* To renovate; to re

311

peat; to begin again. pr. par. *renewing;* past, *renewed:* adj. *renewable:* s. *renewal, renewedness.*

REN'NET. *s.* See RUNNET.

REN'NET, REN'NETING. *s.* A kind of apple.

RENOUNCE'. *v.* To disown; to quit upon oath. pr. par. *renouncing;* past, *renounced.*

REN'OVATE. *v.* To renew; to restore to the first state. pr. par. *renovating;* past, *renovated.* s. *renovation.*

RENOWN'. *s.* Fame; praise widely spread. adj. *renowned.*

RENT. *s.* A break; a laceration.

RENT. *s.* Revenue; periodical payment. pr. par. *renting;* past, *rented:* s. *rental, renter, rent-roll.*

RENUNCIA'TION. *s.* Act of renouncing.

REPAIR'. *v.* To restore after injury or dilapidation; to mend. pr. par. *repairing;* past, *repaired:* s. *repair.*

REP'ARABLE. *adj.* Capable of being repaired. s. *reparation.*

REPARTEE'. *s.* A smart reply.

REPASS'. *v.* To pass again; to pass or travel back. pr. par. *repassing;* past, *repassed.*

REPAST'. *s.* A meal; act of taking food; victuals.

REPAY'. *v.* To pay back; to compensate; to requite. pr. par. *repaying;* past, *repayed:* s. *repayment.*

REPEAL'. *v.* To revoke; to abrogate. pr. par. *repealing;* past, *repealed:* s. *repeal.*

REPEAT. *v.* To iterate, to use again; to do, speak, or try again; to recite. pr. par. *repeating;* past, *repeated·* s. *repeater,* one that *repeats;* a watch that strikes the hours.

REPEL. *v.* To drive back. pr. par. *repelling;* past, *repelled:* adj. *repellent.*

REPENT'. *v.* To think on any thing past with sorrow; to change the mind. pr. par *repenting;* past, *repented:* s. *repentance:* adj. and s *repentant.*

REPEO'PLE. *v* To stock with people anew. pr. par. *repeopling;* past, *repeopled.*

REPERCUS'SION. *s.* Rebound. adj. *repercussive.*

REP'ERTORY. *s.* A magazine; a book in which any thing is to be found. pl. *repertories.*

REPETI'TION. *s.* Act of repeating; thing repeated.

REPI'NE. *v.* To fret; to be discontented. pr. par. *repining;* past, *repined:* s. *repiner:* adv. *repiningly.*

REPLA'CE. *v.* To put into the former place; to put into a new place. pr. par. *replacing;* past, *replaced.*

REPLANT'. *v.* To plant anew. pr. par. *replanting;* past, *replanted.*

REPLEN'ISH. *v.* To fill again; to stock; to furnish. pr. par. *replenishing;* past, *replenished.*

REPLE'TE. *adj.* Full; full to exuberance. s. *repletion:* adj. *repletive.*

REPLEV'IN. *v.* To take back or set at liberty any thing seized. pr. par. *replevining;* past, *replevined:* s. *replevin.*

REPLICA'TION. *s.* Act of replying; answer to a plea in law.

REPLY'. *v.* To answer. pr. par. *replying;* past, *replied:* s. *reply,* pl. *replies, replyer.*

REPORT'. *v.* To cause a rumour; to give repute; to give an account of; to return; to rebound. pr. par. *reporting;* past, *reported:* s. *report, reporter.*

REPO'SE. *v.* To lay to rest; to be at rest; to confide. pr. par. *reposing;* past, *reposed:* s. *repose, reposal, reposedness.*

REPOS'ITORY. *s.* A place where any thing is safely deposited. s. *repositories.*

REPREHEND'. *v.* To reprove; to censure. pr. par. *reprehending;* past, *reprehended:* adj. *reprehensible, reprehensive:* adv. *reprehensibly.*

REPRESENT'. *v.* To exhibit as if

312

present; to describe; to personate. pr. par. *representing;* past, *represented:* s. *representation:* adj. and s. *representative.*

REPRESS'. *v.* To crush; to subdue. pr. par. *repressing;* past, *repressed:* s. *repression:* adj. *repressive.*

REPRIEVE'. *v.* To respite, after sentence of death; to respite. pr. par. *reprieving;* past, *reprieved:* s. *reprieve, reprieval.*

REPRIMAND'. *v.* To chide; to reprove. pr. par. *reprimanding;* past, *reprimanded:* s. *rep'rimand.*

REPRINT'. *v.* To print again. pr. par. *reprinting;* past, *reprinted:* s. *reprint.*

REPRI'SAL. *s.* Act of seizing, by way of retaliation; thing seized.

REPROACH'. *v.* To censure in opprobrious terms; to upbraid. pr. par. *reproaching;* past, *reproached:* s. *reproach:* adj. *reproachable, reproachful:* adv. *reproachfully.*

REP'ROBATE. *adj.* Lost to virtue; lost to grace; abandoned. s. *reprobate.*

REP'ROBATE. *v.* To disallow; to reject; to abandon. pr. par. *reprobating;* past, *reprobated:* s. *reprobation.*

REPRODUCE'. *v.* To produce again. pr. par. *reproducing;* past, *reproduced.*

REPRODUC'TION. *s.* Act of reproducing; thing reproduced.

REPROVE. *v.* To blame; to censure; to check. pr. par. *reproving;* past, *reproved:* adj. *reprovable:* s. *reprover, reproof.*

REP'TILE. *adj.* Creeping upon many feet. s. *reptile.*

REPUB'LIC. *s.* Commonwealth; popular government. adj. and s. *republican:* s. *republicanism.*

REPUB'LISH. *v.* To publish anew. pr. par. *republishing;* past, *republished:* s. *republication.*

REPU'DIATE. *v.* To put away; to reject; to divorce. pr. par. *repudiating;* past, *repudiated:* adj. *repudiable:* s. *repudiation.*

REPUG'NANT. *adj.* Contrary, opposite, inconsistent. s. *repugnance, repugnancy:* adv. *repugnantly.*

REPULSE'. *s.* Act of driving back; state of being driven back; defeat. *v. repulse;* pr. par. *repulsing;* past, *repulsed:* adj. *repulsive.*

REPU'TE. *s.* Character; reputation; established opinion. v. *repute;* pr. par. *reputing;* past, *reputed:* adj. *reputable:* s. *reputation.*

REQUEST'. *s.* Petition; entreaty; demand; state of being desired. pr. par. *requesting;* past, *requested.*

RE'QUIEM. *s.* A hymn in which rest is implored for the dead.

REQUI'RE. *v.* To demand; to mak necessary; to need; to request pr. par. *requiring;* past, *required*

REQ'UISITE. *adj.* Needful; necessary; required. s. *requisite.*

REQUISI'TION. *s.* Demand; application for a thing, as of right.

REQUI'TE. *v.* To repay; to retaliate; to recompense. pr. par. *requiting;* past, *requited:* s. *requital.*

RESCIND'. *v.* To cut off; to abrogate. pr. par. *rescinding;* past *rescinded.*

RESCIS'SION. *s.* Act of rescinding

RE'SCRIPT. *s.* Written answer edict of an emperor.

RES'CUE. *v.* To set free from violence, confinement, or danger pr. par. *rescuing;* past, *rescued:* s *rescue, rescuer.*

RESEARCH'. *s.* Inquiry, search.

RESEM'BLE. *v.* To compare; to be like; to have likeness to. pr. par *resembling;* past, *resembled:* s. *resemblance.*

RESENT'. *v.* To take ill; to consider as injury or affront. pr. par. *resenting;* past, *resented:* adj. *resentful:* s. *resentment.*

RESERVE'. *v.* To keep in store; to save for some other purpose; to retain. pr. par. *reserving;* past, *reserved:* s. *reservation, reserve, reservedness:* adv *reservedly.*

RE'SERVOIR. *s.* A place where any

thing is kept in store; an artificial pond.

RESI'DE. *v.* To have abode; to dwell; to sink; to subside. pr. par. *residing*; past, *resided*: s. *residence*: adj. and s. *resident*.

RES'IDUE. *s.* The remaining part; that which is left. adj. *residuary*.

RESIGN'. *v.* To give up; to yield; to submit. pr. par. *resigning*; past, *resigned*: s. *resignation*: adv. *resignedly*.

RESIL'IENCE. *s.* The act of starting or leaping back. adj. *resilient*.

RES'IN. *s.* A vegetable substance that easily ignites. adj. *resinous*.

RESIST'. *v.* To oppose, not to admit impression or force. pr. par. *resisting*; past, *resisted*: s. *resistance*: adj. *resistible*: s. *resistibility*.

RES'OLUTE. *adj.* Determined; fixed; constant. adv. *resolutely*: s. *resolution*.

RESOLVE'. *v.* To free from doubt or difficulty; to solve; to determine; to analyze; to reduce. pr. par. *resolving*; past, *resolved*: adj. *resolvable*: adv. *resolvedly*.

RE'SONANT. *adj.* Resounding. s. *resonance*.

RESORT'. *v.* To have recourse; to repair to. pr. par. *resorting*; past, *resorted*: s. *resort, resorter*.

RESOUND'. *v.* To echo; to sound back; to be much and loudly mentioned; pr. par. *resounding*; past, *resounded*: s. *resound*.

RESOURCE'. *s.* New or unexpected means; resort; expedient.

RESPECT'. *v.* To regard; to reverence in a moderate degree; to have relation to. pr. par. *respecting*; past, *respected*: s. *respect*: adj. *respectful*: adv. *respectfully*.

RESPECT'ABLE. *adj.* Venerable; meriting respect. s. *respectability*: adv. *respectably*.

RESPECT'IVE. *adj.* Particular; relative; not absolute. adv. *respectively*.

RESPI'RE. *v.* To breathe; to catch breath. pr. par *respiring*; past, *respired*: s. *respiration*: adj. *respirable, respiratory*.

RES'PITE. *s.* Reprieve; suspension of a capital sentence; pause; interval. *v.* respite; pr. par. *respiting*; past, *respited*.

RESPLEN'DENT. *adj.* Bright; shining. s. *resplendence, resplendency*: adv. *resplendently*.

RESPOND'. *v.* To answer; to correspond; to suit. pr. par. *responding*; past, *responded*: s. *respondent*.

RESPONSE'. *s.* An answer; answer made by a congregation, speaking alternately with the priest. adj. *responsive, responsory*.

RESPON'SIBLE. *adj.* Answerable; accountable; capable of discharging an obligation. s. *responsibility*, pl. *responsibilities*.

REST. *s.* Repose; cessation or absence of motion; quiet; peace; pause; remainder. v. *rest*; pr. par *resting*; past, *rested*: adj. *restless*: adv. *restlessly*: s. *restlessness*.

RESTAURA'TION. *s.* Act of recovering to the former state.

RES'TIFF, RES'TIVE. *adj.* Unwilling to stir; stubborn. s. *restiveness*.

RESTITU'TION. *s.* Act of restoring; retribution.

RESTORE'. *v.* To give back to the owner; to bring back; to retrieve; to cure; to recover from disease. pr. par. *restoring*; past, *restored*: s. *restoration*: adj. and s. *restorative*.

RESTRAIN'. *v.* To hold back; to withhold; to repress; to hinder to limit. pr. par. *restraining*; past, *restrained*: adj. *restrainable*: s. *restraint*.

RESTRICT'. *v.* To limit; to confine. pr. par. *restricting*; past, *restricted*. s. *restriction*: adj. *restrictive*.

RESULT'. *v.* To leap back; to arise as a consequence; to be produced as an effect. pr.par. *resulting*; past, *resulted*: s. *result*.

RESU'ME. *v.* To take back; to be

gin again. pr. par. *resuming;* past, *resumed.*

RESUMP'TION. *s.* Act of resuming. adj. *resumptive.*

RESURREC'TION. *s.* Revival from the dead; return from the grave.

RESUS'CITATE. *v.* To stir up again; to revive. pr. par. *resuscitating;* past, *resuscitated:* s. *resuscitation:* adj. *resuscitative.*

RETAIL'. *v.* To sell in small quantities; to tell in broken parts, or at second-hand. pr. par. *retailing;* past, *retailed:* s. *re'tail, retailer.*

RETAIN'. *v.* To keep; not to dismiss; to keep in pay; to withhold. pr. par. *retaining;* past, *retained:* s. *retainer.*

RETA'KE. *v.* To take again. pr. par. *retaking;* past, *retaken;* pret. *retook.*

RETAL'IATE. *v.* To return, by giving like for like; to requite. pr. par. *retaliating;* past, *retaliated:* s. *retaliation.*

RETARD'. *v.* To delay, to hinder. pr. par. *retarding;* past, *retarded:* s. *retardation, retarder.*

RETCH. *v.* To force up from the stomach. pr. par. *retching;* past, *retched.*

RETEN'TION. *s.* Act of retaining. adj. *retentive:* s. *retentiveness.*

RET'ICLE. *s.* A small net. adj. *reticular, reticulated, retiform.*

RET'INUE. *s.* A number attending upon a principal person; a train.

RETI'RE. *v.* To retreat, to withdraw. pr. par. *retiring;* past, *retired:* s. *retiredness, retirement.*

RETORT'. *v.* To throw back; to curve back; to return any argument, censure, or incivility. pr. par. *retorting;* past, *retorted:* s. *retort, retorter.*

RETOUCH'. *v.* To improve by new touches. pr. par. *retouching;* past, *retouched.*

RETRA'CE. *v.* To trace back; to trace again. pr. par. *retracing;* past, *retraced.*

RETRACT'. *v.* To take back; to recall; to recant. pr. par. *retracting* past, *retracted:* s. *retraction:* adj. *retractive.*

RETREAT'. *s.* Act of retiring; retirement; place of privacy. *v.* retreat; pr. par. *retreating;* past, *retreated.*

RETRENCH'. *v.* To cut off; to lessen. pr. par. *retrenching;* past, *retrenched:* s. *retrenchment.*

RETRIBU'TION. *s.* Repayment; return accommodated to the action. adj. *retributive, retributory.*

RETRIE'VE. *v.* To recover; to restore; to repair. pr. par. *retrieving,* past, *retrieved:* s. *retrieve:* adj. *retrievable.*

RETROAC'TIVE. adj. Having a backward action; acting upon the past. s. *retroaction.*

RET'ROGRADE. adj. Going backward; contrary. *v. retrograde,* pr. par. *retrograding;* past, *retrograded:* s. *retrogression:* adj. *retrogressive.*

RET'ROSPECT. *s.* Backward view. s. *retrospection:* adj. *retrospective.*

RETURN'. *v.* To turn back; to come again to the same place; to make answer; to retort. pr. par. *returning;* past, *returned:* s. *return:* adj. *returnable.*

REUNI'TE. *v.* To join again. pr. par *reuniting;* past, *reunited:* s. *reunion.*

REVEAL'. *v.* To discover; to show; to lay open. pr. par. *revealing;* past, *revealed:* s. *revelation, revealer.*

REVEI'LLE, REVEILLE'. *s.* The morning beat of drum.

REV'EL. *v.* To feast with loose and clamorous merriment. pr. par. *reveling;* past, *reveled:* s. *reveller, revelry,* pl. *revelries.*

REVENGE'. *v.* To return an injury pr. par. *revenging;* past, *revenged:* s. *revenge, revenger:* adj. *revengeful:* adv. *revengefully.*

REV'ENUE. *s.* Income; annual prof its.

REVER'BERATE. *v.* To beat back; to be driven back; to resound. pr.

par. *reverberating;* past, *reverberated:* adj. *reverberant, reverberatory:* s. *reverberation.*

REVE'RE. *v.* To reverence; to honour. pr. par. *revering;* past, *revered:* s. *reverer.*

REV'ERENCE. *s.* Veneration, respect; act of obeisance; title of the clergy. *v. reverence;* pr. par. *reverencing;* past, *reverenced:* adj. *reverend, reverent, reverential:* adv. *reverently.*

REVERSE. *v.* To turn upside down; to overturn; to turn back; to repeal; to put each in the place of the other. pr. par. *reversing;* past, *reversed:* s. *reverse, reversal:* adv. *reversely:* adj. *reversible.*

REVER'SION. *s.* Act of reverting; estate reverted. adj. *reversionary.*

REVERT. *v.* To return; to fall back. pr. par. *reverting;* past, *reverted.*

REV'ERY. *s.* Loose musing; irregular thought. pl. *reveries.*

REVEST. *v.* To clothe again; to vest again in a possession or office. pr. par. *revesting;* past, *revested.*

REVIEW'. *v.* To look back; to view again; to survey; to examine. pr. par. *reviewing;* past, *reviewed:* s. *review, reviewer.*

REVI'LE. *v.* To vilify; to reproach; pr. par. *reviling;* past, *reviled:* s. *reviler, revilement.*

REVI'SE. *v.* To review. pr. par. *revising;* past, *revised:* s. *revisal, revise, reviser, revision.*

REVIS'IT. *v.* To visit again. pr. par. *revisiting;* past, *revisited.*

REVI'VE. *v.* To return to life; to reanimate; to renew. pr. par. *reviving;* past, *revived:* s. *revival, reviver.*

REVOKE. *v.* To call back; to repeal; to annul; to renounce at cards. pr. par. *revoking;* past, *revoked:* s. *revoke, revocation.*

REVOLT. *v.* To fall off from one to another; to turn; to rebel. pr. par. *revolting;* past, *revolted:* s. *revolt, revolter.*

REVOLU'TION. *s.* Act of revolving; rotation; change. adj. *revolutionary:* s. *revolutionist.*

REVOLVE'. *v.* To roll in a circle, to perform a revolution; to consider. pr. par. *revolving;* past, *revolved.*

REVUL'SION. *s.* Act of withhold ing or drawing back.

REWARD'. *v.* To give in return; to repay; to compensate. pr. par. *rewarding;* past, *rewarded:* s. *reward, rewarder.*

RHAP'SODY. *s.* A collection of songs or verses; thoughts joined together without necessary dependence or necessary connexion pl. *rhapsodies:* adj. *rhapsodical* s. *rhapsodist.*

RHET'ORIC. *s.* The act of speaking with propriety and elegance: power of persuasion; oratory. 's *rhetorician:* adj. *rhetorical:* adv *rhetorically.*

RHEUM. *s.* A thin, watery matter, oozing through the glands.

RHEUMAT'IC. adj. Proceeding from rheum; denoting the pain which attacks the joints, &c. s. *rheumatism.*

RHINO'CEROS. *s.* A species of quadruped. pl. *rhinoceroses.*

RHODODEN'DRON. *s.* A kind of plant.

RHOMB. *s.* A term in geometry. s *rhomboid;* adj. *rhomboidal.*

RHU'BARB. *s.* A kind of medicinal plant.

RHYME. *s.* An harmonical succession of sounds; the correspondence of the last sound of one verse to the last sound or syllable of another. *v. rhyme;* pr. par. *rhyming;* past, *rhymed:* s. *rhymer, rhymester.*

RHYTH'M. *s.* Metre; verse; proportion applied to any motion whatever. adj. *rhythmical.*

RI'AL. *s.* A Spanish coin.

RIB. *s.* One of the bones which en compass the body, &c. adj. *ribbed*

RIB'ALD. adj. Base, mean, lewd, scandalous. s. *ribaldry.*
RIB'AND, RIBBON. *s.* A fillet of silk.
RICE. *s.* One of the esculent grains.
RICH. adj. Wealthy; opulent; precious; splendid; plentiful; fertile. s. *riches, richness :* adv. *richly.*
RICK. *s.* A pile of corn or hay, regularly heaped up.
RICK'ETS. *s.* A distemper in children. adj. *rickety.*
RID. *v.* To set free; to clear; to disencumber. pr. par. *ridding ;* past, *ridded :* s. *riddance.*
RID'DEN. Past par. of the v. *to ride.*
RID'DLE. *s.* An enigma; a puzzling question; a coarse sieve. pr. par. *riddling ;* past, *riddled :* s. *riddler.*
RIDE. *v.* To travel on horseback; to travel in a vehicle ; to be on the water ; to be supported by something subservient. pr. par. *riding;* past, *ridden :* s. *ride, rider, riding.*
RID'ICULE. *s.* Wit of that species that provokes laughter; folly. v. *ridicule;* pr. par. *ridiculing;* past, *ridiculed:* adj. *ridiculous:* adv. *ridiculously.*
RI'DINGHABIT. *s.* A dress worn by women, when they ride on horseback.
RIFF'RAFF. *s.* Refuse.
RI'FLE. *v.* To rob; to plunder. pr. par. *rifling ;* past, *rifled :* s. *rifler.*
RI'FLE. *s.* A kind of whetstone; a sort of gun, having within its barrel indented lines. s. *rifleman,* pl. *riflemen.*
RIG. *s.* A small ridge, made by digging, in a field; form of the sails and spars of a ship.
RIG. *v.* To dress; to accoutre; to fix the masts, spars, and sails, of a ship. pr. par. *rigging;* past, *rigged :* s. *rig, rigger, rigging.*
RIGADOON'. *s.* A kind of brisk dance.
RIGHT. adj. Fit, proper, suitable, true, just, straight ; not left. s. *right:* adv. *right, rightly:* v. *right;* pr. par. *righting* past, *righted.*
RIGHT'EOUS. adj. Just, honest agreeing with right. adv. *righteously :* s. *righteousness.*
RI'GID. adj. Stiff; not to be bent; strict; severe. s. *rigidity.* adv. *rigidly:* s. *rigidness.*
RIG'MAROLE. *s.* A repetition of idle words.
RIG'OUR, RIG'OR. *s.* Cold, stiffness, severity, austerity, strictness. adj. *rigorous:* adv. *rigorously.*
RILL. *s.* A little streamlet.
RIM. *s.* A border, a margin.
RIM'PLE. *s.* A wrinkle, a fold, a pucker. v. *rimple;* pr. par. *rimpling;* past, *rimpled.*
RIND. *s.* Bark, husk.
RING. *s.* A circle; a circle of metal; a number of bells harmoniously tuned; the sound of bells, &c. pr. par. *ringing;* past, *rung:* s. *ringer.*
RING'DOVE. *s.* A kind of pigeon.
RING'LEADER. *s.* One who leads the ring ; the head of a riotous body.
RING'LET. *s.* A small ring; a curl.
RING'STREAKED. adj. Circularly streaked.
RING'WORM. *s.* A circular tetter
RINSE. *v.* To wash slightly. pr. par *rinsing ;* past, *rinsed:* s. *rinser.*
RIOT. *s.* An uproar; a disturbance caused by three or more persons. v. *riot;* pr. par. *rioting;* past, *rioted:* s. *rioter :* adj. *riotous:* adv. *riotously :* s. *riotousness.*
RIP. *v.* To tear; to lacerate ; to cut asunder. pr. par. *ripping;* past, *ripped.*
RIPE. adj. Brought to perfection in growth; mature. s. *ripeness:* v. *ripen;* pr. par. *ripening;* past, *ripened.*
RIP'PLE. *v.* To fret on the surface, to clean flax. pr. par. *rippling,* past, *rippled:* s. *ripple.*
RISE. *v.* To become erect, to get up from rest; to advance; to

swell; to ascend; to make an insurrection. pr. par. *rising;* past, *risen;* pret. *rose: s. rise, riser.*
RIS'IBLE. *adj.* Having the faculty or power of laughing; exciting laughter. s. *risibility.*
RISK. *s.* Hazard; danger. v. *risk;* pr. par. *risking;* past, *risked: s. risker.*
RITE. *s.* Solemn act of religion; external observance. s. and adj. *ritual.*
RI'VAL. *s.* A competitor. adj. *rival:* v. *rival;* pr. par. *rivaling;* past, *rivaled: s. rivalry.*
RIVE. *v.* To split; to cleave. pr. par. *riving;* past, *riven.*
RIV'ER. *s.* A land current of water, of the first class.
RIV'ET. *s.* A fastening pin, clenched at both ends. v. *rivet;* pr. par. *riveting;* past, *riveted.*
RIV'ULET. *s.* A small river; a brook.
RIXA'TION. *s.* A quarrel; a brawl.
RIX'DOLLAR. *s.* A German coin, worth about four shillings and sixpence sterling.
ROACH *s.* A kind of fish. pl. *roaches.*
ROAD. *s.* A large way; a path.
ROAD'STEAD. *s.* A place in which ships can anchor.
ROAM. *v.* To ramble; to rove. pr. par. *roaming;* past, *roamed: s. roamer.*
ROAN. *adj.* Bay, sorrel, or black colour, mixed with gray or white spots.
ROAR. *v.* To cry as a lion, or any other wild beast; to make a loud noise. pr. par. *roaring;* past, *roared: s. roar. roarer.*
ROAST. *v.* To dress meat by turning it round before the fire. pr. par. *roasting;* past, *roasted: s. roast, roaster.*
ROB. *v.* To take forcibly from the person; to plunder. pr. par. *robbing;* past, *robbed: s. robber, robbery,* pl. *robberies.*
ROBE. *s.* A gown of state; a dress of dignity. v. *robe;* pr. par. *robing* past, *robed.*
ROB'IN, ROBIN-RED'-BREAST. *s* A kind of bird.
ROBUST'. *adj.* Strong; vigorous.
ROCK. *s.* A vast mass of stone, fixed in the earth; a distaff. adj *rocky: s. rockiness.*
ROCK. *v.* To shake; to move backwards and forwards. pr. par. *rocking;* past, *rocked: s. rocker.*
ROCK'ET. *s.* A kind of fire-work, a species of plant.
ROD. *s.* A long twig, &c.
RODE. Pret of the v. *to ride.*
RODOMONTA'DE. *s.* An empty, noisy bluster or boast; a rant. v. *rodomontade;* pr. par. *rodomontading;* past, *rodomontaded: s. rodomontador.*
ROE. *s.* A species of deer;—the eggs of fish.
ROGA'TION. *s.* Litany, supplication.
ROGUE. *s.* A vagabond; a knave; a villain. adj. *roguish:* adv. *roguishly: s. roguishness.*
ROIST, ROIS'TER. *v.* To behave turbulently; to be at free quarters; to bluster. pr. par. *roisting, roistering;* past, *roisted, roistered: s. roister.*
ROLL. *v.* To move by volutation; to move round on its axis; to wrap round upon itself; to involve in bandage; to run on wheels. pr. par. *rolling;* past, *rolled: s. roll, roller.*
ROL'LINGPIN. *s.* A round piece of wood, used by bakers.
RO'MAN. *s.* A native or citizen of Rome; a papist. adj. *Roman: s. Romanist.*
ROMANCE'. *s.* The ancient corrupt Latin language, such as was spoken, during the middle ages, in France; a military fable of the middle ages; a tale of wild adventures, in war and love; a lie, a fiction. v. *romance;* pr. par. *romancing;* past, *romanced: s. romancer.*

ROMAN'TIC. *adj.* Resembling a romance; wild; false; full of wild scenery.

ROMP. *s.* A rude, awkward, boisterous, untaught girl; rough, rude play v. *romp,* pr. par. *romping;* past, *romped:* adj. *rompish.*

RON'DEAU. *s.* A kind of ancient poetry; a kind of jig, or lively tune, which ends with the first strain repeated.

ROOD. *s.* The fourth part of an acre; a pole; a measure of 16½ feet.

ROOF. *s.* The cover of a house. v. *roof;* pr. par. *roofing;* past, *roofed:* adj. *roofless.*

ROOK. *s.* A species of small crow; one of the pieces used in the game of chess. s. *rookery,* pl. *rookeries.*

ROOM. *s.* Space; sufficient space; chamber; place of another. adj. *roomy.*

ROOST. *s.* That on which a bird sits, to sleep. v. *roost;* pr. par. *roosting;* past, *roosted.*

ROOT. *s.* That part of a plant which rests in the ground. v. *root;* pr. par. *rooting;* past, *rooted:* adj. *rooty.*

ROPE. *s.* A cord; a string. s. *ropiness:* adj. *ropy:* s. *rope-dancer, rope-ladder.*

RO'SARY. *s.* A bunch of beads, on which the Romanists number their prayers; a place where roses grow. pl. *rosaries.*

ROS'CID. *adj.* Dewy.

ROSE. *s.* A kind of flower. adj. *rosy;* s. *rosiness, rosewater.*

ROSE. Pret of the v. *to rise.*

RO'SEATE. *adj.* Rosy; blooming; purple as a rose.

ROSE'MARY. *s.* A kind of plant.

ROS'IN. *s.* Inspissated turpentine; juice of the pine. v. *rosin;* pr. par. *rosining;* past, *rosined.*

ROS'TRUM. *s.* The beak of a bird: the beak of a ship: the scaffold whence orators harangued.

ROT. *v.* To putrefy; to lose the cohesion of its parts. pr. par. *rotting;* past, *rotted:* s. *rot* adj. *rotten · s. rottenness.*

RO'TARY, RO'TATORY. *adj.* Whirling as a wheel.

ROTA'TION. *s.* Act of whirling round like a wheel; revolution.

ROTE. *s.* A musical instrument; words uttered by mere memory, without judgment; memory of words, without comprehension of the sense.

ROTUND'. *adj.* Round, spherical. s. *rotundity.*

ROTUN'DA, ROTUN'DO. *s.* A circular building, such as the Pantheon at Rome.

ROUGE. *s.* Red paint. pronounced *rooje.* v. *rouge;* pr. par. *rouging;* past, *rouged.*

ROUGH. *adj.* Rugged; having inequalities on the surface; coarse; tempestuous. adv. *roughly:* s. *roughness:* v. *roughen;* pr. par. *roughening;* past, *roughened.*

ROUGH'CAST. *v.* To mould without nicety or elegance; to form with asperities and inequalities; to dash with pebbles and mortar. pr. par. *roughcasting;* past, *roughcasted:* s. *roughcast.*

ROUGH'RIDER. *s.* One who breaks horses for riding.

ROUGH'SHOD. *adj.* Having roughened shoes, to prevent slipping.

ROUND. *adj.* Circular; spherical; whole; not broken. v. *round;* pr. par. *rounding;* past, *rounded:* s. *round:* adv. *round, roundly:* prep. *round:* adj. *roundish:* s. *roundness*

ROUND'ABOUT. *adj.* Indirect.

ROUND'ELAY. *s.* A rondeau.

ROUND'HEAD. *s.* A puritan; so named from the practice of cropping the hair round.

ROUND-ROB'IN. *s.* A written petition or remonstrance, signed by several persons, around a ring or circle

ROUSE. *v.* To wake from rest, to excite. pr. par. *rousing;* past, *roused:* s. *rouser.*

ROUT. *s.* A clamorous multitude, a rabble; confusion of a defeated

army. v. *rout;* pr. par. *routing;* past, *routed.*
ROUTE. s. Road, way.
ROUTI'NE. s. Custom, practice.
ROVE. v. To ramble; to range; to wander over. pr. par. *roving;* past, *roved:* s. *rover.*
ROW. s. A number of things ranged in a line; a rank or file.
ROW. s. A riotous noise; a drunken debauch.
ROW. v. To impel by oars. pr. par. *rowing;* past, *rowed:* s. *rower.*
ROW'EL. s. A little, flat ring or wheel, in horses' bits; the points of a spur, turning on an axis; a seton.
ROY'AL. adj. Kingly; regal. s. *royalist, royalty,* pl. *royalties:* adv. *royally.*
RUB. v. To move one body upon another; to wipe; to remove by friction. pr. par. *rubbing;* past, *rubbed:* s. *rub, rubber.*
RUB'BISH. s. Ruins of building; fragments of matter used in building; any thing vile and worthless.
RU'BICUND. adj. Inclining to redness. s. *rubicundity.*
RU'BRIC. s. Directions printed in books of law, and in prayerbooks; so called, because they were originally distinguished by being in red ink.
RU'BY. s. A precious stone, of a red colour. adj. *ruby.*
RUCTA'TION. s. Belching.
RUD'DER. s. A helm.
RUD'DY. adj. Approaching to redness. s. *ruddiness.*
RUDE. adj. Raw; barbarous; untaught; uncivil; unpolished; artless. adv. *rudely:* s. *rudeness.*
RU'DIMENT. s. First principles; first elements of a science; beginning. adj. *rudimental.*
RUE. v. To grieve for; to regret. pr. par. *ruing;* past, *rued:* adj. *rueful:* adv. *ruefully:* s. *ruefulness.*
RUFF. s. A puckered linen or muslin ornament, for the neck; a state of roughness.
RUF'FIAN. s. A brutal, boisterous, mischievous fellow; a cut-throat; a robber. adj. *ruffianly, ruffianlike.*
RUF'FLE. v. To disorder; to put out of form; to make less smooth; to grow rough or turbulent. pr. par. *ruffling;* past, *ruffled:* s. *ruffle.*
RUG. s. A coarse, nappy, woollen cloth.
RUG'GED. adj. Rough; full of unevenness and asperity. adv. *ruggedly:* s. *ruggedness.*
RU'IN. s. Fall, destruction, overthrow; thing fallen. v. *ruin;* pr. par. *ruining;* past, *ruined:* s. *ruiner:* adj. *ruinous:* adv. *ruinously.*
RULE. s. Government; sway; canon, &c. v. *rule;* pr. par. *ruling,* past, *ruled:* s. *ruler.*
RUM. s. A kind of spirits, distilled from molasses.
RUM'BLE. v. To make a hoarse, low, continued noise. pr. par. *rumbling;* past, *rumbled:* s. *rumbler.*
RU'MINATE. v. To chew the cud; to muse. pr. par. *ruminating;* past, *ruminated:* adj. *ruminant:* s. *rumination, ruminator.*
RUM'MAGE. v. To search rudely. pr. par. *rummaging;* past, *rummaged.*
RU'MOUR. s. Flying or popular report. v. *rumour;* pr. par. *rumouring;* past, *rumoured.*
RUMP. s. The end of the back bone; the buttocks.
RUM'PLE. s. A pucker; a rude plait. v. *rumple;* pr. par. *rumpling* past, *rumpled.*
RUN. v. To move swiftly; to make haste, &c. pr. par. *running;* past, *run;* pret. *ran:* s. *run, runner.*
RUN'AGATE. s. A fugitive, an apostate.
RUN'DLE. s. A step of a ladder, something put round an axis.
RUN'DLET. s. A small barrel.
RUNG. Past par. of the v. *to ring.*

320

RUNG. *s.* A round or step of a ladder, &c.

RU'NIC. *adj.* Denoting the letters and language of the ancient northern nations.

RUN'NET. *s.* A liquor made by steeping the stomach of a calf in hot water, and used to coagulate milk for curds and cheese; sometimes written *rennet.*

RUNT. *s.* A dwarf animal.

RUPEE'. *s.* An East Indian silver coin, worth about two shillings and four-pence sterling.

RUP'TURE. *s.* The act of breaking; state of being broken; hernia. v. *rupture;* pr. par. *rupturing;* past, *ruptured:* s. *ruption.*

RU'RAL. *adj.* Relating or belonging to the country. adv. *rurally:* s. *ruralness.*

RUSH. *s.* A kind of plant. pl. *rushes:* adj. *rushy* · s. *rushiness.*

RUSH. *v.* To enter or move with violence. pr. par. *rushing;* past, *rushed:* s. *rush.*

RUSK. *s.* Hard bread, made from rye.

RUS'SET. *adj.* Reddishly brown; gray; homespun. s. *russet.*

RUST. *s.* Oxide of iron; tarnished surface of any metal; matter bred by corruption or degeneration. v. *rust;* pr. par. *rusting;* past, *rusted:* adj. *rusty:* s. *rustiness.*

RUS'TIC. *adj.* Rural; rude; untaught. s. *rusticity.*

RUS'TICATE. *v.* To reside in the country; to banish into the country. pr. par. *rusticating;* past, *rusticated:* s. *rustication.*

RUT. *s.* The track of a carriage wheel.

RUTH'FUL. *adj.* Merciful; sorrowful. adv. *ruthfully:* adj. *ruthless:* s. *ruthlessness.*

RYE. A kind of esculent grain.

S

SAB'BATH. *s.* A day appointed for public worship, and rest from labour. adj. *sabbatic, sabbatical.*

SA'BLE. *s.* A kind of fur.

SA'BLE. *adj.* Black.

SABOT'. *s.* A sort of wooden shoe.

SA'BRE. *s.* A cimetar; a short sword with a convex edge. v. *sabre;* pr. par. *sabring;* past, *sabred.*

SAC'CHARINE. *adj.* Having the taste or any other of the chief qualities of sugar.

SACERDO'TAL. *adj.* Priestly; belonging to the priesthood.

SACH'EL. *s.* A small sack or bag.

SACH'EM. *s.* The title of some American chiefs.

SACK. *s.* A bag, a pouch, a large bag; a kind of sweet wine.

SACK. *v.* To take by storm; to pillage. pr. par. *sacking,* past, *sacked:* s. *sack, sacker.*

SACK'BUT. *s.* A kind of trumpet.

SACK'CLOTH. *s.* Cloth of which sacks are made; coarse cloth sometimes worn in mortification.

SA'CRAMENT. *s.* An oath; any ceremony producing an obligation, the eucharist. adj. *sacramental:* adv. *sacramentally.*

SA'CRED. *adj.* Immediately relating to God; devoted to religious uses; holy; consecrated. adv. *sacredly:* s. *sacredness.*

SAC'RIFICE. *v.* To offer to heaven; to immolate as an atonement or propitiation; to destroy; to kill. pr. par. *sacrificing;* past, *sacrificed:* s. *sacrifice, sacrificer:* adj. *sacrific, sacrifical, sacrificatory, sacrificial.*

SAC'RILEGE. *s.* The crime of appropriating to one's-self what is devoted to religion; the crime of robbing heaven. adj. *sacrilegious:* adv. *sacrilegiously:* s. *sacrilegiousness.*

SACRIS'TY. *s.* An apartment where

SAD—SAI   SAK—SAL

the consecrated vessels or movables of a church are deposited. pl. *sacristies*: s. *sacristan*.

SAD. *adj.* Sorrowful; gloomy; serious. v. *sadden;* pr. par. *saddening* past, *saddened:* adv. *sadly,* s. *sadness*.

SAD'DLE. *s.* The seat which is put upon a horse, for the accommodation of the rider. v. *saddle;* pr. par. *saddling;* past, *saddled:* s. *saddler*.

SAD'DUCEE. *s.* One of the most ancient sects amongst the Jews.

SAFE. *adj.* Free from danger free from hurt. adv. *safely:* s. *safeness, safety,* pl. *safeties*.

SAFECON'DUCT. *s.* Convoy; guard through an enemy's country; pass.

SAFE'GUARD. *s.* Defence, protection, convoy.

SAF'FLOWER. *s.* A species of plant.

SAF'FRON. *s.* A kind of plant.

SAGA'CIOUS. *adj.* Of quick scent; of quick thought. adv. *sagaciously*: s. *sagacity,* pl. *sagacities*.

SAGE. *s.* A species of plant.

SAGE. *adj.* Wise, grave, prudent. adv. *sagely:* s. *sage, sageness.*

SAGIT'TAL. *adj.* Belonging to an arrow.

SAGITTA'RIUS. *s.* One of the signs of the zodiac.

SA'GO. *s.* The granulated juice of an East-India plant.

SAID. Pret. and past par. of the v. *to say:* adj. aforesaid, declared, shown.

SAIL. *s.* The expanded sheet which catches the wind, and propels a vessel on the water. v. *sail;* pr. par. *sailing;* past, *sailed*.

SAIL'ER, SAIL'OR. *s.* A seaman; one who practises or understands navigation.

SAIN'FOIN, SAINT'FOIN. *s.* A kind of herb.

SAINT. *s.* A person eminent for piety and virtue. v. *saint;* pr. par. *sainting;* past, *sainted* adj *saintly, saintlike*.

SAKE. *s.* Final cause, end; purpose; account.

SAL. *s.* Salt.

SAL'AD. *s.* Food of raw herbs; a kind of vegetable.

SALAMAN'DER. *s.* An animal supposed to live in the fire.

SAL'ARY. *s.* Stated hire; annual or periodical payment. pl. *salaries*.

SALE. *s.* The act of selling; vent; market. adj. *saleable:* s. *saleableness:* adv. *saleably*.

SALES'MAN. *s.* One who sells. pl. *salesmen*.

SAL'IENT. *adj.* Leaping, bounding.

SALIQUE'. *adj.* Belonging to the law, by virtue of which males only inherit.

SALI NE. *adj.* Consisting of salt; constituting salt.

SALI'VA. *s.* The juice which is separated by the salival glands. adj. *salivous*.

SAL'IVATE. *v.* To purge by the salival glands. pr. par. *salivating,* past, *salivated:* s. *salivation*.

SAL'LOW. *s.* A tree of the genus of willow.

SAL'LOW. *adj.* Sickly, yellow. s. *sallowness*.

SAL'LY. *s.* Eruption; issue from a place besieged; quick egress. pl. *sallies:* v. *sally;* pr. par. *sallying;* past, *sallied*.

SAL'LYPORT. *s.* A gate from which sallies are made.

SALMAGUN'DI. *s.* A mixture of chopped meats.

SALM'ON. *s.* A species of fish.

SALOON'. *s.* A spacious hall or room; a sort of state-room.

SALT. *s.* A substance used to preserve meat, fish, and other things from corrupting. v. *salt;* pr. par. *salting;* past, *salted:* adj. *salt, saltish:* s. *saltness*.

SAL'TANT. *adj.* Jumping, dancing. s. *saltation*.

SALT'CELLAR. *s.* A vessel of salt, set on the table.

SALU'BRIOUS. *adj.* Wholesome,

healthful, promoting health. s. *salubrity*.

SAL'UTARY. *adj.* Wholesome, healthful, safe, advantageous. s. *salutariness*.

SALU'TE. *v.* To greet, to hail, to address. pr. par. *saluting*; past, *saluted:* s. *salute, salutation, salutatory,* pl. *salutatories*.

SALUTIF'EROUS. *adj.* Healthy, bringing health.

SAL'VABLE. *adj.* Possible to be saved.

SAL'VAGE. *s.* Recompense allowed by the law, for saving goods from a wreck.

SALVA'TION. *s.* Act of saving; preservation from eternal death; reception to the happiness of heaven.

SALVE. *s.* A glutinous matter, applied to wounds and hurts; help; remedy. v. *salve;* pr. par. *salving;* past, *salved*.

SAL'VER. *s.* A plate on which any thing is presented.

SAL'VO. *s.* An exception; a reservation; an excuse. pl. *salvoes*.

SAME. *adj.* Not different; identical; not another. s. *sameness*.

SAMPH'IRE. *s.* A plant preserved in pickle.

SAM'PLE. *s.* A specimen, an example.

SAM'PLER. *s.* A pattern of work, a specimen.

SAN'ABLE. *adj.* Curable; susceptive of remedy; remediable.

SAN'ATIVE. *adj.* Powerful to cure; healing. s. *sanativeness*.

SANC'TIFY. *v.* To make holy; to free from the power of sin for the time to come. pr. par. *sanctifying;* past, *sanctified:* s. *sanctification, sanctifier*.

SANCTIMO'NIOUS. *adj.* Saintly; having the appearance of sanctity. adv. *sanctimoniously:* s. *sanctimoniousness, sanctimony,* pl. *sanctimonies*.

SANC'TION. *s.* The act of confirmation, which gives to any thing its obligatory power; ratification. v. *sanction;* pr. par. *sanctioning,* past, *sanctioned*.

SANC'TITY. *s.* Holiness; the state of being holy. pl. *sanctities*.

SANC'TUARY. *s.* A holy place; a sacred asylum. pl. *sanctuaries*.

SAND. *s.* Particles of stone not conjoined, or stone broken to powder. v. *sand;* pr. par. *sanding;* past, *sanded:* s. *sandiness:* adj. *sandy*.

SAN'DAL. *s.* A loose shoe.

SAND'BLIND. *adj.* Having a defect in the eyes, by which small particles appear to fly before them.

SANE. *adj.* Sound, healthy.

SANG. Pret. of the v. *to sing*.

SAN'GUINE. *adj.* Red; having the colour of blood; warm; ardent; confident. adj. *sanguineous:* s. *sanguineness, sanguinity*.

SANG'UINARY. *adj.* Cruel, bloody murderous.

SANHE'DRIM. *s.* The chief council among the Jews.

SAN'ITY. *s.* Soundness of mind. pl. *sanities*.

SANK. Pret. of the v. *to sink*.

SAP. *s.* The vital juice of plants; the juice that circulates in trees and herbs. adj. *sapless, sappy:* s. *sappiness*.

SAP. *v.* To undermine; to enter under ground. pr. par. *sapping* past, *sapped:* s. *sap, sapper*.

SA'PIENCE. *s.* Wisdom, sageness, knowledge. adj. *sapient*.

SAP'LING. *s.* A young tree; a young plant.

SAPONA'CEOUS. *adj.* Soapy; resembling soap; having the qualities of soap.

SAP'PHIC. *adj.* Denoting a kind of verse, after the manner of Sappho.

SAP'PHIRE. *s.* A precious stone, of a blue colour.

SAR'CASM. *s.* A keen reproach; a taunt; a gibe. adj. *sarcastic, sarcastical:* adv. *sarcastically*.

SAR'CENET. *s.* Fine, thin, woven silk.

SARCOPH'AGUS. *s.* A sort of stone coffin or grave, in which the ancients laid those bodies which were not to be burned. Latin pl. *sarcophagi.*

SARDON'IC. *adj.* Forced or feigned, as applied to laughter, smiles, or grins.

SAR'DONYX. *s.* A kind of precious stone. pl. *sardonyxes.*

SARSAPARIL'LA. *s.* A kind of tree; a kind of herb.

SASH. *s.* A belt, worn by way of distinction; a ribbon worn round the waist, by ladies; a window, so formed as to let up and down, by pulleys.

SAS'SAFRAS. *s.* A kind of tree.

SAT. Pret. and past par. of the v. *to sit.*

SA'TAN. *s.* The devil. adj. *satanic, satanical;* adv. *satanically.*

SATCH'EL. *s.* A little bag; commonly a bag used by school-boys.

SATE. *v.* To satiate, to glut, to pall. pr. par. *sating;* past, *sated.*

SAT'ELLITE. *s.* A small planet, revolving round a larger.

SA'TIATE. *v.* To satisfy, to fill, to glut, to pall. pr. par. *satiating;* past, *satiated;* s. *satiety.*

SAT'IN. *s.* A soft, close, and shining silk.

SAT'INET'. *s.* A sort of slight satin.

SATIRE. *s.* A poem, in which wickedness or folly is censured. adj. *satirical;* adv. *satirically;* s. *satirist;* v. *satirize;* pr. par. *satirizing;* past, *satirized.*

SATISFAC'TION. *s.* The act of satisfying; the state of being pleased; gratification; amends; atonement for a crime. adj. *satisfactory;* adv. *satisfactorily;* s. *satisfactoriness.*

SAT'ISFY. *v.* To content; to please to such a degree, that nothing more is desired. pr. par. *satisfying;* past, *satisfied;* s. *satisfier.*

SA'TRAP. *s.* In Persia, a governor of a district; a kind of viceroy; a nobleman in power.

SAT'URATE. *v.* To impregnate till no more can be received or imbibed. pr. par. *saturating;* past, *saturated;* s. *saturation.*

SAT'URDAY. *s.* The last day of the week.

SAT'URN. *s.* A remote planet of the solar system.

SATURNA'LIAN. *adj.* Sportive, loose; like the feasts of Saturn.

SATUR'NIAN. *adj.* Happy, golden.

SATUR'NINE. *adj.* Gloomy, grave, melancholy.

SAT'YR. *s.* A sylvan god.

SAUCE. *s.* Something eaten with food, to improve its taste.

SAUCE'PAN. *s.* A small skillet, with a long handle, in which sauce or small things are boiled.

SAU'CER. *s.* A small pan or platter, in which sauce is set on a table; a piece of china, into which a tea cup is set.

SAU'CY. *adj.* Pert, petulant, insolent, impudent. adv. *saucily;* s. *sauciness.*

SAUN'TER. *v.* To wander about idly; to loiter; to linger. pr. par. *sauntering;* past, *sauntered;* s. *saunterer.*

SAUS'AGE. *s.* A roll or ball of meat, minced very small, and sometimes stuffed into skins.

SAV'AGE. *adj.* Wild, uncultivated, untamed, barbarous. s. *savage;* adv. *savagely;* s. *savageness.*

SAVAN'NA. *s.* An open meadow, without a wood.

SAVE. *v.* To preserve from danger or destruction; not to spend or lose. pr. par. *saving;* past, *saved.* s. *saver, saving, savingness;* adv. *savingly.*

SAVE. *prep.* Except, not including.

SAVE'ALL. *s.* A small pan, inserted into a candlestick, to save the ends of candles.

SAV'IN. *s.* A species of plant.

SA'VIOUR. *s.* The Redeemer; Christ.

SA'VORY. *s.* A kind of plant. pl *savories.*

324

SA'VOUR. *s.* A scent, odour, taste. *v. savour;* pr. par. *savouring;* past, *savoured:* adj. *savoury:* s. *savouriness.*

SAVOY'. *s.* A sort of colewort.

SAW. Pret. of the v. *to see.*

SAW. *s.* A dentated instrument, by the attrition of which, wood or metal is cut. *v. saw;* pr. par. *sawing;* past, *sawed:* s. *sawer, sawyer.*

SAW'DUST. *s.* Dust made by the attrition of a saw.

SAW'PIT. *s.* A pit, over which timber is laid to be sawed.

SAX'ON. *s.* One of the people who inhabited the northern part of Germany. adj. *Saxon.*

SAY. *v.* To speak; to utter in words; to tell. pr. par. *saying;* past, *said:* s. *say, saying.*

SCAB. *s.* An incrustation, formed over a sore, by dried matter. adj. *scabbed, scabby, scabious:* s. *scabbedness, scabbiness.*

SCAB'BARD. *s.* The sheath of a sword.

SCAB'ROUS. adj. Rough; rugged; pointed on the surface; harsh. s. *scabrousness.*

SCAF'FOLD. *s.* A temporary gallery or stage, raised either for shows or spectators; the gallery raised for the execution of great malefactors; frames of timber erected on the side of a building, for the workmen. *v. scaffold;* pr. par. *scaffolding;* past, *scaffolded:* s. *scaffolding.*

SCALA'DE. *s.* The act of storming a place, by raising ladders against the walls.

SCALD. *v.* To burn with hot liquid. pr. par. *scalding,* past, *scalded:* s. *scald.*

SCALE. *s.* A balance; a vessel suspended by a beam, against another vessel; the small shells or crusts, which, lying over another, make the coats of fishes. *v. scale;* pr. par. *scaling;* past, *scaled:* adj. *scaled, scaly:* s. *scaliness.*

SCAL'LION. *s.* A kind of onion

SCAL'LOP. *s.* A fish with a hollow, pectinated shell.

SCAL'LOP. *v.* To mark on the edge with segments of circles. pr par. *scalloping;* past, *scalloped.*

SCALP. *s.* The skull; the cranium; the bone that encloses the brain. *v. scalp;* pr. par. *scalping,* past, *scalped.*

SCAM'PER. *v.* To fly with speed and trepidation. pr. par. *scampering;* past, *scampered.*

SCAN. *v.* To examine a verse by counting the feet; to examine nicely. pr. par. *scanning;* past, *scanned.*

SCAN'DAL. *s.* Offence given by the faults of others; reproachful aspersion; opprobrious censure; infamy. *v. scandalize;* pr. par. *scandalizing;* past, *scandalized:* adj. *scandalous:* adv. *scandalously:* s. *scandalousness.*

SCANT. *v.* To limit, to straiten. pr. par. *scanting;* past, *scanted:* adj. *scant, scanty:* adv. *scantily, scantly:* s. *scantiness, scantness.*

SCANT'LING. *s.* A quantity cut for a particular purpose; a certain proportion.

SCAPE'GOAT. *s.* The goat set at liberty by the Jews, on the day of solemn expiation.

SCAPE'MENT. *s.* A general term for the manner of communicating the impulse of the wheels to the pendulum.

SCAP'ULARY. *s.* Part of the habit of a friar, consisting of two narrow slips of cloth, covering the back and the breast. pl. *scapularies.*

SCAR. *s.* A mark made by a hurt or fire; a cicatrix. *v. scar;* pr. par. *scarring;* past, *scarred.*

SCAR'AMOUCH. *s.* A buffoon in motley dress.

SCARCE. adj. Not plentiful; rare; not common. adv. *scarcely:* s. *scarceness. scarcity,* pl. *scarcities.*

SCARE. *v.* To frighten, to terrify. pr. par. *scaring;* past, *scared.*

SCARECROW. s. An image or clapper, set up to frighten birds.

SCARF. s. Any thing that hangs loose upon the shoulders or dress.

SCARF'SKIN. s. The cuticle; the epidermis; the outer scaly integuments of the body.

SCAR'IFY. v. To let blood by the incisions of the skin, commonly after the application of cuppingglasses. pr. par. *scarifying;* past, *scarified:* s. *scarification, scarificator, scarifier.*

SCAR'LET. s. A colour compounded of red and yellow. adj. *scarlet.*

SCARP. s. The slope on that side of a ditch which is next to a fortified place, and looks towards the fields.

SCATE. s. A kind of wooden shoe, with a steel plate underneath, used to slide on the ice. v. *scate;* pr. par. *scating;* past, *scated.*

SCATE. s. A fish of the species of thornback.

SCAT'TER. v. To throw loosely about; to sprinkle; to disperse; to spread thinly. pr. par. *scattering;* past, *scattered:* adv. *scatteringly.*

SCAV'ENGER. s. A person whose province is to keep the streets clean, more commonly employed to remove the dirt.

SCENE. s. The stage; the general appearance of any action; a display; part of a play. s. *scenery:* pl. *sceneries:* adj. *scenic.*

SCENT. s. The power of smelling; the smell; odour, good or bad. v. *scent;* pr. par. *scenting;* past, *scented:* adj. *scentless.*

SCEP'TIC. s. See SKEPTIC.

SCEP'TRE. s. The ensign of royalty, borne in the hand. adj. *sceptered.*

SCHED'ULE. s. A writing, additional or appendant; a small scroll; a little inventory.

SCHEME. s. A plan; a combination of various things in one view; a project; a contrivance. v. *scheme;* pr. par. *scheming;* past, *schemed:* s *schemer*

SCHISM. s. A separation or division in the church of God. s. *schismatic.* adj. *schismatical:* adv. *schismatically:* v. *schismatize;* pr. par *schismatizing;* past, *schismatized.*

SCHOL'AR. s. One who learns of a master; a disciple; a man of letters. adj. *scholastic, scholastical:* adv. *scholastically.*

SCHO'LIAST. s. A writer of explanatory notes.

SCHO'LIUM. s. A note; an explanatory observation.

SCHOOL. s. A house of discipline and instruction; a place of literary education. v. *school;* pr. par. *schooling;* past, *schooled:* s. *schooling.*

SCHOOL'FELLOW. s. One bred at the same school.

SCHOOL'MAN. s. One versed in the niceties and subtleties of academical disputation. pl. *schoolmen.*

SCHOOL'MASTER. s. A man who presides and teaches in a school.

SCHOOL'MISTRESS. s. A woman who governs a school. pl. *schoolmistresses.*

SCHOON'ER. s. A small vessel with two masts.

SCI'ENCE. s. Knowledge; certainty grounded on demonstration; any art or species of knowledge. adj. *scientific.*

SCIENTIF'IC, SCIENTIF'ICAL. adj. Producing demonstrative knowledge; producing certainly.

SCIM'ITAR. s. A short sword, with a convex edge.

SCIN'TILLATE. v. To sparkle; to emit sparks. pr. par. *scintillating* past, *scintillated:* adj. *scintillant* s. *scintillation.*

SCI'OLISM. s. Superficial knowledge; not sound knowledge. s *sciolist.*

SCI'ON. s. A small twig, taken from one tree, to be engrafted in to another.

SCIS'SORS. s. A small pair of shears, or blades moving on a pivot.

SCLAVO'NIC, SCLAVO'NIAN. adj

Relating to the language or manners of the Sclavi, or people of Sclavonia.

SCOFF. *v.* To treat with insolent ridicule, or contumelious language. pr. par. *scoffing;* past, *scoffed:* s. *scoff, scoffer:* adv. *scoffingly.*

SCOLD. *v.* To quarrel clamorously and rudely. pr. par. *scolding;* past, *scolded:* s. *scold, scolder, scolding:* adv. *scoldingly.*

SCOL'LOP. *s.* A pectinated shell-fish.

SCONCE. *s.* A fort; a bulwark; the head; a pensile candlestick, generally with a mirror to reflect the light. *v. sconce;* pr. par. *sconcing;* past, *sconced.*

SCOOP. *s.* A kind of large ladle; a vessel with a long handle, used to throw out liquor; a sweep; a stroke. *v. scoop;* pr. par. *scooping;* past, *scooped:* s. *scooper.*

SCOPE. *s.* Aim, intention, drift, room, space, liberty, license.

SCOP'ULOUS. *adj.* Full of rocks.

SCORBU'TIC, SCORBU'TICAL. *adj.* Diseased with the scurvy. adv. *scorbutically.*

SCORCH. *v.* To burn superficially. pr. par. *scorching;* past, *scorched: v. scorch.*

SCORE. *s.* A notch or long incision; a line drawn; an epoch; an era; debt imputed; sake; twenty. *v. score;* pr. par. *scoring;* past, *scored.*

SCO'RIA. *s.* Dross, recrement. adj. *scorious.*

SCORN. *v.* To despise, to slight, to revile, to contemn. pr. par. *scorning;* past, *scorned:* s. *scorn, scorner:* adj. *scornful:* adv. *scornfully.*

SCOR'PION. *s.* A reptile with a venomous sting; one of the signs of the zodiac.

SCOT. *s.* Shot, payment, parish payments.

SCOT. *s.* A native of Scotland. *adj. Scotch, Scottish:* s. *Scotticism.*

SCOT'-FREE. *adj.* Without payment, untaxed, unhurt.

SCOUN'DREL. *s.* A mean rascal a low, petty villain.

SCOUR. *v.* To rub hard with any thing rough, in order to clean the surface; to cleanse; to whiten; to rove; to range. pr. par. *scouring,* past, *scoured:* s. *scourer.*

SCOURGE. *s.* A whip, a lash, a punishment. *v. scourge;* pr. par. *scourging;* past, *scourged:* s. *scourger.*

SCOUT. *s.* One who is sent privily to observe the motions of an enemy. *v. scout;* pr. par. *scouting,* past, *scouted.*

SCOW. *s.* A large flat boat.

SCOWL. *v.* To frown; to look angry, sour, or sullen. pr. par. *scowling;* past, *scowled:* s. *scowl:* adv. *scowlingly*

SCRAB'BLE. *v.* To make unmeaning or idle marks. pr. par. *scrabbling;* past, *scrabbled.*

SCRAG. *s.* Any thing thin or lean; the small end of the neck. adj. *scraggy:* s. *scraggedness, scragginess.*

SCRAM'BLE. *v.* To catch at any thing, eagerly and tumultuously, with the hands; to catch with haste. pr. par. *scrambling;* past, *scrambled:* s. *scramble, scrambler.*

SCRAP. *s.* A small particle; a little piece; a fragment; crumb.

SCRAPE. *v.* To deprive of the surface, by the light action of a sharp instrument; to erase. pr. par. *scraping;* past, *scraped:* s. *scrape, scraper.*

SCRATCH. *v.* To tear or mark with slight incisions; to tear with the nails. pr. par. *scratching;* past, *scratched:* s. *scratch, scratcher*

SCRATCH'ES. *s.* Cracked ulcers or scabs, in a horse's foot

SCRAWL. *v.* To draw or mark irregularly or clumsily. pr. par. *scrawling;* past, *scrawled:* s. *scrawl, scrawler.*

SCREAK. *v.* To make a shrill or loud noise. pr. par. *screaking;* past, *screaked.*

SCREAM. *v.* To cry out shrilly, as in agony or terror. pr. par. *screaming;* past, *screamed:* s. *scream, screamer.*

SCREECH. *v.* To cry out as in terror or anguish. pr. par. *screeching;* past, *screeched:* s. *screech,* pl. *screeches.*

SCREEN. *s.* Any thing that affords shelter or concealment. v. *screen;* pr. par. *screening;* past, *screened.*

SCREW. *s.* One of the mechanical powers. v. *screw;* pr. par. *screwing;* past, *screwed.*

SCRIB'BLE. *v.* To fill with artless or worthless writing; to write without use or elegance. pr. par. *scribbling;* past, *scribbled:* s. *scribble, scribbler.*

SCRIBE. *s.* A writer; a public notary; a Jewish teacher or doctor of the law.

SCRIMP. *adj.* Short, scanty.

SCRIP. *s.* A small bag; a satchel.

SCRIP'TURE. *s.* Writing; sacred writing; the Bible. adj. *scriptural.*

SCRIV'ENER. *s.* One who draws contracts; one who engrosses writings first drawn by a lawyer.

SCROF'ULA. *s.* A depravation of the humours of the body, which breaks out in sores, commonly called the king's evil.

SCROLL. *s.* A writing wrapped up.

SCRUB. *v.* To rub hard with something coarse and rough. pr. par. *scrubbing;* past, *scrubbed.*

SCRUB. *s.* A mean fellow; any thing mean or despicable; a worn-out broom. adj. *scrubby.*

SCRUF. *s.* The same with *scurf.*

SCRU'PLE. *s.* Doubt; difficulty of determination; perplexity; twenty grains. v. *scruple;* pr. par. *scrupling;* past, *scrupled:* s. *scrupler.*

SCRU'PULOUS. *adj.* Nicely doubtful; hard to satisfy in determinations of conscience; captious. s. *scrupulosity.*

SCRU'TINY. *s.* Inquiry, search, examination with nicety. pl. *scrutinies:* v. *scrutinize;* pr. par. *scrutinizing;* past, *scrutinized.*

SCRUTOI'RE. *s.* A case of drawers for writing.

SCUD. *v.* To flee; to run away with precipitation. pr. par. *scudding,* past, *scudded.*

SCUD. *s.* A cloud swiftly driven by the wind.

SCUF'FLE. *s.* A confused quarrel a tumultuous broil. v. *scuffle;* pr par. *scuffling;* past, *scuffled:* s *scuffler.*

SCULK. *v.* To lurk in hiding places; to lie close. pr. par. *sculking;* past, *sculked:* s. *sculker.*

SCULL. *s.* The bone which incases and defends the head; the arched bone of the head.

SCULL. *v.* To propel a boat by means of a single oar, at the stern. pr. par. *sculling;* past, *sculled.*

SCULL'CAP. *s.* A head-piece; a night-cap.

SCUL'LER. *s.* A cock-boat; a boat in which there is but one rower; one that rows a cock-boat.

SCUL'LERY. *s.* The place where common utensils, as kettles or dishes, are cleaned and kept. pl. *sculleries.*

SCUL'LION. *s.* The lowest domestic servant.

SCULP'TOR. *s.* A carver; one who cuts wood or stone into images.

SCULP'TURE. *s.* The art of carving wood, or hewing stone, into images; carved work. v. *sculpture,* pr. par. *sculpturing;* past, *sculptured.*

SCUM. *s.* That which rises to the top of any liquor; the dross; the refuse. v. *scum;* pr. par. *scumming;* past, *scummed:* s. *scummer*

SCUP'PER. *s.* In a ship, a small hole in the side, above the deck, by which water is discharged.

SCURF. *s.* A kind of dry, miliary scab; any thing sticking on the surface. adj. *scurfy:* s. *scurfiness.*

SCUR'RILOUS. *adj.* Grossly opprobrious; lewdly jocular, vile; low adv *scurrilously*. s. *scurrility*, pl. *scurrilities*.

SCUR'VY. *adj.* Scabbed; covered with scabs; diseased with the scurvy; vile; bad. s. *scurvy*, pl. *scurvies*.

SCUTCH'EON. *s.* The shield represented in heraldry; the ensigns armorial of a family. See ESCUTCHEON.

SCU'TIFORM. *adj.* Shaped like a shield.

SCUT'TLE. *s.* A wide, shallow basket; a small grate; a quick pace.

SCUT'TLE. *v.* To cut holes in the deck or sides of a ship, for the purpose of sinking her. pr. par. *scuttling;* past, *scuttled*.

SCYTHE. *s.* An instrument for cutting grass.

SEA. *s.* The ocean; the water; a collection of water.

SEA'BOARD. *s.* The land near the sea.

SEA'BOAT. *s.* A vessel capable of resisting a rough sea.

SEA BREEZE. *s.* Wind blowing from the sea.

SEA'CALF. *s.* The seal. pl. *sea-calves*.

SEA'COAL. *s.* Coal, so called, not because found in the sea, but because brought to London by sea; pitcoal.

SEA COAST. *s.* Shore; edge of the sea.

SEA'-COMPASS. *s.* The card and needle of mariners. pl. *sea-compasses*.

SEA'FARING. *adj.* Travelling by sea.

SEA'GIRT. *adj.* Girded or encircled by the sea.

SEA'GREEN. *adj.* Resembling the colour of the distant sea; cerulean.

SEA'GULL. *s.* A bird common on the sea-coasts.

SEA'HORSE. *s.* A kind of fish.

SEA'MAN. *s.* A sailor, a navigator, a mariner. pl. *seamen*: s. *seamanship*.

SEA'MEW. *s.* A fowl that frequents the sea.

SEA'PIECE. *s.* A picture representing any thing at sea.

SEA'PORT. *s.* A harbour.

SEA'ROOM. *s.* Open sea; spacious main.

SEA'ROVER. *s.* A pirate.

SEA'SERVICE. *s.* Service at sea.

SEA'-SHORE. *s.* The coast of the sea.

SEA'SICK. *adj.* Sick, as new voyagers on the sea.

SEA'-SIDE. *s.* The edge of the sea.

SEA'-TERM. *s.* A word of art used by the seamen.

SEA'WORTHY. *adj.* Fit to go to sea; applied to a ship. s. *seaworthiness*.

SEAL. *s.* The sea-calf.

SEAL. *s.* A stamp engraved with a particular impression; the impression made in wax. v. *seal;* pr. par. *sealing;* past, *sealed:* s. *sealer*.

SEAL'ING-WAX. *s.* Hard wax, used to seal letters.

SEAM. *s.* The suture where the two edges of cloth are sewed together; a cicatrix; a scar. v. *seam;* pr. par. *seaming;* past, *seamed*. adj. *seamless*.

SEAMS'TRESS. *s.* A woman whose occupation is to sew. pl. *seamstresses*.

SEA'POY. *s.* See SEPOY.

SEAR. *v.* To burn, to cauterize. pr. par. *searing;* past, *seared*.

SEARCH. *v.* To examine, to explore, to inquire. pr. par. *searching;* past, *searched:* s. *search*, pl *searches*, *searcher*.

SEA'SON. *s.* One of the four parts of the year; a fit time. adj. *seasonable:* adv. *seasonably*. s. *seasonableness*.

SEA'SON. *v.* To mix with food any thing that gives a high relish; to qualify by admixture of another ingredient; to inure to another climate. pr. par. *seasoning;* past, *seasoned:* s. *seasoning*.

SEAT. *s.* A chair; any thing on

which one may sit. v. *seat;* pr. par. *seating;* past, *seated.*
SECE'DE. *v.* To withdraw from; to leave. pr. par. *seceding;* past, *seceded:* s. *seceder, secession.*
SECLU'DE. *v.* To confine from; to shut up apart. pr. par. *secluding;* past, *secluded:* s. *seclusion.*
SEC'OND. *adj.* The next in order to the first; next in order or dignity. adj. *secondary:* adv. *secondly, secondarily.*
SEC'OND. *s.* One who accompanies another in a duel; one who supports or maintains; the sixtieth part of a minute. v. *second;* pr. par. *seconding;* past, *seconded.*
SE'CRET. *adj.* Hidden, not revealed, concealed, retired. s. *secrecy, secret:* adv. *secretly.*
SEC'RETARY. *s.* One intrusted with the management of business; one who writes for another. pl. *secretaries.*
SECRE'TE. *v.* To hide; to conceal; to separate. pr. par. *secreting;* past, *secreted:* s. *secretion:* adj. *secretory.*
SECT. *s.* Men united in certain tenets. s. *sectary,* pl. *sectaries.*
SECTA'RIAN. *adj.* Belonging to sectaries. s. *sectarian, sectarianism.*
SEC'TION. *s.* The act of cutting or dividing; a part divided from the rest. adj. *sectional.*
SEC'TOR. *s.* A geometrical instrument.
SEC'ULAR. *adj.* Not spiritual; relating to the affairs of the present world. s. *secularity, secularization:* v. *secularize;* pr. par. *secularizing;* past, *secularized:* adv. *secularly.*
SECU'RE. *adj.* Free from fear; exempt from terror; confidential; safe. v. *secure;* pr. par. *securing;* past, *secured:* adv. *securely:* s. *security,* pl. *securities.*
SEDAN' *s.* A kind of portable coach; a chair.
SEDA'TE. *adj.* Calm, quiet, unruffled. adv. *sedately:* s. *sedateness:* adj. *sedative.*
SED'ENTARY. *adj.* Wanting motion or action; inactive. s. *sedentariness.*
SEDGE. *s.* A growth of narrow flags, a narrow flag. adj. *sedgy.*
SED'IMENT. *s.* That which settles at the bottom.
SEDI'TION. *s.* A tumult, an insurrection. adj. *seditious:* adv. *seditiously:* s. *seditionary,* pl. *seditionaries, seditiousness.*
SEDU'CE. *v.* To draw aside from the right; to tempt; to corrupt. pr. par. *seducing;* past, *seduced:* s. *seducer, seduction:* adj. *seductive.*
SED'ULOUS. *adj.* Assiduous, industrious, diligent. adv. *sedulously:* s. *sedulousness.*
SEE. *s.* The diocese of a bishop.
SEE. *v.* To perceive by the eye; to observe. pr. par. *seeing;* past, *seen.*
SEED. *s.* The organized particle produced by plants and animals, from which new plants and animals are generated. v. *seed;* pr. par. *seeding;* past, *seeded:* s. *seedling, seedplot.*
SEED'PEARL. *s.* Small grains of pearl.
SEEDS'MAN. *s.* One who sells seed. pl. *seedsmen.*
SEEK. *v.* To search for; to solicit. pr. par. *seeking;* past, *sought:* s. *seeker.*
SEEM. *v.* To appear; to make a show; to have semblance. pr. par. *seeming;* past, *seemed:* adv. *seemingly:* s. *seemingness.*
SEEM'LY. *adj.* Decent, becoming, fit. adv. *seemly:* s. *seemliness.*
SEER. *s.* A prophet; one who foresees future events.
SEE'SAW. *s.* A reciprocating motion. v. *seesaw;* pr. par. *seesawing,* past, *seesawed.*
SEETHE. *v.* To boil; to be hot. pr. par. *seething;* past, *seethed.*
SEGAR', CIGAR'. *s.* A little roll of tobacco, smoked without a pipe.
SEG'MENT. *s.* A figure contained between a chord and an arc of a circle, or so much of a circle as is cut off by that chord.

SE'GREGATE. *v.* To set apart; to separate. pr. par. *segregating;* past, *segregated:* s. *segregation.*

SEI'GNIOR. *s.* A lord; the title of honour given by Italians.

SEI'GNIORY. *s.* A lordship, a territory. pl. *seigniories.*

SEINE. *s.* A large net, used in fishing.

SEIZE. *v.* To take hold of; to grasp; to take by force. pr. par. *seizing;* past, *seized:* s. *seizure.*

SEL'DOM. *adv.* Rarely, not often.

SELECT'. *v.* To choose in preference to others rejected. pr. par. *selecting;* past, *selected:* adj. *select:* s. *selection, selectness.*

SELENOG'RAPHY. *s.* A description of the moon.

SELF. One of the pronouns. pl. *selves:* adj. *selfsame.*

SELF'ISH. *adj.* Attentive only to one's own interest. adv. *selfishly:* s. *selfishness.*

SELL. *v.* To give for a price; to vend. pr. par. *selling;* past, *sold:* s. *seller.*

SEL'VAGE, SEL'VEDGE. *s.* The edge of cloth, &c. adj. *selvedged.*

SEM'BLANCE. *s.* Likeness, resemblance.

SEM'I. *s.* A word which, used in composition, signifies *half.*

SEM'IBREVE. *s.* A note in music, containing half the quantity of a breve.

SEM'ICIRCLE. *s.* Half a circle. adj. *semicircular.*

SEM'ICOLON. *s.* Half a colon (;).

SEMIDIAM'ETER. *s.* Half a diameter.

SEM'IMETAL. *s.* A half metal; an imperfect metal.

SEM'INAL. *adj.* Belonging to seed; contained in the seed.

SEM'INARY. *s.* A seed plot; a place of education. pl. *seminaries.*

SEM'IQUAVER. *s.* A note in music, containing half the quantity of a quaver.

SEM'ITONE. *s.* In music, half a tone.

SEM'IVOWEL. *s.* A consonant which makes an imperfect sound they are six in number, f, l, m, n, r, s.

SEN'ATE. *s.* An assembly of counsellors, who share in the govern ment; a parliament. s. *senator:* adj. *senatorial.*

SEND. *v.* To despatch, to commission, &c. pr. par. *sending;* past, *sent.*

SENES'CENCE. *s.* The state of growing old; decay.

SEN'ESCHAL. *s.* The judge of a certain court of justice.

SE'NILE. *adj.* Relating or belonging to old age. s. *senility.*

SE'NIOR. *s.* One older than another. s. *seniority,* pl. *seniorities, seniory,* pl. *seniories.*

SEN'NA. *s.* A kind of medicinal tree.

SEN'NIGHT. *s.* The space of seven nights and days; a week.

SENSA'TION. *s.* Perception by the senses.

SENSE. *s.* Faculty of perceiving; perception by the senses; understanding, meaning, import. adj. *sensible:* s. *sensibility:* adv. *sensibly:* adj. *senseless:* adv. *senselessly:* s. *senselessness.*

SEN'SITIVE. *adj.* Having sense or perception, but not reason; easily affected. adv. *sensitively.*

SENSO'RIUM. *s.* The part where the senses transmit their perceptions to the mind; the seat of sense.

SEN'SUAL. *adj.* Pleasing to the senses; carnal. s. *sensualist, sensuality:* adv. *sensually.*

SEN'TENCE. *s.* Determination or decision, as of a judge; doom; a maxim; a short paragraph. v. *sentence;* pr. par. *sentencing;* past *sentenced.*

SENTEN'TIOUS. *adj.* Short and energetic. adv. *sententiously:* s. *sententiousness.*

SEN'TIENT. *adj.* Perceiving, having perception.

SEN'TIMENT. *s.* Thought, notion, opinion, sensibility. adj. *sentimental:* s. *sentimentality, sentimentalist*

331

SENTINEL, SENTRY. *s.* One who watches or keeps guard to prevent surprise. pl. *sentinels, sentries.*

SEPARABLE. *adj.* Susceptive of disunion. *s. separability.*

SEPARATE. *v.* To divide into parts; to disunite. pr. par. *separating;* past, *separated:* adj. *separate:* adv. *separately:* s. *separation, separator.*

SEPOY. *s.* An Indian native, who is a soldier in the infantry of the East India Company.

SEPTANGULAR. *adj.* Having seven corners or angles.

SEPTEMBER. *s.* The ninth month of the year.

SEPTENNIAL. *adj.* Lasting seven years; happening once in seven years.

SEPTENTRIONAL. *adj.* Northern. *s. septentrionality.*

SEPTIC. *adj.* Having the power to promote putrefaction.

SEPTILATERAL. *adj.* Having seven sides.

SEPTUAGENARY. *adj.* Consisting of seventy.

SEPTUAGESIMA. *s.* The third Sunday before Lent.

SEPTUAGINT. *s.* The ancient Greek version of the Old Testament.

SEPTUPLE. *adj.* Seven times as much.

SEPULCHRE. *s.* A grave; a tomb. adj. *sepulchral.*

SEPULTURE. *s.* Interment, burial.

SEQUACIOUS. *adj.* Following; attendant. *s. sequaciousness.*

SEQUEL. *s.* Succeeding part; consequence; event.

SEQUESTER. *v.* To separate from others, for the sake of privacy, to put aside; to remove. pr. par. *sequestering;* past, *sequestered.*

SEQUESTRATE. *v.* To sequester; to separate; to take away. pr. par. *sequestrating;* past, *sequestrated:* s. *sequestration.*

SERAGLIO. *s.* In the east, a house for concubines. pronounced *seralio.*

SERAPH. *s.* One of the order of angels. pl. *seraphim:* adj. *seraphic.*

SERENADE. *s.* Music or songs with which ladies are entertained, by their lovers, in the night. v. *serenade;* pr. par. *serenading;* past, *serenaded.*

SERENE. *adj.* Calm, placid, quiet. *s. serene, serenity:* adv. *serenely.*

SERF. *s.* A slave; one bound to the soil.

SERGE. *s.* A kind of woollen cloth.

SERJEANT. *s.* A degree in law, next below a judge; a petty officer in the army, &c. s. *sergeantry.*

SERIES. *s.* Sequence, order, succession.

SERIOUS. *adj.* Grave, solemn, important. adv. *seriously:* s. *seriousness.*

SERMON. *s.* A discourse pronounced by a divine.

SEROUS. *adj.* Thin, watery. s. *serosity.*

SERPENT. *s.* A kind of venomous animal.

SERPENTINE. *adj.* Winding like a serpent; curvilinear.

SERRATED. *adj.* Formed with indentures like the edge of a saw s. *serration.*

SERVE. *v.* To work for; to attend at command; to assist. pr. par. *serving;* past, *served:* s. *servant, service, servitude:* adj. *serviceable:* adv. *serviceably.*

SERVILE. *adj.* Slavish, mean, fawning. adv. *servilely:* s. *servility.*

SESQUIPEDAL, SESQUIPEDALIAN. *adj.* Containing a foot and a half.

SESS. *s.* Rate; cess charged; tax. pl. *sesses.*

SESSION. *s.* The act of sitting; the space during which an assembly sits.

SET. *v.* To place; to put in any situation or place, &c. pr. par. *setting;* past, *set:* adj. *set:* s. *set, setter.*

SETACEOUS. *adj.* Bristly.

SET-OFF. *s.* Any counterbalance; a recommendation, a decoration

SE'TON. s. An issue; a rowel.
SETTEE'. s. A long seat, with a back.
SET'TLE. v. To place in any certain state; to establish; to fix. pr. par. *settling;* past, *settled:* s. *settledness, settlement, settler.*
SEV'EN. adj. Four and three. ordinal adj. *seventh:* adv. *seventhly:* adj. *sevenfold.*
SEV'ENTEEN. adj. Seven and ten. ordinal adj. *seventeenth.*
SEV'ENTY. adj. Seven times ten. ordinal adj. *seventieth.*
SEV'ER. v. To part by violence, to force asunder. pr. par. *severing;* past, *severed:* s. *severance.*
SEV'ERAL. adj. Different; distinct from one another; divers. adv. *severally:* s. *severalty.*
SEVE'RE. adj. Sharp, censorious, rigorous. adv. *severely:* s. *severity,* pl. *severities.*
SEW. v. To join by the use of a needle. pr. par. *sewing;* past, *sewed:* s. *sewer.*
SEW'ER. s. A passage for water.
SEX. s. The property by which any animal is male or female. pl. *sexes:* adj. *sexual.*
SEXAGEN'ARY. adj. Threescore.
SEXAGES'IMA. s. The second Sunday before Lent. adj. *sexagesimal.*
SEXAN'GULAR. adj. Having six corners or angles.
SEXEN'NIAL. adj. Lasting six years; happening once in six years.
SEX'TANT. s. The sixth part of a circle; an astronomical instrument.
SEX'TON. s. An under officer of a church.
SEX'TUPLE. adj. Sixfold.
SHAB'BY. adj. Mean, paltry. adv. *shabbily:* s. *shabbiness.*
SHACK'LE. v. To chain, to fetter, to bind. pr. par. *shackling;* past, *shackled:* s. *shackle.*
SHAD. s. A kind of fish.
SHADE. s. The cloud or opacity made by interception of the light: darkness; obscurity. v. *shade;* pr. par. *shading;* past, *shaded:* s *shadiness:* adj. *shady.*
SHAD'DOCK. s. A kind of orange.
SHAD'OW. s. The representation of a body by which the light is intercepted; opacity; shade. v. *shadow;* pr. par. *shadowing;* past, *shadowed:* adj. *shadowy.*
SHAFT. s. An arrow; the handle of a weapon; the pole of a carriage, &c. adj. *shafted.*
SHAG. s. Rough hair; a kind of cloth. adj. *shaggy:* s. *shaggedness.*
SHA'GREEN. s. The skin of a kind of fish.
SHAKE. v. To put into a vibrating motion, to agitate. pr. par. *shaking;* past, *shaken:* s. *shake, shaker.*
SHALL. v. A defective verb.
SHALLOON'. s. A slight woollen stuff.
SHAL'LOP. s. A small boat.
SHALLOT'. s. See Eschalot.
SHAL'LOW. adj. Not deep. s. *shallowness.*
SHAM. v. To trick; to cheat, to delude. with false pretences. pr. par. *shamming;* past, *shammed:* s. *sham:* adj. *sham.*
SHAM'BLES. s. The place where butchers kill or sell their meat.
SHAM'BLING. adj. Moving awkwardly and irregularly.
SHAME. s. The passion felt when reputation is supposed to be lost; ignominy; disgrace. v. *shame;* pr. par. *shaming;* past, *shamed:* adj *shameful, shameless:* adv. *shamefully, shamelessly:* adj. *shamefaced.*
SHAM'ROCK. s. A three-leaved clover.
SHANK. s. The middle joint of the leg; the handle.
SHAN'TY. adj. Showy, gay.
SHAPE. v. To form, to mould. pr par. *shaping;* past, *shaped;* s. *shapes shapeliness:* adj. *shapeless, shapely.*
SHARE. v. To divide, to part, to partake. pr. par. *sharing;* past, *shared:* s. *share, sharer.*
SHARK. s. A kind of fish.
SHARP. adj. Keen, piercing, cut

ting. *s. sharp;* pr. par. *sharping;* past, *sharped:* s. *sharper, sharpness:* adv. *sharply.*

SHARP'EN. *v.* To make keen; to point; to edge. pr. par. *sharpening;* past, *sharpened.*

SHARP'-SIGHTED. *adj.* Having quick sight.

SHARP-WITTED. *adj.* Having an acute mind.

SHAT'TER. *v.* To break into pieces; to impair. pr. par. *shattering;* past, *shattered.*

SHAVE. *v.* To pare off with a razor; to pare close to the surface. pr. par. *shaving;* past, *shaved:* s. *shaveling, shaver, shaving.*

SHAWL. *s.* A part of modern female dress.

SHE. The female pron. personal.

SHEAF. *s.* A bundle of stalks of corn bound together. pl. *sheaves.*

SHEAR. *v.* To clip or cut. pr. par. *shearing;* past, *sheared, shorn:* s. *shears, shearer.*

SHEATH. *s.* The case of any thing; the scabbard. *v. sheath, sheathe;* pr. par. *sheathing;* past, *sheathed.*

SHED. *s.* A shelter made of boards.

SHED. *v.* To pour out; to spill. pr. par. *shedding;* past, *shed:* s. *shedder.*

SHEEP. *s.* A species of animal. adj. *sheepish:* adv. *sheepishly:* s. *sheepishness, sheepcot, sheepfold, sheepwalk.*

SHEER. adj. Pure, clear, unmingled.

SHEET. *s.* Any thing broad and thin, such as linen or paper. *v. sheet;* pr. par. *sheeting;* past, *sheeted:* s. *sheeting.*

SHEET-ANC'HOR. *s.* The largest anchor.

SHEK'EL. *s.* An ancient Jewish coin.

SHELF. *s.* A board fixed against a wall, &c. to place things on; a sand-bank or rock in the sea. pl. *shelves* adj. *shelvy.*

SHELL. *s.* The external crust. *v. shell;* pr. par. *shelling;* past, *shelled:* adj *shelly:* s. *shellfish.*

SHELL-BARK. *s.* A kind of hickory nut.

SHEL'TER. *s.* A cover from injury protection. *v. shelter;* pr. par. *sheltering;* past, *sheltered:* adj. *sheltery.*

SHEL'TIE. *s.* A Scotch pony.

SHELVE. *v.* To place on shelves; to furnish with shelves; to slope. pr. par. *shelving;* past, *shelved:* adj. *shelving, shelvy.*

SHEP'HERD. *s.* One who tends sheep. fem. *shepherdess,* pl. *shepherdess.*

SHER'BET. *s.* A kind of drink.

SHER'IFF. *s.* An officer to whom is intrusted, in each county, the execution of the laws. s. *shrievalty,* the office or jurisdiction of a sheriff.

SHER'RY. *s.* A kind of Spanish wine.

SHIELD. *s.* A buckler; defence; protection. *v. shield;* pr. par. *shielding;* past, *shielded.*

SHIFT. *v.* To change place; to change; to find some expedient pr. par. *shifting;* past, *shifted:* s *shift, shifter,* adj. *shiftless.*

SHIL'LING. *s.* A coin, equal to 12 pence.

SHIN. *s.* The fore-part of the leg.

SHINE. *v.* To glitter, to glisten pr. par. *shining;* past, *shone.*

SHIN'GLE. *s.* A thin board, to cover houses. *v. shingle;* pr. par. *shingling;* past, *shingled.*

SHIP. *s.* A large vessel of burden, with sails. *v. ship;* pr. par. *shipping;* past, *shipped:* s. *shipping, shipwreck, shipwright.*

SHIP'BOARD. adv. In a ship.

SHIRE. *s.* A division of a kingdom; a county.

SHIRK. *v.* To practise mean or artful tricks. pr. par. *shirking;* past, *shirked.*

SHIRT. *s.* The under garment of a man. *v. shirt;* pr. par. *shirting;* past, *shirted.*

SHIV'ER. *v.* To break at once into many parts; to quake; to tremble. pr. par. *shivering;* past, *shivered*

SHOAL. *s.* A great multitude; a throng; a shallow place. adj. *shoal.*

SHOCK. *s.* Conflict; concussion; offence; a pile of sheaves of corn. v. *shock;* pr. par. *shocking;* past, *shocked:* adv. *shockingly.*

SHOD. Pret. and past par. of the v. *to shoe.*

SHOE. *s.* The outer cover of the foot. v. *shoe;* pr. par. *shoeing;* past, *shod:* s. *shoer, shoeblack, shoemaker.*

SHONE. Pret. and past par. of the v. *to shine.*

SHOOK. Pret. of the v. *to shake.*

SHOOT. *v.* To discharge any thing, so as to make it fly with speed or violence; to strike with any thing shot. pr. par. *shooting;* past, *shot:* s. *shoot, shooter.*

SHOP. *s.* A place in which goods are sold by retail; a place for work. v. *shop;* pr. par. *shopping;* past, *shopped:* s. *shopper, shopboard, shopkeeper, shopman,* pl. *shopmen.*

SHOPLIFTER. *s.* One who, under pretence of buying, steals goods out of a shop.

SHORE. Pret. of the v. *to shear.* past par. *shorn.*

SHORE. *s.* The coast of the sea; the bank of a river; a drain; the support of a building. v. *shore;* pr. par. *shoring;* past, *shored.*

SHORT. adj. Not long; defective: scanty. v. *shorten;* pr. par. *shortening;* past, *shortened:* adv. *shortly:* s. *shortness:* adj. *shortlived, shortsighted.*

SHORTHAND. *s.* A method of writing in compendious characters; stenography.

SHOT. Pret. and past par. of the v. *to shoot.*

SHOT. *s.* The act of shooting; the missile weapon emitted by any instrument.

SHOULD. Pret. of the v. *shall.*

SHOULDER. *s.* The joint which connects the arm to the body. v. *shoulder;* pr. par. *shouldering;* past, *shouldered.*

SHOUT. *s.* A loud cry of triumph or exultation, &c. v. *shout;* pr. par. *shouting;* past, *shouted:* s. *shouter.*

SHOVE. v. To push. pr. par. *shoving;* past, *shoved:* s. *shove.*

SHOVEL. *s.* An instrument for lifting earth, &c. v. *shovel;* pr. par. *shoveling;* past, *shoveled.*

SHOW. v. To exhibit to view; to prove. pr. par. *showing;* past, *shown:* s. *show:* adj. *showy.*

SHOWER. *s.* A fall of rain; a storm of any thing, falling thick. v. *shower;* pr. par. *showering,* past, *showered:* adj. *showery.*

SHRED. v. To tear into small pieces. pr. par. *shredding;* past, *shredded:* s. *shred.*

SHREW. *s.* A peevish, malignant, clamorous woman. adj. *shrewish:* adv. *shrewishly:* s. *shrewishness*

SHREWD. adj. Cunning, smart. adv. *shrewdly:* s. *shrewdness.*

SHRIEK. v. To scream. pr. pa. *shrieking;* past, *shrieked:* s. *shriek.*

SHRIEVALTY. *s.* The office of a sheriff. pl. *shrievalties.*

SHRILL. adj. Sounding with a piercing, tremulous, or vibratory sound. s. *shrillness:* adv. *shrilly.*

SHRIMP. *s.* A small fish.

SHRINE. *s.* A case in which some thing sacred is deposited.

SHRINK. v. To contract; to shrivel pr. par. *shrinking;* past, *shrunk.*

SHRIVEL. v. To contract into wrinkles. pr. par. *shriveling;* past, *shriveled.*

SHROUD. *s.* A dress for the dead; a shelter; the ropes which support a mast. v. *shroud;* pr. par. *shrouding;* past, *shrouded.*

SHROVETIDE, SHROVE-TUESDAY. *s.* The day before Ash-Wednesday, or Lent.

SHRUB. *s.* A bush; a small tree; a kind of drink. s. *shrubbery,* p. *shrubberies.*

SHRUG. v. To express horror or dissatisfaction by motion of the

335

shoulders. pr. par. *shrugging;* past, *shrugged:* s. *shrug.*

SHRUNK. Pret. and past par. of the v. *to shrink.*

SHUD'DER. *v.* To quake with fear, or aversion. pr. par. *shuddering;* past, *shuddered:* s. *shudder.*

SHUF'FLE. *v.* To throw into disorder; to play mean tricks; to evade. pr. par. *shuffling;* past, *shuffled;* s. *shuffle, shuffler.*

SHUN. *v.* To avoid; to endeavour to escape. pr. par. *shunning;* past, *shunned.*

SHUT. *v.* To close; to confine; to exclude. pr. par. *shutting;* past, *shut.* s. *shutter.*

SHUT'TLE. *s.* An instrument used in weaving.

SHUT'TLECOCK. *s.* A cork stuck with feathers, and beaten backward and forward.

SHY. *adj.* Wary, cautious, reserved. adv. *shyly;* s. *shyness.*

SIB'ILANT. *adj.* Hissing. s. *sibilation.*

SIB'YL. *s.* A prophetess amongst the pagans. adj. *sibylline.*

SICCA'TION. *s.* The act of drying.

SICK. *adj.* Afflicted with disease; disgusted. v. *sicken;* pr. par. *sickening;* past, *sickened:* s. *sickliness, sickness:* adv. and adj. *sickly.*

SICK'LE. *s.* A reaping-hook.

SIDE. *s.* The parts of animals fortified by the ribs; edge; party; faction. adj. *side:* v. *side;* pr. par. *siding;* past, *sided.*

SIDE'BOARD. *s.* The side-table on which conveniences are placed.

SIDE'LONG. *adj.* Lateral, oblique. adv. *sidelong.*

SI'DERAL, SIDE'REAL. *adj.* Starry, astral.

SIDE'SADDLE. *s.* A woman's saddle.

SIDE'WAYS, SIDE'WISE. *adv.* Laterally; on one side.

SI'DLE. *v.* To go with the side foremost pr. par. *sidling;* past, *sidled.*

SIEGE. *s.* The act of besetting a fortified place.

SIEVE. *s* A bolter; hair, &c. strained upon a hoop, to sift through.

SIFT. *v.* To separate by a sieve. pr. par. *sifting;* past, *sifted:* s. *sifter.*

SIGH. *v.* To emit the breath audibly, as in grief. pr. par. *sighing;* past, *sighed:* s. *sigh.*

SIGHT. *s.* Perception by the eye; view, &c. adj. *sightless, sightly;* s. *sightliness.*

SIGN. *s.* A token; that by which any thing is shown; a constellation. v. *sign;* pr. par. *signing;* past, *signed:* s. *signer.*

SIG'NAL. *s.* Notice given by a sign, a sign that gives notice. adj. *signal.*

SIG'NAL. *adj.* Eminent; remarkable. v. *signalize;* pr. par. *signalizing* past, *signalized:* adv. *signally.*

SIG'NATURE. *s.* A sign or mark, amongst printers, a letter or number, to distinguish different sheets

SIG'NET. *s.* A seal.

SIGNIF'ICANT. *adj.* Expressive, betokening, important. adv. *significantly:* s. *significance.*

SIG'NIFY. *v.* To declare by some sign or token; to mean; to express. pr. par. *signifying;* past, *signified:* s. *signification:* adj *significative.*

SI'GNIOR. *s.* A title of honour amongst the Italians; with the Turks, the *grand signior* is the emperor.

SI'LENCE. *s.* Stillness, taciturnity, secrecy. v. *silence;* pr. par. *silencing;* past, *silenced:* adj. *silent:* adv. *silently.*

SILI'CIOUS. *adj.* Partaking of the nature of flint.

SILK. *s.* The thread of a certain worm; the cloth made from the thread. adj. *silken, silky:* s. *silkiness, silkworm.*

SILK'MERCER. *s.* A dealer in silk.

SILL. *s.* The foot of a door-case, &c.

SIL'LABUB. *s.* A liquor made of milk and wine, or cider and sugar.

SIL'LY. *adj.* Foolish, simple, weak adv *sillily* s. *silliness.*

336

SIL'VAN *adj.* Woody: full of woods; belonging to a wood.

SIL'VER. *s.* One of the metals. *v. silver;* pr. par. *silvering;* past, *silvered:* adj. *silvery:* s. *silversmith.*

SIM'ILAR *adj.* Resembling. s. *similarity,* pl. *similarities:* adv. *similarly.*

SIM'ILE. *s.* A comparison by which any thing is illustrated. pronounced *sim'-il-e.*

SIMIL'ITUDE. *s.* Likeness, resemblance, comparison.

SIM'MER. *v.* To boil gently. pr. par. *simmering;* past, *simmered.*

SI'MONY. *s.* The crime of buying or selling church preferments. pl. *simonies:* adj. *simoniacal:* s. *simoniac:* adv. *simoniacally.*

SIM'PER. *v.* To smile foolishly. pr. par. *simpering;* past, *simpered:* s. *simper:* adv. *simperingly.*

SIM'PLE. *adj.* Single, uncompounded, artless, harmless, silly. s. *simple, simplicity:* adv. *simply.*

SIM'PLETON. *s.* A silly person.

SIM'PLIFY. *v.* To render plain; to bring back to simplicity. pr. par. *simplifying;* past, *simplified:* s. *simplification.*

SIM'ULATE. *v.* To feign; to counterfeit. pr. par. *simulating;* past, *simulated:* s. *simulation.*

SIMULTA'NEOUS. *adj.* Acting together; existing at the same time. adv. *simultaneously.*

SIN. *s.* An act against the laws of God. *v. sin;* pr. par. *sinning;* past, *sinned:* adj. *sinful:* adv. *sinfully:* s. *sinfulness, sinner.*

SINCE. *conj.* Because that, from the time that. prep. *since.*

SINCE'RE. *adj.* Candid, honest, uncorrupt. adv. *sincerely:* s. *sincerity.*

SINE. *s.* A term in geometry.

SI'NECURE. *s.* An office which yields revenue, without any employment.

SIN'EW. *s.* A tendon; the ligament by which the joints are moved. adj. *sinewed, sinewy.*

SING. *v.* To form the voice to melody; to articulate musically. pr. par. *singing;* past, *sung:* s. *singer, singing.*

SINGE. *v.* To scorch, to burn slightly or superficially. pr. par. *singing,* past, *singed:* s. *singe.*

SIN'GLE. *adj.* One; not double particular; alone. *v. single;* pr par. *singling;* past, *singled:* s *singleness:* adv. *singly.*

SING'SONG. *s.* A contemptuous expression, for bad singing.

SING'ULAR. *adj.* Single; not plural, particular; rare; remarkable. s. *singularity,* pl. *singularities:* adv. *singularly.*

SIN'ISTER. *adj.* Being on the left hand; deceitful; bad. adj. *sinistrous:* adv. *sinistrously.*

SINK. *v.* To fall gradually; to decline. pr. par. *sinking;* past, *sunk.*

SINK. *s.* A drain; a place of filth.

SIN'UATE. *v.* To bend in and out. pr. par. *sinuating;* past, *sinuated.* s. *sinuation, sinuosity,* pl. *sinuosities:* adj. *sinuous.*

SIP. *v.* To drink by small draughts. pr. par. *sipping;* past, *sipped:* s. *sip.*

SI'PHON, SY'PHON. *s.* A pipe through which liquors are conveyed.

SIR. *s.* A word of respect, to men, a title applied to a knight.

SIRE. *s.* A father; a title given to a monarch.

SI'REN. *s.* A goddess who enticed men by singing.

SIR'LOIN. *s.* The loin of beef.

SIR'NAME. *s.* The family name.

SIROC'CO. *s.* The south-east or Syrian wind.

SIR'RAH. *s.* An appellation of reproach and insult.

SIR'UP, SYR'UP. *s.* A vegetable juice, boiled with sugar.

SIS'TER. *s.* A woman born of the same parents. adj. *sisterly:* s. *sisterhood.*

SIS'TER-IN-LAW. *s.* A husband or wife's sister.

SIT. *v.* To repose on a seat; to

incubate. pr. par. *sitting;* past, *sat.*
SITE. *s.* Situation; local position.
SITUA'TION. *s.* Position, condition, state.
SIX. *adj.* Twice three. ordinal adj. *sixth:* adv. *sixthly.*
SIXTEEN'. *adj.* Six and ten. ordinal adj. *sixteenth.*
SIX'TY. *adj.* Six times ten. ordinal adj. *sixtieth.*
SIZE. *s.* Bulk; comparative magnitude; any viscous or glutinous substance. v. *size;* pr. par. *sizing;* past, *sized.*
SIZ'ER, SER'VITOR. *s.* A certain rank of students in the university of Cambridge, and in some other colleges.
SKATE. *s.* A sort of shoe armed with iron, for sliding on the ice. v. *skate;* pr. par. *skating;* past, *skated:* s. *skater.*
SKATE. *s.* A flat fish.
SKEIN. *s.* A knot of thread or silk, wound and doubled.
SKEL'ETON. *s.* Bones preserved, as in their natural situation.
SKEP. *s.* A little coniform house for bees.
SKEP'TIC, SCEP'TIC. *s.* One who assents or believes only after seeing unquestionable evidence. adj. *skeptical:* adv. *skeptically:* s. *skepticism.*
SKETCH. *v.* To draw a plan, by tracing the outline. pr. par. *sketching;* past, *sketched:* s. *sketch.*
SKEW'ER. *s.* A wooden or iron pin, used to keep meat in form. v. *skewer;* pr. par. *skewering;* past, *skewered.*
SKIFF. *s.* A small, light boat.
SKILL. *s.* Knowledge of any practice or art. adj. *skilful, skilled:* adv. *skilfully:* s. *skilfulness.*
SKIL'LET. *s.* A small kettle or boiler.
SKIM. *v.* To clear off from the upper part; to glide along. pr. par. *skimming,* past, *skimmed:* s. *skimmer, scum.*

SKIMMILK'. *s.* Milk from which the cream has been taken.
SKIN. *s.* The natural covering of the flesh; a hide; a pelt; a husk. v *skin;* pr. par. *skinning;* past, *skinned:* s. *skinner, skinniness:* adj. *skinny.*
SKIN'FLINT. *s.* A niggardly person: a very low word.
SKIP. *v.* To pass by quick leaps; to bound lightly and joyfully. pr. par. *skipping;* past, *skipped:* s. *skip, skipper.*
SKIP'PER. *s.* The captain of a small vessel; a kind of worm.
SKIR'MISH. *s.* A slight fight; a contest. v. *skirmish;* pr. par. *skirmishing;* past, *skirmished:* s. *skirmisher.*
SKIRT. *s.* That part of a garment which hangs loose below the waist; edge; margin. v. *skirt;* pr. par *skirting;* past, *skirted.*
SKIT'TISH. *adj.* Shy; easily frightened; volatile. adv. *skittishly:* s. *skittishness.*
SKIT'TLES. *s.* Ninepins.
SKREEN. *s.* A riddle or coarse sieve; a shade; shelter or concealment. v. *skreen;* pr. par. *skreening;* past, *skreened.*
SKULK. *v.* To hide; to lurk in fear or malice. pr. par. *skulking;* past, *skulked.*
SKULL. *s.* The bone that encloses the head.
SKULL'CAP. *s.* A headpiece.
SKY. *s.* The region which appears to surround this earth beyond the atmosphere; the heavens. pl. *skies* adj. *skycoloured:* s. *skylark, skylight, skyrocket.*
SLAB. *s.* A plane of stone; the outside piece of timber, when sawed into boards.
SLAB'BER. *v.* To daub when suppling; to smear with spittle. pr. par. *slabbering;* past, *slabbered* s. *slabberer.*
SLAB'BY. *adj.* Thick; viscous; wet.
SLACK. *adj.* Not tense; relaxed,

loose; remiss. v. *slack, slacken;* pr. par. *slacking, slackening;* past, *slacked, slackened:* adv. *slackly:* s. *slackness.*

SLACK. *s.* Coal broken into small parts.

SLAIN. The past par. of the v. *to slay.*

SLAKE. *v.* To quench; to extinguish. pr. par. *slaking;* past, *slaked.*

SLAM. *v.* To push violently; to shut rudely. pr. par. *slamming;* past, *slammed.*

SLAM'KIN, SHAM'MERKIN. *s.* A slatternly woman; a trollop.

SLAN'DER. *v.* To censure falsely; to scandalize. pr. par. *slandering;* past, *slandered:* s. *slander, slanderer, slanderousness:* adj. *slanderous:* adv. *slanderously.*

SLANG. *s.* Vulgar cant.

SLANT. *adj.* Oblique; not perpendicular. v. *slant;* pr. par. *slanting;* past, *slanted:* adv. *slantwise.*

SLAP. *s.* A blow with the open hand. v. *slap;* pr. par. *slapping;* past, *slapped:* adv. *slapdash.*

SLASH. *v.* To cut; to lash; to cut with long cuts. pr. par. *slashing;* past, *slashed:* s. *slash, slasher.*

SLATE. *s.* A kind of flat, fissile stone. v. *slate;* pr. par. *slating;* past, *slated:* s. *slater.*

SLATTERN. *s.* A slovenly woman.

SLAUGHT'ER. *s.* Massacre; act of slaying. v. *slaughter;* pr. par. *slaughtering;* past, *slaughtered:* s. *slaughterer, slaughter-house.*

SLAVE. *s.* One held to involuntary servitude. s. *slavery, slavishness:* adj. *slavish:* adv. *slavishly.*

SLAV'ER. *s.* Spittle running from the mouth. v. *slaver;* pr. par. *slavering;* past, *slavered:* s. *slaverer.*

SLAY. *v.* To kill; to butcher. pr. par. *slaying:* past, *slayed:* s. *slayer.*

SLED, SLEDGE. *s.* A carriage drawn without wheels.

SLEDGE. *s.* A smith's large hammer.

SLEEK. *adj.* Smooth, glossy. adv. *sleekly:* s. *sleekness.*

SLEEP. *v.* To take rest, by suspension of the mental and corporal powers; to be motionless. pr. par. *sleeping;* past, *slept:* s. *sleep, sleeper, sleepiness, sleeplessness:* adj. *sleepless, sleepy.*

SLEET. *s.* A kind of smooth, small hail or snow. v. *sleet;* pr. par. *sleeting;* past, *sleeted:* adj. *sleety.*

SLEEVE. *s.* The part of a garment that covers the arms.

SLEIGHT. *s.* Artful trick; dextrous practice.

SLEN'DER. *adj.* Thin; small; not bulky; sparing. adv. *slenderly:* s. *slenderness.*

SLEPT. Pret. and past par. of the v. *to sleep.*

SLEW. Pret. of the v. *to slay.*

SLEY. *s.* The frame which contains a weaver's reed.

SLICE. *v.* To cut into flat pieces. pr. par. *slicing;* past, *sliced:* s. *slice.*

SLIDE. *v.* To pass along smoothly; to slip; to glide. pr. par. *sliding,* past, *slid, slidden:* s. *slide, slider.*

SLIGHT. *adj.* Small, weak, worthless. s. *slightness:* adv. *slightly.*

SLIGHT. *s.* Neglect; contempt; act of scorn; artifice. v. *slight;* pr. par. *slighting;* past, *slighted:* s *slighter:* adv. *slightingly.*

SLIM. *adj.* Slender, weak, slight. *s slimness.*

SLIME. *s.* Viscous mire; any glutinous substance. s. *sliminess:* adj *slimy.*

SLING. *s.* A missive weapon, made by a strap and two strings; a throw; a kind of hanging bandage. v. *sling,* pr. par. *slinging;* past, *slung:* s. *slinger.*

SLINK. *v.* To steal; to sneak out of the way. pr. par. *slinking;* past, *slunk:* adj. *slink,* produced before its time; unfed; applied to the young of a beast.

SLIP. *v.* To slide; to glide; to sneak; to make a false step. pr. par. *slipping;* past, *slipped:* s. *slip.*

SLIPPER. *s.* A loose shoe. adj. *slippered.*

SLIPPERY. *adj.* Smooth, glib; not

339

affording firm footing. s. *slipperiness*.

SLIP'PY. adj. Slippery; easily sliding. s. *slippiness*.

SLIP'SHOD. adj. Having the shoes not pulled up at the heels.

SLIT. v. To cut longwise. pr. par. *slitting*; past, *slit:* s. *slit*.

SLI'VER. s. A branch torn off.

SLOATS. s. The under parts of a cart.

SLOB'BER. v. To slaver; to spill upon; to slabber. pr. par. *slobbering*; past, *slobbered:* s. *slobberer:* adj. *slobbery*.

SLOE. s. The fruit of the black thorn.

SLOOP. s. A small ship, commonly with one mast; *sloop of war*, a small frigate, with three masts.

SLOP. v. To drink grossly and greedily; to soil by spilling liquor. pr. par. *slopping;* past, *slopped:* s. *slop:* adj. *sloppy*.

SLOP'-SHOP. s. A place where coarse, ready-made clothes are sold.

SLOPE. s. An oblique direction; declivity. v. *slope;* pr. par. *sloping;* past, *sloped:* adv. *slopingly*.

SLOTH. s. Slowness, laziness, idleness; a kind of stupid animal. adj. *slothful:* adv. *slothfully:* s. *slothfulness*.

SLOUCH. s. An idle fellow; an ungainly, clownish gait or manner. v. *slouch;* pr. par. *slouching;* past, *slouched*.

SLOUGH. s. A deep miry place.

SLOV'EN. s. One dirtily or carelessly dressed. s. *slovenliness:* adj. and adv. *slovenly*.

SLOW. adj. Not swift; tardy. adv. *slowly:* s. *slowness*.

SLUDGE. s. Mire.

SLUG. s. A kind of snail; a piece of shapeless metal, to shoot from a gun. adj. *sluggish:* adv. *sluggishly:* s. *sluggishness*.

SLUICE. s. A water-gate.

SLUM'BER. v. To sleep lightly; to sleep; to repose. pr. par. *slumbering;* past, *slumbered:* s. *slumber, slumberer*.

SLUNG. Pret. and past par. of the v. *to sling*.

SLUNK. Pret. and past par. of the v. *to slink*.

SLUR. s. A faint reproach; a slight disgrace; a slight : in musi:, a mark denoting a connexion of one note with another. v. *slur;* pr. par. *slurring;* past, *slurred*.

SLUT. s. A dirty woman. adj. *sluttish:* adv. *sluttishly:* s. *sluttishness*.

SLY. adj. Meanly artful; secretly insidious; cunning. adv. *slyly:* s *slyness*.

SMACK. v. To have a taste, or savour; to make a noise by separation of the lips strongly pressed together. pr. par. *smacking*, past *smacked:* s. *smack*.

SMACK. s. A kind of ship.

SMALL. adj. Little, slender, minute s. *smallness*.

SMALL'CRAFT. s. Vessels less than ships.

SMALL'POX. s. A kind of eruptive distemper.

SMALTS. s. A blue substance, used by bleachers.

SMART. adj. Pungent, quick, acute, brisk. v. *smart;* pr. par. *smarting*, past, *smarted:* s. *smart, smartness*. adv. *smartly*.

SMAT'TER, SMAT'TERING. s. Superficial knowledge. s. *smatterer*.

SMEAR. v. To overspread with something viscous and adhesive; to soil. pr. par. *smearing;* past, *smeared:* adj. *smeary*.

SMELL. v. To perceive by the nose. pr. par. *smelling;* past, *smelled:* s *smell, smeller*.

SMELT. v. To melt ore, so as to extract the metal. pr. par. *smelting;* past, *smelted:* s. *smelter*.

SMILE. v. To contract the face with pleasure. pr. par. *smiling;* past, *smiled:* s. *smile:* adv. *smilingly*.

SMIRK. v. To look affectedly soft or kind. pr. par. *smirking;* past, *smirked*.

SMITE. v. To strike; to kill; to

340

destroy; to blast. pr. par. *smiting;* past, *smitten:* s. *smile, smiter.*

SMITH. *s.* One who works in metals. s. *smithery, smithy.*

SMIT'TEN. Past par. of the v. *to smite.*

SMOCK. *s.* The under garment of a woman; a shift.

SMOCK'FACED. adj. Beardless, maidenly, pale.

SMOKE. *s.* The visible effluvium, or sooty exhalation, from any thing burning. v. *smoke;* pr. par. *smoking;* past, *smoked:* s. *smoker, smokiness:* adj. *smokeless, smoky.*

SMOOTH. adj. Even on the surface; level. v. *smooth;* pr. par. *smoothing;* past, *smoothed:* adv. *smoothly:* s. *smoothness.*

SMOOTH'FACED. adj. Mild looking; having a smooth air.

SMOTE. *v.* Pret. of the v. *to smite.*

SMOTH'ER. *v.* To suffocate. pr. par. *smothering;* past, *smothered.*

SMOUL'DERING. par. adj. Burning and smoking without vent.

SMUG. adj. Nice; spruce; dressed with affectation of niceness. s. *smugness.*

SMUG'GLE. *v.* To import or export goods, without paying the customs. pr. par. *smuggling;* past, *smuggled:* s. *smuggler.*

SMUT. *s.* A spot made with soot or coal; obscenity. v. *smut;* pr. par. *smutting;* past, *smutted:* adv. *smuttily:* s. *smuttiness:* adj. *smutty.*

SNACK. *s.* A share; a part taken by compact; a slight, hasty repast.

SNAF'FLE. *s.* A bridle which crosses the nose.

SNAG. *s.* A jag, or short protuberance; in the United States, the trunk of a tree, lying in a river, with its top towards the stream.

SNAIL. *s.* A kind of slimy animal.

SNAKE. *s.* A species of serpent.

SNAKE'ROOT. *s.* A species of plant.

SNAP. *v.* To break at once; to break short; to bite suddenly. pr. par. *snapping;* past, *snapped:* s. *snap,*

snapper, snappishness: adj. *snappish:* adv. *snappishly.*

SNAP'DRAGON. *s.* A kind of plant.

SNARE. *s.* A gin, a net, a trap, a noose. v. *snare;* pr. par. *snaring;* past, *snared:* s. *snarer.*

SNARL. *v.* To growl as an angry animal; to gnarl; to entangle. pr. par. *snarling;* past, *snarled:* s. *snarler.*

SNATCH. *v.* To seize hastily; to catch eagerly. pr. par. *snatching,* past, *snatched:* s. *snatch, snatcher.*

SNEAK. *v.* To creep slyly; to come or go as if afraid to be seen; to hide. pr. par. *sneaking;* past, *sneaked:* adj. *sneaking:* adv. *sneakingly.*

SNECK. *s.* The latch of a door.

SNEER. *v.* To show contempt by looks; to insinuate contempt by covert expressions. pr. par. *sneering;* past, *sneered:* s. *sneer, sneerer:* adv. *sneeringly.*

SNEEZE. *v.* To emit wind audibly by the nose. pr. par. *sneezing;* past, *sneezed:* s. *sneeze.*

SNIP. *v.* To cut at once with scissors. pr. par. *snipping;* past, *snipped:* s. *snip, snipper.*

SNIPE. *s.* A small fowl of game.

SNIV'EL. *v.* To run at the nose; to cry as a child. pr. par. *sniveling,* past, *sniveled:* s. *sniveler.*

SNORE. *v.* To breathe hard through the nose. pr. par. *snoring;* past, *snored:* s. *snore, snorer.*

SNORT. *v.* To blow through the nose, as a high-mettled horse. pr. par. *snorting;* past, *snorted:* s. *snorter.*

SNOUT. *s.* The nose of a beast; the nosle. adj. *snouted.*

SNOW. *s.* Small particles of water, frozen before they unite into drops. v. *snow;* pr. par. *snowing;* past, *snowed:* adj. *snowy:* s. *snowball.*

SNOW'DROP. *s.* An early flower.

SNUB. *s.* A jag, a snag, a knot in wood.

SNUB'NOSED. adj. Having a flat or short nose.

SNUFF. *s.* The burnt wick of a

candle; powdered tobacco, to be taken up the nose. v. *snuff;* pr. par. *snuffing;* past, *snuffed:* s. *snuffer, snuffers.* adj. *snuffy.*

SNUF'FLE. *v.* To speak or breathe hard through the nose. pr. par. *snuffling;* past, *snuffled;* s. *snuffler.*

SNUG. *adj.* Close; free from any inconvenience. adv. *snugly:* s. *snugness.*

SO. One of the adverbs.

SOAK. *v.* To steep, to drench. pr. par. *soaking;* past, *soaked.*

SOAP. *s.* A substance used in washing. adj. *soapy:* s. *soapiness, soap-boiler.*

SOAR. *v.* To fly aloft; to tower. pr. par. *soaring;* past, *soared:* s. *soar.*

SOB. *v.* To sigh convulsively, in weeping, &c. pr. par. *sobbing;* past, *sobbed:* s. *sob.*

SO'BER. *adj.* Temperate; not drunk; serious; solemn. adv. *soberly:* s. *sobriety.*

SO'CIABLE. *adj.* Inclined to company; friendly; familiar. s. *sociability,* pl. *sociabilities, sociableness:* adv. *sociably.*

SO'CIAL. *adj.* Fit for society; companionable. s. *sociality:* adv. *socially.*

SOCI'ETY. *s.* Union of many in one general interest; community; company. pl. *societies.*

SOCIN'IAN. *s.* A follower of the doctrines of Socinus. adj. *socinian:* s. *socinianism.*

SOCK. *s.* Something put between the foot and shoe; the shoe of the ancient comic actors.

SOCK'ET. *s.* Any hollow pipe, that receives something inserted; the receptacle of the eye.

SOCRATIC', SOCRAT'ICAL. *adj.* After the manner or doctrine of Socrates.

SOD. *s.* A turf, a clod.

SO'DA. *s.* A fixed alkali.

SOD'DEN. Past par. of the v. *to seethe.*

SOEV'ER. One of the adverbs.

SO'FA *s.* A kind of seat.

SOFT. *adj.* Not hard; ductile; simple; gentle. v. *soften;* (pronounced *sof''-n;*) pr. par. *softening;* past, *softened:* adv. *softly:* s. *softener, softness.*

SOHO'. *int.* A form of calling from a distant place.

SOIL. *v.* To foul, to pollute, to sully. pr. par. *soiling;* past, *soiled* s. *soil.*

SOIL. *s.* Ground; earth, considered in relation to its vegetative qualities.

SOJOURN'. *v.* To dwell any where for a time. pr. par. *sojourning;* past, *sojourned:* s. *so'journ, so'journer.*

SOL'ACE. *v.* To comfort, to cheer pr. par. *solacing;* past, *solaced:* s *solace.*

SOL'ANDER. *s.* A disease in horses.

SO'LAR. *adj.* Relating or belonging to the sun.

SOLD. Pret. and past par. of the v. *to sell.*

SOLD'ER. *v.* To unite or fasten with metallic cement. pronounced *sod'der.* pr. par. *soldering;* past, *soldered:* s. *solder, solderer.*

SOL'DIER. *s.* One who fights for pay, a warrior. adj. *soldierlike, soldierly* s. *soldiery.*

SOLE. *s.* The bottom of the foot; the bottom of the shoe; a kind of fish. v. *sole;* pr. par. *soling;* past, *soled.*

SOLE. *adj.* Single; only. adv. *solely.*

SO'LECISM. *s.* An impropriety in language.

SOL'EMN. *adj.* Religiously grave, awful; formal. s. *solemnity,* pl. *so-lemnities:* adv. *solemnly.*

SOL'EMNIZE. *v.* To dignify by particular formalities; to celebrate. pr. par. *solemnizing:* past, *solemnized:* s. *solemnization.*

SOLI'CIT. *v.* To importune; to implore; to ask. pr. par. *soliciting,* past, *solicited:* s. *solicitation, solicitor.*

SOLI'CITOUS. *adj.* Anxious, care-

SOL—SON

ful, concerned. adv. *solicitously:* s. *solicitude.*

SOL'ID. adj. Not fluid; compact; strong. s. *solid, solidity,* pl. *solidities:* adv. *solidly.*

SOLIDUNG'ULOUS. adj. Wholehoofed.

SOLIL'OQUY. s. A discourse made by one, in solitude, to himself. pl. *soliloquies:* v. *soliloquize;* pr. par. *soliloquizing;* past, *soliloquized.*

SOL'IPEDE. s. An animal whose feet are not cloven.

SOL'ITARY. adj. Living alone; retired; single. adv. *solitarily:* s. *solitude.*

SO'LO. s. A tune played or sung by one person.

SOL'STICE. s. The tropical point of the sun. adj. *solstitial.*

SOL'UBLE. adj. Capable of dissolution or separation. s. *solubility,* pl. *solubilities.*

SOLU'TION. s. The act of solving; separation; explanation. adj. *solutive.*

SOLVE. v. To clear; to explain. pr. par. *solving;* past, *solved:* adj. *solvable.*

SOL'VENT. adj. Having the power to cause solution; able to pay debts contracted.

SOM'BRE. adj. Dark, gloomy.

SOME. adj. More or less; noting an indeterminate quantity, or thing. s. *somebody, something:* adv. *sometime, somewhere.*

SOM'ERSET. s. A leap by which a jumper throws himself from a height, and turns over his head.

SOMNAM'BULIST. s. One who walks in his sleep. s. *somnamoulism.*

SOMNIF'EROUS. adj. Causing sleep. adj. *somnific.*

SOM'NOLENCE, SOM'NOLENCY. s. Sleepiness, inclination to sleep. adj. *somnolent.*

SON. s. A male child; a male descendant.

SONA'TA s. A tune.

SON—SOR

SON'-IN-LAW. s. A man married to one's daughter.

SONG. s. A poem to be modulated by the voice. s. *songster, songstress,* pl. *songstresses.*

SONIF'EROUS. adj. Giving or bringing sound.

SON'NET. s. A short poem. s. *sonnetteer.*

SO'NOROUS. adj. Loud-sounding. adv. *sonorously:* s. *sonorousness:* adj. *sonorific.*

SOON. adv. Before long time be passed; early.

SOOT. s. Condensed or embodied smoke. s. *sootiness:* adj. *sooty.*

SOOTH. s. Truth, reality.

SOOTHE. v. To flatter, to calm, to soften. pr. par. *soothing;* past, *soothed:* s. *soother:* adv. *soothingly.*

SOOTH'SAY. v. To predict, to foretel. pr. par. *soothsaying;* past, *soothsaid:* s. *soothsayer.*

SOP. s. Any thing steeped in liquor. v. *sop;* pr. par. *sopping;* past, *sopped.*

SO'PHIST. s. A professor of philosophy; a subtle, caviling disputer. s. *sophism, sophister, sophistry:* adj. *sophistic, sophistical:* adv. *sophistically.*

SOPHIS'TICATE. v. To adulterate; to debase. pr. par. *sophisticating;* past, *sophisticated:* s. *sophistication, sophisticator.*

SOPORIF'EROUS, SOPORIF'IC. adj Causing sleep, narcotic.

SOR'CERER. s. A conjurer, an enchanter, a magician. fem. *sorceress,* pl. *sorceresses:* s. *sorcery,* pl *sorceries.*

SOR'DID. adj. Foul, gross, filthy, mean. adv. *sordidly:* s. *sordidness.*

SORE. s. A place tender and painful; an ulcer. adj. *sore:* adv. *sorely:* s. *soreness.*

SOROR'OCIDE. s. The murder of a sister; one who commits the murder.

SOR'REL. s. A species of acid plant a reddish colour. adj. *sorrel.*

343

SOR'RILY. adv. Meanly, poorly, despicably. s. sorriness.
SOR'ROW. v. To grieve; to be sad. pr. par. sorrowing; past, sorrowed: s. sorrow, sorrowfulness: adj. sorrowful: adv. sorrowfully.
SOR'RY. adj. Grieved for something past; melancholy; vile.
SORT. s. A kind; a species. v. sort; pr. par. sorting; past, sorted.
SOT. s. A drunkard; a dolt; a wretch stupified by drinking. adj. sottish: adv. sottishly: s. sottishness.
SOUCHONG'. s. A kind of tea.
SOUGHT. Pret. and past par. of the v. to seek.
SOUL. s. The immaterial and immortal spirit of man. adj. soulless.
SOUND. adj. Healthy; salutary; stout; unbroken. adv. soundly: s. soundness.
SOUND. s. A shallow sea, such as may be sounded. v. sound; pr. par. sounding; past, sounded.
SOUND. s. Any thing audible; a noise. v. sound; pr. par. sounding; past, sounded.
SOUND'BOARD. s. The board which propagates the sound in organs, &c.
SOUP. s. Strong decoction of flesh.
SOUR. adj. Acid, austere. v. sour; pr. par. souring; past, soured: adj. sourish: adv. sourly: s. sourness.
SOURCE. s. Spring, fountain, original.
SOUS. s. A French penny. pronounced soo.
SOUSE. s. Pickle made of salt and water. v. souse; pr. par. sousing; past, soused.
SOUSE. v. To fall with violence. pr. par. sousing; past, soused: adv. souse.
SOUTH. s. One of the four cardinal points, opposite the north. adj. south, southerly, southern, southernmost: adv. southward.
SOUTHEAST'. s. The point midway between the east and south.
SOUTHWEST' s. The point midway between the south and west.

SOV'EREIGN. adj. Supreme in power. s. sovereign, sovereignty, pl sovereignties.
SOW. s. A female pig.
SOW. v. To scatter seed. pr. par sowing; past, sowed, sown: s. sower
SOW'INS. s. Flummery.
SPACE. s. Room; local extension, quantity of time.
SPA'CIOUS. adj. Wide, extensive. roomy. adv. spaciously: s. spaciousness.
SPADE. s. An instrument for digging.
SPAN. s. Nine inches; any short duration. v. span; pr. par. spanning; past, spanned.
SPAN'GLE. s. A small plate of shining metal. v. spangle; pr. par. spangling; past, spangled.
SPAN'IEL. s. A kind of dog.
SPAN'ISH. s. The language or people of Spain.
SPANK. v. To strike with the open hand. pr. par. spanking; past, spanked.
SPANK'ER. s. A person that takes long steps with agility.
SPAR. s. A small beam; a sparkling mineral.
SPAR. v. To fight for amusement. pr. par. sparring; past, sparred.
SPAR'ABLE. s. A small nail.
SPARE. v. To use frugally; not to waste; to have unemployed; to do without. pr. par. sparing; past, spared: adj. spare: adv. sparely, sparingly: s. spareness.
SPARE'RIB. s. Ribs having spare or little flesh.
SPARGEFAC'TION. s. The act of sprinkling.
SPARK. s. A small particle of fire. v. spark; pr. par. sparking; past, sparked.
SPARK'LE. v. To emit sparks; to issue in sparks; to shine. pr. par. sparkling; past, sparkled · s. sparkle, sparkler, sparklingness: a Iv. sparklingly.
SPAR'ROW. s. A small bird.

SPAR'ROWHAWK. *s.* A kind of small hawk.

SPARSE. *adj.* Scattered; far apart. *adv. sparsely.*

SPASM. *s.* Convulsion; violent and involuntary contraction. *adj. spasmodic.*

SPAT'TER. *v.* To sprinkle with dirt, or any thing offensive. *pr. par. spattering; past, spattered.*

SPAT'TERDASHES. *s.* Coverings for the legs.

SPAV'IN. *s.* A disease in the limbs of horses. *adj. spavined.*

SPAW. *s.* A mineral water; the place famous for mineral water.

SPAWN. *s.* The eggs of fish or frogs. *v. spawn; pr. par. spawning; past, spawned: s. spawner.*

SPEAK. *v.* To utter articulate sounds; to express thoughts by words. *pr. par. speaking; past, spoken: s. speaker.*

SPEAR. *s.* A long pointed weapon; a lance. *v. spear; pr. par. spearing; past, speared.*

SPEAR'GRASS. *s.* Long, stiff grass.

SPEAR'MINT. *s.* A species of mint.

SPE'CIAL. *adj.* Noting a sort or species; peculiar; designed for a particular purpose. *s. speciality, specialty: adv. specially.*

SPE'CIES. *s.* A sort; a single order of beings.

SPECIF'IC, SPECIF'ICAL. *adj.* That which distinguishes one sort from another; appropriated to the cure of some particular distemper. *s. specific. adv. specifically.*

SPE'CIFY. *v.* To particularize; to show by some particular marks of distinction. *pr. par. specifying; past, specified: s. specification.*

SPE'CIMEN. *s.* A sample.

SPE'CIOUS. *adj.* Showy; plausible, false. *adv. speciously: s. speciousness.*

SPECK. *s.* A small discoloration; a spot. *v. speckle; pr. par. speckling; past, speckled: s. speckle, speckledness.*

SPEC'TACLE. *s.* A show; any thing exhibited as eminently remarkable. *adj. spectacular.*

SPEC'TACLES. *s.* Glasses to assist the sight. *adj. spectacled.*

SPECTA'TOR. *s.* A looker-on; a beholder.

SPEC'TRE. *s.* An apparition.

SPEC'TRUM. *s.* An image; a visible form. Latin pl. *spectra.*

SPEC'ULATE. *v.* To meditate; to contemplate; to look forward. *pr. par. speculating; past, speculated: s. speculation, speculator: adj. speculative: adv. speculatively.*

SPEC'ULUM. *s.* A mirror; a looking-glass; a surgical instrument. Latin pl. *specula: adj. specular.*

SPED. Pret. and past par. of the v. *to speed.*

SPEECH. *s.* Articulate utterance; talk. pl. *speeches: adj. speechless.*

SPEED. *v.* To make haste; to have good success; to aid, &c. *pr. par speeding; past, sped: s. speed, speediness: adv. speedily: adj. speedy.*

SPELL. *s.* A charm; a turn of work.

SPELL. *v.* To form words of letters. *pr. par. spelling; past, spelled.*

SPEL'TER. *s.* A kind of semi-metal.

SPEN'CER. *s.* A coat without skirts.

SPEND. *v.* To consume, to exhaust, to waste. *pr. par. spending; past, spent: s. spender, spendthrift.*

SPERM. *s.* Seed. *adj. spermatic.*

SPERMACET'I. *s.* A particular sort of whale oil.

SPERMOL'OGIST. *s.* One who gathers or treats of seeds.

SPEW. *v.* To vomit; to eject. *pr. par. spewing; past, spewed.*

SPHERE. *s.* A globe; an orb; circuit. *adj. spherical: adv. spherically.*

SPHE'ROID. *s.* A body oblong or oblate, approaching to the form of a sphere. *adj. spheroidal.*

SPHINX. *s.* A famous monster in Egypt, having the face of a virgin, and the body of a lion. pl. *sphinxes.*

SPICE. *s.* An aromatic substance, such as the nutmeg, &c. *v. spice; pr. par. spicing; past, spiced: spicery: adj. spicy.*

345

SPITER. *s* A kind of insect.
SPIG'OT. *s.* A pin or peg, put into a faucet.
SPIKE. *s.* An ear of corn; a long nail of metal. *v. spike*; pr. par. *spiking*; past, *spiked*.
SPIKE'NARD. *s.* A species of balsamic plant.
SPILE. *s.* A peg or pin, to stop a hole in a cask.
SPILL. *v.* To shed; to lose by shedding; to waste. pr. par. *spilling*; past, *spilled*.
SPIN. *v.* To draw out into a thread; to move quickly round. pr. par. *spinning*; past, *spun*: *s. spinner*.
SPIN'ACH, SPIN'AGE. *s.* A species of plant.
SPIN'DLE. *s.* The pin by which a thread is twisted; a long, slender stalk. *v. spindle*; pr. par. *spindling*; past, *spindled*.
SPINE. *s.* The back-bone.
SPINET. *s.* A small harpsichord.
SPI'NOUS, SPI'NY. *adj.* Thorny; full of thorns. *s. spinosity*: adj. *spiniferous*.
SPIN'STER. *s.* A woman that spins; the legal term for a girl or maiden woman.
SPIR'ACLE. *s.* A breathing-hole; a vent.
SPIRE. *s.* A curve line; any thing wreathed or contorted; a steeple. adj. *spiral*: adv. *spirally*.
SPIR'IT. *s.* Breath; an immaterial substance; the soul; an apparition; temper; ardour; sentiment. *v. spirit*; pr. par. *spiriting*; past, *spirited*: adv. *spiritedly*: *s. spiritedness*: adj. *spiritless*.
SPIR'ITUAL. *adj.* Distinct from matter; immaterial; incorporeal; not temporal. s. *spirituality*, pl. *spiritualities*: *v. spiritualize*; pr. par. *spiritualizing*; past, *spiritualized*: adv. *spiritually*.
SPIR'ITUOUS. *adj.* Having the quality of a vinous spirit.
SPIRT. *v.* To spring out in a sudden stream; to stream out by intervals. pr. par. *spirting*; past, *spirted*: s. *spirt*
SPIS'SITUDE. *s.* Grossness, thickness.
SPIT. *s.* A long prong for roasting meat. *v. spit*; pr. par. *spitting*, past, *spitted*.
SPIT. *v.* To eject from the mouth. pr. par. *spitting*; past, *spit*: *s. spitter, spittle*.
SPITE. *s.* Malice; rancour; malevolence. *v. spite*; pr. par. *spiting*, past, *spited*: adj. *spiteful*: adv. *spitefully*: *s. spitefulness*.
SPLASH. *v.* To daub with water or filth. pr. par. *splashing*; past, *splashed*: *s. splash*: adj. *splashy*.
SPLEEN. *s.* The milt; spite; ill-humour. adj. *splenetic*.
SPLEN'DID. *adj.* Showy, magnificent, sumptuous. adv. *splendidly*: *s. splendour*.
SPLICE. *v.* To join the two ends of a rope, without a knot. pr. par. *splicing*; past, *spliced*.
SPLINT. *s.* A thin piece of wood, used by surgeons.
SPLIN'TER. *s.* A fragment, broken with violence; a thin piece of wood. *v. splinter*; pr.par. *splintering*; past, *splintered*.
SPLIT. *v.* To cleave, to divide, to burst asunder. pr. par. *splitting*, past, *split*: *s. splitter*.
SPLUT'TER. *s.* Bustle, tumult. *v. splutter*; pr. par. *spluttering*; past, *spluttered*.
SPOIL. *v.* To rob; to plunder; to corrupt; to make useless. pr. par. *spoiling*; past, *spoiled*: *s. spoil, spoiler*.
SPOKE. *s.* The bar of a wheel.
SPOKE. Pret. of the v. *to speak*: past par. *spoken*.
SPOKES'MAN. *s.* One who speaks for another. pl. *spokesmen*.
SPOLIA'TION. *s.* The act of robbery or privation.
SPON'DEE. *s.* A metrical foot of two long syllables.
SPONGE. *s.* A soft, porous substance, remarkable for absorbing water. *v.*

sponge; pr. par. *sponging*; past, *sponged:* s. *sponger, sponginess:* adj. *spongy.*

SPON'SOR. *s.* A surety; one who makes a promise, or gives security for another.

SPONTA'NEOUS. *adj.* Voluntary, not compelled. adv. *spontaneously:* s. *spontaneousness.*

SPONTOON'. *s.* A kind of pike or halberd.

SPOOL. *s.* A weaver's quill.

SPOON. *s.* A vessel used in eating liquids.

SPOON. *v.* To scud before the wind, in a storm. pr. par. *spooning;* past, *spooned.*

SPORT. *s.* Play, diversion, game. v. *sport;* pr. par. *sporting;* past, *sported:* s. *sporter, sportfulness, sportiveness:* adj. *sportful, sportive:* adv. *sportfully, sportingly, sportively.*

SPORTS'MAN. *s.* One who pursues the recreations of the field. pl. *sportsmen.*

SPOT. *s.* A blot; a taint; a disgrace; a certain place. v. *spot;* pr. par. *spotting;* past, *spotted:* adj. *spotless:* s. *spotlessness, spottiness.*

SPOUSE. *s.* A husband or wife.

SPOUT. *s.* A wooden gutter; a pipe; a cataract. v. *spout;* pr. par. *spouting;* past, *spouted.*

SPRAIN. *v.* To stretch the ligaments of a joint, without dislocation of the bone. pr. par. *spraining;* past, *sprained:* s. *sprain.*

SPRANG. Pret. of the v. *to spring.*

SPRAT. *s.* A small sea-fish.

SPRAWL. *v.* To struggle as in the convulsions of death; to tumble; to creep. pr. par. *sprawling;* past, *sprawled.*

SPRAY. *s.* The extremity of a branch; flying foam of the sea.

SPREAD. *v.* To extend, to expand, to cover by extension. pr. par. *spreading;* past, *spread:* s. *spread, spreader.*

SPRIG *s.* A small branch, a brad or nail without a head. v. *sprig;* pr. par. *sprigging;* past, *sprigged.*

SPRIGHT. *s.* See SPRITE.

SPRIGHT'LY. *adj.* Lively, brisk, gay.

SPRING. *v.* To grow by vegetative power; to arise; to bound; to start; to fire a mine. pr. par. *springing;* past, *sprung.*

SPRING. *s.* A season of the year; elastic force; bound; fountain, &c.

SPRINGE. *s.* A gin, a noose.

SPRING'TIDE. *s.* The high tide at the new moon.

SPRINK'LE. *v.* To disperse in small masses; to scatter in drops. pr. par. *sprinkling;* past, *sprinkled.*

SPRITE. *s.* A spirit; an incorporeal agent.

SPRIT'SAIL. *s.* The sail on a ship's bowsprit.

SPROUT. *v.* To shoot by vegetation; to germinate. pr. par. *sprouting;* past, *sprouted:* s. *sprout.*

SPRUCE. *adj.* Nice; trim; neat, without elegance. adv. *sprucely:* s. *spruceness.*

SPRUCE. *s.* A species of fir.

SPRUNG. Pret. and past par. of the v. *to spring.*

SPUME. *s.* Foam, froth. v. *spume,* pr. par. *spuming;* past, *spumed:* adj. *spumous, spumy.*

SPUN. Pret. and past par. of the v. *to spin.*

SPUNGE. *s.* See SPONGE.

SPUN'GING-HOUSE. *s.* A house to which debtors are taken, before commitment to prison.

SPUNK. *s.* Touchwood; rotten wood spirit; courage. adj. *spunky:* adv. *spunkily.*

SPUR. *s.* A sharp point fixed to the heel; stimulus; incitement. v. *spur;* pr. par. *spurring;* past, *spurred.*

SPU'RIOUS. *adj.* Not genuine, counterfeit. adv. *spuriously:* s. *spuriousness.*

SPURN. *v.* To kick, to reject, to scorn. pr. par. *spurning;* past, *spurned.* s. *spurn, spurner.*

SPUR'RIER. *s.* One who makes spurs.

SPURT. *v.* To fly out with a quick

stream. pr. par. *spurting;* past, *spurted.*

SPUT'TER. *v.* To spit much; to speak hastily and thickly. pr. par. *sputtering;* past, *sputtered:* s. *sputter, sputterer.*

SPY. *s.* One sent to watch the conduct or motions of others. pl. *spies:* v. *spy;* pr. par. *spying;* past, *spied.*

SPY'GLASS. *s.* A small telescope. pl. *spyglasses.*

SQUAB. *adj.* Unfeathered; thick and short. s. *squab:* adj. *squabbish.*

SQUAB'BLE. *v.* To quarrel; to debate peevishly. pr. par. *squabbling;* past, *squabbled:* s. *squabble, squabbler.*

SQUAD. *s.* A company of armed men: generally applied to awkward soldiers.

SQUAD'RON. *s.* A part of an army or fleet.

SQUAL'ID. *adj.* Foul, nasty, filthy. s. *squalidity, squalidness.*

SQUALL. *s.* A sudden gust of wind. adj. *squally.*

SQUALL. *v.* To scream. pr. par. *squalling;* past, *squalled:* s. *squall, squaller.*

SQUA'MOUS. *adj.* Scaly; rough.

SQUAN'DER. *v.* To spend profusely; to waste. pr. par. *squandering;* past, *squandered:* s. *squanderer.*

SQUARE. *adj.* Having right angles: cornered; equal; honest; fair. s. *square, squareness:* v. *square;* pr. par. *squaring;* past, *squared.*

SQUASH. *s.* A kind of plant. pl. *squashes.*

SQUAT. *v.* To sit cowering; to sit close to the ground. pr. par. *squatting;* past, *squatted:* s. *squatter,* one who settles upon land without a title.

SQUAT. *adj.* Cowering down; thick and short.

SQUAW. *s.* The Indian name for woman.

SQUEAK. *v.* To set up a sudden, dolorous cry. pr. par. *squeaking;* past, *squeaked:* s. *squeak, squeaker.*

SQUEAL. *v.* To cry with a shrill, sharp voice. pr. par. *squealing* past, *squealed.*

SQUEA'MISH. *adj.* Having a weak stomach; fastidious; easily disgusted. adv. *squeamishly:* s. *squeamishness.*

SQUEEZE. *v.* To press; to crush between two bodies. pr. par. *squeezing;* past, *squeezed:* s. *squeeze.*

SQUIB. *s.* A small pipe of paper, filled with combustible matter; any sudden flash, a lampoon.

SQUILL. *s.* A kind of plant.

SQUINT. *s.* An oblique look. v. *squint;* pr. par. *squinting;* past, *squinted:* adv. *squintingly.*

SQUIRE. *s.* A gentleman next in rank to a knight; an attendant on a knight. v. *squire;* pr. par. *squiring;* past, *squired.*

SQUIR'REL. *s.* A kind of small quadruped.

SQUIRT. *v.* To throw out in a quick stream. pr. par. *squirting;* past, *squirted:* s. *squirt, squirter.*

STAB. *v.* To pierce with a pointed weapon. pr. par. *stabbing;* past, *stabbed:* s. *stab, stabber.*

STA'BLE. *adj.* Fixed; able to stand; steady; constant. s. *stability,* pl *stabilities.*

STA'BLE. *s.* A house for beasts. v. *stable;* pr. par. *stabling;* past, *stabled.*

STACK. *s.* A large heap of hay, corn, &c. v. *stack;* pr. par. *stacking;* past, *stacked.*

STADT'HOLDER. *s.* Formerly the chief magistrate of the United Provinces.

STAFF. *s.* A support in walking; a prop; an ensign of office. pl *staves.*

STAG. *s.* A male deer.

STAGE. *s.* A raised floor, on which any show is exhibited; a place in which rest is taken on a journey. s. *stagecoach,* pl. *stagecoaches.*

STAG'GER. *v.* To reel; not to stand or walk steadily; to hesitate. pr. par. *staggering;* past, *staggered* s. *staggers,* a disease of horses.

STAG'NATE. *v.* To lie motionless; to have no course or stream. pr. par. *stagnating;* past, *stagnated:* adj. *stagnant:* s. *stagnation.*

STAID. *adj.* Sober, grave, composed. s. *staidness.*

STAIN. *v.* To blot, to spot, to tinge. pr. par. *staining;* past, *stained:* s. *stain, stainer:* adj. *stainless.*

STAIR. *s.* A succession of flat steps, to ascend a building, &c. s. *staircase.*

STAKE. *s.* A post, wager, pledge, hazard. v. *stake;* pr. par. *staking;* past, *staked.*

STALAC'TITES. *s.* Spar in the shape of an icicle. adj. *stalactical.*

STALE. *adj.* Old; long kept; nearly obsolete. s. *staleness.*

STALK. *v.* To walk stately. pr. par. *stalking;* past, *stalked:* s. *stalk, stalker.*

STALK. *s.* A stem.

STALK'INGHORSE. *s.* A horse, real or fictitious, by which a fowler shelters himself from the sight of the game; a mask; a pretence.

STALL. *s.* A crib for horses, &c. a booth. adj. *stallfed.*

STAL'LION. *s.* A horse not castrated.

STAM'INA. *s.* The first principles of any thing; the solids of a human body; the fine threads which grow within the flowers of plants. adj. *stamineous.*

STAM'MER. *v.* To stutter; to falter. pr. par. *stammering;* past, *stammered:* s. *stammerer:* adv. *stammeringly.*

STAMP. *v.* To strike, by pressing the foot hastily downwards; to pound; to impress. pr. par. *stamping;* past, *stamped:* s. *stamp, stamper.*

STANCH, STAUNCH. *adj.* Sound, firm, tight, trusty.

STANCH, STAUNCH. *v.* To stop blood, &c. from running. pr. par. *stanching;* past, *stanched:* adj. *stanch:* s. *stancher.*

STANCH'ION. *s.* A prop, a support.

STAND. *v.* To be upon the feet; to remain erect; to stop; to halt; to endure; to await. pr. par. *standing;* past, *stood:* s. *stand, standing.*

STAN'DARD. *s.* An ensign in war; undoubted authority; a settled rate; a measure.

STAN'DISH. *s.* A case for pens and ink. pl. *standishes.*

STAN'NARY. *s.* A tin mine. pl. *stannaries.*

STAN'ZA. *s.* A subdivision of a poem.

STA'PLE. *s.* A settled mart; material; chief article of commerce; a loop of iron. adj. *staple.*

STA'PLER. *s.* A dealer,—as a *wool stapler.*

STAR. *s.* One of the luminous bodies of the heavens. adj. *starless starred, starry:* s. *stargazer.*

STAR'BOARD. *s.* The right side of a ship, when one stands with one's face towards the bow.

STARCH. *s.* A kind of viscous matter, made of flour or potatoes. *v. starch;* pr. par. *starching;* past, *starched:* s. *starchedness.*

STARE. *v.* To look with wonder &c. pr. par. *staring;* past, *stared.* s. *stare, starer.*

STARK. *adv.* A word used to augment the signification of another word;—as *stark* mad.

STAR'LING. *s.* A kind of bird.

START. *v.* To rise or move suddenly; to alarm; to propose. pr par. *starting;* past, *started:* s. *start.*

START'ING-POST. *s.* The barrier from which a race begins.

STAR'TLE. *v.* To move, on feeling a sudden impression of alarm or terror; to fright. pr. par. *startling,* past, *startled:* s *startle.*

STARVE. *v.* To kill with hunger or cold. pr. par. *starving;* past, *starved.*

STARVELING. *s.* An animal thin and weak for want of nourishment.

STATE. *s.* Condition; circumstances of nature or fortune; a kingdom; a commonwealth; pomp; dignity

STATE. *v.* To settle; to represent; to narrate. pr. par. *stating;* past, *stated:* adv. *statedly:* s. *statement.*

STATES'MAN. *s.* One versed in the arts of government. pl. *statesmen.*

STAT'ICS. *s.* The science which considers the weight of bodies. adj. *static, statical.*

STA'TION. *s.* The act of standing; post assigned; situation; rank. v. *station;* pr. par. *stationing;* past, *stationed:* adj *stationary.*

STA'TIONER. *s.* A bookseller; a seller of paper, &c. s. *stationary.*

STA'TIST. *s.* A statesman, a politician.

STATIS'TICS. *s.* That part of municipal philosophy, which states and defines the situation, strength, and resources of a nation. adj. *statistic, statistical.*

STAT'UARY. *s.* The art of carving images or representations of life; one that practises the art of making statues. pl. *statuaries.*

STAT'UE. *s.* An image; a solid representation of any living being.

STAT'URE. *s.* The height of any animal.

STAT'UTE. *s.* A law; an edict of a legislator. adj. *statutable, statutory.*

STAUNCH. *v.* See Stanch.

STAVE. *s.* One of the pieces which form a barrel or tub; a metrical portion.

STAVE. *v.* To break into staves; to wreck. pr. par. *staving;* past, *staved* or *stove.*

STAY. *v.* To continue in a place; to stop; to prop. pr. par. *staying;* past, *stayed:* s. *stay.*

STAYS. *s.* Bodice for women; ropes in a ship to support the mast. s. *staymaker.*

STEAD. *s.* Place, room, use, help, frame.

STEAD'FAST. *adj.* Fast in place; firm; fixed; constant. adv. *steadfastly:* s. *steadfastness.*

STEADY. *adj* Firm; not tottering constant. v. *steady;* pr. par. *steadying;* past, *steadied:* adv. *steadily* s. *steadiness.*

STEAK. *s.* A slice of flesh.

STEAL. *v.* To take by theft; to pass silently. pr. par. *stealing;* past, *stolen:* s. *stealer:* adv. *stealingly.*

STEALTH. *s.* The act of stealing; secret act. adj. *stealthy.*

STEAM. *s.* The vapour of hot liquor. v. *steam;* pr. par. *steaming;* past, *steamed:* s. *steamer.*

STEAM'ER. *s.* A vessel driven by steam.

STEED. *s.* A horse for state or war

STEEL. *s.* Iron, refined and hardened. v. *steel;* pr. par. *steeling,* past, *steeled.*

STEEL'YARD. *s.* A kind of balance.

STEEP. *adj.* Rising or descending with great inclination; precipitous. s. *steep, steepness.*

STEEP. *v.* To soak in liquor. pr. par. *steeping;* past, *steeped.*

STEE'PLE. *s.* A turret of a church a spire. adj. *steepled.*

STEER. *s.* A young bullock.

STEER. *v.* To guide a ship. pr. par. *steering;* past, *steered:* s. *steersman,* pl. *steersmen.*

STEER'AGE. *s.* The act or practice of steering; the stern or hinder part of a ship.

STEGANOG'RAPHY. *s.* The art of secret writing.

STEL'LATE. *adj.* Pointed as a star

STEM. *s.* The stalk.

STEM. *v.* To oppose or stop; to pass cross or forward, notwithstanding the stream. pr. par. *stemming;* past, *stemmed.*

STENCH. *s.* A bad smell.

STENOG'RAPHY. *s.* The art of writing in short-hand.

STENTO'RIAN. *adj.* Loud; uncommonly loud.

STEP. *v.* To move with the feet; to walk. pr. par. *stepping* past, *stepped:* s. *step, stepper.*

STEP. *adj.* Prefixed to a term of relation, signifies one who is related only by marriage.

STEP'PING-STONE. s. A stone laid for the foot to step on.

STERCORA'CEOUS. adj. Belonging or relating to dung. s. *stercoration*.

STEREOG'RAPHY. s. The art of drawing the forms of solids upon a plane. adj. *stereographic*.

STEREOM'ETRY. s. The art of measuring solid bodies.

STE'REOTYPE. s. Stereotype printing is by types cast together, in a solid plate; not by types, each of which can be separated from the others. v. *stereotype*; pr. par. *stereotyping*; past, *stereotyped*.

STER'ILE. adj. Barren, unfruitful. s. *sterility*, pl. *sterilities:* v. *sterilize;* pr. par. *sterilizing;* past, *sterilized*.

STER'LING. adj. An epithet by which genuine English money is discriminated; genuine. s. *sterling*.

STERN. adj. Of severe countenance or manners; harsh; unrelenting. adv. *sternly:* s. *sternness*.

STERN. s. The hind part of a ship.

STEW. v. To seethe in a slow, moist heat. pr. par. *stewing;* past, *stewed:* s. *stew*.

STEW'ARD. s. One who manages the affairs of another.

STEW'PAN. s. A pan used for stewing.

STICK. s. A piece of wood, small and long: a thrust; a stab.

STICK. v. To fasten; to adhere; to remain; to stab. pr. par *sticking;* past, *stuck:* s. *stick, stickiness:* adj. *sticky*.

STICK'LE. v. To take part with one side or other; to contest. pr. par. *stickling;* past, *stickled:* s. *stickler*.

STIFF. adj. Rigid, inflexible, formal. v. *stiffen;* pr. par. *stiffening;* past, *stiffened:* adv. *stiffly:* s. *stiffness*.

STIFF'NECKED. adj. Stubborn, obstinate.

STI'FLE. v. To suffocate; to suppress. pr. par. *stifling;* past, *stifled*.

STIG'MA. s. A brand; a mark of infamy. adj. *stigmatic:* v. *stigmatize;* pr. par. *stigmatizing;* past *stigmatized*.

STILE. s. A set of steps to pass from one enclosure to another, the pin of a sun-dial.

STILET'TO. s. A small dagger.

STILL. v. To silence; to quiet; to appease. pr. par. *stilling;* past. *stilled:* adj. *still:* s. *stillness*.

STILL. adv. To this time; till now, nevertheless; notwithstanding.

STILL. s. A vessel for distillation; an alembic.

STILL LI'FE. s. Things that have only vegetable life.

STILL'BORN. adj. Born lifeless.

STILTS. s. Supports on which boys raise themselves when they walk.

STIM'ULATE. v. To prick; to prick forward; to excite. pr. par. *stimulating;* past, *stimulated:* adj. *stimulant, stimulative:* s. *stimulant, stimulation, stimulator*.

STING. v. To pierce or wound with a point darted out as that of a scorpion, or bee; to pain acutely. pr. par. *stinging;* past, *stung:* s. *sting, stinger*.

STIN'GO. s. Old beer.

STIN'GY. adj. Niggardly, avaricious. adv. *stingily:* s. *stinginess*.

STINK. v. To emit an offensive smell. pr. par. *stinking;* past, *stunk:* s. *stink*.

STINT. v. To bound, to limit, to confine. pr. par. *stinting;* past, *stinted:* s. *stint*.

STI'PEND. s. Wages; settled pay. adj. and s. *stipendiary*, pl. *stipendiaries*.

STIP'TIC. s. See STYPTIC.

STIP'ULATE. v. To contract; to bargain; to settle terms. pr. par. *stipulating;* past, *stipulated:* s. *stipulation, stipulator*.

STIR. v. To move, to agitate, to incite. pr. par. *stirring;* past, *stirred:* s. *stir, stirrer*.

STIRK. s. A young ox or heifer.

351

STIR'RUP. *s.* An iron for a horseman's foot.

STITCH. *v.* To sew with a needle; to join. pr. par. *stitching;* past, *stitched:* s. *stitch.*

STITCH. *s.* A sharp pain in the side, &c. pl. *stitches.*

STIVER. *s.* A Dutch coin.

STOCCA'DE. *s.* An enclosure or fence, made with pointed stakes.

STOCK. *s.* The trunk; the body of a plant; a breed; a quantity, &c. *v.* stock; pr. par. *stocking;* past, *stocked.*

STOCK'BROKER. *s.* One who deals in stock, or the public funds. s. *stockjobber.*

STOCK'DOVE. *s.* A ringdove.

STOCK'FISH. *s.* Dried cod.

STOCK'ING. *s.* A covering for the leg.

STOCKS. *s.* An instrument to confine the legs; wooden-work upon which ships are built.

STOCKSTILL'. *adj.* Motionless as logs.

STO'IC. *s.* A disciple of the sect of Zeno. adj. *stoic, stoical:* adv. *stoically:* s. *stoicism.*

STOLE. *s.* A long vest.

STOLE. Pret. of the v. *to steal.* past par. *stolen.*

STOM'ACH. *s.* The ventricle in which food is digested. adj. *stomachic.*

STOM'ACHER. *s.* An ornamental covering worn by women on the breast.

STONE. *s.* A kind of mineral, &c. v. *stone;* pr. par. *stoning;* past, *stoned:* s. *stonecutter, stonecast, stonethrow, stonework.*

STOOD. Pret. and past par. of the v. *to stand.*

STOOK. *s.* A shock of corn, containing twelve sheaves. v. *stook;* pr. par. *stooking;* past, *stooked.*

STOOL. *s.* A seat without a back.

STOOP. *v.* To bend down; to bend forward. pr. par. *stooping;* past, *stooped:* s. *stoop:* adv. *stoopingly.*

STOP. *v.* To hinder from progressive motion; to intercept; to staunch. pr. par. *stopping;* past, *stopped:* s. *stop, stopper, stopcock, stopgap, stopple, stupper.*

STORE. *s.* A large quantity; a stock accumulated; a warehouse. v. *store;* pr. par. *storing;* past, *stored.* s. *storehouse.*

STORK. *s.* A kind of bird.

STORM. *s.* A tempest; an assault against a fortified place. v. *storm,* pr. par. *storming;* past, *stormed* s. *storminess:* adj. *stormy.*

STO'RY. *s.* History; account of things past; a short tale. pl. *stories:* adj. *storied.*

STO'RY. *s.* A floor; a flight of rooms. pl. *stories.*

STOUT. *adj.* Strong, lusty, brave, bold. adv. *stoutly:* s. *stoutness.*

STOVE. *s.* A hot-house; a thing in which fire is made. v. *stove;* pr par. *stoving;* past, *stoved.*

STOW. *v.* To lay up in order, and close. pr. par. *stowing;* past, *stowed:* s. *stowage.*

STRAD'DLE. *v.* To stand or walk with the feet astride. pr. par. *straddling;* past, *straddled.*

STRAG'GLE. *v.* to wander; to stray: to rove. pr. par. *straggling;* past, *straggled:* s. *straggler.*

STRAIGHT. *adj.* Not crooked; right; direct. adv. *straight, straightly:* v. *straighten;* pr. par. *straightening;* past, *straightened:* s. *straightness.*

STRAIN. *v.* To purify by filtration; to sprain, to force. pr. par. *straining;* past, *strained:* s. *strain, strainer.*

STRAIT. *adj.* Narrow, close, strict. s. *strait, straitness:* v. *straiten,* pr. par. *straitening,* past, *straitened:* adv. *straitly.*

STRAIT'LACED. *adj.* Griped with stays; stiff; constrained.

STRAKE *s.* A long mask; a streak.

STRAMINE'OUS. *adj.* Strawy; consisting of straw; light.

STRAND. *s.* The beach of the sea.

ʼr of any water; a ply. v. *strand*, ʼr. par. *stranding;* past, *stranded.*

STRANGE. *adj.* Foreign; of another country; singular; wonderful. adv. *strangely:* s. *strangeness, stranger,*

STRANG'LE. *v.* To choke, to suffocate. pr. par. *strangling;* past, *strangled:* s. *strangler, strangulation.*

STRANG'LES. *s.* Swellings in a horse's throat.

STRANG'URY. *s.* A difficulty of urine, with pain.

STRAP. *s.* A narrow, long slip of cloth or leather. v. *strap;* pr. par. *strapping;* past, *strapped.*

STRAP'PING. *adj.* Large; well grown.

STRAT'AGEM. *s.* An artifice in war; a trick.

STRAT'IFY. *v.* To range in beds or layers. pr. par. *stratifying;* past, *stratified:* s. *stratification.*

STRATOG'RAPHY. *s.* Description of whatever relates to an army.

STRATUM. *s.* A layer of earth, &c. pl. *strata.*

STRAW. *s.* The stalk on which corn grows.

STRAW'BERRY. *s.* A species of fruit. pl. *strawberries.*

STRAY. *v.* To wander; to go beyond the proper limits. pr. par. *straying;* past, *strayed:* s. *stray.*

STREAK. *s.* A line of colour different from that of the ground. v. *streak;* pr. par. *streaking;* past, *streaked.*

STREAM. *s.* A running water; a current. v. *stream;* pr. par. *streaming;* past, *streamed.*

STREAM'ER. *s.* An ensign; a flag.

STREAM'LET. *s.* A small stream.

STREET. *s.* A paved way, between two rows of houses, &c.

STRENGTH. *s.* Force; vigour; power of the body; firmness. v. *strengthen;* pr. par. *strengthening;* past, *strengthened:* s. *strengthener, strengthner.*

STREN'UOUS. *adj.* Active; zealous; ardently laborious. adv. *strenuously:* s. *strenuousness.*

STRESS. *s.* Importance; important part; weight; force.

STRETCH. *v.* To extend; to spread out; to expand. pr. par. *stretching,* past, *stretched:* s. *stretch, stretcher.*

STREW. *v.* To scatter loosely. pr. par. *strewing;* past, *strewed.*

STRI'Æ. *s.* Small channels in cockle shells, &c. adj. *striate, striated.*

STRICK'EN. The ancient past par. of the v. *to strike.*

STRICK'LE. *s.* That which strikes the corn in a measure, to level it; an instrument used to whet scythes.

STRICT. *adj.* Exact, rigorous, severe, confined. adv. *strictly:* s. *strictness.*

STRIC'TURE. *s.* A contraction; a critical comment.

STRIDE. *s.* A long step; a step taken with great violence. v. *stride;* pr. par. *striding;* past, *stridden.*

STRIFE. *s.* Contention, discord. adj. *strifeful.*

STRIKE. *v.* To hit with a blow; to impress; to stamp; to lower, as an ensign. pr. par. *striking;* past, *struck:* adv. *strikingly:* s. *strikingness.*

STRING. *s.* A slender rope; a small cord. v. *string;* pr. par. *stringing;* past, *strung:* adj. *stringy.*

STRIN'GENT. *adj.* Binding, contracting.

STRING'HALT. *s.* A sudden twitching and snatching up of the hinder legs of a horse.

STRIP. *v.* To make naked; to deprive of covering; to divest; to take the last milk from a cow. pr. par. *stripping;* past, *stripped:* s. *strip, stripper, strippings.*

STRIPE. *v.* To variegate with lines; to beat. pr. par. *striping;* past, *striped:* s. *stripe.*

STRIPLING. *s.* A youth.

STRIVE. *v.* To struggle; to make an effort. pr. par. *striving;* past, *striven:* s. *striver.*

STROKE. *s.* A blow; a knock; the touch of a pencil; a masterly or eminent effort. v. *stroke;* pr. par. *stroking;* past, *stroked:* s. *stroker.*

STROLL. *v.* To ramble, to rove. pr. par. *strolling;* past, *strolled:* s. *stroll, stroller.*

STRONG. *adj.* Vigorous, forceful, powerful. adv. *strongly.*

STROP. *s.* See STRAP.

STROPHE. *s.* A stanza.

STROVE. Pret. of the v. *to strive.*

STRUCK. Pret. and past par. of the v. *to strike.*

STRUG'GLE. *v.* To labour; to be embarrassed; to strive. pr. par. *struggling;* past, *struggled:* s. *struggle, struggler.*

STRUM'PET. *s.* A prostitute.

STRUNG. Pret. and past par. of the v. *to string.*

STRUT. *v.* To walk with affected dignity. pr. par. *strutting;* past, *strutted:* s. *strut, strutter;* adv. *struttingly.*

STUB. *s.* A thick, short stock, left when the rest is cut off. v. *stub;* pr. par. *stubbing;* past, *stubbed.*

STUB'BLE. *s.* The stalks of corn left in the field by the reaper.

STUB'BORN. *adj.* Obstinate, inflexible, contumacious. adv. *stubbornly:* s. *stubbornness.*

STUB'NAIL. *s.* A nail broken off; a short, thick nail.

STUC'CO. *s.* A kind of fine plaster, for walls. v. *stucco;* pr. par. *stuccoing;* past, *stuccoed.*

STUCK. Pret. and past par. of the v. *to stick.*

STUD. *s.* A stock of breeding mares; a nail with a large head, driven for ornament. v. *stud;* pr. par. *studding;* past, *studded.*

STU'DENT. *s.* One who studies; a scholar.

STU'DIOUS. *adj.* Diligent; contemplative. adv. *studiously:* s. *studiousness.*

STUDY. *s.* Application of mind to books and learning; deep cogitation; the chamber where one studies. pl. *studies:* v. *study;* pr. par. *studying;* past, *studied.*

STUFF. *s.* Any matter or body; materials out of which any thing is made.

STUFF. *v.* To fill very full. pr. par. *stuffing;* past, *stuffed:* s. *stuffing.*

STUL'TIFY. *v.* To make stupid or foolish. pr. par. *stultifying;* past, *stultified.*

STUM'BLE. *v.* To trip in walking. pr. par. *stumbling;* past, *stumbled.* s. *stumble, stumbler:* adv. *stumblingly:* s. *stumbling-block.*

STUMP. *s.* The part of any solid body remaining after the rest is taken away. v. *stump;* pr. par. *stumping;* past, *stumped:* adj. *stumpy.*

STUMP. *v.* To walk about heavily or clumsily. pr. par. *stumping* past, *stumped.*

STUN. *v.* To confound or make dizzy with noise. pr. par. *stunning,* past, *stunned.*

STUNG. Pret. and past par. of the v. *to sting.*

STUNT. *v.* To hinder from growth. pr. par. *stunting;* past, *stunted.*

STUPE. *s.* Warm medicaments for a sore. v. *stupe;* pr. par. *stuping,* past, *stuped.*

STUPEN'DOUS. *adj.* Prodigious, amazing, astonishing. adv. *stupendously:* s. *stupendousness.*

STU'PID. *adj.* Dull; wanting sensibility. s. *stupidity,* pl. *stupidities;* adv. *stupidly:* s. *stupor.*

STU'PIFY. *v.* To make stupid. pr. par. *stupifying;* past, *stupified:* s. *stupifier, stupefaction.*

STUR'DY. *adj.* Hardy, stout, obstinate. adv. *sturdily:* s. *sturdiness.*

STUR'GEON *s.* A kind of fish.

STURK, STIRK. *s.* A young ox or heifer.

STUT'TER. *v.* To speak with hesitation; to stammer. pr. par. *stuttering;* past, *stuttered:* s. *stutter:* adv. *stutteringly.*

STY. *s.* A cabin for hogs; a humour in the eyelid. pl. *sties.*

STY'GIAN. *adj.* Hellish, infernal.

STYLE. *s.* A pointed iron, used anciently in writing on tables of wax; manner of writing, with regard to language; title, &c. *adj. styled, stylish:* adv. *stylishly.*

STYP'TIC, STYP'TICAL. *adj.* Having the power to stop blood. s. *styptic, stypticity.*

SUA'SIVE. *adj.* Having the power to persuade.

SUAV'ITY. *s.* Sweetness to the senses, or to the mind. pl. *suavities.*

SUBA'CID. *adj.* Sour in a small degree.

SUBAC'RID. *adj.* Sharp and pungent in a small degree.

SUBAL'TERN. *adj.* Inferior; subordinate. s. *subaltern.*

SUBA'QUEOUS. *adj.* Lying under water.

SUBDIVI'DE. *v.* To divide a part into yet more parts. pr. par. *subdividing;* past, *subdivided:* s. *subdivision.*

SUBDU'CE, SUBDUCT. *v.* To withdraw; to take away. pr. par. *subducing, subducting;* past, *subducted, subducted:* s. *subduction.*

SUBDUE'. *v.* To crush, to oppress, to conquer. pr. par. *subduing;* past, *subdued:* s. *subduer.*

SUBJA'CENT. *adj.* Lying under.

SUBJECT'. *v.* To put under; to reduce to submission; to expose. pr. par. *subjecting;* past, *subjected:* adj. *sub'ject, subjective:* s. *subject, subjection.*

SUBJOIN'. *v.* To add at the end; to add afterwards. pr. par. *subjoining;* past, *subjoined.*

SUBJU'GATE. *v.* To conquer, to subdue. pr. par. *subjugating;* past, *subjugated:* s. *subjugation.*

SUBJUNC'TION. *s.* The state of being subjoined; the act of subjoining. adj. *subjunctive.*

SUB'LIMATE. *v.* To raise by the force of chymical fire; to exalt. pr. par. *sublimating;* past, *sublimated:* s. *sublunate, sublimation:* adj. *sublimate.*

SUBLI'ME. *adj.* High in place; exalted; lofty; grand. s. *sublime, sublimity,* pl. *sublimities:* v. *sublime,* pr. par. *subliming;* past, *sublimed;* adv. *sublimely.*

SULING'UAL. *adj.* Placed under the tongue.

SUBLU'NAR, SUBLU'NARY. *adj.* Situated beneath the moon; earthly; terrestrial.

SUBMARI'NE. *adj.* Lying or acting under the sea.

SUBMERGE'. *v.* To put under water. pr. par. *submerging;* past, *submerged.*

SUBMERSE'. *v.* To put under water. pr. par. *submersing;* past, *submersed:* s. *submersion.*

SUBMIS'SION. *s.* Act of submitting; acknowledgment of inferiority or dependence; resignation. adj. *submissive:* adv. *submissively.* s. *submissiveness.*

SUBMIT. *v.* To yield; to refer; to subject; to resign without resistance. pr. par. *submitting;* past, *submitted.*

SUBOR'DINATE. *adj.* Inferior in order; subject. s. *subordinate, subordination:* v. *subordinate;* pr. par. *subordinating;* past, *subordinated:* adv. *subordinately.*

SUBORN'. *v.* To procure by indirect and illegal means. pr. par. *suborning;* past, *suborned:* s. *subornation, suborner.*

SUBPŒNA. *s.* A writ commanding attendance in a court, under a penalty. v. *subpœna;* pr. par. *subpœnaing;* past, *subpœnaed.*

SUBSCRI'BE. *v.* To underwrite the name; to promise or engage in writing. pr. par. *subscribing:* past, *subscribed:* s. *subscriber, subscription.*

SUBSEC'TION. *s.* A subdivision of a larger section.

SUB'SEQUENT. *adj.* Following in train: not preceding. adv. *subsequently:* s. *subsequence.*

SUBSERVE'. *v.* To serve in subordination. pr. par. *subserving:* past, *subserved: s. subservience, subserviency:* adj. *subservient.*

SUBSI'DE. *v.* To sink; to tend downwards. pr. par. *subsiding;* past, *subsided: s. subsidence.*

SUB'SIDY. *s.* Aid, commonly such as is given in money. pl. *subsidies;* adv. *subsidiarily:* adj. *subsidiary: s. subsidiary; v. subsidize;* pr. par. *subsidizing;* past, *subsidized.*

SUBSIST'. *v.* To be; to have existence; to continue; to be sustained. pr. par. *subsisting;* past, *subsisted: s. subsistence:* adj. *subsistent.*

SUB'STANCE. *s.* Something existing; something real; the essential part.

SUBSTAN'TIAL. *adj.* Real; actually existing; solid; firm. s. *substantiality, substantials:* adv. *substantially.*

SUBSTAN'TIATE. *v.* To make to exist; to prove by evidence. pr. par. *substantiating;* past, *substantiated.*

SUB'STANTIVE. *s.* A noun; the name of any thing that exists. adj. *substantive:* adv. *substantively.*

SUB'STITUTE. *v.* To put in the place of. pr. par. *substituting;* past, *substituted: s. substitute, substitution.*

SUBSTRA'TUM. *s.* A layer of earth, or any other substance lying under another. pl. *substrata.*

SUBSTRUC'TURE. *s.* A foundation.

SUBTEND'. *v.* To be extended under. pr. par. *subtending;* past, *subtended.*

SUBTENSE'. *s.* The chord of an arch.

SUBTERFLU'ENT, SUBTER'FLUOUS. *adj.* Flowing under.

SUB'TERFUGE. *s.* A shift, an evasion, a trick.

SUBTERRA'NEAN, SUBTERRA'NEOUS. *adj.* Lying under the earth; under ground.

SUB'TILE. *adj.* Thin, cunning, artful. adv. *subtilely: s. subtilty,* pl. *subtilties.*

SUBTILIZE. *v.* To make thin; to volatilize; to refine. pr. par. *subtilizing;* past, *subtilized: s. subtilization.*

SUB'TLE. *adj.* Sly, artful, cunning. pronounced *sut-tle. s. subtlety,* pl *subtleties:* adv. *subtly.*

SUBTRACT'. *v.* To take a part from the rest. pr. par. *subtracting;* past, *subtracted: s. subtraction.*

SUB'URBS. *s.* Buildings, &c. belonging to a city, but without the walls. adj. *suburban.*

SUBVEN'TION. *s.* The act of coming under; the act of supporting.

SUBVERT'. *v.* To overthrow, to overturn. pr. par. *subverting;* past, *subverted: s. subversion, subverter:* adj. *subversive.*

SUCCEDA'NEUM. *s.* That which is put to serve for something else. adj. *succeedaneous.*

SUCCEED'. *v.* To follow in order; to prosper. pr. par. *succeeding;* past, *succeeded: s. succession, successor:* adj. *successive:* adv. *successively.*

SUCCESS'. *s.* Happy termination of any affair. pl. *successes:* adj. *successful* · adv. *successfully.*

SUCCINCT'. *adj.* Short, concise, brief adv. *succinctly: s. succinctness.*

SUC'CORY. *s.* A species of plant. pl. *succories.*

SUC'COTASH. *s.* A mixture of green or unripe maize and beans, boiled.

SUC'COUR. *v.* To help, to relieve. pr. par. *succouring;* past, *succoured: s. succour, succourer.*

SUC'CULENT. *adj.* Juicy, moist. s. *succulence.*

SUCCUMB'. *v.* To yield; to sink under difficulty. pr. par. *succumbing;* past, *succumbed.*

SUCH. *adj.* Of that kind; of the like kind.

SUCK. *v.* To draw in; to imbibe, to extract. pr. par. *sucking;* past, *sucked: s. suck, sucker, suction.*

SUCK'LE. *v.* To nurse at the breast pr par. *suckling;* past, *suckled:* s. *suckling.*

SUDA'TION. *s.* Sweating. *adj. su-datory.*

SUD'DEN. *adj.* Without notice; hasty. *s. sudden, suddenness: adv. suddenly.*

SUDORIF'IC. *adj.* Provoking or causing sweat. *s. sudorific.*

SUDS. *s.* A lixivium of soap and water.

SUE. *v.* To prosecute by law; to entreat. *pr. par. suing; past, sued.*

SUET. *s.* Hard fat; particularly about the kidneys.

SUF'FER. *v.* To bear, to undergo, to endure, to allow. *pr. par. suffering; past, suffered: adj. sufferable: adv. sufferably: s. sufferance, sufferer, suffering.*

SUFFI'CE. *v.* To be sufficient. *pr. par. sufficing; past, sufficed: s. sufficiency: adj. sufficient: adv. sufficiently.*

SUF'FOCATE. *v.* To choke by exclusion or interception of air. *pr. par. suffocating; past, suffocated: s. suffocation.*

SUF'FRAGAN. *s.* A bishop, considered as subject to his metropolitan. *adj.* and *s. suffragant.*

SUF'FRAGE. *s.* Vote, voice, approbation.

SUFFU'SE. *v.* To spread over. *pr. par. suffusing; past, suffused: s. suffusion.*

SU'GAR. *s.* The salt of the sugar-cane. *v. sugar; pr. par. sugaring; past, sugared: s. sugarcandy.*

SUGGEST'. *v.* To hint, to intimate, to propose. *pr. par. suggesting; past, suggested: s. suggester, suggestion.*

SU'ICIDE. *s.* Self-murder; a self-murderer.

SUIT. *s.* A petition; courtship; process; a set; a number of things correspondent one to another; a retinue. *v. suit; pr. par. suiting; past, suited: adj. suitable: adv. suitably.*

SUITE. *s.* Consecution; series; regular order; retinue. pronounced *sweet.*

SUIT'ER, SUIT'OR. *s.* One that sues; a petitioner; a wooer. *fem. suitress, pl. suitresses.*

SUL'CATED. *adj.* Furrowed.

SULK. *v.* To be sluggishly discontented; to be silently sullen. *pr. par. sulking; past, sulked: adv. sulkily: s. sulkiness: adj. sulky.*

SUL'LEN. *adj.* Gloomy, dismal, obstinate. *adv. sullenly: s. sullenness.*

SUL'LY. *v.* To soil; to tarnish. *pr. par. sullying; past, sullied.*

SUL'PHATE, SUL'PHUR. *s.* Brimstone. *adj. sulphureous, sulphurous.*

SUL'PHURET. *s.* A term in chymistry.

SUL'TAN. *s.* The Turkish emperor. *fem. sultana, sultaness.*

SUL'TRY. *adj.* Hot without ventilation. *s. sultriness.*

SUM. *s.* The whole; compendium; the amount. *v. sum; pr. par. summing; past, summed.*

SU'MACH. *s.* A species of plant.

SUM'MARY. *adj.* Short, brief, compendious. *adv. summarily: s. summary, pl. summaries.*

SUM'MER. *s.* The second season.

SUM'MERSET. *s.* A leap, heels over head.

SUM'MIT. *s.* The top; the utmost height.

SUM'MON. *v.* To call with authority; to cite. *pr. par. summoning, past, summoned: s. summons, pl. summonses.*

SUMP'TER. *s.* A horse that carries clothes or furniture.

SUMP'TUARY. *adj.* Relating to expense.

SUMP'TUOUS. *adj.* Costly, expensive, splendid. *adv. sumptuously: s. sumptuousness.*

SUN. *s.* The luminary that makes the day. *v. sun; pr. par. sunning, past, sunned: adj. sunny: s. sunbeam: adj. sunburned, sunburnt: s. sunflower, sunrise, sunset, sunshine.*

SUN'DAY. *s.* The first day of the week.

SUN'DER. *v.* To part; to separate. pr. par. *sundering;* past, *sundered.*

SUN'DIAL. *s.* A marked plate, on which the shadow points the hour.

SUN'DRY. *adj.* Several; more than one. *s. sundries.*

SUNG. Pret. and past par. of the v. *to sing.*

SUNK. Pret. and past par. of the v. *to sink.*

SUP. *v.* To eat by mouthfuls; to drink by little at a time; to eat the evening meal. pr. par. *supping;* past, *supped: s. sup, supper.*

SU'PER. *s.* In composition, notes either more than another, or more than enough, or on the top.

SU'PERABLE. *adj.* Conquerable. adv. *superably.*

SUPERABOUND'. *v.* To be exuberant. pr. par. *superabounding;* past, *superabounded: s. superabundance:* adj. *superabundant:* adv. *superabundantly.*

SUPERADD'. *v.* To add over and above. pr. par. *superadding;* past, *superadded: s. superaddition.*

SUPERAN'NUATE. *v.* To impair or disqualify by age or length of time. pr. par. *superannuating;* past, *superannuated: s. superannuation.*

SUPERB'. *adj.* Grand, pompous, magnificent. adv. *superbly.*

SUPERCAR'GO. *s.* An officer in a ship, whose business is to manage the trade. pl. *supercargoes.*

SUPERCIL'IOUS. *adj.* Proud, haughty, dogmatical. adv. *superciliously: s. superciliousness.*

SUPEREM'INENT. *adj.* Eminent in a high degree. adv. *supereminently: s. supereminence.*

SUPERER'OGATE. *v.* To do more than duty requires. pr. par. *supererogating;* past, *supererogated: s. supererogation:* adj. *supererogatory.*

SU'PERFICE, SUPERFI'CIES. *s.* Outside, surface.

SUPERFI'CIAL. *adj.* Lying on the surface; not reaching below the surface. *s. superficiahty:* adv. *superficially.*

SUPERFI'NE. *adj.* Eminently fine.

SUPER'FLUOUS. *adj.* Exuberant; more than enough; unnecessary. *s. superfluity,* pl. *superfluities.*

SUPERHU'MAN. *adj.* Above the nature or power of man.

SUPERINCUM'BENT. *adj.* Lying on the top of something else.

SUPERINDU'CE. *v.* To bring in as an addition. pr. par. *superinducing;* past, *superinduced: s. superinduction.*

SUPERINTEND'. *v.* To oversee; to overlook. pr. par. *superintending;* past, *superintended: s. superintendence:* adj. and s. *superintendent.*

SUPE'RIOR. *adj.* Higher; greater in dignity or excellence. *s. superior, superiority,* pl. *superiorities.*

SUPER'LATIVE. *adj.* Implying or expressing the highest degree. adv. *superlatively: s. superlativeness.*

SUPER'NAL. *adj.* Having a higher position; celestial.

SUPERNA'TANT. *adj.* Swimming above. *s. supernatation.*

SUPERNATURAL. *adj.* Being above the powers of nature. adv. *supernaturally.*

SUPERNU'MERARY. *adj.* Above a stated number.

SUPERSCRI'BE. *v.* To write upon the top or outside. pr. par. *superscribing;* past, *superscribed: s. superscription.*

SUPERSE'DE. *v.* To make void; to suspend. pr. par. *superseding;* past, *superseded.*

SUPERSTI'TION. *s.* False devotion or religion. adj. *superstitious:* adv. *superstitiously.*

SUPERSTRUCT'. *v.* To build upon any thing. pr. par. *superstructing,* past, *superstructed: s. superstruction, superstructure.*

SUPERVE'NE. *v.* To come as an extraneous addition. pr. par. *su* *pervening;* past, *supervened:* adj. *supervenient:* s. *supervention.*

SUPERVI'SE. *v.* To overlook, to oversee. pr. par. *supervising;* past, *supervised:* s. *supervision, supervisor.*

SUPI'NE. adj. Lying with the face upward; negligent, careless, indolent. adv. *supinely:* s. *supineness.*

SU'PINE. *s.* A particular kind of verbal noun.

SUP'PER. *s.* The last meal of the day. adj. *supperless.*

SUPPLANT'. *v.* To displace by stratagem; to turn out. pr. par. *supplanting;* past, *supplanted:* s. *supplanter.*

SUP'PLE. adj. Yielding, soft, not obstinate. *v. supple;* pr. par. *suppling;* past, *suppled:* s. *suppleness.*

SUP'PLEMENT. *s.* Addition to any thing by which its defects are supplied. adj. *supplemental, supplementary.*

SUP'PLETORY. adj. Brought in to fill up deficiencies. s. *suppletory.*

SUP'PLIANT. adj. Entreating; beseeching. s. *suppliant:* adv. *suppliantly.*

SUP'PLICATE. *v.* To implore, to entreat. pr. par. *supplicating;* past, *supplicated:* adj. *supplicatory:* s. *supplicant.*

SUPPLY'. *v.* To fill up, as any deficiencies happen; to furnish. pr. par. *supplying;* past, *supplied:* s. *supply,* pl. *supplies.*

SUPPORT'. *v.* To sustain, to prop. pr. par. *supporting;* past, *supported:* s. *support, supporter:* adj. *supportable.*

SUPPO'SE. *v.* To lay down without proof; to imagine. pr. par. *supposing;* past, *supposed:* s. *supposer, supposition:* adj. *suppositive:* adv. *suppositively.*

SUPPRESS'. *v.* To crush, to overpower, to overwhelm, to conceal. pr. par. *suppressing;* past, *suppressed:* s. *suppression, suppressor:* adj. *suppressive.*

SUP'PURATE. *v.* To generate pus or matter. pr. par. *suppurating,* past, *suppurated:* s. *suppuration* adj. *suppurative.*

SUPRE'ME. adj. Highest in dignity or authority. adv. *supremely:* s. *supremacy,* pl. *supremacies.*

SUR'BASE. *s.* A kind of skirt, border, or moulding, above the base adj. *surbased.*

SURCHARGE'. *v.* To overload, to overcharge. pr. par. *surcharging* past, *surcharged:* s. *sur'charge.*

SUR'CINGLE. *s.* A girth which is put over the saddle.

SURE. adj. Certain, infallible. adv. *sure, surely:* s. *sureness.*

SUREFOOT'ED. adj. Treading firmly; not apt to stumble.

SU'RETY. *s.* Certainty, security, bail. pl. *sureties.*

SURF. *s.* The swell or dashing of the sea.

SUR'FACE. *s.* Superficies, outside.

SUR'FEIT. *v.* To feed with meat or drink to satiety and sickness. pr. par. *surfeiting;* past, *surfeited.* s. *surfeit.*

SURGE. *s.* A swelling sea. v. *surge,* pr. par. *surging;* past, *surged.* adj. *surgy.*

SUR'GEON. *s.* One who cures by manual operation. s *surgery:* adj. *surgical:* adv. *surgically.*

SUR'LY. adj. Morose, rough, un civil. adv. *surlily:* s. *surliness.*

SURMI'SE. *v.* To suspect; to imagine imperfectly. pr. par. *surmising;* past, *surmised:* s. *surmisal, sur'mise, surmiser.*

SURMOUNT'. *v.* To rise above; to overcome. pr. par. *surmounting;* past, *surmounted:* adj. *surmountable.*

SUR'NAME, SIR'NAME. *s.* The name of the family. v. *surname:* pr. par. *surnaming;* past, *surnamed.*

SURPASS'. *v.* To excel; to exceed. pr. par. *surpassing;* past, *surpassed:* adj. *surpassable:* adv. *surpassingly.*

359

SUR'PLICE. *s.* A clergyman's white garment.

SUR'PLUS. *s.* A supernumerary part; overplus. s. *surplusage.*

SURPRI'SE. *v.* To take unawares; to fall upon unexpectedly. pr. par. *surprising;* past, *surprised:* s. *surprisal, surprise:* adv. *surprisingly.*

SURREN'DER. *v.* To yield; to deliver. pr. par. *surrendering;* past, *surrendered:* s. *surrender.*

SURREPTI'TIOUS. *adj.* Done by stealth; gotten or produced fraudulently. adv. *surreptitiously:* s. *surreption.*

SUR'ROGATE. *s.* A deputy; the deputy of an ecclesiastical judge.

SURROUND'. *v.* To environ; to encompass. pr. par. *surrounding;* past, *surrounded.*

SURTOUT'. *s.* A large upper coat.

SURVEY'. *v.* To overlook; to view; to measure land or buildings. pr. par. *surveying;* past, *surveyed:* s. *sur'vey, surveyor.*

SURVI'VE. *v.* To live after the death of another. pr. par. *surviving;* past, *survived:* s. *survival, survivor.*

SUSCEP'TIBLE. *adj.* Capable of admitting; disposed to admit. s. *susceptibility,* pl. *susceptibilities:* adj. *susceptive.*

SUSPECT'. *v.* To imagine guilty without proof; to doubt. pr. par. *suspecting;* past, *suspected.*

SUSPEND'. *v.* To hang, to interrupt, to delay. pr. par. *suspending;* past, *suspended:* s. *suspender, suspension.*

SUSPENSE'. *s.* Uncertainty; delay of certainty or determination. adj. *suspensive.*

SUSPI'CION. *s.* The act of suspecting; surmise of guilt. adj. *suspicious:* adv. *suspiciously:* s. *suspiciousness.*

SUSTAIN'. *v.* To bear, to prop, to support. pr. par. *sustaining;* past, *sustained:* adj. *sustainable:* s. *sustainer, sustenance, sustentation.*

SUT'LER. *s.* A man that sells provisions and liquor, in a camp.

SWAB. *s.* A kind of mop, to clean floors. v. *swab;* pr. par. *swabbing,* past, *swabbed.* s. *swabber.*

SWAD'DLE. *v.* To swathe; to bind in clothes. pr. par. *swaddling;* past, *swaddled.*

SWAG. *v.* To sink down by its weight; to hang heavy. pr. par. *swagging;* past, *swagged.*

SWAG'GER. *v.* To bluster, to bully. pr. par. *swaggering;* past, *swaggered:* s. *swaggerer.*

SWAIN. *s.* A young man; a pastoral youth.

SWAL'LOW. *s.* A kind of migratory bird.

SWAL'LOW. *v.* To take down the throat. pr. par. *swallowing;* past, *swallowed:* s. *swallow.*

SWAM. Pret. of the v. *to swim.*

SWAMP. *s.* A marsh, a bog. v. *swamp;* pr. par. *swamping;* past, *swamped:* adj. *swampy.*

SWAN. *s.* A kind of water-fowl.

SWAN'SKIN. *s.* A kind of soft flannel.

SWAP. *v.* To exchange. pr. par. *swapping;* past, *swapped.*

SWARD. *s.* A green turf.

SWARM. *s.* A great body or number of bees, &c.; a crowd. v. *swarm;* pr. par. *swarming;* past, *swarmed.*

SWARTH'Y. *adj.* Of dark complexion; tawny. s. *swarthiness.*

SWATHE. *v.* To bind, to confine. pr. par. *swathing;* past, *swathed.*

SWAY. *v.* To wave in the hand; to bias; to govern. pr. par. *swaying;* past, *swayed:* s. *sway.*

SWEAR. *v.* To obtest some superior power; to utter an oath. pr. par. *swearing;* past, *sworn:* s. *swearer.*

SWEAT. *s.* The matter evacuated at the pores, by heat or labour. . *sweat;* pr. par. *sweating;* past, *sweated:* s. *sweater, sweatiness* adj. *sweaty.*

SWE'DISH. *adj.* Belonging or relating to Sweden.
SWEEP. *v.* To clean with a besom; to drive or carry off with celerity and violence. pr. par. *sweeping;* past, *swept:* s. *sweep, sweeper, sweepings.*
SWEEP'STAKE. *s.* One who wins all that is staked.
SWEET. *adj.* Luscious to the taste; mild; soft; not stale. s. *sweet, sweetness, sweetener:* v. *sweeten;* pr. par. *sweetening;* past, *sweetened;* adj. *sweetish:* adv. *sweetly:* s. *sweetbriar, sweetheart, sweetmeat.*
SWEET'BREAD. *s.* The pancreas of the calf.
SWEETMAR'JORAM. *s.* See MARJORAM.
SWEETWIL'LIAM. *s.* A species of plant.
SWELL. *v.* To grow bigger; to extend the parts. pr. par. *swelling;* past, *swelled:* s. *swell, swelling.*
SWEL'TER. *v.* To be pained with heat. pr. par. *sweltering;* past, *sweltered:* adj. *sweltry.*
SWEPT. Pret. and past par. of the v. *to sweep.*
SWERVE. *v.* To wander, to rove, to deviate. pr. par. *swerving;* past, *swerved.*
SWIFT. *adj.* Quick, fleet, rapid. adv. *swiftly:* s. *swiftness.*
SWIG. *v.* To drink by large draughts. pr. par. *swigging;* past, *swigged:* s. *swig.*
SWILL. *v.* To drink luxuriously and grossly. pr. par. *swilling;* past, *swilled:* s. *swill, swiller.*
SWIM. *v.* To float; to glide along. pr. par. *swimming;* past, *swum:* s. *swim, swimmer:* adv. *swimmingly.*
SWIN'DLE. *v.* To cheat. pr. par. *swindling;* past, *swindled:* s. *swindler.*
SWINE. *s.* A hog, a pig pl. *swine:* adj. *swinish.*
SWING. *v.* To wave to and fro. pr. par. *swinging,* past, *swung:* s. *swing.*
SWIN'GING. *adj.* Great, huge. pronounced *swin-jing:* adv. *swingingly.*
SWISS, SWIT'ZER. *s.* A native of Switzerland.
SWITCH. *s.* A small, flexible twig. pl. *switches:* v. *switch;* pr. par. *switching;* past, *switched.*
SWIV'EL. *s.* Something fixed in another body, so as to turn round in it.
SWOB'BER. *s.* A sweeper of a ship's deck; a term in a game of cards.
SWOL'LEN, SWOLN. Past par. of the v. *to swell.*
SWOON. *v.* To suffer a suspension of thought and sensation. pr. par *swooning;* past, *swooned:* s. *swoon.*
SWOOP. *s.* The fall of a bird of prey upon his quarry.
SWOP. *v.* To exchange. pr. par. *swopping;* past, *swopped:* s. *swop.*
SWORD. *s.* A sharp pointed weapon. s. *swordfish, swordknot.*
SWORE. Pret. of the v. *to swear.*
SWUNG. Pret. and past par. of the v. *to swing.*
SYC'AMORE. *s.* A kind of tree.
SYC'OPHANT. *s.* A parasite; a flatterer. s. *sycophancy:* adj. *sycophantic.*
SYL'LABLE. *s.* As much of a word as is uttered by the help of one vowel, or one articulation. adj *syllabic, syllabical:* adv. *syllabically.*
SYL'LABUB. *s.* Milk and acids.
SYL'LABUS. *s.* An abstract; a compendium containing the heads of a discourse. pl. *syllabuses.*
SYL'LOGISM. *s.* An argument composed of three propositions. adj. *syllogistic, syllogistical:* adv. *syllogistically:* s. *syllogization, syllogizer:* v. *syllogize;* pr. par. *syllogizing;* past, *syllogized.*
SYLPH. *s.* A fabled being of the air.
SYL'VAN. *adj.* Woody; relating or belonging to a wood.
SYM'BOL. *s.* A type; a figurative representation. adj. *symbolical:* adv. *symbolically* s. *symbolization*

SYM—SYN

v. *symbolize;* pr. par. *symbolizing;* past, *symbolized.*

SYM'METRY. *s.* Adaptation of parts to each other; proportion; harmony. pl. *symmetries:* adj. *symmetrical.*

SYM'PATHY. *s.* Fellow-feeling; mutual sensibility. pl. *sympathies:* adj. *sympathetic, sympathetical:* adv. *sympathetically:* v. *sympathize;* pr. par. *sympathizing;* past, *sympathized.*

SYM'PHONY. *s.* A harmony of mingled sounds. pl. *symphonies:* adj. *symphonious.*

SYMP'TOM. *s.* A sign, a token, an indication. adj. *symptomatic.*

SYN'AGOGUE. *s.* An assembly of the Jews, to worship. adj. *synagogical.*

SYN'COPE. *s.* Fainting fit; contraction of a word, by cutting off a part in the middle. pronounced *sin'-co-pe.*

SYN'DIC. *s.* A kind of chief magistrate; a curator.

SYNEC'DOCHE. *s.* A figure, by which a part is substituted for the whole, or the whole for a part. pronounced *si-nek'-do-ke.*

SY'NOD. *s.* An assembly, particularly of ecclesiastics. adj. *synodal, synodic, synodical:* adv. *synodically.*

SYN'ONYME. *s.* A word of the same meaning as some other word. adj. *synonymous:* adv. *synonymously.*

SYNOP'SIS. *s.* A general view; all the parts brought under one view. pl. *synopses:* adj. *synoptical:* adv. *synoptically.*

SYN'TAX. *s.* A system; that part of grammar which teaches the construction of words. pl. *syntaxes:* adj. *syntactical.*

SYN'THESIS. *s.* The act of joining, opposed to analysis. pl. *syntheses:* adj. *synthetic, synthetical:* adv. *synthetically.*

SY'PHON. *s.* A tube, a pipe.

SY'REN. *s.* See SIREN.

SYR'IAC. *s.* The Syriac language. adj. *syriac.*

SYR'INGE. *s.* A pipe through which a liquid is squirted. v. *syringe;* pr. par. *syringing;* past, *syringed.*

SYR'TIS. *s.* A quicksand; a bog. pl. *syrtes.*

SYR'UP. *s.* The juice of vegetables, boiled with sugar.

SYS'TEM. *s.* Combination of many things acting together; scheme; mode. adj. *systematic, systematical:* adv. *systematically:* v. *systematize:* pr. par. *systematizing;* past, *systematized.*

SYS'TOLE. *s.* In anatomy, the contraction of the heart; in grammar, the shortening of a long syllable. pronounced *sis'-to-le.*

T

TAB—TAB

TAB'BY. *s.* A kind of waved silk.

TAB'BY. *adj.* Brindled; varied with different colours.

TAB'ERNACLE. *s.* A temporary habitation; a sacred place; a place of worship.

TAB'ID. *adj.* Wasted by disease. *s. tabidness.*

TAB'LATURE. *s.* In painting, a single piece, comprehended in one view, and formed according to one single intelligence, meaning, or design.

TA'BLE. *s.* A flat or level surface; an index, &c. *s. tablecloth, table talk.*

TAB'LET. *s.* A small table. a surface written on, or painted.

TA'BOUR. *s.* A small drum, generally beaten with one stick. *s. tabouret,* a small tabour.

TAB'ULAR. *adj.* Set down in the

form of tables or synopses; formed in laminæ; set in squares.

TA'CIT. *adj.* Silent; implied, not expressed. *adv. tacitly.*

TA'CITURN. *adj.* Silent; uttering little. *s. taciturnity.*

TACK. *v.* To fasten; to join; to stitch together; to turn a ship. *pr. par. tacking; past, tacked: s. tack.*

TACK'LE. *s.* Weapons; the ropes, &c. of a ship. *v. tackle; pr. par. tackling; past, tackled: s. tackling.*

TACT. *s.* Touch; technical character; something which marks a particular trade or profession. *s. taction.*

TACT'IC, TACT'ICAL. *adj.* Relating to the art of ranging men in the field of battle. *s. tactics, tactician.*

TAD'POLE. *s.* A young shapeless frog.

TAF'FETA. *s.* A thin silk.

TAF'FEREL. *s.* The upper part of the stern of a ship.

TAG. *s.* A point of metal, put to the end of a string; any thing paltry and mean. *pr. par. tagging; past, tagged.*

TAIL. *s.* That which terminates an animal behind; the lower part; any thing hanging long.

TAIL'OR. *s.* One whose business is to make clothes. *fem. tailoress, pl. tailoresses: v. tailor; pr. par. tailoring; past, tailored.*

TAINT. *v.* To imbue or impregnate; to stain; to sully; to infect; to corrupt. *pr. par. tainting; past, tainted: s. taint.*

TAKE. *v.* To receive; to seize; to captivate with pleasure, &c. *pr. par. taking; past, taken.*

TALE. *s.* A narrative; a story; reckoning.

TAL'ENT. *s.* A certain weight or sum of money; faculty; power; quality.

TAL'ISMAN. *s.* A magical character. *adj. talismanic.*

TALK. *v.* To speak in conversation;
to prattle. *pr. par. talking; past, talked: s. talk, talker: adj. talkative: s. talkativeness.*

TALL. *adj.* High in stature; lofty *s. tallness.*

TAL'LOW. *s.* The grease or fat of an animal.

TAL'LY. *s.* A stick notched and cut in conformity with another stick, and used for keeping account; any thing made to suit another. *pl. tallies: v. tally; pr. par. tallying; past, tallied.*

TAL'MUD. *s.* The book containing the Jewish traditions, the rabinical constitutions, and explications of the law.

TAL'ON. *s.* The claw of a bird of prey.

TAM'ARIND. *s.* A species of tree, and also its fruit.

TAM'ARISK. *s.* A species of flowering tree.

TAM'BOUR. *s.* A tambourine; a frame on which embroidery is worked. *pr. par. tambouring; past, tamboured.*

TAMBOURI'NE. *s.* A kind of drum.

TAME. *adj.* Not wild; domestic; subdued; spiritless. *pr. par. taming; past, tamed: adj. tameable adv. tamely: s. tameness, tamer.*

TAM'PER. *v.* To meddle; to deal to practise upon secretly. *pr. par. tampering; past, tampered: s. tamperer.*

TAN. *v.* To impregnate and imbue with bark; to imbrown by the sun *pr. par. tanning; past, tanned: s. tan, tanner, tanpit.*

TAN'GENT. *s.* A term in geometry.

TAN'GIBLE. *adj.* Perceptible by the touch; capable of being touched. *s. tangibility.*

TAN'GLE. *v.* To implicate; to knit together; to ravel. *pr. par. tangling; past, tangled.*

TAN'IST. *s.* A kind of captain or governor. *s. tanistry*, a succession made up of inheritance and election.

TANK. *s.* A large cistern or basin

TANK'ARD. *s.* A kind of drinking cup.
TAN'SY. *s.* A kind of odorous plant.
TAN'TALIZE. *v.* To torment by the show of pleasures which cannot be reached. pr. par. *tantalizing;* past, *tantalized:* s. *tantalization, tantalizer.*
TAN'TAMOUNT. *adj.* Equivalent.
TANTIV'Y. *adv.* A hunting cry. pl. *tantivies.*
TAP. *v.* To touch lightly; to pierce a vessel. pr. par. *tapping;* past, *tapped:* s. *tap.*
TAPE. *s.* A narrow fillet of linen or cotton.
TA'PER. *s.* A wax candle; a light.
TA'PER. *adj.* Regularly narrowed from the bottom to the top; pyramidical. v. *taper;* pr. par. *tapering;* past, *tapered.*
TAPESTRY. *s.* Cloth woven in regular figures.
TAP'ROOT. *s.* The principal stem of the root.
TAP'STER. *s.* One whose business is to draw beer, in an alehouse.
TAR. *s.* Liquid pitch. v. *tar;* pr. par. *tarring;* past, *tarred:* adj. *tarry.*
TAR'DY. *adj.* Slow; sluggish. adv. *tardily:* s. *tardiness.*
TARE. *s.* A weed that grows amongst corn; the common vetch; the weight of a package in which any commodity is contained.
TAR'GET. *s.* A kind of shield; a circular board to shoot at.
TAR'IFF. *s.* A cartel of commerce; a scale of custom duties.
TAR'NISH. *v.* To sully; to make not bright; to lose brightness. pr. par. *tarnishing;* past, *tarnished.*
TARPAWL'ING. *s.* Hempen cloth smeared with tar.
TAR'RY. *v.* To stay; to loiter; to wait. pr. par. *tarrying;* past, *tarried:* s. *tarrier.*
TART. *adj.* Sour; sharp; severe. adj. *tartish:* adv. *tartly:* s. *tart, tartness.*
TARTAN. *s.* The plaid of Scotland.

TAR'TAR. *s.* A species of vinous salt. adj. *tartarous.*
TARTA'REAN. *adj.* Hellish.
TASK. *s.* Work imposed by another employment. v. *task;* pr. par. *tasking;* past, *tasked:* s. *tasker, taskmaster.*
TAS'SEL. *s.* An ornamental bunch of silk, or glittering substances. adj. *tasseled.*
TASTE. *v.* To perceive and distinguish by the palate; to have a smack; to try the relish. pr. par. *tasting;* past, *tasted:* s. *taste, taster:* adj. *tasteless, tasty.*
TAT'TER. *s.* A rag; a fluttering rag. adj. *tattered.*
TATTERDEMAL'ION. *s.* A ragged fellow.
TAT'TLE. *v.* To prate; to talk idly. pr. par. *tattling;* past, *tattled:* s. *tattle, tattler.*
TATTOO'. *s.* The beat of drum, by which soldiers are warned to their quarters.
TATTOO'. *v.* To mark the skin, as Indians. pr. par. *tattooing;* past, *tattooed.*
TAUGHT. Pret. and past par. of the v. *to teach.*
TAUNT. *v.* To reproach; to insult; to ridicule. pr. par. *taunting;* past, *taunted:* s. *taunt, taunter:* adv. *tauntingly.*
TAU'RUS. *s.* The bull; the second sign in the zodiac.
TAUTOL'OGY. *s.* Repetition of the same words, or of the same sense in different words. pl. *tautologies:* adv. *tautological:* s. *tautologist:* v. *tautologize;* pr. par. *tautologizing:* past, *tautologized.*
TAUTOPH'ONY. *s.* A successive repetition of the same sound.
TAV'ERN. *s.* A house where wine is sold, and drinkers entertained.
TAW. *s.* A marble to play with.
TAW'DRY. *adj.* Meanly showy. adv. *tawdrily:* s. *tawdriness.*
TAW'NY. *adj.* Yellow, like things tanned.
TAX. *s.* An impost, an excise;

364

charge; censure. pl. *taxes:* v. *tax;* pr. par. *taxing;* past, *taxed:* adj. *taxable:* s. *taxation.*

TEA. *s.* A species of Chinese plant; the infusion of the plant.

TEACH. *v.* To instruct; to inform. pr. par *teaching;* past, *taught:* s. *teacher:* adj. *teachable.*

TEAL. *s.* A wild fowl, of the duck kind.

TEAM *s.* A number of horses or oxen, drawing at once the same carriage.

TEAR. *s.* The water which drops from the eyes.

TEAR. *v.* To pull into pieces; to rend; to take away by sudden violence, &c. pr. par. *tearing;* past, *torn:* s. *tear.*

TEASE. *v.* To comb or unravel wool or flax; to scratch cloth, in order to level the nap; to torment; to vex. pr. par. *teasing;* past, *teased:* s. *teaser.*

TEA'SEL. *s.* A plant used for teasing.

TEAT. *s.* A dug, a pap.

TECH'NICAL. *adj.* Belonging to arts; not in common or popular use. s. *technicality,* pl. *technicalties*· adv. *technically.*

TECHNOL'OGY. *s.* A description of, or a discourse upon arts.

TECTON'IC. *adj.* Pertaining to building.

TED. *v.* To spread new-mown grass. pr. par. *tedding;* past, *tedded.*

TE DEUM. *s.* A hymn of the church, so called from the two first words of the Latin.

TE'DIOUS. *adj.* Wearisome by continuance; irksome. adv. *tediously:* s. *tediousness.*

TEEM. *v.* To bring young; to be pregnant; to be full; to produce. pr. par. *teeming;* past, *teemed.*

TEENS. *s.* The years reckoned by the termination *teen.*

TEETH. *s.* The pl. of *tooth.* v. *teeth,* to bring teeth: pr par. *teething;* past, *teethed.*

TEG'UMENT. *s.* In anatomy, a cover.

TEL'EGRAPH. *s.* An instrument which conveys intelligence by signals. v. *telegraph;* pr. par. *telegraphing;* past, *telegraphed.*

TEL'ESCOPE. *s.* A long glass, by which distant objects are viewed. adj. *telescopic.*

TELL. *v.* To utter; to express: to inform; to betray. pr. par. *telling;* past, *told:* s. *teller,* one who numbers; one who pays out money, at a bank.

TEMER'ITY. *s.* Rashness; unreasonable contempt of danger.

TEM'PER. *v.* To mix, so as that one part qualifies the other; to modify; to soften; to calm; to form metals to a proper degree of hardness. pr. par. *tempering;* past, *tempered:* s. *temper, temperament, temperature.*

TEM'PERANCE. *s.* Moderation, opposed to *gluttony* and *drunkenness;* calmness; moderation of passion. adj. *temperate:* adv. *tem perately:* s. *temperateness.*

TEM'PERATURE. *s.* Constitution of nature; degree of any qualities; due balance of contrarieties; degree of heat.

TEM'PEST. *s.* The utmost violence of the wind; commotion; perturbation. adj. *tempestuous:* adv. *tempestuously:* s. *tempestuousness.*

TEM'PLAR. *s.* A student of law, at the Temple in London; a knight of a certain order.

TEM'PLE. *s.* A place appropriated to acts of religion; the upper part of the sides of the head.

TEM'PORAL. *adj.* Measured by time; not eternal; secular; not ecclesiastical; not spiritual; placed at the temples. s. *temporality,* pl. *temporalities, temporalty:* adv. *temporally.*

TEM'PORARY. *adj.* Lasting only for a limited time.

TEM'PORIZE. *v.* To procrastinate; to comply with the times or oc-

cusions. pr. par. *temporizing;* past, *temporized:* s. *temporizer.*
TEMPT. *v.* To solicit to ill; to incite by offering some pleasure or advantage; to provoke. pr. par. *tempting;* past, *tempted:* s. *temptation, tempter:* adv. *temptingly.*
TEN. *adj.* Twice five. adj. *tenfold.*
TEN'ABLE. *adj.* Capable of being held against an attack.
TENA'CIOUS. *adj.* Grasping hard; inclined to hold fast; retentive; glutinous. adv. *tenaciously:* s. *tenacity,* pl. *tenacities.*
TEN'ANT. *s.* One who holds of another: correlative to *landlord:* one who resides in any place. s. *tenancy:* adj. *tenantable:* s. *tenantry,* pl. *tenantries.*
TENCH. *s.* A kind of fish.
TEND. *v.* To watch; to guard; to attend; to move towards; to contribute. pr. par. *tending;* past, *tended:* s. *tendance, tendence, tendency,* pl. *tendencies.*
TEN'DER. *adj.* Soft; sensible; easily pained; delicate; compassionate; gentle. adv. *tenderly:* s. *tenderness, tender-hearted.*
TEN'DER. *v.* To offer; to propose for acceptance. pr. par. *tendering;* past, *tendered:* s. *tender.*
TEN'DINOUS. *adj.* Sinewy; containing tendons.
TEN'DON. *s.* A sinew; a ligature by which the joints are moved.
TEN'DRIL. *s..* The clasp of a vine, &c.
TEN'EBROUS. *adj.* Dark, gloomy. s. *tenebrosity.*
TEN'EMENT. *s.* Any thing held by a tenant.
TEN'ET. *s.* Position, principle, opinion.
TEN'NIS. *s.* A play, at which a ball is driven with a racket.
TEN'ON. *s.* The end of a timber, cut to be fitted into another timber
TEN'OR. *s.* Continuity of state; constant mode; sense contained; a sound in music.

TENSE. *s.* A variation of the verb, to signify time.
TENSE. *adj.* Stretched, stiff. s. *tenseness, tension:* adj. *tensile.*
TENT. *s.* A soldier's movable lodging place, commonly made of canvas, extended on poles; a species of wine. adj. *tented*
TEN'TER. *s.* A hook on which things are stretched.
TENTH. *adj.* Just after the ninth adv. *tenthly.*
TENU'ITY. *s.* Thinness, smallness, slenderness. adj. *tenuous.*
TEN'URE. *s.* The manner whereby tenements are holden of their lords.
TEPEFAC'TION. *s.* The act of warming to a small degree.
TEP'ID. *adj.* Lukewarm; warm in a small degree. s. *tepidity.*
TER'APIN. *s.* A kind of tortoise.
TERGIVER'SATE. *v.* To change from one party or opinion, to the opposite. pr. par. *tergiversating* past, *tergiversated:* s. *tergiversation.*
TERM. *s.* Limit; boundary; the word by which a thing is expressed; stipulation; time during which any thing lasts. v. *term;* pr. par. *terming;* past, *termed.*
TER'MAGANT. *adj.* Quarrelsome; scolding; furious. s. *termagant, termagancy.*
TER'MINATE. *v.* To limit; to put an end to; to cease. pr. par. *terminating;* past, *terminated* adj. *terminable:* s. *termination.*
TER'NARY. *adj.* Proceeding by threes; consisting of three.
TER'RACE. *s.* A mount of earth, covered with grass or gravel.
TERRA'QUEOUS. *adj.* Composed of land and water.
TERRE'NE. *adj.* Earthly, terrestrial.
TERRES'TRIAL. *adj.* Earthly.
TER'RIBLE. *adj.* Dreadful; formidable; causing fear. adv. *terribly.*
TER'RIER. *s.* A dog that follows his game under ground.

TER'RIFY. *v.* To fright; to make afraid. pr. par. *terrifying;* past, *terrified:* adj. *terrific.*

TER'RITORY. *s.* Land, country, dominion. pl. *territories:* adj. *territorial.*

TER'ROR. *s.* Fear communicated; fear received.

TERSE. *adj.* Smooth; cleanly written; neat. adv. *tersely:* s. *terseness.*

TER'TIAN. *adj.* Returning every third day.

TES'SELATED. *adj.* Variegated by squares.

TEST. *s.* Trial; means of trial; discriminative characteristic. v. *test;* pr. par. *testing;* past, *tested.*

TESTA'CEOUS. *adj.* Consisting of shells; having continuous, not jointed shells: opposed to *crustaceous.*

TES'TAMENT. *s.* A written will; the name of each of the volumes of Scripture. adj. *testamentary.*

TES'TATE. *adj.* Having made a will.

TESTA'TOR. *s.* One who leaves a will. fem. *testatrix,* pl. *testatrixes.*

TES'TER. *s.* The cover of a bed.

TES'TIFY. *v.* To witness; to give evidence. pr. par. *testifying;* past, *testified:* s. *testifier, testification.*

TES'TY. *adj.* Fretful; peevish; apt to be angry. adv. *testily:* s. *testiness.*

TES'TIMONY. *s.* Evidence, proof. pl. *testimonies:* s. *testimonial.*

TESTU'DINOUS. *adj.* Resembling the shell of a tortoise.

TETH'ER. *s.* A string by which cattle are restrained, at pasture. pr. par. *tethering;* past, *tethered*

TETRAGONAL. *adj.* Square.

TETRAM'ETER. *adj.* Having four metrical feet.

TE'TRARCH. *s.* A Roman governor of the fourth part of a province. s. *tetrarchate.*

TETRAS'TIC. *s.* An epigram or stanza of four verses.

TET'RASTYLE. *s.* A building with four pillars in front.

TET'TER. *s.* A scab, a ringworm.

TEUTON'IC. *adj.* Spoken by the Teutones, or ancient Germans.

TEXT. *s.* That on which a comment is written; a sentence of Scripture.

TEXT-HAND. *s.* A particular kind of large hand-writing: so called because the *text* was always written in a large hand, and the comment in a small.

TEX'TILE. *adj.* Woven; capable of being woven.

TEX'TURE. *s.* The act of weaving, a thing woven; combination of parts.

THAN. One of the conjunctions.

THANE. *s.* An old title of honour, equivalent to gentleman.

THANK. *v.* To return acknowledgments for any favour or kindness pr. par. *thanking;* past, *thanked:* s. *thanks:* adj. *thankful, thankless.* adv. *thankfully:* s. *thankfulness, thanksgiving.*

THAT. A word which sometimes performs the office of a pronoun, and sometimes of a conjunction.

THATCH. *s.* A straw roof. v. *thatch,* pr. par. *thatching;* past, *thatched* s. *thatcher.*

THAW. *v.* To grow liquid after congelation; to melt. pr. par. *thawing;* past, *thawed:* s. *thaw.*

THE. The definite article.

THE'ATRE. *s.* A place in which shows are exhibited: a play-house. adj. *theatrical:* adv. *theatrically.*

THEE. *pron.* The objective case of *thou.*

THEFT. *s.* The act of stealing; the thing stolen.

THEIR. The pronoun possessive from *they.*

THE'ISM. *s.* Deism; the acknowledgment of a God, as opposed to *atheism.* s. *theist:* adj. *theistical.*

THEM. *pron.* The objective case of *they.* pron. *themselves.*

THEME. *s.* A subject on which one speaks or writes.

THEN. One of the adverbs.

THENCE. *adv.* From that place; from that time. *adv.* *thenceforth, thenceforward.*

THEOC'RACY. *s.* Government immediately superintended by God. pl. *theocracies.*

THEOD'OLITE. *s.* A mathematical instrument, for measuring heights and distances.

THEOG'ONY. *s.* The generation of the gods.

THEOL'OGY. *s.* Divinity. s. *theologian:* adj. *theological:* adv. *theologically.*

THE'OREM. *s.* A position laid down as an acknowledged truth; a position proposed to be demonstrated.

THE'ORY. *s.* Speculation; not practice. pl. *theories:* adj. *theoretical:* adv. *theoretically:* s. *theorist.*

THERAPEU'TIC. *adj.* Curative; teaching the cure of diseases.

THERE. *adv.* In that place. *adv.* *thereabouts, thereafter, thereat, thereby, therefore, therefrom, therein, thereof, thereon, thereout, thereto, thereunto, thereupon, therewith.*

THER'MAL. *adj.* Relating to warm baths.

THERMOM'ETER. *s.* An instrument for measuring degrees of heat. adj. *thermometrical.*

THESE. *pron.* The plural of *this.*

THE'SIS. *s.* A position; a subject; something laid down, affirmatively or negatively. pl. *theses.*

THEY. *pron.* The plural of *he, she,* and *it.*

THICK. *adj.* Dense; not rare; gross: muddy; great in circumference, &c. adv. *thickly:* s. *thickness:* v. *thicken;* pr. par. *thickening;* past, *thickened.*

THICK'ET. *s.* A close knot or tuft of trees; a close wood or copse.

THICK'SKULLED. *adj.* Dull, stupid.

THICK'SET. *adj.* Closely planted.

THIEF. *s.* One who steals. pl. *thieves.*

THIEVE. *v.* To steal; to practise theft. pr. par. *thieving;* past, *thieved:* adj. *thievish:* adv. *thievishly:* s. *thievishness.*

THIGH. *s.* A limb of the body, including all between the groin and the knee.

THILL. *s.* The shafts of a wagon or cart.

THIM'BLE. *s.* A metal cover for the finger, used when sewing.

THIN. *adj.* Not thick; rare; not dense; not close, &c. comp. *thinner:* sup. *thinnest:* v. *thin;* pr. par. *thinning;* past, *thinned:* adv. *thinly:* s. *thinness.*

THINK. *v.* To have ideas; to reason; to cogitate. pr. par. *thinking;* past, *thought.*

THIRD. *adj.* The first after the second. s. *third:* adv. *thirdly.*

THIRST. *s.* The pain suffered for want of drink; vehement desire. adj. *thirsty:* s. *thirstiness:* v. *thirst;* pr. par. *thirsting;* past, *thirsted.*

THIR'TEEN. *adj.* Ten and three; ordinal adj. *thirteenth.*

THIR'TY. *adj.* Thrice ten. ordinal adj. *thirtieth.*

THIS. *pron.* That which is present; what is now mentioned. pl. *these.*

THIS'TLE. *s.* A kind of prickly plant. adj. *thistly,*

THITH'ER. *adv.* To that place: it is opposed to *hither:* to that end; to that point. adv. *thitherto, thitherward.*

THONG. *s.* A strap or string of leather.

THO'RAL. *adj.* Relating to the bed.

THO'RAX. *s.* The breast; the chest. adj. *thoracic.*

THORN. *s.* A species of prickly tree. adj. *thorny.*

THOR'OUGH. *adj.* Complete; full; perfect; passing through. adv. *thoroughly.*

THOR'OUGHFARE. *s.* A passage through; a passage without any stop or let.

THOR'OUGHPACED. *adj.* Perfect, complete.

THOSE. *pron.* The plural of *that.*

THOU. *pron.* The second pronoun personal. pl. *ye,* or *you.*

THOUGH. *conj.* Notwithstanding that; although.

THOUGHT. Pret. and past par. of the v. *to think.*

THOUGHT. *s.* The operation of the mind; the act of thinking; idea; solicitude; concern. *adj. thoughtful, thoughtless: adv. thoughtfully: s. thoughtfulness.*

THOU'SAND. *s.* The number of ten hundred. ordinal adj. *thousandth.*

THRAL'DOM. *s.* Slavery; servitude.

THRAPPLE, THROT'TLE. *s.* The windpipe of any animal.

THRASH, THRESH. *v.* To beat corn, to free it from the chaff; to beat; to drub. pr. par. *thrashing;* past, *thrashed: s. thrasher.*

THREAD. *s.* A small line; the rudiment of cloth. v. *thread;* pr. par. *threading;* past, *threaded.*

THREAD'BARE. *adj.* Deprived of the nap; worn out.

THREAP. *v.* To argue; to contend. pr. par. *threaping;* past, *threaped.*

THREATEN. *v.* To menace; to denounce evil. pr. par. *threatening;* past, *threatened: s. threat, threatener: adv. threateningly.*

THREE. *adj.* Two and one. adj. *threefold.*

THRESH. *v.* See THRASH.

THRESH'OLD. *s.* The ground or step under a door; entrance.

THREW. Pret. of the v. *to throw.*

THRICE. *adv.* Three times.

THRIFT. *s.* Profit; state of prosperity; frugality. adv. *thriftily: s. thriftiness: adj. thrifty.*

THRILL. *v.* To pierce; to feel a sharp, tingling sensation. pr. par. *thrilling;* past, *thrilled: s. thrill.*

THRIVE. *v.* To prosper; to grow rich; to grow up. pr. par. *thriving;* past, *thriven: adv. thrivingly.*

THROAT. *s.* The passages of nutriment and breath.

THROB. *v.* To heave; to beat; to palpitate. pr. par. *throbbing;* past, *throbbed.*

THROE. *s.* The pain of travail, any extreme agony.

THRONE. *s.* A royal seat; the seat of a bishop. adj. *throned.*

THRONG. *s.* A crowd; a multitude pressing against each other. v. *throng;* pr. par. *thronging;* past, *thronged.*

THROS'TLE. *s.* The thrush; a machine for spinning cotton twist.

THROT'TLE. *s.* The windpipe. v *throttle;* to choke; to suffocate pr. par. *throttling;* past, *throttled*

THROUGH. One of the prepositions. adv. *through:* prep. *throughout.*

THROVE. Pret. of the v. *to thrive.*

THROW. *v.* To fling; to cast; to toss, &c. pr. par. *throwing;* past, *thrown: s. throw, thrower.*

THRUM. *s.* The ends of weavers' threads.

THRUM. *v.* To grate; to play coarsely. pr. par. *thrumming;* past, *thrummed.*

THRUSH. *s.* A species of singing bird; a disease appearing in small, round ulcerations. pl. *thrushes.*

THRUST. *v.* To push; to stab; to compress; to intrude. pr. par. *thrusting;* past, *thrust: s. thrust.*

THUMB. *s.* The short, strong finger. v. *thumb;* pr. par. *thumbing,* past, *thumbed.*

THUMB'STALL. *s.* A sheath of leather, to put on the thumb.

THUMP. *s.* A hard, heavy, dead blow. v. *thump;* pr. par. *thumping;* past, *thumped: s. thumper.*

THUN'DER. *s.* The noise made by the explosion of electric matter in the clouds. v. *thunder;* pr. par. *thundering;* past, *thundered:* s. *thunderer, thunderbolt.*

THURS'DAY. *s.* The fifth day of the week.

THUS. *adv.* In this manner; to this degree.

THWACK. *v.* To strike with something blunt and heavy; to bang

pr. par. *thwacking;* past, *thwacked:* s. *thwack.*
THWART. *adj.* Transverse; cross, in relation to something else; perverse. v. *thwart;* pr. par. *thwarting;* past, *thwarted.*
THY. *pron.* The possessive adj. of *thou:* pron. *thyself.*
THYME. *s.* A kind of odoriferous plant.
TIA'RA. *s.* A dress for the head; a diadem.
TICK. *s.* Score; trust; a kind of small insect; the case which holds the stuffing of a bed.
TICK. *v.* To note by regular vibration, as a watch or clock. pr. par. *ticking;* past, *ticked:* s. *tick.*
TICK'EN, TICK'ING. *s.* Cloth used to make a bed-tick.
TICK'ET. *s.* A written token of any right or debt. v. *ticket;* pr. par. *ticketing;* past, *ticketed.*
TICK'LE. *v.* To affect with a prurient sensation, by slight touches. pr. par. *tickling;* past, *tickled:* s. *lickler:* adj. *ticklish:* s. *ticklishness.*
TIDE. *s.* Alternate ebb and flow of the sea; stream; season. v. *tide;* pr. par. *tiding;* past, *tided.*
TIDE'WAITER. *s.* An officer who watches the landing of goods, at the custom-house.
TI'DINGS. *s.* News; incidents related.
TI'DY. *adj.* Neat. adv. *tidily:* s. *tidiness.*
TIE, TYE. *v.* To bind; to fasten with a knot. pr. par. *tying;* past, *tied:* s. *tie, tye.*
TIER. *s.* A row; a rank. pronounced *teer.*
TIERCE. *s.* A vessel that holds the third part of a pipe.
TIF'FANY. *s.* Very thin silk. pl. *tiffanies.*
TIG. *s.* A play in which children try to touch each other last.
TI'GER. *s.* A fierce beast, of the leonine kind. fem. *tigress,* pl. *tigresses.*
TIGHT. *adj.* Tense; close; neat.

v. *tighten;* pr. par. *tightening;* past, *tightened:* adv. *tightly:* s. *tightness.*
TILE. *s.* A thin plate of baked clay, used to cover houses, and corn kilns. v. *tile;* pr. par. *tiling;* past, *tiled:* s. *tiler.*
TILL. *s.* A money-box in a shop.
TILL. *adv.* To the time of; to; until.
TILL. *v.* To cultivate; to plough. pr. par. *tilling;* past, *tilled:* s. *tiller, tillage:* adj. *tillable.*
TIL'LER. *s.* The beam by which a helm is moved.
TILT. *s.* A tent; any support of covering over head; a kind of military sport; a thrust; inclination forward. v. *tilt;* pr. par. *tilting;* past, *tilted:* s *tilter.*
TILTH. *s.* Culture; tillage; tilled ground.
TIM'BER. *s.* Wood fit for building; the main beams of a fabric. v. *timber;* pr. par. *timbering;* past, *timbered.*
TIM'BREL. *s.* A kind of musical instrument, played by pulsation.
TIME. *s.* The measure of duration; interval; season; age, &c. v. *time;* pr. par. *timing;* past, *timed:* adj. and adv. *timely.*
TIME'KEEPER, TIME'PIECE. *s.* A watch or clock that keeps good time; a chronometer.
TIME'SERVER. *s.* One who meanly complies with present power. par adj. and s. *timeserving.*
TIM'ID. *adj.* Fearful, timorous. s. *timidity.*
TIM'OROUS. *adj.* Fearful; full of fear and scruple. adv. *timorously.*
TIN. *s.* One of the primitive metals; thin plates of iron, covered with tin. v. *tin;* pr. par. *tinning;* past, *tinned:* s. *tinman, tinner.*
TINC'TURE. *s.* Colour or taste superadded by something; extract of some drug, made in spirits. v. *tincture;* pr. par. *tincturing;* past, *tinctured.*
TIN'DER. *s.* Any thing highly inflammable, placed to catch fire.

TINE. *s.* The tooth of a harrow; the spike of a fork.
TINGE. *v.* To impregnate or imbue with a colour or taste. pr. par. *tinging;* past, *tinged:* s. *tinge.*
TIN'GLE. *v.* To feel a sound, or the continuance of a sound, in the ears; to feel a sharp, quick pain, with a sensation of motion. pr. par. *tingling;* past, *tingled.*
TINK'ER. *s.* A mender of old vessels of metal.
TIN'KLE. *v.* To make a sharp, quick noise; to clink. pr. par. *tinkling;* past, *tinkled:* s. *tinkle.*
TIN'SEL. *s.* A kind of shining cloth; any thing shining with false lustre. *v. tinsel;* pr. par. *tinseling;* past, *tinseled.*
TINT. *s.* A dye; a colour.
TINY. *adj.* Little, small, puny.
TIP. *s.* The top; the end; the point. *v. tip;* pr. par. *tipping;* past, *tipped.*
TIP'PET. *s.* Something worn about the neck.
TIP'PLE. *v.* To drink luxuriously; to drink habitually to excess. pr. par. *tippling;* past, *tippled:* s. *tipple, tippler.*
TIP'STAFF. *s.* One of the officers of a court of justice. pl. *tipstaves.*
TIP'SY. *adj.* Slightly drunk.
TIP'TOE. *s.* The end of the toe.
TIP'TOP. *s.* The very top.
TIRA'DE. *s.* An invective, delivered in a long train of words.
TIRE. *v.* To fatigue; to harass; to fail with weariness. pr. par. *tiring;* past, *tired:* s. *tiredness.* adj. *tiresome.*
TIRE'WOMAN. *s.* A woman who makes dresses for her mistress's head. pl. *tirewomen.*
TIS'SUE. *s.* Cloth interwoven with gold, &c.
TIT. *s.* A small horse: generally in contempt: a titmouse, or tomtit.
TIT'BIT. *s.* A nice bit.
TITHE. *s.* The tenth part; the part assigned for the maintenance of the clergy. *v. tithe;* pr. par. *tithing;* past, *tithed:* adj. *tithable:* s. *tither.*

TITH'ING. *s.* According to the institution of Alfred, the number or company of ten men, with their families.
TITILLA'TION. *s.* The act of tickling; the state of being tickled.
TI'TLE. *s.* A general head, comprising particulars; an appellation of honour, a name; a claim of right. adj. *titled:* s. *titlepage.*
TIT'TER. *v.* To laugh with restraint. pr. par. *tittering;* past, *tittered:* s. *titter.*
TIT'TLE. *s.* A small particle; a point.
TIT'ULAR. *adj.* Nominal; having or conferring only the title. adj. *titulary.*
TO. One of the prepositions.
TOAD. *s.* An animal resembling a frog.
TOAD'EATER. *s.* A fawning parasite; a servile sycophant.
TOAST. *v.* To scorch at the fire; to name when a health is drunk. pr. par. *toasting;* past, *toasted:* s. *toast, toaster.*
TOBAC'CO. *s.* A species of aromatic plant. s. *tobacconist.*
TOC'SIN. *s.* An alarm-bell.
TOD'DY. *s.* In low language, a kind of punch, or mixture of spirits sugar, and water.
TOE. *s.* One of the divided extremities of the foot.
TOGETH'ER. *adv.* In company: in the same place; in concert; in continuity.
TOIL. *v.* To labour; to fatigue one's self. pr. par. *toiling;* past, *toiled* s. *toil, toilsomeness:* adj. *toilsome.*
TOIL'ET. *s.* A dressing-table.
TOKAY'. *s.* A kind of Hungarian wine.
TO'KEN. *s.* A sign; a mark; a memorial; an evidence.
TOLD. Pret. and past par of the v. *to tell.*
TOLE'DO. *s.* A sword of the finest Toledo temper. pl. *toledoes.*
TOL'ERATE. *v.* To allow, so as not to hinder; to suffer; to pass un-

censured. pr. par. *tolerating;* past, tolerated: s. tolerance, toleration: adj. *tolerable, tolerant.*

TOLL. s. An excise of goods; a part taken as an impost; the sound of a bell. v. *toll;* pr. par. *tolling;* past, *tolled:* s. toller.

TOLL BOOTH. s. In Scotland, a prison, properly a *custom-house,* where toll is received.

TOMB. s. A monument in which the dead are enclosed.

TOM'BOY. s. A hoyden; a romping girl.

TOM'TIT. s. A titmouse; a small bird.

TON. s. A weight consisting of twenty cwt. avoirdupois; a measure containing two pipes. s. *tonnage.*

TONE. s. Sound, note, accent.

TONGS. s. An instrument by which hold is taken of any thing.

TONGUE. s. The instrument of speech, in human beings; the organ by which animals lick; speech; a language. v. *tongue;* pr. par. *tonguing;* past, *tongued.*

TONGUE'TIED. adj. Having the tongue fastened underneath by the muscle, so as to impede speech.

TON'IC. adj. In medicine, bracing, strengthening.

TON'SURE. s. The act of clipping the hair; the state of being shorn.

TOO. adv. Over and above; overmuch; also.

TOOK. Pret. of the v. *to take.*

TOOL. s. An instrument.

TOOT. v. To sound; to make a noise. pr. par. *tooting;* past, *tooted:* s. tooter.

TOOTH. s. One of the small bones used in mastication and articulation, &c. pl. *teeth:* adj. *toothed, toothless:* s. *toothache, toothpick.*

TOP. s. The highest part; the surface; the highest place or degree; an inverted conoid, used by children as a plaything. v. *top;* pr. par. *topping;* past, *topped.*

TOP'ARCH. s. The principal mar in a place. s. *toparchy.*

TO'PAZ. s. A ye
TOPE. v. To dri par. *toping;* pa
TOP'FUL. adj. F
TOPGAL'LANT. est sails.
TOP'IC. s. A gen as generally ap ticular part; pr sion. adj. *topic*
TOP'KNOT. s. A top of the head
TOP'MOST. adj. est.
TOPOG'RAPHY. particular plac *ies:* s. *topogr graphic, topogr*
TOP'SAIL. s. O sails.
TOPSYTUR'VY. tom upwards.
TORCH. s. A la flambeau. pl. *to*
TOR'MENT. s. E ture. v. *tormen ing;* past, *torme*
TORN. Past par.
TORNA'DO. s. A ricane. pl. *torn*
TORPE DO. s. A fish. pl. *torped*
TORPES'CENT. pid.
TOR'PID. adj. Nu sluggish. s. *to torpor.*
TOR'REFY. v. T the fire. pr. par *torrefied:* s. *tor*
TOR'RENT. s. An
TOR'RID. adj. S violently hot.
TORT. s. A wror *tious:* adv. *tort*
TOR'TOISE. s. A covered with a
TOR'TUOUS. adj ed, winding. s.
TOR'TURE. s. T inflicted; angui

ture; pr. par. *torturing;* past, *tortured:* s. *torturer.*

TO'RY. *s.* A robber; one of the political party, opposed to the *whigs;* one who advocates high-handed monarchy. pl. *tories:* s. *toryism.*

TOSS. *v.* To throw up into the air; to throw with violence; to agitate. pr. par. *tossing;* past, *tossed:* s. *toss,* pl. *tosses, tosser.*

TO'TAL. *adj.* Whole, complete. s. *totality:* adv. *totally.*

TOT'TER. *v.* To shake, so as to threaten a fall; to stagger. pr. par. *tottering;* past, *tottered.*

TOUCH. *v.* To perceive by the sense of feeling; to come slightly in contact with, &c. pr. par. *touching;* past, *touched:* s. *touch, touchiness:* adv. *touchingly:* adj. *touchy.*

TOUCH'-HOLE. *s.* The hole through which the fire is conveyed to the powder in a gun.

TOUCH'STONE. *s.* Stone by which metals are examined; any test or criterion.

TOUCH'WOOD. *s.* Decayed wood, used to catch the fire struck from a flint.

TOUGH. *adj.* Yielding to flexure or extension, without fracture; not brittle; stiff; clammy; tenacious. *v. toughen;* pr. par. *toughening;* past, *toughened:* s. *toughness.*

TOUPEE, TOUPET'. *s.* A kind of foretop; natural or artificial hair, dressed particularly on the forehead.

TOUR. *s.* Ramble; roving journey. s. *tourist.*

TOUR'NAMENT *s.* Tilt, joust, military sport.

TOUR'NIQUET. *s.* A bandage which can be straitened or relaxed by turning a handle, to prevent the blood from issuing.

TOW. *s.* The coarse part of flax or hemp.

TOW. *v.* To draw by a rope, through the water. pr. par. *towing;* past, *towed.*

TOW'ARD. *adj.* Ready to do or learn; not froward. adv. *towardly* s. *towardliness, towardness.*

TOW'ARDS. *adv.* In a direction to.

TOW'EL. *s.* A cloth with which the hands, &c. are wiped.

TOW'ER. *s.* A high building; a fortress; high flight. v. *tower;* pr. par. *towering;* past, *towered.*

TOWN. *s.* A collection of houses, larger than a village. s. *township, townsman,* pl. *townsmen.*

TOY. *s.* A petty commodity; a trifle; a plaything. v. *toy;* pr. par. *toying,* past, *toyed:* adj. *toyish:* s. *toyishness.*

TRACE. *s.* Mark left by any thing passing; track; path; that part of the harness by which the draught is given. v. *trace;* pr. par. *tracing,* past, *traced:* s. *trace:* adj. *traceable.*

TRA'CERY. *s.* Ornamental stonework.

TRACK. *s.* Mark left; a road; a beaten path. v. *track;* pr. pa. *tracking;* past, *tracked:* adj. *trackless.*

TRACT. *s.* A region; a quantity of land; continuity; a treatise; a small book.

TRACT'ABLE. *adj.* Manageable; docile. s. *tractability:* adv. *tractably.*

TRAC'TILE. *adj.* Ductile. s. *tractility.*

TRAC'TION. *s.* Act of drawing, state of being drawn.

TRADE. *s.* Traffic; commerce; occupation. v. *trade;* pr. par. *trading;* past, *traded:* s. *trader, tradesman,* pl. *tradesmen.*

TRADE'-WIND. *s.* The monsoon, the periodical wind between the tropics.

TRADI'TION. *s.* The act or practice of delivering accounts, from mouth to mouth, without written memorials. adj. *traditional, traditionary:* adv. *traditionally.*

TRADU'CE. *v.* To calumniate; to censure. pr. par. *traducing;* past, *traduced* s. *traducement, traducer,* adj. *traducible.*

TRADUC'TION. s. Derivation from one of the same kind; propagation; tradition; transmission. adj. *traductive.*

TRAF'FIC. s. Commerce; exchange of commodities. v. *traffic;* pr. par. *trafficking;* past, *trafficked:* s. *trafficker.*

TRA'GEDY. s. A dramatic representation of a serious action; any mournful or dreadful event. pl. *tragedies:* s. *tragedian:* adv. *tragically.*

TRAGICOM'EDY. s. A drama, composed of merry and serious events. pl. *tragicomedies:* adj. *tragicomical.*

TRAIL. v. To draw along the ground; to drag. pr. par. *trailing;* past, *trailed:* s. *trail.*

TRAIN. v. To draw by artifice or stratagem; to educate; to exercise. pr. par. *training,* past, *trained.*

TRAIN. s. The part of a gown that falls behind upon the ground; a series; a consecution; process; retinue; a procession; a line of powder leading to a mine. s. *trainer.*

TRAIN'-OIL. s. Oil drawn by boiling, from the fat of a whale.

TRAIT. s. A stroke; a touch; a peculiarity. pronounced *tray,* or *trate.*

TRAIT'OR. s. One who, being trusted, betrays. adj. *traitorous:* adv. *traitorously.*

TRAIT'RESS. s. A woman who betrays. pl. *traitresses.*

TRAJECT'. v. To cast through; to throw across. pr. par. *trajecting;* past. *trajected:* s. *traject, trajection.*

TRAM'MEL. s. A net in which animals are caught; a kind of shackles, in which horses are taught to pace. v. *trammel;* pr. par. *trameling;* past, *trameled.*

TRAMP. v. To tread heavily. pr. par. *tramping;* past, *tramped:* s. *tramper.*

TRAM'PLE. v. To tread under foot, with pride or contempt; to tread quick and loudly. pr. par. *trampling;* past, *trampled:* s. *trampler.*

TRANCE. s. An ecstacy; a state in which the soul is rapt into visions of distant or future things.

TRAN'QUIL. adj. Quiet; undisturbed. s. *tranquility:* v. *tranquilize;* pr. par. *tranquilizing;* past, *tranquilized:* s. *tranquilizer.*

TRANSACT'. v. To negotiate; to perform; to do; to carry on. pr. par. *transacting;* past, *transacted:* s. *transaction, transactor.*

TRANSAL'PINE. adj. Situated beyond the Alps.

TRANSCEND'. v. To pass; to overpass; to surpass. pr. par. *transcending;* past, *transcended;* s. *transcendence:* adj. *transcendent.*

TRANSCENDENT'AL. adj. General; pervading many particulars; supereminent.

TRANSCRI'BE. v. To copy; to write from an exemplar. pr. par. *transcribing;* past, *transcribed:* s. *transcriber, transcript, transcription.*

TRAN'SEPT. s. A cross aisle.

TRANSFER'. v. To convey; to assign from one to another; to remove. pr. par. *transferring;* past, *transferred:* s. *transfer, transferrer:* adj. *transferrable.*

TRANSFIG'URE. v. To transform. pr. par. *transfiguring;* past, *transfigured:* s. *transfiguration.*

TRANSFIX'. v. To pierce through, and fasten to something at the other side. pr. par. *transfixing;* past, *transfixed.*

TRANSFORM'. v. To metamorphose; to change with regard to external form. pr. par. *transforming;* past, *transformed:* s. *transformation.*

TRANSFUSE'. v. To pour out of one thing into another. pr. par. *transfusing;* past, *transfused:* s. *transfusion:* adj. *transfusible.*

TRANSGRESS'. v. To pass beyond;

374

to violate. pr. par. *transgressing;* past, *transgressed:* s. *transgression, transgressor.*

TRAN'SIENT. *adj.* Passing; soon passed; momentary; not durable. adv. *transiently.*

TRANSIL'IENCE. *s.* Leap from one thing to another.

TRAN'SIT. *s.* In astronomy, the passing of any planet just by or under a fixed star.

TRANSI'TION. *s.* Removal; passage from one state or thing to another; change. adj. *transitive.*

TRAN'SITORY. *adj.* Continuing only a short time. adv. *transitorily.*

TRANSLATE'. *v.* To transport; to remove; to change; to interpret to another language. pr. par. *translating;* past, *translated:* s. *translation, translator.*

TRANSLOCA'TION. *s.* Reciprocal removal.

TRANSLU'CENT, TRANSLU'CID. *adj.* Transparent; giving a passage to the light. s. *translucency.*

TRANSMARI'NE. *adj.* Lying on the other side of the sea; found beyond sea.

TRANSMIGRA'TION. *s.* Passage from one state or place into another.

TRANSMIT'. *v.* To send from one person or place to another. s. *transmission:* adj. *transmittible, transmissive.*

TRANSMU'TE. *v.* To change from one nature or substance into another. pr. par. *transmuting;* past, *transmuted:* adj. *transmutable:* s. *transmutation, transmuter.*

TRANSPA'RENT. *adj.* Pervious to the light; clear, not opaque. s. *transparency,* pl. *transparencies.*

TRANSPIERCE'. *v.* To pierce through. pr. par. *transpiercing;* past, *transpierced.*

TRANSPI'RE. *v.* To emit in vapour; to escape from secrecy to notice. pr. par. *transpiring;* past, *transpired.*

TRANSPLANT'. *v.* To remove and plant in a new place. pr. par. *transplanting;* past, *transplanted:* s. *transplantation.*

TRANSPORT'. *v.* To carry from one place to another; to carry into banishment, as a felon; to hurry by violence of passion; to put into ecstacy. pr. par. *transporting;* past, *transported:* s. *trans'port, transportation.*

TRANSPO'SE. *v.* To put each into the place of another; to remove. pr. par. *transposing;* past, *transposed:* s. *transposal, transposition.*

TRANSUBSTANTIA'TION. *s.* A miraculous operation, believed in the Roman church, in which the elements of the eucharist are supposed to be changed into the real body and blood of Christ.

TRANSU'DE. *v.* To pass through in sweat or vapour. pr. par. *transuding;* past, *transuded:* s. *transudation.*

TRANSVERSE'. *adj.* Being in a cross direction. adv. *transversely.*

TRAP. *s.* A kind of snare; a stratagem to betray or catch unawares; a kind of game. pr. par. *trapping* past, *trapped.*

TRAPDOOR'. *s.* A door that opens vertically.

TRAP'PINGS. *s.* Ornaments appendant to a saddle; embellishments; superficial and trifling decorations

TRASH. *s.* Any thing worthless.

TRAV'AIL. *v.* To labour; to toil; to be in labour. pr. par. *travailing,* past, *travailed:* s. *travail.*

TRAV'EL. *v.* To make journeys; to pass; to move. pr. par. *traveling,* past, *traveled:* s. *travel, traveller.*

TRAVERSE'. *v.* To cross; to lay athwart; to thwart with obstacles; to oppose; to wander over. pr. par *traversing;* past, *traversed:* adj. *traverse':* s. *tra'verse:* adj. *traversable.*

TRAV'ESTY. *s.* A burlesque performance; a literary work turned into ridicule. pl. *travesties:* v. *trav*
375

esty; pr. par. *travestying*; past, *travestied.*

TRAY. *s.* A shallow wooden vessel; a salver.

TREACH'ERY. *s.* Perfidy; breach of faith. pl. *treacheries:* adj. *treacherous:* adv. *treacherously.*

TREA'CLE. *s.* Molasses.

TREAD. *v.* To set the foot; to trample; to walk with form or state, &c. pr. par. *treading;* past, *trodden:* s. *tread.*

TREAD'LE. *s.* A part of an engine on which the feet act, to put it in motion.

TREA'SON. *s.* An offence committed against the safety of a national government. adj. *treasonable:* adv. *treasonably.*

TREAS'URE. *s.* Wealth hoarded. v. *treasure;* pr. par. *treasuring;* past, *treasured:* s. *treasurer, treasury,* pl. *treasuries.*

TREAT. *v.* To negotiate; to settle; to discourse on; to use in any manner, good or bad; to make a gratuitous entertainment, &c. s. *treat, treaty,* pl. *treaties, treatment.*

TREAT'ISE. *s.* A written discourse.

TRE'BLE. *adj.* Threefold; triple. v. *treble;* pr. par. *trebling;* past, *trebled:* adv. *trebly.*

TRE'BLE. *s.* The highest or acutest part in music; a sharp sound.

TREE. *s.* A large vegetable, rising with one woody stem, to a considerable height.

TRE'FOIL. *s.* A kind of plant.

TREM'BLE. *v.* To shake as with fear or cold; to totter. pr. par. *trembling;* past, *trembled:* s. *trembler:* adv. *tremblingly.*

TREMEN'DOUS. *adj.* Dreadful; horrible; astonishingly terrible. adv. *tremendously.*

TREM'OUR, TREM'OR. *s.* The state of trembling; quivering or vibratory motion.

TREM'ULOUS. *adj.* Trembling; fearful; vibrating. adv. *tremulously.*

TRENCH. *v.* To cut; to cut or dig into pits or ditches: to encroach.

pr. par. *trenching;* past, *trenched* s. *trench.*

TRENCH'ANT. *adj.* Cutting, sharp

TRENCH'ER. *s.* A wooden platter.

TREPAN'. *s.* An instrument by which surgeons cut out round pieces of the skull; a snare. v *trepan;* pr. par. *trepanning;* past, *trepanned.*

TREPIDA'TION. *s.* State of trembling or quivering; state of terror

TRES'PASS. *v.* To transgress; to offend; to enter unlawfully upon another's ground. pr. par. *trespassing;* past, *trespassed:* s. *trespass,* pl. *trespasses, trespasser.*

TRESS. *s.* A lock or curl of hair pl. *tresses.*

TRES'TLE. *s.* The frame of a table; a movable form by which any thing is supported; a three-legged stool.

TRET. *s.* An allowance made by merchants to retailers.

TREV'ET. *s.* Any small thing that stands on three 'egs.

TREY. *s.* A three at cards.

TRI'ANGLE. *s.* A figure of three angles. adj. *triangular.*

TRIBE. *s.* A distinct body of the people, as divided by family or nation.

TRIBULA'TION. *s.* Persecution; distress; vexation.

TRIBU'NAL. *s.* The seat of a judge, a court of justice.

TRIB'UNE. *s.* An officer of Rome, chosen by the people; the commander of a Roman legion.

TRIB'UTE. *s.* Payment made in acknowledgment of subjection. adj *tributary.*

TRICE. *s.* A short time; an instant

TRICK. *s.* A sly fraud; a dextrous artifice; a vicious practice; a habit; a number of cards laid regularly up, at play. v. *trick;* pr. par. *tricking;* past, *tricked:* adv. *trickish.*

TRICK'LE. *v.* To fall in drops; to rill in a slender stream. pr. par. *trickling;* past, *trickled.*

TRI'DENT. *s.* The three-forked sceptre of Neptune.

TRID'UAN. *adj.* Lasting three days; happening every third day.

TRIEN'NIAL. *adj.* Lasting three years; happening every third year.

TRI'FLE. *v.* To act or talk without weight or dignity; to indulge in light amusement; to idle. pr. par. *trifling;* past, *trifled:* s. *trifle, trifler:* adv. *triflingly.*

TRIFO'LIATE. *adj.* Having three leaves.

TRI'FORM. *adj.* Having a triple shape.

TRIG. *s.* The mark at which a person stands or stops, before leaping for amusement.

TRIG'GER. *s.* The catch, that, being pulled, looses the cock of a gun.

TRIG'ONAL. *adj.* Triangular; having three corners.

TRIGONOM'ETRY. *s.* The art of measuring triangles.

TRILL. *s.* A quaver. *v. trill;* pr. par. *trilling;* past, *trilled.*

TRIM. *adj.* Nice, snug, dressed up.

TRIM. *s.* Dress; ornaments; a word of slight contempt.

TRIM. *v.* To dress; to decorate; to shave; to clip; to adjust; to balance a vessel; to fluctuate between two parties. pr. par. *trimming;* past, *trimmed:* adv. *trimly:* s. *trimmer, trimness.*

TRIN'ITY. *s.* The incomprehensible union of three persons in the Godhead. s. and adj. *trinitarian.*

TRINKET. *s.* A toy; an ornament of dress.

TRI'O. *s.* A piece of music, consisting of three harmonic parts; three persons, in derision.

TRIP. *v.* To throw by striking the feet from the ground; to fail; to err; to move lightly; to take a short journey or voyage. pr. par. *tripping;* past, *tripped:* s. *trip:* adv. *trippingly.*

TRIP'ARTITE. *adj.* Divided into three parts; consisting of three parts.

TRIPE. *s.* The intestines

TRIP'EDAL. *adj.* Having three feet

TRIPER'SONAL. *adj.* Consisting of three persons.

TRIPET'ALOUS. *adj.* Having a flower consisting of three leaves

TRIPH'THONG. *s.* A coalition of three vowels to form one sound

TRIP'LE. *adj.* Threefold; treble; three times repeated.

TRIP'LET. *s.* Three verses rhyming together.

TRIP'LICATE. *adj.* Thrice as much: trebled. s. *triplication.*

TRI'POD. *s.* A seat with three feet.

TRIP'TOTE. *s.* A noun used only in three cases.

TRI'REME. *s.* A galley with three benches of oars on each side.

TRISEC'TION. *s.* Division into three equal parts.

TRIS'YLLABLE. *s.* A word consisting of three syllables. adj. *trisyllabical.*

TRITE. *adj.* Worn out; stale; common. adv. *tritely:* s. *triteness.*

TRIT'URATE. *v.* To reduce to powder. pr. par. *triturating;* past. *triturated:* s. *trituration.*

TRI'UMPH. *s.* The pomp with which a victory is celebrated; state of being victorious; victory. *v. triumph;* pr. par. *triumphing;* past, *triumphed:* adj. *triumphal, triumphant:* adv. *triumphantly.*

TRIUM'VIRATE, TRIUM'VIRI. *s.* A coalition or concurrence of three men.

TRIU'NE. *adj.* At once three and one. s. *triunity.*

TRIV'ET. *s.* Something supported by three feet.

TRIV'IAL. *adj.* Trifling, unimportant. adv. *trivially:* s. *trivialness.*

TROD, TROD'DEN. Past par. of the v. *to tread.*

TROL'LOP. *s.* A slattern.

TROOP. *s.* A company; a body of soldiers; a small body of cavalry. v. *troop;* pr. par. *trooping;* past, *trooped:* s. *trooper.*

TROPE. *s.* A metaphor. s. *tropist.*

TROPHY *s.* Something shown or preserved, in token of victory. pl. *trophies:* adj. *trophied.*

TROPIC. *s.* One of the lines distant 23½ degrees from the equator. adj. *tropical*, situated within, or belonging to the tropics.

TROT. *v.* To move with a high, jolting pace. pr. par. *trotting;* past, *trotted:* s. *trot, trotter.*

TROTH. *s.* Belief, faith, verity.

TROUBADOUR. *s.* An early poet of Provence.

TROUBLE. *v.* To disturb, to perplex, to afflict, to grieve, to teaze. pr. par. *troubling;* past, *troubled:* s. *trouble, troubler:* adj. *troublesome.*

TROUGH. *s.* Any thing hollowed, and open longitudinally on the upper side.

TROUNCE. *v.* To punish severely. pr. par. *trouncing;* past, *trounced.*

TROU'SERS, TROW'SERS. *s.* Long, wide breeches.

TROUT. *s.* A kind of fresh-water fish.

TROVER. *s.* An action instituted for the delivery or value of goods, found by a person who refuses to deliver them, on demand.

TROW'EL. *s.* An instrument used chiefly by masons, to lift the mortar.

TROY, TROY'-WEIGHT. *s.* A kind of weight, having twelve ounces in a pound.

TRU'ANT. *s.* An idler; one who wanders idly about, neglecting his duty or employment. adj. *truant:* adv. *truantly.*

TRUCE. *s.* A temporary peace; a cessation of hostilities.

TRUCK. *v.* To traffic by exchange; to give in exchange. pr. par. *trucking;* past, *trucked:* s. *truck.*

TRUCK. *s.* Wooden wheels for carriage of cannon; a kind of carriage, with low wheels, for heavy weights.

TRUCKLE. *v.* To be in a state of subjection or inferiority; to yield; to creep. pr. par. *truckling;* past, *truckled.*

TRUCK'LEBED, TRUN'DLEBED *s.* A bed that runs on wheels, under a higher bed.

TRUDGE. *v.* To travel laboriously, to march heavily on. pr. par. *trudging;* past, *trudged.*

TRUE. adj. Agreeing with fact, or with the nature of things; veracious; genuine; real; faithful; exact; conformable to a rule. s. *truism, truth:* adv. *truly:* adj. *truehearted.*

TRUF'FLE. *s.* A subterraneous mushroom.

TRULL. *s.* A vagrant strumpet.

TRUMP. *s.* A trumpet; a card that has particular privileges in a game.

TRUMP. *v.* To win with a trump card; to obtrude; to trump *up*, to invent. pr. par. *trumping;* past, *trumped.*

TRUMP'ERY. *s.* Something fallaciously splendid; falsehood; something of no value. pl. *trumperies.*

TRUMP'ET. *s.* An instrument of martial music; one who praises. pr. par. *trumpeting;* past, *trumpeted:* s. *trumpeter.*

TRUNC'ATE. *v.* To cut short; to maim. pr. par. *truncating;* past, *truncated:* s. *truncation.*

TRUNCH'EON. *s.* A short staff; a staff of command.

TRUN'DLE. *v.* To roll; to bowl along. pr. par. *trundling;* past, *trundled:* s. *trundle*, any round, rolling thing.

TRUNK. *s.* The body without the limbs; a chest for clothes; the proboscis of an elephant, &c.

TRUN'NIONS. *s.* The knobs or bunchings of a gun, that bear it on the cheeks of a carriage.

TRUSS. *s.* A bandage for ruptures; a bundle. pl. *trusses:* v. *truss;* pr. par. *trussing;* past, *trussed.*

TRUST. *s.* Confidence, reliance, credit, deposit. v. *trust;* pr. par. *trusting;* past, *trusted:* s. *trustee, trustiness:* adv. *trustily:* adj. *trusty.*

TRY. *v.* To examine; to make experiment of; to endeavour; to examine; to inquire into the guilt or innocence of. adj. *triable:* s. *trial, trier.*

TUB. *s.* A large open vessel of wood.

TUBE. *s.* A pipe; a long, hollow body. adj. *tubular.*

TU'BERCLE. *s.* A pimple.

TU'BULATED, TU'BEROUS. *adj.* Having prominent knots or excrescences.

TUCK. *s.* A kind of fold. v. *tuck;* pr. par. *tucking;* past, *tucked:* s. *tucker.*

TUES'DAY. *s.* The third day of the week.

TUFT. *s.* A number of threads or ribbons, or any small bodies, joined together; a cluster. adj. *tufted.*

TUG. *v.* To pull with strength, long continued; to struggle; to pluck. pr. par. *tugging;* past, *tugged:* s. *tug, tugger.*

TUI'TION. *s.* Guardianship; superintendent care.

TU'LIP. *s.* A kind of flower.

TUM'BLE. *v.* To fall; to roll about. pr. par. *tumbling;* past, *tumbled:* s. *tumble, tumbler.*

TUM'BREL. *s.* A kind of cart.

TU'MEFY. *v.* To swell; to make to swell. pr. par. *tumefying;* past, *tumefied:* s. *tumefaction.*

TU'MOUR. *s.* A morbid swelling.

TU'MULOSE. *adj.* Full of hills. s. *tumulosity.*

TU'MULT. *s.* A promiscuous commotion in a multitude; an irregular violence. adj. *tumultuary, tumultuous:* adv. *tumultuously.*

TUN. *s.* A large cask; the measure of four hogsheads; 20 cwt. v. *tun;* pr. par. *tunning;* past, *tunned:* s. *tunnage*

TUN'-DISH. *s.* A tunnel. pl. *tun-dishes.*

TUNE. *s.* A diversity of notes put together; harmony; concert of parts; fit temper. v. *tune;* pr. par. *tuning;* past, *tuned:* adj. *tuneful, tuneless:* s. *tuner.*

TU'NIC. *s.* Part of the Roman dress; integument.

TUN'NEL. *s.* The shaft of a chimney; a funnel; a pipe by which liquor is poured into vessels. v. *tunnel;* pr. par. *tunneling;* past, *tunneled.*

TUN'NY. *s.* A kind of sea-fish. pl. *tunnies.*

TUP. *s.* A ram.

TUR'BAN. *s.* The cover worn by the Turks, on their heads. adj. *turbaned.*

TUR'BARY. *s.* The right of digging turf; the place where turf is dug

TUR'BID. *adj.* Muddy; thick. s. *turbidness.*

TUR'BOT. *s.* A kind of sea-fish.

TUR'BULENCE. *s.* Tumult; confusion. adj. *turbulent:* adv. *turbulently.*

TURF. *s.* A clod covered with grass; peat. adj. *turfy.*

TUR'GENT. *adj.* Swelling, tumid, pompous.

TURGES'CENCE. *s.* Act of swelling; state of being swollen; empty magnificence.

TUR'GID. *adj.* Swelling; bloated; pompous; vainly magnificent. s. *turgidity.*

TUR'KEY. *s.* A large fowl, supposed to have been first brought from Turkey.

TUR'MERIC. *s.* An Indian root which makes a yellow die.

TUR'MOIL. *s.* Trouble, disturbance.

TURN. *v.* To put into a circular motion; to revolve; to invert; to change; to transform, &c. pr. par. *turning;* past, *turned:* s. *turn, turner, turnery.*

TURN'COAT. *s.* One who forsakes his party or principles.

TUR'NIP. *s.* A kind of esculent root.

TURN'KEY. *s.* One who opens and locks the doors of a prison.

TURN'PIKE. *s.* A revolving cross, fixed to hinder horses from entering; a gate where toll is collected. to repair the road. In the United States, a *turnpike* signifies an artificial road, covered with stones and gravel. v. *turnpike;* pr. par. *turnpiking;* past, *turnpiked.*

TURN'SOL. *s.* A kind of plant.

TURN'STILE. *s.* A kind of turnpike, in a foot-path.

TUR'PENTINE. *s.* The gum exuded by the pine.

TUR'PITUDE. *s.* Inherent vileness; badness.

TUR'RET. *s.* A little tower. adj. *turreted.*

TUR'TLE, TUR'TLEDOVE. *s.* A species of dove: *turtle,* the sea-tortoise.

TUS'CAN. *adj.* Relating to one of the orders of architecture.

TUSK. *s.* The long tooth of a pugnacious animal; the fang. adj. *tusked.*

TU'TANAG. *s.* A kind of mixed metal, compounded of lead and tin.

TU'TELAGE. *s.* Guardianship; state of being under a guardian. adj. *tutelar, tutelary.*

TU'TOR. *s.* One who has the care of another's learning and morals; a teacher. v. *tutor;* pr. par. *tutoring;* past, *tutored:* fem. *tutoress,* pl. *tutoresses:* s. *tutorage.*

TWANG. *v.* To sound with a quick, sharp noise; to speak or sing with an affected modulation of the voice. pr. par. *twanging;* past, *twanged:* s. *twang.*

TWEAK. *v.* To pinch; to squeeze between the fingers. pr. par. *tweaking;* past, *tweaked.*

TWEE'DLE. *v.* To handle lightly: used of awkward fiddling. pr. par. *tweedling;* past, *tweedled.*

TWEE'ZERS. *s.* Nippers, or small pincers to pluck off hairs.

TWELVE. *adj.* Two and ten. ordinal adj. *twelfth.*

TWELVE'MONTH. *s.* A year.

TWEN'TY. *adj.* Twice ten. ordinal adj. *twentieth.*

TWICE. *adv.* Two times; doubly.

TWIG. *s.* A small shoot of a branch; a switch. v *twig;* pr. par. *twigging;* past, *twigged.*

TWI'LIGHT. *s.* The dubious or faint light, before sunrise, and after sunset. adj. *twilight.*

TWIN. *s.* One of two born at the same birth; one born at the same birth.

TWINE. *v.* To twist two bodies, in order to unite them; to wind. pr par. *twining;* past, *twined:* s. *twine*

TWINGE. *v.* To torment with sudden and short pain; to tweak. pr. par. *twinging;* past, *twinged* · s. *twinge.*

TWINK'LE. *v.* To shine faintly; to open and shut the eyes by turns. pr. par. *twinkling;* past, *twinkled.*

TWIRL. *v.* To turn round; to revolve with a quick motion. pr. par. *twirling;* past, *twirled:* s. *twirl.*

TWIST. *v.* To form by complication, or convolution; to contort; to writhe, &c. pr. par. *twisting,* past, *twisted:* s. *twist, twister.*

TWIT. *v.* To sneer, to flout, to reproach. pr. par. *twitting;* past, *twitted;* adv. *twittingly.*

TWITCH. *v.* To pull with a quick motion; to snatch. pr. par. *twitching;* past, *twitched:* s. *twitch.*

TWIT'TER. *v.* To make a sharp, tremulous, intermitted noise; to simper. pr. par. *twittering;* past, *twittered:* s. *twitter.*

TWO. *adj.* One and one. adj. *two-edged, two-fold, two-handed.*

TYE. *v.* See TIE.

TY'GER. *s.* See TIGER.

TYMPAN'UM. *s.* A drum; a part of the ear, so called from its resemblance to a drum.

TYPE. *s.* Emblem; mark; that by which something future is prefigured; a printing letter. adj. *typical:* adv. *typically.*

TYP'IFY. *v.* To figure; to snow in emblem. pr. par. *typifying;* past, *typified.*

TYPOG'RAPHY. *s.* Emblematical, figurative, or hieroglyphical representation; the art of printing. adj. *typographical;* adv. *typographically*

TY'RANT. *s.* An absolute monarch,

TYR—TYR

governing imperiously; a cruel and despotic master. adj. *tyrannical:* adv. *tyrannically:* s. *tyranny,* pl. *tyrannies.*
TYR'ANNISE. *v.* To act as a ty-

TYR—TYT

rant. pr. par. *tyrannizing;* past, *tyrannized.*
TY'RO. *s.* One not yet master of his art; one in his rudiments.
TYTHE. *s.* See TITHE.

U

UBI—UNA

UBI'QUITY. *s.* Omnipresence; existence at the same time, in all places.
UD'DER. *s.* The dugs of a cow.
UG'LY. *adj.* Deformed; offensive to the sight. s. *ugliness.*
UL'CER. *s.* An inveterate sore. v. *ulcerate;* pr. par. *ulcerating;* past, *ulcerated;* s. *ulceration:* adj. *ulcerous.*
UL'LAGE. *s.* The quantity which a cask wants of being full.
ULTE'RIOR. *adj.* Lying on the further side.
UL'TIMATE. *adj.* Intended as the last resort; being the last in the train of consequences. adv. *ultimately:* s. *ultimatum.*
ULTRAMARI'NE. *adj.* Beyond the sea; foreign.
ULTRAMON'TANE. *adj.* Beyond the mountains.
UM'BER. *s.* A yellow colour; a fish.
UM'BRAGE. *s.* Shade, shadow; resentment.
UMBRA'GEOUS. *adj.* Shady; obscure.
UMBREL'LA. *s.* A screen from the sun or rain.
UMBROS'ITY. *s.* Shadiness.
UM'PIRE. *s.* An arbitrator; one who, as a common friend, decides disputes. s. *umpirage.*
UNABASH'ED. *adj.* Not ashamed; not confused by modesty.
UNABA'TED. *adj.* Undiminished.
UNA'BLE. *adj.* Not having ability; weak.
UNACCENT'ED. *adj.* Having no accent.
UNACCOM'PANIED. *adj.* Not attended.

UNA—UNA

UNACCOM'PLISHED. *adj.* Not accomplished.
UNACCOUNT'ABLE. *adj.* Not explicable; not to be solved by reason; not subject. adv. *unaccountably.*
UNACCUS'TOMED. *adj.* Not accustomed.
UNACKNOWL'EDGED. *adj.* Not owned.
UNACQUAINT'ED. *adj.* Not acquainted. s. *unacquaintance.*
UNADMI'RED. *adj.* Not admired.
UNADORN'ED. *adj.* Not adorned.
UNADUL'TERATED. *adj.* Genuine, not spoiled by spurious mixtures.
UNADVI'SED. *adj.* Imprudent; done without thought. s. *unadvisedness.* adv. *unadvisedly.*
UNAFFECT'ED. *adj.* Real; free from affectation; candid; not laboured; not moved. adv. *unaffectedly.*
UNAFFECT'ING. *adj.* Not pathetic.
UNAID'ED. *adj.* Not assisted.
UNA'LIENABLE. *adj.* Not to be transferred.
UNAL'TERABLE. *adj.* Unchangeable; immutable. s. *unalterableness:* adv. *unalterably:* adj. *unaltered.*
UNAMBI'TIOUS. *adj.* Free from ambition.
UNA'MIABLE. *adj.* Not amiable.
UNAN'IMOUS. *adj.* Being of one mind; agreeing in design or opinion. s. *unanimity:* adv. *unanimously.*
UNAN'SWERABLE. *adj.* Not to be refuted. adv. *unanswerably:* adj. *unanswered.*
UNAPPAL'LED. *adj.* Not impressed by fear.

381

UNAPPEAS'ED. *adj.* Not pacified.
UNAPPRIZ'ED. *adj.* Not informed.
UNAPPRO'PRIA'TED. *adj.* Having no particular application.
UNAPPROV'ED. *adj.* Not approved.
UNAPT'. *adj.* Dull; not ready; unfit; improper. *s. unaptness:* adv. *unaptly.*
UNARRAY'ED. *adj.* Not dressed.
UNASK'ED. *adj.* Not courted by solicitation; not sought by entreaty or care.
UNASPI'RING. *adj.* Not ambitious.
UNASSAIL'ABLE. *adj.* Not to be assaulted. *adj. unassailed.*
UNASSIST'ED. *adj.* Not helped. *adj. unassisting.*
UNASSU'MING. *adj.* Not arrogant; modest.
UNATTAIN'ABLE. *adj.* Not to be attained.
UNATTEMPT'ED. *adj.* Untried.
UNATTEND'ED. *adj.* Having no retinue; unaccompanied.
UNAU'THORIZED. *adj.* Not supported by authority.
UNAVAIL'ABLE. *adj.* Useless; vain with respect to any purpose. *adj. unavailing.*
UNAVENG'ED. *adj.* Not avenged.
UNAVOID'ABLE. *adj.* Inevitable; not to be shunned. adv. *unavoidably.*
UNAWA'RE, UNAWA'RES. *adv.* Without thought; unexpectedly.
UNAW'ED. *adj.* Unrestrained by fear or reverence.
UNBAR'. *v.* To open, by removing the bars; to unbolt. pr. par. *unbarring;* past, *unbarred.*
UNBECOM'ING. *adj.* Indecent; unsuitable; indecorous. *s. unbecomingness:* adv. *unbecomingly.*
UNBEFRIEND'ED. *adj.* Wanting friends; without friends.
UNBELIEV'ER. *s.* An infidel; one who does not entertain the same belief as another.
UNBEND'. *v.* To free from flexure; to relax. pr. par. *unbending;* past, *unbent.*
UNBESEEM'ING. *adj.* Unbecoming.

UNBI'AS. *v.* To free from bias. pr par. *unbiasing;* past, *unbiased.*
UNBID'DEN. *adj.* Uninvited; uncommanded.
UNBIND'. *v.* To loose; to untie. pr. par. *unbinding;* past, *unbound.*
UNBLEM'ISHED. *adj.* Free from blemish.
UNBLEND'ED. *adj.* Not mingled.
UNBLEST'. *adj.* Wretched; ac cursed.
UNBLUSH'ING. *adj.* Not having the sense of shame.
UNBOLT'. *v.* To unbar. pr. par. *un bolting;* past, *unbolted.*
UNBORN'. *adj.* Not yet brought into life.
UNBO'SOM. *v.* To reveal in confidence; to open. pr. par. *unbosoming;* past, *unbosomed.*
UNBOUND'. *adj.* Loose; wanting a cover: used of books.
UNBOUND'ED. *adj.* Infinite; interminable. adv. *unboundedly.*
UNBRA'CE. *v.* To loose; to relax. pr. par. *unbracing;* past, *unbraced.*
UNBRI'DLED. *adj.* Not bridled, licentious; not restrained.
UNBRO'KEN. *adj.* Unsubdued; not violated.
UNBUCK'LE. *v.* To loose from buckles. pr. par. *unbuckling;* past, *unbuckled.*
UNBUILT'. *adj.* Not yet erected.
UNBUR'IED. *adj.* Not interred.
UNBUR'THEN. *v.* To rid of a load. pr. par. *unburthening;* past, *unburthened.*
UNBUT'TON. *v.* To loose any thing buttoned. pr. par. *unbuttoning;* past, *unbuttoned.*
UNCAL'LED. *adj.* Not summoned.
UNCAN'DID. *adj.* Void of candour.
UNCA'SE. *v.* To disengage from any covering. pr. par. *uncasing;* past, *uncased.*
UNCEAS'ING. *adj.* Continual.
UNCEREMO'NIOUS. *adj.* Not attended with ceremony.
UNCER'TAIN. *adj.* Doubtful; un

382

settled. s. *uncertainty*, pl. *uncertainties:* adv. *uncertainly.*
UNCHAIN'. *v.* To free from chains. pr. par. *unchaining;* past, *unchained.*
UNCHANG'ED. *adj.* Not altered. adj. *unchangeable, unchanging:* adv. *unchangeably.*
UNCHAR'ITABLE. *adj.* Not charitable. s. *uncharitableness:* adv. *uncharitably.*
UNCHASTE'. *adj.* Not chaste.
UNCHRIS'TIAN. *adj.* Contrary to the laws of Christianity.
UNCIR'CUMCISED. *adj.* Not circumcised.
UNCIR'CUMSCRIBED. *adj.* Unbounded.
UNCIR'CUMSPECT. *adj.* Not cautious.
UNCIV'IL *adj.* Unpolite; rude. adv. *uncivilly.*
UNCIV'ILIZED. *adj.* Not reclaimed from barbarity.
UNCLAIM'ED. *adj.* Not claimed.
UNCLASP'. *v.* To open what is shut with clasps. pr. par. *unclasping;* past, *unclasped.*
UNCLAS'SIC, UNCLAS'SICAL. *adj.* Not classic.
UNCLE. *s.* The brother of one's father or mother.
UNCLEAN'. *adj.* Foul; dirty. s. *uncleanness:* adv. *uncleanly:* s. *uncleanliness.*
UNCLOTHE'. *v.* To strip; to make naked. pr. par. *unclothing;* past, *unclothed.*
UNCOM'FORTABLE. *adj.* Affording no comfort; dismal. s. *uncomfortableness:* adv. *uncomfortably.*
UNCOM'MON. *adj.* Not frequent; rare. s. *uncommonness:* adv. *uncommonly.*
UNCOMMU'NICATED. *adj.* Not communicated. adj. *uncommunicative.*
UNCOMPLAISANT'. *adj.* Not civil.
UNCOMPLY'ING. *adj.* Not complying.
UNCOMPOUND'ED. *adj.* Simple; not mixed. s. *uncompoundedness.*

UNCONDI'TIONAL. *adj.* Not limited by terms.
UNCONFI'NED. *adj.* Free from restraint. adv. *unconfinedly.*
UNCONFIRM'ED. *adj.* Not confirmed.
UNCONFORM'ABLE. *adj.* Inconsistent. s. *unconformity.*
UNCONNECT'ED. *adj.* Not coherent; loose.
UNCONQ'UERABLE. *adj.* Not to be subdued. adj. *unconquered.*
UNCON'SCIONABLE. *adj.* Forming unreasonable expectations. adv. *unconscionably.*
UNCON'SCIOUS. *adj.* Having no mental perception; unknowing.
UNCONSTRAIN'ED. *adj.* Free from constraint. s. *unconstraint:* adv. *unconstrainedly.*
UNCONSU'MED. *adj.* Not wasted
UNCONTRADICT'ED. *adj.* Not contradicted.
UNCONTROL'LABLE. *adj.* Resistless. adv. *uncontrollably:* adj. *uncontrolled.*
UNCONTROVERT'ED. *adj.* Not disputed; not contradicted.
UNCONVERT'ED. *adj.* Not converted.
UNCONVIN'CED. *adj.* Not convinced.
UNCORD'. *v.* To loose a thing bound with cords. pr. par. *uncording;* past, *uncorded.*
UNCORRUPT'. *adj.* Honest; not tainted by wickedness. adj. *uncorrupted, uncorruptible.*
UNCOU'PLE. *v.* To loose from couples; to disjoin. pr. par. *uncoupling;* past, *uncoupled.*
UNCOUR'TEOUS. *adj.* Uncivil. adv. *uncourteously.*
UNCOURT'LY. *adj.* Inelegant of manners; uncivil. s. *uncourtliness.*
UNCOUTH'. *adj.* Strange; unusual awkward. s. *uncouthness:* adv. *uncouthly.*
UNCOV'ER. *v.* To divest of covering. pr. par. *uncovering;* past, *uncovered.*

UNCREAT'ED. *adj.* Not yet created; not produced by creation.

UNC'TION. *s.* The act of anointing; ointment.

UNC'TUOUS. *adj.* Fat; clammy. *s. unctuosity.*

UNCUL'TIVATED. *adj.* Not cultivated; not instructed.

UNCURL'. *v.* To loose from ringlets or convolutions. pr. par. *uncurling;* past, *uncurled.*

UNCUR'RENT. *adj.* Not current; out of credit.

UNDAUNT'ED. *adj.* Unsubdued by fear. adv. *undauntedly:* adj. *undaunted.*

UNDECEIVE'. *v.* To set free from the influence of fallacy. pr. par. *undeceiving;* past, *undeceived.*

UNDECI'DED. *adj.* Not decided.

UNDEFA'CED. *adj.* Not disfigured.

UNDEFI'LED. *adj.* Not polluted.

UNDEFI'NABLE. *adj.* Not to be defined. adj. *undefined.*

UNDENI'ABLE. *adj.* Not to be denied. adv. *undeniably.*

UN'DER. One of the prepositions.

UNDERGO'. *v.* To suffer; to sustain. pr. par. *undergoing;* past, *undergone.*

UN'DERHAND. *adj.* Secretly; clandestinely.

UNDERLI'NE. *v.* To mark with lines below the words. pr. par. *underlining;* past, *underlined.*

UN'DERLING. *s.* An inferior agent.

UNDERMI'NE. *v.* To dig cavities under any thing; to injure by clandestine means. pr. par. *undermining;* past, *undermined:* s. *underminer.*

UN'DERMOST. *adj.* Lowest in place.

UNDERNEATH'. *prep.* Under; below.

UN'DERPART. *s.* Subordinate or unessential part.

UN'DERPLOT. *s.* The secondary plot; a clandestine scheme.

UNDERRA'TE. *v.* To undervalue. pr. par. *underrating;* past, *underrated.*

UNDERSELL'. *v.* To sell cheaper. pr. par. *underselling;* past, *undersold.*

UNDERSTAND'. *v.* To comprehend; to know the meaning of. pr. par. *understanding;* past, *understood:* s. *understanding.*

UN'DERSTRAPPER. *s.* An inferior agent.

UNDERTA'KE. *v.* To attempt; to engage in. pr. par. *undertaking,* past, *undertaken:* pret. *undertook.*

UNDERTA'KER. *s.* One who undertakes; one who provides necessaries for a funeral.

UNDERVAL'UE. *v.* To rate too low; to esteem lightly. pr. par. *undervaluing;* past, *undervalued.*

UNDERWENT'. Pret. of the v. *undergo.*

UN'DERWOOD. *s.* The low trees that grow among timber.

UNDERWRI'TE. *v.* To write under; to subscribe to a policy of insurance. pr. par. *underwriting;* past, *underwritten:* s. *underwriter.*

UNDESCRIB'ED. *adj.* Not described.

UNDESERV'ED. *adj.* Not merited. adv. *undeservedly.*

UNDESIGN'ING. *adj.* Not acting with any set purpose; sincere. adj. *undesigned.*

UNDETER'MINED. *adj.* Unsettled, undecided.

UNDEV'IATING. *adj.* Regular; not crooked.

UNDIGEST'ED. *adj.* Not concocted crude; not digested.

UNDIMIN'ISHED. *adj.* Not lessened, entire.

UNDIS'CIPLINED. *adj.* Not disciplined.

UNDISGUIS'ED. *adj.* Open, artless.

UNDISMAY'ED. *adj.* Not discouraged.

UNDISSEM'BLING. *adj.* Not dissembling. adj. *undissembled.*

UNDISTURB'ED. *adj.* Calm; tranquil.

UNDO'. *v.* To ruin; to loose; to unravel. pr. par. *undoing;* past, *undone:* pret. *undid.*

UNDOUBTED. *adj.* Indubitable; indisputable. *adv. undoubtedly.*
UNDRAWN. *adj.* Not drawn.
UNDRESS.' *v.* To strip; to divest of ornaments. *pr. par. undressing; past, undressed:* s. *un'dress,* pl. *undresses.*
UNDUE. *adj.* Not right; illegal; not agreeable to duty.
UNDULATE. *v.* To roll as waves. *pr. par. undulating; past, undulated:* s. *undulation:* adj. *undulary, undulatory.*
UNDU'TIFUL. *adj.* Not obedient; not reverent. s. *undutifulness:* adv. *undutifully:* adj. *unduteous.*
UNEARTHED. *adj.* Driven from a den in the ground.
UNEARTH'LY. *adj.* Not terrestrial.
UNEA'SY. *adj.* Painful; disturbed; not at ease. s. *uneasiness:* adv. *uneasily.*
UNEA'TEN. *adj.* Not eaten.
UNED'UCATED. *adj.* Not having received education.
UNEL'IGIBLE. *adj.* Not proper to be chosen.
UNEMPLOY'ED. *adj.* Not busy; at leisure.
UNENLIGHT'ENED. *adj.* Not illuminated.
UNENTERTAINING. *adj.* Giving no delight.
UNEN'VIED. *adj.* Exempt from envy.
UNE'QUAL. *adj.* Not equal; disproportioned. adv. *unequally:* adj. *unequalled.*
UNEQUIV'OCAL. *adj.* Not equivocal.
UNER'RING. *adj.* Committing no mistake. adv. *unerringly.*
UNESSAY'ED. *adj.* Unattempted.
UNESSEN'TIAL. *adj.* Not important; not constituting essence.
UNE'VEN. *adj.* Not even; not level. s. *unevenness.*
UNEXAM'INED. *adj.* Not examined.
UNEXAM'PLED. *adj.* Not known by any precedent.
UNEXCEP'TIONABLE *adj.* Not liable to any objection.
UNEX'ECUTED. *adj.* Not executed.

UNEXHAUS'TED. *adj.* Not spent
UNEXPECT'ED. *adj.* Not expected. adv. *unexpectedly.*
UNEXPLOR'ED. *adj.* Not searched out.
UNEXPOS'ED. *adj.* Not exposed.
UNEXTING'UISHABLE. *adj.* Unquenchable. adj. *unextinguished.*
UNFA'DING. *adj.* Not withering adj. *unfaded.*
UNFA'IR. *adj.* Not fair; dishonest. s. *unfairness:* adv. *unfairly.*
UNFAITH'FUL. *adj.* Perfidious; treacherous. s. *unfaithfulness:* adv. *unfaithfully.*
UNFASH'IONABLE. *adj.* Not fashionable. adv. *unfashionably.*
UNFAST'EN. *v.* To loose; to unfix. *pr. par. unfastening; past, unfastened.*
UNFATH'OMABLE. *adj.* Not to be sounded by a line. adj. *unfathomed.*
UNFA'VOURABLE. *adj.* Not favourable. adv. *unfavourably.*
UNFEAS'IBLE. *adj.* Impracticable.
UNFED'. *adj.* Not supplied with food.
UNFEEL'ING. *adj.* Void of sensibility. s. *unfeelingness:* adv. *unfeelingly.*
UNFEIGN'ED. *adj.* Not counterfeited; real. adv. *unfeignedly.*
UNFELT'. *adj.* Not felt.
UNFET'TER. *v.* To unchain. *pr. par. unfettering; past, unfettered.*
UNFIN'ISHED. *adj.* Incomplete.
UNFIT'. *adj.* Improper; unsuitable v. *unfit;* pr. par. *unfitting;* past, *unfitted:* s. *unfitness:* adv. *unfitly.*
UNFIX'. *v.* To loosen; to unfasten. pr. par. *unfixing;* past, *unfixed.*
UNFLEDG'ED. *adj.* Not completely feathered; young.
UNFOLD'. *v.* To expand; to spread; to discover. pr. par. *unfolding;* past, *unfolded.*
UNFORESEEN'. *adj.* Not foreseen.
UNFORGIV'ING. *adj.* Relentless.
UNFOR'TIFIED. *adj.* Not fortified.
UNFORTUNATE. *adj.* Not successful; unprosperous. adv. *unfortunately.*

UNFOUGHT. *adj.* Not fought.
UNFOUND'ED. *adj.* Void of foundation.
UNFREQUENT'ED. *adj.* Rarely visited.
UNFRE'QUENTLY. *adv.* Not commonly.
UNFRIEND'LY. *adj.* Not benevolent; not kind. *s. unfriendliness.*
UNFRUIT'FUL. *adj.* Not fruitful. *s. unfruitfulness.*
UNFURL'. *v.* To expand; to unfold. pr. par. *unfurling;* past, *unfurled.*
UNGAIN'LY. *adj.* Awkward; uncouth.
UNGAIN'FUL. *adj.* Unprofitable.
UNGAR'RISONED. *adj.* Without a garrison.
UNGEN'EROUS. *adj.* Niggardly, mean, not liberal. *adv. ungenerously.*
UNGE'NIAL. *adj.* Not congenial.
UNGENTEEL'. *adj.* Not genteel.
UNGEN'TLEMANLIKE. *adj.* Unlike a gentleman. *adj. ungentlemanly.*
UNGIRD'. *v.* To loose any thing bound with a girdle. pr. par. *ungirding;* past, *ungirded:* adj. *ungirt.*
UNGOD'LY. *adj.* Wicked; negligent of God. *s. ungodliness: adv. ungodlily.*
UNGOV'ERNABLE. *adj.* Not to be ruled; not to be restrained. *adv. ungovernably.*
UNGOV'ERNED. *adj.* Without government; unbridled.
UNGRACE'FUL. *adj.* Wanting elegance. *s. ungracefulness.*
UNGRA'CIOUS. *adj.* Wicked, odious, offensive, unpleasing. *adv. ungraciously.*
UNGRAMMAT'ICAL. *adj.* Not according to grammar. *adv. ungrammatically.*
UNGRATE'FUL. *adj.* Not grateful. *s ungratefulness: adv. ungratefully.*
UNGRAT'IFIED. *adj.* Not gratified.
UNGROUND ED. *adj.* Having no foundation

UNGUARD'ED. *adj.* Undefended; careless; imprudent. *adv. unguardedly.*
UNG'UENT. *s.* Ointment.
UNGUID'ED. *adj.* Not directed.
UNHAL'LOWED. *adj.* Unholy profane.
UNHAND'SOME. *adj.* Ungraceful illiberal. *s. unhandsomeness: adv unhandsomely.*
UNHAN'DY. *adj.* Awkward.
UNHANG'. *v.* To divest of hangings; to take down from a hook pr. par. *unhanging;* past, *unhung.*
UNHANG'ED. *adj.* Not put to death by the gallows.
UNHAP'PY. *adj.* Wretched; miserable; unfortunate. *s. unhappiness: adv. unhappily.*
UNHARM'ED. *adj.* Unhurt.
UNHARMO'NIOUS. *adj.* Unmusical, harsh, discordant.
UNHAR'NESS. *v.* To loose from the traces; to disarm. pr. par. *unharnessing;* past, *unharnessed.*
UNHEALTH'Y. *adj.* Sickly. *s. in healthiness.*
UNHEARD'. *adj.* Not perceived by the ear; not vouchsafed an audience.
UNHEED'ED. *adj.* Disregarded.
UNHEED'FUL. *adj.* Incautious. *adj unheeding.*
UNHEWN'. *adj.* Not hewn.
UNHINGE'. *v.* To throw from the hinges; to disorder. pr. par. *unhinging;* past, *unhinged.*
UNHO'LY. *adj.* Profane; impious *s. unholiness.*
UNHON'OURED. *adj.* Not venerated; not celebrated.
UNHORSE'. *v.* To throw from the saddle. pr. par. *unhorsing;* pas *unhorsed.*
UNHURT'. *adj.* Free from harm adj. *unhurtful.*
U'NICORN. *s.* A beast that has only one horn.
U'NIFORM. *adj.* Similar to itself; conforming to one rule. *s. uniformity: adv. uniformly.*

386

UNI—UNJ

UNIMPAIR'ED. *adj.* Not diminished; not injured.
UNIMPAS'SIONED. *adj.* Not endowed with passions; not pathetic.
UNIMPEACH'ABLE. *adj.* Not accusable. adj. *unimpeached.*
UNIMPOR'TANT. *adj.* Not momentous.
UNIN'FLUENCED. *adj.* Not influenced.
UNINFORM'ED. *adj.* Ignorant.
UNINJURED. *adj.* Unhurt.
UNINSTRUCT'ED. *adj.* Not taught.
UNINSTRUC'TIVE. *adj.* Not conferring any improvement.
UNINTEL'LIGIBLE. *adj.* That cannot be understood. s. *unintelligibility;* adv. *unintelligibly.*
UNINTEN'TIONAL. *adj.* Not designed. adv. *unintentionally.*
UNINTERESTING. *adj.* Exciting no interest.
UNINTERMIT'TING. *adj.* Continuing. par. adj. *unintermitted.*
UNINTERRUPT'ED. *adj.* Not interrupted. adv. *uninterruptedly.*
UNINVI'TED. *adj.* Not asked.
U'NION. *s.* The act of joining in one; concord; federation.
UNIP'AROUS. *adj.* Bringing one at a birth.
UNIQUE'. *adj.* Sole; without an equal.
U'NISON. *adj.* Sounding alone. s. *unison,* an exact agreement of sound.
U'NIT. *s.* One; the least number.
UNITA'RIAN. *s.* One of a sect which believes in the unity of God.
UNI'TE. *v.* To join in one; to make agree or adhere. pr. par. *uniting;* past. *united:* s. *uniter, unity,* pl. *unities;* adv. *unitedly.*
UNIVER'SAL. *adj.* General; total. s. *universality;* adv. *universally.*
U'NIVERSE. *s.* The general system of things.
UNIVER'SITY. *s.* A school where all the arts are taught. pl. *universities.*
UNJUST. *adj.* Iniquitous; contrary to justice. adv. *unjustly.*
UNJUS'TIFIABLE. *adj.* Not to be justified. adv. *unjustifiably;* adj *unjustified.*

UNK—UNM

UNKEN'NEL. *v.* To drive from his hole; to rouse from his retreat. pr. par. *unkenneling;* past, *unkenneled.*
UNKIND'. *adj.* Not favourable; not kind. s. *unkindness, unkindliness.* adv. *unkindly.*
UNKNOW'INGLY. *adv.* Ignorantly
UNKNOWN'. *adj.* Not known.
UNLA'CE. *v.* To loose any thing fastened with a lace. pr. par. *Un lacing;* past, *unlaced.*
UNLA'DE. *v.* To remove from that which carries. pr. par. *unlading,* past, *unladed.*
UNLAMENT'ED. *adj.* Not deplored.
UNLATCH'. *v.* To open by lifting up the latch. pr. par. *unlatching;* past, *unlatched.*
UNLAW'FUL. *adj.* Contrary to law. s. *unlawfulness;* adv. *unlawfully.*
UNLEARN'. *v.* To forget or disuse what has been learned. pr. par. *unlearning;* past, *unlearned.*
UNLEAV'ENED. *adj.* Not fermented.
UNLESS'. *conj.* Except; if not.
UNLET'TERED. *adj.* Unlearned.
UNLI'CENSED. *adj.* Having no permission.
UNLI'KE. *adj.* Dissimilar; improbable. adv. *unlikely;* s. *unlikeness, unlikelihood, unlikeliness.*
UNLIM'ITED. *adj.* Having no limits. adv. *unlimitedly.*
UNLOAD'. *v.* To disburthen. pr. par. *unloading;* past, *unloaded.*
UNLOCK'. *v.* To open a lock. pr. par. *unlocking;* past, *unlocked.*
UNLOOK'ED, UNLOOK'ED FOR *adj.* Unexpected.
UNLOOSE'. *v.* To loose. pr. par. *unloosing;* past, *unloosed.*
UNLUCK'Y. *adj.* Unfortunate; unhappy; inauspicious. s. *unluckiness;* adv. *unluckily.*
UNMAN'. *v.* To make irresolute to deject. pr. par. *unmanning,* past, *unmanned.*
UNMAN'AGEABLE. *adj.* Not manageable.

387

UNMAN'AGED. *adj.* Not tutored; not educated.
UNMAN'LY. *adj.* Unsuitable to a man; effeminate.
UNMAN'NERED. *adj.* Ill-bred; rude. *adv. unmannerly: s. unmannerliness.*
UNMAR'RIED. *adj.* Not married.
UNMASK'. *v.* To strip of a disguise. pr. par. *unmasking;* past, *unmasked.*
UNMATCH'ED. *adj.* Matchless; having no equal.
UNMEAN'ING. *adj.* Having no meaning.
UNMEANT'. *adj.* Not intended.
UNMED'ITATED. *adj.* Not previously thought of.
UNMER'CHANTABLE. *adj.* Unsaleable.
UNMER'CIFUL. *adj.* Cruel; severe. *s. unmercifulness:* adv. *unmercifully.*
UNMER'ITED. *adj.* Not deserved. *s. unmeritedness.*
UNMIND'ED. *adj.* Not heeded.
UNMIND'FUL. *adj.* Negligent. s. *unmindfulness:* adv. *unmindfully.*
UNMOLEST'ED. *adj.* Undisturbed.
UNMO'VED. *adj.* Not moved; not affected.
UNNA'MED. *adj.* Not named; not mentioned.
UNNAT'URAL. *adj.* Contrary to nature; forced. adv. *unnaturally.*
UNNE'CESSARY. *adj.* Needless. adv. *unnecessarily.*
UNNEIGH'BOURLY. *adj.* Unkind.
UNNERVE'. *v.* To enfeeble. pr. par. *unnerving;* past, *unnerved.*
UNNO'TED. *adj.* Not observed.
UNNUM'BERED. *adj.* Not counted.
UNOBJEC'TIONABLE. *adj.* Not to be objected to.
UNOBSER'VANT. *adj.* Not attentive.
UNOBSERV'ED. *adj.* Not regarded; unseen. adv. *unobservedly:* adj. *unobserving.*
UNOBSTRUCT'ED. *adj.* Not hindered.
UNOBTRU'SIVE. *adj.* Not obtrusive.

UNOC'CUPIED. *adj.* Unpossessed.
UNOR'GANIZED. *adj.* Not organized.
UNPA'CIFIED. *adj.* Not composed.
UNPACK'. *v.* To open things packed up. pr. par. *unpacking:* past, *unpacked.*
UNPAID'. *adj.* Not paid.
UNPAL'ATABLE. *adj.* Nauseous; disagreeable.
UNPAR'ALLELED. *adj.* Not to be equalled.
UNPAR'DONABLE. *adj.* Not to be forgiven. adv. *unpardonably:* adj. *unpardoned.*
UNPARLIAMEN'TARY. *adj.* Contrary to the usage or constitution of parliament.
UNPA'TRONIZED. *adj.* Having no patron.
UNPEO'PLE. *v.* To depopulate. pr. par. *unpeopling;* past, *unpeopled.*
UNPERCEIV'ED. *adj.* Not observed.
UNPERFORM'ED. *adj.* Undone.
UNPIN'. *v.* To open any thing fastened with a pin. pr. par. *unpinning;* past, *unpinned.*
UNPIT'YING. *adj.* Without pity. adj. *unpitied:* adv. *unpitifully.*
UNPLEAS'ANT. *adj.* Not pleasant; uneasy. s. *unpleasantness:* adv. *unpleasantly.*
UNPLEAS'ING. *adj.* Offensive. s *unpleasingness.*
UNPOL'ISHED. *adj.* Not smoothed; not refined.
UNPOLI'TE. *adj.* Not elegant; not civil. s. *unpoliteness.*
UNPOLLU'TED. *adj.* Not corrupted.
UNPOP'ULAR. *adj.* Not popular; disliked. s. *unpopularity.*
UNPOR'TIONED. *adj.* Not endowed with a fortune.
UNPRAC'TISED. *adj.* Not habituated: not skilful.
UNPRECEDENT'ED. *adj.* Without an example.
UNPRE'JUDICED. *adj.* Free from prejudice.
UNPREMED'ITATED. *adj.* Not premeditated.

388

UNPREPA'RED. *adj.* Not prepared. s. *unpreparedness.*
UNPRETEND'ING. *adj.* Not claiming any distinction.
UNPREVENT'ED. *adj.* Not hindered.
UNPRIN'CIPLED. *adj.* Without settled principles; nefarious.
UNPRINT'ED. *adj.* Not printed.
UNPRODUC'TIVE. *adj.* Not efficient; barren.
UNPROF'ITABLE. *adj.* Not profitable. *adv. unprofitably.*
UNPROLIF'IC. *adj.* Barren.
UNPROM'ISING. *adj.* Giving no promise of excellence.
UNPROPI'TIOUS. *adj.* Inauspicious.
UNPROTECT'ED. *adj.* Not protected.
UNPROVI'DED. *adj.* Not provided.
UNPROVOK'ING. *adj.* Giving no offence. *adj. unprovoked.*
UNPUB'LISHED. *adj.* Not published; secret; unknown.
UNPUN'ISHED. *adj.* Not punished.
UNQUAL'IFY. *v.* To disqualify; to divest of qualification. *pr. par. unqualifying;* past, *unqualified.*
UNQUES'TIONABLE. *adj.* Indubitable. *adv. unquestionably:* adj. *unquestioned.*
UNQUI'ET. *adj.* Not calm; not disturbed.
UNRAV'EL. *v.* To disentangle; to extricate. *pr. par. unraveling;* past, *unraveled.*
UNREAD'. *adj.* Not read.
UNREAD'Y. *adj.* Not prepared; not prompt. *s. unreadiness.*
UNRE'AL. *adj.* Unsubstantial.
UNREAS'ONABLE. *adj.* Not agreeable to reason; exorbitant. s. *unreasonableness:* adv. *unreasonably.*
UNRECLAIM'ED. *adj.* Not tamed; not reformed.
UNREFI'NED. *adj.* Not refined.
UNRELENT'ING. *adj.* Cruel; relentless.
UNREMIT'TING. *adj.* Not abating; persevering.
UNREPEAL'ED. *adj.* Not revoked.
UNRESIST'ING. *adj.* Not opposing. adj. *unresisted.*

UNREST'. *s.* Disquiet.
UNRESTRAIN'ED. *adj.* Not confined; unlimited.
UNREVEAL'ED. *adj.* Not discovered.
UNREVENG'ED. *adj.* Not revenged.
UNREWARD'ED. *adj.* Not rewarded.
UNRID'DLE. *v.* To solve an enigma. *pr. par. unriddling;* past, *unriddled:* s. *unriddler.*
UNRIGHT'EOUS. *adj.* Unjust; wicked. s. *unrighteousness:* adv. *unrighteously.*
UNRI'PE. *adj.* Immature. s. *unripeness.*
UNRI'VALED. *adj.* Having no rival; unequaled.
UNRO'BE. *v.* To undress. pr. par *unrobing;* past, *unrobed.*
UNROLL'. *v.* To open any thing rolled. *pr. par. unrolling;* past, *unrolled.*
UNROOF'. *v.* To strip off the roof. *pr. par. unroofing;* past, *unroofed*
UNRUF'FLE. *v.* To cease from agitation. *pr. par. unruffling;* past, *unruffled.*
UNRU'LY. *adj.* Turbulent; ungovernable. s. *unruliness.*
UNSAD'DLE. *v.* To take off the saddle. *pr. par. unsaddling;* past, *unsaddled.*
UNSA'FE. *adj.* Not secure; dangerous. adv. *unsafely.*
UNSA'LEABLE. *adj.* Not merchantable.
UNSANC'TIFIED. *adj.* Unholy.
UNSATISFAC'TORY. *adj.* Not giving satisfaction.
UNSAT'ISFIED. *adj.* Not contented
UNSAV'OURY. *adj.* Tasteless; unpleasing. s. *unsavouriness:* adv. *unsavourily.*
UNSAY'. *v.* To retract; to recant *pr. par. unsaying;* past, *unsaid.*
UNSCREW'. *v.* To loosen a screw *pr. par. unscrewing;* past, *unscrewed.*
UNSCRIP'TURAL. *adj.* Not defensible by Scripture.
UNSEARCH ABLE. *adj.* Inscrutable.
UNSEAS'ONABLE. *adj.* Ill-timed,

unfit. s. unseasonableness: adv. unseasonably.
UNSEEM'LY. adj. Indecent; unbecoming. s. unseemliness.
UNSEEN'. adj. Not seen; invisible.
UNSER'VICEABLE. adj. Useless.
UNSET'TLE. v. To make uncertain; to overthrow. pr. par. unsettling; past, unsettled: s. unsettledness.
UNSHA'KEN. adj. Unmoved.
UNSHEATH'. v. To draw from the scabbard. pr. par. unsheathing; past, unsheathed.
UNSHIP'. v. To take out of a ship. pr. par. unshipping; past, unshipped.
UNSHOD'. adj. Having no shoes.
UNSHORN'. adj. Not clipped.
UNSIGHT'LY. adj. Disagreeable to the sight. s. unsightliness.
UNSKIL'FUL. adj. Wanting skill. s. unskilfulness: adv. unskilfully: adj. unskilled.
UNSO'CIABLE. adj. Not sociable. adv. unsociably.
UNSO'CIAL. adj. Not social.
UNSOLD'. adj. Not sold.
UNSOL'DIERLIKE, UNSOL'DIERLY. adj. Unbecoming a soldier.
UNSOLI'CITED. adj. Not solicited.
UNSOPHIS'TICATED. adj. Not adulterated; not counterfeit.
UNSORT'ED. adj. Not separated; not suitable.
UNSOUGHT'. adj. Not sought for.
UNSOUND'. adj. Not sound. s. unsoundness.
UNSOWN'. adj. Not sown.
UNSPEAK'ABLE. adj. Unutterable. adv. unspeakably.
UNSPE'CIFIED. adj. Not specified.
UNSPOT'TED. adj. Unstained; immaculate.
UNSTA'BLE. adj. Not fixed; inconstant.
UNSTAID'. adj. Not cool; not steady. s. unstaidness.
UNSTEAD'Y. adj. Inconstant; mutable. s. unsteadiness: adv. unsteadily.
UNSTU'DIED. adj. Unpremeditated.
UNSUBSTAN'TIAL. adj. Not solid.

UNSUCCESS'FUL. adj. Not successful. s. unsuccessfulness: adv. unsuccessfully.
UNSUIT'ABLE. adj. Not suitable. s. unsuitableness.
UNSUL'LIED. adj. Not disgraced; pure.
UNSUNG'. adj. Not celebrated in verse.
UNSUPPORT'ED. adj. Not supported.
UNSU'RE. adj. Not fixed; not certain.
UNSURMOUNT'ABLE. adj. Insuperable.
UNSUSCEP'TIBLE. adj. Not liable to admit impression.
UNSUSPECT'ING. adj. Not imagining that any ill is designed. adj. unsuspected.
UNSUSPI'CIOUS. adj. Having no suspicion.
UNSWORN'. adj. Not bound by an oath.
UNTA'MEABLE. adj. Not to be tamed. adj. untamed.
UNTAUGHT'. adj. Uninstructed.
UNTEN'ABLE. adj. Not to be held in possession; not maintainable.
UNTEN'ANTED. adj. Having no tenant.
UNTEND'ED. adj. Not having any attendance.
UNTHANK'FUL. adj. Ungrateful. s. unthankfulness: adv. unthankfully.
UNTHINK'ING. adj. Thoughtless.
UNTHRIF'TY. adj. Prodigal; wasteful; not improving. s. unthriftiness: adv. unthriftily.
UNTI'DY. adj. Not tidy; slovenly.
UNTIE'. v. To unbind; to unfasten. pr. par. untying; past, untied.
UNTIL'. adv. and prep. To the time that.
UNTIME'LY. adj. Happening before the natural time; illtimed.
UN'TO. One of the prepositions.
UNTOLD'. adj. Not told; not revealed.
UNTO'WARD. adj. Froward; awkward; vexatious. adv. untowardly. s. untowardness.

390

UNTRAIN'ED. *adj.* Not educated; not disciplined.
UNTRAV'ELED. *adj.* Never trodden by passengers; never having seen foreign countries.
UNTRI'ED. *adj.* Not yet attempted; not having passed trial.
UNTROD'DEN. *adj.* Not marked by the foot.
UNTROUB'LED. *adj.* Not disturbed by care; transparent.
UNTRUE'. *adj.* False. *s. untruth:* adv. *untruly.*
UNTU'TORED. *adj.* Uninstructed.
UNTWI'NE. *v.* To open what is wrapped on itself; to separate that which clasps round any thing.
UNU'SED. *adj.* Not put to use; not accustomed.
UNU'SUAL. *adj.* Uncommon; rare. *s. unusualness:* adv. *unusually.*
UNUT'TERABLE. *adj.* Inexpressible.
UNVAL'UED. *adj.* Not prized; inestimable.
UNVAR'NISHED. *adj.* Not varnished.
UNVA'RYING. *adj.* Unchanging. *adj. unvaried.*
UNVERS'ED. *adj.* Unacquainted.
UNVIS'ITED. *adj.* Not resorted to; never yet visited.
UNWAR'RANTABLE. *adj.* Not defensible; not allowed. adv. *unwarrantably.*
UNWAR'RANTED. *adj.* Not certain; not ascertained.
UNWA'RY. *adj.* Imprudent; unexpected. *s. unwariness:* adv. *unwarily.*
UNWEL'COME. *adj.* Not pleasing; not well received.
UNWELL'. *adj.* Not well; slightly indisposed.
UNWEPT'. *adj.* Not lamented.
UNWHOLE'SOME. *adj.* Insalubrious; corrupt. *s. unwholesomeness.*
UNWIEL'DY. *adj.* Unmanageable; bulky. adv. *unwieldily.*
UNWIL'LING. *adj.* Not inclined; not complying by inclination. *s. unwillingness:* adv. *unwillingly.*

UNWI'SE. *adj.* Defective in wisdom, injudicious. adv. *unwisely.*
UNWISH'ED. *adj.* Not sought; not desired.
UNWIT'NESSED. *adj.* Wanting testimony.
UNWIT'TINGLY. *adv.* Without knowledge.
UNWOM'ANLY. *adj.* Unbecoming a woman.
UNWON'TED. *adj.* Uncommon; unused.
UNWOR'THY. *adj.* Not worthy. *s. unworthiness:* adv. *unworthily.*
UNWRIT'TEN. *adj.* Not written; oral; traditional.
UNWROUGHT. *adj.* Not laboured.
UNYIELD'ING. *adj.* Not giving place; obstinate.
UNYO'KE. *v.* To loose from the yoke. pr. par. *unyoking;* past, *unyoked.*
UP. One of the prepositions. adv. *up.*
UPBRAID'. *v.* To charge contemptuously with any thing disgraceful; to reproach. pr. par. *upbraiding*, past, *upbraided:* s. *upbraider.* adv. *upbraidingly.*
UPHEAVE'. *v.* To heave up. pr. par. *upheaving;* past, *upheaved.*
UPHILL'. *adj.* Difficult; laborious.
UPHOLD'. *v.* To lift on high; to support; to continue. pr. par. *upholding;* past, *upheld:* s. *upholder.*
UPHOL'STERER. *s.* One who furnishes houses with beds, curtains, &c. *s. upholstery.*
UP'LAND. *s.* High ground. *adj. upland.*
UPLIFT'. *v.* To raise aloft. pr. par *uplifting;* past, *uplifted.*
UPON'. *prep.* Not under, not within; on.
UP'PER. *adj.* Superior in place; higher. sup. *uppermost.*
UP'RIGHT. *adj.* Perpendicularly erect: honest. *s. uprightness:* adv *uprightly.*
UP'ROAR. *s.* Tumult; disturbance.
UPSET'. *v.* To overturn. pr. par *upsetting:* past, *upset.*
UP'SHOT. *s.* Conclusion; final event.

391

UP'START. *s.* One suddenly raised to wealth, power, or honour. *adj. upstart.*

UPTURN'. *v.* To throw up; to furrow. pr. par. *upturning;* past, *upturned.*

UPWARD. *adv.* Directed to a higher part. *adv. upwards.*

URBA'NE. *adj.* Civil; courteous. *s. urbanity.*

URCH'IN. *s.* A hedge-hog.

URGE. *v.* To incite; to push; to provoke. pr. par. *urging;* past, *urged: s. urger, urgency:* adj. *urgent:* adv. *urgently.*

U'RINE. *s.* Animal water. *adj. urinary.*

URN. *s.* A vessel used for the ashes of the dead, &c.

UR'SULINE. *adj.* Denoting an order of nuns.

US. *pron.* The objective case of *we.*

U'SAGE. *s.* Treatment; custom.

U'SANCE. *s.* A term used by merchants.

USE. *s.* Usage; custom; habit; convenience. *v. use;* pr. par. *using;* past, *used:* adj. *useful, useless: s. user, usefulness, uselessness:* adv. *usefully, uselessly.*

USH'ER. *s.* An introducer; an under-teacher. *v. usher,* pr. par. *ushering;* past, *ushered.*

USQUEBAUGH'. *s.* A compounded distilled spirit.

U'SUAL. *adj.* Common, customary, frequent. adv. *usually.*

U'SUFRUCT. *s.* The temporary use. adj. *usufructuary.*

USURP'. *v.* To seize without right. pr. par. *usurping;* past, *usurped: s. usurpation, usurper:* adv. *usurpingly.*

U'SURY. *s.* Money paid for the use of money; interest; illegal interest. *s. usurer:* adj. *usurious:* adv. *usuriously.*

UTEN'SIL. *s.* An instrument for use.

U'TERINE. *adj.* Belonging to the womb.

UTIL'ITY. *s.* Usefulness; profit.

UT'MOST. *adj.* Extreme; in the highest degree. *s. utmost.*

UTO'PIAN. *adj.* Ideal; not real.

UT'TER. *adj.* Situated on the outside; extreme; excessive. sup. *uttermost: s. uttermost:* adv. *utterly.*

UT'TER. *v.* To speak; to pronounce; to publish. pr. par. *uttering;* past, *uttered: s. utterer.*

UXO'RIOUS. *adj.* Submissively fond of a wife. *s. uxoriousness:* adv. *uxoriously.*

V

VA'CANT. *adj.* Empty; unfilled; unoccupied. *v. vacate;* pr. par. *vacating;* past, *vacated: s. vacation, vacancy,* pl. *vacancies.*

VAC'CINATE. *v.* To inoculate with vaccine matter. pr. par. *vaccinating;* past, *vaccinated: s. vaccination, vaccinator.*

VAC'CINE. *adj.* Of or belonging to a cow.

VA'CILLATE. *v.* To waver; to be inconstant. pr. par. *vacillating;* past, *vacillated: s. vacillation.*

VACU'ITY. *s.* Emptiness. pl. *vacuities.*

VAC'UUM. *s.* Space unoccupied by matter.

VAG'ABOND. *adj.* Wandering; vagrant. *s. vagabond.*

VAGA'RY. *s.* A wandering; a capricious freak. pl. *vagaries.*

VA'GRANT. *adj.* Wandering; unsettled. *s. vagrant, vagrancy.*

VAGUE. *adj.* Unmeaning, undetermined.

VAIL. *s.* A curtain; a cover; money given to servants. *v. vail;* pr. par *vailing;* past, *vailed.*

VAIN. *adj.* Fruitless; unreal; meanly proud; showy. adv. *vainly.*

VALE. *s.* A wide, open space, between hills.
VALEDIC'TION. *s.* A farewell. *adj. valedictory.*
VAL'ENTINE. *s.* A sweetheart, chosen on Valentine's day; a letter sent on Valentine's day.
VALE'RIAN. *s.* A kind of plant.
VALET'. *s.* A waiting servant.
VALETUDINA'RIAN, VALETU'DINARY. *adj.* Weakly; sickly. *s. valetudinarian.*
VAL'IANT. *adj.* Stout; brave. *adv. valiantly.*
VAL'ID. *adj.* Efficacious, weighty, conclusive. *s. validity.*
VAL'LEY. *s.* A low ground or a hollow between two hills. *pl. valleys.*
VALLI'SE. *s.* A portmanteau.
VAL'OUR. *s.* Personal bravery; strength. *adj. valorous: adv. valorously.*
VAL'UE. *s.* Price; worth; high rate. *v. value: pr. par. valuing; past, valued; r. valuation, valuator: adj. valuable.*
VALVE. *s.* A folding door; any thing that opens over the mouth of a vessel.
VAMP. *v.* To mend old things; to piece. *pr. par. vamping; past, vamped: s. vamper.*
VAMP. *s.* The upper leather of a shoe: a sock.
VAM'PIRE. *s.* A pretended demon; a kind of bat.
VAN. *s.* The front of an army or fleet: the first line. *s. vanguard.*
VANDAL'IC. *adj.* Barbarous; resembling the character of the Vandals. *s. vandalism.*
VANE. *s.* A plate turned with the wind.
VAN'ISH. *v.* To lose perceptible existence; to disappear. *pr. par. vanishing; past, vanished.*
VAN'ITY. *s.* Emptiness; uncertainty; idle show; ostentation; petty pride. *pl. vanities.*
VAN'QUISH. *v.* To conquer; to overcome. *pr. par. vanquishing; past, vanquished: s. vanquisher: adj. vanquishable.*

VAP'ID. *adj.* Dead; spiritless. *s. vapidness.*
VA'POUR. *s.* Any thing exhalable, fume; steam; vain imagination in the plural, hypochondriacal maladies. *adj. vaporous.*
VA'POUR. *v.* To emit fumes; to bully *pr. par. vapouring; past, vapoured s. vapourer: adv. vapouringly.*
VA'RIABLE. *adj.* Changeable; inconstant. *s. variableness: adv. variably: s. variation.*
VA'RIANCE. *s.* Disagreement; discord.
VA'RIEGATE. *v.* To diversify; to stain with different colours. *pr. par. variegating; past, variegated. s. variegation.*
VARI'ETY. *s.* Change; succession of one thing to another. *pl. varieties.*
VARI'OLOID. *s.* A modification of the smallpox.
VARI'OLOUS. *adj.* Relating to the disease called the smallpox.
VA'RIOUS. *adj.* Different; several; changeable. *adv. variously.*
VAR'LET. *s.* A servant or attendant, a term of reproach.
VAR'NISH. *s.* A shining liquid substance. *v. varnish; pr. par. varnishing; past, varnished: s. varnisher.*
VA'RY. *v.* To change; to diversify. *pr. par. varying; past, varied.*
VAS'CULAR. *adj.* Consisting of vessels. *s. vascularity.*
VASE. *s.* A vessel; generally rather for show than use.
VAS'SAL. *s.* One who holds of a superior lord; a subject; a servant. *s. vassalage.*
VAST. *adj.* Very large; immensely great. *s. vastness: adv. vastly.*
VAT. *s.* A large tub, used by brewers, &c.
VAUDE'VILLE. *s.* A ballad; a musical drama.
VAULT. *s.* A continued arch; a cellar, a cave. *adj. vaulted.* pronounced *vaut.*
VAULT. *v.* To leap; to jump. pronounced *vaut. pr. par. vaulting; past, vaulted: s. vaulter.*
VAUNT. *v.* To boast; to brag. pr
393

par. *vaunting;* past, *vaunted:* s. *vaunter:* adv. *vauntingly.*

VEAL. *s.* The flesh of a calf.

VEER. *v.* To turn about; to change. pr. par. *veering;* past, *veered.*

VEGETABLE. *s.* Any thing that has growth without sensation, as plants. adj. *vegetable:* v. *vegetate;* pr. par. *vegetating;* past, *vegetated:* s. *vegetation:* adj. *vegetative.*

VEHEMENT. *adj.* Violent; ardent. s. *vehemence:* adv. *vehemently.*

VEHICLE. *s.* That in which any thing is carried. adj. *vehicular.*

VEIL. *s.* A cover to conceal the face; a disguise. v. *veil;* pr. par. *veiling;* past, *veiled.*

VEIN. *s.* A blood-vessel; course of metal in a mine; tendency or turn of the mind or genius. adj. *veined, veiny.*

VELLUM. *s.* A fine kind of parchment.

VELOCITY. *s.* Speed; swiftness. pl. *velocities.*

VELVET. *s.* Silk with a short fur or pile. adj. *velvet.*

VELVETEEN. *s.* A kind of stuff made in imitation of velvet.

VENAL. *adj.* Mercenary; prostitute. s. *venality.*

VENATIC, VENATICAL. *adj.* Used in hunting.

VEND. *v.* To sell. pr. par. *vending;* past, *vended:* s. *vender, vendor, vendee:* adj. *vendible.*

VENDUE. *s.* Auction.

VENEER. *v.* To cover with thin wood, &c. pr. par. *veneering;* past, *veneered:* s. *veneering.*

VENERATE. *v.* To reverence; to regard with awe. pr. par. *venerating;* past, *venerated:* s. *veneration, venerator:* adj. *venerable:* adv. *venerably.*

VENEREAL. *adj.* Relating to love, or rather lust.

VENESECTION. *s.* Blood-letting, by cutting a vein.

VENGEANCE. *s.* Punishment, avengement. adj. *vengeable, vengeful.*

VENIAL. *adj.* Pardonable.

VENISON. *s.* The flesh of deer. pronounced *ven'-zon.*

VENOM. *s.* Poison. adj. *venomous.* adv. *venomously.*

VENT. *s.* A small aperture; a passage at which any thing is let out emission. v. *vent;* pr. par. *venting* past, *vented.*

VENTIDUCT. *s.* A passage for the wind.

VENTILATE. *v.* To cool or purify, by the admission of wind. pr. par *ventilating;* past, *ventilated:* s. *ventilation, ventilator.*

VENTRAL. *adj.* Belonging to the belly.

VENTRICLE. *s.* Any small cavity in an animal body, particularly those of the heart; the stomach.

VENTRILOQUISM. *s.* The act of speaking inwardly, so that the sound seems to issue from the belly; and so modifying the tones, as to induce a belief, that the sound issues from any place to which the attention of the auditors is directed. s. *ventriloquist.*

VENTURE. *s.* A hazard; an undertaking of chance and danger. v. *venture;* pr. par. *venturing;* past, *ventured:* s. *venturer:* adj. *venturous:* adv. *venturously.*

VERACITY. *s.* Moral truth; honesty of report. adj. *veracious.*

VERANDA. *s.* A kind of open portico.

VERB. A part of speech, defined as signifying "to be, to do, or to suffer."

VERBAL. *adj.* spoken: not written; oral; consisting of mere words; having word corresponding to word. adv. *verbally.*

VERBATIM. *adv.* Word for word.

VERBERATE. *v.* To beat; to strike. pr. par. *verberating;* past, *verberated:* s. *verberation.*

VERBIAGE. *s.* Verbosity; bombast.

VERBOSE. *adj.* Exuberant in words prolix. s. *verbosity.*

394

VER'DANT. *adj.* Green. *s. verdancy.*
VER'DERER. *s.* An officer in the forest.
VER'DICT. *s.* The determination of a jury; decision.
VER'DIGRIS. *s.* The green rust of copper.
VER'DITER. *s.* Chalk made green.
VERGE. *s.* A rod, or something resembling it, carried as an emblem of authority; the mace of a dean; the brink; the edge.
VERGE. *v.* To bend downwards; to tend. pr. par. *verging;* past, *verged.*
VER'GER. *s.* He that carries the mace before a dean.
VER'IFY. *v.* To justify against a charge of falsehood; to confirm. pr. par. *verifying;* past, *verified: s. verification, verifier:* adj. *verifiable.*
VER'ILY. *adv.* In truth; certainly.
VERISIMIL'ITUDE. *s.* Probability. adj. *verisimilar.*
VER'ITY. *s.* Truth. adj. *veritable.*
VER'JUICE. *s.* Acid liquor expressed from crab-apples.
VERMICEL'LI. *s.* A paste rolled and broken in the form of worms. pronounced *ver-me-chel·e.*
VERMIC'ULAR. *adj.* Acting like a worm; spiral.
VER'MICULE. *s.* A little grub or worm.
VER'MIFORM. *adj.* Having the shape of a worm.
VER'MIFUGE. *s.* A medicine that destroys worms.
VERMIL'ION. *s.* A beautiful red colour.
VER'MIN. *s.* Any noxious animal: used commonly for small creatures.
VERMIP'AROUS. *adj.* Producing worms.
VERNAC'ULAR. *adj.* Of one's own country.
VER'NAL. *adj.* Belonging to the spring.
VER'SATILE. *adj* Changeable variable. *s. versatility,* pl. *versatilities.*
VERSE. *s.* Language restrained to harmonic sounds, or to a regular number of syllables; a line of verse; a portion of Scripture, contained in one numerical division.
VERSED. *adj.* Skilled in; acquainted with.
VER'SIFY. *v.* To make verses; to turn into verse. pr. par. *versifying;* past, *versified: s. versifier, versification.*
VER'SION. *s.* Change; transformation: translation.
VERST. *s.* A Russian measure, equal to about three quarters of an English mile.
VER'TEBRE. *s.* A joint of the back adj. *vertebral.*
VER'TEX. *s.* The point over head the top. pl. *vertices, vertexes.*
VER'TICAL. *adj.* Placed in the zenith; perpendicular to the horizon. adv. *vertically.*
VERTI'GINOUS. *adj.* Rotatory giddy.
VER'TIGO. *s.* A giddiness.
VER'Y. *adv.* True; in a great degree; in an eminent degree.
VES'ICLE. *s.* A small cuticle inflated; a blister.
VES'PERS. *s.* The evening service of the Roman church.
VES'SEL. *s.* Any thing in which liquids or other things are put; a ship.
VEST. *s.* An outer garment; a kind of coat. *s. vestment, vesture.*
VEST. *v.* To dress; to make possessor of. pr. par. *vesting;* past, *vested.*
VES'TAL. *s.* A virgin consecrated to Vesta; a pure virgin. adj. *vestal.*
VES'TIBULE. *s.* The porch or first entrance of a house.
VES'TIGE. *s.* Mark left behind in passing.
VES'TRY. *s.* A room appendant to a church, in which the sacerdotal garments, &c. are kept; a parochial

assembly, commonly convened in the vestry. pl. *vestries.*
VETCH. *s.* A kind of pea. pl. *vetches.*
VET'ERAN. *s.* An old soldier; one long practised in any thing. adj. *veteran.*
VET'ERINARY. *adj.* Pertaining to science in the diseases of cattle.
VEX. *v.* To plague, to disquiet, to torment. pr. par. *vexing;* past, *vexed:* s. *vexation:* adj. *vexatious:* adv. *vexatiously.*
VI'AL. *s.* A small bottle.
VI'AND. *s.* Food; meat dressed.
VIAT'ICUM. *s.* Provision for a journey; the last rite of the Roman church.
VI'BRATE. *v.* To move to and fro. pr. par. *vibrating;* past, *vibrated:* s. *vibration:* adj. *vibrative, vibratory.*
VIC'AR. *s.* A substitute; a clergyman of the episcopal church, next in degree below a rector. adj. *vicarial, vicarious:* s. *vicarage:* adv. *vicariously.*
VICE. *s.* Depravity; wickedness; a kind of small iron press, with screws.
VICEAD'MIRAL. *s.* The second commander of a fleet.
VICECHAN'CELLOR. *s.* The second magistrate of the universities.
VICE'ROY. *s.* He who governs in place of the king. s. *viceroyalty,* pl. *viceroyalties.*
VI'CINAGE. *s.* Neighbourhood.
VICIN'ITY. *s.* Nearness; neighbourhood. pl. *vicinities.*
VI'CIOUS. *adj.* Corrupt; devoted to vice. s. *viciousness:* adv. *viciously.*
VICIS'SITUDE. *s.* Change, revolution.
VIC'TIM. *s.* A sacrifice, something destroyed.
VIC'TOR. *s.* A conqueror. adj. *victorious:* adv. *victoriously:* s. *victory.*
VIC'TUALS. *s.* Provision of food; sustenance. pronounced *vit'-als.* v.

victual; pr. par. *victualing;* past, *victualed:* s. *victualler.*
VIDEL'ICET. *adv.* To wit, that is generally written *viz.*
VID'UAL. *adj.* Belonging to the state of a widow. s. *viduity.*
VIE. *v.* To contest; to strive for superiority. pr. par. *vying;* past, *vied.*
VIEW. *v.* To survey; to see. pr. par. *viewing;* past, *viewed:* s. *view, viewer.*
VI'GIL. *s.* Watch; devotions performed in the customary hours of rest.
VI'GILANT. *adj.* Watchful; circumspect. s. *vigilance:* adv. *vigilantly.*
VIGNETTE'. *s.* An ornamental assemblage of leaves and flowers. pronounced *vin-yet*.
VIG'OUR, VIGOR. *s.* Force, strength, energy. adj. *vigorous:* adv. *vigorously.*
VILE. *adj.* Base; worthless; sordid. s. *vileness:* adv. *vilely.*
VIL'IFY. *v.* To debase; to make vile; to defame. pr. par. *vilifying;* past, *vilified:* s. *vilification, vilifier.*
VIL'LA. *s.* A country-seat.
VIL'LAGE. *s.* A small collection of houses, less than a town. s. *villager.*
VIL'LAIN. *s.* One who held by a base tenure; a wicked wretch. s. *villanage, villany.*
VIMIN'EOUS. *adj.* Made of twigs.
VINDE'MIAL. *adj.* Belonging to a vintage.
VIN'DICATE. *v.* To justify; to revenge; to clear. pr. par. *vindicating;* past, *vindicated:* s. *vindication, vindicator:* adj. *vindicative, vindicatory.*
VINDIC'TIVE. *adj.* Revengeful. s. *vindictiveness:* adv. *vindictively.*
VINE. *s.* The plant that bears the grape. s. *vineyard.*
VIN'EGAR. *s.* Wine, &c. grown sour.
VI'NOUS. *adj.* Having the qualities of wine. s. *vinosity.*

VIN'TAGE. *s.* The produce of the vine for a year; the time in which grapes are gathered. *s. vintager.*

VINT'NER. *s.* One who sells wine.

VI'OL. *s.* A stringed instrument of music.

VI'OLATE. *v.* To injure; to hurt; to infringe. pr. par. *violating*; past, *violated*. *s. violation, violator*: adv. *violable*.

VI'OLENCE. *s.* Force; unjust force; outrage; eagerness. adj. *violent*: adv. *violently*.

VI'OLET. *s.* A kind of flower.

VI'OLIN. *s.* A fiddle.

VIOLINCEL'LO. *s.* A bass violin.

VI'PER. *s.* A serpent, of that species which brings forth its young alive. adj. *viperine, viperous*.

VIRAG'O *s.* An impudent, turbulent woman.

VIR'GIN. *s.* A maid. adj. *virgin, virginal*: *s. virginity*.

VIR'GO. *s.* The sixth sign of the Zodiac.

VIRID'ITY. *s.* Greenness.

VIR'ILE. adj. Belonging to man. *s. virility*.

VIR'TUAL. adj. Having the efficacy, without the material part. adv. *virtually*.

VIR'TUE. *s.* Moral goodness; efficacy. adj. *virtuous*: adv. *virtuously*.

VIRTUO'SO. *s.* A man skilled in antique or natural curiosities.

VIR'ULENT. adj. Poisonous, venomous, bitter. *s. virulence*: adv. *virulently*.

VIS-A-VIS'. *s.* A carriage which holds only two persons, who sit face to face. pronounced *ve-za-ve'*.

VIS'AGE. *s.* Face, look.

VIS'CID. adj. Glutinous. *s. viscidity*.

VIS'COUNT. *s.* A degree of nobility next to an earl. pronounced *vi'count*. fem. *viscountess*, pl. *viscountesses*.

VIS'COUS. adj. Glutinous. *s. viscosity*.

VIS'IBLE. adj. Perceptible to the eye; apparent. *s. visibility*: adv *visibly*.

VIS'ION. *s.* Sight; the faculty of seeing; a dream.

VIS'IONARY. adj. Affected by phantoms; imaginary. *s. visionary*.

VIS'IT. *v.* To go to see. (In Scriptural language,) to send good or evil judicially. pr. par. *visiting*, past, *visited*: *s. visit, visitant, visitation, visiter, visitor*.

VIS'OR. *s.* A mask; part of a helmet. adj. *visored*.

VIS'TA. *s.* View; prospect through an avenue.

VIS'UAL. adj. Used in sight; instrumental to sight.

VI'TAL. adj. Contributing to life necessary to life. *s. vitality*: pl *vitals*: adv. *vitally*.

VI'TIATE. *v.* To deprave; to spoil pr. par. *vitiating*; past, *vitiated*.

VIT'RIFY. *v.* To change into glass. pr. par. *vitrifying*; past, *vitrified*: *s. vitrification*: adj. *vitreous*.

VIT'RIOL. *s.* A kind of mineral salt. See the Etymological Dictionary.

VIT'ULINE. adj. Belonging to a calf, or to veal.

VITU'PERATE. *v.* To blame; to censure. pr. par. *vituperating*; past, *vituperated*: *s. vituperation* adj. *vituperative*.

VIVA'CIOUS. adj. Long-lived; sprightly; gay. *s. vivacity*.

VIV'ID. adj. Lively; quick; striking. *s. vividness*: adv. *vividly*.

VIV'IFY. *v.* To animate. pr. par. *vivifying*; past, *vivified*: *s. vivification*.

VIVIP'AROUS. adj. Bringing forth the young alive.

VIX'EN. *s.* A scolding woman; a shrew.

VIZ'ARD. *s.* A mask used for disguise.

VIZ'IER. *s.* The prime-minister of the Turkish empire.

VOCAB'ULARY. *s.* A dictionary; a book of words. pl. *vocabularies*.

VO'CAL. adj. Having a voice; ut

tered or modulated by the voice. adv. *vocally.*

VOCA'TION. *s.* Calling by the will of God; employment; trade.

VOC'ATIVE. *s.* The grammatical case used in calling or speaking to.

VOCIF'ERATE. *v.* To clamour; to make an outcry. pr. par. *vociferating;* past, *vociferated:* s. *vociferation:* adj. *vociferous.*

VOGUE. *s.* Fashion; popular reception.

VOICE. *s.* Sound emitted by the mouth; vote; suffrage.

VOID. *adj.* Empty; vacant; vain; ineffectual. *v. void;* pr. par. *voiding;* past, *voided:* s. *void, voidance, voider, voidness.*

VOITU'RE. *s.* A sort of carriage.

VOL'ATILE. *adj.* Flying; having the power to pass off by spontaneous evaporation; lively, fickle. s. *volatility.*

VOLCA'NO. *s.* A burning mountain. pl. *volcanoes.*

VOLI'TION. *s.* The act of willing; power of choice exerted.

VOL'LEY. *s.* A flight of shot; an emission of many at once. pl. *vollies.*

VOL'UBLE. *adj.* Rolling; moving quickly; active or fluent, (applied to the tongue, or speech.) adv. *volubly:* s. *volubility.*

VOL'UME. *s.* Something rolled, or convolved; a book; circumference. adj. *voluminous.*

VOL'UNTARY. *adj.* Acting without compulsion; willing. adv. *voluntarily.*

VOLUNTEE'R. *s.* One who enters into any service, of his own accord. *v. volunteer;* pr. par. *volunteering,* past, *volunteered.*

VOLUP'TUOUS. *adj.* Given to excess of pleasure; luxurious. s. *voluptuousness:* adv. *voluptuously:* s. *voluptuary,* pl. *voluptuaries.*

VOM'IT. *v.* To throw up from the stomach; to throw up with violence from any hollow. pr. par. *vomiting;* past, *vomited:* s. *vomit.*

VORA'CIOUS. *adj.* Greedy; ravenous; rapacious. s. *voracity:* adv *voraciously.*

VOR'TEX. *s.* Any thing whirled round. Latin pl. *vortices;* English, *vortexes:* adj. *vortical.*

VO'TARY. *s.* One devoted to any particular service, &c. pl. *votaries;* fem. *votaress,* pl. *votaresses.*

VOTE. *s.* Suffrage; wish expressed in favour of any person or thing. *v. vote;* pr. par. *voting;* past, *voted:* s. *voter.*

VO'TIVE. *adj.* Given by vow.

VOUCH. *v.* To call to witness; to attest; to warrant. pr. par. *vouching;* past, *vouched:* s. *voucher.*

VOUCHSA'FE. *v.* To deign; to condescend. pr. par. *vouchsafing;* past, *vouchsafed:* s. *vouchsafement.*

VOW. *s.* A solemn and religious promise. *v. vow;* pr. par. *vowing;* past, *vowed.*

VOW'EL. *s.* A letter utterable by itself.

VOY'AGE. *s.* A travel by sea. *v voyage;* pr. par. *voyaging;* past, *voyaged:* s. *voyager.*

VUL'GAR. *adj.* Plebeian; practised amongst the common people; (in relation to a language,) national: also, mean, unfashionable. s. *vulgar, vulgarism, vulgarity:* adv. *vulgarly.*

VUL'GATE. *s.* An ancient Latin translation of the Bible.

VUL'NERABLE. *adj.* Susceptible of wounds.

VUL'NERARY. *adj.* Useful in the cure of wounds.

VUL'PINE. *adj.* Belonging or relating to a fox.

VUL'TURE. *s.* A large bird of prey

W

WAB'BLE. *v.* To move from side to side. pr. par. *wabbling;* past, *wobbled.*

WAD. *s.* A bundle of straw or other loose matter, thrust close together. *s. wadding.*

WAD'DLE. *v.* To shake, in walking, from side to side. pr. par. *waddling;* past, *waddled.*

WADE. *v.* To walk through water. pr. par. *wading;* past, *waded.*

WA'FER. *s.* A thin cake; paste made to close letters.

WAFT. *v.* To carry through the air, or on the water. pr. par. *wafting;* past, *wafted.*

WAG. *v.* To move lightly; to shake slightly. pr. par. *wagging;* past, *wagged.*

WAG. *s.* Any one ludicrously mischievous. s. *waggery,* pl. *waggeries, waggishness:* adj. *waggish:* adv. *waggishly.*

WAGE. *v.* To lay a wager; to carry on. pr. par. *waging;* past, *waged:* s. *wage.*

WA'GER. *s.* A bet. *v. wager;* pr. par. *wagering;* past, *wagered.* s. *wagerer.*

WA'GES. *s.* Hire, pay.

WAG'GLE. *v.* To waddle. pr. par. *waggling;* past, *waggled.*

WAG'ON, WAG'GON. *s.* A heavy carriage, for burthens. s. *wagonage, wagoner.*

WAG'TAIL. *s.* A kind of bird.

WAIL. *v.* To moan, to lament. pr. par. *wailing;* past, *wailed:* s. *wail.*

WAIN. *s.* A carriage.

WAIN'SCOT. *s.* The inner wooden covering of a wall. v. *wainscot;* pr. par. *wainscotting;* past, *wainscotted.*

WAIST. *s.* The smallest part of the body. s. *waistband, waistcoat.*

WAIT. *v.* To expect, to stay for. pr. par. *waiting;* past, *waited:* s. *wait, waiter.*

WAIVE. *v.* To put off, to quit [r. par. *waiving;* past, *waived.*

WAKE. *v.* To watch; not to sleep, to be roused. pr. par. *waking,* past, *waked:* s. *wake, wakefulness, wakener:* adj. *wakeful.*

WA'KEN. *v.* To wake; to rouse from sleep. pr. par. *wakening,* past, *wakened.*

WALK. *v.* To move by leisurely steps; to travel on foot. pr. par. *walking;* past, *walked:* s. *walk, walker.*

WALL. *s.* A partition of brick or stone. v. *wall;* pr. par. *walling,* past, *walled:* s. *wallflower, wallfruit.*

WAL'LET. *s.* A small bag; a knapsack.

WALL'EYED. *adj.* Having white eyes.

WAL'LOP. *v.* To move violently; to strike. pr. par. *walloping;* past, *walloped.*

WAL'LOW. *v.* To roll in mire, &c. pr. par. *wallowing;* past, *wallowed.* s. *wallower.*

WAL'NUT. *s.* A kind of fruit.

WAN. *adj.* Pale, as with sickness. s. *wanness.*

WAND. *s.* A long rod; a charming rod.

WAN'DER. *v.* To rove, to deviate pr. par. *wandering;* past, *wandered:* s. *wanderer.*

WANE. *v.* To grow less; to decrease. pr. par. *waning;* past, *waned:* s. *wane.*

WANT. *v.* To be without; to need; to fail. pr. par. *wanting;* past, *wanted:* s. *want.*

WAN'TON. *adj.* Lascivious, licentious, gay v. *wanton;* pr. par. *wantoning,* past, *wantoned·* adv. *wantonly:* s. *wanton, wantonness.*

WAR. *s.* Hostility, fighting, combat. v. *war;* pr. par. *warring,* past, *warred:* adj. *warlike, worworn·* s. *warfare, warrior.*

WAR'BLE. *v.* To quaver; to utter musically. pr. par. *warbling;* past, *warbled:* s. *warble, warbler.*

WARD. *v.* To guard, to watch, to defend. pr. par. *warding;* past, *warded:* s. *ward, warden, warder.*

WARES. *s* Merchandise.

WARE'HOUSE. *s.* A storehouse for merchandise.

WARM. *adj.* Heated to a small degree; zealous; ardent. v. *warm;* pr. par *warming;* past, *warmed:* adv. *warmly:* s. *warmth.*

WARN. *v.* To caution; to admonish. pr. par. *warning;* past, *warned:* s. *warner, warning.*

WARP. *s.* The thread that lies parallel to the selvage. v. *warp;* pr. par. *warping;* past, *warped.*

WARP. *v.* To turn, to contract, to shrivel. pr. par. *warping;* past, *warped.*

WAR'RANT. *v.* To support or maintain; to attest; to justify. pr. par. *warranting;* past, *warranted:* s. *warrant, warranty,* pl. *warranties:* adj. *warrantable.*

WAR'REN. *s.* A kind of park for rabbits.

WART. *s.* A corneous excrescence on the flesh.

WA'RY. *adj.* Cautious, scrupulous. adv. *warily:* s. *wariness.*

WAS. Pret. of the v. *to be.*

WASH. *v.* To cleanse by ablution. pr. par. *washing;* past, *washed:* s. *wash,* pl. *washes, washer:* adj. *washy.*

WASH'BALL. *s.* Ball made of soap.

WASP. *s.* A stinging insect. adj. *waspish:* adv. *waspishly:* s. *waspishness.*

WASTE. *v.* To diminish, to squander, to destroy. pr. par. *wasting;* past, *wasted:* s. *waste, wastefulness, waster:* adj. *waste, wasteful:* adv. *wastefully.*

WATCH. *s.* Forbearance of sleep; attention; guard; a period of the night; a pocket clock. v. *watch;* pr. par. *watching;* past, *watched:* s. *watcher, watchfulness:* adj.

watchful: adv. *watchfully:* s. *watchhouse, watchman,* pl. *watchmen, watchtower.*

WATCH'WORD. *s.* The word given to sentinels, in order to know their friends.

WAT'ER. *s.* A transparent colourless fluid. v. *water;* pr. par. *watering;* past, *watered:* adj. *watery:* s. *watercress,* pl. *watercresses, waterfall, watering-place, watermelon.*

WATERCOL'OURS. *s.* Colours made into a soft consistence with water.

WAT'ERLOGGED. *adj.* Heavy and unmanageable, from the weight of water.

WAT'ERMAN. *s.* A ferryman; a boatman. pl. *watermen.*

WAT'ERMARK. *s.* The utmost limit of the rise of the flood.

WAT'ERMILL. *s.* A mill turned by water.

WAT'ERTIGHT. *adj* That will not admit or discharge water.

WAT'ERWORK. *s.* Play of fountains; any hydraulic performance.

WAT'TLE. *v.* To bind or make firm with twigs. pr. par. *wattling* past, *wattled.*

WAVE. *s.* A billow; an inequality. v. *wave;* pr. par. *waving;* past, *waved:* adj. *wavy.*

WA'VER. *v.* To play to and fro; to be unsettled. pr. par. *wavering* past, *wavered:* s. *waverer.*

WAX. *s.* A thick matter gathered by the bee. v. *wax;* pr. par. *waxing;* past, *waxed.* adj. *waxen, waxy*

WAX. *v.* To grow, to increase. pr par. *waxing;* past, *waxed.*

WAY. *s.* A road, a course, a method.

WAY'FARER. *s.* A passenger, a traveller. adj. *wayfaring.*

WAY'LAY. *v.* To beset by ambush. pr. par. *waylaying;* past, *waylaid:* s. *waylayer.*

WAY'WARD. *adj.* Froward, peevish. adv. *waywardly:* s. *waywardness.*

WE. A pronoun; pl. of *I.*

WEAK. *adj.* Feeble, not strong, infirm. *v. weaken;* pr. par. *weakening;* past, *weakened:* s. *weakener, weakness:* adv. and adj. *weakly.*
WEAL. *s.* Happiness, prosperity; republic.
WEALTH. *s.* Riches. adv. *wealthily:* s. *wealthiness:* adj. *wealthy.*
WEAN. *v.* To put from the breast; to withdraw from any habit or desire. pr. par. *weaning;* past, *weaned.*
WEAP'ON. *s.* An instrument of offence. adj. *weaponed, weaponless.*
WEAR. *v.* To waste; to consume tediously. pr. par. *wearing;* past, *worn:* s. *wear, wearer.*
WEA'RY. *adj.* Subdued by fatigue; tired. *v. weary;* pr. par. *wearying,* past, *wearied:* s. *weariness:* adj. *wearisome.*
WEA'SEL. *s.* A small quadruped.
WEATH'ER. *s.* State of the air; a storm. *v. weather;* pr. par. *weathering;* past, *weathered:* adj. *weatherbeaten, weatherproof.*
WEATH'ERCOCK. *s.* A cock, set on the top of a spire, to show the point from which the wind blows.
WEATH'ERGLASS. *s.* A barometer, a thermometer. pl. *weatherglasses.*
WEAVE. *v.* To form by texture; to unite by intermixture. pr. par. *weaving;* past, *woven:* s. *weaver.*
WEB. *s.* Texture; any thing woven.
WEB'FOOTED. *adj.* Having films between the toes.
WED. *v.* To marry; to unite for ever. pr. par. *wedding;* past, *wedded:* s. *wedding, wedlock.*
WEDGE. *s.* A body with a sharp edge. *v. wedge;* pr. par. *wedging;* past, *wedged.*
WED'NESDAY. *s.* The fourth day of the week.
WEED. *s.* A noxious or useless herb; a mourning garment. *v. weed;* pr. par. *weeding;* past, *weed:* s. *weeder:* adj. *weedy.*
WEEK. *s.* The space of seven days. adv. and adj. *weekly.*
WEEK'DAY. *s.* Any day not Sunday.
WEEP. *v.* To shed tears. pr. par. *weeping;* past, *wept:* s. *weeper.*
WEE'VIL. *s.* A grub.
WEFT. *s.* The woof of cloth.
WEIGH. *v.* To ascertain the weight of. pr. par. *weighing;* past, *weighed:* s. *weigher.*
WEIGHT. *s.* Quantity measured by the balance; ponderous mass, gravity, pressure. adv. *weightily.* s. *weightiness:* adj. *weighty.*
WEL'COME. *adj.* Received with gladness; admitted willingly. *v. welcome;* pr. par. *welcoming;* past, *welcomed:* s. *welcome.*
WELD. *s.* A plant which dies yellow.
WELD. *v.* To beat one mass of iron into another. pr. par. *welding;* past, *welded.*
WEL'FARE. *s.* Happiness, success, prosperity.
WELL. *s.* A fountain, a deep narrow pit of water.
WELL. *adj.* Not sick, in health, happy; advantageous. adv. *well.* adj. *wellborn, wellbred, wellmannered, wellmeaning, wellspent, wellspoken:* s. *wellmeaner, wellwisher.*
WELLFA'VOURED. *adj.* Comely
WELSH. *adj.* Relating to the people or country of Wales.
WELT. *s.* A border; an edging; a raised stripe. *v. welt;* pr. par. *welting;* past, *welted.*
WEL'TER. *v.* To roll in blood, mire, &c. pr. par. *weltering;* past, *weltered.*
WEN. *s.* A fleshy protuberance.
WENCH. *s.* A young woman; a strumpet. pl. *wenches:* s. *wencher.*
WENT. Pret. of the *v. to go.*
WEPT. Pret. and past par. of the *v. to weep.*
WERE. Pret. of the *v. to be:* second person, *wert.*
WE'SAND. *s.* The windpipe.
WEST. *s.* The point or region opposite to the east. adj. *west, westerly, western:* adv. *westward.*
WET. *s.* Water, moisture. adj. *wet,*

v. wet; pr. par. *wetting;* past, *wet, wetted:* s. *wetness.*
WETH'ER. *s.* A ram castrated.
WETSHOD'. *adj.* Wet over the shoes.
WHACK. *v.* To strike. pr. par. *whacking;* past, *whacked:* s. *whack.*
WHALE. *s.* A large fish. s. *whalebone*
WHANG. *s.* A leather thong.
WHAP'PER. *s.* Any thing uncommonly large.
WHARF. *s.* A perpendicular bank raised for lading or emptying vessels; a quay. pl. *wharves:* s. *wharfage, wharfinger.*
WHAT. One of the pronouns. adv. *whatever, whatsoever.*
WHEAT. *s.* A species of grain. adj. *wheaten.*
WHEED'LE. *v.* To entice by soft words; to flatter. pr. par. *wheedling;* past, *wheedled:* s. *wheedler.*
WHEEL. *s.* A circular body, that turns round upon an axis. *v. wheel;* pr. par. *wheeling;* past, *wheeled:* s. *wheeler, wheelbarrow, wheelwright.*
WHEEZE. *v.* To breathe with noise. pr. par. *wheezing;* past, *wheezed.*
WHELP. *s.* The young of a dog, or of any beast of prey. *v. whelp;* pr. par. *whelping;* past, *whelped.*
WHEN. *adv.* At the time that, &c. adv. *whenever, whensoever.*
WHENCE. *adv.* From what place, &c.
WHERE. *adv.* At which place or places. adv. *whereabout, whereas, whereat, whereby, wherefore, wherein, whereof, whereon, wheresoever, whereunto, wherever, whereupon, wherewith, wherewithal.*
WHER'RY. *s.* A light boat, generally with two masts. pl. *wherries.*
WHET. *v.* To sharpen by attrition; to edge. pr. par. *whetting;* past, *whetted:* s. *whet, whetter.*
WHETH'ER. One of the adverbs.
WHET'STONE. *s.* A sharpening stone.
WHEY. *s.* The thin or serous part of milk.

WHICH. One of the pronouns. adv. *whichsoever.*
WHIFF. *s.* A puff of wind.
WHIG. *s.* A kind of sour or thin milk; one of the political party opposed to the tories.
WHILE. *s.* Time; space of time adv. *while, whilst.*
WHILE. *v.* To loiter; to draw out pr. par. *whiling;* past, *whiled.*
WHIM. *s.* A freak; a caprice.
WHIM'PER. *v.* To cry without any loud noise. pr. par *whimpering* past, *whimpered.*
WHIM'SICAL. *adj.* Freakish, capricious. adv. *whimsically.*
WHIN. *s.* Furze, gorse.
WHINE. *v.* To lament in low murmurs. pr. par. *whining;* past, *whined:* s. *whine, whiner.*
WHIP. *v.* To strike with any thing tough and flexible; to sew slightly. pr. par. *whipping;* past, *whipped.* s. *whip, whipper, whipcord.*
WHIP'HAND. *s.* Advantage over, &c.
WHIP'SAW. *s.* A large saw, for two persons.
WHIRL. *v.* To turn rapidly round. pr. par. *whirling;* past, *whirled:* s. *whirl, whirligig, whirlpool, whirlwind.*
WHISK. *s.* A small besom, or brush; a quick violent motion. *v. whisk,* pr. par. *whisking;* past, *whisked.*
WHIS'KER. *s.* The hair growing on the upper lip or cheek, unshaven; a mustachio. adj. *whiskered.*
WHIS'KEY. *s.* A spirit distilled from grain.
WHIS'PER. *v.* To speak with a low voice. pr. par. *whispering;* past, *whispered:* s. *whisper, whisperer.*
WHIST. *int.* Be still! be silent!
WHIST. *s.* A game at cards.
WHIS'TLE. *v.* To form a kind of musical modulation of the breath. pronounced *whis'-l.* pr. par. *whistling;* past, *whistled:* s. *whistle, whistler.*
WHIT. *s.* A point, a jot.
WHITE. *adj.* Snowy, pale. s. *white, whitener, whiteness:* v. *whiten;* pr.

par *whitening;* past, *whitened:* adj. *wh:tish*

WHITELEAD'. *s.* Oxide of lead.

WHITETHORN. *s.* A species of thorn.

WHITEWASH. *s.* A kind of liquid plaster, with which walls are whitened. v. *whitewash;* pr. par. *whitewashing;* past, *whitewashed.*

WHITH'ER. *adv.* To what place. adv. *whithersoever.*

WHI'TING. *s.* A kind of fish; a soft chalk.

WHIT'LOW. *s.* A swelling on the finger.

WHIT'SUNTIDE. *s.* The feast of Pentecost.

WHIZ. *v.* To make a loud, humming noise. pr. par. *whizzing;* past, *whizzed:* s. *whiz.*

WHO. One of the pronouns. possessive case, *whose;* objective, *whom:* pron. *whoever, whosoever.*

WHOLE. *adj.* All, total, complete. s. *whole:* adv. *wholly.*

WHOLE'SALE. *s.* Sale of a large quantity at once. adj. *wholesale.*

WHOLE'SOME. *adj.* Sound; contributing to health. adv. *wholesomely:* s. *wholesomeness.*

WHOOP. *s.* A shout of pursuit. v. *whoop;* pr. par. *whooping;* past, *whooped.*

WHOR'TLEBERRY. *s.* A species of fruit. pl. *whortleberries.*

WHY. *adv.* For what reason.

WICK. *s.* The substance round which is applied the wax or tallow of a torch or candle.

WICK'ED. *adj.* Vicious, criminal, flagitious. adv. *wickedly:* s. *wickedness.*

WICK'ER. *s.* Made of small sticks.

WICK'ET. *s.* A small gate.

WIC'LIFFITE. *s.* One of the followers of the great religious reformer, Wicliffe.

WIDE. *adj.* Broad, extended far each way. adv *wide, widely:* v. *widen;* pr. par. *widening;* past, *widened:* s. *wideness.*

WID'GEON. *s.* A kind of water-fowl.

WID'OW. *s.* A woman whose husband is dead. s. *widowhood.*

WID'OWER. *s.* One who has lost his wife.

WIDTH. *s.* Breadth, wideness.

WIELD. *v.* To use with full command; to handle. pr. par. *wielding:* past, *wielded:* adj. *wieldy*

WIFE. *s.* A married woman. pl. *wives.*

WIG. *s.* An artificial covering for the head, made of hair.

WIGHT. *s.* A person, a being.

WILD. *adj.* Not tame; savage; propagated by nature. adv. *wildly:* s. *wild, wildness.*

WIL'DER. *v.* To lose or puzzle in an unknown or pathless tract. pr. par. *wildering;* past, *wildered.*

WIL'DERNESS. *s.* A desert. pl. *wildernesses.*

WILD'FIRE. *s.* A kind of inflammable composition.

WILD'GOOSECHASE. *s.* A fruitless pursuit.

WILE. *s.* A deceit, a fraud, a trick v. *wile;* pr. par. *wiling;* past, *wiled* adv. *wilily:* s. *wiliness:* adj. *wily.*

WILK. *s.* A kind of periwinkle.

WILL. *s.* That power by which we desire, and purpose; choice; a testament. v. *will;* pr. par. *willing;* past, *willed:* adj. *wilful:* adv. *wilfully:* s. *wilfulness.*

WIL'LING. *adj.* Inclined to any thing; consenting. adv. *willingly:* s. *willingness.*

WIL'LOW. *s.* A kind of tree.

WIN. *v.* To gain by conquest; to obtain; to gain by play. pr. par. *winning;* past, *won:* s. *winner.*

WINCE. *v.* To shrink from pain. pr par. *wincing;* past, *winced.*

WINCH. *s.* A windlass. pl. *winches.*

WIND. *s.* A strong current of air s. *windiness:* adj. *windy.*

WIND. *v.* To blow; to sound by inflation; to turn round; to twist. pr. par. *winding;* past, *wound.*

WIND'BOUND. *adj.* Confined by contrary winds

403

WIND'FALL. *s.* Fruit blown down from the tree. adj. *windfallen.*
WIND'GALL. *s.* A disease of a horse.
WIND'INGSHEET. *s.* A sheet in which the dead are wrapped.
WIND'LASS. *s.* A handle by which a rope is coiled around a cylinder. pl. *windlasses.*
WIND'MILL. *s.* A mill turned by the wind.
WIN'DOW. *s.* An aperture in a building, by which air and light are admitted.
WIND'PIPE. *s.* The passage for the breath.
WIND'WARD. *adv.* Towards the wind. adj. *windward.*
WINE. *s.* The fermented juice of the grape.
WING. *s.* The limb of a bird, by which it flies, &c. v. *wing;* pr. par. *winging;* past, *winged.*
WINK. *v.* To shut the eyes. pr. par. *winking;* past, *winked:* s. *wink.*
WIN'NOW. *v.* To separate by means of the wind; to sift. pr. par. *winnowing;* past, *winnowed:* s. *winnower.*
WIN'TER. *s.* The cold season of the year. v. *winter;* pr. par. *wintering;* past, *wintered:* adj. *winterly, wintry.*
WIPE. *v.* To cleanse by rubbing with something soft. pr. par. *wiping;* past, *wiped:* s. *wipe, wiper.*
WIRE. *s.* Metal drawn into a slender thread. adj. *wiry.*
WIRE'DRAW. *v.* To spin into wire; to draw out into length. pr. par. *wiredrawing;* past, *wiredrawn:* s. *wiredrawer.*
WIS'DOM. *s.* Sapience; the power of judging rightly.
WISE. *adj.* Sapient; judging rightly; judicious. adv. *wisely.*
WISE'ACRE. *s.* A fool, a simpleton.
WISH. *v.* To have strong desire; to long. pr. par. *wishing;* past, *wished:* s. *wish,* pl. *wishes, wisher.*
WISP. *s.* A small bundle of hay or straw. v. *wisp;* pr. par. *wisping;* past, *wisped.*

WIST'FUL. *adj.* Attentive, earnest. adv. *wistfully.*
WIT. *s.* The powers of the mind; quickness of fancy. adj. *witless, witted, witty:* s. *witticism, wittiness:* adv. *wittily.*
WITCH. *s.* A woman accused of sorcery. pl. *witches:* s. *witchery,* pl. *witcheries, witchcraft.*
WITH. One of the prepositions. adv. *withal:* prep. and adv. *within, without.*
WITHDRAW'. *v.* To take back; to retire; to bereave. pr. par. *withdrawing;* past, *withdrawn.*
WITHE. *s.* A willow twig.
WITH'ER. *v.* To fade, to grow sapless. pr. par. *withering;* past, *withered:* s. *witheredness.*
WITH'ERS. *s.* The joint which unites the neck and shoulders of a horse.
WITHHOLD'. *v.* To restrain, to keep back, to hinder. pr. par. *withholding;* past, *withheld.*
WITHSTAND'. *v.* To oppose, to resist. pr. par. *withstanding;* past, *withstood:* s. *withstander.*
WIT'LING. *s.* A pretender to wit.
WIT'NESS. *s.* Testimony; evidence, one who gives testimony. pl. *witnesses:* v. *witness;* pr. par. *witnessing;* past, *witnessed.*
WIT'TINGLY. *adv.* Knowingly, not ignorantly.
WIZ'ARD. *s.* A male witch.
WIZ'EN. *v.* To wither; to become dry. pr. par. *wizening;* past, *wizened.*
WO, WOE. *s.* Grief, sorrow, misery. adj. *woful:* adv. *wofully:* s. *wofulness.*
WOAD. *s.* A species of plant, used by dyers.
WO'BEGONE. *adj.* Lost in wo; distracted in wo.
WOLD. *s.* A plain open country; downs.
WOLF. *s.* A species of voracious animal. pl. *wolves.*
WOLF'DOG. *s.* A dog kept to guard sheep.

WOM'AN. *s.* The female of the human race. pl. *women:* adj. *womanly, womanish:* adv. *womanly.*
WOMB. *s.* The place of the fœtus.
WON. Pret. and past par. of the v. *to win.*
WON'DER. *v.* To be astonished, &c. pr. par. *wondering;* past, *wondered·* s. *wonder, wonderer:* adj. *wonderful, wonderous, wondrous:* adv. *wonderfully, wondrously.*
WONT'ED. *part.* Accustomed, usual.
WOO. *v.* To court; to sue to for love. pr. par. *wooing;* past, *wooed:* s. *wooer:* adv. *wooingly.*
WOOD. *s.* A large thick collection of trees; timber. adj. *wooded, wooden, woody.*
WOOD'BINE. *s.* Honeysuckle.
WOOD'COCK. *s.* A species of bird.
WOOD'LAND. *s.* Ground covered with woods.
WOOD'NOTE. *s.* Wild music.
WOOD'NYMPH. *s.* A fabled goddess of the woods.
WOOD'PECKER. *s.* A species of bird.
WOOF. *s.* The weft.
WOOL. *s.* The fleece of sheep. adj. *woollen, woolly:* s. *wooliness, woolcomber.*
WOOL STAPLER. *s.* One who deals largely in wool.
WORD. *s.* A single part of speech; oral expression. *s. wordiness:* adj. *wordy.*
WORE. Pret. of the v. *to wear.*
WORK. *v.* To labour, to ferment. pr. par. *working;* past, *worked:* s. *work, worker, workhouse, workman,* pl. *workmen, workmanship.*
WORLD. *s.* System of beings; the earth. s. *worldliness:* adj. and adv. *worldly.*
WORM. *s.* A kind of insect; any thing spiral. v. *worm;* pr. par. *worming;* past, *wormed:* adj. *wormy, wormeaten.*
WORM'WOOD. *s.* A species of plant.
WORN. Past par. of the v. *to wear.*
WOR'RY. *v.* To tear, to mangle, to harass. pr. par. *worrying;* past, *worried:* s. *worrier.*
WORSE. adj. The comp. of *bad.* adv. *worse:* sup. *worst:* s. *worst.*
WOR'SHIP. *s.* Dignity, eminence, adoration; a term of honour. v. *worship;* pr. par. *worshiping;* past, *worshiped:* adj. *worshipful:* adv *worshipfully:* s. *worshiper.*
WORST. *v.* To defeat, to overthrow. pr. par. *worsting;* past, *worsted.*
WORST'ED. *s.* Woollen yarn.
WORT. *s.* A species of herb; beer not fermented.
WORTH. *s.* Price, value, excellence. adj. *worth, worthless:* s *worthlessness.*
WOR'THY. adj. Deserving, valuable. s. *worthy, worthiness:* adv. *worthily.*
WOULD. Pret. of the v. *to will.*
WOUND. *s.* A hurt given by violence. pronounced *woond:* v. *wound;* pr. par. *wounding,* past, *wounded.*
WOUND. Pret. and past par. of the v. *to wind.* pronounced as written.
WOVE. Pret. of the v. *to weave.* past par. *woven.*
WRAITH. *s.* The fabled apparition of a person about to die.
WRAN'GLE. *v.* To dispute peevishly; to altercate. pr. par. *wrangling;* past, *wrangled:* s. *wrangle, wrangler.*
WRAP. *v.* To roll together; to involve. pr. par. *wrapping;* past, *wrapped:* s. *wrapper.*
WRATH. *s.* Anger, rage.
WREAK. *v.* To revenge; to execute. pr. par. *wreaking;* past, *wreaked.*
WREATH. *s.* Any thing curled or twisted; a garland. v. *wreath;* pr. par. *wreathing;* past, *wreathed.* adj. *wreathy.*
WRECK. *s.* Destruction by sea; ruin; the thing wrecked. v. *wreck;* pr. par. *wrecking;* past, *wrecked.*
WREN. *s.* A kind of small bird.
WRENCH. *v.* To pull by violence

WRE—WRI

to wrest; to sprain. pr. par. *wrenching*; past, *wrenched*: s. *wrench*.

WREST. *v.* To twist by violence; to extort by force; to distort. pr. par. *wresting*; past, *wrested*.

WRES'TLE. *v.* To struggle; to contend. pr. par. *wrestling*; past, *wrestled*: s. *wrestler*.

WRETCH. *s.* A miserable or worthless mortal. pl. *wretches*: adj. *wretched*: s. *wretchedness*: adv. *wretchedly*.

WRIG'GLE. *v.* To move to and fro with short motions. pr. par. *wriggling*; past, *wriggled*.

WRING. *v.* To twist; to turn round with violence. pr. par. *wringing*; past, *wrung*.

WRINK'LE. *s.* A furrow of the skin or face; a rumple of cloth. v. *wrinkle*; pr. par. *wrinkling*; past, *wrinkled*.

WRI—WRY

WRIST. *s.* The joint by which the hand is joined to the arm. s. *wristband*.

WRIT. *s.* Something written; a legal process.

WRITE. *v.* To express by means of letters. pr. par. *writing*; past, *written*: s. *writing*, *writer*.

WRITHE. *v.* To distort; to deform by distortion. pr. par. *writhing*; past, *writhed*.

WRONG. *s.* An injury; injustice; error. v. *wrong*; pr. par. *wronging*; past, *wronged*: adj. *wrong*, *wrongful*: s. *wrongness*: adv. *wrongly*, *wrongfully*.

WROTE. Pret. of the v. *to write*.

WROUGHT. One of the participles of the v. *to work*.

WRUNG. Pret. and past par. of the v. *to wring*.

WRY. *adj.* Crooked; distorted.

X Y Z

XEB—YEA

XEBEC'. *s.* A kind of small three-masted vessel.

YACHT. *s.* A small ship for carrying passengers.

YAM. *s.* A kind of esculent root.

YARD. *s.* Enclosed ground adjoining a house; a measure of three feet; the support of the sails.

YARN. *s.* Thread made of wool, &c.

YAW. *s.* The unsteady motion which a ship makes in a great swell. v. *yaw*; pr. par. *yawing*; past, *yawed*.

YAWL. *s.* A little boat, sharp at both ends.

YAWN. *v.* To gape. pr. par. *yawning*; past, *yawned*: s. *yawn*.

YE. *pron.* One of the nominatives plural of *thou*.

YEA. *adv.* Yes.

YEAR. *s.* Twelve months, or three hundred and sixty five days. adj. and adv. *yearly*.

YEAR'LING. *adj.* Being a year old. s. *yearling*.

YEA—YIE

YEARN. *v.* To feel great internal uneasiness. pr. par. *yearning*; past, *yearned*.

YEAST. *s.* Barm.

YELL. *v.* To cry out with horror and agony. pr. par. *yelling*; past, *yelled*: s. *yell*.

YEL'LOW. *adj.* One of the primitive colours. s. *yellow*: adj. *yellowish*.

YELP. *v.* To bark as a beagle hound after his prey pr par. *yelping*; past, *yelped*.

YEO'MAN. *s.* A man of a small estate in land; a farmer. pl. *yeomen*: s. *yeomanry*.

YES. *adv.* A term of affirmation.

YES'TERDAY. *s.* The day next before to-day.

YET. One of the conjunctions; one of the adverbs.

YEW. *s.* A kind of tree.

YIELD. *v.* To produce; to afford; to concede; to submit. pr. par. *yielding*; past, *yielded*: s. *yielder*

YOKE. *s.* The bandage placed on the neck of draught oxen; a mark of servitude; a chain; bond; couple. *v. yoke;* pr. par. *yoking;* past, *yoked: s. yokefellow.*

YOLK. *s.* The yellow part of an egg.

YON. *adj.* That: used when pointing towards. *adv. yonder.*

YORE. *adv.* Of old time; long ago.

YOU. One of the pronouns.

YOUNG. *adj.* Being in the first part of life; not old. *s. young.*

YOUNG'STER, YOUN'KER. *s.* A young person: in contempt.

YOUR. *pron.* Belonging to you. emphatic, *yourself.*

YOUTH. *s.* The part of life succeeding childhood; a young man. *adj. youthful: adv. youthfully.*

ZA'NY. *s.* A merry-andrew; a buffoon. *pl. zanies.*

ZEAL. *s.* Passionate ardour. *adj. zealless, zealous: s. zealot: adv. zealously.*

ZE'BRA. *s.* An Indian ass.

ZE'NITH. *s.* The point over head, opposite to the nadir.

ZEPH'YR. *s.* The west wind; poetically, any calm, soft wind.

ZEST. *s.* The peel of an orange squeezed into wine; a relish; a taste added.

ZEUG'MA. *s.* A figure in grammar.

ZIG'ZAG. *adj.* Having sharp and quick turns.

ZINC. *s.* One of the metals.

ZO'DIAC. *s.* A great circle of the sphere, containing the twelve signs.

ZONE. *s.* A girdle; a division of the earth.

ZOOG'RAPHY. *s.* A description of the forms, natures, and properties of animals. *s. zoographer.*

ZOOL'OGY. *s.* A treatise concerning living creatures. *s. zoologist: adj. zoological.*

ZO'OPHYTE. *s.* Certain vegetables or substances, which partake of the nature both of vegetables and animals.

ZOOT'OMY. *s.* Dissection of the bodies of beasts. *s. zootomist.*

407

THE END.

www.ingramcontent.com/pod-product-compliance
Lightning Source LLC
Chambersburg PA
CBHW022122290426
44112CB00008B/767